Reading(s)

GEOFFREY SUMMERFIELD
New York University

JUDITH SUMMERFIELD
Queens College, The City University of New York

RANDOM HOUSE NEW YORK

First Edition
98765432
Copyright © 1989 by Random House, Inc.

Library of Congress Cataloging-in-Publication Data
Summerfield, Geoffrey.
   Reading (s)

   Includes index.
   1. College readers.   2. English language—Rhetoric.
I. Summerfield, Judith, 1941–   .   II. Title.
PE1417.S85 1989   808'.0427   88–33837

MANUFACTURED IN THE UNITED STATES OF AMERICA

ISBN–0–394–36290–X

COPYRIGHTS AND ACKNOWLEDGMENTS

Introduction
Seamus Heaney, "'Villanelle." Reprinted by permission of Faber and Faber Ltd. from uncollected poems of Seamus Heaney.
Diagram from Frank Smith, *Understanding Reading*, Harcourt Brace Jovanovich, Inc. Reprinted by permission of the author.
Edwin Morgan, "Advice to a Corkscrew," in *Poems of Thirty Years*, Carcanet Press Limited.

Chapter One
From Steven Millhauser, *Edwin Mullhouse, The Life and Death of an American Writer 1943–1954* by Jeffrey Cartwright. Copyright © 1972 by Steven Millhauser. Reprinted by permission of McIntosh and Otis, Inc.
From Johnny Connors, *Gypsies*, by Johnny Connors and Jeremy Sandford.
From Arthur Hopcraft, *The Great Apple Raid*. Reprinted by permission of A. P. Watt Ltd. on behalf of Arthur Hopcraft.
From *As the Twig Is Bent* by Winifred Foley. Copyright © 1974. Reprinted by permission of Taplinger Publishing Company. Reproduced from *A Child in the Forest* by Winifred Foley with the permission of BBC Ltd.

From *A Tree Grows in Brooklyn* by Betty Smith. Copyright 1943, 1947 by Betty Smith. Reprinted by permission of Harper & Row, Publishers, Inc.
From *An Unfinished Woman* by Lillian Hellman. Copyright © 1969 by Lillian Hellman. By permission of Little Brown and Company.
From Eudora Welty, *One Writer's Beginnings*. Reprinted by permission of the publishers from *One Writer's Beginnings* by Eudora Welty, Cambridge, Mass.: Harvard University Press, Copyright © 1983, 1984 by Eudora Welty.

Chapter Two
From Sherwood Anderson, *A Story Teller's Story*. Reprinted by permission of Harold Ober Associates Incorporated. Copyright 1924 by B. W. Huebsch, Inc. Copyright renewed 1951 by Eleanor Copenhaver Anderson.
Fiona Pitt-Kethley, "Ghost Stories," from *Sky Ray Lolly*. Reprinted by permission from Chatto & Windus.

Copyrights and Acknowledgments continue on page 442.

Introduction

Villanelle for an Anniversary

A spirit moved. John Harvard walked the yard.
The atom lay unsplit, the west unwon.
The books stood open and the gates unbarred.

The maps dreamt on like moondust. Nothing stirred.
The future was a verb in hibernation.
A spirit moved, John Harvard walked the yard.

Before the classic style, before the clapboard,
All through the small hours of an origin,
The books stood open and the gates unbarred.

Night passage of a migratory bird.
Wingbeat. Gownflap. Like a homing pigeon,
A spirit moved, John Harvard walked the yard.

Was that his soul (look!) sped to its reward
By grace or works? A shooting star? An omen?
The books stood open and the gates unbarred.

Begin again where frosts and tests were hard.
Find yourself or founder. Here. Imagine
A spirit moves, John Harvard walks the yard,
The books stand open and the gates unbarred.

SEAMUS HEANEY

Reading in college in America can be said to have started in 1636, when John Harvard opened a college in Cambridge, Massachusetts. In 1976, for the 350th anniversary of that occasion, Seamus Heaney, Boylston Professor of Rhetoric and Oratory at Harvard, wrote the preceding lines, a celebration of the right to read and of the reader's responsibility for making meaning.

To pick up Heaney's metaphor:* *Reading(s)* invites you, the reader, to "find yourself or founder." That's a "tough" and hard directive, yet also exhilarating and energizing. Don't expect someone else to do your reading for you and don't expect "easy" answers. Exercise your mind and take risks; no one will blame you for "floundering." As with swimming, you may well flounder at first and get out of your depth! But never blame others for barring you from the pursuit of knowledge or light: the books *are* open, and it's up to you to enter.

Reading(s), as you will see, invites you to read print and to read the world. Reading is, literally, reading print; "reading," a larger term, is the act of construing and making sense of everything that is in the world.

The Sequence of Readings

The book is divided into three sections. The medium, throughout, is literature, broadly understood. The themes of Part One are growing up as a reader, the variety of other worlds that we can enter through reading, and how these other worlds modify our relationship with our actual world. The theme of Part Two is the relationship between nature and culture: how we learn to "read" these two interacting, and often opposing, worlds. The theme of Part Three is the constant activity we all engage in of renegotiating our relationship with our culture and its values, with other cultures, and with people who may represent values other than our own.

We provide an introduction to each text, then a text, and then our reading of some of the key features and issues that the text offers. In addition to these contexts, we also include occasional brief commentaries on important aspects of reading and of "reading." Under the heading "Consider This," we provide suggestions for discussion and reflection, both inside your own head and with others in class. "Your Writings for Others to Read" at the end of chapters offers various prompts for your own writing.

Interactions

The text of this book is woven from *seven* strands:

1. A variety of different kinds of texts, inviting different ways of reading.
2. A continuous interaction of two different kinds of reading: reading texts about our inner and outer worlds; and "reading" and "rereading" those worlds.

---

* Our reading of Heaney's "Villanelle" would include the following observations: A villanelle is a traditional pattern for light verse, such as might be commissioned for a wedding or celebration. The rhyme scheme is very strict, and the skill of the poet is committed to making it look easy.

Seamus Heaney constructs his rhyme scheme neatly, weaving the poem together, and thus weaves together the past and the present, so that while John Harvard literally *walked* the yard 350 years ago, his spirit now *walks* the same yard, a benign and exemplary ghost. The name of the place, Harvard Yard, is memorable due to its accidental (?) phonic patterning: three identical vowel patterns, and the neat rhyme of *-vard* and *yard*. The music of the poem is in its variations: un*won*, hiberna*tion*, ori*gin*, pi*geon*, om*en*, and finally—most importantly—ima*gine*.

3. A presentation of various, sometimes conflicting, ways in which people in various cultures "read" the world, and express these ways of "reading" in their beliefs, values, assumptions, and ideologies.
4. The interactions between reading and other ways of living in the lives of individuals at various stages of their growth.
5. The interactions between what we find in texts and what we, ourselves, bring to the act of reading.
6. A selective representation of the ways in which various cultures read "nature" and sometimes mis-read elements of their own culture as if they were part of "nature."
7. A selection of texts which show how particular minds achieve a *critical* reading of the ideology of their own dominant culture.

These are the strands that we have deliberately worked to weave into the book. If you, the reader, find more than these, we shall be delighted.

The underlying bias of *Reading(s)* should be quite clear; we value literature. We value its power to move, to change minds, its strength, its subtlety, vividness, particularity, specificity, and density. We construe reading as a way of living, and the texts in this book as offering good "ways of being." But we construe literature as a field that includes more than fiction, poetry, and drama; for us, literature is inclusive rather than exclusive. We see literature, above all, as an integral enlivening part of a continuing *conversation*, within ourselves and between ourselves and others. We believe that it is always worth talking about, but, first, it *must* be allowed to do *its own uninterrupted work*. We need to have the space, the protected space, in which to become vicarious *participants*, before we change gear to do all the other things that we do as *spectators*, thinking, and talking, about *what we have experienced*.

How to Read

Here we would like to offer you a copy of Frank Smith's book, *Understanding Reading*: since that is not practicable, let us just say this: a useful guide to reading is Smith's diagram on page vi.

It's useful because it clearly demonstrates some of the elements of good reading—intelligent, active reading.

Different kinds of texts set up different kinds of expectations and require different kinds of reading: hence the old joke about a naive reader who waded through every word of a telephone directory. Coming to the end, he said, "There were lots of characters, but the plot wasn't very interesting." That's an extreme case of inappropriate expectations. The difference between an immature reader and a mature reader, or a naive and a canny reader, is that the latter in each case starts to construct appropriate expectations even before they read a word of the text: they open a novel with novel-expectations and a book of essays with essay-expectations. The most fundamental and largest of these is, in Smith's diagram, the great curve that encompasses the whole book. Within that overarching curve

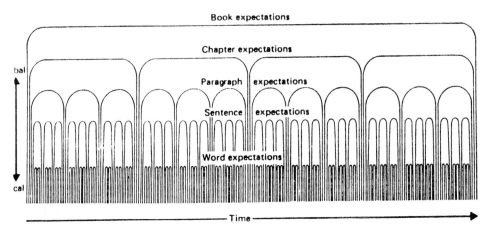

Figure A   Layers of prediction in reading a book.

is a hierarchy of diminishing spans of units, the smallest of which usually operates
at the level of the shortest segment, the phrase or the segment that one act of
looking can pass to the mind to be processed.*

A life-history of congenial readings, of reading that has yielded various
satisfactions, is a story of *satisfied expectations*. That so few adults enjoy poetry
can be explained in terms of a consistent paucity of satisfactions, giving rise to
expectations so miserable, so demoralized, that poetry is cast into outer darkness.
We have tried to repair this damage in two ways: by including relatively direct
and strong poems and by including hints of what kinds of expectations are
appropriate to poetry. Both of these will work better if the necessary *silence* of
the printed word is overcome by *reading aloud*. Reading aloud well is far more
difficult than silent reading; every occasion of reading aloud should, therefore,
be adequately *rehearsed* so that the text is familiar, and the reader can enjoy the
privilege and the protection of being in control, of possession. "To appreciate,"
said Henry James, means "to make it one's own." This is true of nothing more
than of poetry, and one cannot read a poem aloud effectively until one has made
it one's own.

Following in Frank Smith's footsteps, we recommend that as you move
through any text in the book, you allow yourself to read *fast*, and keep up with
the momentum, the continuity of the inclusive top curve, so as to take the text
whole. This holistic reading can be followed by any number or variety of slower,
more disjointed readings, but it should always come first. If possible, it should
also be repeated, last, so that as you "leave" a text, you leave it with a memory
of the whole rather than the fragments.

As you move through the book, we hope that you will build up an intuitive
sense of textual varieties, varieties in structure, tone, procedure, effect, and will

* See Frank Smith, p. 204.

therefore come to grasp how Text A is different from, and so interacts with, Text B, C, and so on. Our sense of what a text is can best be expressed in terms of its differences from other texts. Hence, the difficulty we all have when confronted by one solitary text, trying to characterize it in isolation.

How to Write from Reading(s)

We believe that every text in the book can provoke/promote/arouse the energy that issues in writing. Our own preference is for you to keep a reading journal, throughout the semester, as a continuing written dialogue with yourself, about what you are reading and rereading. On the basis of this, especially if you make contributions to discussion by reading from your journals, many possibilities for writing will emerge. We hope that your own texts will be as various as those you have read; that is, that you are encouraged to write in a variety of forms, genres, roles, and voices.

Contact

Even if we have been smart in editing this book, making the selections, providing contexts for the texts, and imagining you, the reader, and responding to our sense of "where you are," we suspect that there may still be texts here that you will find it difficult to make contact with. This may even be true of the text that is about this very problem!

When you come into the classroom, you leave the society in which *you* call most of the shots, and you enter a different society, in which someone else calls the shots, makes the choices, and says "Read this." On the whole, colleges haven't been too clever about this, and too many students have left college hating reading, at worst, or giving up on it or tolerating it, at best.

As you will see when you read Malcolm Cowley (p. 137) this is a problem that some people have already recognized and deplored: not simply because it really isn't necessary to bore anybody, but because the question of *contact* is rarely discussed or even considered.

We hope that when a text fails to connect with you, you will say so: our hope is that you will try to fool neither yourself nor your instructor, but admit that this or that text simply fails to *touch* you; that, with the best will in the world, you find it impossible (at *this* time, in *this* place) to make contact with it.

This will leave more room for the texts that *do* work for you, that animate your mind and arouse your energies; and will alert your instructors to the texts with which they may be able to help you to make contact. This process is rather like your social life. You say to a friend, "*You* obviously enjoy So-and-so's company, but *I* don't know what you see in them." If your friend is so inclined, they will then represent to you their perceptions of So-and-so; if they do this well, you will come to understand—even if you can't altogether share—their point of view.

We would like to thank our friends, our colleagues, and our students, for sharing with us their pleasure in reading and to acknowledge the satisfactions that so many writers, past and present, published and unpublished, have brought to our lives.

Our work on this book has been consistently felicitous, not least because of the genial collaboration of Steve Pensinger, our editor, and the professionalism of the Random House staff: Lorraine Hohman, who designed the book and Valerie Sawyer who shepherded it through the production process. Carolyn Viola-John edited our text with scrupulous care, and for this we are most grateful.

We also wish to express our thanks to Barry M. Maid, University of Arkansas at Little Rock; David Rosenwasser, Muhlenberg College; Charles Schuster, University of Wisconsin—Milwaukee; and Michael Vivion, University of Missouri, whose readings of a deplorably inchoate early draft of this book proved extremely helpful.

Geoffrey and Judith Summerfield

Contents

Introduction   iii
Villanelle for an Anniversary   *Seamus Heaney*   iii
Illustrations   xiv
Advice to a Corkscrew   *Edwin Morgan*   xvi

PART ONE *Entering a Language*   1

CHAPTER ONE *Early Words*   3

Gurshes, Jurbles, Fliffs . . .   *Steven Millhauser*   4
A bee a noppity: assa question!   *Steven Millhauser*   6
Captain Murderer   *Charles Dickens*   9
The Man That Spelt KNIFE Was a Fool   *Johnny Connors*   13
The First Book to Impress Me   *Arthur Hopcraft*   16
Poe's Murderers and Corpses Were Gathering
    in Our Kitchen   *Winifred Foley*   17
If I Were King   *Betty Smith*   19
In the Fig Tree I Learned to Read   *Lillian Hellman*   24
Did You Have *Our Wonder World?*   *Eudora Welty*   26

CHAPTER TWO *Possessed by Words*   32

I Had Thought I Understood How a Murder
    Could Happen   *Sherwood Anderson*   33
Ghost Stories   *Fiona Pitt-Kethley*   40
Literature   *Colette*   41
Through the Eyes of Men   *Simone de Beauvoir*   44
How We Comprehend   *Frank Smith*   46

CHAPTER THREE *Creating an Inner Life* 59

The Winds	*Eudora Welty* 60
I Sat Up All Night . . .	*Seamus Heaney* 78
The Lone Ranger	*Thomas Frosch* 83
A Boy's Head	*Miroslav Holub* 84
When You Open a Book, Anything Can Happen	*Annie Dillard* 85
Growing Up	*Ursula Fanthorpe* 91

CHAPTER FOUR *Transitions* 95

Tragedy	*Fiona Pitt-Kethley* 96
Fifteen	*William Stafford* 97
It's Called the Universe	*Frank Conroy* 99
Where Are You Now, Batman?	*Brian Patten* 108
I Sank into Other Streets and Universes	*Steven Millhauser* 109
Autobiographical Notes	*James Baldwin* 111
My Life in Fiction	*Rachel Brownstein* 112

PART TWO *Losing Nature? Gaining Culture?* 117

CHAPTER FIVE *Losses and Gains* 119

Reading for Another Life and Liberation	*Richard Wright* 120
I Want to Be an Honest Man	*James Baldwin* 128
The First Day of School	*Cynthia Ozick* 131
The World Is Too Much With Us	*William Wordsworth* 136
Destroying the Roots	*Malcolm Cowley* 137
Realizing What You Don't Know and Never Will	*Anna Quindlen* 143
What Do 47-Year-Olds Know?	*Benjamin Barber* 146
Psalm Concerning the Castle	*Denise Levertov* 148

CHAPTER SIX *Nature . . .* 151

O Taste and See	*Denise Levertov* 152
Sunrise	*Eudora Welty* 154
Cock-Crow	*Edward Thomas* 156
Out of the Sea, Early	*May Swenson* 156
Memories of Waves	*Walt Whitman* 158
How Everything Happens (Based on the Study of the Wave)	*May Swenson* 160
The Wonder I Felt	*Richard Wright* 162

This Lucky Situation of Joy   *James Agee* 163
I Know Green Apples   *Mark Twain* 164
The River Was Turned to Blood *Mark Twain* 166

CHAPTER SEVEN *Nature and Culture* **168**

Snake   *D. H. Lawrence* 171
Bad Mouth   *Margaret Atwood* 175
Snake-Phobia   *Alan Moorehead* 178
Pigeon Season   *Mark Twain* 184
Take a Chicken to Lunch   *Associated Press* 185
Song of the Hen's Head   *Margaret Atwood* 186
The Early Purges   *Seamus Heaney* 187
Animals and Human Obligations *Peter Medawar and Jean
              Medawar* 188
Pigs, Dogs and People: Clash in Jersey *The New York Times* 192
Capturing Animals   *Ted Hughes* 195
The Animals in That Country *Margaret Atwood* 202
Predictions and Intentions—Global and Focal *Frank Smith* 204

CHAPTER EIGHT *Tracks* **209**

Excerpts from *Tracks*   *Robyn Davidson* 210

PART THREE *Negotiations and Renegotiations* **245**

CHAPTER NINE *Reading Culture* **247**

I Think There are Too Many Trees *D. H. Lawrence* 248
Stopping by Woods on a Snowy Evening *Robert Frost* 251
No Longer Lovely, Nor Dark, Nor Deep *Michael Patrick Doyle* 253
On a Certain Blindness in Human Beings *William James* 254
My Uncle Harry Said . . .   *Wright Morris* 256
A Wagner Matinée   *Willa Cather* 259
Rhymes   *Seamus Heaney* 265
Mending Wall   *Robert Frost* 270
Seminar: Felicity and Mr. Frost *Ursula Fanthorpe* 272
Down by the Salley Gardens   *W. B. Yeats* 274
The Song of Wandering Aengus *W. B. Yeats* 275
Seminar: Life; Early Poems   *Ursula Fanthorpe* 276

CHAPTER TEN *Reading Differences* *279*

It Takes Courage to Say Things Differently   *Kay Boyle*   280
The Castaways, or Vote for Caliban   *Adrian Mitchell*   283
A Schism Between Mothers   *Anna Quindlen*   286
Rating the Kids   *Ellen Goodman*   288
Beset by Mediocrity   *Russell Baker*   290
Robert Called Me "Baby"   *Anna Quindlen*   292
Sheep and Women   *Robyn Davidson*   296
Some Say Frontier Is Still There . . .   *Peter Appleborne*   299
About Men   *Gretel Ehrlich*   302

CHAPTER ELEVEN *Reading Roles and Relationships* *306*

Waitress   *Thom Gunn*   306
Backdrop Addresses Cowboy   *Margaret Atwood*   307
Of Roles and Robes   *Ellen Goodman*   309
Live-In Myths   *Ellen Goodman*   311
Spells   *Fiona Pitt-Kethley*   314
My Secret Advice   *Ellen Willis*   314
Vowing to Get Married   *Ellen Goodman*   319
U/S and Marriage   *Andrew Hacker*   321
The Secret Museum   *Walter Kendrick*   327
On Reading Fiction   *Philip Roth*   332
How I Met My Husband   *Alice Munro*   333

CHAPTER TWELVE *Interpretations* *346*

Questions About a Child   *John Berger and Jean Mohr*   348
Waiting for the Idiot to Go Away   *Peter Sharpe*   355
Disclosing, Uncovering, Reading, Inferring   *Arthur Conan Doyle*   356
How Conan Doyle Learned to Read   *Joseph Bell*   361
Near a Church   *James Agee*   363
Stranger on a Train   *Virginia Woolf*   366
Painkillers   *Thom Gunn*   370
Where Were You When Elvis Died?   *Lester Bangs*   371
Then I Will Be Elvis!   *Lester Bangs*   376
It's All the Art of Impersonation   *Philip Roth*   382
The Death of Marilyn Monroe   *Edwin Morgan*   383

CHAPTER THIRTEEN *Values and Evaluations (I)* *387*

Anxiety   *Grace Paley*   388
After the Beep   *Alan Devenish*   390
What a Sweet Name!   *Oscar Wilde*   392

Fashion   *Edward Sapir* 394
Thoughts on a Shirtless Cyclist, Robin Hood
    and One or Two Other Things   *Russell Hoban* 405

CHAPTER FOURTEEN *Values and Evaluations (II)* *413*

Six Feet of the Country   *Nadine Gordimer* 414
The Family of Man   *Edward Steichen* 423
                                                                Carl Sandburg 426
The Great Family of Man   *Roland Barthes* 428
Mr. Cogito on the Need for Precision   *Zbigniew Herbert* 430
A Poem for Vida Hadjebi Tabrizi   *Kay Boyle* 436
My Sad Captains   *Thom Gunn* 439
Critique   *William Stafford* 440

INDEX OF AUTHORS   446
INDEX OF TITLES   447

Illustrations

The illustrations in this volume serve a variety of purposes. In some cases, they are included on the basis of the old adage that a picture is worth a thousand words—they provide an explanation or a relevant bit of information more economically or more vividly than words would.

In other cases they provide a *complement* to the text: here, in the picture, is how the same subject matter or topic has been presented *visually*, or *graphically*. By comparing the text and the picture, you will be able to recognize the distinctive and characteristic strengths of a verbal language and, by contrast, of a visual medium.

Underlying all this is a prior reason, and that is our belief that since the subject of the book is *reading*, it will do its work all the better for offering the reader a *variety* of texts and images that invite a variety of ways of reading and of "reading."

Title page. Louis Jou for Anatole France, *Les opinions de M. Jérôme Coignard*.
13. After Vierge for Victor Hugo, *Les Travailleurs de la mer*.
15. Photograph: The Bettmann Archive.
16. Gustave Doré for Lodovico Ariosto, *Roland furieux*, 1879.
18. Arthur B. Frost for Lewis Carroll, *Rhyme? and Reason?*, London, 1890.
30. Robert Massin, *Letter and Image*, p. 123, Fig. 444.
40. Arthur B. Frost for Lewis Carroll, *Rhyme? and Reason?*, London, 1890.
47. Drawing by Roz Chast; © 1987. The New Yorker Magazine.
65. Walter Crane for Jacob and Wilhelm Grimm, *Household Stories*, 1882.
74. Frederick Sandys, "Danae in the Brazen Chamber," 1867.
81. Lionel Feininger, "Wee Willie Winkie's World," 1906.
100. Photograph: Barbara Rios/Photo Researchers.
149. Edward Calvert, *Eleven Engravings*, Plate IV, Cambridge, 1966.
157. Rockwell Kent, "Get Up," 1920.
158. August Lepère for Joris Karl Huysmans, *A rebours*, 1903.
159. Eduoard Manet for Charles Cros, *Le fleuve*, 1874.
161. From *Alice's Adventures Underground* by Charles Lutwidge Dodgson, McMillan, 1887.
176. From *The Pictorial Museum of Animated Nature*, c. 1840.
178. G. J. Grandville, "April Fish."
183. Pierre Choffard for Joseph-Louis Desormeaux, *Histoire de la Maison de Bourbon*, 1772–1788.
193, 195. Photographs: William E. Sayre/NY Times Pictures.

202. Gwendolen Raverat, for A. G. Street, *Farmer's Glory*, 1934.
208. Arthur Boyd Houghton for Miguel de Cervantes, *Adventures of Don Quixote de la Mancha*, 1866.
210, 220, 224, 231, 240. Photographs: Rick Smolan/ContactPress/Woodfin Camp and Associates.
244. "Slow but sure" in George Wither, *A Collection of Emblemes with Metricall Illustrations, both Moral and Divine*, London, 1635.
259. Photographs: From *Photographs and Words*, by Wright Morris, 1982, plate number 62.
264. From *Illustrated London News*, May 8, 1875.
269. Photograph: Jan Lukas/Photo Researchers.
276. Photograph: The Bettmann Archive.
282. Photograph: Julio Donoso/Sygma.
295. G. J. Grandville, *The Public and Private Life of Animals*, 1877.
296. Photograph: Audrey Gottlieb/Monkmeyer Press.
297. Photograph: Collection of Bob Gallagher.
312, 321. Arthur B. Frost for Lewis Carroll, *Rhyme? and Reason?*.
323. Edward Calvert, *Eleven Engravings*, Plate XI, Cambridge, 1966.
347. Arthur B. Frost for Charles Dickens, *American Notes*, c. 1870s.
348, 349, 351, 353. Photographs: From *Another Way of Telling* by John Berger and Jean Mohr, Pantheon, 1982.
354. Photograph: The Imperial War Museum, London.
360. George du Maurier for "The Notting Hill Mystery," 1862.
372. Frederick Sandys for Thornbury, *Historical and Legendary Ballads*, 1876.
376. Frederick Sandys, "Amor Mundi," 1865.
381. Photograph: Slick Lauson/People Weekly © 1987 Time, Inc.
384. Movie Still Archives.
393, 394. Photographs: Culver Pictures.
422. Photograph: Michael Evans/Contact Press/Woodfin Camp and Associates.
423. Photograph: Ted Castle.
424. Photograph: Richard Harrington/Superstock/Three Lions.
425. Photograph: Frank Scherschel/Life Magazine, © 1947, Time, Inc.
426. Photograph: Werner Bischof/Magnum.
427. Photograph: Constance Stuart/Black Star
428. Photograph: Tana Hoban.
429. Photograph: Hans Wild/Life Magazine, © Time, Inc.
430. Photograph: Ernst Haas/Magnum.
431. Gustave Doré for Lodovico Ariosto, *Roland furieux*, 1879.
440. Photograph: Lick Observatory, University of California, Mt. Hamilton, CA.

GET
IИ
IT

Edwin Morgan, "Advice to a Corkscrew"

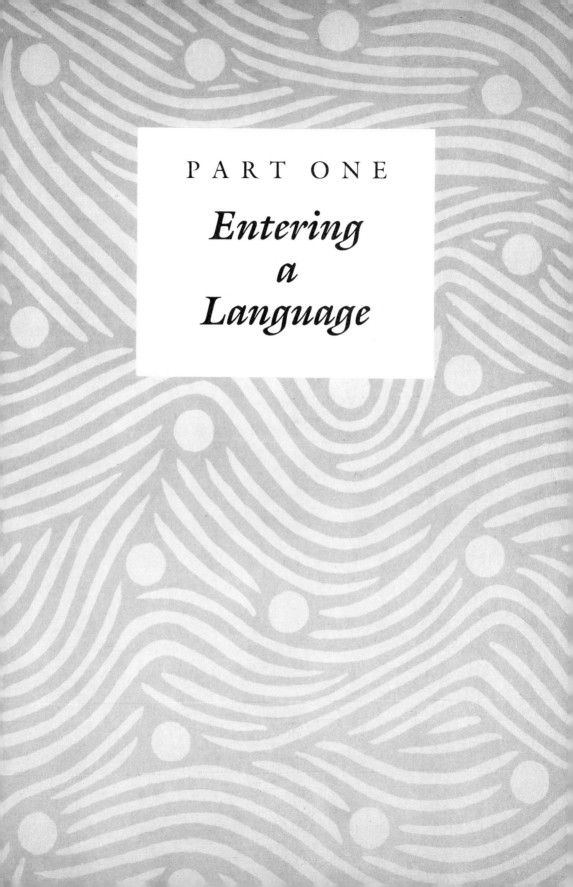

PART ONE

Entering a Language

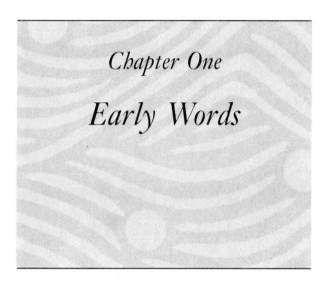

Chapter One

Early Words

We cannot know directly who we were before we possessed the power of speech, for our memory of that time is null and void. But those wordless months are amply compensated by the unprecedented growth of our mind, of our social selves, once we begin to speak and interact with others through their language, which becomes, in turn, our own.

Then comes the gift of understanding. We enter into the "other world" of stories, where as if by magic we become other selves, powerful, exotic, unkill-able, immortal; and also learn to give shape and form to our fears and anxieties. So we learn to laugh and to weep, to shout and to shudder for these other selves with all their victories, trials, and tribulations.

Soon, we can take an object, a rectangular thing, from a shelf, open it, and scan the signs on the page: lo and behold, we ourselves can *make* the story *happen*, unaided by any parent or sibling, aunt or grandparent.

And so begins that extraordinary other life, the limitless life of the imagi-nation. From now on, no day is too long, no weather too miserable, for by simply extending a hand and turning the pages, we can have another life, a life in which we can become more, far more, than merely a son or daughter, a brother or sister. Behind our eyes, who could ever guess who we really are in that transmogrifying other world?

STEVEN MILLHAUSER

Gurshes, Jurbles, Fliffs . . .

*In this first text, an extract from a novel by Steven Millhauser (b. 1943), we invite
you to take a journey. It would be a journey down "memory lane," if only you could
remember what it was like to be an infant. (The word* infant *originally meant "without
speech, without language.") Steven Millhauser's fiction depends on two assumptions:
one, that the narrator—Edwin's friend, Jeffrey Cartwright—can remember so far back
in time, to when he was only a year old. And two, that the story is written, not by
the* actual *writer (Steven Millhauser) but by the narrator, Jeffrey Cartwright, someone
who was always intensely interested in his friend Edwin, even when Edwin irritated
or annoyed him almost beyond endurance.*

Edwin was like that: he resisted all change violently, but as soon as the change
became part of his normal scheme of things he clung to it violently, resisting all
change. We developed an intimate speechless friendship. Through the mist of years
I look back upon that time as upon a green island of silence from which I set forth
forever onto a tempestuous sea. In green and blue August we stared at one another
through the lacquered bars of his crib. In orange and blue October we rode side by
side in our carriage along Benjamin Street, a yellow leaf came down out of the sky
onto Edwin's blanket. In white and blue December I gave him a snowball, which
he tried to eat. He liked his father to hold him upside down and blow on his feet.
On my first birthday (February is a gray month) I gave him a piece of cake; he
threw it up in the air, where I shall leave it. April showers bring May flowers. Time,
as Edwin would never have said, passed.

   Not that we were literally silent. Before Speech the Intruder came crashing into
our private party he made quite a preliminary ruckus, pounding on the door and
rattling the knob and tossing snowballs at the windows. That is to say, in the early
months we had an elaborate system of gasps, purrs, chuckles, burbles, sniffs, smacks,
snorts, burps, clicks, plops, clucks, yelps, puffs, gulps, slurps, squeals, ho's, hums,
buzzes, whines, chirrups, grunts, hisses, hollers, yowls, rasps, gurgles, gargles,
glugs, and giggles, not to mention a vast number of hitherto unclassified sounds:
gurshes, jurbles, fliffs, cloffs, whizzles, mishes, nists, wints, bibbles, chickles, plips,
and chirkles, to name a few, as well as occasional norples, nufts, and snools. Edwin's
pre-speech vocabulary was impressive and I bitterly regret that I was unable to
record his earliest experiments with language. I do remember a number of them,
however, for from the beginning I observed him with the fond solicitude of an elder
brother and the scrupulous fascination of a budding biographer. I can confidently
state that the following utterances issued from the mouth of Edwin before he had
attained the age of three months:

   aaaaa (crying)
   nnnnn (complaining)
   kkkkk (giggling)

ggggg (giggling)
cheeeooo (sneezing)
hp hp hp (hiccuping)
haaaooo (yawning)
tatata (singing)
fsssss (drooling)
eeeee (screaming; singing)
b-b-b-b-b (unknown)

By six months (I was a year old and walking) Edwin had achieved more elaborate combinations:

kakooka
pshhh
dam dam dam
chfff (an early version of Jeffrey?)
keeee (accompanied by a grin and flapping hands)
kfffk
dknnnnz
shksp-p-p-p
kaloo
kalay
aaaaaeeeee (singing)

Some of his bolder adventures in the realm of sound were later suppressed by the polite requirements of civilized noise. I refer not so much to his intricate belches and exquisite winds as to his astonishing salivary achievements. How I long to convey to the adult reader his breathtaking combinations of the buzz and drool, his dribbles and drizzles, his bubbles and burbles—whole salivary sonatas enhanced by gushing crescendos and hissing fortissimi, gurgling glissandi and trickling pianissimi, streaming prestissimos, spouting arpeggios, those slurps and slops, those drips and drops, those spluttering splattering splurts of sputum and drippy splish-splashings of melodious spittle. Adult speech, Edwin used to say, is ridiculously exclusive.

The questing biographer gazes with fondness upon this slightly damp picture of brighteyed baby Edwin sporting among sounds, a happy porpoise, untouched by purpose, diving blissfully in the moneybins of language like a latterday Scrooge McDuck. Surely Edwin's later and highly sophisticated delight in language may be traced back to these early months, when sound was not yet a substitute for things but rather a thing itself, the gayest of his toys: a toy that could be rolled and bounced and licked and swallowed and twisted into a thousand delightful shapes. In general, language for little Edwin combined the virtues of rubber dogs, rattles, and breasts. Later Edwin tried to recapture by a variety of methods this early experience of what I shall call the thingness of speech. Thus, extracting from the mahogany bookcase a fat volume which he said was written in Hebrew, he would open to the first page and begin reading very slowly in a voice as solemn and deep as possible:

Tiurf eht dna ecneidebosid tsrif snam fo.
Etsat latrom esohw eert neddibrof taht fo.
Eow—

losing control at "neddibrof," gaining it at "taht fo," and sputtering into helpless laughter at "eow," which he pronounced in imitation of a rocket in a war movie: eeeeeeowwwww. And he would torment his mother, who was concerned for her daughter's intellectual development, by speaking to eighteen-month-old Karen for hours on end in carefully enunciated nonsense syllables, to which Karen would respond as in a secret code in solemn or laughing nonsense noises of her own.

STEVEN MILLHAUSER

A bee a noppity: assa question!

For our second text, we stay with Edwin, and discover—possibly to our surprise—that he enjoys the sounds *his father makes, reading aloud, even though he understands not a word.*

The reasons may well be that (a) Edwin enjoyed the sounds of any *voice, since it was evidence of the reassuring presence of others: the opposite of solitude; (b) Edwin's father* performed*—he didn't just "talk," using his normal speaking voice, but "put on," assumed, an especially expressive reading voice.*

. . . every evening Mr. Mullhouse read aloud to Edwin from books without pictures, while Edwin, understanding nothing, listened in fascination to his father's voice. It was the sound alone that held him, undistorted by meaning; and the sense I think of a special occasion, a sacred rite requiring in the profane listener a hush of awe. Mr. Mullhouse's reading voice was not his everyday voice but a formal, artificial, ideal version of it; a voice, you might say, that formed literature out of the dust of speech and breathed into its nostrils the breath of life. For the next few months Edwin experienced the great passages of English literature as a feast of babbling. Besides a few standard courses in English Composition, Mr. Mullhouse was teaching a course called Survey of English Literature from Beowulf to Joyce and another called Victorian Fiction. Edwin's favorite poets at this time were Chaucer, Spenser, Shakespeare, and Milton; he showed a special interest in medieval alliterative verse; and in prose, aside from his beloved Dickens, he listened with pleasure to passages from *Le Morte D'Arthur*, Boswell's *Life of Johnson*, and *Finnegans Wake*. In the months that followed, as sounds increasingly came to be associated with things, Edwin lost his interest in adult literature, which curiously enough ceased to have any meaning whatsoever as the words themselves began to acquire meanings.

For his second birthday I gave Edwin a tall child's dictionary with a glossy cover. "Say thank you," said Mrs. Mullhouse. "You wackum," said Edwin. He was making excellent progress. The nightly readings from Dickens or the Survey anthology stirred Edwin to imitate the fine sounds he heard, so that in a sense his interest in speech was really an interest in reading. By his second birthday he knew numerous passages by heart and loved to recite them with all the gusto of a budding actor:

A bee a noppity: assa question!

It wuzza besta time, it wuzza wussa time, it wuzza age a whiz, it wuzza age a foo!

Wanna opril wishes sure as soda!

At the same time, try as he might, he could no longer avoid the knowledge that sounds had meanings, and so at first reluctantly, then resignedly, at last passionately, he began to acquire a vocabulary. He became obsessed by the notion that there was a name for everything; perhaps he felt that the world contained a finite number of things and that to learn the names of all of them was to define the universe. Or perhaps he felt a sense of discovery and even invention, as if objects he had never noticed before were springing into existence by virtue of being named. Indeed in the Late Years, during the era of long moonlit conversations that followed the completion of *Cartoons,** Edwin once claimed that to name things is to invent the universe; the more names, the larger the universe, or some such nonsense; and when I reminded him drily of his initial resistance to language, he turned to me with a puzzled expression and said: "But I was always advanced for my age. You must be wrong, Jeffrey." For of course he had forgotten everything.

His favorite word between the ages of two and three was "Wussat?" accompanied by a pointing finger; his favorite game was to search for objects without names. "Wussat?" he would cry, pointing to his foot. "Shoe," Mrs. Mullhouse would say. "Unless of course you mean foot. Or did you mean toe, Edwin?" "Wussat?" he would say, bending over and pointing again. "Shoelace," Mrs. Mullhouse would answer. "You know: shoelace. A lace for your shoesy-woozies." "Wussat?" "That's a whatchamacallit, Edwin. You know: a whoosiewhatsits. Oh what is the name of that stupid tongue. Oh: tongue. Only it's not a real tongue, Edwin, it's a shoe tongue." "Wussat?" "Oh dear, Edwin, I really—it doesn't have a name, it's just a sort of hole for the shoelace to go through. You'd better ask daddy." Daddy was the real test. Daddy knew everything, or almost everything, and what he didn't know he knew how to find out. "Wussat?" "Window." "Wussat?" "Windowsill." "Wussat?" "Frame. All of this is called the frame, boys. This piece here is called the sash; it holds the glass. This is a rail. Look: top rail, bottom rail. These things are stiles. And up here too: top rail, bottom rail, stile, stile." "Wussat?" "Damned if I know." There followed a search through the mahogany bookcase, interrupted by cries of "Helen, have you seen my carpentry book, you know, the one with the blue and red cover?" and at last pulling out a book Mr. Mullhouse sat crosslegged on the floor before the bookcase and turned pages wildly until he came to a picture of a window. "Aha!" he cried, looking up and raising a finger. "The correct term, gents, is: sash bar." He sighed and shook his head. "You'd think it would have a more splendid name."

There is a picture of Edwin from this period showing him seated on the armchair, leaning forward with a frown and pointing a finger. Under the picture, in Mr. Mullhouse's small neat print, is the single mysterious word: "Tripod."

---

* The book that Edwin himself wrote.

How on earth could Jeffrey Cartwright remember all those details if he himself was only about six months older than Edwin? Impossible, surely? By posing the question, we simply remind ourselves that Millhauser's (or Jeffrey's) biography of Edwin is *not actually* a biography, but a fiction.

CONSIDER THIS

★ How exactly would anyone go about the task of actually writing *your* biography, including an account of your earliest years or months? You would be able to provide them with very little information from your own recollections, but perhaps you have a little store of your parents' recollections? (Reinforced by photographs in the family album.) But how do you know that your parents' memories are reliable? Isn't there an almost universal tendency to sentimentalize childhood? Would that tendency not distort their version?

★ Imagine, then, if you set to write your best friend's biography: how exactly would you go about it?

Sounds as Meaning

"Adult speech," Edwin used to say, "is ridiculously exclusive": certainly, as we grow up, we learn to make fewer extravagant, sloppy, or explosive sounds. For Edwin, "language . . . combined the virtues of rubber dogs, rattles, and breasts": it was as if he could touch it, feel its weight (or lightness), its texture, its solidity.

Early in life, every infant begins to hear and to read the sounds of social interaction: at best, the soothing, loving, delightful sounds of parental affection and care. And, lo and behold, it begins to reciprocate. So it enters the conversation that is family life, first as a spectator, then as a participant; and in so doing, it begins to invent its own protolanguage, a little repertoire of sounds: through a closed door, these could be mistaken for English, but on closer listening, they turn out to be quite different: *nyanya, shumshum, bubububub, mimimimim* . . . and so on.

But we can make sense of this protolanguage, even though it is not English or French or Russian or Spanish. We can make sense of it—"read" it—because (a) it occurs in a *context* that promotes our reading, that offers many clues; (b) its elements are repeated, consistently; and (c) the infant quickly establishes two recognizable *functions* for its soundings, and clearly differentiates two distinct patterns of sound to express these functions. It finishes on a rising tone if it is demanding action, and on a falling tone if it is merely making a sound to signify the pleasure of perceiving something that it recognizes, remembers, or is closely attending to. The infant, then, reads its world in two distinct ways: (a) as something that it wants to control or regulate or interact with; and (b) as something that it is pleased to muse on, recognize, or signify. (It is possible that you, dear reader, will be a parent in a few years' time: we are hereby giving you fair warning: don't expect your baby to start life by speaking your language!)

As the infant grows, it discovers two facts about language: one, that its first language (an invented one) didn't get it very far, so that around the age of eighteen months, it abandons it, and buys into the language of the family; and two, that words (like *dog, cat, milk, shoe*) are *not* the things themselves, but are perfectly efficient signs whereby it can get other people to understand its needs, desires, interests, likes and dislikes.

As soon as the child has done this, parents and siblings can extend its "readings" of the environment by reading that environment with the child, guiding or leading its attention to aspects of the world that are simultaneously signified in their speaking and their other signs (e.g., gestures, touching, etc.). Then, lo and behold, the child is more than ready to listen to stories.*

If we have a lucky childhood, people tell us stories, and they read stories to us. In both cases, part of our pleasure is to register and savor the expressiveness of the *sounds* that their telling/reading-aloud voices make. We relish not only the sounds of individual words—*plop! scrunch! terrifying! FEE! FI! FO! FUM! transmogrify!*—but also the larger patterns of sound: acceleration, deceleration; crescendo, diminuendo; and the suggestive pauses that precede some kind of "crunch" or climax. To use an obvious metaphor, we enjoy the various kinds of "music" that good acts of telling/reading-aloud provide: we *feel* the drama through the music, which is fundamentally *expressive*.

But as we ourselves learn to read, and as we become fluent in reading, the music of the language tends to disappear. Sometimes this doesn't matter: there's not much music in a railway schedule! But with some other kinds of texts, the loss of sound (actually heard, or imagined by the "mind's ear") is a serious loss. As you read on, you should be able to identify the texts in which the "sounds" of the text are a significant part of the pleasure.

CHARLES DICKENS

Captain Murderer

As soon as we can understand enough of the language, then, we mostly delight in listening to stories, even if they frighten us. Charles Dickens (1812–1870) in the next text recalls how he was frequently frightened out of his wits by a young woman baby sitter who had a large repertoire of terrible stories.

Were you ever frightened, as a child, by a terrifying story? Did anyone in particular seem to take pleasure in frightening you? Or did you frighten yourself by asking for a story that gave you "a shudder and cold beads on the forehead"?

The first diabolical character who intruded himself on my peaceful youth (as I called to mind that day at Dullborough), was a certain Captain Murderer. This wretch

---

* This account of language is derived from the extraordinary work of M. A. K. Halliday, especially his book *Learning How to Mean*.

must have been an offshoot of the Blue Beard family, but I had no suspicion of the consanguinity in those times. His warning name would seem to have awakened no general prejudice against him, for he was admitted into the best society and possessed immense wealth. Captain Murderer's mission was matrimony, and the gratification of a cannibal appetite with tender brides. On his marriage morning, he always caused both sides of the way to church to be planted with curious flowers; and when his bride said, "Dear Captain Murderer, I never saw flowers like these before: what are they called?" he answered, "They are called Garnish for house-lamb," and laughed at his ferocious practical joke in a horrid manner, disquieting the minds of the noble bridal company, with a very sharp show of teeth, then displayed for the first time. He made love in a coach and six, and married in a coach and twelve, and all his horses were milk-white horses with one red spot on the back which he caused to be hidden by the harness. For, the spot *would* come there, though every horse was milk-white when Captain Murderer bought him. And the spot was young bride's blood. (To this terrific point I am indebted for my first personal experience of a shudder and cold beads on the forehead.) When Captain Murderer had made an end of feasting and revelry, and had dismissed the noble guests, and was alone with his wife on the day after their marriage, it was his whimsical custom to produce a golden rolling-pin and a silver pie-board. Now, there was this special feature in the Captain's courtships, that he always asked if the young lady could make piecrust; and if she couldn't by nature or education, she was taught. Well. When the bride saw Captain Murderer produce the golden rolling-pin and silver pie-board, she remembered this, and turned up her lace-silk sleeves to make a pie. The Captain brought out a silver pie-dish of immense capacity, and the Captain brought out flour and butter and eggs and all things needful, except the inside of the pie; of materials for the staple of the pie itself, the Captain brought out none. Then said the lovely bride, "Dear Captain Murderer, what pie is this to be?" He replied, "A meat pie." Then said the lovely bride, "Dear Captain Murderer, I see no meat." The Captain humorously retorted, "Look in the glass." She looked in the glass, but still she saw no meat, and then the Captain roared with laughter, and suddenly frowning and drawing his sword, bade her roll out the crust. So she rolled out the crust, dropping large tears upon it all the time because he was so cross, and when she had lined the dish with crust and had cut the crust all ready to fit the top, the Captain called out, "*I* see the meat in the glass!" And the bride looked up at the glass, just in time to see the Captain cutting her head off; and he chopped her in pieces, and peppered her, and salted her, and put her in the pie, and sent it to the baker's, and ate it all, and picked the bones.

   Captain Murderer went on in this way, prospering exceedingly, until he came to choose a bride from two twin sisters, and at first didn't know which to choose. For, though one was fair and the other dark, they were both equally beautiful. But the fair twin loved him, and the dark twin hated him, so he chose the fair one. The dark twin would have prevented the marriage if she could, but she couldn't; however, on the night before it, much suspecting Captain Murderer, she stole out and climbed his garden wall, and looked in at his window through a chink in the shutter, and saw him having his teeth filed sharp. Next day she listened all day, and heard him make his joke about the house-lamb. And that day month, he had the paste rolled out, and cut the fair twin's head off, and chopped her in pieces, and peppered her, and salted her, and put her in the pie, and sent it to the baker's, and ate it all, and picked the bones.

Now, the dark twin had had her suspicions much increased by the filing of the Captain's teeth, and again by the house-lamb joke. Putting all things together when he gave out that her sister was dead, she divined the truth, and determined to be revenged. So, she went up to Captain Murderer's house, and knocked at the knocker and pulled at the bell, and when the Captain came to the door, said: "Dear Captain Murderer, marry me next, for I always loved you and was jealous of my sister." The Captain took it as a compliment, and made a polite answer, and the marriage was quickly arranged. On the night before it, the bride again climbed to his window, and again saw him having his teeth filed sharp. At this sight she laughed such a terrible laugh at the chink in the shutter, that the Captain's blood curdled, and he said: "I hope nothing has disagreed with me!" At that, she laughed again, a still more terrible laugh, and the shutter was opened and search made, but she was nimbly gone, and there was no one. Next day they went to church in a coach and twelve, and were married. And that day month, she rolled the piecrust out, and Captain Murderer cut her head off, and chopped her in pieces, and peppered her, and salted her, and put her in the pie, and sent it to the baker's, and ate it all, and picked the bones.

But before she began to roll out the paste she had taken a deadly poison of a most awful character, distilled from toads' eyes and spiders' knees; and Captain Murderer had hardly picked her last bone, when he began to swell, and to turn blue, and to be all over spots, and to scream. And he went on swelling and turning bluer, and being more all over spots and screaming, until he reached from floor to ceiling and from wall to wall; and then, at one o'clock in the morning, he blew up with a loud explosion. At the sound of it, all the milk-white horses in the stables broke their halters and went mad, and then they galloped over everybody in Captain Murderer's house (beginning with the family blacksmith who had filed his teeth) until the whole were dead, and then they galloped away.

Hundreds of times did I hear this legend of Captain Murderer, in my early youth, and added hundreds of times was there a mental compulsion upon me in bed, to peep in at his window as the dark twin peeped, and to revisit his horrible house, and look at him in his blue and spotty and screaming stage, as he reached from floor to ceiling and from wall to wall. The young woman who brought me acquainted with Captain Murderer had a fiendish enjoyment of my terrors, and used to begin, I remember—as a sort of introductory overture—by clawing the air with both hands, and uttering a long low hollow groan. So acutely did I suffer from this ceremony in combination with this infernal Captain, that I sometimes used to plead I thought I was hardly strong enough and old enough to hear the story again just yet. But, she never spared me one word of it, and indeed commended the awful chalice to my lips as the only preservative known to science against "The Black Cat"—a weird and glaring-eyed supernatural Tom, who was reputed to prowl about the world by night, sucking the breath of infancy, and who was endowed with a special thirst (as I was given to understand) for mine.

CONSIDER THIS

★ If our act of "remembering" is at least in part an act of *reconstruction* (rather than merely a matter of scanning a movie version of an old family photograph album), do you think it is possible that Dickens actually remembered all of those details?

★ Charles Lamb, the English writer, whose sister murdered their mother, once claimed that there is no point in trying to protect children from nocturnal fears; even if they don't hear frightening stories, they will still feel these fears, because—he argued—"the archetypes are within us."

   The poet W. H. Auden, a writer who was fascinated by this subject, agreed that "there are well authenticated cases of children being dangerously terrified by some fairy story. Often, however, this arises from the child having only heard the story once. Familiarity with the story by repetition turns the pain of fear into the pleasure of a fear faced and mastered." How find you, convincing or unconvincing?

Johnny Connors

The Man That Spelt KNIFE Was a Fool

Gypsies have always been misfits: they usually lead a nomadic life, living in horse-drawn wagons, outside the mainstream of society. Many of them have preserved at least some of their old Romany language. As a result, they are regarded with suspicion or contempt by many people: Hitler marked them for extermination during World War II; in England and Ireland, the police often give them a difficult time and order them to move on. Gypsy children rarely go to school for more than a few days a year.

Johnny Connors, an Irish gypsy, tells how he was desperate to learn to read and went to an evening class run by sympathetic nuns.

About four weeks had passed and I could write my name JOHN.

And nearly every minute during the day I would be saying, "ZABQAZXOUWZ. ACB792Y14MN2Q," and so on.

I would sing it all day, "ABCDEFG HIJKLMNO PQRST UVWXYZ."

Six weeks had passed and I could tell the time of the clock myself.

That was six weeks at night-school. Then the Nun asked me, would I like to go to a real classroom with little girls, because it was a girls' school. I said I would, so the next day for the first time in my life I was in a classroom. When the girls of the class saw me I could hear them whispering to one another, "He is a gyppo."

I was nearly mad. I shouted, "Ah, shut up your big mouths." I know it was wrong of me to treat young ladies that way, but they had started it.

After a while that day I got settled down to the class. And then I asked the teacher, "Could I go to the toilet?"

"Yes, John, go right ahead out to the yard."

I went into the toilet and I bolted one of the doors, and two girls came in.

It was a girls' toilet I was in.

"Hurry on, Mary, and pull your bloomers up when you leave."

I made a burst for the door and my trousers tripped me up. I ran out the gate of the school. As I was going out I met the Reverend Mother.

"What's wrong, John?" said the Reverend Mother.

"Those girls followed me into the toilet, the dirty things. They should be ashamed of themselves."

I could see a smile on the Reverend Mother's face.

"You go back to your class, John, and I will sort it all out."

I was ashamed of my life. Then it was playtime and the girls became to like me. I would skip with them, play ball with them. They became great pals of mine. The big bully girls were afraid of me, because when the big bully girls would bully the little girls I would stop them.

There was one big girl: I christened her, Young Elephant. She was a very fat girl and she would bump into the little girls and the little girls would fall flat on their faces. So one day she was bullying all the other little girls. "Hold on there, you overgrown young elephant, don't be pushing any of the little girls." So from that day onwards she never pushed any of the little girls, and if she tried to the little girls would say, "I will get John to call you more names."

I really enjoyed being at school. But the police and corporation gave my Daddy three days' notice and I had to leave school.

That night when I came back to the wagon, my Daddy said, "Johnny, tomorrow is your last day at school."

"What?" I said, "I am not going to stop going to school."

"Well, if you don't you will have to follow the wagons a very long road."

"Why?" I said.

"Because we are being shifted on Saturday."

I could not sleep that night, I was fed up.

The next morning I went to school, and I told the teacher that this was my last day at school. She was very upset.

"Why must you stop going to school, John?" said the teacher.

"Because we are getting shifted."

"Oh, I am sorry to hear that, John."

At playtime all the girls gathered round me, "Please don't leave, John." Some of them was crying.

That evening I was forced to say good luck to all.

I was a very happy little boy and I wanted to go to school and I would not be able to go to school. So I said to myself, "I will learn myself how to read proper." Every sweet-paper with writing on it I would collect them all day. Tea bags, sugar bags and butter wrappers. I would stay at shop windows reading everything that was in the windows. And big words like "Palmolive," I would split them up, Pal-mo-live. And "Corporation," Cor-por-ation. The only words that had me beat were medical words. "Physician" was a killer. I did really lose my temper with that word PHY-SICIAN. What really was making me angry was that words like PHYSICIAN, LAMB or KNIFE had silent letter words, and I would say to myself, the man that spelt KNIFE was a fool.

When I would be sent to the shops on errands, I would be hours reading everything in the shop. My Mammy often told me to get Lyons' tea. Instead I would get some other strange brand of tea so as I could read the strange words on the packet. Because I knew every word on the Lyons' tea packet.

The same way when my Daddy would send me for cigarettes. He would say to me, "Make sure you get Woodbines," and I would say, "Maybe they have no Woodbines, what kind will I get if they have no Woodbines?" My Daddy would say, "Get any kind." I would get the strangest packet of cigarettes the shop had in stock so as I could read the writing on the packet. And if I was beaten at a word, I would go back into the shop and ask the person in the shop what the word meant. There were times people got angry with me over me asking so many questions. And they would simply say, "Buzz off, you are a nuisance."

Sweets with strange wrappings was the sweets I liked very much, even if they

were horrible sweets. I don't think I ever enjoyed a sweet in them times, because I was not interested in the sweets, the wrapping was what I got more enjoyment out of. In other words, strange things were more helpful to me.

Also milestones, finger-posts, and most of all the rubbish-dumps were my teacher. When I would see a dump I would rather collect the old newspapers, comics and books out of the dump than go to the movies. Furthermore, I had been locked up on many occasions by the police and convicted for taking old books and papers and educational articles of my own choosing from dumps. So you could say I paid the hard way for the little bit of knowledge I have.

Johnny Connors *did* learn to read; and he also learned to write. As a result, he was able to write his life story and help us to understand a different way of life: to see it *from the inside*.

As a learner, did he make things difficult for himself?

ARTHUR HOPCRAFT

The First Book to Impress Me

Arthur Hopcraft, who writes plays for television, tells us of his first important book.

The first book to impress me was roughly twice the size of my chest. I was then, at a guess, aged five. It had stiff, shiny covers with needle-sharp corners, and contained pictorial horror-stories. They concerned small animals, and big animals, and they were parables whose message was that small creatures had to do as they were told, otherwise they got beaten or eaten or, at the very least, chased through dark woods whose trees were in league with the big creatures and tripped the small ones up as they ran or swiped them with branches from behind. This book frightened me, but I guarded it like treasure. After a while I stopped being afraid of all the episodes except for the one involving the chase. There was a special power in the drawing of the black roots and tendrils and the terror in the face of the animal/child running away. I ran in my dreams. Shapes, vague and faceless, converged on me. I would wake just as they were about to touch me.

CONSIDER THIS

★ Notice how "after a while I stopped being afraid of all the episodes": is this support for Auden's view (p. 12)?
★ "This book frightened me, but I guarded it like treasure." How do you explain this contradiction?

WINIFRED FOLEY

Poe's Murderers and Corpses Were Gathering in Our Kitchen

One day, Winifred Foley, who worked in a small village post office in the west of England, was listening to the radio when the announcer invited listeners to send in stories of their early years. Winifred, on impulse, sat down that evening and wrote some pages about her childhood. A few weeks later, she heard her own words on the radio, and her life was transformed: she went on to write her autobiography, from which we have chosen her account of how, as a child, she was "both repelled and fascinated" by Edgar Allan Poe's tales of mystery and imagination. Through reading, Foley entered another world, very different from the actual poverty-stricken life of her family home.

For once I had the house, the fire, and a book to read, all to myself!

I spread some newspapers on the table, tipped the contents of the kitchen drawer on to it, got the brickdust and rags from the back-kitchen, and gave our odd assortment of cutlery an enthusiastic, if not very thorough, rubbing over. I banked up the fire; lumps in the front, small at the back; then I stood up on a chair to reach down the book.

Very little printed matter that came into our house was censored from us, but obviously Dad had considered *Coffin Island and Other Stories* by Edgar Allan Poe, a little macabre for young readers. It had been printed like a thick magazine, with a lurid cover illustration of a skeleton hanging from a dead tree, near a church, on a moonlit night; and lurking in the shadows were weird, ghoulish creatures.

A bit scary, but nothing to worry about, with the lovely autumn sunshine streaming in through the window, and a cheerful fire to sit by. Not time to put the potatoes in the oven yet.

Feeling as lucky as a cat shut up in a dairy, I pulled my chair up to the fire, rested my feet on the steel fender, and plunged into my feast of horror.

Very soon I was both repelled and fascinated. I feared to go on reading, yet dared not stop. Even the dancing flames of the fire could bring no cheer to the black mood of every page, although they brought enough for my young eyes to read by. What kind of mind could the author of this horror have possessed? The warm entrails of a fresh-killed corpse could have been his inkwell.

Only when the flames began to flicker down, did I notice that the daylight had quietly gone. The window was no longer a frame for the sunlit garden and distant trees; it now framed the black mourning of the night.

Outside the reach of the fire the little room had grown dark. Fool, greedy fool! So anxious to settle down with my book, I had not had the forethought to bring the lamp in from the back-kitchen, or to put a spare bucket of coal by the hearth in

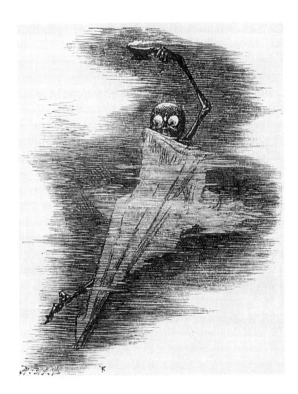

readiness for making up the fire. Nor had I fetched the potatoes from the box in the back-kitchen to go in the oven.

And now I couldn't! Not only Poe's murderers and corpses were gathering in our little dark back-kitchen, but all the witches and ogres from my own mind's store had joined them. They might even now be coming behind my chair, waiting to pounce; to put their claw-like talons round my throat.

Mam, Mam, hurry home Mam, before the flame from the fire dies down, and I am left in the black pit of darkness, and they can carry me away! If only Granny had not moved from next door, or the young couple who had taken the cottage had not gone out for the evening!

Somehow I must find the courage to lift the poker from the fender and break the last bits of black coal into more flames, but take care not to turn my head or take my eyes from the printed page to acknowledge "them," who I could now sense were in the darkening corners.

. . . our cottages were breeding grounds for cockroaches. Though, periodically, Mam attacked every crack and crevice with Keating's powder, Jeyes' fluid, and boiling soda water, she could not stay the infestation of these pests.

They never emerged in daylight, or by lamplight, and never came up to the bedrooms. But when the family were in bed, and all was dark, out they came, to forage up the walls, in the rag mats, and even across the clothes line on the ceiling. We children hated them, and would never come downstairs in the dark, unless Mam or Dad preceded us with a lighted candle. Mam made her wallpaper paste with a flour mix. Now as the cockroaches looked for sustenance, their movements made faint crackles behind the paper. Only, to me, it wasn't cockroaches; it was the stiff black cloaks of fearsome witches brushing against the wall.

All the time, the glow of the fire went down, down, until there was barely enough to read by. Concentrating on the printed page was less horrific than allowing my mind to dwell on the lurking horrors, crowding now right up round my chair. The draught from under the back-kitchen door came straight from graves freshly opened by fiendish vandals; I could almost smell the bodies.

Old Auntie's corpse had been laid out in the little narrow room adjoining. Now her spirit knew all about my wicked sins. Now she knew how I had crouched down on the mat by the fire, slyly waiting to steal the remainder of the sodden chewed crust from my little brother's hand, while he lay asleep on her lap. Now she knew that I had dipped my finger in her sugar basin. All my bad deeds came to the surface of my memory. Perhaps old Auntie didn't love me any more, now that immortality had opened her eyes to my sins.

I dared not raise my eyes, for old Auntie's ghost would not lurk behind the chair, or in the corner. No, she would come white and wraithlike, and scold me with a forbidding skeletal finger, to my face.

The fire was almost out. Only Mam could save me now, and it seemed that Mam would never come. Never? Wasn't that the creak of the garden gate? Wasn't that sound the sound of voices? The dear, familiar tones of Mam and the little ones? Yet not till Mam's hand closed on the doorknob to enter, did I find the courage to move.

Dispirited by the high price of boots, tired out, with aching arms and painful varicosed legs, hungry, her patience tried by the weary whimpering of the little ones, Mam's misery flared into righteous anger, as I scurried to light the lamp and fill the coal bucket.

The dead fire, the oven empty of the warm, roast potatoes she had used to encourage the little ones as they soldiered on through the woods, the selfish thoughtlessness of a daughter old enough to know better—all this should have got me the sort of hiding I deserved, if Mam had found the strength to give it me.

But she was almost in tears. "Whatever 'ave you bin doin'?" she wailed. Mam never read a book herself. Her own life was too full of conflicts and troubles, work and excitement. It was no use trying to explain.

BETTY SMITH

If I Were King

We all want more than one life, and before the arrival of movies and TV, the main way to enjoy the illusion of another life was through reading. Most ordinary families could not afford to buy books; hence, the immeasurable importance of public libraries, where readers could enter thousands of other lives through novels, autobiographies, biographies, and travel books.

Here in a passage from Betty Smith's (b. 1906) A Tree Grows in Brooklyn *we see Francie, who has set herself the task of moving through the library shelves in alphabetical order! Like Johnny Connors, Francie was a compulsive reader. She read everything she could find: trash, classics, timetables, and the grocer's price list. To read meant escape—from the dailiness of her city block, where the boys were forever fighting.*

A second story window flew open and a woman clutching a crepe-paperish kimono around her sprawling breasts, yelled out,

"Leave him alone and get off this block, you lousy bastards."

Francie's hands flew to cover her ears so that at confession she would not have to tell the priest that she had stood and listened to a bad word.

"We ain't doing nothing, Lady," said Neeley with that ingratiating smile which always won over his mother.

"You bet your life, you ain't. Not while I'm around." Then without changing her tone she called to her son, "And get upstairs here, you. I'll learn you to bother me when I'm taking a nap." The pretzel boy went upstairs and the gang ambled on.

"That lady's tough." The big boy jerked his head back at the window.

"Yeah," the others agreed.

"My old man's tough," offered a smaller boy.

"Who the hell cares?" inquired the big boy languidly.

"I was just saying," apologized the smaller boy.

"My old man ain't tough," said Neeley. The boys laughed.

They ambled along, stopping now and then to breathe deeply of the smell of Newtown Creek which flowed its narrow tormented way a few blocks up Grand Street.

"God, she stinks," commented the big boy.

"Yeah!" Neeley sounded deeply satisfied.

"I bet that's the worst stink in the world," bragged another boy.

"Yeah."

And Francie whispered yeah in agreement. She was proud of that smell. It let her know that nearby was a waterway, which, dirty though it was, joined a river that flowed out to the sea. To her, the stupendous stench suggested far-sailing ships and adventure, and she was pleased with the smell.

Just as the boys reached the lot in which there was a ragged diamond tramped out, a little yellow butterfly flew across the weeds. With man's instinct to capture anything running, flying, swimming or crawling, they gave chase, throwing their ragged caps at it in advance of their coming. Neeley caught it. The boys looked at it briefly, quickly lost interest in it and started up a four-man baseball game of their own devising.

They played furiously, cursing, sweating and punching each other. Every time a stumble bum passed and loitered for a moment, they clowned and showed off. There was a rumor that the Brooklyn's had a hundred scouts roaming the streets of a Saturday afternoon watching lot games and spotting promising players. And there wasn't a Brooklyn boy who wouldn't rather play on the Brooklyn's team than be president of the United States.

After a while, Francie got tired of watching them. She knew that they would play and fight and show off until it was time to drift home for supper. It was two o'clock. The librarian should be back from lunch by now. With pleasant anticipation, Francie walked back towards the library.

*   *   *

"When I get big," she thought, "I will have such a brown bowl and in hot August there will be nasturtiums in it."

She put her hand on the edge of the polished desk liking the way it felt. She looked at the neat row of freshly-sharpened pencils, the clean green square of blotter, the fat white jar of creamy paste, the precise stack of cards and the returned books waiting to be put back on the shelves. The remarkable pencil with the date slug above its point was by itself near the blotter's edge.

"Yes, when I get big and have my own home, no plush chairs and lace curtains for me. And *no* rubber plants. I'll have a desk like this in my parlor and white walls and a clean green blotter every Saturday night and a row of shining yellow pencils always sharpened for writing and a golden-brown bowl with a flower or some leaves or berries always in it and books . . . books . . . books. . . ."

She chose her book for Sunday; something by an author named Brown. Francie figured she had been reading on the Brown's for months. When she thought she was nearly finished, she noticed that the next shelf started up again with Browne. After that came Browning. She groaned, anxious to get into the C's where there was a book by Marie Corelli that she had peeped into and found thrilling. Would she *ever* get to that? Maybe she ought to read two books a day. Maybe. . . .

She stood at the desk a long time before the librarian deigned to attend to her.

"Yes?" inquired that lady pettishly.

"This book. I want it." Francie pushed the book forward opened at the back with the little card pushed out of the envelope. The librarians had trained the children to present the books that way. It saved them the trouble of opening several hundred books a day and pulling several hundred cards from as many envelopes.

She took the card, stamped it, pushed it down a slot in the desk. She stamped Francie's card and pushed it at her. Francie picked it up but she did not go away.

"Yes?" The librarian did not bother to look up.

"Could you recommend a good book for a girl?"

"How old?"

"She is eleven."

Each week Francie made the same request and each week the librarian asked the same question. A name on a card meant nothing to her and since she never looked up into a child's face, she never did get to know the little girl who took a book out every day and two on Saturday. A smile would have meant a lot to Francie and a friendly comment would have made her so happy. She loved the library and was anxious to worship the lady in charge. But the librarian had other things on her mind. She hated children anyhow.

Francie trembled in anticipation as the woman reached under the desk. She saw the title as the book came up: *If I Were King* by McCarthy. Wonderful! Last week it had been *Beverly of Graustark* and the same two weeks before that. She had had the

McCarthy book only twice. The librarian recommended these two books over and over again. Maybe they were the only ones she herself had read; maybe they were on a recommended list; maybe she had discovered that they were sure fire as far as eleven-year-old girls were concerned.

Francie held the books close and hurried home, resisting the temptation to sit on the first stoop she came to, to start reading.

Home at last and now it was the time she had been looking forward to all week: fire-escape-sitting time. She put a small rug on the fire-escape and got the pillow from her bed and propped it against the bars. Luckily there was ice in the icebox. She chipped off a small piece and put it in a glass of water. The pink-and-white peppermint wafers bought that morning were arranged in a little bowl, cracked, but of a pretty blue color. She arranged glass, bowl and book on the window sill and climbed out on the fire-escape. Once out there, she was living in a tree. No one upstairs, downstairs or across the way could see her. But she could look out through the leaves and see everything.

It was a sunny afternoon. A lazy warm wind carried a warm sea smell. The leaves of the tree made fugitive patterns on the white pillow-case. Nobody was in the yard and that was nice. Usually it was pre-empted by the boy whose father rented the store on the ground floor. The boy played an interminable game of graveyard. He dug miniature graves, put live captured caterpillars into little match boxes, buried them with informal ceremony and erected little pebble headstones over the tiny earth mounds. The whole game was accompanied by fake sobbings and heavings of his chest. But today the dismal boy was away visiting an aunt in Bensonhurst. To know that he was away was almost as good as getting a birthday present.

Francie breathed the warm air, watched the dancing leaf shadows, ate the candy and took sips of the cooled water in-between reading the book.

> If I were King, Love,
> Ah, if I were King. . . .

The story of François Villon was more wonderful each time she read it. Sometimes she worried for fear the book would be lost in the library and she'd never be able to read it again. She had once started copying the book in a two-cent notebook. She wanted to own a book so badly and she had thought the copying would do it. But the penciled sheets did not seem like nor smell like the library book so she had given it up, consoling herself with the vow that when she grew up, she would work hard, save money and buy every single book that she liked.

As she read, at peace with the world and happy as only a little girl could be with a fine book and a little bowl of candy, and all alone in the house, the leaf shadows shifted and the afternoon passed.

Francie groans at the prospect of forcing herself to read Browning; on the other hand, she can't wait to read Marie Corelli. What *difference* does it make to your reading of Francie's story, if you yourself have *no* idea of who exactly Robert Browning and Marie Corelli were? (Not to mention Villon!)

Surely, the text offers enough information to allow you to guess or infer that Francie doesn't want to read Browning, but will force herself to, whereas she is excited by the prospect of Corelli, since she had already peeped and found her book thrilling. Your contact with Betty Smith, in the 1980s, is much weaker than the contact Betty Smith's readers made with her when *A Tree Grows in Brooklyn* was first published in 1943. Then, many of her older readers would still *recognize* that Browning was a very popular poet before World War I, and that Marie Corelli was then a sensationally popular romantic novelist. The effect is similar to that of books entitled "Whatever Happened to. . . .?" which offer up-to-date information about the present lives of people who *used to be* famous. When your own children come to watch videotapes of your favorite movies or TV programs, again the effect will be similar: they will not recognize the actors, what their characters represent, and the situations. The passage of time has changed the patterns of recognition. If, now, we explained to you who Danielle Steel is, you would rightly think us crazy. But what will be needed in the year 1999, 2099, 2199 . . .?

François Villon (a fifteenth-century Parisian, whose romantic life story was very popular in the late nineteenth and early twentieth centuries) wrote some exciting love poems. His most famous line is, "Where are the snows of yesteryear?" which can be translated as meaning "Who on earth is the Lone Ranger?" or "Where are you now, Batman?"

Reading is unlike talking or listening in matters of *reference*. When we talk with people we know, we *recognize* almost all of their references, because we are living in the same time and place. And, if we don't recognize a reference, we can always ask: who exactly is Batman?

In reading, however, the situation is very different: we can say that every writer writes for a reader who *will* recognize all the references—this reader is the writer's *ideal* or *implied* reader. But anyone else will not necessarily recognize all of the references. When younger readers have this experience, it sometimes makes them feel ignorant or inadequate or frustrated. If you know what we are talking about, take heart from the fact that *everyone* has this experience, however much they have read, however long they have been reading. In general, by the time you reach a reference you don't recognize, you will have gathered enough from the text to be able to make a reasonable guess, surmise, or inference. We advise you very strongly *not to break off your first reading* to go in search of a reference book: complete your first reading *with as few interruptions as possible*. When you have got the drift of the whole passage, section, or chapter, *then* you can stop reading and check on references that you're not sure about.

CONSIDER THIS

★ It seems that Betty Smith, in this passage from *A Tree Grows in Brooklyn*, is setting up a contrast between the boys, with their baseball and butterfly hunt, their gregarious tribal life, and the solitary Francie, the girl-reader. But the picture is made less obvious, more complicated, by the dismal boy engaged in strange funeral games. Is he, also, like Francie, exercising his imagination? Or is he just pretending, trying to fool himself? The word *fake* seems to suggest as much: "The whole game was accompanied by fake sobbings and heavings of his chest." Are we supposed to infer that the boy is "weird" because his emotions are not genuine?

LILLIAN HELLMAN

In the Fig Tree I Learned to Read

Francie sat on the fire escape when she needed to be alone, undisturbed; Lillian Hellman sat in a fig tree. For much of her childhood, Hellman (1905–1984) was shuttled between two worlds, New Orleans and New York, while her father tried to earn a living. An only child, she lived in fear and confusion among grown-ups—parents, grandparents, aunts, and uncles. It was in those early years that she found an outlet: in reading she discovered that she could be alone, and not *lonely. In this passage from* An Unfinished Woman *Hellman reassuringly admits that before we know our way around books and can choose those that are likely to be right for us, much of our early experience of reading is very confusing, full of false starts and frustrations: "bewildered by almost all of what I read, sweating in the attempt to understand a world of adults I fled from in real life but desperately wanted to join in books."*

There was a heavy fig tree on the lawn where the house turned the corner into the side street, and to the front and sides of the fig tree were three live oaks that hid the fig from my aunts' boardinghouse. I suppose I was eight or nine before I discovered the pleasures of the fig tree, and although I have lived in many houses since then, including a few I made for myself, I still think of it as my first and most beloved home.

I learned early, in our strange life of living half in New York and half in New Orleans, that I made my New Orleans teachers uncomfortable because I was too far ahead of my schoolmates, and my New York teachers irritable because I was too far behind. But in New Orleans, I found a solution: I skipped school at least once a week and often twice, knowing that nobody cared or would report my absence. On those days I would set out for school done up in polished strapped shoes and a prim hat against what was known as "the climate," carrying my books and a little basket filled with delicious stuff my Aunt Jenny and Carrie, the cook, had made for my school lunch. I would round the corner of the side street, move on toward St. Charles Avenue, and sit on a bench as if I were waiting for a streetcar until the boarders and the neighbors had gone to work or settled down for the post-breakfast rest that all Southern ladies thought necessary. Then I would run back to the fig tree, dodging in and out of bushes to make sure the house had no dangers for me. The fig tree was heavy, solid, comfortable, and I had, through time, convinced myself that it wanted me, missed me when I was absent, and approved all the rigging I had done for the happy days I spent in its arms: I had made a sling to hold the school books, a pulley rope for my lunch basket, a hole for the bottle of afternoon cream-soda pop, a fishing pole and a smelly little bag of elderly bait, a pillow embroidered with a picture of Henry Clay on a horse that I had stolen from Mrs. Stillman, one of my aunts' boarders, and a proper nail to hold my dress and shoes to keep them neat for the return to the house.

It was in that tree that I learned to read, filled with the passions that can only come to the bookish, grasping, very young, bewildered by almost all of what I read, sweating in the attempt to understand a world of adults I fled from in real life but desperately wanted to join in books. (I did not connect the grown men and women in literature with the grown men and women I saw around me. They were, to me, another species.)

It was in the fig tree that I learned that anything alive in water was of enormous excitement to me. True, the water was gutter water and the fishing could hardly be called that: sometimes the things that swam in New Orleans gutters were not pretty, but I didn't know what was pretty and I liked them all. After lunch—the men boarders returned for a large lunch and a siesta—the street would be safe again, with only the noise from Carrie and her helpers in the kitchen, and they could be counted on never to move past the back porch, or the chicken coop. Then I would come down from my tree to sit on the side street gutter with my pole and bait. Often I would catch a crab that had wandered in from the Gulf, more often I would catch my favorite, the crayfish, and sometimes I would, in that safe hour, have at least six of them for my basket. Then, about 2:30, when house and street would stir again, I would go back to my tree for another few hours of reading or dozing or having what I called the ill hour. It is too long ago for me to know why I thought the hour "ill," but certainly I did not mean sick. I think I meant an intimation of sadness, a first recognition that there was so much to understand that one might never find one's way and the first signs, perhaps, that for a nature like mine, the way would not be easy. I cannot be sure that I felt all that then, although I can be sure that it was in the fig tree, a few years later, that I was first puzzled by the conflict which would haunt me, harm me, and benefit me the rest of my life: simply, the stubborn, relentless, driving desire to be alone as it came into conflict with the desire not to be alone when I wanted not to be. I already guessed that other people wouldn't allow that, although, as an only child, I pretended for the rest of my life that they would and must allow it to me.

"I cannot be sure that I felt all that then." If you ever choose to write about your own early years, you can opt for fiction or for autobiography: if you choose autobiography, as Hellman does, then you will soon find yourself admitting "I cannot be sure. . . ." If your attempts are overwhelmed by too much uncertainty (which would irritate you and any reader of your text!), you can do as Betty Smith did, and transform your life story into fiction and admit as much: look, I've written a novel or a short story!

In any event, the dividing line between such fiction and autobiography is a blurred and shifting one. Fiction will give you more freedom and detachment, and will save you from having to admit "I cannot be sure . . ." Autobiography, on the other hand, will give you the pleasure of rendering your version of what actually happened as vividly and accurately as possible, even if you have to invent some of it!

EUDORA WELTY

Did You Have Our Wonder World?

Winifred Foley had to wait until her family went out before she had peace and quiet for reading; Betty Smith's Francie escaped to a fire escape, Lillian Hellman to a fig tree; Eudora Welty was probably the luckiest: "any room in our house, at any time of day, was there to read in, or to be read to." She was born in 1909, in Jackson, Mississippi, and still lives there in the house the family moved into when she was sixteen.

Her father taught her to "read" the sky in order to forecast the weather; little did he know that he was helping her prepare herself to use weather effectively in her fiction. For her brothers, there were model trains, signs of technological progress. It was her mother who led her into reading fiction; and when she started to write she brought her meteorological sensibility and the inner life of fiction together: "Commotion in the weather and the inner feelings aroused by such a hovering disturbance emerged connected in dramatic form."

In time, a barometer was added to our dining room wall; but we didn't really need it. My father had the country boy's accurate knowledge of the weather and its skies. He went out and stood on our front steps first thing in the morning and took a look at it and a sniff. He was a pretty good weather prophet.

"Well, I'm *not*," my mother would say with enormous self-satisfaction.

He told us children what to do if we were lost in a strange country. "Look for where the sky is brightest along the horizon," he said. "That reflects the nearest river. Strike out for a river and you will find habitation." Eventualities were much on his mind. In his care for us children he cautioned us to take measures against such things as being struck by lightning. He drew us all away from the windows during the severe electrical storms that are common where we live. My mother stood apart, scoffing at caution as a character failing. "Why, I always loved a storm! High winds never bothered me in West Virginia! Just listen at that! I wasn't a bit afraid of a little lightning and thunder! I'd go out on the mountain and spread my arms wide and *run* in a good big storm!"

So I developed a strong meteorological sensibility. In years ahead when I wrote stories, atmosphere took its influential role from the start. Commotion in the weather and the inner feelings aroused by such a hovering disturbance emerged connected in dramatic form. (I tried a tornado first, in a story called "The Winds.")*

* See page 60.

From our earliest Christmas times, Santa Claus brought us toys that instruct boys and girls (separately) how to build things—stone blocks cut to the castle-building style, Tinker Toys, and Erector sets. Daddy made for us himself elaborate kites that needed to be taken miles out of town to a pasture long enough (and my father was not afraid of horses and cows watching) for him to run with and get up on a long cord to which my mother held the spindle, and then we children were given it to hold, tugging like something alive at our hands. They were beautiful, sound, shapely box kites, smelling delicately of office glue for their entire short lives. And of course, as soon as the boys attained anywhere near the right age, there was an electric train, the engine with its pea-sized working headlight, its line of cars, tracks equipped with switches, semaphores, its station, its bridges, and its tunnel, which blocked off all other traffic in the upstairs hall. Even from downstairs, and through the cries of excited children, the elegant rush and click of the train could be heard through the ceiling, running around and around its figure eight.

All of this, but especially the train, represents my father's fondest beliefs—in progress, in the future. With these gifts, he was preparing his children.

And so was my mother with her different gifts.

I learned from the age of two or three that any room in our house, at any time of day, was there to read in, or to be read to. My mother read to me. She'd read to me in the big bedroom in the mornings, when we were in her rocker together, which ticked in rhythm as we rocked, as though we had a cricket accompanying the story. She'd read to me in the diningroom on winter afternoons in front of the coal fire, with our cuckoo clock ending the story with "Cuckoo," and at night when I'd got in my own bed. I must have given her no peace. Sometimes she read to me in the kitchen while she sat churning, and the churning sobbed along with *any* story. It was my ambition to have her read to me while *I* churned; once she granted my wish, but she read off my story before I brought her butter. She was an expressive reader. When she was reading "Puss in Boots," for instance, it was impossible not to know that she distrusted *all* cats.

It had been startling and disappointing to me to find out that story books had been written by *people*, that books were not natural wonders, coming up of themselves like grass. Yet regardless of where they came from, I cannot remember a time when I was not in love with them—with the books themselves, cover and binding and the paper they were printed on, with their smell and their weight and with their possession in my arms, captured and carried off to myself. Still illiterate, I was ready for them, committed to all the reading I could give them.

Neither of my parents had come from homes that could afford to buy many books, but though it must have been something of a strain on his salary, as the youngest officer in a young insurance company, my father was all the while carefully selecting and ordering away for what he and Mother thought we children should grow up with. They bought first for the future.

Besides the bookcase in the livingroom, which was always called "the library," there were the encyclopedia tables and dictionary stand under windows in our diningroom. Here to help us grow up arguing around the dining room table were the Unabridged Webster, the Columbia Encyclopedia, Compton's Pictured Encyclopedia, the Lincoln Library of Information, and later the Book of Knowledge. And the year we moved into our new house, there was room to celebrate it with the new 1925 edition of the Britannica, which my father, his face always deliberately turned toward the future, was of course disposed to think better than any previous edition.

In "the library," inside the mission-style bookcase with its three diamond-latticed glass doors, with my father's Morris chair and the glass-shaded lamp on its table beside it, were books I could soon begin on—and I did, reading them all alike and as they came, straight down their rows, top shelf to bottom. There was the set of Stoddard's Lectures, in all its late nineteenth-century vocabulary and vignettes of peasant life and quaint beliefs and customs, with matching halftone illustrations: Vesuvius erupting, Venice by moonlight, gypsies glimpsed by their campfires. I didn't know then the clue they were to my father's longing to see the rest of the world. I read straight through his other love-from-afar: the Victrola Book of the Opera, with opera after opera in synopsis, with portraits in costume of Melba, Caruso, Galli-Curci, and Geraldine Farrar, some of whose voices we could listen to on our Red Seal records.

My mother read secondarily for information; she sank as a hedonist into novels. She read Dickens in the spirit in which she would have eloped with him. The novels of her girlhood that had stayed on in her imagination, besides those of Dickens and Scott and Robert Louis Stevenson, were *Jane Eyre, Trilby, The Woman in White, Green Mansions, King Solomon's Mines*. Marie Corelli's name would crop up but I understood she had gone out of favor with my mother, who had only kept *Ardath* out of loyalty. In time she absorbed herself in Galsworthy, Edith Wharton, above all in Thomas Mann of the *Joseph* volumes.

St. Elmo was not in our house; I saw it often in other houses. This wildly popular Southern novel is where all the Edna Earles in our population started coming from. They're all named for the heroine, who succeeded in bringing a dissolute, sinning roué and atheist of a lover (St. Elmo) to his knees. My mother was able to forgo it. But she remembered the classic advice given to rose growers on how to water their bushes long enough: "Take a chair and *St. Elmo*."

To both my parents I owe my early acquaintance with a beloved Mark Twain. There was a full set of Mark Twain and a short set of Ring Lardner in our bookcase, and those were the volumes that in time united us all, parents and children.

Reading everything that stood before me was how I came upon a worn old book without a back that had belonged to my father as a child. It was called *Sanford and Merton*. Is there anyone left who recognizes it, I wonder? It is the famous moral tale written by Thomas Day in the 1780s, but of him no mention is made on the title page of *this* book; here it is *Sanford and Merton in Words of One Syllable* by Mary Godolphin. Here are the rich boy and the poor boy and Mr. Barlow, their teacher and interlocutor, in long discourses alternating with dramatic scenes—danger and rescue allotted to the rich and the poor respectively. It may have only words of one syllable, but one of them is "quoth." It ends with not one but two morals, both engraved on rings: "Do what you ought, come what may," and "If we would be great, we must first learn to be good."

This book was lacking its front cover, the back held on by strips of pasted paper, now turned golden, in several layers, and the pages stained, flecked, and tattered around the edges; its garish illustrations had come unattached but were preserved, laid in. I had the feeling even in my heedless childhood that this was the only book my father as a little boy had had of his own. He had held onto it, and might have gone to sleep on its coverless face: he had lost his mother when he was seven. My father had never made any mention to his own children of the book, but he had brought it along with him from Ohio to our house and shelved it in our bookcase.

My mother had brought from West Virginia that set of Dickens; those books looked sad, too—they had been through fire and water before I was born, she told me, and there they were, lined up—as I later realized, waiting for *me*.

I was presented, from as early as I can remember, with books of my own, which appeared on my birthday and Christmas morning. Indeed, my parents could not give me books enough. They must have sacrificed to give me on my sixth or seventh birthday—it was after I became a reader for myself—the ten-volume set of Our Wonder World. These were beautifully made, heavy books I would lie down with on the floor in front of the diningroom hearth, and more often than the rest volume 5, *Every Child's Story Book*, was under my eyes. There were the fairy tales—Grimm, Andersen, the English, the French, "Ali Baba and the Forty Thieves"; and there was Aesop and Reynard the Fox; there were the myths and legends, Robin Hood, King Arthur, and St. George and the Dragon, even the history of Joan of Arc; a whack of *Pilgrim's Progress* and a long piece of *Gulliver*. They all carried their classic illustrations. I located myself in these pages and could go straight to the stories and pictures I loved; very often "The Yellow Dwarf" was first choice, with Walter Crane's Yellow Dwarf in full color making his terrifying appearance flanked by turkeys. Now that volume is as worn and backless and hanging apart as my father's poor *Sandford and Merton*. The precious page with Edward Lear's "Jumblies" on it has been in danger of slipping out for all these years. One measure of my love for Our Wonder World was that for a long time I wondered if I would go through fire and water for it as my mother had done for Charles Dickens; and the only comfort was to think I could ask my mother to do it for me.

I believe I'm the only child I know of who grew up with this treasure in the house. I used to ask others, "Did you have Our Wonder World?" I'd have to tell them The Book of Knowledge could not hold a candle to it.

I live in gratitude to my parents for initiating me—and as early as I begged for it, without keeping me waiting—into knowledge of the word, into reading and spelling, by way of the alphabet. They taught it to me at home in time for me to begin to read before starting to school. I believe the alphabet is no longer considered an essential piece of equipment for traveling through life. In my day it was the keystone to knowledge. You learned the alphabet as you learned to count to ten, as you learned "Now I lay me" and the Lord's Prayer and your father's and mother's name and address and telephone number, all in case you were lost.

My love for the alphabet, which endures, grew out of reciting it but, before that, out of seeing the letters on the page. In my own story books, before I could read them for myself, I fell in love with various winding, enchanted-looking initials drawn by Walter Crane at the heads of fairy tales. In "Once upon a time," an "O" had a rabbit running it as a treadmill, his feet upon flowers. When the day came, years later, for me to see the Book of Kells, all the wizardry of letter, initial, and word swept over me a thousand times over, and the illumination, the gold, seemed a part of the word's beauty and holiness that had been there from the start.

We grow up in a little world of family and home; and this is what we come to think of as *natural*. Eudora Welty was startled to discover that story books—which felt, like everything else at home, *natural*—"were not natural wonders, coming up of themselves like grass." So she experienced the first glimmerings of a deep difference: there is nature, and there is *culture*. If skies, clouds, rainstorms, winds, sunrise and sunset are part of the *natural* world, what, then, is *culture*?

In the words of the celebrated psychologist Jerome Bruner, "Culture is passed on as the child learns to see the world as the adult does." But since we are not clones of our parents, and since circumstances change—technology, the economy, the international situation, the environment, health, institutions—we both learn from our parents' culture, beginning to replicate it, and also modify it. At times of crisis, as in the 1960s, one generation may deliberately invent a counterculture, to promote values directly opposed to those of the elders.

The most important element of human culture—the foundation and the medium—is language. As we in turn sustain the language of our parents, so we internalize their values. Eudora Welty herself recognizes this, as she acknowledges the deep influences of both mother and father, and realizes, as she "looks back," that "those were the volumes that in time united us all, parents and children."

Note again, in Welty's text, the question of recognition that we discussed when reading Betty Smith's references to Browning, Corelli, and Villon. Welty's mother had read Dickens, passionately, Scott, Stevenson, Charlotte Brontë, and many more. Marie Corelli also puts in an appearance, and when your eyes encountered her name again, you *recognized*.

One of the crucial features of reading is that it involves the use of two kinds of knowledge: one is the visual information on the page and the second is all the nonvisual information that *you* bring inside your mind to the act of reading. Now that you have already met the name "Marie Corelli," it becomes part of what *you* bring to the texts you read.

YOUR WRITING(S) FOR OTHERS TO READ

It has been said that there can be no action without reaction: whenever we are aroused or animated by something we have read, the best outlets for our energies are probably (a) to talk about what has enlivened us, and so share it with others; (b) to write *our own text*, has in some way been "provoked," released, suggested, or nudged into existence by what we have read.

Here now are a few suggestions for ways in which you may feel disposed to write as a result of reading Chapter 1.

1. An informal account of your own early interactions with language, using information provided by your parents, grandparents, uncles, and aunts.
2. A commentary on words or phrases whose sound(s) give you particular or special pleasure.
3. A brief memoir of your own early experiences of reading and of being read to. (Again, you may need to draw information from your parents and so on.)
4. An account of your experience of a particular story, film, or TV program that scared you in childhood.
5. An account of how you yourself first became aware of some of the distinctions between nature and culture.

Chapter Two
Possessed by Words

Without being taught by anyone else, we build up a resourceful competence. One glance at a page, and we may know whether or not a book is "right" for us. And when it is, we learn to perform amazingly complicated tricks with our minds. It is as if the book takes hold of—possesses—us, so that it feels as if *we* are inventing the text! Not only can we guess the likely meanings of words we never met before, but we can predict with remarkable confidence what is probably going to happen on the next page; we can form a reasonable idea of what may well happen in the next chapter; we can even offer ourselves a forecast of what the weather will be like on the book's last page—sunny for us, for we *are* the hero(ine), and gloomy for all the villains, if indeed they will still be alive to tell the tale.

And when we are not in the mood for a real book, we can dig out the comics, the technicolor pages of derring-do, romance, of astro-exploration, of weird aliens—and coast hair-raisingly through all manner of alternative worlds, even beyond the bounds of space!

Thus, without knowing it, we develop our notions of what constitutes courage, daring, enterprise, cool nerve, and many other parts of the repertoire of human possibility. As for the inhuman "baddies," they are driven out to outer space and splattered with a laser. But they will be back tomorrow to fight another day.

SHERWOOD ANDERSON

I Had Thought I Understood How a Murder Could Happen

In Sherwood Anderson's (1876–1941) autobiography, we learn how two boys, he and his brother, were intensely aroused by Cooper's novel The Last of the Mohicans *(1826), in which the French settlers and the native Americans (Indians) do battle. Anderson's phrase for reading is "cramming ourselves with"—a very different experience from being crammed with undigestible or alien "food" by someone in authority.*

    In this episode, the young Anderson takes on the role of the white "leather-stocking" scout, Natty Bumppo, whom the English call Hawkeye (a name later borrowed by "M·A·S·H"), and whom the French know as "La Longue Carabine,"* while his brother is the Delaware Indian Uncas, "Le Cerf Agile,"† son of the great and wise chief, Chingachgook. Their enemy is a neighboring boy whom they dislike, and he, without his knowledge, becomes "Le Renard Subtil" (The Cunning Fox), a "dirty Huron."

    In Cooper's novel, as in history, the plight of the Indians is a tragic one; they are "scattered, like herds of broken deer." Their only consolation is a vision of a life-after-death in the "happy hunting-ground." Anderson and his brother turn the world of their childhood, their bit of this world, into a happy "hunting-ground," by acting out or performing their fantasy, which they derive from Cooper's novel, translating the fiction into action, and their lives into romantic adventure. It is a consolation for the fact that they know they were born too late: if only they had been born a few generations earlier, when their local landscape—a rather shabby little village—had been a part of "God's wilderness"!

One of the boys in the bed has had a fight with the son of a neighbor. He, the third son of the family, has taken a hatchet out of the neighbor boy's hands. We had been cramming ourselves with the contents of a book, "The Last of the Mohicans," and the neighbor boy, whose father is the town shoemaker, had the hatchet given him as a Christmas present. He would not lend it, would not let it go out of his hands and so my brother, the determined one, has snatched it away.

    The struggle took place in a little grove of trees half a mile from the house. "Le Renard Subtil," cries my brother jerking the hatchet out of the neighbor boy's hand. The neighbor boy did not want to be the villain—"Le Renard Subtil."

    And so he went crying off toward his home, on the farther side of the field. He lived in a yellow house just beyond our own and near the end of the street at the edge of the town.

    My brother now had possession of the hatchet and paid no more attention to him but I went to stand by a fence to watch him go.

    It is because I am a white man and understand the whites better than he. I am Hawkeye the scout, "La Longue Carabine," and as I stand by the fence *la longue*

---

* The long or large carbine.

† Quick-footed deer.

carabine is lying across the crook of my arm. It is represented by a stick. "I could pick him off from here, shall I do it?" I ask, speaking to my brother with whom I fight viciously every night after we have got into bed but who, during the day, is my sworn comrade in arms.

Uncas—"Le Cerf Agile"—pays no attention to my words and I rest the stick over the fence, half determined to pick off the neighbor boy but at the last withholding my fire. "He is a little pig, never to let a fellow take his hatchet. Uncas was right to snatch it out of his hand."

As I withhold my fire and the boy goes unscathed and crying across the snow-covered field I feel very magnanimous—since at any moment I could have dropped him like a deer in flight. And then I see him go crying into his mother's house. Uncas has, in fact, cuffed him a couple of times in the face. But was it not justified? "Dare a dirty Huron—a squaw man—dare such a one question the authority of a Delaware? Ugh!"

And now "Le Renard Subtil" has gone into his mother's house and has blabbed on us, and I tell Uncas the news but, with the impenetrable stoicism of a true savage, he pays no attention. He is as one sitting by the council fire. Are words to be wasted on a dog of a Huron?

And now "Le Cerf Agile" has an idea. Drawing a line in the snow, he stands some fifty feet from the largest of the trees in the grove and hurls the hatchet through the air.

What a determined fellow! I am of the paleface race myself and shall always depend for my execution upon *la longue carabine* but Uncas is of another breed. Is there not painted on his breast a crawling tortoise? In ink I have traced it there myself from a drawing he has made.

During the short winter afternoon the hatchet will be thrown not once but a hundred, perhaps two hundred, times. It whirls through the air. The thing is to throw the hatchet so that, at the end of its flight, the blade goes, just so, firmly into the soft bark of the tree. And it must enter the bark of the tree at just a particular spot.

The matter is of infinite importance. Has not Uncas, "The Last of the Mohicans," broad shoulders? He will later be a strong man. Now is the time to acquire infinite skill.

He has measured carefully the spot on the body of the tree where the blade of the hatchet must enter with a soft chug, deep into the yielding bark. There is a tall warrior, a hated Huron, standing by the tree and young Uncas has measured carefully so that he knows just where the top of the warrior's head should come. An idea has come to him. He will just scalp the unsuspecting warrior with the blade of the tomahawk; and has not he, Uncas, crept for many weary miles through the forest, going without food, eating snow for his drink? A skulking Huron has dared creep into the hunting grounds of the Delawares and has learned the winter abiding place of our tribe. Dare we let him go back to his squaw-loving people, bearing such knowledge? Uncas will show him!

He, Uncas, is absorbed in the problem before him and has not deigned to look off across the fields to where the neighbor boy has gone crying to his mother. "Le Renard Subtil" will be heard from again but for the present is forgotten. The foot must be advanced just so. The arm must be drawn back just so. When one hurls the hatchet the body must be swung forward just so. An absolute silence must be maintained. The skulking Huron who has dared come into our hunting grounds is unaware of the presence of the young Uncas. Is he, Uncas, not one whose feet leave no traces in the morning dew?

Deep within the breasts of my brother and myself there is a resentment that we were born out of our time. By what a narrow margin in the scroll of time have we missed the great adventure! Two, three, at the most a dozen generations earlier and we might so well have been born in the virgin forest itself. On the very ground where we now stand Indians have indeed stalked one another in the forest, and how often Uncas and myself have discussed the matter. As for our father, we dismiss him half contemptuously. He is born to be a dandy of the cities and has turned out to be a village house-painter, in the dwelling places of the paleface. The devil!— with luck he might have turned out to be an actor, or a writer or some such scum of earth but never could he have been a warrior. Why had not our mother, who might have been such a splendid Indian princess, the daughter of a great chief, why had she also not been born a few generations earlier? She had just the silent stoicism needed for the wife of a great warrior. A deep injustice had been done us, and something of the feeling of that injustice was in the stern face of Uncas as he crept each time to the line he had marked out in the snow and sent the hatchet hurtling through the air.

The two boys, filled with scorn of their parentage, on the father's side, are in a little grove of trees at the edge of an Ohio town. In later days the father—also born out of his place and time—will come to mean more to them but now he has little except their contempt. Now Uncas is determined—absorbed—and I, who have so little of his persistence, am impressed by his silent determination. It makes me a little uncomfortable for, since he has snatched the hatchet out of the neighbor boy's hand, saying, "Go on home, crybaby," no word has passed his lips. There is but a small grunting sound when the hatchet is hurled and a scowl on his face when it misses the mark.

And "Le Renard Subtil" has gone home and blabbed to his mother, who in turn has thrown a shawl over her head and has gone to our house, no doubt to blab, in her turn, to our mother. "La Longue Carabine," being a paleface, is a little intent on disturbing the aim of "Le Cerf Agile." "We'll catch hell," he says, looking at the hatchet thrower who has not so far unbent from the natural dignity of the Indian as to reply. He grunts and taking his place solemnly at the line poises his body. There is the quick abrupt swing forward of the body. What a shame Uncas did not later become a professional baseball player. He might have made his mark in the world. The hatchet sings through the air. Well, it has struck sideways. The Huron is injured but not fatally, and Uncas goes and sets him upright again. He has marked the place where the Huron warrior's head should be by pressing a ball of snow into the wrinkled bark of the tree and has indicated the dog's body by a dead branch.

And so Hawkeye the scout—"La Longue Carabine"—has gone creeping off among the trees to see if there are any more Hurons lurking about and has come upon a great buck, pawing the snow and feeding on dry grass at the edge of a small creek. Up goes *la longue carabine* and the buck pitches forward, dead, on the ice. Hawkeye runs forward and swiftly passes his hunting knife across the neck of the buck. It will not do to build a fire now that there are Hurons lurking in the hunting ground of the Delawares so Uncas and he must feed upon raw meat. Well, the hunter's life for the hunter! What must be must be! Hawkeye cuts several great steaks from the carcass of the buck and makes his way slowly and cautiously back to Uncas. As he approaches he three times imitates the call of a catbird and an answering call comes from the lips of "Le Cerf Agile."

"Aha! the night is coming on," Uncas now says, having at last laid the Huron low. "Now that the dirty lover of squaws is dead we may build a fire and feast. Cook the venison ere the night falls. When darkness has come we must show no fire. Do not make much smoke—big fires for the paleface, but little fires for us Indians."

Uncas stands for a moment, gnawing the bone of the buck, and then of a sudden becomes still and alert. "Aha! I thought so," he says, and goes back again to where he has drawn the mark in the snow. "Go," he says; "see how many come."

And now Hawkeye must creep through the thick forests, climb mountains, leap canyons. Word has come that "Le Renard Subtil" only feigned when he went off crying, across the field—fools that we were! While we have been in the forest he has crept into the very teepee of our people and has stolen the princess, the mother of Uncas. And now "Le Renard Subtil," with subtle daring, drags the stoical princess right across the path of her warrior son. In one moment from a great height Hawkeye draws the faithful Deer Killer to his shoulder and fires, and at the same moment the tomahawk of Uncas sinks itself in the skull of the Huron dog.

" 'Le Renard Subtil' had drunk firewater and was reckless," says Uncas, as the two boys go homeward in the dusk.

The older of the two boys now homeward bound is somewhat afraid but Uncas is filled with pride. As they go homeward in the gathering darkness and come to the house, where lives "Le Renard Subtil," to which he has gone crying but a few hours before, an idea comes to him. Uncas creeps in the darkness, halfway between the house and the picket fence in front and, balancing the hatchet in his hand, hurls it proudly. Well for the neighbor's family that no one came to the door at that moment for Uncas' long afternoon of practicing has got results. The hatchet flies through the air and sinks itself fairly and deeply into the door panel as Uncas and Hawkeye run away home.

And now they are in the bed and the mother is rubbing the warm grease into their chapped hands. Her own hands are rough, but how gentle they are! She is thinking of her sons, of the one already gone out into the world and most of all at the moment of Uncas.

There is something direct brutal and fine in the nature of Uncas. It is not quite an accident that in our games he is always the Indian while I am the despised white, the paleface. It is permitted me to heal my misfortune a little by being, not a storekeeper or a fur trader but that man nearest the Indian's nature of all the palefaces who ever lived on our continent, "La Longue Carabine"; but I cannot be an Indian and least of all an Indian of the tribe of the Delawares. I am not persistent patient and determined enough. As for Uncas, one may coax and wheedle him along any road and I am always clinging to that slight sense of leadership that my additional fifteen months of living gives me, by coaxing and wheedling, but one may not drive Uncas. To attempt driving him is but to arouse a stubbornness and obstinacy that is limitless. Having told a lie to mother or father, he will stick to the lie to the death while I—well, perhaps there is in me something of the doglike, the squaw man, the paleface, the very spirit of "Le Renard Subtil"—if the bitter truth must be told. In all my after years I shall have to struggle against a tendency toward slickness and plausibility in myself. I am the tale-teller, the man who sits by the fire waiting for listeners, the man whose life must be led in the world of his fancies, I am the one destined to follow the little, crooked words of men's speech through the uncharted paths of the forests of fancy. What my father should have been I am to become. Through long years of the baffling uncertainty, that only such men as myself can ever know, I am to creep with trembling steps forward in a strange land, following the little words, striving to learn all the ways of the ever-changing words, the smooth-lying little words, the hard, jagged, cutting words, the round, melodious, healing words. All the words I am in the end to come to know a little and to attempt to use for my purpose have, at the same time, the power in them both to heal and to destroy. How often am I to be made sick by words, how often am I to be healed by words, before I can come at all near to man's estate!

And so as I lie in the bed putting out my chapped hands to the healing touch of mother's hands I do not look at her. Already I am often too conscious of my own inner thoughts to look directly at people and now, although I am not the one who has cuffed the neighbor boy and jerked the hatchet out of his hands, I am nevertheless busily at work borrowing the troubles of Uncas. I cannot let what is to be be, but must push forward striving to change all by the power of words. I dare not thrust my words forward in the presence of mother, but they are busily getting themselves said inside myself.

There is a consciousness of Uncas also within me. Another curse that is to lie heavily on me all through my life has its grip on me. I am not one to be satisfied to act for myself, think for myself, feel for myself but I must also attempt to think and feel for Uncas.

At the moment slick plausible excuses for what has happened during the afternoon are rising to my lips, struggling for expression. I am not satisfied with being myself and letting things take their course, but must be inside the very body of Uncas, striving to fill his stout young body with the questioning soul of myself.

As I write this I am remembering that my father, like myself, could never be singly himself but must always be playing some rôle, everlastingly strutting on the stage of life in some part not his own. Was there a rôle of his own to be played? That I do not know and I fancy he never knew, but I remember that he once took it into his head to enact the rôle of the stern and unyielding parent to Uncas and what came of it.

The tragic little comedy took place in the woodshed back of one of the innumerable houses to which we were always moving when some absurd landlord took it into his head that he should have some rent for the house we occupied, and Uncas had just beaten with his fists a neighbor boy who had tried to run away with a baseball bat belonging to us. Uncas had retrieved the bat and had brought it proudly home, and father, who happened along the street at that moment, had got the notion fixed in his mind that the bat belonged, not to us, but to the neighbor boy. Uncas tried to explain, but father, having taken up the rôle of the just man, must needs play it out to the bitter end. He demanded that Uncas return the bat into the hands of the boy from whom he had just ravaged it and Uncas, growing white and silent, ran home and hid himself in the woodshed where father quickly found him out.

"I won't," declared Uncas; "the bat's ours"; and then father—fool that he was for ever allowing himself to get into such an undignified position—began to beat him with a switch he had cut from a tree at the front of the house. As the beating did no good and Uncas only took it unmoved, father, as always happened with him, lost his head.

And so there was the boy, white with the sense of the injustice being done, and no doubt father also began to feel that he had put his foot into a trap. He grew furious and, picking up a large stick of wood from a woodpile in the shed, threatened to hit Uncas with it.

What a moment! I had run to the back of the shed and had thrown myself on the ground where I could look through a crack and as long as I live I shall never forget the next few moments—with the man and the boy, both white, looking at each other; and, that night, in the bed later, when mother was rubbing my chapped hands and when I knew there was something to be settled between her and Uncas, that picture danced like a crazy ghost in my fancy.

I trembled at the thought of what might happen, at the thought of what had happened that day in the shed.

Father had stood—I shall never know how long—with the heavy stick upraised, looking into the eyes of his son, and the son had stared, with a fixed determined stare, back into the eyes of his father.

At the moment I had thought that—boy as I was—I understood how such a strange unaccountable thing as a murder could happen. Thoughts did not form themselves definitely in my mind but after that moment I knew that it is always the weak, frightened by their own weakness, who kill the strong, and perhaps I also knew myself for one of the weak ones of the world. At the moment, as father stood with the stick upraised, glaring at Uncas, my own sympathies (if my own fancy has not tricked me again) were with father. My heart ached for him.

He was saved by mother. She came to the door of the shed and stood looking at him and his eyes wavered, and then he threw the stick back upon the pile from which he had taken it and went silently away. I remembered that he tramped off to Main Street and that, later in the evening when he came back to the house, he was drunk and went drunken to bed. The trick of drunkenness had saved him from the ordeal of looking into the eyes of Uncas or of mother, as so often words have later saved me from meeting fairly some absurd position into which I have got myself.

And so there was I now, in the bed and up to one of father's tricks: upstart that I was, dog of a Huron myself, I was trembling for mother and for Uncas—two people very well able to take care of themselves.

Mother dropped my hand and took the outstretched hand of my brother.

"What happened?" she asked.

And Uncas told her, fairly and squarely. "He was a cry-baby and a big calf and

I walloped him one. I wanted the hatchet and so I took it—that's what I did. I banged him one on the nose and jerked it out of his hand."

Mother laughed—a queer unmirthful little laugh. It was the kind of laugh that hurts. There was irony in it and that got to Uncas at once. "It doesn't take much of a fellow to snatch a hatchet out of the hands of a cry-baby," she said.

That was all. She kept on rubbing his hands and now it was my eyes, and not the eyes of Uncas, that could look directly into our mother's eyes.

Perhaps it was in that moment, and not in the moment when I lay on the ground peaking through the crack into the shed, that the first dim traces of understanding of all such fellows as father and myself came to me. I looked at mother with adoration in my own eyes, and when she had taken the kerosene lamp and had gone away, and when we boys were all again curled quietly like sleeping puppies in the bed, I cried a little, as I am sure father must have cried sometimes when there was no one about. Perhaps his getting drunk, as he did on all possible occasions, was a way of crying too.

And I cried also, I suppose, because in Uncas and mother there was a kind of directness and simplicity that father and all fellows, who like myself are of the same breed with him, can never quite achieve.

What is so odd about Anderson's narrative? Is it that the narrator switches without warning from the fantasy-romance world of Cooper's adventure back to the ordinary world in which children blab to their mothers, and mothers complain to their neighbors? And then switches back again, so fast, that as we read we have to move quickly to keep up with all these odd transitions? One of the most incongruous is surely "What a shame Uncas [fiction] did not later become a professional baseball player" [actual world]!

The crucial shift in our reading of Anderson's story presumably comes as we "move into" the mother's mind, and see the boys as her sons, rather than as they see themselves, that is, as adventurous, fantasizing boys or as romantic heroes in a better time. And then the text switches back again, and we see "Uncas" through his older brother's eyes. So Anderson reaches his reflections on himself, not as he was when a boy, but as he is now, a professional writer: "I am the tale-teller . . ." following "the uncharted paths of the forests of fancy." So the *actual* trees of Anderson's backyard became the romantic forests of early America, and now become a metaphor for the mind where fiction is made. And Anderson switches, again unpredictably, between the thoughts of his mind then, to his present reflections, and back again to the ideas, hopes, and fears of his childhood. And, like Lillian Hellman in the fig tree, he knew that he was "over the hill" even as his mother rubbed his boyish hands. He had discovered *self-consciousness*, had begun to monitor his own thoughts and feelings, and had become a *spectator* even when he seemed to be a *participant*. There was no going back to the "innocence" of childhood: words were "busily getting themselves said inside" himself, the words, for example, that he would soon have to say to his mother and her neighbor to explain exactly what he had been playing at. So he has learned not only to reexamine, scrutinize, and interpret his past experience, but also to anticipate and rehearse the future moment that inescapably approaches: "slick plausible excuses" rise to his lips, words that if properly controlled can get him out of trouble.

Even in boyhood, Anderson had begun to "read" his father, to read him critically and sympathetically, as someone who had missed the road, lost his way, failed to match up to his possibilities. And now, as an adult, reconstructing those long-ago moments, he knows how weak his father was, but he also knows that his "own fancy" could have "tricked him again," and that he could have misinterpreted those past experiences. Anderson finally recognizes that he has lost—if ever he had it—a state of "simplicity," which is another name for "innocence," otherwise known as the "Garden of Eden."

The next text, "Ghost Stories," by Fiona Pitt-Kethley (b. 1954), *may* disappoint you. On the other hand, it may give you a pleasant surprise. It all depends on your expectations, and on how you react to something that doesn't quite match them.

FIONA PITT-KETHLEY

Ghost Stories

'Don't peep or the Bogey Man will get you!'
my great grandmother'd say as she held kids
under her shawl, but I looked in vain from
my mother's cardigan and no-one came.

At school, I told others ghost stories—
but could feel no frisson of fear myself—   5   frisson: thrill

James, Poe, Le Fanu, with added horrors.
'Have you heard the one' I'd start over lunch
'about the rotting nun?'

There were two odd handles in the front rooms   10
of our Victorian house. One was painted
pale grey like the Study's walls, the other—
brass-plated wearing thin. 'Some sort of bell
to call servants in the old days.'

When I was on my own I'd take a breath   15
and slowly move one of the handles up,
imagine *them*, turning the knob softly,
opening the door and coming in.

I'd visualise a pair—maid and butler
perhaps, in black going a little green,   20
their hair and eyebrows white, aged farcically
beyond old age, like the oldest members
of dynasties in epic film sagas.

Then, I'd put the handle back down again   25
and make them go away.

❦

What an interesting surprise to discover that, over lunch at school, the "I" of this text trotted out all the old clichés of horror stories, but, when alone, entered into a quite different kind of fantasy, in which she recreated a sense of how it might have been, in that same house, a few generations earlier.

The nice twist is that she engages in a piece of social and historical reconstruction and then builds into it the awesome fantasy that those two servants never died: look, here they come now! How incredibly old they are as they stagger in!

COLETTE

Literature

While the boys are enacting their fantasies of the Lone Ranger, Uncas, and Davy Crockett and blazing paths of glory, what kinds of fantasies are the girls living, as a result of their reading? What are they reading? The French writer Colette (Sidonie Gabrielle Claudine, 1873–1954) provides an answer in the following story, written in a form she called "Dialogue for One Voice."

"Godmother?"

"   "

"What are you doing, Godmother? A story for the papers? Is it a sad story?"

"   . . . ?"

"Because you look so unhappy!"

"   . . .   "

"Ah, it's because you're late? It's like a composition: you have to turn in your work on the day they tell you to? . . . What would they say if you turned in your notebook without anything in it?"

"   . . . ?"

"The men who judge it at the paper!"

"   . . .   "

"They wouldn't pay you? That's so boring. It's the same thing for me; but Mama only gives me two sous for each composition. She says I'm mercenary. Well, work hard. Can I see your page? That's all you have? You'll never be ready!"

"   . . . !"

"What! you don't have a subject? Don't they give you an outline, like us at school, for French composition? That way at least you have a chance!"

"   . . .   "

"What I'd like is for Mademoiselle to let us write whatever comes into our heads. Oh boy, if I was a writer!"

"   . . . ?"

"What would I do? I'd write a hundred thousand million things, and stories for children."

"   . . .   "

"I *know* there's lots of them; but they're enough to make you sick of being a child. How many more am I going to get as presents? You know, too many people take us for idiots! When I see in a catalogue: 'For Young Readers,' I say to myself, 'Well, that's just great! more grownups knocking themselves out to come down to our level, as they say!' I don't know why grownups use a special tone to come down to our level. Do we children get to write books for grownups?"

"   . . .   "

"That's fair, isn't it? I'm for what's fair. For example, I want a book for teaching you things to be a book for teaching you things, and a book for fun, I want it to be fun. I don't want them mixed up. For years, you saw, in children's books, a car drive up, and there was always a man in the story to pass along to you his opinion about the progress of machines . . . Now you're sure to see a dashing aviator descend from the sky, but he talks about the conquest of the air . . . and of the . . . the glorious dead who lead the way. You see, there are constantly things breaking in on the story in children's books, things that smell of a grownup giving a lesson. It's no use for Papa to repeat, 'A child must understand everything he reads . . .' I think that's grotexque . . ."

"   . . .   "

"Grotesque? Are you sure? Grotexque is prettier."

"   . . . ?"

"I think it's grotexque because grownups never seem to remember about when they were little. I think things that I don't understand everything about are terrific. I like beautiful words that sound pretty, words you don't use in talking. I never ask what they mean, because I would rather think about them and look at them until they make me a little scared. And I like books without pictures too."

" . . . ?"

"Yes, you see, Godmother, when they say, for example, in the history book I'm reading, 'There once was a beautiful young girl in a castle, on the edge of a lake . . .' I turn the page, and I see a drawing of the castle, and the young girl and the lake. Oh brother!"

" . . . ?"

"I can't really explain, but it never, never looks like my young girl, or my castle or my lake . . . I can't put it in words. If I knew how to paint . . . That's why I prefer your books, your yellow books without any pictures. You understand me, Godmother?"

" . . . "

"You say 'yes' but I'm not sure . . . And also, they don't talk enough about love in books for children."

" . . . !"

"What did I say now? Is love a bad word?"

" . . . "

"On top of that, I don't know what it is! I'm very much in love."

" . . . ?"

"Nobody. I know I'm only ten and that it would be ridiculous to be in love with somebody, at my age. But I am in love, that's all, just like that. I'm waiting. That's why I like love stories so much, terrifying stories, but that end happy."

" . . . "

"Because with stories that end sad, you go on feeling sad afterward, you're not hungry, you think about it for a long time, and when you look at the book's cover, you say to yourself, 'They just go on being unhappy in there . . .' You think about what you could do to make things right, you imagine writing the next story where everything would work out . . . I like it so much when people get married!"

" . . . ?"

"Yes, but only after they've been very unhappy before, each in his own way. It isn't that I like it, all the unhappiness, but it's necessary."

" . . . ?"

"For there to be a beginning, middle, and an end. And also because love, the way I see it, is being very sad at first, and then very happy after."

" . . . "

"No, no, not at all, it's not often the opposite! Who's asking you that? Don't bother me with your grown-up opinions! And now try to write a beautiful story in your newspaper, a story for *me*, not for children. A story where people cry and adore each other and get married . . . And put words I like in it, too, yes, like 'foment,' 'surreptitious,' and 'pro rata' and 'corroborate' and 'premonitory' . . . And then when you start a new paragraph you'll say, 'At this juncture . . .' "

" . . . ?"

"I don't know exactly what it means, but I think it makes it very elegant."

Here, we find one of the most powerful myths of girlhood and womanhood: that women *wait*. They wait to fall in love and, eventually, to get married. That is what women *do*. Men fight enemies out in the world. Men conquer mountains. Men brave the wilderness. But women wait. The god-daughter/narrator in this one-sided dialogue is ready—at ten. She shuns books with morals (books that "teach you things" about cars and aviators—nonfiction in the guise of fiction?). She wants *real* fictions: books that give her the plot of unhappiness first (unhappiness is not only necessary but desired!) and then, at last, after the couple have suffered, grant them happiness in the form of *marriage*.

CONSIDER THIS

★ Where do you suppose the ten-year-old acquired her ideas about womens' roles, love, and marriage? What books might she have already read at ten? What had you read at ten? What other myths about reading and *gender* do you recognize in the story?

★ How long did it take you to catch on to what Colette is doing in this "dialogue"? How long did it take you to fill in the gaps?

SIMONE DE BEAUVOIR

Through the Eyes of Men

Gender differences, from the forms of our bodies to the ways we dream, work, play, make love, raise children, and read books, are the subject of Simone de Beauvoir's classic of the women's movement, The Second Sex. *De Beauvoir (1908–1986) reads her sex, in history, politics, economics, and biology. Do little girls read differently than little boys? Of course they do: they read themselves as they are expected to be, in a world where the accepted hierarchy places them beneath, below, subordinate to men.*

Everything helps to confirm this hierarchy in the eyes of the little girl. The historical and literary culture to which she belongs, the songs and legends with which she is lulled to sleep, are one long exaltation of man. It was men who built up Greece, the Roman Empire, France, and all other nations, who have explored the world and invented the tools for its exploitation, who have governed it, who have filled it with sculptures, paintings, works of literature. Children's books, mythology, stories, tales, all reflect the myths born of the pride and the desires of men; thus it is that through the eyes of men the little girl discovers the world and reads therein her destiny.

The superiority of the male is, indeed, overwhelming: Perseus, Hercules, David, Achilles, Lancelot, the old French warriors Du Guesclin and Bayard, Napoleon— so many men for one Joan of Arc; and behind her one descries the great male figure of the archangel Michael! Nothing could be more tiresome than the biographies of famous women: they are but pallid figures compared with great men; and most of them bask in the glory of some masculine hero. Eve was not created for her own sake but as a companion for Adam, and she was made from his rib. There are few women in the Bible of really high renown: Ruth did no more than find herself a husband. Esther obtained favor for the Jews by kneeling before Ahasuerus, but she was only a docile tool in the hands of Mordecai; Judith was more audacious, but she was subservient to the priests, and her exploit, of dubious aftertaste, is by no means to be compared with the clean, brilliant triumph of young David. The goddesses of pagan mythology are frivolous or capricious, and they all tremble before Jupiter. While Prometheus magnificently steals fire from the sun, Pandora opens her box of evils upon the world.

There are in legend and story, to be sure, witches and hags who wield fearful powers. Among others, the figure of the Mother of the Winds in Andersen's *Garden of Paradise* recalls the primitive Great Goddess: her four gigantic sons obey her in fear and trembling, she beats them and shuts them up in sacks when they misbehave. But these are not attractive personages. More pleasing are the fairies, sirens, and undines, and these are outside male domination; but their existence is dubious, hardly individualized; they intervene in human affairs but have no destiny of their own: from the day when Andersen's little siren becomes a woman, she knows the yoke of love, and suffering becomes her lot.

In modern tales as in ancient legends man is the privileged hero. Mme de Ségur's books are a curious exception: they describe a matriarchal society where the husband, when he is not absent, plays a ridiculous part; but commonly the figure of the father, as in the real world, is haloed with glory. The feminine dramas of *Little Women* unfold under the ægis of a father deified by absence. In novels of adventure it is the boys who take a trip around the world, who travel as sailors on ships, who live in the jungle on breadfruit. All important events take place through the agency of men. Reality confirms what these novels and legends say. If the young girl reads the papers, if she listens to the conversation of grownups, she learns that today, as always, men run the world. The political leaders, generals, explorers, musicians, and painters whom she admires are men; certainly it is men who arouse enthusiasm in her heart.

De Beauvoir offers here not just a woman's *opinion:* what she offers is history. Hard facts about the historical and literary culture. This is the way things are: histories in the dominant culture are, primarily, about "men who built up Greece, the Roman Empire. . ." They are *not* about what the *women* did while the men built up Greece and the Roman Empire.

CONSIDER THIS

★ Pull out your histories—try to combat de Beauvoir's facts with facts. How many other Joan of Arc's do you find in the history books? And how many of them "bask in the glory of some masculine hero"? What, in fact, constitutes a *heroine*? Male characteristics? Or female characteristics? And how do you distinguish one from the other?

★ How *are* women portrayed in the literary culture? Can you think of other Biblical figures than the ones de Beauvoir mentions? How are they represented in the Bible? How are they to be *read* as role models? Do you think that men and women are raised, from childhood, to *read* the world differently? How so?

FRANK SMITH

How We Comprehend

Even while we are still small children, we have begun to construct a "theory of the world," which we carry with us in our minds. Some of the most important parts of this theory are binary categories: asleep/awake, hungry/full, hard/soft, permitted/forbidden, dark/light, past/future, heavy/light, here/there, near/distant, nice/nasty, liquid/solid, dog/cat, horse/cow, town/country. Others categories are things we drink out of, liquids to drink, liquids to drink first thing in the morning, liquids to drink when sick, liquids drunk only by grown-ups, and so on.

Our theory of the world also includes an increasingly effective sense of the relationships between categories: if you look again at the categories above, you will see that some are social or moral categories, others are categories of physical properties. Here, now, Frank Smith explains how these relationships are the crucial part of our ways of understanding and our ways of learning.

[Here is] a provisional definition of comprehension: relating what we attend to in the world around us—the visual information of print in the case of reading—to what we already have in our heads. And here is a provisional definition of learning: modifying what we already have in our heads as a consequence of attending to the world around us. We learn to read, and we learn through reading, by adding to what we know already. If we are to develop and make use of these two provisional definitions, and go on to discuss reading in a meaningful way, then we must first consider what it is that "we already have in our heads."

I have employed two quite different terms to refer to the knowledge that we carry around all the time. I spoke in the first chapter about "nonvisual information," the knowledge we have stored behind the eyes that enables the brain to make sense of the visual information that comes through the eyes while reading. And in the last

IT'S THE MIRACLE BOOK!

- It will help you be a better you!
- You will lose 30 pounds in 30 days!
- You will buy real estate with no money down!
- You will win friends and influence people!
- Contains lots of gossip!
- Contains tons of historical facts!
- You will be able to closely identify with every single character!
- You will experience every emotion known to mankind!

YOU NEED NEVER BUY ANOTHER BOOK AGAIN FOR THE REST OF YOUR LIFE !!!

R. Chast

chapter I talked about long-term memory, our permanent source of information about the world. These are not two distinct parts or aspects of the brain. The nonvisual information that we depend on to understand written language (like the "nonacoustic information" that we need to understand speech) must be long-term memory, our only source of prior knowledge about language and the world. In more general contexts this source of prior knowledge is also referred to by psychologists by a third term—*cognitive structure*. This is a particularly apt term since "cognitive" means knowledge and "structure" implies an organization, and that indeed is what we have in our heads, an organization of knowledge.

Certainly it would be simplistic to suggest that what we carry around in our heads is just "memories." The brain is not an audiovisual souvenir album filled with an assortment of snapshots and tape recordings of bits of the past. At the very least we would have to say that the brain contains memories-with-a-meaning; our memories are related to everything else that we know. Cognitive structure is much more like a summary of our past experience. I do not want to remember that on 16 July I sat on a chair, and that on 17 July I sat on a chair, and on 18 July I sat on a chair. I want to remember that chairs are for sitting on, a summary of my experience. We remember specific events only when they are exceptions to our summary rules or when they have some particularly dramatic or powerful or emotional significance. And even then our memories, when we "recall" them, turn out to be highly colored by our present intentions and perspectives about the world (Bartlett, 1932). Specific memories that cannot be related to our summary, to our present general understanding, will make little sense, which may be the reason we can recall so little of our childhood.

But it would also be an oversimplification to suggest that our heads are filled with an accumulation of facts and rules. The brain is not like a library or encyclopedia where useful information and procedures are filed away under appropriate headings for possible future reference. And certainly the human brain is not like a bank in which nuggets of instruction are deposited by our teachers and our textbooks. Instead, the system of knowledge in our heads is organized into an intricate and internally consistent working model of the world, built up through our interactions with the world and integrated into a coherent whole. We know far more than we were ever taught.

THE THEORY OF THE WORLD IN OUR HEADS

What we have in our heads is a *theory* of what the world is like, a theory that is the basis of all our perceptions and understanding of the world, the root of all learning, the source of all hopes and fears, motives and expectancies, reasoning and creativity. And this theory is all we have. If we can make sense of the world at all, it is by interpreting our interactions with the world in the light of our theory. The theory is our shield against bewilderment.

As I look around my world, I distinguish a multiplicity of meaningful objects that have all kinds of complicated relations to each other and to me. But neither these objects nor their interrelations are self-evident. A chair does not announce itself to me as a chair; I have to recognize it as such. Chairs are a part of my theory. I recognize a chair when my brain decides that a chair is what I am looking at. A chair does not tell me that I can sit on it, or put my coat or books or feet on it, or stand on it to reach a high shelf, or wedge it against a door that I do not wish to be opened. All this is also part of my theory. I can only make sense of the world in terms of what I know already. All of the order and complexity that I perceive in the world around me must reflect an order and complexity in my own mind. Anything I cannot relate to the theory of the world in my head will not make sense to me. I shall be bewildered.

The fact that bewilderment is an unusual state for most of us despite the complexity of our lives is a clear indication that our theory of the world in the head is very efficient. The reason we are usually not aware of the theory is that it works so well. Just as a fish takes water for granted until deprived of it, so we become aware of our dependence on the theory in our head only when it proves inadequate, and the world fails to make sense. That we can occasionally be bewildered only serves to demonstrate how efficiently our theory usually functions. When were you last bewildered by something that you heard or read? Our theory of the world seems ready even to make sense of almost everything we are likely to experience in spoken and written language—a powerful theory indeed.

And yet, when was the last time you saw a bewildered baby? Infants have theories of the world too, not as complex as those of adults, but then children have not had as much time to make their theories complex. But children's theories seem to work very well for their needs. Even the smallest children seem able most of the time to make sense of their world in their own terms; they rarely appear confused or uncertain. The first time many children run into a situation that they cannot possibly relate to anything they know already is when they arrive at school, a time when they may be consistently bewildered, or if they are confronted with events that make no sense. We often deny children credit for knowing very much. But, in fact, most of our knowledge of the world—of the kind of objects it contains and the way they can be related—and most of our knowledge of language, is in our heads before we arrive at school. At five or six the framework is there, and the rest is mainly a matter of filling in the details.

For the remainder of this chapter I shall talk a little more about how this theory in the head is organized, and then discuss how it is used so that we can comprehend the world. . . .

. . . it would appear that learning is considered to come before comprehension in school—children must learn in order to understand. But I want to show that learning is more a result of comprehension than its cause. When we eventually get to considering reading in detail I intend to argue that, for a child, learning to read is literally a matter of "understanding reading."

But to do all this I must first explain the nature of comprehension, which will require a short discussion of the way in which our theory of the world is organized, and some detailed consideration of how we put that theory to use.

THE STRUCTURE OF KNOWLEDGE

The system of knowledge that is the theory of the world in our heads has a structure just like any other theory or system of organizing information, such as a library. Information systems have three basic components—a set of categories, some rules for specifying membership of the categories, and a network of interrelations among the categories—and I shall briefly examine each component in turn.

Categories

To categorize means to treat some objects or events as the same, yet as different from other objects or events. All human beings categorize, instinctively, starting at birth. There is nothing remarkable about this innate propensity to categorize, since living organisms could not survive if they did not in fact treat some objects or events as the same, yet as different from the other objects and events.

No living organism could survive if it treated everything in its experience as the same; there would be no basis for differentiation and therefore no basis for learning. There would be no possibility of being systematic. Just as a librarian cannot treat all books as the same when putting them on the shelves, so all human beings must differentiate throughout their lives. In our culture at least, everyone is expected to be able to distinguish dogs from cats, tables from chairs, and the letter *A* from the letter *B*.

But similarly, no living organism could survive if it treated everything in its experience as different. If there is no basis for similarity there is still no basis for learning. Thus the librarian must treat some books as the same in some senses—so that all chemistry books are stacked in the same area—even though these books may differ in size, color, and author's name. In the same way everyone, in our culture at least, is expected to ignore many differences in order to treat all dogs as the same, all cats as the same, and many different shapes like A, **A**, $\mathscr{A}$, *a*, **a**, a as the letter "a".

In other words, the basis of survival and of learning is the ability to ignore many potential differences so that certain objects* will be treated as the same, yet as different from other objects. All objects that belong to one category are treated as the same, yet as different from objects belonging to other categories.

The categories that we all observe, which are part of our theories of the world, are visually quite arbitrary; they are not generally imposed on us by the world itself. The world does not force us to categorize animals into dogs and cats and so forth— we could divide them up in other ways, for example treating all green-eyed animals as the same, in contrast to those with other eye colors, or differentiating those over fifteen inches in height from those under fifteen inches. The librarian could very nearly organize books on the basis of the color of their covers, or their size, or the number of pages. But we cannot usually invent categories for ourselves—hence the qualification "in our culture at least" in previous paragraphs. The reason we divide animals on a cat and dog basis and not on the basis of size or eye color is that the categories we have are part of our culture. In part, to share a culture means to share the same categorical basis for organizing experience. Language reflects the way a culture organizes experience, which is why many of the words in our language are a clue to the categories in our shared theories of the world. We have the words "dog" and "cat" but not a word for animals with green eyes or less than fifteen inches in height. When we have to learn new categories, the existence of a name in the language tends often to be the first clue that a category exists.

Not that words are essential prerequisites for the establishment of categories. Quite the reverse—categories can exist for which we have no names. I can easily distinguish certain mottled brown and grey birds that come to my garden every morning, but I do not know a name for them. To know a name without an understanding of the category that it labels is meaningless. In fact, the existence of a category is a prerequisite for learning how to use words, since words label categories rather than specific objects. What we call a dog is any individual animal that we put in the category with the name "dog."

The category system that is part of our theory of the world in our heads is essential for making sense of the world. Anything we do that we cannot relate to a category will not make sense; we shall be bewildered. Our categories, in other words, are the basis of our perception of the world. As I have explained, perception

---

* From this point on, I shall refrain from the cumbersome practice of talking all the time about "objects or events." But every reference to "objects" applies in general to "events" as well.

can be regarded as a decision-making process. The brain "sees" what it decides it is looking at, which means the category to which visual information is allocated. If I see a chair in front of me, then I must have a category for chairs in my theory of the world and have decided that what I am looking at is an example of that category. If I can see the word *cat* when I read, then I must have a category for that word quite independent of my knowledge of its name or possible meanings, just as I must have categories for the letters *c*, *a*, and *t* if I can distinguish those in the word. Interestingly, we cannot see things in more than one category at a time; it is not possible to see the letters "c", "a", and "t" *and* the word "cat" simultaneously in the visual information *cat*, which is one reason why children may find learning to read more difficult if they have to concentrate on the individual letters in words. Usually you only see what you are looking for, and you are quite unaware of other possible meanings or interpretations. If I ask you to read the address 410 LION STREET you will probably not notice that the numerals 10 in 410 are exactly the same visual information as the letters IO in LION. When you look for the category of numbers you see numbers and when you look for the category of letters you see letters. Even now that you are aware of what I am doing, you cannot look at 10 and see both letters and numbers simultaneously, any more than you can see the faces and the vase simultaneously in Figure A. The brain can only make decisions about one category at a time when processing the same visual information (although we could see the faces and vase simultaneously if they did not have a common contour). Unless there is one category to which incoming information can be related, the brain can make no decision at all; the world will not make sense. The brain, like every other executive, needs categories in order to make decisions.

Rules for Category Membership

But categories in themselves are not enough. The category "chemistry books" is useless if a librarian has no way of recognizing a chemistry book when confronted by one, just as a child can make no use of the information that there are cats and dogs in the world without some notion of how to distinguish one from the other. A child who can recite the alphabet has established a set of 26 categories but may not be able to recognize a single letter. For every category that we employ there must be at least one way of recognizing members of that category. Every category must have at least one set of rules, a specification, that determines whether an object (or an event) belongs in that category. Sometimes a single category may have more than one set of rules—we can distinguish an object as an onion by its appearance, feel, smell, and taste. We can recognize the letter "a" in a number of different guises. But just as we must have a category for every object we can distinguish in the world, so we must have at least one set of rules—called *distinctive features*—for allocating that object to the particular category. These are not usually rules that we can put into words, any more than we can open a window into our minds and inspect the categories we have there. Knowledge of this kind is called *implicit*—we only know we have the categories or the rules by the fact that we can make use of them.

The question of what constitutes the rules that differentiate the various categories that we employ in reading and language generally will demand a good deal of

Figure A

attention in later chapters—especially when we see that "teaching" is often little more than telling children that a category exists, leaving them to discover for themselves what the rules are.

Category Interrelations

Rules permit the categories in a system to be used, but they do not ensure that the system makes sense. A library does not make sense simply because all the chemistry books are stacked together in one place and all the poetry books in another. What makes a library a system is the way in which the various categories are related to each other, and this is the way the system in our brains makes sense as well.

I cannot attempt to list all the different interrelations among the categories in the theory of the world in our heads. To do so would be to attempt to document the complexity of the world as we perceive it. As I said when I discussed the content of our minds from the point of view of memory, everything that we know is directly or indirectly related to everything else, and any attempt to illustrate these relationships risks becoming interminable.

For example, consider again an onion. We know what that particular object is called—in more than one language perhaps—and also the names of several kinds of onion. All these are relations of the particular object to language. We also know what an onion looks, feels, smells, and tastes like, again perhaps in more than one way. We know where an onion comes from—how it is grown—and we probably have a good idea about how it gets to the place where we know we can buy one. We know roughly what we have to pay to buy one. We know how an onion can be used in cooking, and probably its other uses as well. We may know half-a-dozen different ways of cooking onions (with different names), and we certainly know a number of things that can be eaten with onions. We know a number of instruments for dealing with onions—knives, graters, and blenders, for example. We not only know what we can do with onions, we also know what onions can do to us, both raw and cooked. We know people who love onions and people who hate them; people who can cook them and people who cannot. We may even know something about the role of onions in history. One enormous ramification of our knowledge of onions is related to the fact that we can call them by more than one name. An onion can also be called a vegetable, which means that everything we know about vegetables in general, applies to onions in particular. Indeed, every time we relate an onion to something else—to a knife, a frying pan, or a particular person—then we discover that what we know about onions is part of what we know about knives, frying pans, and people. There is no end.

Many interrelations are part of the system of language that is such an important part of our theory of the world. One complex set of interrelations is called *syntax*, which is the way elements of language are related to each other. Another set of interrelations is called *semantics*, which is the way language is related to the rest of our theory of the world. Both of these important topics will be considered in the next chapter, which will be devoted to language and in particular to language comprehension.

But just as our knowledge of language is based on our knowledge of the world, so our ability to comprehend language is based on our ability to comprehend the world. The final section of the present chapter will illustrate how we use our theory of the world to comprehend the world.

PREDICTION AND COMPREHENSION

Cognitive structure, the theory of the world in our heads, may so far have seemed rather a static place, not much different in essence from an encyclopedia. But the theory of the world in our heads is *dynamic*, and not just in the sense that it is constantly being added to and changed, particularly during that lively period of intense learning and growth we call childhood. Time and change are an essential part of the way we perceive the world—how otherwise could we understand language, music, or even a football match?—and also of the way we operate upon the world. Our skills are the part of our theory of the world that enables us to interact with the world, to take the initiative in our transactions with our environment. And every skill involves delicate temporal organization. Our theory of the world is indeed dynamic.

Besides, we can do even more with the theory in our heads than make sense of the world and interact with it. We can live in the theory of the world itself. Within this theory we can exercise our imagination to invent and create, to test the possible solutions to problems and examine the consequences of possible behaviors. We can explore new worlds of our own and can be led into other worlds by writers and artists. But the aspect of imagination with which we shall be most concerned is more mundane, though at first encounter it may sound quite exotic. We can use the theory of the world in our heads *to predict the future*. This ability to predict is both pervasive and profound, because it is the basis of our comprehension of the world.

The Pervasiveness of Prediction

Everyone predicts—including children—all the time. Our lives would be impossible, we would be reluctant even to leave our beds in the morning, if we had no expectation about what the day will bring. We would never go through a door if we had no idea of what might be on the other side. And all our expectations, our predictions, can be derived from only one source, the theory of the world in our heads.

We are generally unaware of our constant state of anticipation for the simple reason once again that our theory of the world works so well. Our theory is so efficient that when our predictions fail, we are surprised. We do not go through life predicting that anything might happen—indeed, that would be contrary to prediction, and in that case nothing could surprise us. The fact that something always could rhinoceros take us by surprise—like the word *rhinoceros* a few words ago—is evidence that indeed we always predict but that our predictions are usually accurate. It is always possible that we could be surprised, yet our predictions are usually so appropriate that surprise is a very rare occurrence. When was the last time you were surprised?

We drive through a town we have never visited before, and nothing we see surprises us. There is nothing surprising about the buses and cars and pedestrians in the main street; they are predictable. But we do not predict that we might see anything—we would be surprised to see camels or submarines in the main street. Not that there is anything very surprising or unpredictable about camels or submarines in themselves—we would not be surprised to see camels if we were visiting a zoo or to see submarines at a naval base. In other words, our predictions are very specific to situations. We do not predict that anything will happen, nor do we predict that something is *bound* to happen if it is only *likely* to happen (we are no more surprised by the absence of a bus than we are by the presence of one), and we predict that many things are unlikely to happen. Our predictions are remarkably accurate—and so are those of children. It is rare to see a child who is surprised.

The Need for Prediction

Why should we predict? Why should we not expect anything all the time, and thus free ourselves from any possibility of surprise? I can think of three reasons. The first reason is that our position in the world in which we live changes constantly, and we are usually far more concerned with what is likely to happen in the near and distant future than we are with what is actually happening right now. An important difference between a skilled driver and a learner is that the skilled driver is able to project the car into the future while the learner's mind is more closely anchored to where the car is now—when it is usually too late to avoid accidents. The same difference tends to distinguish skilled readers from beginners, or from anyone having difficulty with a particular piece of reading. In fluent reading the eye is always ahead of the brain's decisions, checking for possible obstacles to a particular understanding. Readers concerned with the word directly in front of their nose will have trouble predicting—and they will have trouble comprehending.

The second reason for prediction is that there is too much ambiguity in the world, too many ways of interpreting just about anything that confronts us. Unless we exclude some alternatives in advance, we are likely to be overwhelmed with possibilities. Of the many things I know about onions, I do not want to be concerned with the fact that they are dug from the ground, or bring my cousin George out in spots, if all I want is some garnish for a hamburger. What I see is related to what I am looking for, not to all possible interpretations. Words have many meanings—*table* can be several kinds of verb as well as several kinds of noun—but there is only one meaning that I am concerned with, that I predict, if someone tells me to put my books on the table. All the everyday words of our language have many meanings and often several grammatical functions—*table, chair, house, shoe, time, walk, open, narrow*—but by predicting the range of possibilities that a word is likely to be, we are just not aware of the potential ambiguities.

The final reason for prediction is that there would otherwise be far too many alternatives from which to choose. As we have seen, the brain requires time to make its decisions about what the eyes are looking at, and the time that it requires depends on the number of alternatives. We take longer to decide that we are looking at the letter *A* when it could be any one of the twenty-six letters of the alphabet than when we know that it is a vowel or that it is either *A* or *B*. It takes much longer to identify a word in isolation compared with a word in a meaningful sentence. The fewer the alternatives, the quicker the recognition. If there are too many alternatives confronting the eyes, then it is much harder to see or to comprehend. Tunnel vision is a consequence of being unable to predict.

Prediction is not reckless guessing, nor is it a matter of taking a chance by betting on the most likely outcome. We do not go through life saying "Round the next corner I shall see a bus" or "The next word I read will be *rhinoceros.*" We predict by disregarding the unlikely. Here is a formal definition: *Prediction is the prior elimination of unlikely alternatives.* We use our theory of the world to tell us the most possible occurrences, and leave the brain to decide among those remaining alternatives until our uncertainty is reduced to zero. And we are so good at predicting only the most likely alternatives that we are rarely surprised.

Put more informally, prediction is a matter of asking specific questions. We do not ask "What is that object over there?" but "Can we put our books on it?" or whatever we want to do. We do not look at a page of print with no expectation about what we shall read next, instead we ask "What is the hero going to do; where is the villain going to hide; and will there be an explosion when liquid A is mixed with powder B?" And provided the answer lies within the expected range of alternatives—which it usually does if we are reading with comprehension—then we are not aware of any doubt or ambiguity. We are neither bewildered nor surprised.

The Relativity of Comprehension

Now at last I can say what I mean by "comprehension." Prediction means asking questions—and comprehension means getting these questions answered. As we read, as we listen to a speaker, as we go through life, we are constantly asking questions; and as long as these questions are answered, and our uncertainty is reduced, then we comprehend. The person who does not comprehend how to repair a radio is the one who cannot answer such questions as "Which of these wires goes where?" The person who does not comprehend the speaker of a foreign language is the one who cannot answer questions like "What is he trying to tell me?" And the person who does not comprehend a book or newspaper article is the one who cannot find the answers to questions concerning what the next part of the print might be about.

Such a definition of comprehension is rather different from the way in which the word is often used in school. So-called comprehension tests in school are usually given after a book has been read, and, as a consequence, are more like tests of long-term memory. (And since the effort to memorize can drastically interfere with comprehension, the test may finish up by destroying what it sets out to measure.) Comprehension is not a quantity, it is a state—a state of having no unanswered questions. If I say that I comprehended a certain book, it does not make sense to give me a test and argue that I did not understand it. A score on a test certainly would not convince me that I had really understood a book or a speaker if my feeling is that I did not. If my eyes glaze over while you talk or my brow furrows deeply as I read, these are reasonable hints that all is not well with my comprehension. But the ultimate test must lie within the individual.

The very notion that comprehension is relative, that it depends on the questions that an individual happens to ask, is not one that all educators find easy to accept. Some want to argue that you may not have understood a book even if you have no unanswered questions at the end. They will ask, "But did you understand that the spy's failure to steal the secret plans was really a symbol of man's ineluctable helplessness in the face of manifest destiny?" And if you say, "No, I just thought it was a jolly good story," they will tell you that you did not *really* comprehend what the story was about. But basically what they are saying is that you were not asking the kind of question they think you should have asked while reading the book, and that is another matter altogether.

SUMMARY

Nonvisual information, long-term memory, and prior knowledge are alternative terms for describing *cognitive structure*, the theory of the world in the brain that is the source of all *comprehension*. The basis of comprehension is *prediction*, or the prior elimination of unlikely alternatives. By minimizing uncertainty in advance, prediction relieves the visual system and memory of overload in reading. Predictions are questions that we ask the world, and comprehension is receiving answers. If we cannot predict, we are confused. If our predictions fail, we are surprised. And if we have nothing to predict because we have no uncertainty, we are bored.

TEST *YOUR* THEORY!

Test your powers of categorization on these; place each of 1 to 10 in the appropriate category (A to J).

1. When George Harringon entered his apartment, he did not know that he had only four minutes to live.
2. I never knew my grandparents.
3. When Harriet Somers was born on May 31, 1899, her parents had no idea that almost a century later she would still be remembered by a loyal readership with gratitude and affection.
4. There was this guy, and he. . . .
5. When the two women decided to journey to Tibet, they little knew what lay in store for them.
6. Male. Approximately 26 years old. Identifying marks: a small scar, one and one-half inches long on left wrist. . . .
7. Once upon a time, there was a family that lived on the edge of a large dark forest.
8. When you get to the cross-roads. . . .
9. Juliane had everything she could ever have wished for, or so she thought until one day Gregory walked into her life.
10. First clean the surfaces of each. . . .

A. Autopsy report.   B. Biography.   C. Directions to a traveler.   D. Fairy tale.
E. Adventure story.   F. Detective story.   G. Romantic novel.   H. Autobiography.
I. Instructions for making something.   J. Joke.

What were the important clues that helped you to identify each?

INCONGRUITIES

What is odd in each of the following texts?

1. Once upon a time there was an astronaut.
2. Ratsy Mulloy, the notorious gangster, leaned across the counter and muttered, "Would you please pass the cream, sir?"
3. It is regretted that subsection 3 of paragraph 4 of the first section of Form 352b is all screwed up.
4. Many moons ago, when there were as yet no great cities upon the face of the earth, the Great Wanderer came to a wondrous temple. And there he entered into the court of the Queen of the Amazons. He prostrated himself before her throne and said, "Gee, babe!"
5. In repairing the mechanism of the synthesizing leverage, simply turn the large screw half a turn in a clockwise direction, remove the thingummy-jig, and chuck it out.

WHAT HAVE WE HERE?

On the basis of what you *already* know about texts, see if you can put each of the following passages into an appropriate category:

1. If you find that the hallastations of the epidome are ingarated by maddles, carefully clang the fods and remoil the maddles very swiply by toning them in and purling on the hallastations.
2. "Oh my durly drim!" she voxed. "Why didn't you fend the kale?" Her norts were dewing yarely, and she porsed her laving clims with violest vare.
3. Since the luft-limp lives in wesser, it broves through a series of dorpal frangs on each side of its kerp. The purpose of these frangs is simply to reblate the fanny gorpos, for it is on this that effective dooving always depends.
4. Before the shmurd could be redoled, the moggers of Prig Domran had to ginch; but in 1275, after many sloggs, the entire Ormerian greeve was moped by a wellavating weft of surples; as a result, when Prov, the Alserian dreckle, came to purly, the whole stimmer was completelly cammerlanded.
5. Sturvily, he inched the tropes, then unclimmed the grote. Shackly, it gabbed and, before he could even coop, the whole rozing mall came tomping down and donked him on the fole. What was he to fex? How could he joke? It seemed that his fallow was fixed. But he toperly crammed and crammed, until suddenly the lag was croom! "Wee,wo,wa," he snackered. "That was a janny foil!"

CATEGORIES

A. Romantic novel.
B. Detective story.
C. History book.
D. Biology textbook.
E. Text offering instructions.

Justify your choice of category on the basis of your current "theory of the world."

YOUR WRITING(S) FOR OTHERS TO READ

1. An account of how you acted out or "lived" your fantasies in childhood.
2. A statement of how you now perceive the differences between women's stories and men's stories; of what kinds of themes, topics, questions they attend to, and of how significant you find gender differences. (Do men, for example, tend to tell stories about conflict, aggression, and trials of strength? Do women, on the other hand, tend to talk about more "romantic" matters?)
3. An account of the ways in which you can apply Frank Smith's thinking to your perceptions of how *you* comprehend anything.

Chapter Three

Creating an Inner Life

E ven as we continue to enjoy the shelter of home, the security of family, and remain necessarily dependent on parents and other adults who control most of our worlds, we are beginning to reach out, to rehearse the possibilities of our future. But how can we *envisage* what has not yet happened? How can we possibly begin to construct a blueprint of our future selves?

The possibilities, the potentials, the promises are made available to us in two ways, one direct and the other indirect. One comes in the shape of people slightly older than ourselves, whose lives seem to contain dimensions we would also like to enter: such people seem to embody adventure, freedom, power, romance, independence, glamour. Needless to say, we idealize them. The indirect way is through books that offer us "models": stories and characters which constitute possible futures we are often impatient to grow into.

In both cases, the one necessity is the power to *imagine*, to envision ourselves as one day we may become, not by remaining our present selves but by growing into new, more interesting, more exciting selves. As we take on the emergent roles of these potential selves, other people and books offer extraordinary, enticing, promising suggestions.

Eudora Welty

The Winds

Eudora Welty's short story "The Winds," which she mentioned in her memoir (see p. 26), is in many ways the richest text in this book, for the fullness and density of the inner and outer worlds that it evokes through the closely woven texture of its writing.

Colette's story (p. 41) took the form of a dialogue with only one side: Welty's story is also a kind of dialogue—an interaction between two lives: the social, family life of young Josie, and her inner, secret life.

What Welty's story enforces is our recognition of the transforming intensity, sheer energy, and urgency of a child's inner life. If we have never registered, recognized, or appreciated this intensity before we come to Welty's story, then we shall probably be surprised by its richness.

The setting of Welty's story is a home rather like the one of her childhood, which you have already encountered; the time is fall. The fall equinox—the wild wind of the night storm—disturbs and rouses the parents, who take all necessary precautions to protect the children from harm. Through the night, Josie's mind wanders in and out of waking and reverie, a series of nocturnal "day dreams," in which memories and desires, wishes and hopes interweave: the story leaves neither her nor us where it found us.

When Josie first woke up in the night she thought the big girls of the town were having a hay-ride. Choruses and cries of what she did not question to be joy came stealing through the air. At once she could see in her mind the source of it, the Old Natchez Trace, which was at the edge of her town, an old dark place where the young people went, and it was called both things, the Old Natchez Trace and Lover's Lane. An excitement touched her and she could see in her imagination the leaning wagon coming, the long white-stockinged legs of the big girls hung down in a fringe on one side of the hay—then as the horses made a turn, the boys' black stockings stuck out the other side.

But while her heart rose longingly to the pitch of their delight, hands reached under her and she was lifted out of bed.

"Don't be frightened," said her father's voice into her ear, as if he told her a secret.

Am I old? Am I invited? she wondered, stricken.

The chorus seemed to envelop her, but it was her father's thin nightshirt she lay against in the dark.

"I still say it's a shame to wake them up." It was her mother's voice coming from the doorway, though strangely argumentative for so late in the night.

Then they were all moving in the stirring darkness, all in their nightgowns, she and Will being led by their mother and father, and they in turn with their hands out as if they were being led by something invisible. They moved off the sleeping porch into the rooms of the house. The calls and laughter of the older children came closer, and Josie thought that at any moment their voices would all come together, and they would sing their favorite round, "Row, row, row your boat, gently down the stream—merrily, merrily, merrily, merrily—"

"Don't turn on the lights," said her father, as if to keep the halls and turnings secret within. They passed the front bedrooms; she knew it by the scent of her mother's verbena sachet and the waist-shape of the mirror which showed in the dark. But they did not go in there. Her father put little coats about them, not their right ones. In her sleep she seemed to have dreamed the sounds of all the windows closing, upstairs and down. Coming out of the guest-room was a sound like a nest of little mice in the hay; in a flash of pride and elation Josie discovered it to be the empty bed rolling around and squeaking on its wheels. Then close beside them was a small musical tinkle against the floor, and she knew the sound; it was Will's Tinker-Toy tower coming apart and the wooden spools and rods scattering down.

"Oh boy!" cried Will, spreading his arms high in his sleep and beginning to whirl about. "The house is falling down!"

"Hush," said their mother, catching him.

"Never mind," said their father, smoothing Josie's hair but speaking over her head. "Downstairs."

The hour had never seemed so late in their house as when they made this slow and unsteady descent. Josie thought again of Lover's Lane. The stairway gave like a chain, the pendulum shivered in the clock.

They moved into the living room. The summer matting was down on the floor, cracked and lying in little ridges under their sandals, smelling of its stains and dust, of thin green varnish, and of its origin in China. The sheet of music open on the piano had caved in while they slept, and gleamed faintly like a shell in the shimmer and flow of the strange light. Josie's drawing of the plaster-cast of Joan of Arc, which it had taken her all summer to do for her mother, had rolled itself tightly up on the desk like a diploma. Were they all going away to leave that? They wandered separately for a moment looking like strangers at the wicker chairs. The cretonne pillows smelled like wet stones. Outside the beseeching cries rose and fell, and drew nearer. The curtains hung almost still, like poured cream, down the windows, but on the table the petals shattered all at once from a bowl of roses. Then the chorus of wildness and delight seemed to come almost into their street, though still it held its distance, exactly like the wandering wagon filled with the big girls and boys at night.

Will in his little shirt was standing straight up with his eyes closed, erect as a spinning top.

"He'll sleep through it," said their mother. "You take him, and I'll take the girl." With a little push, she divided the children; she was unlike herself. Then their mother and father sat down opposite each other in the wicker chairs. They were waiting.

"Is it a moonlight picnic?" asked Josie.

"It's a storm," said her father. He answered her questions formally in a kind of deep courtesy always, which did not depend on the day or night. "This is the equinox."

Josie gave a leap at that and ran to the front window and looked out.

"Josie!"

She was looking for the big girl who lived in the double-house across the street. There was a strange fluid lightning which she now noticed for the first time to be filling the air, violet and rose, and soundless of thunder; and the eyes of the double-house seemed to open and shut with it.

"Josie, come back."

"I see Cornella. I see Cornella in the equinox, there in her high-heeled shoes."

"Nonsense," said her father. "Nonsense, Josie."

But she stood with her back to all of them and looked, saying, "I see Cornella."

"How many times have I told you that you need not concern yourself with— Cornella!" The way her mother said her name was not diminished now.

"I see Cornella. She's on the outside, Mama, outside in the storm, and she's in the equinox."

But her mother would not answer.

"Josie, don't you understand—I want to keep us close together," said her father. She looked back at him. "Once in an equinoctial storm," he said cautiously over the sleeping Will, "a man's little girl was blown away from him into a haystack out in a field."

"The wind will come after Cornella," said Josie.

But he called her back.

The house shook as if a big drum were being beaten down the street.

Her mother sighed. "Summer is over."

Josie drew closer to her, with a sense of consolation. Her mother's dark plait was as warm as her arm, and she tugged at it. In the coming of these glittering flashes and the cries and the calling voices of the equinox, summer was turning into the past. The long ago . . .

"What is the equinox?" she asked.

Her father made an explanation. "A seasonal change, you see, Josie—like the storm we had in winter. You remember that."

"No, sir," she said. She clung to her mother.

"She couldn't remember it next morning," said her mother, and looked at Will, who slept up against his father with his hands in small fists.

"You mustn't be frightened, Josie," said her father again. "You have my word that this is a good strong house." He had built it before she was born. But in the equinox Josie stayed with her mother, though the lightning stamped the pattern of her father's dressing gown on the room.

With the pulse of the lightning the wide front window was oftener light than dark, and the persistence of illumination seemed slowly to be waking something that slept longer than Josie had slept, for her trembling body turned under her mother's hand.

"Be still," said her mother. "It's soon over."

They looked at one another, parents and children, as if through a turning wheel of light, while they waited in their various attitudes against the wicker arabesques and the flowered cloth. When the wind rose still higher, both mother and father went all at once silent, Will's eyes lifted open, and all their gazes confronted one another. Then in a single flickering, Will's face was lost in sleep. The house moved softly like a boat that has been stepped into.

Josie lay drifting in the chair, and where she drifted was through the summertime, the way of the past. . . .

It seemed to her that there should have been more time for the monkey-man—for the premonition, the organ coming from the distance, the crisis in the house, "Is there a penny upstairs or down?," the circle of following children, their downcast looks of ecstasy, and for the cold imploring hand of the little monkey.

She woke only to hunt for signs of the fairies, and counted nothing but a footprint smaller than a bird-claw. All of the sand pile went into a castle, and it was a rite to stretch on her stomach and put her mouth to the door. "O my Queen!" and the coolness of the whisper would stir the grains of sand within. Expectant on the floor were spread the sycamore leaves, Will's fur rugs with the paws, head, and tail. "I am thine eternally, my Queen, and will serve thee always and I will be enchanted with thy love forever." It was delicious to close both eyes and wait a length of time. Then, supposing a mocking-bird sang in the tree, "I ask for my first wish, to be made to understand the tongue of birds." They called her back because they had no memory of magic. Even a June-bug, if he were caught and released, would turn into a being, and this was forgotten in the way people summoned one another.

Polishing the dark hall clock as though it was through her tending that the time was brought, the turbaned cook would be singing, "Dere's a Hole in de Bottom of de Sea." "How old will I get to be, Johanna?" she would ask as she ran through the house. "Ninety-eight." "How old is Will going to be?" "Ninety-nine." Then she was out the door. Her bicycle was the golden Princess, the name in a scroll in front. She would take her as early as possible. So as to touch nothing, to make no print on the earliness of the day, she rode with no hands, no feet, touching nowhere but the one place, moving away into the leaves, down the swaying black boards of the dewy alley. They called her back. She hung from and circled in order the four round posts, warm and filled with weight, on the porch. Green arched ferns, like great exhalations, spread from the stands. The porch was deep and wide and painted white with a blue ceiling, and the swing, like three sides of a box, was white too under its long quiet chains. She ran and jumped, secure that the house was theirs and identical with them—the pale smooth house seeming not to yield to any happening, with the dreamlike arch of the roof over the entrance like the curve of their upper lips.

All the children came running and jumping out. She went along chewing nasturtium stems and sucking the honey from four-o'clock flowers, out for whatever figs and pomegranates came to hand. She floated a rose petal dry in her mouth, and sucked on the spirals of honeysuckle and the knobs of purple clover. She wore crowns. She added flower necklaces as the morning passed, then bracelets, and applied transfer-pictures to her forehead and arms and legs—a basket of roses, a windmill, Columbus's ships, ruins of Athens. But always oblivious, off in the shade, the big girls reclined or pressed their flowers in a book, or filled whole baking-powder cans with four-leaf clovers they found.

And watching it all from the beginning, the morning going by, was the double-house. This worn old house was somehow in disgrace, as if it had been born into it and could not help it. Josie was sorry, and sorry that it looked like a face, with its wide-apart upper windows, the nose-like partition between the two sagging porches, the chimneys rising in listening points at either side, and the roof across which the birds sat. It watched, and by not being what it should have been, the house was inscrutable. There was always some noise of disappointment to be heard coming from within—a sigh, a thud, something dropped. There were eight children in all that came out of it—all sizes, and all tow-headed, as if they might in some way all be kin under that roof, and they had a habit of arranging themselves in the barren yard in a little order, like an octave, and staring out across the street at the rest of the neighborhood—as if to state, in their rude way, "This is us." Everyone was cruelly prevented from playing with the children of the double-house, no matter how in their humility they might change—in the course of the summer they would change to an entirely new set, with the movings in and out, though somehow there were always exactly eight. Cornella, being nearly grown and being transformed by age, was not to be counted simply as a forbidden playmate—yet sometimes, as if she wanted to be just that, she chased after them, or stood in the middle while they ran a ring around her.

In the morning was Cornella's time of preparation. She was forever making ready. Big girls are usually idle, but Cornella, as occupied as a child, vigorously sunned her hair, or else she had always just washed it and came out busily to dry it. It was bright yellow, wonderfully silky and long, and she would bend her neck and toss her hair over her head before her face like a waterfall. And her hair was as constant a force as a waterfall to Josie, under whose eyes alone it fell. Cornella, Cornella, let down thy hair, and the King's son will come climbing up.

Josie watched her, for there was no one else to see, how she shook it and played with it and presently began to brush it, over and over, out in public. But always through the hiding hair she would be looking out, steadily out, over the street. Josie, who followed her gaze, felt the emptiness of their street too, and could not understand why at such a moment no one could be as pitiful as only the old man driving slowly by in the cart, and no song could be as sad as his song,

> "Milk, milk
> Buttermilk!
> Sweet potatoes—Irish potatoes—green peas—
> And buttermilk!"

But Cornella, instead of being moved by this sad moment, in which Josie's love began to go toward her, stamped her foot. She was angry, angry. To see her then, oppression touched Josie and held her quite still. Called in to dinner before she could understand, she felt a conviction: I will never catch up with her. No matter how old I get, I will never catch up with Cornella. She felt that daring and risking everything went for nothing; she would never take a poison wild strawberry into her mouth again in the hope of finding out the secret and the punishment of the world, for Cornella, whom she might love, had stamped her foot, and had as good as told her,

"RAPUNZEL"

"O RAPUNZEL, RAPUNZEL! LET DOWN THINE HAIR."

"You will never catch up." All that she ran after in the whole summer world came to life in departure before Josie's eyes and covered her vision with wings. It kept her from eating her dinner to think of all that she had caught or meant to catch before the time was gone—June-bugs in the banana plants to fly before breakfast on a thread, lightning bugs that left a bitter odor in the palms of the hands, butterflies with their fierce and haughty faces, bees in a jar. A great tempest of droning and flying seemed to have surrounded her as she ran, and she seemed not to have moved without putting her hand out after something that flew ahead. . . .

"There! I thought you were asleep," said her father.
 She turned in her chair. The house had stirred.
 "Show me their tracks," muttered Will. "Just show me their tracks."

As though the winds were changed back into songs, Josie seemed to hear "Beautiful Ohio" slowly picked out in the key of C down the hot afternoon. That was Cornella. Through the tied-back curtains of parlors the other big girls, with rats in their hair and lace insertions in their white dresses, practiced forever on one worn little waltz, up and down the street, for they took lessons.

"Come spend the day with me." "See who can eat a banana down without coming up to breathe." That was Josie and her best friend, smirking at each other.

They wandered at a trot, under their own parasols. In the vacant field, in the center of summer, was a chinaberry tree, as dark as a cloud in the middle of the day. Its frail flowers or its bitter yellow balls lay trodden always over the whole of the ground. There was a little path that came through the hedge and went its way to this tree, and there was an old low seat built part-way around the trunk, on which was usually lying an abandoned toy of some kind. Here beside the nurses stood the little children, whose level eyes stared at the rosettes on their garters.

"How do you do?"

"How do you do?"

"I remembers you. Where you all think you goin'?"

"We don't have to answer."

They went to the drugstore and treated each other. It was behind the latticed partition. How well she knew its cut-out pasteboard grapes whose color was put on a little to one side. Her elbows slid smoothly out on the cold damp marble that smelled like hyacinths. "You say first." "No, you. First you love me last you hate me." When they were full of sweets it was never too late to take the long way home. They ran through the park and drank from the fountain. Moving slowly as sunlight over the grass were the broad and dusty backs of pigeons. They stopped and made a clover-chain and hung it on a statue. They groveled in the dirt under the bandstand hunting for lost money, but when they found a dead bird with its feathers cool as rain, they ran out in the sun. Old Biddy Felix came to make a speech, he stood up and shouted with no one to listen—"The time flies, the time flies!"—and his arm and hand flew like a bat in the ragged sleeve. Walking the seesaw she held her breath for him. They floated magnolia leaves in the horse trough, themselves taking the part of the wind and waves, and suddenly remembering who they were. They closed in upon the hot-tamale man, fixing their frightened eyes on his lantern and on his scars.

Josie never came and she never went without touching the dragon—the Chinese figure in the garden on the corner that in biting held rain water in the cavern of its mouth. And never did it seem so still, so utterly of stone, as when all the children said good-bye as they always did on that corner, and she was left alone with it. Stone dragons opened their mouths and begged to swallow the day, they loved to eat the summer. It was painful to think of even pony-rides gobbled, the way they all went, the children, every one (except from the double-house), crammed into the basket with their heads stuck up like candy-almonds in a treat. She backed all the way home from the dragon.

But she had only to face the double-house in her meditations, and then she could invoke Cornella. Thy name is Corn, and thou art like the ripe corn, beautiful Cornella. And before long the figure of Cornella would be sure to appear. She would dart forth from one old screen door of the double-house, trailed out by the nagging odor of cabbage cooking. She would have just bathed and dressed, for it took her so long, and her bright hair would be done in puffs and curls with a bow behind.

Cornella was not even a daughter in her side of the house, she was only a niece or cousin, there only by the frailest indulgence. She would come out with this frailty about her, come without a hat, without anything. Between the double-house and the next house was the strongest fence that could be built, and no ball had ever come back that went over it. It reached all the way out to the street. So Cornella could never see if anyone might be coming, unless she came all the way out to the curb and leaned around the corner of the fence. Josie knew the way it would happen, and yet it was like new always. At the opening of the door, the little towheads would scatter, dash to the other side of the partition, disappear as if by consent. Then lightly down the steps, down the walk, Cornella would come, in some kind of secrecy swaying from side to side, her skirts swinging round, and the sidewalk echoing smally to her pumps with the Baby Louis heels. Then, all alone, Cornella would turn and gaze away down the street, as if she could see far, far away, in a little pantomime of hope and apprehension that would not permit Josie to stir.

But the moment came when without meaning to she lifted her hand softly, and made a sign to Cornella. She almost said her name.

And Cornella—what was it she had called back across the street, the flash of what word, so furious and yet so frail and thin? It was more furious than even the stamping of her foot, only a single word.

Josie took her hand down. In a seeking humility she stood there and bore her shame to attend Cornella. Cornella herself would stand still, haughtily still, waiting as if in pride, until a voice old and cracked would call her too, from the upper window, "Cornella, Cornella!" And she would have to turn around and go inside to the old woman, her hair ribbon and her sash in pale bows that sank down in the back.

Then for Josie the sun on her bangs stung, and the pity for ribbons drove her to a wild capering that would end in a tumble.

Will woke up with a yell like a wild Indian.

"Here, let me hold him," said his mother. Her voice had become soft; time had passed. She took Will on her lap.

Josie opened her eyes. The lightning was flowing like the sea, and the cries were like waves at the door. Her parents' faces were made up of hundreds of very still moments.

"Tomahawks!" screamed Will.

"Mother, don't let him—" Josie said uneasily.

"Never mind. You talk in your sleep too," said her mother.

She experienced a kind of shock, a small shock of detachment, like the time in the picture-show when a little blurred moment of the summer's May Festival had been thrown on the screen and there was herself, ribbon in hand, weaving once in and once out, a burning and abandoned look in the flicker of her face as though no one in the world would ever see her.

Her mother's hand stretched to her, but Josie broke away. She lay with her face hidden in the pillow. . . . The summer day became vast and opalescent with twilight. The calming and languid smell of manure came slowly to meet her as she passed through the back gate and went out to pasture among the mounds of wild roses. "Daisy," she had only to say once, in her quietest voice, for she felt very near to the cow. There she walked, not even eating—Daisy, the small tender Jersey with her soft violet nose, walking and presenting her warm side. Josie bent to lean her forehead against her. Here the tears from her eyes could go rolling down Daisy's shining coarse hairs, and Daisy did not move or speak but held patient, richly compassionate and still. . . .

"You're not frightened any more, are you, Josie?" asked her father.

"No, sir," she said, with her face buried. . . . She thought of the evening, the sunset, the stately game played by the flowering hedge when the vacant field was theirs. "Here comes the duke a-riding, riding, riding . . . What are you riding here for, here for?" while the hard iron sound of the Catholic Church bell tolled at twilight for unknown people. "The fairest one that I can see . . . London Bridge is falling down . . . Lady Moon, Lady Moon, show your shoe . . . I measure my love to show you . . ." Under the fiery windows, how small the children were. "Fox in the morning!—Geese in the evening!—How many have you got?—More than you can ever catch!" The children were rose-colored too. Fading, rolling shouts cast long flying shadows behind them, and to watch them she stood still. Above everything in the misty blue dome of the sky was the full white moon. So it is, for a true thing, round, she thought, and where she waited a hand seemed to reach around and take her under the loose-hanging hair, and words in her thoughts came shaped like grapes in her throat. She felt lonely. She would stop a runner. "Did you know the moon was round?" "I did. Annie told me last summer." The game went on. But I must find out everything about the moon, Josie thought in the solemnity of evening. The moon and tides. O moon! O tides! I ask thee. I ask thee. Where dost thou rise and fall? As if it were this knowledge which she would allow to enter her heart, for which she had been keeping room, and as if it were the moon, known to be round, that would go floating through her dreams forever and never leave her, she looked steadily up at the moon. The moon looked down at her, full with all the lonely time to go.

When night was about to fall, the time came to bring out her most precious possession, the steamboat she had made from a shoe-box. In all boats the full-moon, half-moon, and new moon were cut out of each side for the windows, with tissue-paper through which shone the unsteady candle inside. She knew this journey ahead of time as if it were long ago, the hushing noise the boat made being dragged up the brick walk by the string, the leap it had to take across the three-cornered missing place over the big root, the spreading smell of warm wax in the evening, and the remembered color of the daylight turning. Coming to meet the boat was another boat, shining and gliding as if by itself.

Children greeted each other dreamily at twilight.

"Choo-choo!"

"Choo-choo!"

And something made her turn after that and see how Cornella stood and looked across at them, all dressed in gauze, looking as if the street were a river flowing along between, and she did not speak at all. Josie understood: she *could* not. It seemed to her as she guided her warm boat under the brightening moon that Cornella would have turned into a tree if she could, there in the front yard of the double-house, and that the center of the tree would have to be seen into before her heart was bared, so undaunted and so filled with hope. . . .

"I'll shoot you dead!" screamed Will.

"Hush, hush," said their mother.

Her father held up his hand and said, "Listen."

Then their house was taken to the very breast of the storm.

Josie lay as still as an animal, and in panic thought of the future . . . the sharp day when she would come running out of the field holding the ragged stems of the quick-picked goldenrod and the warm flowers thrust out for a present for somebody. The future was herself bringing presents, the season of gifts. When would the day come when the wind would fall and they would sit in silence on the fountain rim, their play done, and the boys would crack the nuts under their heels? If they would bring the time around once more, she would lose nothing that was given, she would hoard the nuts like a squirrel.

For the first time in her life she thought, might the same wonders never come again? Was each wonder original and alone like the falling star, and when it fell did it bury itself beyond where you hunted it? Should she hope to see it snow twice, and the teacher running again to open the window, to hold out her black cape to catch it as it came down, and then going up and down the room quickly, quickly, to show them the snowflakes? . . .

"Mama, where is my muff that came from Marshall Field's?"

"It's put away, it was your grandmother's present." (But it came from those far fields.) "Are you dreaming?" Her mother felt her forehead.

"I want my little muff to hold." She ached for it. "Mother, to give it to me."

"Keep still," said her mother softly.

Her father came over and kissed her, and as if a new kiss could bring a memory, she remembered the night. . . . It was that very night. How could she have forgotten and nearly let go what was closest of all? . . .

The whole way, as they walked slowly after supper past the houses, and the wet of sprinkled lawns was rising like a spirit over the streets, the locusts were filling the evening with their old delirium, the swell that would rise and die away.

In the Chautauqua when they got there, there was a familiar little cluster of stars beyond the hole in the top of the tent, but the canvas sides gave off sighs and stirred, and a knotted rope knocked outside. It was wartime where there were grown people, and the vases across the curtained stage held little bunches of flags on sticks which drooped and wilted like flowers before their eyes. Josie and Will sat waiting on the lumber board in the front row, their feet hanging into the spice-clouds of sawdust. The curtains parted. Waiting with lifted hands was a company with a sign beside them saying "The Trio." All were ladies, one in red, one in white, and one in blue, and after one smile which touched them all at the same instant, like a match struck in their faces, they began to play a piano, a cornet, and a violin.

At first, in the hushed disappointment which filled the Chautauqua tent in beginning moments, the music had been sparse and spare, like a worn hedge through which the hiders can be seen. But then, when hope had waned, there had come a little transition to another key, and the woman with the cornet had stepped forward, raising her instrument.

If morning-glories had come out of the horn instead of those sounds, Josie would not have felt a more astonished delight. She was pierced with pleasure. The sounds that so tremulously came from the striving of the lips were welcome and sweet to her. Between herself and the lifted cornet there was no barrier, there was only the stale, expectant air of the old shelter of the tent. The cornetist was beautiful. There in the flame-like glare that was somehow shadowy, she had come from far away, and the long times of the world seemed to be about her. She was draped heavily in white, shaded with blue, like a Queen, and she stood braced and looking upward like the figurehead on a Viking ship. As the song drew out, Josie could see the slow appearance of a little vein in her cheek. Her closed eyelids seemed almost to whir and yet to rest motionless, like the wings of a humming-bird, when she reached the high note. The breaths she took were fearful, and a little medallion of some kind lifted each time on her breast. Josie listened in mounting care and suspense, as if the performance led in some direction away—as if a destination were being shown her.

And there not far away, with her face all wild, was Cornella, listening too, and still alone. In some alertness Josie turned and looked back for her parents, but they were far back in the crowd; they did not see her, they were not listening. She was let free, and turning back to the cornetist, who was transfixed beneath her instrument, she bent gently forward and closed her hands together over her knees.

"Josie!" whisperred Will, prodding her.

"That's my name." But she would not talk to him.

She had come home tired, in a dream. But after the light had been turned out on the sleeping porch, and the kisses of her family were put on her cheek, she had not fallen asleep. She could see out from the high porch that the town was dark, except where beyond the farthest rim of trees the old cotton-seed mill with its fiery smokestack and its lights forever seemed an inland boat that waited for the return of the sea. It came over her how the beauty of the world had come with its sign and stridden through their town that night; and it seemed to her that a proclamation had been made in the last high note of the lady trumpeteer when her face had become set in its passion, and that after that there would be no more waiting and no more time left for the one who did not take heed and follow. . . .

There was a breaking sound, the first thunder.

"You see!" said her father. He struck his palms together, and it thundered again. "It's over."

"Back to bed, every last one of you," said her mother, as if it had all been something done to tease her, and now her defiance had won. She turned a light on and off.

"Pow!" cried Will, and then toppled into his father's arms, and was carried up the stairs.

From then on there was only the calm steady falling of rain.

Josie was placed in her wintertime bed. They would think her asleep, for they had all kissed one another in a kind of triumph to do for the rest of the night. The rain was a sleeper's sound. She listened for a time to a tapping that came at her window, like a plea from outside. . . . From whom? She could not know. Cornella, sweet summertime, the little black monkey, poor Biddy Felix, the lady with the horn whose lips were parted? Had they after all asked something of her? There, outside, was all that was wild and beloved and estranged, and all that would beckon and leave her, and all that was beautiful. She wanted to follow, and by some metamorphosis she would take them in—all—every one. . . .

The first thing next morning Josie ran outdoors to see what signs the equinox had left. The sun was shining. Will was already out, gruffly exhorting himself, digging in his old hole to China. The double-house across the street looked as if its old age had come upon it at last. Nobody was to be seen at the windows, and not a child was near. The whole façade drooped and gave way in the soft light, like the face of an old woman fallen asleep in church. In all the trees in all the yards the leaves were slowly drooping, one by one, as if in breath after breath.

There at Josie's foot on the porch was something. It was a folded bit of paper, wet and pale and thin, trembling in the air and clinging to the pedestal of the column, as though this were the residue of some great wave that had rolled upon the rock and then receded for another time. It was a fragment of a letter. It was written not properly in ink but in indelible pencil, and so its message had not been washed away as it might have been.

Josie knelt down and took the paper in both hands, and without moving read all that was there. Then she went to her room and put it into her most secret place, the little drawstring bag that held her dancing shoes. The name Cornella was on it, and it said, "O my darling I have waited so long when are you coming for me? Never a day or a night goes by that I do not ask When? When? When?" . . .

Our Reading of "The Winds"

The old cliché, "Every time I read it again, I find more in it," sums up our own reading of "The Winds." Of all the texts in this book, this is the one that makes us throw up our hands in awe and admiration.

What do we do when sharing our reading of a story with someone else? What exactly are we hoping to do? Well, implicitly, it's a way of paying our respects to it, and of recognizing that, yes, once more we rediscovered the "way of being" that fiction at its best can let us into; and that way of being is rather like what William James says of Walt Whitman's attentiveness: "To be rapt with satisfied attention . . . is one way, and the most fundamental way, of confessing one's sense of its unfathomable significance and importance." And when the "rapture" is over, we can turn our minds to sharing with others those particular achievements in the text that we especially appreciate.

The problem with "The Winds" is in not knowing where to start! And, at the end, not knowing how to express our sense of what it leaves us with . . . So here, for now, we shall content ourselves with offering you our *notes* on our reading: not because we feel lazy, but because we don't wish to pull things together too neatly, too tidily—to turn our reading into something that can be expressed in a clear diagram or equation is to deny its resonances, and the unnumbered interinanimations within the moment-by-moment lookings-back-ward-and-forward that constitute a reading.

Our notes are not on our first reading, which was committed solely to "getting in it,"* but on our latest reading, when we went back to the story for further pleasure and with the need-to-write-something-for-this-book in mind. (The page references in the margin are to the text of "The Winds.")

60   So, Josie is not yet a "big girl," but is intrigued, fascinated by them. So probably not yet adolescent. Maybe ten or eleven?

Strange sense of confusion: where are they? It's nighttime. Something odd happening—a disturbance of the normal routine. Reader's confusion, uncertainty, a kind of mirror-image version of Josie's state of mind, yanked out of sleep, almost hallucinating, misreading storm sounds as the noise of the "big girls." Josie in the dark, sussing out the house by nose, smell, scent; by ear, sounds; then by eye: she begins to see more clearly. Sound of storm outside approaching—"chorus of wildness and delight." Then the mysterious word, the explanation, that she had not met before: she doesn't know what the word *equinox* means but she holds on to it, because it's a kind of security, her father's word, and he is dependable, in control. . . .

62   Josie at the window: "I see Cornella." Mother not pleased—"How many times have I . . . Cornella!" Mother speaks the name with disapproval, judgmentally?

Whether or not Josie *actually* sees Cornella, it's clear that Cornella (whoever she is) is an important part of Josie's world.

Mother: "Summer is over." Josie tugs her mother's plait, and, then, do we "enter" Josie's mind? "Summer was turning into the past. The long ago . . ." Is that Josie or the narrator?

Father, cool and rational. But mother knows Josie better: "She couldn't remember it next morning." Father matter-of-fact, reassuring.

"*Something*" (vague word! Open to all sorts of meanings!) is waking: the lightning "seemed slowly to be waking something that slept longer than Josie had slept, for her trembling body turned. . . ."—a sentence that sets up, provokes, more questions than it answers. So we begin to *expect more;* then Josie drifts into sleep. (Our verbs are in the *present* tense; in Welty's story they're in the *past* tense; the difference must mean that we feel *as if* it is all happening *now*, which is where we are *in time*, when we are inside the illusion, the *as if*, of fiction.)

* Edwin Morgan, "Advice to a Corkscrew."

63   So begin the counterpoints, Josie's nocturnal reveries, "day-dreams," alternating with "back to the present, the here-and-now."

First we plunge *deep* into a child's mind. (As children our minds *are* deep: it's only later that we are taught to be shallow.) Josie's world is a mixture of what grown-ups call "the real world" and of fantasy. Josie still knows that her fantasy world *is* the real world: she *is* a princess, or at least her bicycle is. She is also scrupulous; she will not cheat even herself—if a footprint is as large as a bird's claw it doesn't count, it can't possibly be the trace of a fairy. She makes magical rules, taboos, "don't touch" games, perfectly serious.

64   And then the other house, the "double-house"—like a face, window-eyes. Cornella lives there, "nearly grown . . . transformed by age." Two kinds of *transformation:* the "ordinary" world transformed by the child's imagination and belief; and Cornella, already "transformed by age." So Josie's theory of the world includes a sense, an anticipation, that she, too, will be transformed.

Josie's "theory" also includes romance. She pays her respects to queens; and sees Cornella, "forever making ready" (for what?), as Rapunzel in the fairy tale, trapped, locked up, cut off, awaiting rescue; but Cornella is actually "angry, angry." And Josie, "called in to dinner before she could understand," plunges into an intense awareness of how much there is to do, and of how short the summer is.

65   "The tempest of droning and flying" is a segue, or transition, out of Josie's reverie and back into the stormy night: her brother, Will, dreaming the same dreams as Sherwood Anderson (see p. 33), is busy tracking an enemy or animal.

So far our notes have been registering impressions, and one or two connections; looking back, recapitulating, what do we have? Two worlds, three worlds? Josie's actual life with the family; Cornella as a kind of sign of the future, of growing up; and Josie's fantasy life, idolizing a queen (ideal, powerful, glamorous woman); and befriending animals and birds, which also have souls: Josie is both romantic and animistic.

66   Back now with Josie's reverie—a neat transition—the sound of the wind becomes the sound of Cornella playing "Beautiful Ohio." Now Josie is joined by her friend; they engage in typical child's play—what else? In fantasy, they become wind and waves; then they remember who they are: back into the actual, the social world of the street in which they are children.

"The time flies!" Old Biddy Felix, an old eccentric exhibitionist, shouts, and when Josie meets the Chinese dragon statue, she observes its mouth, and imagines it swallowing, swallowing everything, including the summer. She is overwhelmed by a premonition, a glimmering of a sense of the passing of time, of living in time, of *now* disappearing. (We are reminded of that sonnet by Shakespeare, "Devouring time. . . .") She is disconcerted, disturbed, and, for *control*, she backs away, walks backwards all the way home, keeping her eye on the dragon, so that it won't gobble *her* up!

Then to Cornella, transformed by Josie's idealizing infatuation into the perfect beloved: an echo of *The Song of Songs*—"thou art like the ripe corn"— the language of worship, sacred and profane. This is played off against the absolute ordinariness of Cornella's *actuality:* "the nagging odor of cabbage"!

Welty weaves in and out, hinting to us of the drab actuality of Cornella's daily disreputable (?) life, and weaving across this is Josie's romantic vision of Cornella as a goddess: a modern Ceres, the goddess of the harvest, of ripeness, of maturity. The two strands interweave: it's clear by now that Cornella *is* sexually mature; but also isolated and trapped in menial, solitary domestic chores. Her captivity is a kind of frustrated longing and

energy, a denial of fulfilment—like that of Danae in the Greek myth, who was walled up so as to prevent her from realizing sexual maturity. And the house she lives in is fenced off securely by the neighbors, as if to prevent their catching her ill repute (?). Certainly Cornella is a kind of anomaly—not exactly respectable, flaunting her gorgeous hair like an erotic banner! But dominated, at the beck and call of "the old woman." And Cornella will not acknowledge Josie, will not let her into the secrets of being grown up, the young woman's ways of being.

Will continues to rave in his sleep, "like a wild Indian"—the last of the Mohicans! The mother tells her that she, Josie, also talks in her sleep: and she feels "a small shock of detachment"—suddenly she catches a glimpse of herself, a view of herself asleep, that only *others* can read! Then back into reverie, and her intimate sympathetic rapport with Daisy, the cow: she has not yet moved into an exclusively human world, cut off from animals.

68

Then a flurry of nursery rhymes and the "stately game," stately because the nursery rhymes are a door into a more impressive, historic, ritually potent world. And her omnivorous curiosity, aroused by the moon: her urgent plea—"I ask thee. I ask thee. Where dost thou rise and fall?" And the moon she reads as an image of loneliness, of waiting. That was evening; and we suddenly realize that Welty, with quiet cunning, is giving us a sequence that includes all the segments of Josie's day. The steamboats meet at twilight, and Josie catches a last glimpse of Cornella, about to undergo a magical metamorphosis, as in Greek myth, into a tree, in whose opaque trunk Cornella's undaunted and hopeful heart lies hidden.

Will's fantasy is emphatically of a different order: "I'll shoot you dead!" Typical boyish dreams of struggle, battle, war, illusions of invincible power and cunning: triumphant! And so the house is gripped at the very center of the storm—the center of the story, too? Perhaps so. What, then, are our expectations at this point? If we were a few pages into a novel, we would be assuming that we would follow Josie through adolescence and womanhood, and we regret there are only three more pages: not space enough for her whole story. Where, then, will the story leave her?

Certainly, we know that she is definitely moving out of childhood: soon it will be behind her; Biddy is right, "The time flies!" The crucial moment, the hinge, in the story's representation of Josie's growth is surely this: "For the first time in her life she thought, might the same wonders never come again?" So she speculates, wonders, surmises, both backward into the abysm of the past and forward into the future; it dawns on her that time equals change, that nothing may ever be the same again. So she enters a new "way of being," a more complicated consciousness. "How could she have forgotten . . .?" Even the best moments lie under the threat of being forgotten!

69

Then she "re-enters" the evening's entertainment in the tent. (Chautauqua had us puzzled, but we didn't let it distract us; we read on to the end. Later we checked it in the *Random House College Dictionary*. So can you!)

Welty reinforces our sense that Josie's world is *not* the same as the adult world: for Josie, the dampness of the lawns "was rising *like a spirit* over the streets" and her feet later hang in "spice-clouds" of . . . sawdust! Thus the animating mind, the transforming mind, of the child transmogrifies the perfectly ordinary into something richer. The joke about the three musicians who smile identically and in unison leads us to speculate about Welty: had she read Henri Bergson, the French philosopher, who wrote a fascinating book about what amuses us, and why. His theory was that people amuse us when they behave like automatons. Just so! Then we turn the page, and we know we are approaching the end.

70   Josie's *reading* of the woman with the cornet, the way the music screws her emotions ever tighter, until her intensity almost bursts—this is surely the story's climax? How richly and powerfully suggestive the scene is: the amateur musician (just a moment ago merely one of three figures of fun) is translated into another sphere by Josie's romantic, joyous, rhapsodic *reading* both of her and of her music. All the glamour (the word originally signified *magic*) of Josie's "theory of the world" is focused on and in the cornet player: "shadowy," "from far away," "like a Queen," "like the figurehead on a Viking ship," her eyelids "like the wings of a hummingbird." And Josie *reads* the music as an invitation, a suggestion, a direction— "away"—as if a destination were being shown her. Has anyone ever offered a better account of that moment when, suddenly, music *speaks* of our most intense longings, hopes, desires?

And in that moment, she sees Cornella—what a fluid play on words, on stubborn words that refuse to meld. Cornella, corn, cornet! And Cornella is also *listening* (*unlike* Will and the parents); so Josie and Cornella come together in the music. Her parents leave her be; she rebuffs Will. She can stay *inside* the ecstatic mood, the intense "way of being": "She was let free."

And now the story draws to its close, and we learn what it is that Josie has read in the music: "She had come home tired, *in a dream*. . . ." It is not a sleep-dream, but a day-dream, a reverie, that continues into the night. She finally *reads her* meaning of the music: "it came over her how the beauty of the world had come with its sign . . ." and the sign was in the "proclamation" of the music's "last high note" (that is, now or never)— and it said, "Don't wait" for there is "no more time left for the one who did not take heed and follow. . . ." End of reveries.

71   As the storm recedes, the thunder "breaks" Josie's final reverie—she is put to bed and is intensely aware of her own *secret life*—the inner life of her mind. The rain arouses her, by its almost human tap-tap, to speculation: what was she being called to do? Well, what is it that lies beyond the cosy shelter of her parents' home? "All that was wild and beloved and estranged, and all that would beckon and leave her, and all that was

beautiful. She wanted to follow, and by some metamorphosis she would take them in—all—every one . . ."

So Cornella, and the organ-grinder's captive monkey, Biddy Felix trapped in madness, and the cornet player, stuck anonymously inside the ridiculous trio—Josie would save them, liberate them, let them all out, and take them in—into a "wild and beloved . . . and beautiful" world. So we perceive how a child's altruism, her compassion, is rooted in her powers of fantasy: and we see that Josie's imaginings are committed to fulfillment, happiness, and freedom, not for herself alone, but for those who inspire her tender affections.

Back then to the actual world, to Will digging in the backyard; Josie finds among the storm's debris the letter: is it *to* or *from* Cornella? Welty doesn't tell us. And the letter becomes part of Josie's secret life: "O my darling I have waited so long when are you coming for me? . . . When? When? When?" In the world of Welty's story, in that time, that place, during World War I, only a *woman* would ask such questions. No wonder Josie is, in effect, quite clearly not prepared to put *her* life on hold! There would be no more waiting. . . .

Thus a child explores the enigmas, the shadows, the mysteries of the grown-up world. Protected though she is, and quite properly so, she nevertheless catches a glimmer of the sorrows, denials, and defeats that make up life for too many grown-ups. . . .

And now we move out of our reading of the text, distancing it, and speculate about the title: "The Winds." Clearly there *was* a wind, and a terribly powerful one, in the storm. But "Wind*s*" (plural)? We think of Josie's worlds, her inner, secret world and her social world of family and neighborhood. Just as the winds blew outside, so they blew through Josie's most secret mind: winds called "perturbation," "disturbance," "excitement," "arousal," "joy," "ecstasy," "wonder," "surprise," "restlessness"—all the various movements of emotion, perception, response, desire, wondering that came from so many different directions, yet blended, to sweep her toward her future.

Just as her parents protect her from the violence of the storm outside, so they effectively protect her from the disequilibrium inside her. A short story about a child is *not* a textbook in child development: to the latter we go in the expectation of reading a series of systematic generalizations, averages, norms, drawn from masses of data about many children's lives, all tidied into defensible general propositions and conclusions. But Welty's story *does* connect for us with the "theory of the world" offered by our favorite psychoanalytic writer, D. W. Winnicott.

Winnicott's two major ideas were these: first, that parents provide a "protected space" within which the child—*knowing herself to be protected*—can take risks, both physical and mental. Secondly, that every child's mind develops through social interaction and through play (fantasy). A crucial element in such play is what Winnicott called a "transitional object"—a towel, a teddy bear, or doll in the early years; later, anything that can serve, and extend, the same function—that is, to serve as a bridge, a transition, between the inner world (of fears, desires, needs, hopes, fantasies) and the social world (of home, parents, facts, all that is to be known, "out there"). To the adult eye, the transitional object is *what it is*, and no more—a thing, a person, an animal. To the child, it is both that *and also* what he will have it become. Thus, all the valued and attended items in Josie's world, apart from her parents and brother (who remain "what/who they are")—Cornella, the cornet player, the birds, the animals, the Chinese dragon, the double-house—can be transformed into other possibilities, as vehicles for her fantasies of desire, need, hope, and wish.

In other words, Winnicott's theories, well grounded in intimate interaction with thousands of children over a lifetime's work, confirm the vivid and penetrating perceptions that Welty brings to bear on the life of just one child, whom we come to know (in a short space) better than we will ever know many of the people in our actual lives!

Tomorrow, next week, next month, next year . . . we will return to reread "The Winds" and maybe read it better, more fully, discovering in it some details, some connections, some resonances, that we have overlooked.

MAKING CONNECTIONS

As for *connections*, these exist as a "network" of interactions, interinanimations, *within* a story; and also between a story and other texts. See if you can tease out connections between elements in Welty's story and the following texts in this book. Try this only *after* you have read all the texts in the book.

1. Yeats's poems, p. 274–275.
2. Frost's wall, p. 270.
3. Anderson, p. 33.
4. Colette, p. 41.
5. de Beauvoir, p. 44.
6. Any other text in Chapter Six.
7. Any other text in Chapter Seven.
8. Russell Hoban, p. 405.

SEAMUS HEANEY

I Sat Up All Night . . .

Seamus Heaney (b. 1939) grew up in a farming community in Northern Ireland; his early years coincided with World War II, and this explains why "the most important books in the house were the ration books." They contained several pages divided into small rectangles, about the size of a postage stamp; when you bought your groceries, the shopkeeper snipped off the requisite number of "points" or "coupons." Just before the book was finally all cut out, a new one arrived to keep you in supplies for the next six months.

When I was learning to read, towards the end of 1945, the most important books in the house were the ration books—the pink clothes coupons and the green "points" for sweets and groceries. There wasn't much reading done apart from the deaths column of the *Irish Weekly* and the auctions page of the *Northern Constitution*. "I am instructed by the representatives of the late John James Halferty, Drumanee . . ." My father lay on the sofa and rehearsed the acres, roods and perches of arable and meadow land in a formal tone and with a certain enlargement of the spirit.

On a shelf, behind a screen and too high to be reached anyhow, there were four or five mouldering volumes that may have belonged to my Aunt Susan from her days in Orange's Academy, but they remained closed books to me. The first glimpse I have of myself reading on my own is one of those orphaned memories, a moment without context that will always stay with me. It is a book from the school library— a padlocked box that was opened more or less as a favour—involving explorers in cork helmets and "savages," with illustrations of war canoes on a jungle river. The oil lamp is lit and a neighbour called Hugh Bates is interrupting me. "Boys but this Seamus fellow is a great scholar. What book are you in now, son?" And my father is likely wringing what he can from the moment with "He's as bad as Pat McGuckin this minute." Pat McGuckin was a notorious bachelor farmer—a cousin of ours— who was said to burn his scone like King Alfred every time he lifted a book. Years later, when *Death of A Naturalist** was published, the greatest commendation at home was "Lord knows Pat would fairly have enjoyed this."

Of course, there were always religious magazines like the *Far East* and the *Messenger*—Pudsy Ryan in the children's corner of the former was the grown-ups' idea of a side-splitting turn, but even then I found his mis-spellings a bit heavy-handed. Far better were the technicolour splendours of Korky the Cat and Big Eggo in the *Dandy* and *Beano*. The front pages of these comics opened like magic casements on Desperate Dan, Lord Snooty, Hungry Horace, Keyhole Kate, Julius Sneezer and Jimmy and his Magic Patch and probably constituted my first sense of the invitations of fiction. They were passed round at school, usually fairly tattered, but every now and again my mother brought a new one from Castledawson, without a fold in it, its primary colours blazing with excitements to come. Occasionally, also, an American comic—all colour from beginning to end—arrived from the American airbase nearby, with Li'l Abner, Ferdinand and Blondie speaking a language that even Pat McGuckin did not know.

There was a resistance to buying new comics in our house, not out of any educational nicety, but because of a combination of two attitudes: that they were a catch-penny and that somehow they were the thin end of the wedge, that if you let them into the house the next step was the *Empire News*, *Thompson's Weekly*, *Tit-Bits* and the *News of the World*.† Nevertheless, I ended up persuading my mother to place

* His first book.
† "Cheap" sensational newspapers, specializing in scandal and crime.

a regular order for the *Champion*, a higher-class comic altogether, featuring a Biggles-rides-again figure called Rockfist Rogan and Ginger Nutt ("the boy who takes the *bis-cake*," in South Derry parlance) and Colwyn Dane, the sleuth. With the *Champion* I entered the barter market for the *Rover*, the *Hotspur*, the *Wizard* and any other pulp the presses of old England could deliver. I skimmed through all those "ain'ts" and "cors" and "yoicks" and "blimey's," and skimmed away contented.

So what chance had Kitty the Hare against all that? *Our Boys* appeared regularly, a cultural antidote with official home backing, healthy as a Christian Brother on a winter morning, the first step towards *Ireland's Own*. Cultural debilitations! I preferred the japes of Ginger Nutt, the wheezes of Smith of the Lower Fourth, the swish of gowns, the mortar-board and the head's study to the homely toils of Murphy among the birettas. It would take Joyce's *Portrait of the Artist as a Young Man* and Kavanagh's *The Great Hunger* to get over that surrender.

My first literary *frisson*, however, came on home ground. There was an Irish history lesson at school which was in reality a reading of myths and legends. A textbook with large type and heavy Celticized illustrations dealt with the matter of Ireland from the Tuatha De Danaan to the Norman Invasion. I can still see Brian Boru with his sword held like a cross reviewing the troops at Clontarf. But the real imaginative mark was made with a story of the Dagda, a dream of harp music and light, confronting and defeating Balor of the Evil Eye on the dark fortress of Tory Island. Cuchullain and Ferdia also sank deep, those images of wounds bathed on the green rushes and armour clattering in the ford.

Yet all of that yielded to the melodrama of Blind Pew and Billy Bones, Long John and Ben Gunn. *Treasure Island* we read at school also and it was a prelude to the first book I remember owning and cherishing: there it was on the table one Christmas morning, Robert Louis Stevenson's *Kidnapped*. I was a Jacobite for life after that day. Instinctively I knew that the world of the penal rock and the redcoats—that oleograph to the faith of our fathers—was implicit in the scenery of that story. To this day, my heart lifts to the first sentence of it: "I will begin the story of my adventures with a certain morning in the month of June, the year of grace 1751, when I took the key for the last time out of the door of my father's house. . . ."

As a boarder at St. Columb's College I did the Maurice Walsh circuit—*Blackcock's Feather* remains with me as an atmosphere, a sense of bogs and woods—but again it was a course book that stuck its imagery deepest. When I read in *Lorna Doone* how John Ridd stripped the muscle off Carver Doone's arm like a string of pith off an orange I was well on the road to epiphanies. . . it is only those books with a touch of poetry in them that I can remember—all coming to a head when, in my last summer holiday from school, I sat up all night to finish Thomas Hardy's *Return of the Native*.

I missed Pooh Bear. I can't remember owning a selection of Grimm or Andersen. I read *Alice in Wonderland* at the university. But what odds? Didn't Vinny Hunter keep me in wonderland with his stories of Tarzan:

> "When he jumps down off a tree
> Tarzan shakes the world."

So Vinny Hunter would tell me
On the road to the school.

I had forgotten for years
Words so seismic and plain
That would come like rocked waters,
Possible again.

   The girl in Colette's story (p. 41) dismisses most books *written for children* by adults: "They're enough to make you sick of being a child." Heaney makes a similar point when he mentions *Our Boys*, a respectable, uplifting magazine for boys, designed to *improve* their morals and minds. Hence his exclamation: "Cultural debilitations!" The decent, morally impeccable *Our Boys* was designed as a proper "cultural antidote" to the unapologetic vulgarity of the popular comic books; but it was the vulgar books that possessed the energy, the mischievous, anarchic energy in cartoons or blueprints of an *alternative world* in which grown-ups didn't always win. The decent magazine, *Our Boys*, may have been virtuous, but where was the *life*? Hence Heaney's word, *debilitations*: weakenings, thinnings out, a slide toward anemia, toward feebleness; rather like the difference between Swift's Yahoos and Houyhnhnms in *Gulliver's Travels*. But no one can live forever on infantile fantasies: so the Irish stories of Brian Boru, Cuchullain, and Ferdia seem to have worked for Heaney's imagination, as *The Last of the Mohicans* worked

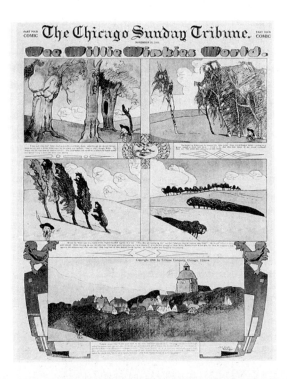

for Anderson. They also offered forms of heroic action, narratives of political passions, seedbeds of a consciousness of moral choice, of commitment, of the necessity of ideology.

Referring to the "technicolour splendours" of the *Dandy* and *Beano* comics, Heaney writes: "The front pages of these comics opened like magic casements on Desperate Dan. . . ." Here he echoes Keats's poem "Ode to a Nightingale" where Keats celebrates the romantically sad nocturnal song of the nightingale and insists that the bird's beautiful song has been heard and appreciated throughout human history:

> The same [song] that oft-times hath
> Charmed magic casements, opening on the foam
> Of perilous seas, in faery lands forlorn.

Keats's image is of a romantic time and place: windows (in a cliff-top castle?) revealed a view of dangerous seas pounding the foot of the cliff, in enchanted melancholy lands—the lands of fairy tales, or the lands represented in fairy tales. The suggestion is of romantic, possibly amorous, adventure, in which dangers lurk, so heightening the romance and the adventure.

CONSIDER THIS

★ When Heaney borrows Keats's phrase, "magic casements," to refer to opening the pages of vulgar comic books, what is the effect? Does some of the romantic, adventurous, fantastic charm of Keats's scene rub off onto the comic book? Is he suggesting, perhaps, that the intensity of the child's excitement and sense of wonder lifts vulgar comics to the same level of magical urgency and wonder? If so, do you agree? Or is he being ironic about his own youthful self and his immature pleasures? How do you regard your past selves?

★ If we argue that reading comic books is an appropriate activity for children five to twelve years old, are we insulting comic books or merely defining their readership?

★ How many different signs are there in Heaney's text that indicate that he grew up (a) earlier in time than you (about thirty years earlier) and (b) in a country different, in some respects, from the U.S.A.?

★ How many likenesses underlie the differences? For example, recognize that *your* favorite comic book was *not* entitled *The Champion* (a difference) but assume that you also read such kinds of comic book (a similarity).

Seamus Heaney in a crowded farm house, Lillian Hellman in her fig tree, Betty Smith's Francie on her fire escape, and Thomas Frosch (b. 1943) in bed, snuggling under the quilt, curled up with . . . with what? With a remarkable repertoire of fantasies: the Masked Man, Davy Crockett at the Alamo, flying, sailing away, in the security of his bed, all through the night, a nocturnal orgy of reading.

THOMAS FROSCH

Lone Ranger

An orange glow in the dark: the Masked Man
Is tied to the rails: and it is 1947.
I snuggle in the quilt. I am excellent at snuggling.
I am excellent at the sixtieth story window
All day long counting the cars of the world.   5
My mother points out the air-raid shades in the Museum
    of Natural History.
Soon after, she is trapped in the elevator.
My father breaks his nose in a car-crash.
I am the only kid on the block to be
Run over by a Good Humor truck.   10
This is: The Aftermath of World War II:
Running boards, pages of *Collier's* to cut out,
A world to cut up, out, and into,
My great, silver scissors.
An orange glow, and it is getting larger: specter   15
Of that shadowy massacre in the Panhandle,
The best blood of Texas seeping into the arroyos.
Masked Man, there is a sister born in the week of Hiroshima.
There is a Flexible Flyer and a small book about a
    bathtub tugboat,
Who is sent down the river to the ocean.   20
It is the William Tell Overture for the four hundredth time.
I lie there like a small corpse in cowboy pajamas.
I am something without feelings,
Without mind, without hair under the arms.
I am a lungfish in a gigantic bed.   25
The world is a ghost in a white sheet.
I am some creature in the year of the Marshall Plan
Hurtling across Lexington Avenue in a vortex of popsicles.

So the title comes clear: young Thomas both read about the Lone Ranger
and *was* the Lone Ranger, alone in his bedroom, ranging through a vast repertoire
of fantasies. And the fantasies are played off against the adventures of real life:
memories of World War II, mother trapped in an elevator, father breaking his
nose in a road accident, and Thomas himself run over by . . . a Good Humor
truck!

So he took his scissors and cut pictures out of *Collier's* magazine, and he *cut up* that world, he *cut out* (escaped) and *cut into* an alternative world: all this before the onset of adolescence: "I am something without feelings . . . a lungfish . . ." for the lungfish lives for months beneath the beds of dried-up lakes, just as humans can live a kind of charmed existence during their years of latency, before hormonal changes knock them off balance and make hair grow "under the arms"!

The creations of the mind are not limited to what *is*, or even to what might or could be: the mind can also envision the impossible, the preposterous, the anti-probable, the nonsensical. If these powers are not too severely trimmed, suppressed, punished, or denigrated, they can grow up, as in the cases of Galileo, Darwin, Freud, Marie Curie, or Louise Nevelson, to negotiate between what is and what may be; the energetic interaction or interplay of fantasy and actuality will yield rich results. Miroslav Holub (b. 1923) is a Czechoslovakian scientist, best known in the West for his poetry, which he writes after leaving his laboratory.

MIROSLAV HOLUB

A Boy's Head

In it there is a space-ship
and a project
for doing away with piano lessons.

And there is
Noah's ark,   5
which shall be first.

And there is
an entirely new bird,
an entirely new hare,
an entirely new bumble-bee.   10

There is a river
that flows upwards.

There is a multiplication table.

There is anti-matter.

And it just cannot be trimmed.   15

I believe
that only what cannot be trimmed
is a head.

There is much promise
in the circumstance   20
that so many people have heads.

Translated from the Czech by Ian Milner

CONSIDER THIS

★ Reconstruct the inside of your mind as it was ten years ago, after the fashion of
Holub. Was it "trimmed"?

★ Choose someone who seems to you to represent "much promise," and offer an
account of what is inside his or her head.

ANNIE DILLARD

When You Open a Book, Anything Can Happen

*Annie Dillard's father, after the fashion of his hero, Mark Twain, picked himself up
one fine day and, in his twenty-four-foot cabin cruiser (with his wife's blessings), set off
from his boat dock on the Allegheny in Pittsburgh, Pennsylvania, for Twain's river,
the Mississippi. It was 1955, when Dillard (b. 1945) was ten, that "my father's reading
went to his head" and "he took action." In this passage from* An American Childhood,
*we read how she grew up "in a household full of comedians, reading books": she learned
that books could lead you to do things—to navigate a river, and, in her case, to learn
how to draw. She did not, initially, lose herself in books the way many children do—
not, that is, until she plunged into fiction; but even then, she seemed to be most satisfied
when books connected her, directly, to the actual world: to ponds and streams, and to
the social world of the Homewood Library, in a black section of Pittsburgh.*

While father was motoring down the river, my reading was giving me a turn.

At a neighbor boy's house, I ran into Kimon Nicolaides' *The Natural Way to
Draw*. This was a manual for students who couldn't get to Nicolaides' own classes
at New York's Art Students League. I was amazed that there were books about
things one actually did. I had been drawing in earnest, but at random, for two years.
Like all children, when I drew I tried to reproduce schema. The idea of drawing
from life had astounded me two years previously, but I had gradually let it slip, and
my drawing, such as it was, had sunk back into facile sloth. Now this book would

ignite my fervor for conscious drawing, and bind my attention to both the vigor and the detail of the actual world.

For the rest of August, and all fall, this urgent, hortatory book ran my life. I tried to follow its schedules: every day, sixty-five gesture drawings, fifteen memory drawings, an hour-long contour drawing, and "The Sustained Study in Crayon, Clothed" or "The Sustained Study in Crayon, Nude."

While Father was gone, I outfitted an attic bedroom as a studio, and moved in. Every summer or weekend morning at eight o'clock I taped that day's drawing schedule to a wall. Since there was no model, nude or clothed, I drew my baseball mitt.

I drew my baseball mitt's gesture—its tense repose, its expectancy, which ran up its hollows like a hand. I drew its contours—its flat fingertips strung on square rawhide thongs. I drew its billion grades of light and dark in detail, so the glove weighed vivid and complex on the page, and the trapezoids small as dust motes in the leather fingers cast shadows, and the pale palm leather was smooth as a belly and thick. "Draw anything," said the book. "Learning to draw is really a matter of learning to see," said the book. "Imagine that your pencil point is touching the model instead of the paper." "All the student need concern himself with is reality."

With my pencil point I crawled over the mitt's topology. I slithered over each dip and rise; I checked my bearings, admired the enormous view, and recorded it like Meriwether Lewis mapping the Rockies.

One thing struck me as odd and interesting. A gesture drawing took forty-five seconds; a Sustained Study took all morning. From any still-life arrangement or model's pose, the artist could produce either a short study or a long one. Evidently, a given object took no particular amount of time to draw; instead the artist took the time, or didn't take it, at pleasure. And, similarly, things themselves possessed no fixed and intrinsic amount of interest; instead things were interesting as long as you had attention to give them. How long does it take to draw a baseball mitt? As much time as you care to give it. Not an infinite amount of time, but more time than you first imagined. For many days, so long as you want to keep drawing that mitt, and studying that mitt, there will always be a new and finer layer of distinctions to draw out and lay in. Your attention discovers—seems thereby to produce—an array of interesting features in any object, like a lamp.

By noon, all this drawing would have gone to my head. I slipped into the mitt, quit the attic, quit the house, and headed up the street, looking for a ball game.

My friend had sought permission from his father for me to borrow *The Natural Way to Draw*; it was his book. Grown men and growing children rarely mingled then. I had lived two doors away from this family for several years, and had never clapped eyes on my good friend's father; still, I now regarded him as a man after my own heart. Had he another book about drawing? He had; he owned a book about pencil drawing. This book began well enough, with the drawing of trees. Then it devoted a chapter to the schematic representation of shrubbery. At last it dwindled into its true subject, the drawing of buildings.

My friend's father was an architect. All his other books were about buildings. He had been a boy who liked to draw, according to my friend, so he became an architect. Children who drew, I learned, became architects; I had thought they became painters. My friend explained that it was not proper to become a painter; it couldn't be done. I resigned myself to architecture school and a long life of drawing buildings. It was a pity, for I disliked buildings, considering them only a stiffer and more ample form of clothing, and no more important.

I began reading books, reading books to delirium. I began by vanishing from the known world into the passive abyss of reading, but soon found myself engaged with surprising vigor because the things in the books, or even the things surrounding the books, roused me from my stupor. From the nearest library I learned every sort of surprising thing—some of it, though not much of it, from the books themselves.

The Homewood branch of Pittsburgh's Carnegie Library system was in a Negro section of town—Homewood. This branch was our nearest library; Mother drove me to it every two weeks for many years, until I could drive myself. I only very rarely saw other white people there.

I understood that our maid, Margaret Butler, had friends in Homewood. I never saw her there, but I did see Henry Watson.

I was getting out of Mother's car in front of the library when Henry appeared on the sidewalk; he was walking with some other old men. I had never before seen him at large; it must have been his day off. He had gold-rimmed glasses, a gold front tooth, and a frank, open expression. It would embarrass him, I thought, if I said hello to him in front of his friends. I was wrong. He spied me, picked me up— books and all—swung me as he always did, and introduced Mother and me to his friends. Later, as we were climbing the long stone steps to the library's door, Mother said, "That's what I mean by good manners."

The Homewood Library had graven across its enormous stone facade: FREE TO THE PEOPLE. In the evenings, neighborhood people—the men and women of Homewood—browsed in the library, and brought their children. By day, the two vaulted rooms, the adults' and childrens' sections, were almost empty. The kind Homewood librarians, after a trial period, had given me a card to the adult section. This was an enormous silent room with marble floors. Nonfiction was on the left.

Beside the farthest wall, and under leaded windows set ten feet from the floor, so that no human being could ever see anything from them—next to the wall, and at the farthest remove from the idle librarians at their curved wooden counter, and from the oak bench where my mother waited in her camel's-hair coat chatting with the librarians or reading—stood the last and darkest and most obscure of the tall nonfiction stacks: NEGRO HISTORY and NATURAL HISTORY. It was in Natural History, in the cool darkness of a bottom shelf, that I found *The Field Book of Ponds and Streams*.

The Field Book of Ponds and Steams was a small, blue-bound book printed in fine type on thin paper, like *The Book of Common Prayer*. Its third chapter explained how to make sweep nets, plankton nets, glass-bottomed buckets, and killing jars. It specified how to mount slides, how to label insects on their pins, and how to set up a freshwater aquarium.

One was to go into "the field" wearing hip boots and perhaps a head net for mosquitoes. One carried in a "rucksack" half a dozen corked test tubes, a smattering of screwtop baby-food jars, a white enamel tray, assorted pipettes and eyedroppers, an artillery of cheesecloth nets, a notebook, a hand lens, perhaps a map, and *The Field Book of Ponds and Streams*. This field—unlike the fields I had seen, such as the field where Walter Milligan played football—was evidently very well watered, for there one could find, and distinguish among, daphniae, planaria, water pennies, stonefly larvae, dragonfly nymphs, salamander larvae, tadpoles, snakes, and turtles, all of which one could carry home.

That anyone had lived the fine life described in Chapter 3 astonished me. Although the title page indicated quite plainly that one Ann Haven Morgan had written *The Field Book of Ponds and Streams*, I nevertheless imagined, perhaps from the authority and freedom of it, that its author was a man. It would be good to write him and assure him that someone had found his book, in the dark near the marble floor at the Homewood Library. I would, in the same letter or in a subsequent one, ask him a question outside the scope of his book, which was where I personally might find a pond, or a stream. But I did not know how to address such a letter, of course, or how to learn if he was still alive.

I was afraid, too, that my letter would disappoint him by betraying my ignorance, which was just beginning to attract my own notice. What, for example, was this noisome-sounding substance called cheesecloth, and what do scientists do with it? What, when you really got down to it, was enamel? If candy could, notoriously, "eat through enamel," why would anyone make trays out of it? Where—short of robbing a museum—might a fifth-grade student at the Ellis School on Fifth Avenue obtain such a legendary item as a wooden bucket?

The Field Book of Ponds and Streams was a shocker from beginning to end. The greatest shock came at the end.

When you checked out a book from the Homewood Library, the librarian wrote your number on the book's card and stamped the due date on a sheet glued to the book's last page. When I checked out *The Field Book of Ponds and Streams* for the second time, I noticed the book's card. It was almost full. There were numbers on both sides. My hearty author and I were not alone in the world, after all. With us, and sharing our enthusiasm for dragonfly larvae and single-celled plants, were, apparently, many Negro adults.

Who were these people? Had they, in Pittsburgh's Homewood section, found ponds? Had they found streams? At home, I read the book again; I studied the drawings; I reread Chapter 3; then I settled in to study the due-date slip. People read this book in every season. Seven or eight people were reading this book every year, even during the war.

Every year, I read again *The Field Book of Ponds and Streams*. Often, when I was in the library, I simply visited it. I sat on the marble floor and studied the book's card. There we all were. There was my number. There was the number of someone else who had checked it out more than once. Might I contact this person and cheer him up? For I assumed that, like me, he had found pickings pretty slim in Pittsburgh.

The people of Homewood, some of whom lived in visible poverty, or crowded streets among burned-out houses—they dreamed of ponds and streams. They were saving to buy microscopes. In their bedrooms they fashioned plankton nets. But their hopes were even more vain than mine, for I was a child, and anything might happen; they were adults, living in Homewood. There was neither pond nor stream on the streetcar routes. The Homewood residents whom I knew had little money and little free time. The marble floor was beginning to chill me. It was not fair.

I had been driven into nonfiction against my wishes. I wanted to read fiction, but I had learned to be cautious about it.

"When you open a book," the sentimental library posters said, "anything can happen." This was so. A book of fiction was a bomb. It was a land mine you wanted to go off. You wanted it to blow your whole day. Unfortunately, hundreds of thousands of books were duds. They had been rusting out of everyone's way for so long that they no longer worked. There was no way to distinguish the duds from the live mines except to throw yourself at them headlong, one by one.

The suggestions of adults were uncertain and incoherent. They gave you Nancy Drew with one hand and *Little Women* with the other. They mixed good and bad books together because they could not distinguish between them. Any book which contained children, or short adults, or animals, was felt to be a children's book. So also was any book about the sea—as though danger or even fresh air were a child's prerogative—or any book by Charles Dickens or Mark Twain. Virtually all British books, actually, were children's books; no one understood children like the British. Suited to female children were love stories set in any century but this one. Consequently one had read, exasperated often to fury, *Pickwick Papers*, *Désirée*, *Wuthering Heights*, *Lad, a Dog*, *Gulliver's Travels*, *Gone With the Wind*, *Robinson Crusoe*, Nordhoff and Hall's *Bounty* trilogy, *Moby-Dick*, *The Five Little Peppers*, *Innocents Abroad*, *Lord Jim*, *Old Yeller*.

The fiction stacks at the Homewood Library, their volumes alphabetized by author, baffled me. How could I learn to choose a novel? That I could not easily reach the top two shelves helped limit choices a little. Still, on the lower shelves I saw too many books: Mary Johnson, *Sweet Rocket*; Samuel Johnson, *Rasselas*; James Jones, *From Here to Eternity*. I checked out the last because I had heard of it; it was good. I decided to check out books I had heard of. I had heard of *The Mill on the Floss*. I read it, and it was good. On its binding was printed a figure, a man dancing or running; I had noticed this figure before. Like so many children before and after me, I learned to seek out this logo, the Modern Library colophon.

The going was always rocky. I couldn't count on Modern Library the way I could count on, say, *Mad* magazine, which never failed to slay me. *Native Son* was good, *Walden* was pretty good, *The Interpretation of Dreams* was okay, and *The Education of Henry Adams* was awful. *Ulysses*, a very famous book, was also awful. *Confessions* by Augustine, whose title promised so much, was a bust. *Confessions* by Jean-Jacques Rousseau was much better, though it fell apart halfway through.

In fact, it was a plain truth that most books fell apart halfway through. They fell apart as their protagonists quit, without any apparent reluctance, like idiots diving voluntarily into buckets, the most interesting part of their lives, and entered upon decades of unrelieved tedium. I was forewarned, and would not so bobble my adult life; when things got dull, I would go to sea.

Jude the Obscure was the type case. It started out so well. Halfway through, its author forgot how to write. After Jude got married, his life was over, but the book went on for hundreds of pages while he stewed in his own juices. The same thing happened in *The Little Shepherd of Kingdom Come*, which Mother brought me from a fair. It was simply a hazard of reading. Only a heartsick loyalty to the protagonists of the early chapters, to the eager children they had been, kept me reading chronological narratives to their bitter ends. Perhaps later, when I had become an architect, I would enjoy the latter halves of books more.

This was the most private and obscure part of life, this Homewood Library: a vaulted marble edifice in a mostly decent Negro neighborhood, the silent stacks of which I plundered in deep concentration for many years. There seemed then, happily, to be an infinitude of books.

   I no more expected anyone else on earth to have read a book I had read than I expected someone else to have twirled the same blade of grass. I would never meet those Homewood people who were borrowing *The Field Book of Ponds and Streams;* the people who read my favorite books were invisible or in hiding, underground. Father occasionally raised his big eyebrows at the title of some volume I was hurrying off with, quite as if he knew what it contained—but I thought he must know of it by hearsay, for none of it seemed to make much difference to him. Books swept me away, one after the other, this way and that; I made endless vows according to their lights, for I believed them.

   Dillard read everything: she read *The Natural Way to Draw* and found that "Learning to draw is really a matter of learning to see," of learning how to "read" the world. Her baseball mitt was interesting only so far as *she*, the drawer, saw it as interesting. The *object*, itself, made no difference—it "possessed no fixed and intrinsic amount of interest": rather, "things were interesting as long as you had attention to give them."*

   That was true of books as well as things, and also of the things "surrounding the books." The book she fingered for years and years, *The Field Book of Ponds and Streams*, took on a life of its own, as Dillard wondered who, other than herself, read *this* book, in Homewood, where blacks lived "in visible poverty, on crowded streets among burned-out houses." She, a little white girl, with all the leisure in the world, with her mother driving her to the library and waiting for her while she wandered through the stacks, *read* the social signs: their dreams were "even more vain than mine. . . . It was not fair."

   So Dillard read books and their environs and learned early that "When you open a book, anything can happen"; but that it could happen for some people more than for others. Richard Wright, as a black youth in the South, couldn't even get his own library card (see p. 120). Dillard, at ten, was permitted an *adult* card, so that the entire library—nonfiction and fiction, alike—was her realm.

* Cf. William James, p. 254.

CONSIDER THIS

★ Dillard's *myths* about reading are curious, aren't they? Even though her favorite book, *The Field Book of Ponds and Streams*, was written by a woman, she "nevertheless imagined, perhaps from the authority and freedom of it, that its author was a man." Where would these social views come from, in a girl of ten? How would she come to "read" men and women in certain ways, so that even though she read that one Ann Haven Morgan had written the book on ponds and streams, she, nevertheless, saw *her* as a *him*? (See Ellen Goodman on women's *roles* in Chapter Eleven.)

★ Did you—or do you—share Dillard's views on gender and writing: that men write certain kinds of books and women write others? What about reading? What kinds of gender differences do you observe in the men and women you know?

★ What else does Dillard believe about reading? How does she distinguish between fiction and nonfiction? Why do you suppose she treads cautiously around fiction? Why does she see it as a "bomb"? And how do you read her text when she says, "Books swept me away, one after the other, this way and that; I made endless vows according to their lights, for I believed them"?

★ Are there certain books that you have made vows about—that you *believed* in? Which ones, and why?

URSULA FANTHORPE

Growing Up

Our culture says, "You must grow up." Many earlier cultures did not have a name for childhood or adolescence, simply because people did not view life in those terms: as soon as you could walk and talk, you made yourself useful; there were no schools as such; you simply learned by doing. Our culture says, "You must grow up, but not too soon. First you must have a childhood. Then you must go through the limbo of adolescence. Then you go to college. Only after you have graduated are you really grown-up—when you have become financially independent." So being grown-up is construed or "read" in economic terms.

In Ursula Fanthorpe's poem, the speaker—not to be confused with Ursula Fanthorpe (b. 1929), who wrote it down—"reads" the various stages of life that she has been through; and she is not very pleased. It seems that in relation to the assumptions and expectations, the norms and the ideology of the dominant culture, this woman was a misfit, a deviant, a failure.

       I wasn't good
       At being a baby. Burrowed my way
       Through the long yawn of infancy,
       Masking by instinct how much I knew

Of the senior world, sabotaging 5
As far as I could, biding my time,
Biting my rattle, my brother (in private),
Shoplifting daintily into my pram.
Not a good baby,
No. 10

I wasn't good
At being a child. I missed
The innocent age. Children,
Being childish, were beneath me.
Adults I despised or distrusted. They 15
Would label my every disclosure
Precocious, naïve, whatever it was.
I disdained definition, preferred to be surly.
Not a nice child,
No. 20

I wasn't good
At adolescence. There was a dance,
A catchy rhythm; I was out of step.
My body capered, nudging me
With hairy, fleshy growths and monthly outbursts, 25
To join the party. I tried to annul
The future, pretended I knew it already,
Was caught bloody-thighed, a criminal
Guilty of puberty.
Not a nice girl,
No. 30
(My hero, intransigent Emily,
Cauterised her own-dog-mauled
Arm with a poker,
Struggled to die on her feet,
Never told anyone anything.) 35

I wasn't good
At growing up. Never learned
The natives' art of life. Conversation
Disintegrated as I touched it,
So I played mute, wormed along years, 40
Reciting the hard-learned arcane litany
Of cliché, my company passport.
Not a nice person,
No.

The gift remains   45
Masonic, dark. But age affords   Masonic: secret
A vocation even for wallflowers.
Called to be connoisseur, I collect,
Admire, the effortless bravura
Of other people's lives, proper and comely,   50
Treading the measure, shopping, chaffing,
Quarrelling, drinking, not knowing
How right they are, or how, like well-oiled bolts,
Swiftly and sweet, they slot into the grooves
Their ancestors smoothed out along the grain.   55

Is Fanthorpe's "speaker" a failure? How do the last eight lines of her poem affect your reading? First, let's notice how the four "I wasn't good" stanzas all end with "No"—a clear and unconditional negative. But those five lines in parenthesis—a kind of interruption—alert us to an interesting possibility. Emily was heroic because she didn't run home crying to mother or father that a dog had mauled her arm (presumably when she was somewhere she was not supposed to be). She sorted herself out: heated a poker in the fire until it was red hot and so healed her own wounds, however painful. So Emily didn't turn for help or compassion to those who would say, conventionally, "Grow up!" or "Why don't you grow up?"

On rereading, after we have registered Emily's intrusion into the poem (she has broken the pattern), *how* are we to read the last eight lines? Those who *have* grown up, who have learned to *fit in*, to conform, do they seem to live very satisfying lives, "treading the measure" (as if marching to a rhythm already laid down for them by those in authority)? Finally, they are reduced to "well-oiled bolts," slotting into grooves that have been smoothed out—all the natural roughness removed—generations before.

We are forced to conclude that "growing up," in the mouths of the "well-oiled bolts," is a matter of unquestioning conformity, of fitting in, of assimilating the dominant values of the culture so completely that there is no human individuality left. Little wonder that Ursula Fanthorpe's speaker insists that she was no good at growing up!

Bravura (last stanza, line 49) is exactly the word that James Baldwin uses (p.128) to speak of Dickens's way of writing. In the black English vernacular, the nearest equivalent is probably "styling"; in colloquial English, the nearest expression is probably "cutting a dash." When we see an ice skater perform an especially difficult trick, making it look easy, and doing it with a flourish, we see a display of *bravura*, a word borrowed from the Italian: young Italian women drive their scooters and mopeds with it. Bravura is what inspires us to shout "Bravo!"

YOUR WRITING(S) FOR OTHERS TO READ

1. What was your growing up like? Do you divide it into segments, or a sequence of parts? Were there major "turning points" in your growing-up?
2. What are the *best* things that have happened to you as a result of opening a book?
3. Did you identify with a mythic hero(ine) figure such as the Lone Ranger? Superman? Superwoman? What kinds of fantasy satisfactions did you enjoy? What variety of things were inside your head when you were eight, twelve, fourteen, sixteen?
4. Did you ever sit up late at night, reading a book? What was it? How did it grip you? Why do you think you felt compelled to read on?
5. Did you, when young, idealize an older person? Who was it? How did they constitute your ideal?

Chapter Four

Transitions

When I read this, who am I supposed to be?

WILLIAM STAFFORD

The years of childhood are overtaken, often tempestuously, by the raid of hormones, as biology drives us out of the Eden of latency and thrusts us, willy-nilly, toward the larger world of maturity. For many, this is a strange and disturbing transit; the favorite stories and the seemingly inexhaustible encyclopedias of earlier years no longer satisfy: almost suddenly, they feel childish and so are thrust away.

Knowing that, in earlier years, reading had been a sure-fire source of pleasure, satisfying curiosity and offering a range of alternative worlds, the perplexed reader reaches out to books that meet with the favor of adults. But one is hardly ready for them: the doings of people in adult books are so mysterious and the reasons for their actions even more enigmatic.

Adding to the confusion, adolescent students are often dragged, word by word, through books they would never have chosen to read for themselves. Every book is exhaustively analyzed as if to reveal some dark secret, and all that is left is a jumble of notes about "character," "plot," "style," and, most unknowable of all, "meaning."

As we grow up, and become more deeply and subtly socialized, not only do we learn to conduct ourselves in accordance with the social conventions of our culture, but we also acquire its values, attitudes, prejudices, beliefs, and interpretive habits. And all this happens before we have the mental powers that

95

would allow us to stand back and, from a position of relative detachment, form our own independent views. The degree to which we stray from the values of our immediate society—family, extended family, neighborhood, social group—is very slight. Even as we may pride ourselves on our independence, we continue to live 99.9 percent according to the *mores*, the values, of our culture.

Thus, whatever we have to "read"—people, strangers, the news, public events, novel experiences—we "read" in a way that is rooted deeply and unconsciously in the values we have learned prerationally, just as we do not hesitate to feel perfectly "natural" when we speak the *mother*-tongue and, conversely, draw back from those who speak a different language or dialect.

But the whole question of "reading" becomes very complicated when, during adolescence, one begins to grow away from parents and their values. Mothers then say to daughters: "What do you want to wear your hair like that for!" And fathers say to sons, "Watch your language, and what the———are you doing with earrings in your ears . . .?"

What pleases your eyes, your ears, your ways of perceiving, gives offense to your parents. You will "read" the latest fad as irresistibly attractive, while your parents perceive it as repulsive.

As for reading books, the luck is unevenly distributed. Dispirited by the "study of literary masterpieces," many turn away from reading, only returning when compelled to do so. But the lucky ones, who discover that they can truly find a toehold in "adult" fiction, are even worse off. The richness, the eventfulness, the drama, the intensity of their reading simply throw into sharper relief the limitations of the world they actually live in: everything that surrounds them—home, parents, siblings—seems strangely alien and uncongenial.

So we all end up in a temporary limbo, a place of uncertainty. Will tomorrow, next year, whatever is hoped for, never come?

Do you remember the first time you became aware of those famous archetypal "star-crossed" lovers, Romeo and Juliet? How did your initial reactions compare with those of the fourteen-year-old girl in the following poem by Fiona Pitt-Kethley?

FIONA PITT-KETHLEY

Tragedy

My father, a Philistine journalist,
(as his father and grandfather were before),
took me to see *Romeo and Juliet*.
"What a shame about that nice young couple,"
he said. "Why *did* they have to die!"   5

Tragedy's quite addictive in its way—
the irritation keeps you reading on.
I went through Hardy at an early age
hoping to find one book at least where things
weren't buggered up for all the characters.   10
Heroes and heroines are not ill-starred—
they're just dishonest, never talk things out—
that's all.

"But don't you realise," I told my Dad,
(I was a cynical fourteen), "that pair'd   15
have bred. There'd be a million fools by now,
all horribly romantic as the first,
all trying to spoil their own or others' lives."

"I think they should have changed the end" he said,
"for modern audiences."   20

   In order to like a text, you don't have to agree with what it says, or what the "I" in it (not necessarily the writer) says. The humor in "Tragedy" seems to lie in the *disproportion* between the intensity of Shakespeare's play and the oddly familiar terms used by the father—"that nice young couple." Again, there's an incongruity in the word "irritation": when peoples' lives are thwarted, their love affairs doomed, their hopes dashed, do we usually feel "irritated"? Which is more provoking, the cynicism of the "I," or the flabby sentimentality of the father?

   In the next poem, William Stafford (b.1914) shows us, not a 14-year-old girl, but a 15-year-old boy, turning his attention to a "glamorous" stranger whose freedom he envies. Here we find, not a precocious cynicism about romantic love, but a romantic fantasy about freedom and power.

WILLIAM STAFFORD

Fifteen

South of the bridge on Seventeenth
I found back of the willows one summer
day a motorcycle with engine running
as it lay on its side, ticking over
slowly in the high grass. I was fifteen.   5

I admired all that pulsing gleam, the
shiny flanks, the demure headlights
fringed where it lay; I led it gently
to the road and stood with that
companion, ready and friendly. I was fifteen.   10

We could find the end of a road, meet
the sky on out Seventeenth. I thought about
hills, and patting the handle got back a
confident opinion. On the bridge we indulged
a forward feeling, a tremble. I was fifteen.   15

Thinking, back farther in the grass I found
the owner, just coming to, where he had flipped
over the rail. He had blood on his hand, was pale—
I helped him walk to his machine. He ran his hand
over it, called me good man, roared away.   20

I stood there, fifteen.

Ursula Fanthorpe (p. 91) had a repeated "No" pattern; William Stafford has a repeated "fifteen" pattern. And each time the sentence, "I was fifteen," occurs, its tone and effect change. Stanza one simply provides the reader with some useful information—useful because we all know that at fifteen you can't have a driving license. So the speaker's excluded, barred from driving off on the motorcycle. In the second, he is excited by his contact with the gleaming, glamorous machine and very close to getting it between his legs. Stanza three tantalizes with its sense of freedom, of escape from pedestrian life: oh, the excitement, the relish, the delirium of going off at speed. No wonder he trembles.

Then the pattern breaks: the rider (the *owner*—the speaker has no claim to the motorcycle) "roared away." Ironically, he had called the boy "good man," not realizing that the boy is impatient to escape boyhood and surge forward into manhood. The pattern breaks, and the "I" is left, standing alone, and "I stood there, fifteen" stands all alone, separated from the fourth stanza, in which the owner has reclaimed his bike, has run "his hand over it" (proprietorial, almost erotic) and roared away, leaving the "I" stuck at fifteen.

The impulse that gives rise to a poem is *not at all* odd or peculiar or different from the impulse that *we all experience*: to consider a moment, an event, an episode, a sight, something observed, a little bit of life (either our own or someone else's) and to pause, taking the time to *read it as a sign*—to read it as significant to our theory of the world. How we discover or invent this significance at any moment seems to vary from day to day: sometimes it *strikes* us, coming unbidden, not thought out; on other occasions, we have to tease it out by thinking, by considering it. Sometimes the inclination to pause in this way comes from a sense that what the moment contained was something special, something worth holding onto, even worth celebrating and sharing with others; sometimes the inclination arises out of a sense of puzzlement or perplexity—"I'm sure that moment was 'important,' but what on earth did it mean?" or "Am *I* crazy?"

So we take time to inscribe on it our sense of its meaning—a meaning that seems to have been given, like a gift, or a meaning that we have to work to construct. However we do it, our meaning will either fit into our existing theory, or will modify it. Occasionally, in extreme cases, it will turn our theory upside down. Psychologists call this a "cognitive crisis."

The impulse is *not* to tell a story (if it were, we would tell a story, or write a short story); and it is not to explain (if it were, we might write an editorial or an essay); it is to offer as much as necessary to the readers, as much as they need in order to be able to "read" what it is that got us going in the first place.

So Stafford offered us as much as we need to reconstruct his experience: the episode of finding the motorcycle. If by the time we read his words we have internalized the conventions of reading, we don't ask, "Well, what day of the week was it?" or "What was the guy's name—the one who owned the bike?" or "Well, what were *you* doing south of the bridge on Seventeenth?" Our reading is itself guided by our tacit knowledge of how to read, and *we build this knowledge up simply by reading*. People who have difficulty reading poetry are simply people who don't read poetry. The only cure is to read lots of poetry, without anxiety, without trying to answer too many questions: in that way, the poetry will do its work of teaching you how to read it. One of the most congenial ways of doing this is simply to share it with a friend. Choose two or three poems from this book that you think might interest or amuse or touch your best friend, your mother, your grandmother. . . .

FRANK CONROY

It's Called the Universe

William Stafford's "I" was left standing, excluded from the brotherhood of those who can roar away on motorcycles. Frank Conroy (b.1936), in the next piece, works very hard, not only to join the tribe of those who have mastered the yo-yo, but also to be the very best, to beat everyone else. He has learned the lessons of a particular culture, has absorbed its ideology: it is not enough to play for fun, for amusement, or to pass the time. You must convert that kind of useless play into a competitive game; then you must practice, hard, as hard as ever you can, and slowly eliminate the opposition: you must, above all, win!

As you read Conroy, see what kinds of expectations and predictions his text leads you to create.

Something was happening in front of the dime store. I could see a crowd of kids gathered at the doors and a policeman attempting to keep order. I slipped inside behind his back. The place was a madhouse, jammed with hundreds of shrieking children, all pressing toward one of the aisles where some kind of demonstration was going on.

"What's happening?" I asked a kid as I elbowed past.

"It's Ramos and Ricardo," he shouted. "The twins from California."

I pushed my way to the front rank and looked up at the raised platform.

There, under a spotlight, two Oriental gentlemen in natty blue suits were doing some amazing things with yo-yos. Tiny, neat men, no bigger than children, they stared abstractedly off into space while yo-yos flew from their hands, zooming in every direction as if under their own power, leaping out from small fists in arcs, circles, and straight lines. I stared open-mouthed as a yo-yo was thrown down and *stayed down*, spinning at the end of its string a fraction of an inch above the floor.

"Walking the Dog," said the twin, and lowered his yo-yo to the floor. It skipped along beside him for a yard or so and mysteriously returned to his palm.

"The Pendulum," said the other twin, and threw down a yo-yo. "Sleeping," he said, pointing to the toy as it spun at the end of its string. He gathered the line like so much loose spaghetti, making a kind of cat's cradle with his fingers, and gently rocked the spinning yo-yo back and forth through the center. "Watch end of trick closely," he said smiling, and suddenly dropped everything. Instead of the tangled mess we'd all expected the yo-yo wound up safely in his palm.

"Loop-the-Loop." He threw a yo-yo straight ahead. When it returned he didn't catch it, but executed a subtle flick of his wrist and sent it back out again. Five, ten, twenty times. "Two Hands Loop-the-Loop," he said, adding another, alternating so that as one flew away from his right hand the other flew in toward his left.

"Pickpocket," said the other twin, raising the flap of his jacket. He threw the yo-yo between his legs, wrapping the string around his thigh. As he looked out over the crowd the yo-yo dropped, perfectly placed, into his trouser pocket. Laughing, the kids applauded.

I spent the whole afternoon in one spot, watching them, not even moving when they took breaks for fear I'd lose my place. When it was over I spent my last money on a yo-yo, a set of extra strings, and a pamphlet explaining all the tricks, starting from the easiest and working up to the hardest.

Walking back to the bike I was so absorbed a mail truck almost ran me down. I did my first successful trick standing by the rack, a simpe but rather spectacular exercise called Around the World. Smiling, I put the yo-yo in my pocket and pulled out the bike. I knew I was going to be good at it.

* * *

The common yo-yo is crudely made, with a thick shank between two widely spaced wooden disks. The string is knotted or stapled to the shank. With such an instrument nothing can be done except the simple up-down movement. My yo-yo, on the other hand, was a perfectly balanced construction of hard wood, slightly weighted, flat, with only a sixteenth of an inch between the halves. The string was not attached to the shank, but looped over it in such a way as to allow the wooden part to spin freely on its own axis. The gyroscopic effect thus created kept the yo-yo stable in all attitudes.

I started at the beginning of the book and quickly mastered the novice, intermediate, and advanced stages, practicing all day every day in the woods across the street from my house. Hour after hour of practice, never moving to the next trick until the one at hand was mastered.

The string was tied to my middle finger, just behind the nail. As I threw—with your palm up, make a fist; throw down your hand, fingers unfolding, as if you were casting grain—a short bit of string would tighten across the sensitive pad of flesh at the tip of my finger. That was the critical area. After a number of weeks I could interpret the condition of the string, the presence of any imperfections on the shank, but most importantly the exact amount of spin or inertial energy left in the yo-yo at any given moment—all from that bit of string on my fingertip. As the throwing motion became more and more natural I found I could make the yo-yo "sleep" for an astonishing length of time—fourteen or fifteen seconds—and still have enough spin left to bring it back to my hand. Gradually the basic moves became reflexes. Sleeping, twirling, swinging, and precise aim. Without thinking, without even looking, I could run through trick after trick involving various combinations of the elemental skills, switching from one to the other in a smooth continuous flow. On particularly good days I would hum a tune under my breath and do it all in time to the music.

Flicking the yo-yo expressed something. The sudden, potentially comic extension of one's arm to twice it's length. The precise neatness of it, intrinsically soothing, as if relieving an inner tension too slight to be noticeable, the way a man might hitch up his pants simply to enact a reassuring gesture. It felt good. The comfortable weight in one's hand, the smooth, rapid descent down the string, ending with a barely audible snap as the yo-yo hung balanced, spinning, pregnant with force and the slave of one's fingertip. That it was vaguely masturbatory seems inescapable. I doubt that half the pubescent boys in America could have been captured by any other means, as, in the heat of the fad, half of them were. A single Loop-the-Loop might represent, in some mysterious way, the act of masturbation, but to break down the entire repertoire into the three stages of throw, trick, and return representing erection, climax, and detumescence seems immoderate.

The greatest pleasure in yo-yoing was an abstract pleasure—watching the dramatization of simple physical laws, and realizing they would never fail if a trick was done correctly. The geometric purity of it! The string wasn't just a string, it was a tool in the enactment of theorems. It was a line, an idea. And the top was an entirely different sort of idea, a gyroscope, capable of storing energy and of interacting with the line. I remember the first time I did a particularly lovely trick, one in which the sleeping yo-yo is swung from right to left while the string is interrupted by an extended index finger. Momentum carries the yo-yo in a circular path around the finger, but instead of completing the arc the yo-yo falls on the taut string between the performer's hands, where it continues to spin in an upright position. My pleasure at that moment was as much from the beauty of the experiment as from pride. Snapping apart my hands I sent the yo-yo into the air above my head, bouncing it off nothing, back into my palm.

I practiced the yo-yo because it pleased me to do so, without the slightest application of will power. It wasn't ambition that drove me, but the nature of yo-yoing. The yo-yo represented my first organized attempt to control the outside world. It fascinated me because I could see my progress in clearly defined stages, and because the intimacy of it, the almost spooky closeness I began to feel with the instrument in my hand, seemed to ensure that nothing irrelevant would interfere. I was, in the language of jazz, "up tight" with my yo-yo, and finally free, in one small area at least, of the paralyzing sloppiness of life in general.

The first significant problem arose in the attempt to do fifty consecutive Loop-the-Loops. After ten or fifteen the yo-yo invariably started to lean and the throws became less clean, resulting in loss of control. I almost skipped the whole thing because fifty seemed excessive. Ten made the point. But there it was, written out in the book. To qualify as an expert you had to do fifty, so fifty I would do.

It took me two days, and I wouldn't have spent a moment more. All those Loop-the-Loops were hard on the strings. Time after time the shank cut them and the yo-yo went sailing off into the air. It was irritating, not only because of the expense (strings were a nickel each, and fabricating your own was unsatisfactory), but because a random element had been introduced. About the only unforeseeable disaster in yo-yoing was to have your string break, and here was a trick designed to do exactly that. Twenty-five would have been enough. If you could do twenty-five clean Loop-the-Loops you could do fifty or a hundred. I supposed they were simply trying to sell strings and went back to the more interesting tricks.

The witty nonsense of Eating Spaghetti, the surprise of The Twirl, the complex neatness of Cannonball, Backwards round the World, or Halfway round the World—I could do them all, without false starts or sloppy endings. I could do every trick in the book. Perfectly.

The day was marked on the kitchen calendar. (God Gave Us Bluebell Natural Bottled Gas). I got on my bike and rode into town. Pedaling along the highway I worked out with the yo-yo to break in a new string. The twins were appearing at the dime store.

I could hear the crowd before I turned the corner. Kids were coming on bikes and on foot from every corner of town, rushing down the streets like madmen. Three or four policemen were busy keeping the street clear directly in front of the store, and in a small open space around the doors some of the more adept kids were running through their tricks, showing off to the general audience or stopping to compare notes with their peers. Standing at the edge with my yo-yo safe in my pocket, it didn't take me long to see I had them all covered. A boy in a sailor hat could do some of the harder tricks, but he missed too often to be a serious threat. I went inside.

As Ramos and Ricardo performed I watched their hands carefully, noticing little differences in style, and technique. Ricardo was a shade classier, I thought, although Ramos held an edge in the showy two-handed stuff. When they were through we went outside for the contest.

"Everybody in the alley!" Ramos shouted, his head bobbing an inch or two above the others. "Contest starting now in the alley!" A hundred excited children followed the twins into an alley beside the dime store and lined up against the wall.

"Attention all kids!" Ramos yelled, facing us from the middle of the street like a drill sergeant. "To qualify for contest you got to Rock the Cradle. You got to rock yo-yo in cradle four time. Four time! Okay? Three time no good. Okay. Everybody happy?" There were murmurs of disappointment and some of the kids stepped out of line. The rest of us closed ranks. Yo-yos flicked nervously as we waited. "Winner receive grand prize. Special Black Beauty Prize Yo-Yo with Diamonds," said Ramos, gesturing to his brother who smiled and held up the prize, turning it in the air so we could see the four stones set on each side. ("The crowd gasped . . ." I want to write. Of course they didn't. They didn't make a sound, but the impact of the diamond yo-yo was obvious.) We'd never seen anything like it. One imagined how the stones would gleam as it revolved, and how much prettier the tricks would be. The ultimate yo-yo! The only one in town! Who knew what feats were possible with such an instrument? All around me a fierce, nervous resolve was settling into the contestants, suddenly skittish as racehorses.

"Ricardo will show trick with Grand Prize Yo-Yo. Rock the Cradle four time!"

"One!" cried Ramos.

"Two!" the kids joined in.

"Three!" It was really beautiful. He did it so slowly you would have thought he had all the time in the world. I counted seconds under my breath to see how long he made it sleep.

"Four!" said the crowd.

"Thirteen," I said to myself as the yo-yo snapped back into his hand. Thirteen seconds. Excellent time for that particular trick.

"Attention all kids!" Ramos announced. "Contest start now at head of line."

The first boy did a sloppy job of gathering his string but managed to rock the cradle quickly four times.

"Okay." Ramos tapped him on the shoulder and moved to the next boy, who fumbled. "Out." Ricardo followed, doing an occasional Loop-the-Loop with the diamond yo-yo. "Out . . . out . . . okay," said Ramos as he worked down the line.

There was something about the man's inexorable advance that unnerved me. His decisions were fast, and there was no appeal. To my surprise I felt my palms begin to sweat. Closer and closer he came, his voice growing louder, and then suddenly he was standing in front of me. Amazed, I stared at him. It was as if he'd appeared out of thin air.

"What happen boy, you swallow bubble gum?"

The laughter jolted me out of it. Blushing, I threw down my yo-yo and executed a slow Rock the Cradle, counting the four passes and hesitating a moment at the end so as not to appear rushed.

"Okay." He tapped my shoulder. "Good."

I wiped my hands on my blue jeans and watched him move down the line. "Out . . . out . . . out." He had a large mole on the back of his neck.

Seven boys qualified. Coming back, Ramos called out, "Next trick Backward Round the World! Okay? Go!"

The first two boys missed, but the third was the kid in the sailor hat. Glancing quickly to see that no one was behind him, he hunched up his shoulder, threw, and just barely made the catch. There was some loose string in his hand, but not enough to disqualify him.

Number four missed, as did number five, and it was my turn. I stepped forward, threw the yo-yo almost straight up over my head, and as it began to fall pulled very gently to add some speed. It zipped neatly behind my legs and there was nothing more to do. My head turned to one side, I stood absolutely still and watched the yo-yo come in over my shoulder and slap into my hand. I added a Loop-the-Loop just to show the tightness of the string.

"Did you see that?" I heard someone say.

Number seven missed, so it was between myself and the boy in the sailor hat. His hair was bleached by the sun and combed up over his forehead in a pompadour, held from behind by the white hat. He was a year or two older than me. Blinking his blue eyes nervously, he adjusted the tension of his string.

"Next trick Cannonball! Cannonball! You go first this time," Ramos said to me.

Kids had gathered in a circle around us, those in front quiet and attentive, those in back jumping up and down to get a view. "Move back for room," Ricardo said, pushing them back. "More room, please."

I stepped into the center and paused, looking down at the ground. It was a difficult trick. The yo-yo had to land exactly on the string and there was a chance I'd miss the first time. I knew I wouldn't miss twice. "Can I have one practice?"

Ramos and Ricardo consulted in their mother tongue, and then Ramos held up his hands. "Attention all kids! Each boy have one practice before trick."

The crowd was silent, watching me. I took a deep breath and threw, following the fall of the yo-yo with my eyes, turning slightly, matador-fashion, as it passed me. My finger caught the string, the yo-yo came up and over, and missed. Without pausing I threw again. "Second time," I yelled, so there would be no misunderstanding. The circle had been too big. This time I made it small, sacrificing beauty for security. The yo-yo fell where it belonged and spun for a moment. (A moment I don't rush, my arms widespread, my eyes locked on the spinning toy. The Trick! There it is, brief and magic, right before your eyes! My hands are frozen in the middle of a deaf-and-dumb sentence, holding the whole airy, tenuous statement aloft for everyone to see.) With a quick snap I broke up the trick and made my catch.

Ramos nodded. "Okay. Very good. Now next boy."

Sailor-hat stepped forward, wiping his nose with the back of his hand. He threw once to clear the string.

"One practice," said Ramos.

He nodded.

"C'mon Bobby," someone said. "You can do it."

Bobby threw the yo-yo out to the side, made his move, and missed. "Damn," he whispered. (He said "dahyum.") The second time he got halfway through the trick before his yo-yo ran out of gas and fell impotently off the string. He picked it up and walked away, winding slowly.

Ramos came over and held my hand in the air. "The winner!" he yelled. "Grand prize Black Beauty Diamond Yo-Yo will now be awarded."

Ricardo stood in front of me. "Take off old yo-yo." I loosened the knot and slipped it off. "Put out hand." I held out my hand and he looped the new string on my finger, just behind the nail, where the mark was. "You like Black Beauty," he said, smiling as he stepped back. "Diamond make pretty colors in the sun."

"Thank you," I said.

"Very good with yo-yo. Later we have contest for whole town. Winner go to Miami for State Championship. Maybe you win. Okay?"

"Okay." I nodded. "Thank you."

A few kids came up to look at Black Beauty. I threw it once or twice to get the feel. It seemed a bit heavier than my old one. Ramos and Ricardo were surrounded as the kids called out their favorite tricks.

"Do Pickpocket! Pickpocket!"

"Do the Double Cannonball!"

"Ramos! Ramos! Do the Turkish Army!"

Smiling, waving their hands to ward off the barrage of requests, the twins worked their way through the crowd toward the mouth of the alley. I watched them moving away and was immediately struck by a wave of fierce and irrational panic. "Wait," I yelled, pushing through after them. "Wait!"

I caught them on the street.

"No more today," Ricardo said, and then paused when he saw it was me. "Okay. The champ. What's wrong? Yo-yo no good?"

"No. It's fine."

"Good. You take care of it."

"I wanted to ask when the contest is. The one where you get to go to Miami."

"Later. After school begins." They began to move away. "We have to go home now."

"Just one more thing," I said, walking after them. "What is the hardest trick you know?"

Ricardo laughed. "Hardest trick killing flies in air."

"No, no. I mean a real trick."

They stopped and looked at me. "There is a very hard trick," Ricardo said. "I don't do it, but Ramos does. Because you won the contest he will show you. But only once, so watch carefully."

We stepped into the lobby of the Sunset Theater. Ramos cleared his string. "Watch," he said, and threw. The trick started out like a Cannonball, and then unexpectedly folded up, opened again, and as I watched breathlessly the entire complex web spun around in the air, propelled by Ramos' two hands making slow circles like a swimmer. The end was like the end of a Cannonball.

"That's beautiful," I said, genuinely awed. "What's it called?"

"The Universe."

"The Universe," I repeated.

"Because it goes around and around," said Ramos, "like the planets." . . .

I spent the last few days before school in the woods, attempting to re-create the trick Ramos had shown me in the lobby of the Sunset Theater. I'd broken it down into three steps, the world, the solar system, and the galaxies, the sum of which was The Universe. The world and the solar system were within my abilities, but in the galaxies stage the yo-yo would run out of gas or the string would tangle. My strategy was to go back and practice the simple Cannonball for duration, snapping my throws out more and more evenly, trying for perfect balance so the string wouldn't touch the inner walls of the yo-yo. At the same time I speeded up the first two stages, attempting to feel The Universe not so much as three separate maneuvers but as one continuous rhythmic statement. Progress was slow but steady, and had I not been interrupted by the opening of school, I might have learned it in a week.

One late afternoon in the woods everything fell into place. I'd been practicing for an hour, running through the easy tricks abstractedly, the way an expert mechanic might shuffle cards while waiting for his victims to take their seats, when I began to realize something special was happening. Never had I yo-yoed so effortlessly. Never had the tricks clicked with such mathematical precision. The yo-yo seemed to be playing itself as I stood waving my hands like a conductor before an invisible orchestra. The time was ripe for an assault on The Universe, not only the separate parts, but the whole trick as one unit.

Unbelievably, it came on the first try. I was flabbergasted. I'd been trying for weeks—for so long, in fact, I was reconciled to creeping up on it slowly, perhaps over a period of months—and suddenly victory was mine. Breathless, hoping it hadn't been a fluke, I threw again. As I watched the trick unfold, it came to me that a ghost or a spirit was controlling the yo-yo's movements, and that to be really good one had simply to give up one's desire to dominate the yo-yo and instead let the ghost take over. It was as if someone spoke to me through the yo-yo. See how easy, was the implication. Just practice till you get over your clumsiness, practice until you can yo-yo without thinking about it and then let me take over. I threw back my head and laughed. I danced a little dance on the sand and shouted out into the pine trees. I knew that in all of Fort Lauderdale and very probably in all of Florida there was not one other boy who could do what I had just done.

I knew I was best. As for what happened, I was no more than moderately disappointed when my supposedly unobtainable Black Beauty went on sale at the five-and-ten for sixty cents. I'd gone as far as one could go on the yo-yo. I'd learned tricks the demonstrators didn't know. So when the final contest arrived and I learned that after one or two extremely easy tricks the choice of champion would be based on the greatest number of consecutive Loop-the-Loops, when I learned that my skill counted for nothing in the eyes of the non-yo-yoing judges, when I found myself screwed once again as my string broke at seventy-three (eleven less than a muscle-bound idiot from the beach who couldn't do a simple Cannonball)—when, to wrap it up, all this reality was finally absorbed by my brain, the knowledge that I was without question the best yo-yo player around kept me from despair. There was no despair, only a mild confusion at the sloppiness of things, and a faint sickness at my own bewilderment.

CONSIDER THIS

★ We wonder if that text gave you as much pleasure as it gives us, still, after many readings. Do you, like us, get caught up in the obsessive passion, the passionate obsessiveness, of Frank's quest? Do you find that an act that you may not be especially interested in (who gives a darn about the yo-yo?) becomes intensely absorbing? That Frank's account of his acquisition of skill, and the persistent improvement and refinement of that skill, grips your attention? That you become caught up in the suspense of the competition?

★ What of the ending? Do you hope for a great climax, like a roll of drums and a blast of trumpets, with Frank triumphant, crowned King of the Yo-yo? Do you wish that the narrator had lied, had bent the narrative, to give you such satisfaction? Or do you think the last paragraph is a remarkably effective way of demonstrating (without saying it too obviously) that Frank was growing up?

We know we have left childhood and moved into the next phase of our lives, when we discover that the fabulous heroes and heroines have lost their power to arouse our imaginations and no longer inspire our loyalty. Just as Heaney left the fantasy of comics behind and moved eventually into the intensely satisfying disturbances of Hardy's *Return of the Native*, so Brian Patten (b.1946) in the following poem looks back at those extraordinary years like the timescape of Thomas Frosch's "Lone Ranger," when heroes walked the earth (p. 83). But where did Patten's heroes come from? Books?

BRIAN PATTEN

Where Are You Now, Batman?

Where are you now, Batman? Now that Aunt Heriot has
    reported Robin missing
And Superman's fallen asleep in the sixpenny childhood seats?
Where are you now that Captain Marvel's SHAZAM! echoes
    round the auditorium,
The magicians don't hear it,
Must all be deaf . . . or dead . . .   5
The Purple Monster who came down from the Purple Planet
    disguised as a man
Is wandering aimlessly about the streets
With no way of getting back.
Sir Galahad's been strangled by the Incredible Living Trees,
Zorro killed by his own sword.   10

Blackhawk has buried the last of his companions
And has now gone off to commit suicide in the disused
    Hangars of Innocence.
The Monster and the Ape still fight it out in a room
Where the walls are continually closing in;
Rocketman's fuel tanks gave out over London.   15
Even Flash Gordon's lost, he wanders among the stars
Weeping over the woman he loved
7 Universes ago.
    My celluloid companions, it's only a few years
Since I knew you. Something in us has faded.   20
    Has the Terrible Fiend, That Ghastly Adversary,
Mr Old Age, Caught you in his deadly trap,
And come finally to polish you off,
His machinegun dripping with years . . . ?

CONSIDER THIS

★ Where was Patten, then, as he wrote those lines? In a land of regret? Of disenchantment? Should we regret the loss of childhood, the expulsion from the paradise garden? "Something in us has faded." What exactly? And doesn't it need to fade, in order to release us from its clutches? To allow us to get on with the hard work of growing up?

The "I" of Stafford's "Fifteen" is in limbo—neither a child nor a man: the limbo we call "adolescence," a word that means "*becoming* adult." In our culture, we enter adulthood across the threshold of adolescence, and the Latin word for threshold is *limen*, which gives us our adjective *liminal*: meaning neither outside nor inside, but poised, one foot raised, one's hand on the doorknob, one's sense of self hanging somewhere in mid-air.

Traditional societies mostly have rituals to mark one's entry into adult status. These rituals involve loss: your previous identity is taken away from you and you gain a new identity (man or woman). In between is the liminal, an experience lasting a few hours or a few days, during which you are *nowhere*, in limbo.

Such liminality is not only a *natural* biological phenomenon, but is also something created by the dominant culture, like the suspended animation of human sperm in a laboratory; a recently invented bookish solution to this unhappy condition is to commission and publish "teenage books," fiction that presents and *deals with* (solves?) teenage problems; this strikes us rather like the idea of giving manuals on how to die gracefully to the very old: a kind of cheap band-aid.

The deeper and more demanding solution is to change the structure of adolescence: it was invented by our culture, and it can be changed by our culture. It is not an unalterable "natural" fact. What changes would you like to see?

STEVEN MILLHAUSER

I Sank into Other Streets and Universes

The "I" of Millhauser's Portrait of a Romantic *is in limbo: nostalgia for childhood draws him back into children's books; impatience for adulthood draws him forward into adult books. The former bore him, drive him to despair; the latter confuse him, and leave him feeling "strange and anxious."*

Spring came, that famous season, and with it a sense of dark withdrawal, as if I sought protection against the growing violence of light. I found myself longing to return from school each day to the cool peacefulness of my room, where on days when William did not come over I would change quickly out of my belted pants, my polished shoes, and my oppressively neat schoolshirt into grass-stained sneakers, faded jeans, and a rumpled playshirt with a torn elbow. Bringing in from the kitchen a tall glass of chocolate milk and a saucer of red pistachio nuts, I would close the blinds and pull out the metal wall-light, and lying down on my stomach on the light-brown bedspread crisscrossed with dark brown and dark green, I would open a book. And as in one of those black-and-white movies that begin with the image of some dusty old-fashioned book, which a mysterious hand opens slowly, with intensely crisp papery sounds, to a page of words so large and thick that they are not real words but cunning imitations, and a mysterious voice that is not a real voice but a British voice begins to read, and slowly, softly, you sink through the page into a sudden street where men in tall hats and bushy side-whiskers stride briskly along: so I too sank through soft pages, down, deep down, into other streets and universes.

Twice a week father drove me to the distant stone library, where I borrowed armfuls of books from the teenage section. I looked for familiar names, like Stevenson and Poe, but I was far more attracted by the completely mysterious and unknown. At times I felt I was searching for a book so violently satisfying that a deep calm would come over me, my internal itching would cease, and at last I could stop reading forever. In the high brown room, under the yellow light, I loved to open some dark old novel with a faded title and many dates stamped in crooked columns on the paper slip in back; and leaning against a shelf I would eagerly read the opening sentences, in the hope of coming upon a phrase that would possess me. My needs were imperative and had nothing to do with taste. What I searched for, what I demanded, was a certain mysterious power of annihilation, of dissolution—and behold! on a sudden street, men in tall hats and bushy side-whiskers stride briskly along.

And yet, that spring, I could not conceal from myself a growing fretfulness. Often, as I read, the men in tall hats would waver and grow dim, and I would see only a page of precise black print, upon which there sometimes lay, like a white scratch, a slanting line of space formed by a hazard of typography, and shutting my book unhappily I would grow sullen with disappointment. Sometimes I felt that I was tired of teenage fiction, and asking father's troubled permission I would look at books in the adult section, in a high brown silent unfamiliar room. I would choose a book and ask him to take it out for me, and he would open it with a frown and turn the pages uncertainly and cough into his fist and push out his lips and scratch his neck and at last, with a sigh, oblige me. At home mother would glare through the bottom of her reading glasses as she turned the pages grimly and asked what in the world I hoped to accomplish by reading adult books before I was an adult. But adult books always bored me to death in the first two pages; and I began to wonder whether I had reached an age for which no books were written. And perhaps it was simply that I longed for the remembered mystery of the vanished books of my childhood, rendered in language not for children. Lying indolently on my lamplit bed, gazing down at a page of print, I would recall with sudden vividness a picture in some forgotten storybook: a green hill where plump watermelons grew on watermelon trees, an orange-and-brown tiger holding in his tail a dark green umbrella, a yellow brick house with a bright red roof. One day I brought home from the library an armful of children's books. In my room I began reading feverishly, with a shock of delight, but my eagerness quickly gave way to boredom and despair. And once, in a dull adult novel, a man and a woman went into a room. The woman sat down on the edge of the bed and began to undo the buttons of her blouse. There was a white space, and the scene changed to a vicarage, and I felt strange and anxious, but they never returned to that troubling room.

CONSIDER THIS

★ ". . . mother would glare through the bottom of her reading glasses as she turned the pages grimly and asked what in the world I hoped to accomplish by reading adult books before I was an adult." Indeed! How would you answer her?

JAMES BALDWIN

Autobiographical Notes

James Baldwin (1924–1987) gives, as part of his title, the word Notes. *What are the probable consequences for the writer and for the reader of this particular sign? How does the word influence your expectations, your predictions? The date of Baldwin's text is 1955; see Kay Boyle, page 280.*

I was born in Harlem thirty-one years ago. I began plotting novels at about the time I learned to read. The story of my childhood is the usual bleak fantasy, and we can dismiss it with the restrained observation that I certainly would not consider living it again. In those days my mother was given to the exasperating and mysterious habit of having babies. As they were born, I took them over with one hand and held a book with the other. The children probably suffered, though they have since been kind enough to deny it, and in this way I read *Uncle Tom's Cabin* and *A Tale of Two Cities* over and over and over again; in this way, in fact, I read just about everything I could get my hands on—except the Bible, probably because it was the only book I was encouraged to read. I must also confess that I wrote—a great deal—and my first professional triumph, in any case, the first effort of mine to be seen in print, occurred at the age of twelve or thereabouts, when a short story I had written about the Spanish revolution won some sort of prize in an extremely short-lived church newspaper. I remember the story was censored by the lady editor, though I don't remember why, and I was outraged.

Also wrote plays, and songs, for one of which I received a letter of congratulations from Mayor La Guardia, and poetry, about which the less said, the better. My mother was delighted by all these goings-on, but my father wasn't; he wanted me to be a preacher. When I was fourteen I became a preacher, and when I was seventeen I stopped. Very shortly thereafter I left home. For God knows how long I struggled with the world of commerce and industry—I guess they would say they struggled with *me*—and when I was about twenty-one I had enough done of a novel to get a Saxton Fellowship. When I was twenty-two the fellowship was over, the novel turned out to be unsalable, and I started waiting on tables in a Village restaurant and writing book reviews—mostly, as it turned out, about the Negro problem, concerning which the color of my skin made me automatically an expert. Did another book, in company with photographer Theodore Pelatowski, about the store-front churches in Harlem. This book met exactly the same fate as my first—fellowship, but no sale. (It was a Rosenwald Fellowship.) By the time I was twenty-four I had decided to stop reviewing books about the Negro problem—which, by this time, was only slightly less horrible in print than it was in life—and I packed my bags and went to France, where I finished, God knows how, *Go Tell It on the Mountain*.

CONSIDER THIS

★ Do you detect any resemblances between Baldwin's text and Fanthorpe's poem "Growing Up"? The *differences* are many and obvious, but they may conceal some strong likenesses.

RACHEL BROWNSTEIN

My Life in Fiction

Rules for reading were set down early in Rachel Brownstein's New York home: facts for men, fiction for women. When her father read "serious" novels, the Russian Dostoevski or Tolstoy, it was to get to "The Facts": "lust and hatred, jealousy and greed." His reading of history brought him to "illustrious actions," where the male psyche should live—a world that was "grand, male, and real."

But what of women? Women, according to her father's rules, should be schooled in delicacy, sensitivity, and subtlety—"The Finer Things." The best way for women to be so educated in this "culture" was through the English novelists and Henry James; so Brownstein locked herself in the bathroom to soak up James and to become, at eleven, an English major—while her brother was to be a scientist. What she read in the bathroom, however, was not only the novels of Henry James.

Of all the departments in literature, fiction is the one to which, by nature and circumstances, women are best adapted.

—G. H. LEWES,

"The Lady Novelists"

The good ended happily, and the bad unhappily. That is what Fiction means.

—Miss Prism, in

OSCAR WILDE'S *The Importance of Being Earnest*

In my house novels were *weibische sachen*, women's things. My father used to read Gibbon, Churchill, the paper, while my mother read a good book. My brother was to be a scientist but I was to major in English, which is not too dangerously far from typing (words on paper, after all), because literature is the high road to assimilation, because culture is okay for the Jewish wife-in-training, because poetry is decorative and harmless, but more profoundly because novels are for women. Most novels. Of course my father's face darkened with respect at the names Tolstoy, Dostoevski, and Mann. Over Balzac, Flaubert—maybe Dickens—he supposed men and women might sometimes meet. But George Eliot? Henry James? Charlotte Brontë and Jane Austen? Kathleen Winsor and Margaret Mitchell? The distinction is made with words like "serious." Women and Englishmen, from my father's Austro-Hungarian perspective, were not serious.

He was an underachieving businessman who cheered himself up by explaining why Rome (also) fell, an armchair philosopher and a connoisseur of hard facts, and deep inside him lived a frustrated foxhunter. He very much admired the English. His attitude toward women, whom he affected to despise, was more complicated than he let on. My father assumed that Thackeray and Henry James were not serious, were not for him, but he thought they were subtle and sensitive and other good things. They were The Finer Things. Dostoevski, whose subjects were lust and hatred, jealousy and greed, wrote about what my father considered The Facts. The English novelists wrote, he supposed, about delicate and elevated feelings, the feelings women have or should have: social, not religious, ecstasies. A misconception, you say, and you are right. But it is also true that reading Henry James, that not-English apogee of English novelists, inspired in me a passion for a social life of complex and rarefied meaning. This aspiration my father dimly imagined to be British, frivolous, feminine, unrealistic, but commendable, an excellent, even a necessary thing in a woman. For while men studied the tragic course of history and read the novelists who revealed the horrors that underlie it, women had to keep alive that aspiration toward Fineness without which both the pleasantness and meaning of private life would disappear. My father luxuriated in his tragic vision from the depths of a doilied armchair. My mother, he vaguely presumed, plumped up the cushions, crocheted and disposed the doilies, because of a countervision of coherence and comfort he needed her to continue to have. He was not wrong to think she derived some of her respect for the value of private life from her novelists.

Susan Ferrier (an English woman) wrote a novel called *Marriage* in 1818, and prefaced it with this epigraph from Dr. Johnson (an English man):

> Life consists not of a series of illustrious actions; the greater part of our time passes in compliance with necessities in the performance of daily duties—in the removal of small inconveniences—in the procurement of petty pleasures; and we are well or ill at ease, as the main stream of life glides on smoothly, or is ruffled by small and frequent interruption.

A sentiment to which my father would subscribe. On the one hand, there is the important world of "illustrious actions," to which his heart thrilled but from which his false friend History had barred him; that world is grand, male, and real. On the other hand, there is ordinary life, and ordinary life is all most of us have. That is the life novels describe, and by giving it form and connecting it with dreams, they make it extraordinary—something no man with visions of Higher Things would stoop to do but something any sensible man is happy to have someone else do, while she's doing for him generally.

So this Jewish daughter listened to her father and became an English major at about eleven. (My neighbors gave to "English major" the stresses proper to, say, "French lieutenant.")

Reading the novels of Henry James at fifteen I experienced a miracle. Behind the locked bathroom door, sitting on the terrycloth-covered toilet seat, I was transformed into someone older, more beautiful and graceful. I moved subtly among people who understood delicate and complex webs of feeling, patterned perceptions altogether foreign to my crude "real" life. Mealtimes, encounters, conversations were precisely as significant in James's world as they were insignificant in mine; and as I read more and more novels, what happened in my actual family came to seem less and less important. My parents were proud of my reading and encouraged it, but I knew this was because they were ignorant of what I felt while I read. For commitment to the world of Henry James—a world ineffably *goyish**—was betrayal of them. I hugged my secret knowledge that they were harboring a viper in their bathroom.

Not until I was twenty did I find out that *The Wings of the Dove* is about money; God knows what I thought it was about. All I knew was that its world was the antithesis of the vulgar one in which I was eating lamb chops and mashed potatoes, overhearing gossip about my aunts in Yiddish, fighting with my brother, and going to school. That my father connected reading Henry James with going to school— that he sanctioned it—was an aspect of the central Miracle in the Bathroom in which I turned into Isabel or Kate or Milly. It enabled me to betray him in safety. We lived in a small apartment; in novels I had a universe, not just a room of my own. I remember knowing I was lucky in having two worlds at once. I could relish my lamb chops as Milly Theale never could hers, and at the same time I could be Milly. I, not she, seemed to me the great creation of Henry James.

The English novelists cannot be said to inflame the girlish heart to rebellion. But they do move the mind to make and to value such distinctions as put one's family in its place. Learning from novels about life and love and goodness and beauty, I learned at the same time the difference between a gentleman and a man whose father was in trade, between a lady and the niece of an earl, and these points seemed implicated in the abstractions. English novelists flatter the reader by assuming she has a sense of class distinctions and their importance, even a sense of their being— in their subtler ramifications—a little absurd. "English fiction without the nieces of Earls and the cousins of Generals would be an arid waste," Virginia Woolf wrote. "It would resemble Russian fiction. It would have to fall back upon the immensity of the soul and upon the brotherhood of man."

* Goyish: non-Jewish.

Rachel Brownstein didn't need to go further than her locked bathroom to be uprooted. In the "Miracle of the Bathroom" she discovered Henry James, the American novelist, who wrote *A Portrait of a Lady*, *The Wings of the Dove*, and *The Ambassadors*, long novels about Americans abroad, discovering the "cultivations" of the Europeans, realizing that Americans were, oh, so barbaric, uncivilized.

Nothing in her "vulgar" world, with its gossip, her noisy brother, her aunts speaking Yiddish, the mashed potatoes and the lamb chops, stands up to the "delicate and complex web of feeling" that she discovers in James: he is so powerful that she feels herself of him: "I . . . seemed to me the great creation of Henry James."

The "finer" points of "culture," of class distinctions, of *gentlemen* and *ladies*— this was what she learned from James and from the "English novelists." Do you know what Brownstein is talking about? Have you read books that enabled you—for better or for worse—to "put one's family in its place"? Was it for better, or for worse?

Like Anderson, Brownstein became aware of the quirks, contradictions, and limitations of her father, and connects that theme neatly with the place of fiction in her family's life. She was encouraged to read, and her reading placed a distance between herself and her parents.

In adolescence, the lives and worlds that we can vicariously enter through our reading (and also through our visits to the cinema and our viewing of TV), often become a kind of "criticism" of our own lives and of those of our family. Brownstein discovered what no one else can tell us, but what we all must discover for ourselves: that we can go on "being ourselves," whatever that means, and also *become* heroines or heroes of fiction. It seems likely that what we will eventually become, in actual life, is fed, shaped, and enriched by such fantasy identifications.

Part of this rich and unsettling experience—the discovery in adolescence of other lives for ourselves—also involves, inevitably, the difficult shift in the mind whereby we *distance* ourselves from our immediate family circle, and look (down?) at our parents with eyes informed by new knowledge, new standards, new alternatives, new criteria, new discernment. It can be painful, because it can involve a sense of guilt, a sense of secret betrayal. But it seems that it is also a valuable part of the necessary move toward increasing independence.

CONSIDER THIS

★ Now construe Rachel Brownstein's representation of her adolescent experience in terms of its likeness or unlikeness to your own. For men, this will be much easier than it is for women: women will have the consolation of knowing that their statements will inevitably be subtler.

YOUR WRITING(S) FOR OTHERS TO READ

1. Do you think it's useful to have a developmental phase labeled "adolescence"? What for you were the distinctive characteristics of your adolescence? In what ways did you pretend to be more grown up than you actually were?
2. What kinds of adult opportunities and freedoms especially intrigued or tantalized you during your adolescence?
3. Do you think adolescence *has to be* a "difficult" phase in everyone's life? If you could change the dominant culture that you grew up in, change its conventions and rules, what changes would you make for the benefit of those who would come after you?

PART TWO

Losing Nature? Gaining Culture?

Chapter Five

Losses and Gains

The irreversible plunge into the chaos of adolescence is one of the great turning points of our lives; so also is the move that occurs for most of us around the age of eighteen: we leave home, either literally—by going to college—or psychologically, by realizing that not much longer are we going to be dependent children in a family, subject to parental authority and protection.

So, in whatever manner we leave, we turn the gaze of our minds outward, and as we begin to move into the larger world we find it quite overwhelming. There is so much to be known! Why were we not better prepared! For Richard Wright, a poor young black man sensitive to all the insults, barbs, and humiliations of a racist society, the way out of the confining culture of the home was the public library. For Malcolm Cowley and Cynthia Ozick it was college: Ozick was both overwhelmed and exhilarated by the more sophisticated world of Washington Square and New York University—so many references, allusions, names that were beyond her ken! Cowley, earlier in the century, was embittered and enraged by the superior culture of Harvard; superior both in its economic wealth and in its patronizing attitudes to the culture of those who came from the wrong side of the tracks.

So we see various young adults getting a toehold in the world beyond home, entering a larger and more complicated culture. At such a time, life can degenerate into a hectic and frantic scramble simply to keep up. Whatever happened to contentment, peace and quiet, tranquillity of soul?

RICHARD WRIGHT

Reading for Another Life and for Liberation

You may recall Sherwood Anderson's recognition of a loss of innocence in his boyhood (p. 37). In the next text, you will see how Richard Wright (1908–1960), the pioneering black American writer, struggled to resist and to defeat those forces in the dominant culture that would have kept him in a state of innocence (i.e., ignorance). It's no casual turn of speech, that the white men addressed their black contemporaries as "boy." Boys, by definition, have no power, have no influence, are still in a state of innocence, of not knowing. The year is about 1925; the city is Memphis.

At the time of this episode in his autobiography, Richard Wright is almost nineteen, and still struggling to repair the damage of years of neglect, of limited opportunity, of living in a world without books. As with Annie Dillard, who was in a happier, easier place and time, Wright turns for hope, for knowledge, to the public library.

When you read Wright's list of the writers H. L. Mencken, an influential journalist, regarded as important in 1927, you will not recognize all the names: the passage of sixty years has swept some of them into near oblivion.

> People who shut their eyes to reality simply invite their own destruction, and anyone who insists on remaining in a state of innocence long after that innocence is dead turns himself into a monster.
>
> —JAMES BALDWIN

One morning I arrived early at work and went into the bank lobby where the Negro porter was mopping. I stood at a counter and picked up the Memphis *Commercial Appeal* and began my free reading of the press. I came finally to the editorial page and saw an article dealing with one H. L. Mencken. I knew by hearsay that he was the editor of the *American Mercury*, but aside from that I knew nothing about him. The article was a furious denunciation of Mencken, concluding with one, hot, short sentence: Mencken is a fool.

I wondered what on earth this Mencken had done to call down upon him the scorn of the South. The only people I had ever heard denounced in the South were Negroes, and this man was not a Negro. Then what ideas did Mencken hold that made a newspaper like the *Commercial Appeal* castigate him publicly? Undoubtedly he must be advocating ideas that the South did not like. Were there, then, people other than Negroes who criticised the South? I knew that during the Civil War the South had hated northern whites, but I had not encountered such hate during my life. Knowing no more of Mencken than I did at that moment, I felt a vague sympathy for him. Had not the South, which had assigned me the role of a non-man, cast at him its hardest words?

Now, how could I find out about this Mencken? There was a huge library near the riverfront, but I knew that Negroes were not allowed to patronise its shelves any more than they were the parks and playgrounds of the city. I had gone into the library several times to get books for the white men on the job. Which of them would now help me to get books? And how could I read them without causing concern to the white men with whom I worked? I had so far been successful in hiding my thoughts and feelings from them, but I knew that I would create hostility if I went about this business of reading in a clumsy way.

I weighed the personalities of the men on the job. There was Don, a Jew; but I distrusted him. His position was not much better than mine and I knew that he was uneasy and insecure; he had always treated me in an offhand, bantering way that barely concealed his contempt. I was afraid to ask him to help me to get books; his frantic desire to demonstrate a racial solidarity with the whites against Negroes might make him betray me.

Then how about the boss? No, he was a Baptist and I had the suspicion that he would not be quite able to comprehend why a black boy would want to read Mencken. There were other white men on the job whose attitudes showed clearly that they were Kluxers or sympathisers, and they were out of the question.

There remained only one man whose attitude did not fit into an anti-Negro category, for I had heard the white men refer to him as a "Pope lover." He was an Irish Catholic and was hated by the white Southerners. I knew that he read books, because I had got him volumes from the library several times. Since he, too, was an object of hatred, I felt that he might refuse me but would hardly betray me. I hesitated, weighing and balancing the imponderable realities.

One morning I paused before the Catholic fellow's desk.

"I want to ask you a favour," I whispered to him.

"What is it?"

"I want to read. I can't get books from the library. I wonder if you'd let me use your card?"

He looked at me suspiciously.

"My card is full most of the time," he said.

"I see," I said and waited, posing my question silently.

"You're not trying to get me into trouble, are you, boy?" he asked, staring at me.

"Oh, no, sir."

"What book do you want?"

"A book by H. L. Mencken."

"Which one?"

"I don't know. Has he written more than one?"

"He has written several."

"I didn't know that."

"What makes you want to read Mencken?"

"Oh, I just saw his name in the newspaper," I said.

"It's good of you to want to read," he said. "But you ought to read the right things."

I said nothing. Would he want to supervise my reading?

"Let me think," he said. "I'll figure out something."

I turned from him and he called me back. He stared at me quizzically.

"Richard, don't mention this to the other white men," he said.

"I understand," I said. "I won't say a word."

A few days later he called me to him.

"I've got a card in my wife's name," he said. "Here's mine."

"Thank you, sir."

"Do you think you can manage it?"

"I'll manage fine," I said.

"If they suspect you, you'll get in trouble," he said.

"I'll write the same kind of notes to the library that you wrote when you sent me for books," I told him. "I'll sign your name."

He laughed.

"Go ahead. Let me see what you get," he said.

That afternoon I addressed myself to forging a note. Now, what were the names of books written by H. L. Mencken? I did not know any of them. I finally wrote what I thought would be a foolproof note: *Dear Madam: Will you please let this nigger boy*—I used the word "nigger" to make the librarian feel that I could not possibly be the author of the note—*have some books by H. L. Mencken?* I forged the white man's signature.

I entered the library as I had always done when on errands for whites, but I felt that I would somehow slip up and betray myself. I doffed my hat, stood a respectful distance from the desk, looked as unbookish as possible, and waited for the white patrons to be taken care of. When the desk was clear of people, I still waited. The white librarian looked at me.

"What do you want, boy?"

As though I did not possess the power of speech, I stepped forward and simply handed her the forged note, not parting my lips.

"What books by Mencken does he want?" she asked.

"I don't know, ma'am," I said, avoiding her eyes.

"Who gave you this card?"

"Mr. Falk," I said.

"Where is he?"

"He's at work, at the M—— Optical Company," I said. "I've been in here for him before."

"I remember," the woman said. "But he never wrote notes like this."

Oh, God, she's suspicious. Perhaps she would not let me have the books? If she had turned her back at that moment, I would have ducked out of the door and never gone back. Then I thought of a bold idea.

"You can call him up, ma'am," I said, my heart pounding.

"You're not using these books, are you?" she asked pointedly.

"Oh, no, ma'am. I can't read."

"I don't know what he wants by Mencken," she said under her breath.

I knew now that I had won; she was thinking of other things and the race question had gone out of her mind. She went to the shelves. Once or twice she looked over her shoulder at me, as though she was still doubtful. Finally she came forward with two books in her hand.

"I'm sending him two books," she said. "But tell Mr. Falk to come in next time, or send me the names of the books he wants. I don't know what he wants to read."

I said nothing. She stamped the card and handed me the books. Not daring to glance at them, I went out of the library, fearing that the woman would call me back for further questioning. A block away from the library I opened one of the books and read a title: *A Book of Prefaces*. I was nearing my nineteenth birthday and I did not know how to pronounce the word "preface." I thumbed the pages and saw strange words and strange names. I shook my head, disappointed. I looked at the other book; it was called *Prejudices*. I knew what that word meant; I had heard it all my life. And right off I was on guard against Mencken's books. Why would a man want to call a book *Prejudices*? The word was so stained with all my memories of racial hate that I could not conceive of anybody using it for a title. Perhaps I had made a mistake about Mencken? A man who had prejudices must be wrong.

When I showed the books to Mr. Falk, he looked at me and frowned.

"That librarian might telephone you," I warned him.

"That's all right," he said. "But when you're through reading those books, I want you to tell me what you get out of them."

That night in my rented room, while letting the hot water run over my can of pork and beans in the sink, I opened *A Book of Prefaces* and began to read. I was jarred and shocked by the style, the clear, clean, sweeping sentences. Why did he write like that? And how did one write like that? I pictured the man as a raging demon, slashing with his pen, consumed with hate, denouncing everything American, extolling everything European or German, laughing at the weaknesses of people, mocking God, authority. What was this? I stood up, trying to realise what reality lay behind the meaning of the words. . . . Yes, this man was fighting, fighting with words. He was using words as a weapon, using them as one would use a club. Could words be weapons? Well, yes, for here they were. Then, maybe, perhaps, I could use them as a weapon? No. It frightened me. I read on and what amazed me was not what he said, but how on earth anybody had the courage to say it.

Occasionally I glanced up to reassure myself that I was alone in the room. Who were these men about whom Mencken was talking so passionately? Who was Anatole France? Joseph Conrad? Sinclair Lewis, Sherwood Anderson, Dostoevski, George Moore, Gustave Flaubert, Maupassant, Tolstoy, Frank Harris, Mark Twain, Thomas Hardy, Arnold Bennett, Stephen Crane, Zola, Norris, Gorky, Bergson, Ibsen, Balzac, Bernard Shaw, Dumas, Poe, Thomas Mann, O. Henry, Dreiser, H. G. Wells, Gogol, T. S. Eliot, Gide, Baudelaire, Edgar Lee Masters, Stendhal, Turgenev, Huneker, Nietzsche, and scores of others? Were these men real? Did they exist or had they existed? And how did one pronounce their names?

I ran across many words whose meanings I did not know, and I either looked them up in a dictionary or, before I had a chance to do that, encountered the word in a context that made its meaning clear. But what strange world was this? I concluded the book with the conviction that I had somehow overlooked something terribly important in life. I had once tried to write, had once revelled in feeling, had let my crude imagination roam, but the impulse to dream had been slowly beaten out of me by experience. Now it surged up again and I hungered for books, new ways of looking and seeing. It was not a matter of believing or disbelieving what I read, but of feeling something new, of being affected by something that made the look of the world different.

As dawn broke I ate my pork and beans, feeling dopey, sleepy. I went to work, but the mood of the book would not die; it lingered, colouring everything I saw, heard, did. I now felt that I knew what the white men were feeling. Merely because I had read a book that had spoken of how they lived and thought, I identified myself with that book. I felt vaguely guilty. Would I, filled with bookish notions, act in a manner that would make the whites dislike me?

I forged more notes and my trips to the library became frequent. Reading grew into a passion. My first serious novel was Sinclair Lewis's *Main Street*. It made me see my boss, Mr. Gerald, and identify him as an American type. I would smile when I saw him lugging his golf bags into the office. I had always felt a vast distance separating me from the boss, and now I felt closer to him, though still distant. I felt now that I knew him, that I could feel the very limits of his narrow life. And this had happened because I had read a novel about a mythical man called George F. Babbitt.

The plots and stories in the novels did not interest me so much as the point of view revealed. I gave myself over to each novel without reserve, without trying to criticise it; it was enough for me to see and feel something different. And for me, everything was something different. Reading was like a drug, a dope. The novels created moods in which I lived for days. But I could not conquer my sense of guilt, my feeling that the white men around me knew that I was changing, that I had begun to regard them differently.

Whenever I brought a book to the job, I wrapped it in newspaper—a habit that was to persist for years in other cities and under other circumstances. But some of the white men pried into my packages when I was absent and they questioned me.

"Boy, what are you reading those books for?"

"Oh, I don't know, sir."

"That's deep stuff you're reading, boy."

"I'm just killing time, sir."

"You'll addle your brains if you don't watch out."

I read Dreiser's *Jennie Gerhardt* and *Sister Carrie* and they revived in me a vivid sense of my mother's suffering; I was overwhelmed. I grew silent, wondering about the life around me. It would have been impossible for me to have told anyone what I derived from these novels, for it was nothing less than a sense of life itself. All my life had shaped me for the realism, the naturalism of the modern novel, and I could not read enough of them.

Steeped in new moods and ideas, I bought a ream of paper and tried to write; but nothing would come, or what did come was flat beyond telling. I discovered that more than desire and feeling were necessary to write and I dropped the idea. Yet I still wondered how it was possible to know people sufficiently to write about them. Could I ever learn about life and people? To me, with my vast ignorance, my Jim Crow* station in life, it seemed a task impossible of achievement. I now

* Jim Crow: discriminatory practices against blacks, which restricted them to segregated sections of buses, restaurants, public restrooms.

knew what being a Negro meant. I could endure the hunger. I had learned to live with hate. But to feel that there were feelings denied me, that the very breath of life itself was beyond my reach, that more than anything else hurt, wounded me. I had a new hunger.

In buoying me up, reading also cast me down, made me see what was possible, what I had missed. My tension returned, new, terrible, bitter, surging, almost too great to be contained. I no longer *felt* that the world about me was hostile, killing; I *knew* it. A million times I asked myself what I could do to save myself, and there were no answers. I seemed forever condemned, ringed by walls.

I did not discuss my reading with Mr. Falk, who had lent me his library card; it would have meant talking about myself and that would have been too painful. I smiled each day, fighting desperately to maintain my old behaviour, to keep my disposition seemingly sunny. But some of the white men discerned that I had begun to brood.

"Wake up there, boy!" Mr. Olin said one day.

"Sir!" I answered for the lack of a better word.

"You act like you've stolen something," he said.

I laughed in the way I knew he expected me to laugh, but I resolved to be more conscious of myself, to watch my every act, to guard and hide the new knowledge that was dawning within me.

If I went north, would it be possible for me to build a new life then? But how could a man build a life upon vague, unformed yearnings? I wanted to write and I did not even know the English language. I bought English grammars and found them dull. I felt that I was getting a better sense of the language from novels than from grammars. I read hard, discarding a writer as soon as I felt that I had grasped his point of view. At night the printed page stood before my eyes in sleep.

Mrs. Moss, my landlady, asked me one Sunday morning:

"Son, what is this you keep on reading?"

"Oh, nothing. Just novels."

"What you get out of 'em?"

"I'm just killing time," I said.

"I hope you know your own mind," she said in a tone which implied that she doubted if I had a mind.

I knew of no Negroes who read the books I liked and I wondered if any Negroes ever thought of them. I knew that there were Negro doctors, lawyers, newspaper-men, but I never saw any of them. When I read a Negro newspaper I never caught the faintest echo of my preoccupation in its pages. I felt trapped and occasionally, for a few days, I would stop reading. But a vague hunger would come over me for books, books that opened up new avenues of feeling and seeing, and again I would forge another note to the white librarian. Again I would read and wonder as only the naïve and unlettered can read and wonder, feeling that I carried a secret, criminal burden about with me each day.

That winter my mother and brother came and we set up housekeeping, buying furniture on the instalment plan, being cheated and yet knowing no way to avoid it. I began to eat warm food and to my surprise found that regular meals enabled me to read faster. I may have lived through many illnesses and survived them, never suspecting that I was ill. My brother obtained a job and we began to save toward the trip north, plotting our time, setting tentative dates for departure. I told none of the white men on the job that I was planning to go north; I knew that the moment they felt I was thinking of the North they would change toward me. It would have made them feel that I did not like the life I was living, and because my life was completely conditioned by what they said or did, it would have been tantamount to challenging them.

I could calculate my chances for life in the South as a Negro fairly clearly now.

I could fight the southern whites by organising with other Negroes, as my grandfather had done. But I knew that I could never win that way; there were many whites and there were but few blacks. They were strong and we were weak. Outright black rebellion could never win. If I fought openly I would die and I did not want to die. News of lynchings were frequent.

I could submit and live the life of a genial slave, but that was impossible. All of my life had shaped me to live by my own feelings and thoughts. I could make up to Bess and marry her and inherit the house. But that, too, would be the life of a slave; if I did that, I would crush to death something within me, and I would hate myself as much as I knew the whites already hated those who had submitted. Neither could I ever willingly present myself to be kicked, as Shorty had done. I would rather have died than do that.

I could drain off my restlessness by fighting with Shorty and Harrison. I had seen many Negroes solve the problem of being black by transferring their hatred of themselves to others with a black skin and fighting them. I would have to be cold to do that, and I was not cold and I could never be.

I could, of course, forget what I had read, thrust the whites out of my mind, forget them; and find release from anxiety and longing in sex and alcohol. But the memory of how my father had conducted himself made that course repugnant. If I did not want others to violate my life, how could I voluntarily violate it myself?

I had no hope whatever of being a professional man. Not only had I been so conditioned that I did not desire it, but the fulfilment of such an ambition was beyond my capabilities. Well-to-do Negroes lived in a world that was almost as alien to me as the world inhabited by whites.

What, then, was there? I held my life in my mind, in my consciousness each day, feeling at times that I would stumble and drop it, spill it forever. My reading had created a vast sense of distance between me and the world in which I lived and tried to make a living, and that sense of distance was increasing each day. My days and nights were one long, quiet, continuously contained dream of terror, tension, and anxiety. I wondered how long I could bear it.

CONSIDER THIS

★ Wright was *aroused* by the Memphis newspaper's attack on Mencken. Wright's quest for Mencken's books starts with a simple desire: to "find out about" him. Sheer curiosity drives him, but the root of the curiosity is that sense that, out there in the unknown world, a world *mediated* by print (he cannot go and actually meet Mencken, face to face), there is someone who may feel the way he himself feels, believe what he believes. Have you ever been aroused in this way, by the sense that there might be a bond of some kind between yourself and a stranger?

★ Do you remember being driven to act by sheer curiosity? What were the emotional roots of your curiosity?

★ Notice how Wright "reads" the men on the job, trying to determine whether or not they are likely to be willing to help him. If you "read" adults, when you were younger, what were your reasons for doing so?

★ Notice how effectively Wright forges the note for the librarian, using language that someone else—a white person—would use in that time and that place. In referring to himself as "this nigger boy," he successfully conceals his own authorship. Did you ever forge notes? How successfully? Were you ever found out? What were your feelings as you wrote your forgery?

★ Wright enters the library, the white folks' building. Can you remember entering places where, for whatever reason, you felt you didn't belong?

★ Notice how Wright, when he encounters the librarian, cunningly degrades himself further by not presuming to speak. He is role-playing very effectively. Can you recall doing such a thing, pretending to be someone you weren't—more modest, more courageous, more whatever?

★ How does Wright build up the tension of his encounter with the librarian? Did you at any moment fear that he would be found out?

★ At eighteen, because of the deprivation of his early life, Wright is still fairly naive. So, when he sees Mencken's title, *Prejudices*, he jumps to an inappropriate conclusion, as a result of mis-reading, mis-interpreting. Can you recall a situation that you mis-interpreted as a result of your immaturity or naiveté?

★ Mr. Falk tells Wright, "When you're through reading those books, I want you to tell me what you get out of them." What benefit to Wright, what benefit to Falk, will this provide?

★ Wright reads Mencken's *Prefaces* until dawn breaks. How many conflicting feelings did he experience? What do you think was his most important discovery that night?

★ ". . . the mood of the book would not die; it lingered, colouring everything I saw, heard, did." Have you had such an experience, in which the mood of a book has affected, changed, the very way you experience life?

★ Reading *Main Street* allowed Wright to see his boss, Mr. Gerald, as a type, to typify him, to see him as typical of a particular element in society. This ability makes Wright smile. Have you ever smiled for such a reason?

★ Reading liberates Wright, offering him a more detailed spectator's view of his situation. But it also enforced his recognition of the limits of his world: ". . . a new hunger . . . forever condemned, ringed by walls." Is this a contradiction? How would you explain it?

★ How does Wright manage to convince us that, having started to read voraciously as a way of escape—escape into knowledge, escape into other worlds, other possibilities—its legacy is, in fact, "terror, tension, and anxiety"?

★ Have you ever been deeply disturbed, upset, or confused, morally or emotionally, by reading a book? Can you write about it, or is it still too close to you?

★ Do you think that some of his needs were distinctive, entirely to do with his situation? What do you think you, at your present age, have in common with him? Are you as hungry for books, as eager to read as he was? If not, why not?

★ "My reading had created a vast sense of distance between me and the world in which I lived . . . and that sense of distance was increasing each day." What effect does your reading seem to have on your sense of distance between yourself and the world you live in? Can you talk to your parents about what you're reading? Grandparents? Brothers? Sisters? Boyfriend? Girlfriend? If you can't, then the chances are that you find yourself feeling rather solitary, alone in a world where others look at you peculiarly—as the one who *wastes time* reading books. Our suggestion: find someone who shares your enthusiasm for books.

JAMES BALDWIN

I Want to Be an Honest Man

James Baldwin was more sophisticated, more worldly, wittier, less innocent than Richard Wright; but, without Wright's example, as a role-model for the black writer, Baldwin would have had more difficulty in shaping his determination to become a writer. We join Baldwin again in "Autobiographical Notes," just where we left him on page 112.

Any writer, I suppose, feels that the world into which he was born is nothing less than a conspiracy against the cultivation of his talent—which attitude certainly has a great deal to support it. On the other hand, it is only because the world looks on his talent with such a frightening indifference that the artist is compelled to make his talent important. So that any writer, looking back over even so short a span of time as I am here forced to assess, finds that the things which hurt him and the things which helped him cannot be divorced from each other; he could be helped in a certain way only because he was hurt in a certain way; and his help is simply to be enabled to move from one conundrum to the next—one is tempted to say that he moves from one disaster to the next. When one begins looking for influences one finds them by the score. I haven't thought much about my own, not enough anyway; I hazard that the King James Bible, the rhetoric of the store-front church, something ironic and violent and perpetually understated in Negro speech—and something of Dickens' love for bravura—have something to do with me today; but I wouldn't stake my life on it. Likewise, innumerable people have helped me in many ways; but finally, I suppose, the most difficult (and most rewarding) thing in my life has been the fact that I was born a Negro and was forced, therefore, to effect some kind of truce with this reality. (Truce, by the way, is the best one can hope for.)

One of the difficulties about being a Negro writer (and this is not special pleading, since I don't mean to suggest that he has it worse than anybody else) is that the Negro problem is written about so widely. The bookshelves groan under the weight of information, and everyone therefore considers himself informed. And this information, furthermore, operates usually (generally, popularly) to reinforce traditional attitudes. Of traditional attitudes there are only two—For or Against—and I, personally, find it difficult to say which attitude has caused me the most pain. I am speaking as a writer; from a social point of view I am perfectly aware that the change from ill-will to good-will, however motivated, however imperfect, however expressed, is better than no change at all.

But it is part of the business of the writer—as I see it—to examine attitudes, to go beneath the surface, to tap the source. From this point of view the Negro problem is nearly inaccessible. It is not only written about so widely; it is written about so badly. It is quite possible to say that the price a Negro pays for becoming articulate is to find himself, at length, with nothing to be articulate about. ("You taught me language," says Caliban to Prospero, "and my profit on't is I know how to curse.") Consider: the tremendous social activity that this problem generates imposes on whites and Negroes alike the necessity of looking forward, of working to bring about a better day. This is fine, it keeps the waters troubled; it is all, indeed, that has made possible the Negro's progress. Nevertheless, social affairs are not generally speaking the writer's prime concern, whether they ought to be or not; it is absolutely necessary that he establish between himself and these affairs a distance which will allow, at least, for clarity, so that before he can look forward in any meaningful sense, he must first be allowed to take a long look back. In the context of the Negro problem neither whites nor blacks, for excellent reasons of their own, have the faintest desire to look back; but I think that the past is all that makes the present coherent, and further, that the past will remain horrible for exactly as long as we refuse to assess it honestly.

I know, in any case, that the most crucial time in my own development came when I was forced to recognize that I was a kind of bastard of the West; when I followed the line of my past I did not find myself in Europe but in Africa. And this meant that in some subtle way, in a really profound way, I brought to Shakespeare, Bach, Rembrandt, to the stones of Paris, to the cathedral at Chartres, and to the Empire State Building, a special attitude. These were not really my creations, they did not contain my history; I might search in them in vain forever for any reflection of myself. I was an interloper; this was not my heritage. At the same time I had no other heritage which I could possibly hope to use—I had certainly been unfitted for the jungle or the tribe. I would have to appropriate these white centuries, I would have to make them mine—I would have to accept my special attitude, my special place in this scheme—otherwise I would have no place in *any* scheme. What was the most difficult was the fact that I was forced to admit something I had always hidden from myself, which the American Negro has had to hide from himself as the price of his public progress; that I hated and feared white people. This did not mean that I loved black people; on the contrary, I despised them, possibly because they failed to produce Rembrandt. In effect, I hated and feared the world. And this meant, not only that I thus gave the world an altogether murderous power over me, but also that in such a self-destroying limbo I could never hope to write.

One writes out of one thing only—one's own experience. Everything depends on how relentlessly one forces from this experience the last drop, sweet or bitter, it can possibly give. This is the only real concern of the artist, to recreate out of the disorder of life that order which is art. The difficulty then, for me, of being a Negro writer was the fact that I was, in effect, prohibited from examining my own experience too closely by the tremendous demands and the very real dangers of my social situation.

I don't think the dilemma outlined above is uncommon. I do think, since writers work in the disastrously explicit medium of language, that it goes a little way towards explaining why, out of the enormous resources of Negro speech and life, and despite the example of Negro music, prose written by Negroes has been generally speaking so pallid and so harsh. I have not written about being a Negro at such length because I expect that to be my only subject, but only because it was the gate I had to unlock before I could hope to write about anything else. I don't think that the Negro problem in America can be even discussed coherently without bearing in mind its context; its context being the history, traditions, customs, the moral assumptions and preoccupations of the country; in short, the general social fabric. Appearances to the contrary, no one in America escapes its effects and everyone in America bears some responsibility for it. I believe this the more firmly because it is the overwhelming tendency to speak of this problem as though it were a thing apart. But in the work of Faulkner, in the general attitude and certain specific passages in Robert Penn Warren, and, most significantly, in the advent of Ralph Ellison, one sees the beginnings—at least—of a more genuinely penetrating search. Mr. Ellison, by the way, is the first Negro novelist I have ever read to utilize in language, and brilliantly, some of the ambiguity and irony of Negro life.

About my interests: I don't know if I have any, unless the morbid desire to own a sixteen-millimeter camera and make experimental movies can be so classified. Otherwise, I love to eat and drink—it's my melancholy conviction that I've scarcely ever had enough to eat (this is because it's *impossible* to eat enough if you're worried about the next meal)—and I love to argue with people who do not disagree with me too profoundly, and I love to laugh. I do *not* like bohemia, or bohemians, I do not like people whose principal aim is pleasure, and I do not like people who are *earnest* about anything. I don't like people who like me because I'm a Negro; neither do I like people who find in the same accident grounds for contempt. I love America more than any other country in the world, and, exactly for this reason, I insist on the right to criticize her perpetually. I think all theories are suspect, that the finest principles may have to be modified, or may even be pulverized by the demands of life, and that one must find, therefore, one's own moral center and move through the world hoping that this center will guide one aright. I consider that I have many responsibilities, but none greater than this: to last, as Hemingway says, and get my work done.

I want to be an honest man and a good writer.

CONSIDER THIS

★ Thus James Baldwin developed his complex, subtle, witty, paradoxical, and intelligent "theory of the world." How does your "theory" resemble Baldwin's? How does it differ?

★ At a time when the ethos of Wall Street is encouraging young people to become single-minded materialists, driven by a monomaniacal greed for money, does Baldwin's last sentence strike you as hopelessly out of step, old fashioned, naive?

CYNTHIA OZICK

The First Day of School
Washington Square, 1946

One of the oldest metaphors for life is the journey: and one of the most difficult stages on that journey is the transit from the limited, familiar environment of home and high school to the world of college.

The novelist Cynthia Ozick (b. 1928), on her first day at college, was so naive that she turned up a day too soon and found the buildings deserted: but there was a fascinating world on the doorstep waiting for her to explore, and, in so doing, to discover how much she didn't know.

> . . . this portion of New York appears to many persons the most delectable. It has a kind of established repose which is not of frequent occurrence in other quarters of the long, shrill city; it has a riper, richer, more honorable look than any of the upper ramifications of the great longitudinal thoroughfare—the look of having had something of a social history.
>
> —HENRY JAMES,
> *Washington Square*

I first came down to Washington Square on a colorless February morning in 1946. I was seventeen and a half years old and was carrying my lunch in a brown paper bag, just as I had carried it to high school only a month before. It was—I thought it was—the opening day of spring term at Washington Square College, my initiation into my freshman year at New York University. All I knew of NYU then was that my science-minded brother had gone there; he had written from the Army that I ought to go there too. With master-of-ceremonies zest he described the Browsing Room on the second floor of the Main Building as a paradisal chamber whose bookish loungers leafed languidly through magazines and exchanged high-principled witticisms between classes. It had the sound of a carpeted Olympian club in Oliver Wendell Holmes's Boston, Hub of the Universe, strewn with leather chairs and delectable old copies of *The Yellow Book*.

On that day I had never heard of Oliver Wendell Holmes or *The Yellow Book*, and Washington Square was a far-away bower where wounded birds fell out of trees. My brother had once brought home from Washington Square Park a baby sparrow with a broken leg, to be nurtured back to flight. It died instead, emitting in its last hours melancholy faint cheeps, and leaving behind a dense recognition of the minute explicitness of mortality. All the same, in the February grayness Washington Square had the allure of the celestial unknown. A sparrow might die, but my own life was luminously new: I felt my youth like a nimbus.

Which dissoves into the dun gauze of a low and sullen city sky. And here I am flying out of the Lexington Avenue subway at Astor Place, just a few yards from Wanamaker's, here I am turning a corner past a secondhand bookstore and a union hall; already late, I begin walking very fast toward the park. The air is smoky with New York winter grit, and on clogged Broadway a mob of trucks shifts squawking gears. But there, just ahead, crosscrossed by paths under high branches, is Washington Square; and on a single sidewalk, three clear omens—or call them riddles, intricate and redolent. These I will disclose in a moment, but before that you must push open the heavy brass-and-glass doors of the Main Building and come with me, at a hard and panting pace, into the lobby of Washington Square College on the earliest morning of my freshman year.

On the left, a bank of elevators. Straight ahead, a long burnished corridor, spooky as a lit tunnel. And empty, all empty. I can hear my solitary footsteps reverberate, as in a radio mystery drama: they lead me up a short staircase into a big dark ghost-town cafeteria. My brother's letter, along with his account of the physics and chemistry laboratories (I will never see them), has already explained that this place is called Commons—and here my heart will learn to shake with the merciless newness of life. But not today; today there is nothing. Tables and chairs squat in dead silhouette. I race back through a silent maze of halls and stairways to the brass-and-glass doors—there stands a lonely guard. From the pocket of my coat I retrieve a scrap with a classroom number on it and ask the way. The guard announces in a sly croak that the first day of school is not yet; come back tomorrow, he says.

A dumb bad joke: I'm humiliated. I've journeyed the whole way down from the end of the line—Pelham Bay, in the northeast Bronx—to find myself in desolation, all because of a muddle: Tuesday isn't Wednesday. The nimbus of expectation fades. The lunch bag in my fist takes on a greasy sadness. I'm not ready to dive back into the subway—I'll have a look around.

Across the street from the Main Building, the three omens. First, a pretzel man with a cart. He's wearing a sweater, a cap that keeps him faceless—he's nothing but the shadows of his creases—and wool gloves with the fingertips cut off. He never moves; he might as well be made of papier-mâché, set up and left out in the open since spring. There are now almost no pretzels for sale, and this gives me a chance to inspect the construction of his bare pretzel-poles. The pretzels are hooked over a column of gray cardboard cylinders, themselves looped around a stick, the way horseshoes drop around a post. The cardboard cylinders are the insides of toilet paper rolls.

The pretzel man is rooted between a Chock Full O' Nuts (that's the second omen) and a newsstand (that's the third).

The Chock Full: the doors are like fans, whirling remnants of conversation. <i>She</i>

will marry him. She will not marry him. Fragrance of coffee and hot chocolate. *We can prove that the senses are partial and unreliable vehicles of information, but who is to say that reason is not equally a product of human limitation?* Powdered doughnut sugar on their lips.

Attached to a candy store, the newsstand. Copies of *Partisan Review*: the table of the gods. Jean Stafford, Mary McCarthy, Elizabeth Hardwick, Irving Howe, Delmore Schwartz, Alfred Kazin, Clement Greenberg, Stephen Spender, William Phillips, John Berryman, Saul Bellow, Philip Rahv, Richard Chase, Randall Jarrell, Simone de Beauvoir, Karl Shapiro, George Orwell! I don't know a single one of these names, but I feel their small conflagration flaming in the gray street: the succulent hotness of their promise. I mean to penetrate every one of them. Since all the money I have is my subway fare—a nickel—I don't buy a copy (the price of *Partisan* in 1946 is fifty cents); I pass on.

I pass on to the row of houses on the north side of the square. Henry James was born in one of these, but I don't know that either. Still, they are plainly old, though no longer aristocratic: haughty last-century shabbies with shut eyelids, built of rosy-ripe respectable brick, down on their luck. Across the park bulks Judson Church, with its squat squarish bell tower; by the end of the week I will be languishing at the margins of a basketball game in its basement, forlorn in my blue left-over-from-high-school gym suit and mooning over Emily Dickinson:

> There's a certain Slant of light,
> Winter Afternoons—
> That oppresses, like the Heft
> Of Cathedral Tunes—

There is more I don't know. I don't know that W. H. Auden lives just down *there*, and might at any moment be seen striding toward home under his tall rumpled hunch; I don't know that Marianne Moore is only up the block, her doffed tricorn resting on her bedroom dresser. It's Greenwich Village—I know *that*—no more than twenty years after Edna St. Vincent Millay has sent the music of her name (her best, perhaps her only, poem) into these bohemian streets: bohemia, the honeypot of poets.

On that first day in the tea-leafed cup of the town I am ignorant, ignorant! But the three riddle-omens are soon to erupt, and all of them together will illumine Washington Square.

Begin with the benches in the park. Here, side by side with students and their looseleafs, lean or lie the shadows of the pretzel man, his creased ghosts or doubles: all those pitiables, half-women and half-men, neither awake nor asleep; the discountable, the repudiated, the unseen. No more notice is taken of any of them than of a scudding fragment of newspaper in the path. Even then, even so long ago, the benches of Washington Square are pimpled with this hell-tossed crew, these Mad Margarets and Cokey Joes, these volcanic coughers, shakers, groaners, tremblers, droolers, blasphemers, these public urinators with vomitous breath and rusted teeth stumps, dead-eyed and self-abandoned, dragging their makeshift junkyard shoes, their buttonless layers of raggedy ratfur. The pretzel man with his toilet paper rolls conjures and spews them all—he is a loftier brother to these citizens of the lower pox, he is guardian of the garden of the jettisoned. They rattle along all the seams of Washington Square. They are the pickled city, the true and universal City-below-Cities, the wolfish vinegar-Babylon that dogs the spittled skirts of bohemia. The toilet paper rolls are the temple columns of this sacred grove.

Next, the whirling doors of Chock Full O' Nuts. Here is the marketplace of Washington Square, its bazaar, its roiling gossip-parlor, its matchmaker's office and arena—the outermost wing, so to speak, evolved from the Commons. On a day like today, when the Commons is closed, the Chock Full is thronged with extra power, a cello making up for a missing viola. Until now, the fire of my vitals has been for the imperious tragedians of the *Aeneid*; I have lived in the narrow throat of poetry. Another year or so of this oblivion, until at last I am hammerstruck with the shock of Europe's skull, the bled planet of death camp and war. Eleanor Roosevelt has not yet written her famous column announcing the discovery of Anne Frank's diary. The term "cold war" is new. The Commons, like the college itself, is overcrowded, veterans in their pragmatic thirties mingling with the reluctant dreamy young. And the Commons is convulsed with politics: a march to the docks is organized, no one knows by whom, to protest the arrival of Walter Gieseking, the German musician who flourished among Nazis. The Communists—two or three readily recognizable cantankerous zealots—stomp through with their daily leaflets and sneers. There is even a Monarchist, a small poker-faced rectangle of a man with secretive tireless eyes who, when approached for his views, always demands, in perfect Bronx tones, the restoration of his king. The engaged girls—how many of them there seem to be!—flash their rings and tangle their ankles in their long New Look skirts. There is no feminism and no feminists: I am, I think, the only one. The Commons is a tide: it washes up the cold war, it washes up the engaged girls' rings, it washes up the several philosophers and the numerous poets. The philosophers are all existentialists; the poets are all influenced by *The Waste Land*. When the Commons overflows, the engaged girls cross the street to show their rings at the Chock Full.

Call it density, call it intensity, call it continuity: call it, finally, society. The Commons belongs to the satirists. Here, one afternoon, is Alfred Chester, holding up a hair, a single strand, before a crowd. (He will one day write stories and novels. He will die young.) "What is that hair?" I innocently ask, having come late on the scene. "A pubic hair," he replies, and I feel as Virginia Woolf did when she declared human nature to have "changed in or about December 1910"—soon after her sister Vanessa explained away a spot on her dress as "semen."

In or about February 1946 human nature does not change; it keeps on. On my bedroom wall I tack—cut out from *Life* magazine—the wildest Picasso I can find: a face that is also a belly. Mr. George E. Mutch, a lyrical young English teacher still in his twenties, writes on the blackboard: "When lilacs last in the dooryard bloom'd," and "Bare, ruined choirs, where late the sweet birds sang," and "A green thought in a green shade"; he tells us to burn, like Pater, with a hard, gemlike flame. Another English teacher—older and crustier—compares Walt Whitman to a plumber; the next year he is rumored to have shot himself in a wood. The initial letters of

Washington Square College are a device to recall three of the seven deadly sins: Wantonness, Sloth, Covetousness. In the Commons they argue the efficacy of the orgone box.* Eda Lou Walton, sprightly as a bird, knows all the Village bards, and is a Village bard herself. Sidney Hook is an intellectual rumble in the logical middle distance. Homer Watt, chairman of the English department, is the very soul who, in a far-off time of bewitchment, hired Thomas Wolfe.

And so, in February 1946, I make my first purchase of a "real" book—which is to say, not for the classroom. It is displayed in the window of the secondhand bookstore between the Astor Place subway station and the union hall, and for weeks I have been coveting it: *Of Time and the River.* I am transfigured; I am pierced through with rapture; skipping gym, I sit among morning mists on a windy bench a foot from the stench of Mad Margaret, sinking into that cascading syrup: "Man's youth is a wonderful thing: It is so full of anguish and of magic and he never comes to know it as it is, until it is gone from him forever. . . . And what is the essence of that strange and bitter miracle of life which we feel so poignantly, so unutterably, with such a bitter pain and joy, when we are young?" Thomas Wolfe, lost, and by the wind grieved, ghost, come back again! In Washington Square I am appareled in the "numb exultant secrecies of fog, fog-numb air filled with solemn joy of nameless and impending prophecy, an ancient yellow light, the old smoke-ochre of the morning . . ."

The smoke-ochre of the morning. Ah, you who have flung Thomas Wolfe, along with your strange and magical youth, onto the ash-heap of juvenilia and excess, myself among you, isn't this a lovely phrase still? It rises out of the old pavements of Washington Square as delicately-colored as an eggshell.

The veterans in their pragmatic thirties are nailed to Need; they have families and futures to attend to. When Mr. George E. Mutch exhorts them to burn with a hard, gemlike flame, and writes across the blackboard the line that reveals his own name,

> The world is too much with us; late and soon,
> Getting and spending, we lay waste our powers,

one of the veterans heckles, "What about getting a Buick, what about spending a buck?" Chester, at sixteen, is a whole year younger than I; he has transparent eyes and a rosebud mouth, and is in love with a poet named Diana. He has already found his way to the Village bars, and keeps in his wallet Truman Capote's secret telephone number. We tie our scarves tight against the cold and walk up and down Fourth Avenue, winding in and out of the rows of secondhand bookshops crammed one against the other. The proprietors sit reading their wares and never look up. The books in all their thousands smell sleepily of cellar. Our envy of them is speckled with longing; our longing is sick with envy. We are the sorrowful literary young.

Every day, month after month, I hang around the newsstand near the candy store, drilling through the enigmatic pages of *Partisan Review.* I still haven't bought

---

* Orgone box: a spurious device invented by an eccentric "prophet" who claimed that it increased your libido.

a copy; I still can't understand a word. I don't know what cold war means. Who is Trotsky? I haven't read *Ulysses*; my adolescent phantoms are rowing in the ablative absolute with *pius* Aeneas. I'm in my mind's cradle, veiled by the exultant secrecies of fog.

Washington Square will wake me. In a lecture room in the Main Building, Dylan Thomas will cry his webwork syllables. Afterward he'll warm himself at the White Horse Tavern. Across the corridor I will see Sidney Hook plain. I will read the Bhagavad-Gita and Catullus and Lessing, and, in Hebrew, a novel eerily called *Whither?* It will be years and years before I am smart enough, worldly enough, to read Alfred Kazin and Mary McCarthy.

In the spring, all of worldly Washington Square will wake up to the luster of little green leaves.

CONSIDER THIS

★ What mental luggage did *you* bring with you when you moved from high school to college? Did you feel underequipped ("Going to climb this mountain, and I didn't even bring a decent rope!")? Did you /do you find that people make references that you don't pick up on, but which they seem to assume you will know at the drop of a hat?

Ozick's quotation, "The world is too much . . . ," is from a poem by William Wordsworth, which is an attack on the effects of what we call "the ethos of Wall Street" (p. 131). Wordsworth's argument was that, in pursuing material satisfactions, we lose touch with the deeper, natural, roots of being: we become "out of tune" with fundamental delight in the natural world—a world that earlier "pagan" cultures (for example, Greece and Rome) had celebrated and even worshipped as deserving our deepest, most awesome, reverence.

WILLIAM WORDSWORTH

The World Is Too Much with Us

The world is too much with us; late and soon,
Getting and spending, we lay waste our powers:
Little we see in Nature that is ours;
We have given our hearts away, a sordid boon!
This Sea that bares her bosom to the moon; 5
The winds that will be howling at all hours,
And are up-gathered now like sleeping flowers;
For this, for everything, we are out of tune;
It moves us not.—Great God! I'd rather be

A Pagan suckled in a creed outworn;   10
So might I, standing on this pleasant lea,
Have glimpses that would make me less forlorn;
Have sight of Proteus rising from the sea;
Or hear old Triton blow his wreathèd horn.

MALCOLM COWLEY

Destroying the Roots

If adolescence is one kind of liminal period (see p. 109), then one's years in college are another. In his autobiography, Exile's Return, *Malcolm Cowley (b. 1898) expresses the matter strongly, and sees his "whole training" as a process of destruction, aimed at "making us homeless citizens of the world." His metaphor of the destruction of roots— "directed toward destroying whatever roots we had in the soil"—is a more vivid, almost painfully palpable way of representing an experience which is rather feebly signaled by the now abstract term* deracination.* *But when he begins to make his specific points, exemplifying what forms this process took, he begins to offer cases that many of us may well recognize. For example, "A definite effort was being made to destroy all trace of local idiom or pronunciation and have us speak 'correctly'—that is, in a standardized Ameringlish as colorless as Esperanto" (a synthetic international language that no one actually lives in).*

It is not long before we realize that, in Cowley's case, the university that wreaked this damage on his identity was none other than Harvard, an institution that other, lesser institutions have often struggled to imitate. Is Cowley, then, biting the hand that fed him? Read on.

It often seems to me that our years in school and after school, in college and later in the army, might be regarded as a long process of deracination. Looking backward, I feel that our whole training was involuntarily directed toward destroying whatever roots we had in the soil, toward eradicating our local and regional peculiarities, toward making us homeless citizens of the world.

In school, unless we happened to be Southerners, we were divested of any local pride. We studied Ancient History and American History, but not, in my own case, the history of western Pennsylvania. We learned by name the rivers of Siberia— Obi, Yenisei, Lena, Amur—but not the Ohio with its navigable tributaries, or why most of them had ceased to be navigated, or why Pittsburgh was built at its forks. We had high-school courses in Latin, German, Chemistry, good courses all of them, and a class in Civics where we learned to list the amendments to the Constitution and name the members of the Supreme Court; but we never learned how Presidents

---

* *Deracination* is derived from what was originally a palpable Latin word for uprooting.

were really chosen or how a law was put through Congress. If one of us had later come into contact with the practical side of government—that is, if he wished to get a street paved, an assessment reduced, a friend out of trouble with the police or a relative appointed to office—well, fortunately the ward boss wouldn't take much time to set him straight.

Of the English texts we studied, I can remember only one, "The Legend of Sleepy Hollow," that gave us any idea that an American valley could be as effectively clothed in romance as Ivanhoe's castle or the London of Henry Esmond. It seemed to us that America was beneath the level of great fiction; it seemed that literature in general, and art and learning, were things existing at an infinite distance from our daily lives. For those of us who read independently, this impression became even stronger; the only authors to admire were foreign authors. We came to feel that wisdom was an attribute of Greece and art of the Renaissance, that glamour belonged only to Paris or Vienna and that glory was confined to the dim past. If we tried, notwithstanding, to write about more immediate subjects, we were forced to use a language not properly our own. A definite effort was being made to destroy all trace of local idiom or pronunciation and have us speak "correctly"—that is, in a standardized Amerenglish as colorless as Esperanto. Some of our instructors had themselves acquired this public-school dialect only by dint of practice, and now set forth its rules with an iron pedantry, as if they were teaching a dead language.

In college the process of deracination went on remorselessly. We were not being prepared for citizenship in a town, a state or a nation; we were not being trained for an industry or profession essential to the common life; instead we were being exhorted to enter that international republic of learning whose traditions are those of Athens, Florence, Paris, Berlin and Oxford. The immigrant into that high disembodied realm is supposed to come with empty hands and naked mind, like a recruit into the army. He is clothed and fed by his preceptors, who furnish him only with the best of intellectual supplies. Nothing must enter that world in its raw state; everything must be refined by time and distance, by theory and research, until it loses its own special qualities, its life, and is transformed into the dead material of culture. The ideal university is regarded as having no regional or economic ties. With its faculty, students, classrooms and stadium, it exists in a town as if by accident, its real existence being in the immaterial world of scholarship—or such, at any rate, was the idea to be gained in those years by any impressionable student.

Take my own experience at Harvard. Here was a university that had grown immediately out of a local situation, out of the colonists' need for trained ministers of the Gospel. It had transformed itself from generation to generation with the transformations of New England culture. Farming money, fishing money, trading money, privateering money, wool, cotton, shoe and banking money, had all contributed to its vast endowment. It had grown with Boston, a city whose records were written on the face of its buildings. Sometimes on Sundays I used to wander through the old sections of Beacon Hill and the North End and admire the magnificent doorways, built in the chastest Puritan style with profits from the trade in China tea. Behind some of them Armenians now lived, or Jews; the Old North Church was in an Italian quarter, near the house of Paul Revere, a silversmith. Back Bay had been reclaimed from marshland and covered with mansions during the prosperous years after the Civil War (shoes, uniforms, railroads, speculation in government bonds). On Brattle Street, in Cambridge, Longfellow's house was open to the public, and I might have visited Brook Farm. All these things, Emerson, doorways, factory hands and fortunes, the Elective System, the Porcellian Club, were bound together into one civilization, but of this I received no hint. I was studying Goethe's *Dichtung und Wahrheit* and the Elizabethan drama, and perhaps, on my way to classes in the morning, passing a Catholic church outside of which two Irish boys stood and looked at me with unfriendly eyes. Why was Cambridge an Irish provincial city, almost like Cork or Limerick? What was the reason, in all the territory round Boston, for the hostility between "nice people" and "muckers"? When a development of houses for nice Cambridge people came out on the main street of Somerville (as one of them did), why did it turn its back on the street, build a brick wall against the sidewalk, and face on an interior lawn where nurses could watch nice children playing? I didn't know; I was hurrying off to a section meeting in European History and wondering whether I could give the dates of the German peasant wars.

I am not suggesting that we should have been encouraged to take more "practical" courses—Bookkeeping or Restaurant Management or Sewage Disposal or any of the hundreds that clutter the curriculum of a big university. These specialized techniques could wait till later, after we had chosen our life work. What we were seeking, as sophomores and juniors, was something vastly more general, a key to unlock the world, a picture to guide us in fitting its jigsaw parts together. It happened that our professors were eager to furnish us with such a key or guide; they were highly trained, earnest, devoted to their calling. Essentially the trouble was that the world they pictured for our benefit was the special world of scholarship—timeless, place-less, elaborate, incomplete and bearing only the vaguest relationship to that other world in which fortunes were made, universities endowed and city governments run by muckers.

It lay at a distance, even, from the college world in which we were doing our best to get ahead. The rigorous methods and high doctrines taught by our professors applied only to parts of our lives. We had to fill in the gaps as best we could, usually by accepting the unspoken doctrines of those about us. In practice the college standards were set, not by the faculty, but by the leaders among the students, and particularly by the rich boys from half-English preparatory schools, for whose benefit the system seemed to be run. The rest of us, boys from public high schools, ran the risk of losing our own culture, such as it was, in our bedazzlement with this new puzzling world, and of receiving nothing real in exchange.

Young writers were especially tempted to regard their own experience as some-thing negligible, not worth the trouble of recording in the sort of verse or prose they were taught to imitate from the English masters. A Jewish boy from Brooklyn might win a scholarship by virtue of his literary talent. Behind him there would lie whole generations of rabbis versed in the Torah and the Talmud, representatives of the oldest Western culture now surviving. Behind him, too, lay the memories of an exciting childhood: street gangs in Brownsville, chants in a Chassidic synagogue, the struggle of his parents against poverty, his cousin's struggle, perhaps, to build a labor union and his uncle's fight against it—all the emotions, smells and noises of the ghetto. Before him lay contact with another great culture, and four years of leisure in which to study, write and form a picture of himself. But what he would write in those four years were Keatsian sonnets about English abbeys, which he had never seen, and nightingales he had never heard.

I remember a boy from my own city, in this case a gentile and a graduate of Central High School, which then occupied a group of antiquated buildings on the edge of the business section. Southeast of it was a Jewish quarter; to the north, across the railroad, was the Strip, home of steelworkers, saloons and small-time politicians; to the east lay the Hill, already inhabited by Negroes, with a small red-light district along the lower slopes of it, through which the boys occasionally wandered at lunchtime. The students themselves were drawn partly from these various slums, but chiefly from residential districts in East Liberty and on Squirrel Hill. They followed an out-of-date curriculum under the direction of teachers renowned for thoroughness and severity; they had every chance to combine four years of sound classical discipline with a personal observation of city morals and sociology and politics in action.

This particular student was brilliant in his classes, editor of the school paper, captain of the debating team; he had the sort of reputation that spreads to other high schools; everybody said he was sure to be famous some day. He entered Harvard two or three years before my time and became a fairly important figure. When I went out for the *Harvard Crimson* (incidentally, without making it) I was sent to get some news about an activity for which he was the spokesman. Maybe he would take an interest in a boy from the same city, who had debated and written for the school paper and won a scholarship like himself. I hurried to his room on Mt. Auburn Street. He was wearing—this was my first impression—a suit of clothes cut by a very good tailor, so well cut, indeed, that it made the features above it seem undistinguished. He eyed me carelessly—my own suit was bought in a department store—and began talking from a distance in a rich Oxford accent put on like his clothes. I want away without my news, feeling ashamed. The story wasn't printed.

Years later I saw him again when I was writing book reviews for a New York newspaper. He came into the office looking very English, like the boss's son. A friendly reporter told me that he was a second-string dramatic critic who would never become first-string. "He ought to get wise to himself," the reporter said. "He's got too much culture for this game."

In college we never grasped the idea that culture was the outgrowth of a situation—that an artisan knowing his tools and having the feel of his materials might be a cultured man; that a farmer among his animals and his fields, stopping his plow at the fence corner to meditate over death and life and next year's crop, might have culture without even reading a newspaper. Essentially we were taught to regard culture as a veneer, a badge of class distinction—as something assumed like an Oxford accent or a suit of English clothes.

Those salesrooms and fitting rooms of culture where we would spend four years were not ground-floor shops, open to the life of the street. They existed, as it were, at the top of very high buildings, looking down at a far panorama of boulevards and Georgian houses and Greek temples of banking—with people outside them the size of gnats—and, vague in the distance, the fields, mines, factories that labored unobtrusively to support us. We never glanced out at them. On the heights, while tailors transformed us into the semblance of cultured men, we exercised happily, studied in moderation, slept soundly and grumbled at our food. There was nothing else to do except pay the bills rendered semi-annually, and our parents attended to that.

College students, especially in the big Eastern universities, inhabit an easy world of their own. Except for very rich people and certain types of childless wives, they have been the only American class that could take leisure for granted. There have always been many among them who earned their board and tuition by tending furnaces, waiting on table or running back kickoffs for a touchdown; what I am about to say does not apply to them. The others—at most times the ruling clique of a big university, the students who set the tone for the rest—are supported practically without efforts of their own. They write a few begging letters; perhaps they study a little harder in order to win a scholarship; but usually they don't stop to think where the money comes from. Above them, the president knows the source of the hard cash that runs this great educational factory; he knows that the stream of donations can be stopped by a crash in the stock market or reduced in volume by newspaper reports of a professor gone bolshevik; he knows what he has to tell his trustees or the state legislators when he goes to them begging for funds. The scrubwomen in the library, the chambermaids and janitors, know how they earn their food; but the students themselves, and many of their professors, are blind to economic forces and they never think of society in concrete terms, as the source of food and football fields and professors' salaries.

The university itself forms a temporary society with standards of its own. In my time at Harvard the virtues instilled into students were good taste, good manners, cleanliness, chastity, gentlemanliness (or niceness), reticence and the spirit of competition in sports; they are virtues often prized by a leisure class. When a student failed to meet the leisure-class standards someone would say, "He talks too much," or more conclusively, "He needs a bath." Even boys from very good Back Bay families would fail to make a club if they paid too much attention to chorus girls. . . . Professor Irving Babbitt . . . and his disciples liked to talk about poise, proportionateness, the imitation of great models, decorum and the Inner Check. Those too were leisure-class ideals and I decided that they were simply the student virtues rephrased in loftier language. The truth was that the New Humanism grew out of Eastern university life, where it flourished as in a penthouse garden.

Nor was it the only growth that adorned these high mansions of culture. There was also, for example, the college liberalism that always drew back from action. There was the missionary attitude of Phillips Brooks House and the college Y.M.C.A.'s, that of reaching down and helping others to climb not quite up to our level. There was later the life-is-a-circus type of cynicism rendered popular by the *American Mercury*: everything is rotten, people are fools; let's all get quietly drunk and laugh at them. . . . The Harvard Aesthetes of 1916 were trying to create in Cambridge, Massachusetts, an after-image of Oxford in the 1890s. . . .

They were apparently very different from the Humanists, who never wrote poems at all, and yet, in respect to their opinions, they were simply Humanists turned upside down. For each of the Humanist virtues they had an antithesis. Thus, for poise they substituted *ecstasy;* for proportionateness, the Golden Mean, a worship of *immoderation;* for imitating great models, the opposite virtue of following each impulse, of *living in the moment.* Instead of decorum, they mildly preached a *revolt* from middle-class standards, which led them toward a sentimental reverence for sordid things; instead of the Inner Check, they believed in the duty of *self-expression.* Yet the Humanist and the Aesthete were both products of the same milieu, one in which the productive forces of society were regarded as something alien to poetry and learning. And both of them, though they found different solutions, were obsessed by the same problem, that of their individual salvation or damnation, success or failure, in a world in which neither was at home.

Whatever the doctrines we adopted during our college years, whatever the illusions we had of growing toward culture and self-sufficiency, the same process of deracination was continuing for all of us. We were like so many tumbleweeds sprouting in the rich summer soil, our leaves spreading while our roots slowly dried and became brittle. Normally the deracination would have ended when we left college; outside in the practical world we should have been forced to acquire new roots in order to survive. But we weren't destined to have the fate of the usual college generation and, instead of ceasing, the process would be intensified. Soon the war would be upon us; soon the winds would tear us up and send us rolling and drifting over the wide land.

When Cowley went to Harvard in 1916 he discovered an alien world. Compare James Baldwin's remark: "These were not really my creations, they did not contain my history; I might search in them in vain forever for any reflection of myself." In a word, neither Baldwin nor Cowley could make *contact* with the dominant culture. Deracination cut deep into Cowley's ties with and loyalty to his own past, the culture in which he had grown up. Like many a first-generation college student he was probably taught, albeit implicity, to feel ashamed of his benighted parents, the folks back home.

But his essay reveals a deeper and more damaging form of deracination: the institution itself, though intimately connected with the local centers of power, influence, and wealth, presented itself as almost floating, suspended in mid-air, in the finer unpolluted air of pure ideas. As a result, it was extremely difficult for the newly uprooted student to locate himself in the world and to understand the relationships between the "world" of business, the "world" of politics, the "world" of the city, and the "world" of higher education: education therefore seemed artificial and disconnected.

In the paragraph beginning, "In college we never grasped . . ." (p. 140), Cowley uses the word *culture.* Be aware that the word has many uses, and that Cowley is protesting against a use that is different from the sense in which we have so far used it in *Reading(s).* The use that offends him relates to a particular form of *cultivation,* that involves a kind of social sophistication and polish, an ability to refer to "highbrow" matters, to show that you have read all the "right books," just as you can tell the difference between an expensive wine and a glass of cheap beer. In this sense, *culture* is indisputably rooted in a certain kind of social snobbery: it is this that annoys and provokes Cowley, just as it offends students who have professors who treat them with contempt because the students speak with accents that come from the wrong side of the tracks.

CONSIDER THIS

★ See if you can extract from your reading of Cowley's text a set of principles or criteria for judging the effectiveness or otherwise of an American college/ university education in the late 1980s and 1990s.

★ More personally, do you feel that all that you have learned from living your life thus far is undervalued by your professors? How would you like them to regard such learning?

★ Do you, again personally, feel that you are losing touch with the good things in your past?

★ And what of the lamentable gaps in your knowledge? What are they? Should you do something about them? Do they matter? Are you indeed ignorant and provincial and proud of it?

★ "The students themselves, and many of their professors, are blind to economic forces and they never think of society in concrete terms." Have things changed since Cowley published these words in 1934?

★ And do the Harvard "virtues" he enumerates on p. 141 still prevail? Cleanliness? Chastity? Competitiveness in sports? Which virtues have outlived their usefulness? Which would you choose to encourage or promote?

★ Finally, Cowley judges his Harvard contemporaries—the posher and smarter of them—as driven by nothing better than selfishness, "obsessed by the same problem, that of their individual salvation or damnation, success or failure . . ." How, then, do you judge your own contemporaries?

ANNA QUINDLEN

Realizing What You Don't Know and Never Will

If we have a reasonable amount of self-respect, we make demands of ourselves, and we are also willing to admit that we could know more: there is no virtue in ignorance.

Anna Quindlen (b. 1953) writes a weekly newspaper column, "Life in the 30's," in which she reflects wittily and wisely on issues in her own life. When reading Mark Twain, she picks up his hint that with more years under your belt comes the consolation of knowing more. Quindlen challenges this assumption, but she goes further, and touches on a crucial and often neglected question: "Yes, but what do we really need to know?"

Some years ago my editors decided that I should write a story about the atmosphere on Wall Street. This was fine except that all I knew for sure about Wall Street was how to get there on the subway. So I sought out a writer who made it his business to know everything on the subject and asked him if he could spend an hour educating me.

"How rudimentary should this be?" he asked kindly.

"Let's start with the Dow Jones industrial average." I said. And so we did.

I have learned a lot about Wall Street since then, particularly by reading the newspaper over the last month. But my education really began that day, when I learned just enough so that I would not make a complete fool of myself when I hit the floor of the New York Stock Exchange. I learned just enough, too, to realize how very little I knew, and how extensive my ignorance was. It was a horrible feeling, like the feeling in high school just before you were handed a test for which you had not studied and looked at the first question.

The older I get, the more often and more deeply I feel like that: the more I learn, the more I realize how little I know. It sounds a bit like something Mark Twain might have said, except that if memory serves—and the point is, I suppose, that it often doesn't—Twain was always hinting that age and knowledge are a double bill. I think this is false.

I don't mean that I was smarter when I was younger. Quite the contrary. But when I was younger I was cockier about how dumb I was. I didn't know Chinese, couldn't do quadratic equations and wasn't sure of the difference between a Bolshevik and a Menshevik. But I did not mind much. If I got good grades in school or made good money after I graduated, I figured I was O.K. I had read a reasonable smattering of the great books, and if cocktail party conversation came around to Plutarch or the point spread in the Broncos game, I could just drift off in search of a fresh drink and a group that was talking about something else.

Now, I'm at once keenly bothered by the enormous gaps in my education and pessimistic about doing anything to remedy them. It is not only the serious stuff, although it irritates me that I cannot speak a foreign language, and that when my child asks why people with brown eyes don't see the world tinted brown I clutch and say, "Beats me." Sometimes during a baseball game, a player will make an error and I will realize that I don't know why, or how, or what it was. One part of me wants to learn. Another part thinks that if I have made it through 35 years—not to mention the particular day in question, which may have included toilet training, sibling rivalry, manuscript revision, separated mayonnaise and other assorted complications—I can live with the abject ignorance.

The unfortunate corollary is that my husband and I are long past the time when he was eager to teach me all the tiniest permutations of organized sports. If I ask about the error, he asks me to wait until the commercials. At the commercials, however, we talk about the kids. Apparently, he is accustomed to the gaps in my knowledge, and I to the gaps in his.

I've talked to people who did something about their ignorance, people who went to college at an age when most of their contemporaries were going to Florida to play mah-jongg or golf; I always had a great admiration for them. They were not what people of my generation, particularly those with an advanced business degree, would call goal-oriented: they were learning for the love of learning and were mature enough to think that was sufficient motivation. I was light years away from that kind of maturity when I went to college.

I remember someone joking that a six-month maternity leave should ideally be in the second six months of your child's life, because the first six months were nothing but a series of misunderstandings between a neckless rag doll with bad digestion and a nervous wreck, while during the second six months both of you were beginning to get interesting.

I see a parallel between this and going to school. Children should not be permitted access to education because they are too unformed to appreciate it. Concentrate on those things you already know something about; avoid those subjects that give you difficulty. Zoom through Psych. 1. Zoom through Poli. Sci. 2. Zoom through the Modern Novel, Renaissance Poetry, Chaucer and Shakespeare to get to the big payoff: Paradise Found. Real life.

It wasn't just us, either. I remember a burning question of my college years: What are you going to do with it? This was frequently asked by the parents of those poor souls who were studying, say, philosophy, or classical Greek and Latin. Now I keep thinking: Do with it? *Do with it?* What do you do with a painting? Nothing. You just have it so you can look at it and feel good.

It's a truism that if you could go back to college, this time you would really pay attention. I'm not likely to do this, however, my life having taken on a momentum of its own. I try to read books that will teach me about something I don't understand, and ask intelligent questions of experts in fields that boggle my mind. I used to think that knowledge is power. (That wasn't Twain, was it?) Now, I think power is overrated and knowledge is knowing things, which is impossible to overrate. Like some art school lesson in perspective (at least I think so; I never learned to draw, either), the farther I get away from formal education, the larger and more important the body of knowledge seems. There are so many things to know, and so little time to learn them, and I am afraid my epitaph will read, "She died dumb."

"What are you going to do with it?"

"*Do with it?*" Quindlen replies. So there is *knowing*, and there is *doing*. But what of the third element—being—on which these two rest? "What do you do with a painting? Nothing. You just have it so you can look at it and feel good."

"Feeling good" is one way of *being*; feeling miserable, or distracted, or disillusioned, or bored, or dissatisfied are also ways of being. Some ways of being are clearly to be preferred to others: but the better they are, the less we can will ourselves into them. . . .

Anna Quindlen raises many fascinating questions about *knowing* and about *being*. In the following essay, Benjamin Barber, a political scientist, pursues some of the questions that periodically come into public attention, often in the form of lamentation: "Young people today are *so* ignorant!" Ingeniously, he throws the question back at the generation of those who are most inclined to raise it.

BENJAMIN BARBER

What Do 47-Year-Olds Know?

We have heard a great deal about what our 17-year-olds do and don't know. About half don't know much of anything, according to Diane Ravitch and Chester E. Finn Jr., who authored the book "What Do Our Seventeen Year Olds Know?"

We have also been lectured by E.D. Hirsch Jr. about the decline of "cultural literacy"—the common vocabulary once provided by Homer, Shakespeare, the Bible, etc.—and by Allan Bloom about how post-Nietzschean nihilists and weak-willed college administrators have conspired with know-nothing kids to close the American mind.

Who is to blame for this alarming illiteracy? The culprit fashionable among conservatives like Secretary of Education William J. Bennett is progressive education and all those teachers of the 60's who value skills over substance, participation in learning over authority, creativity over memorization, social justice over high standards and relevance over the timeless classics.

With the complicity of the kids themselves, these dewey-eyed liberals are charged with creating a generation of cultural morons.

But there is ample evidence to suggest that the kids are smart, not stupid—smarter than we give them credit for. They are society-smart rather than school-smart. They are adept readers—but not of books. What they read so acutely are the social signals that emanate from the world in which they will have to make a living. Their teachers in this world—the nation's true pedagogues—are television, advertising, movies, politics and the celebrity domains they define.

What our 17-year-olds know is exactly what our 47-year-olds know and, by their example, teach them. Thus the test we need to administer to find out whether the young are good learners is a test of what our 47-year-olds know and are teaching. To ask who wrote "The Iliad" or what the dates of the French Revolution were or the identity of the philosopher David Hume is beside the point. Rather, we should ask: What do our 47-year-olds know? This is a multiple-choice quiz.

1. One-third of Yale's 1985 graduating class applied for positions as: (a) kindergarten teachers; (b) citizen soldiers in the volunteer Army; (c) doctoral students in philosophy; (d) trainees at the First Boston Corporation?

2. The signals coming from TV and magazine advertising teach you that happiness depends on: (a) the car you drive; (b) the clothes you wear; (c) the income you earn; (d) the way you smell; (e) the books you read?

3. The American most likely to have recently read "The Iliad" is: (a) a member of Congress; (b) an arbitrager; (c) a real estate developer; (d) a cosmetic surgeon; (e) one of those illiterate students who can't read or write?

4. The Reagan Administration has worked to get Government off the backs of the people through deregulation and privatization in order to: (a) unleash business; (b) encourage market competition; (c) increase productivity; (d) foster trickle-down prosperity by helping the rich to get richer; (e) give the young plenty of private space in which to paint, sculpt and read the classics?

5. To be hired by a top corporation, the most important credential is: (a) a doctorate of divinity from Harvard; (b) an honors degree in classics from Oxford; (c) a Yale Younger Poets award; (d) a comparative literature degree from the Sorbonne; (d) an M.B.A. from just about anywhere?

6. If you were running for President, you would devote many hours of study to: (a) the Bible; (b) Shakespeare's plays; (c) "The Federalist Papers"; (d) Plutarch's "Lives of the Romans"; (e) "How To Master Television Makeup"?

7. To sell a screen play to Hollywood you should: (a) adapt a play by Ibsen; (b) retell the story of Jean-Jacques Rousseau's dramatic encounter with David Hume; (c) dramatize "The Aeneid," paying careful attention to its poetic cadences; (d) novelize the life story of Donald Trump, paying careful attention to fiscal cadences?

8. Familiarity with "Henry IV, Part II" is likely to be of great importance in: (a) planning a corporate takeover; (b) evaluating budget cuts at the Department of Education; (c) initiating a medical liability suit; (d) writing an impressive job résumé; (e) taking a test on "What Our Seventeen-Year-Olds Know?"

9. Book publishers are financially rewarded for publishing: (a) cookbooks; (b) cat books; (c) how-to books; (d) popular pot-boilers; (e) critical editions of Immanuel Kant's early writings?

10. Universities are financially rewarded for: (a) supporting quality football teams; (b) forging research links with large corporations; (c) sustaining professional schools of law, medicine and business; (d) stroking wealthy alumni; (e) developing strong philosophy departments?

For extra credit: Name the 10 living poets who most influence your life, and recite a favorite stanza. Well, never mind the stanza, just name the poets. O.K., not 10, just five. Two? So who's your favorite running back?

My sample of 47-year-olds scored extremely well on this test—as did the 17-year-olds who took it (in every case the correct answer is the last, or, all but the last). Test results (nobody did the extra credit question!) reveal a deep strain of hypocrisy in the lamentations of the educational and cultural critics. They want our kids to know things the country at large doesn't give a hoot about.

We honor ambition, we reward greed, we celebrate materialism, we worship acquisitiveness, we commercialize art, we cherish success and then we bark at the young about the gentle arts of the spirit. The kids know that if we really valued learning, we would pay their teachers what we pay our lawyers and stock brokers. If we valued art, we would not measure it by its capacity to produce profits. If we regarded literature as important, we would remove it from the celebrity sweepstakes and spend a little money on our libraries.

Kids just don't care much for hypocrisy, and if they are illiterate, their illiteracy is merely ours, imbibed by them with a scholarly ardor. They are learning well the lesson we are teaching—namely, that there is nothing in all the classics in their school libraries that will be of the slightest benefit to them in making their way to the top of our competitive society.

Their neglect of the classical sources of Western civilization is thus a sad but appropriate tribute not to their ignorance but to their adaptive intelligence, and though we can hardly be proud of ourselves for what we are teaching them, we should at least be proud of them for how well they are learning it.

DENISE LEVERTOV

Psalm Concerning the Castle

Denise Levertov's poem meditates on ways of being; one of the best ways of being is to be absorbed, possessed, by something that is simultaneously inside *us* and *outside us: music, for example. You can't* will *yourself to enjoy it, but simply hope that it will work its magic as before.*

Denise Levertov's way of hoping takes the form of a prayer, a psalm. The state of being involves a rich variety of experiences, but they are united by their center, a way of being tranquil, centered, at peace, in a good place: the place is where we are; it is also inside us.

Let me be at the place of the castle.
Let the castle be within me.
Let it rise foursquare from the moat's ring.
Let the moat's waters reflect green plumage of ducks, let
    the shells of swimming turtles break the surface or be   5
    seen through the rippling depths.
Let horsemen be stationed at the rim of it, and a dog,
    always alert on the brink of sleep.
Let the space under the first storey be dark, let the water
    lap the stone posts, and vivid green slime glimmer upon   10
    them; let a boat be kept there.
Let the caryatids* of the second storey be bears upheld on
    beams that are dragons.
On the parapet of the central room, let there be four
    archers, looking off to the four horizons. Within, let   15
    the prince be at home, let him sit in deep thought, at
    peace, all the windows open to the loggias.   loggias: arcades
Let the young queen sit above, in the cool air, her child in
    her arms; let her look with joy at the great circle, the
    pilgrim shadows, the work of the sun and the play of   20
    the wind. Let her walk to and fro. Let the columns uphold
    the roof, let the storeys uphold the columns, let there
    be dark space below the lowest floor, let the castle rise
    foursquare out of the moat, let the moat be a ring and
    the water deep, let the guardians guard it, let there be   25
    wide lands around it, let that country where it stands be
    within me, let me be where it is.

Amidst the hurly-burly, the rushing around, the hectic pressures of our life "in the world," most of us desire a place into which to retreat—either literally

---

*Caryatids: pillars carved in the form of human or animal figures.

or metaphorically—a still center, where we can find refreshment and re-creation. For Denise Levertov, the image is a castle; for many of us it is some version of nature: the countryside, a riverbank, a day's fishing, a leisurely stroll, a week of backpacking.

As soon as most people had become city dwellers, the countryside, nature, became an important *idea:* it gathered to itself visions of an unspoiled past, nostalgic dreams of Eden or paradise, "idyllic" or "pastoral." At its richest, the idea of nature took on a religious resonance: so we go there hoping to be inspired, renewed by something beyond ourselves, something larger and deeper than our petty money-grubbing business, and more benign than the clamor of crowded city streets. As we left behind the hard reality of country life, we began to dream romantic rural dreams.

YOUR WRITING(S) FOR OTHERS TO READ

1. Do you ever feel yourself to be "in limbo"? What do you think gave rise to that feeling? How did you manage to come out of it?
2. How do you recall *your* first day at college? Was it "good": exhilarating, exciting—or "bad": depressing, confusing? Can we *prepare ourselves* for "first days"? Can we help others to prepare themselves?
3. What are the crucial differences between the culture of your home, street, or town, and the culture in which you now find yourself?

4. If Denise Levertov's "castle" is a good place to be, a metaphor for happiness, well-being, and a sense of wholeness, what are your metaphors? How would you characterize an ideal place to be in your life? Have you known such moments of well-being? How did they come about? How do you use your memories of them?
5. If growing up involves both gain and loss, what do you see yourself as having lost? Gained?

Chapter Six

Nature . . .

It came over her how the beauty of the world had come
with its sign. . . . There, outside, was all that was wild and
beloved and estranged, and all that would beckon her and
leave her, and all that was beautiful. She wanted to follow,
and by some metamorphosis she would take them in—all—
every one . . .

EUDORA WELTY

Before these fields were shorn and tilled,
    Full to the brim our rivers flowed;
The melody of rivers filled
    The fresh and boundless wood;
And torrents dashed, and rivulets played,
And fountains spouted in the shade.

WILLIAM CULLEN BRYANT

I looked back as we crossed the crest of the foothills—with
the air so clear you could see the leaves on Sunset Mountains
two miles away. It's startling to you sometimes just air,
unobstructed, uncomplicated air.

F. SCOTT FITZGERALD

151

W hat is the *natural* world like? What are its colors, textures, rhythms, sounds, spectacles? If you live in a city or a suburb, you may never know, unless you have the opportunity to travel. (Even then, to find sheer untouched nature, you will have to leave your plane, your car, your bicycle, your moped, and plunge in on foot, leaving all roads behind. Even then you may still hear and see aircraft, signs of our modern technocratic culture.)

One way, a good way, is the *vicarious* way of traveling via a text. There are thousands of books written by enterprising, restless, discontented, bored, or simply adventurous individuals who found it impossible to resist the deep and seductive lure of a vision of paradise: to find the earth as it was before we started to fix it up, improve it, mechanize it, render it tamed, civilized, urbanized, and unnatural.

In this chapter, we share with you a few texts that offer a brief glimmering of the distinctive delights of a return to a more primal scene.

DENISE LEVERTOV

O Taste and See

The world is
not with us enough.
O taste and see

the subway Bible poster said,
meaning *The Lord*, meaning   5
if anything all that lives
to the imagination's tongue,

grief, mercy, language,
tangerine, weather, to
breathe them, bite,   10
savor, chew, swallow, transform

into our flesh our
deaths, crossing the street, plum, quince,
living in the orchard and being

hungry, and plucking   15
the fruit.

In her poem Denise Levertov was reacting to Wordsworth's "The World Is Too Much with Us" (see p. 136). But her reaction was triggered by an ad: a religious poster, urging people to "taste and see . . . the Lord." To love is to absorb, to take in, to digest, to savor, to imbibe. Parents, loving a baby, exclaim, "I could *eat* you!" Even crossing the street—an ordinary enough act—can offer an opportunity to take pleasure in the world as "sensational," as something that always has the potential to enliven our senses. If our towns and cities are ugly—not worth looking at—is it because they were designed and built by people who had lost their capacity to "taste and see"?

How did you read Levertov's poem? If you tried to read it as you would a logical argument or a reasoned piece of persuasion, then you are missing the pleasure it conveys. If, on the other hand, you read it with your ears, and heard the *rush*, the piling up, of the enthusiasm, of the mood of exaltation, then you came much closer to feeling that pleasure.

Try reading it (preferably aloud) *not* for the "meaning" but for the *effect*: then try to register, to feel, to sense what that effect was. The effect of someone communicating an intense sense of pleasure—their eyes darting quickly from one thing to another, their minds from one thought to another, so intensely that they almost lose control, until, out of breath, they slow down to come to rest in the orchard and pluck an apple? Try reading it again, *fast*, then eat an apple!

CONSIDER THIS

★ In what sense is Levertov's use of the word *world* different from Wordsworth's?

The texts of stories move as words along the line, like this one, but the events of stories move in *time* and *space*.

Read, now, the words that follow.

When the rooster crowed . . .

What do you *expect* to follow, now that you've read them and constructed the beginning of a meaning? Time? Morning? Early morning? Not sure where? Does the rooster offer a clue? Middle of a city? Unlikely . . . A farm house or a house in the country? Probably. In far far less time than it took you to read all those questions, your eyes picked up the visual information "When the rooster crowed . . ." The time taken was actually between 10 and 50 milliseconds, or between one-hundredth and one-twentieth of a second; the message then went from your eyes to your brain, and your brain "recognized" the words and made its decisions. One of those decisions would be to expect something to *follow* because it perceived "When" as a sign that the-rooster-crows-and-when-it-crows, then . . . So the mind is already beginning to form the outline, the approximate form, of what must come next. Sure enough, we meet the following words:

When the rooster crowed, the moon had still not left the world but . . .

and our expectation is satisfied. It's a recognizable English sentence (unlike "still left not world moon the had the," which would take much longer to read) and its meaning fits in well with the early morning crowing of the rooster. As for "but," this signaled to you that there's more to come (possibly still dealing with the moon) and that there will be some kind of relationship between what's already been understood and what is going to be read next, a relationship rather different from what would follow "and." Now read on:

> When the rooster crowed, the moon had still not left the world but was going down on flushed cheek, one day short of the full. A long thin cloud . . .

When you meet the period after "full," you understand it to be signaling that one segment is complete and the next segment is about to follow: this expectation is immediately confirmed—in less than the twinkling of an eye—by the arrival of "A," the capital letter announcing the start of a new sentence.

By the time you reach "full," you are constructing a sense of early morning. Why, then, did the author, Eudora Welty, not simply write "It was early morning"? We do *not* know the answer to the question, but we can guess: Welty wanted to *affect* us, her readers, in certain ways; to give us, through words, an *illusion* of the experiences of early morning. She wanted us to have an experience by putting us there in the moment of things happening, of things unfolding, rather than *telling* us it was early morning.

Now, go on to read the whole passage, from the beginning of Welty's novel, *Losing Battles*.

Eudora Welty

Sunrise

When the rooster crowed, the moon had still not left the world but was going down on flushed cheek, one day short of the full. A long thin cloud crossed it slowly, drawing itself out like a name being called. The air changed, as if a mile or so away a wooden door had swung open, and a smell, more of warmth than wet, from a river at low stage, moved upward into the clay hills that stood in darkness.

Then a house appeared on its ridge, like an old man's silver watch pulled once more out of its pocket. A dog leaped up from where he'd lain like a stone and began barking for today as if he meant never to stop.

Then a baby bolted naked out of the house. She monkey-climbed down the steps and ran open-armed into the yard, knocking at the walls of flowers still colorless as faces, tagging in turn the four big trees that marked off the corners of the yard, tagging the gatepost, the well-piece, the birdhouse, the bell post, a log seat, a rope swing, and then, rounding the house, she used all her strength to push over a crate that let a stream of white Plymouth Rocks loose on the world. The chickens rushed ahead of the baby, running frantic, and behind the baby came a girl in a petticoat. A wide circle of curl-papers, paler than the streak of dawn, bounced around her head, but she ran on confident tiptoe as though she believed no eye could see her. She caught the baby and carried her back inside, the baby with her little legs still running like a windmill.

The distant point of the ridge, like the tongue of a calf, put its red lick on the sky. Mists, voids, patches of woods and naked clay, flickered like live ashes, pink and blue. A mirror that hung within the porch on the house wall began to flicker as at the striking of kitchen matches. Suddenly two chinaberry trees at the foot of the yard lit up, like roosters astrut with golden tails. Caterpillar nets shone in the pecan tree. A swollen shadow bulked underneath it, familiar in shape as Noah's Ark—a school bus.

Then as if something came sliding out of the sky, the whole tin roof of the house ran with new blue. The posts along the porch softly bloomed downward, as if chalk marks were being drawn, one more time, down a still misty slate. The house was revealed as if standing there from pure memory against a now moonless sky. For the length of a breath, everything stayed shadowless, as under a lifting hand, and then a passage showed, running through the house, right through the middle of it, and at the head of the passage, in the center of the front gallery, a figure was revealed, a very old lady seated in a rocking chair with head cocked, as though wild to be seen.

Then Sunday light raced over the farm as fast as the chickens were flying. Immediately the first straight shaft of heat, solid as a hickory stick, was laid on the ridge.

As readers, our only data (apart from the visual information—the words on the page) is our own nonvisual information (which we carry in our minds into our acts of reading). We remember the actual crowing of roosters; we have occasionally seen a glow of sunrise on the moon, as darkness fades; and we have a pretty clear mental image of an almost full moon. For us, it so happens that listening to/looking at such things is in itself a form of pleasure. As we respond to the sequences of words on the page, we recognize their meanings, and almost automatically *envision* mental images which more or less correspond to our sense of what the text expects of us.

All of this activity is enclosed within a frame that itself helps the whole thing to work: that frame is our choice of a *story* by Eudora Welty. Our memories of our previous experiences as readers (our nonvisual information) guide us to *expect* the kinds of sentences Welty gives us. And part of our knowledge of novels and short stories is this: that we don't go to their sentences for *information*. If we need information we go to the kinds of books that give it: encyclopedias, and various other kinds of reference books. So what do we go to a novel or short story for? What do we expect of it? Simply the experience of an *illusion*—the sense that our eyes and ears and noses are *somewhere else* (that is, not in *this* room, reading *this* book) where it is *as if* they can see, hear and smell: if the illusion is vivid, we even imagine that our fingers can touch.

Imagine, however, that we are actually standing near a farm house at sunrise: unless we were setting out to *note* what happened, *selecting* details that would contribute to the *effect* that we desired to convey to our notebook, our next short story, our diary, or our next writing class, our observations would be *haphazard*, unordered, jumbled.

When, therefore, we experience the *illusion* of Eudora Welty's sunrise, we experience it in a way that is controlled, guided, oriented by her mind's control over the effects of her sequences of words. This is not to deny that people who hate roosters will react slightly differently from those who love them, but neither will be able to exclude the rooster from their visual and aural envisioning.

Let's, then, offer you a piece of useful shorthand: Welty's writing is *presentational*. It *presents* us with a sequence of illusory images which draw on our past experiences of the actual things. Our illusion, then, is one of sensation and of perception.

Here are two other views of sunrise:

EDWARD THOMAS

Cock-Crow

Out of the wood of thoughts that grows by night
To be cut down by the sharp axe of light,—
Out of the night, two cocks together crow,
Cleaving the darkness with a silver blow:
And bright before my eyes twin trumpeters stand,   5
Heralds of splendour, one at either hand,
Each facing each as in a coat of arms:
The milkers lace their boots up at the farms.

MAY SWENSON

OUT OF THE SEA, EARLY

A bloody
egg yolk. A burnt hole
spreading in a sheet. An enraged rose threatening to bloom.
A furnace hatchway opening, roaring.
A globular bladder filling with immense
juice. I start to scream. A red hydrocepha-
lic head is born, teetering on the stump of
its neck. When it separates, it leaks rasp-
berry from the horizon down the wide esca-
lator. The cold blue boiling waves cannot
scour out that band, that broadens, sliding toward me up the wet sand slope. The
fox-hair grows, grows thicker on the
upfloating head. By six o'clock,
diffused to ordinary gold,
it exposes each silk thread and rumple in the carpet.

Edward Thomas (1878–1917) *hears* the roosters crowing in the dark: the *sound* creates in his mind a *visual* image, as bright as the "axe" of the sunrise will be when it comes. The vision in his mind then metamorphoses, changing its form into that of two trumpeting heralds as in a coat of arms: the crowing music of the roosters is like the sound of trumpeters playing "Reveille." Already, even as he continues to lie in bed, envisioning these, the milkers are up and preparing for work.

Thomas *defamiliarizes* the mere noise of roosters by allowing us to "see" the dazzling images inside his head. May Swenson (b. 1919) defamiliarizes sunrise by writing as if she had never seen it before: to make sense of it, she draws on her knowledge of familiar things—egg yolk, hole in a sheet, rose, furnace, and so on. In so doing, she creates a sense of a powerful and wonderful spectacle.

As with Welty, these texts are vividly *presentational*. They don't *discuss*, or *explain*, or *analyze*; they present!

Some elements of the world soak so deeply into us that they become an invisible and mysterious part of our own characters—sights and sounds transformed into some influence, or disposition.

Go to a West Coast fishing port, and talk to people who spend their lives in small boats on surging water; go to a remoter corner of Montana and find a real cowboy; talk to a Pennsylvania miner, a Nebraska ploughman, or a New Jersey nurseryman. The differences are striking: somehow, they have imbibed and incorporated some natural element, some distinctive rhythm into their personalities, and it is reflected in their gestures, their speech, and their idiosyncratic ways of looking at the world.

WALT WHITMAN

Memories of Waves

Even as a boy, I had the fancy, the wish, to write a piece, perhaps a poem, about the sea-shore—that suggesting, dividing line, contact, junction, the solid marrying the liquid—that curious, lurking something, (as doubtless every objective form finally becomes to the subjective spirit,) which means far more than its mere first sight, grand as that is—blending the real and ideal, and each made portion of the other. Hours, days, in my Long Island youth and early manhood, I haunted the shores of Rockaway or Coney island, or away east to the Hamptons or Montauk. Once, at the latter place, (by the old lighthouse, nothing but sea-tossings in sight in every direction as far as the eye could reach,) I remember well, I felt that I must one day write a book expressing this liquid, mystic theme. Afterward, I recollect, how it came to me that instead of any special lyrical or epical or literary attempt, the sea-shore should be an invisible *influence*, a pervading gauge and tally for me, in my composition. (Let me give a hint here to young writers. I am not sure but I have unwittingly follow'd out the same rule with other powers besides sea and shores—avoiding them, in the way of any dead set at poetizing them, as too big for formal handling—quite satisfied if I could indirectly show that we have met and fused, even if only once, but enough—that we have really absorb'd each other and understand each other.)

There is a dream, a picture, that for years at intervals, (sometimes quite long ones, but surely again, in time,) has come noiselessly up before me, and I really believe, fiction as it is, has enter'd largely into my practical life—certainly into my writings, and shaped and color'd them. It is nothing more or less than a stretch of interminable white-brown sand, hard and smooth and broad, with the ocean perpetually, grandly, rolling in upon it, with slow-measured sweep, with rustle and hiss and foam, and many a thump as of low bass drums. This scene, this picture, I say, has risen before me at times for years. Sometimes I wake at night and can hear and see it plainly.

Walt Whitman (1819–1892) was possessed, haunted, saturated by the rhythms of the sea: it helped to shape his sensibility.

CONSIDER THIS

★ What goes to shape the sensibility of someone who grows up in the city? What has gone into the shaping of your sensibility? Farmlands? City streets? Shopping malls? Airplanes? Subway trains?

The poet May Swenson, a century after Whitman, turns to waves for something else—the structure of the sequence, of the eventfulness, of a wave rising, cresting, and breaking—and then the same again, and then the same again, and then . . .

MAY SWENSON

HOW EVERYTHING HAPPENS (Based on a study of the Wave)

                                                                happen.
                                                        to
                                                up
                                        stacking
                                    is
                            something
    When nothing is happening

    When it happens
                        something
                                pulls
                                    back
                                        not
                                            to
                                                happen.

    When   has happened.
            pulling back   stacking up
                    happens

            has happened   stacks up
    When it   something   nothing
                                    pulls back while

    Then nothing is happening.

                                                    happens.
                                                and
                                        forward
                                pushes
                            up
                        stacks
                something
    Then

May Swenson's poems fall into a distinct category, known as "concrete poetry," which flourished throughout much of the world during the 1960s and 1970s. As you will have noticed, concrete poetry breaks away from line-by-line writing, preferring to offer a pattern, a typographic form, that appeals to the eye as an image, even before the eye homes in on the business of reading in a conventional sense. Hold up a concrete poem at arm's length, and you will be able to make a fairly good guess about its subject. *Isomorphic* is the technical term for such texts: like the tail of the mouse in Lewis Carroll's *Alice in Wonderland*.

May Swenson's title is "How Everything Happens": *everything?* Test her claim against anything that moves in space or persists through time: a conversation, driving a car, a gymnast working, doing woodwork, thinking and writing, meeting someone, fixing a meal, putting up a tent, wrestling, performing an operation, a dentist filling one of your teeth . . .

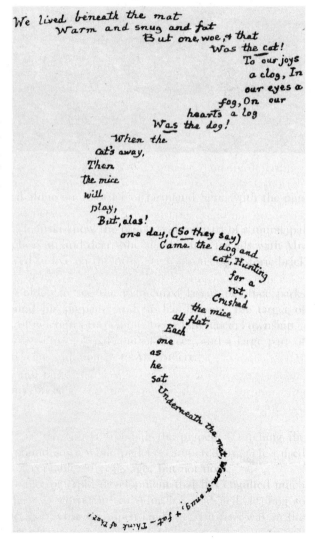

RICHARD WRIGHT

The Wonder I Felt

How and when do the moments of your life "reveal their meanings"? When are events "cryptic"? As they happen? For a vivid example—a flood of examples—we turn again to Richard Wright.

Each event spoke with a cryptic tongue. And the moments of living slowly revealed their coded meanings. There was the wonder I felt when I first saw a brace of mountainlike, spotted, black-and-white horses clopping down a dusty road through clouds of powdered clay.

There was the delight I caught in seeing long straight rows of red and green vegetables stretching away in the sun to the bright horizon.

There was the faint, cool kiss of sensuality when dew came on to my cheeks and shins as I ran down the wet green garden paths in the early morning.

There was the vague sense of the infinite as I looked down upon the yellow, dreaming waters of the Mississippi River from the verdant bluffs of Natchez.

There were the echoes of nostalgia I heard in the crying strings of wild geese winging south against a bleak, autumn sky.

There was the tantalising melancholy in the tingling scent of burning hickory wood.

There was the teasing and impossible desire to imitate the petty pride of sparrows wallowing and flouncing in the red dust of country roads.

There was the yearning for identification loosed in me by the sight of a solitary ant carrying a burden upon a mysterious journey.

There was the disdain that filled me as I tortured a delicate, blue-pink crawfish that huddled fearfully in the mudsill of a rusty tin can.

There was the aching glory in masses of clouds burning gold and purple from an invisible sun.

There was the liquid alarm I saw in the blood-red glare of the sun's afterglow mirrored in the squared panes of whitewashed frame houses.

There was the languor I felt when I heard green leaves rustling with a rainlike sound.

There was the incomprehensible secret embodied in a whitish toadstool hiding in the dark shade of a rotting log.

There was the experience of feeling death without dying that came from watching a chicken leap about blindly after its neck had been snapped by a quick twist of my father's wrist.

There was the great joke that I felt God had played on cats and dogs by making them lap their milk and water with their tongues.

There was the thirst I had when I watched clear, sweet juice trickle from sugar cane being crushed.

There was the hot panic that welled up in my throat and swept through my blood when I first saw the lazy, limp coils of a blue-skinned snake sleeping in the sun.

There was the speechless astonishment of seeing a hog stabbed through the heart, dipped into boiling water, scraped, split open, gutted, and strung up gaping and bloody.

There was the love I had for the mute regality of tall, moss-clad oaks.

There was the hint of cosmic cruelty that I felt when I saw the curved timbers of a wooden shack that had been warped in the summer sun.

There was the saliva that formed in my mouth whenever I smelt clay dust pitted with fresh rain.

There was the cloudy notion of hunger when I breathed the odour of new-cut, bleeding grass.

And there was the quiet terror that suffused my senses when vast hazes of gold washed earthward from star-heavy skies on silent nights . . .

We live *in time* and, as we *participate* in any event, while it is actually happening, the pressure of participation, the work we do unconsciously to continue to play our part—listening, watching, responding, doing—these make demands of us, of our energy, and of our powers of attention. It is only *afterwards*, when the event has been swept into the past, when we are *spectators* of our own past lives, that we can make sense of it: then, and only then, can we say it was an *experience* rather than a mere *event*. True or untrue?

We watch a bird swoop fast to avoid a car's fender; we watch a cat stalking a bird or a mouse; we watch whatever catches our attention and arrests us. Only afterwards can we say "That was exciting!" or "That was fascinating!" or "That was wonderful!" True or untrue?

If we are deeply absorbed can we say *anything*, even to ourselves?

As Mark Twain put it, "I stood like one bewitched. I drank it in, in a speechless rapture."

JAMES AGEE

This Lucky Situation of Joy

When we really pay attention to something outside ourselves, we lose awareness of self; it is as if we have ceased to exist: we are "all eyes" or "all ears." So we can say of someone, "She lost herself in a book," meaning that she was so deeply, so intensely absorbed that she lost all awareness of herself or of her surroundings.

The writer and film critic James Agee's (1909–1955) word for this way of being is "joy": "an illusion of personal wholeness or integrity" achieved through an apparent escape from the endless to-and-fro of the conversations that we hold with ourselves in our minds.

This lucky situation of joy, this at least illusion of personal wholeness or integrity, can overcome one suddenly by any one of any number of unpredictable chances: the fracture of sunlight on the façade and traffic of a street; the sleaving up of chimneysmoke; the rich lifting of the voice of a train along the darkness; the memory of a phrase of an inspired trumpet; the odor of scorched cloth, of a car's exhaust, of a girl, of pork, of beeswax on hot iron, of young leaves, of peanuts; the look of a toy fire engine, or of a hundred agates sacked in red cheesecloth; the oily sliding sound as a pumpgun is broken; the look of a child's underwaist with its bone buttons loose on little cotton straps; the stiffening of snow in a wool glove; the odor of kitchen soap, of baby soap, of scorched bellybands: the flexion of a hand; the twist of a knee; the modulations in a thigh as someone gets out of a chair: the bending of a speeding car round a graded curve: the swollen, blemished feeling of the mouth and the tenacity and thickness of odor of an unfamiliar powder, walking sleepless in high industrial daybreak and needing coffee, the taste of cheap gin mixed with cheap ginger ale without much ice: the taste of turnip greens; of a rotted seed drawn from between the teeth; of rye whiskey in the green celluloid glass of a hotel bathroom: the breath that comes out of a motion-picture theater: the memory of the piccolo notes which ride and transfix Beethoven's pastoral storm: the odor of a freshly printed newspaper; the stench of ferns trapped in the hot sunlight of a bay window; the taste of a mountain summer night: the swaying and shuffling beneath the body of a benighted train; the mulled and branny earth beneath the feet in fall . . .

After Judith Condon, an English student, had read *Let Us Now Praise Famous Men*, the book from which this extract was taken, she wrote: "It is the kind of book that comes to mean something to you which you can ultimately only communicate by saying you have read it, and bits of it follow you around . . . so that you can't remember what it felt like not to have known them before."

MARK TWAIN

I Know . . . Green Apples

By the time he came to write his Autobiography, *Mark Twain (1835–1910) was world famous. Why should he presume to write a book in which he wrote about such "trivial" matters as his love of roasted apples?*

I know the look of green apples and peaches and pears on the trees, and I know how entertaining they are when they are inside of a person. I know how ripe ones look when they are piled in pyramids under the trees, and how pretty they are and how vivid their colors. I know how a frozen apple looks in a barrel down cellar in the wintertime, and how hard it is to bite and how the frost makes the teeth ache, and yet how good it is notwithstanding. I know the disposition of elderly people to select the specked apples for the children and I once knew ways to beat the game. I know the look of an apple that is roasting and sizzling on a hearth on a winter's evening, and I know the comfort that comes of eating it hot, along with some sugar and a drench of cream. I know the delicate art and mystery of so cracking hickory-nuts and walnuts on a flatiron with a hammer that the kernels will be delivered whole, and I know how the nuts, taken in conjunction with winter apples, cider, and doughnuts, make old people's old tales and old jokes sound fresh and crisp and enchanting, and juggle an evening away before you know what went with the time. I know the look of Uncle Dan'l's kitchen as it was on privileged nights when I was a child, and I can see the children grouped on the hearth, with the firelight playing on their faces and the shadows flickering upon the walls clear back toward the cavernous gloom of the rear, and I can hear Uncle Dan'l telling the immortal tales which Uncle Remus Harris was to gather into his book and charm the world with, by and by. And I can feel again the creepy joy which quivered through me when the time for the ghost story was reached—and the sense of regret too which came over me, for it was always the last story of the evening and there was nothing between it and the unwelcome bed.

I can remember the bare wooden stairway in my uncle's house and the turn to the left above the landing, and the rafters and the slanting roof over my bed, and the squares of moonlight on the floor and the white cold world of snow outside, seen through the curtainless window. I can remember the howling of the wind and the quaking of the house on stormy nights, and how snug and cozy one felt under the blankets, listening; and how the powdery snow used to sift in around the sashes and lie in little ridges on the floor, and make the place look chilly in the morning and curb the wild desire to get up—in case there was any. I can remember how very dark that room was in the dark of the moon, and how packed it was with ghostly stillness when one woke up by accident away in the night, and forgotten sins came flocking out of the secret chambers of the memory and wanted a hearing; and how ill-chosen the time seemed for this kind of business and how dismal was the hoo-hooing of the owl and the wailing of the wolf, sent mourning by on the night wind.

I remember the raging of the rain on that roof, summer nights, and how pleasant it was to lie and listen to it and enjoy the white splendor of the lightning and the majestic booming and crashing of the thunder. It was a very satisfactory room, and there was a lightning rod which was reachable from the window, an adorable and skittish thing to climb up and down, summer nights when there were duties on hand of a sort to make privacy desirable . . .

Who cares . . . ? If we did not know how other people express their joys and sorrows, we would be incapable of expressing our own.

If someone never told us about the raging of the rain on the roof, the darkness of their childhood bedroom, and the coziness of their bed, we might never recall our own. As they "read" their own lives, and share these readings with us, so are we better able to read our lives, our joys and sorrows, as both *like* theirs and *unlike* theirs.

Here Mark Twain sits down to try to give us a vivid illusion of "seeing" a river at sunset, as he once saw it.

MARK TWAIN

The River Was Turned to Blood

I still kept in mind a certain wonderful sunset which I witnessed when steamboating was new to me. A broad expanse of the river was turned to blood; in the middle distance the red hue brightened into gold, through which a solitary log came floating, black and conspicuous; in one place a long, slanting mark lay sparkling upon the water; in another the surface was broken by boiling, tumbling rings, that were as many-tinted as an opal; where the ruddy flush was faintest, was a smooth spot that was covered with graceful circles and radiating lines, ever so delicately traced; the shore on our left was densely wooded and the somber shadow that fell from this forest was broken in one place by a long, ruffled trail that shone like silver; and high above the forest wall a clean-stemmed dead tree waved a single leafy bough that glowed like a flame in the unobstructed splendor that was flowing from the sun. There were graceful curves, reflected images, woody heights, soft distances, and over the whole scene, far and near, the dissolving lights drifted steadily, enriching it every passing moment with new marvels of coloring.

I stood like one bewitched. I drank it in, in a speechless rapture. The world was new to me and I had never seen anything like this at home.

CONSIDER THIS

★ Note that last sentence in the long paragraph: "There were . . . coloring," how it pulls the whole paragraph together, summarizing it and reaffirming it. And then the contrasted short paragraph which explains why it is only now, later, after the eventfulness, that he can express it in words. And how he finally explains, justifies, his enthusiasm: "I had never seen anything like this at home." When we encounter something that we could not predict, what happens to our powers of speech, our command of language?

★ Mark Twain was celebrated for his dry and satirical sense of humor: why do you think it is absent from this passage about the river?

Knowing Better

What can we learn from the writers in this chapter? Perhaps their most important lesson is about something that comes before writing—"before" in time, and "before" in terms of a deeper, less rational activity. It's difficult to name it, but it involves vigilance, concentration, attentiveness, a kind of submission to what simply is. Keats called it "negative capability"—a state of mind in which you switch off striving and trying, explaining and analyzing, and simply allow yourself to be engrossed so intently in what you see or hear that you come close to the "illusion" that you are possessed by whatever is the focus of your attention, and even feel that you have become it. People who are deeply involved in music know this experience, and so, apparently, do the great mystics.

If you are blessed with a language adequate to what your attention has discovered, then the relationship between the signifier and what it signifies becomes very intimate, almost one: thus arises the quality of a language that seems to feel no distance from what it represents, a language that itself can create the sense of having emanated from its subject—a water language spoken by the river. Our reason tells us that, of course, water *has no language*, but there are moments when we simply don't have to place too much stress on what our reason tells us.

As Twain says, "I stood like one bewitched." In reading such texts as these, one can enjoy the privilege of sharing some of that bewitchment.

In creating texts that may convey something of the intensity, vividness, and power of one's perceptions one simply cannot fall back on buzz words—*wonderful, marvelous, terrific*—but must find a language that will, in its rhythms, its vowels and consonants, itself seem to create the effects of the rhythms and textures of what is to be represented: a language of sheer mimesis.

In reading such texts, one does not hope to come out at the end *knowing more:* but, rather, to end up *knowing better,* more intimately, more vividly, more powerfully. If your hair stands on end, or you feel goose-pimples or a faint shudder, count your blessings. Reading, like writing, can be a way of living.

YOUR WRITING(S) FOR OTHERS TO READ

1. How important is the sky to you? For what reason do you ever look up at it?
2. What is your best time of day? Are you a "night person" or a "day person"?
3. Do you think it's possible to express pleasure in natural phenomena (e.g., a sunset) without using clichés?
4. Are there aspects of nature that frighten you? Lightning? Thunder? Dark nights?
5. Does the weather affect your moods? How so? If you apply May Swenson's "How Everything Happens" to *anything* you know or do, does her generalization work? Is her claim justified?
6. Does nature bore you? Leave you indifferent? What kinds of pleasures does a city give you that you couldn't find in the backwoods? Conversely, do you occasionally need to "get out"? What do you think you are going in search of?

Chapter Seven
Nature and Culture

" . . . dominion over the fowl of the air and over every
living thing that moveth upon the earth."

GENESIS

There was never a king like Solomon
Not since the world began
Yet Solomon talked to a butterfly
As a man would talk to a man.

RUDYARD KIPLING

Y ou, like us, cannot remember your first act of "reading": it probably
occurred when your mother smiled at you when you were a young baby,
and *you smiled back;* or it was when your parents made gurgling sounds,
close up, and *you gurgled back.* Such actions indicated the beginnings of the
development of your mind, nothing less.

From these very early interactions, you began to be a member of a family, a
social being, someone capable of participating in relationships, and that beginning
was a momentous step for, more than your actual biological birth, it could be
said to be your entry into the human race.*

Since those early moments, you have never stopped "reading" the world—
especially the people with whom you interact. Fundamental to this unending

*We introduced this topic on p. 8. Without looking back, how much of that text can you recall/reconstruct?

and purposeful activity of "reading" is the tacit assumption or presupposition that "things make sense," that your observing—listening and watching, especially—is rooted in the *prior* belief that the world has meaning, in your discovery that through observation and interaction you can make sense of others, your environment, and your relationship with those others and that environment; and you adjust, as necessary, your "theory of the world."

You don't learn to do this unaided; on the contrary, for most of us our mother is the great teacher or, better, the great enabler of learning. Inexhaustibly, persistently, patiently, mothers set up "formats" which promote our learning.

What, then, have we all been "reading" up to this moment in our lives? A conveniently simple answer is: the world, which includes our own bodies, since we observe them when things go wrong inside or when we want to improve them outside. But that general term, *the world*, doesn't take us very far.

Let us, then, divide the world into two parts—the given and the made; that is, nature and culture. By nature we mean such things as the weather; by culture, air conditioning. The following two columns illustrate our distinction:

NATURE	CULTURE
rivers	canals
lakes	reservoirs
rain	sprinkler systems
sunshine	electric lights
bodies	clothes
trees	hedgerows
horses	automobiles
forest fire caused by lightning	central heating
barking	talking

Some things—nature—are already there; others—culture—human beings have created. But the difference is blurred in several ways. Horses, for example, have been chosen and bred for specific purposes: for pulling brewery wagons, for example, or for racing. Human beings have *intervened* in natural processes; so horses started as "nature," but now, with very few exceptions, have been radically modified by "culture."

More important, as we grow up from infancy in a given culture, we tend to assume that our particular culture is "natural": it is "the way things are." Alternative cultures are seen as deviant, odd, or even perverse. At worst, members of a culture can be so convinced that their culture is indeed Nature—God-given—that they will set out to destroy different cultures as aberrant, wicked, savage, immoral, and so on.

We are all inclined to reserve the term *natural* to describe *our* culture, and dismiss other, different cultures as "unnatural." And to compound the problem, politicians work hard to convince us that the culture that they endorse is indeed the only "natural" one. Not content to appeal to "nature," they argue that their culture is the "Nature" intended or given by God. The best way to resist such preposterous claims is simply to hold before you a clear distinction between "nature" and "culture."

At certain times in the history of cultures, the interrelatedness of culture and nature has been mis-read as identity: culture *is* nature, *is* God-given, *is* a cosmic fact. At such moments, there has been a strong tendency to argue for cause-and-effect relationships, a deep inscrutable interdependency, between the human world, culture (the microcosm) and the natural universe (the macrocosm). When, for example, in Shakespeare's plays, things go badly wrong in the family or in the state, you can expect some character soon to invoke the deep correspondence between microcosm and macrocosm. In 1600, Shakespeare's audiences would not dream of questioning such a claim, for it was part and parcel of their own way of "reading" the world. If the small world of human culture is disrupted, breaking down, in chaos, that is a *sign* of cosmic disorder. This assumption persists in the superstitions out of which astrologers continue to make money, and for many centuries was reinforced by the prestige of one of the first writers to affirm it, the Greek philosopher Plato. It could be used, and was indeed used, to justify extreme actions: when the body was in a fever, you relieved the fever by bloodletting; so if the "body" of the state was in a fever (that is, troubled by rebellion or dissent), then the solution was to make the blood flow.

The modern world—since the scientific revolution of the seventeenth century—has witnessed not only an "explosion" of culture and a corresponding destruction of nature but also the unprecedented development of devices for extending our power or capacity to "read." Our powers of observation have been extended both down and up, both in and out, by the electron microscope and the radio telescope; the activity of the human brain can be "read" with remarkable vividness by the CAT scan. Lenses can penetrate the deepest interior of the living body and provide startling images of internal activity, both healthy and unhealthy. Television has given us a ringside seat to watch people walking on the moon and exploring the deepest oceans. And all of these extraordinary technological extensions of "reading" have derived in large part from our ability to read: to read what our predecessors have written, to "read" the "worlds" they have revealed, and to stand on their shoulders. All such advances as these may be termed *prosthetic*, that is, artificial extensions of our basic biological resources such as eyes, ears, and hands. With the invention of writing, the invention of printing, the spread of literacy, and the diffusion of print, the world of any person capable of reading was extended immeasurably: there is virtually no limit to the range and variety of worlds that we can "read" through being able to read.

This capacity doesn't in itself save us from the naive mistake of assuming when we open a book or newspaper that what we read is the real thing. The cynical tradition says, "Don't believe anything you read"; the naive tradition says, "It's in print so it *must* be true." The middle way is to avoid both of these extremes, and to recognize that no text *is* the world it represents. Imagine a history of alcoholism written by a tea-totaller, one written by an alcoholic, and one written by someone who drinks moderately; the probable differences among those three texts will be obvious. No one text will be able to tell the whole truth, to offer the world as it has in fact been; but of the three, is the third not likely to be the most reliable?

Naive realism is a name we give to the point of view, the state of mind, of people who believe that soap operas, for example, *are* or *represent* "real life." In extreme cases, naive realism borders on madness, as in the case of an old man we knew, who used to put on his best clothes when watching important people on television. How, then, do we develop a satisfactory alternative to such naiveté? A useful way to begin is to recognize, and to remind ourselves as often as possible, that we live in a world of signs, signs produced by others for the satisfaction of their needs or desires.

It's possible that the greatest benefit to be derived from a college education is not a degree of any kind, or the acquisition of professional skills, but the condition of relative freedom or independence that allows one to reconsider the values that one has taken for granted, the "culture" that one has accepted without question as "natural."

When we "read" the world, there can be no such thing as an innocent or neutral "reading," for whatever we perceive is determined by the unconscious assumptions and values that we bring to every act of perceiving. When a psychopathic Nazi saw a concentration camp, he presumably smiled; and that smile was enough to convict him of a probably incurable moral lunacy. When a child in a hospital sees a hypodermic needle, she sees something very different from what an elderly nurse sees. When young people see a cheerfully noisy TV commercial for beer, they see something very different from what the parents of a child killed by a drunken driver see.

Is *everything* in the world to be construed as *culture*? Is there any nature remaining? Is there any such thing as "human nature"? These are questions we hope you will be provoked to consider as you read the texts in this chapter.

One clear focus for the relationship between culture and nature is offered by humans' relationships with animals: these can be both benign and exploitive, even destructive. The texts in this chapter explore some of the complex pleasures and pains of such encounters.

D. H. LAWRENCE

Snake

In the first text, D. H. Lawrence (1885–1930) offers a version of his encounter with a snake. He could have written it as an episode in a novel, as a short story, or as an essay; being versatile, he also had poetry up his sleeve, and decided/discovered that a poem would work. It is written in his own kind of free verse, which suited him very well: each little section or paragraph marks a stage in the development of the event and in the movement of Lawrence's thought. He discovers that there is more than one voice inside his head, talking insistently, telling him how to deal with the threat of the snake. (The reference to the albatross, eight lines from the end, harks back to S. T. Coleridge's ballad, "The Ancient Mariner," in which a sailor needlessly kills the greatest of the sea birds and is ever after haunted by guilt.)

A SNAKE came to my water-trough
On a hot, hot day, and I in pyjamas for the heat,
To drink there.

In the deep, strange-scented shade of the great dark carob tree   5
I came down the steps with my pitcher
And must wait, must stand and wait, for there he was at the
          trough before me.

He reached down from a fissure in the earth-wall in the gloom
And trailed his yellow-brown slackness soft-bellied down,
          over the edge of the stone trough
And rested his throat upon the stone bottom,
And where the water had dripped from the tap, in a small
          clearness,   10
He sipped with his straight mouth,
Softly drank through his straight gums, into his slack long
          body,
Silently.

Someone was before me at my water-trough,
And I, like a second-comer, waiting.   15

He lifted his head from his drinking, as cattle do
And looked at me vaguely, as drinking cattle do,
And flickered his two-forked tongue from his lips, and mused
          a moment,
And stooped and drank a little more,
Being earth-brown, earth-golden from the burning bowels of
          the earth   20
On the day of Sicilian July, with Etna smoking.

The voice of my education said to me
He must be killed,
For in Sicily the black, black snakes are innocent, the gold are
          venomous.

And voices in me said, If you were a man   25
You would take a stick and break him now, and finish him off.

But must I confess how I liked him,
How glad I was he had come like a guest in quiet, to drink at
    my water-trough
And depart peaceful, pacified, and thankless,
Into the burning bowels of this earth?   30

Was it cowardice, that I dared not kill him?
Was it perversity, that I longed to talk to him?
Was it humility, to feel so honoured?
I felt so honoured.

And yet those voices: 35
If you were not afraid, you would kill him!

And truly I was afraid, I was most afraid,
But even so, honoured still more
That he should seek my hospitality
From out the dark door of the secret earth.   40

He drank enough
And lifted his head, dreamily, as one who has drunken,
And flickered his tongue like a forked night on the air, so
black,
Seeming to lick his lips,
And looked around like a god, unseeing, into the air,   45
And slowly turned his head,
And slowly, very slowly, as if thrice adream,
Proceeded to draw his slow length curving round
And climb again the broken bank of my wall-face.

And as he put his head into that dreadful hole,   50
And as he slowly drew up, snake-easing his shoulders, and
    entered farther,
A sort of horror, a sort of protest against his withdrawing into that horrid
    black hole,
Deliberately going into the blackness, and slowly drawing
    himself after,
Overcame me now his back was turned.

I looked round, I put down my pitcher,   55
I picked up a clumsy log
And threw it at the water-trough with a clatter.

I think it did not hit him,
But suddenly that part of him that was left behind convulsed in
    undignified haste,

Writhed like lightning, and was gone　　　　　　　　　　　　60
Into the black hole, the earth-lipped fissure in the wall-front,
At which, in the intense still noon, I stared with fascination.

And immediately I regretted it.
I thought how paltry, how vulgar, what a mean act!
I despised myself and the voices of my accursed human　　　65
　　　education.

And I thought of the albatross,
And I wished he would come back, my snake.

For he seemed to me again like a king,
Like a king in exile, uncrowned in the underworld,　　　　70
Now due to be crowned again.

And so, I missed my chance with one of the lords
Of life.
And I have something to expiate:
A pettiness.

Animals have always occupied an odd place in human culture: cats are mostly easy enough—they can be housebroken, deprived of their sex, and used to decorate a window sill or to keep the mice down. Dogs can be used for companionship, even for emotional satisfactions—how many lonely people need to fondle dogs! But dogs can also be unruly, fly off the handle, bite visitors, and bark in the early hours. And what of foxes, wolves, owls, eagles, crows, bears?

The history of human culture provides many examples of animal worship, a recognition of a mysterious, even awesome, vividly alive *otherness* in the animal. But ever since the eighteenth century, we have learned to be far more enlightened and rational; as wild animals were wiped out or driven to eke out some meager, bare survival in the wilderness, our view of them slowly changed. Now, we know what it is to feel nostalgia for the old ways, when people rubbed shoulders nervously with all manner of creatures living either within or on the edge of human settlements. Nostalgia is not distant from sentimentality: so now, as they move toward extinction, we use exotic and rare animals, confined in hygienic pens and dosed with the appropriate additives and vitamins, to rouse in us sentimental, uninformed, exploitive feelings of absurd and contradictory tenderness, protectiveness, and affection.

Their more numerous cousins we cultivate and destroy for our tables.

The "voices" of Lawrence's "education*" said . . ." that he must kill the snake.

---

*That is, his "theory of the world" as shaped by his family's culture, his community's values, and the lessons of his schooling.

The ideology of the culture that had shaped his beliefs and values was in no doubt at all: anything that threatens the supremacy of man must yield to man's right to defend his position at the top of the heap. The voices clamor inside Lawrence's head, appealing to his manliness. Lawrence, however, feels affection for the snake, is glad to receive it as a guest; note, here, Lawrence does not say, "I thought that I felt . . . that I was glad": his impulsive, intuitive feelings are not a matter of thinking . . . but the voices persist, with their culturally sanctioned messages of contempt, loathing, and destructiveness.

So the debate continues, as the warring elements in Lawrence's psyche struggle to dominate.

No one is totally dominated, absolutely possessed, by the values and ideology of the culture that shapes their education; we all live somewhere along a spectrum: at one end is absolutely uncritical, unthinking submission to that domination; at the other is total opposition, absolute rejection. Most of us live somewhere between these two extremes, and it is experiences that raise crucial moral and ethical questions that force us to make the effort to find out where we stand. And this involves us in a strenuous task: to try to identify the social values, the ideology, that directed our parents and our teachers who worked to shape us, to form our minds, before we could know what they were doing; and to try, also, to characterize the values, the implicit ideology, of those parts of our world, of our society—role models, the media, advertising, soap operas, those in authority, influential people—that continue even at this moment to exert influence, often subtle, sometimes blatant, on us, and thereby have power over us.

CONSIDER THIS

★ What is it that engages our interest, that concerns us, as we read Lawrence's "Snake"? The intensity of the quarrel inside the man, or the suspense: will he kill it or let it be? Or is it both?

MARGARET ATWOOD

Bad Mouth

For the past four hundred years, travelers' tales have generally exaggerated the "wildness" of wild animals. (Notice how the cliché "wild animal" conveys an effect quite different from "free animal" or "natural animal," as opposed to tamed, trained, captive, or domesticated.)

When travelers returned home from their exotic journeys, they exaggerated the dangers and spread myths about wild animals in order to heighten their audiences' or readers' sense of the traveler's courage and daring enterprise. Only in the last thirty years, for example, has the scrupulous field work of George Schaller demolished the ridiculous myths about the "savagery" of gorillas. Snakes have always had a bad press, ever since people became acquainted with the Book of Genesis. In the next text, Margaret Atwood (b. 1939) offers representations of various snakes, combining superstitions, loathing, and dread: so "Bad Mouth" refers to the snake—every snake has a "bad" mouth. It is only when we reach her last four lines that we begin to realize that she has played a cunning game.

There are no leaf-eating snakes.
All are fanged and gorge on blood.
Each one is a hunter's hunter,
nothing more than an endless gullet
pulling itself on over the still-alive prey   5
like a sock gone ravenous, like an evil glove,
like sheer greed, lithe and devious.

Puff adder buried in hot sand
or poisoning the toes of boots,
for whom killing is easy and careless   10
as war, as digestion,
why should you be spared?

And you, *Constrictor constrictor*,
sinuous ribbon of true darkness,
one long muscle with eyes and an anus,   15
looping like thick tar out of the trees
to squeeze the voice from anything edible,
reducing it to scales and belly.

And you, pit viper
with your venomous pallid throat
and teeth like syringes   20
and your nasty radar
homing in on the deep red shadow
nothing else knows it casts . . .
Shall I concede these deaths?   25

Between us there is no fellow feeling,
as witness: a snake cannot scream.
Observe the alien
chainmail skin, straight out
of science fiction, pure   30
shiver, pure Saturn.
Those who can explain them
can explain anything.

Some say they're a snarled puzzle
only gasoline and a match can untangle.   35
Even their mating is barely sexual,
a romance between two lengths
of cyanide-colored string.
Despite their live births and squirming nests
it's hard to believe in snakes loving.   40

Alone among the animals
the snake does not sing.
The reason for them is the same
as the reason for stars, and not human.

So whose is the "bad mouth"? Surely it is ours, it is human; only humans have a language in which to "bad mouth" the snakes. So her last two lines insist on our recognizing the sheer alien-ness, the unknowability of "the reason for them": if the reason for their being is *not* human, and surely it is not, then how can we ever presume to claim that we understand them? Claim not only to understand them, but to understand them as *inherently* evil? The ugliness, the loathsomeness, is in the language we use to signify them.

ALAN MOOREHEAD

Snake-Phobia

By the time Alan Moorehead (1910–1983), the Australian writer, visited Eric Worrell's snake farm at Gosford, near Sydney in Australia, he had already been acculturated by the "voice of his education" into a fearful loathing of snakes. See what happens to him as he is persuaded to approach the snakes, nervously getting closer and closer . . .

In the part of Australia where I grew up we used to come across snakes quite often when we were walking in the bush, and our fear and loathing of them was something more than the usual thing, mainly, I suppose, because very occasionally some of us really did get bitten. I never saw a snake—that furtive sliminess, that mad, hating eye—without a sudden instinctive constriction of the heart, and after the first moment of panic was over we children had just one thought in our minds: "Kill it. Do not let it get away." And so we would grab a stick and in a spasm of furious terror we would beat at the hideous twisting thing until at last it lay inert in the dust. Even then we would not dare to touch it; we would hook it up with the stick and toss it away out of sight into the long grass where ants were bound to demolish it within a day or two.

We all knew what to do if we got bitten, and most of us carried about with us a little tin box in which were one of father's razor blades and a phial of permanganate of potash crystals. First you tied your handkerchief round the arm or the leg *above* the bite and tightened it by twisting the knot with a piece of stick. This slowed the flow of the poison to the heart. Next you made an incision between the two punctures caused by the snake's fangs, and provided you had no hollow teeth you sucked out as much blood as you could. Then you rubbed the crystals into the wound, and with luck all would be well.

We knew all about snakes. There was the ferocious tiger snake that automatically attacked and could run as fast as you could. Then there were the brown snakes and the taipans and many other varieties, all of them deadly, and they lurked among rotten logs, and in the bracken and on the edges of swamps waiting to strike; and if they did strike and you did nothing about it you were dead within half an hour. The pythons and carpet-snakes were not poisonous, but they would drop on you from an overhanging branch and suffocate you by wrapping themselves around your neck. Many of the lizards were also poisonous, and those that were not inflicted a sore that continued to suppurate for years. Snakes could be calmed by music, and one way of getting them into the open so that they could be killed was to lay out a saucer of milk—a drink they could never resist.

These notions I have lived with all my life, and it never occurred to me to question them until I returned to Australia last year and spent some time with Eric Worrell, a self-taught herpetologist who runs a snake farm at a place called Gosford, which is a little to the north of Sydney in New South Wales. Now I do not suggest that my experiences at this place came to me as a revelation, that overnight my revulsion turned to love, yet it was quite a sharp shock to learn that almost everything I thought I knew about reptiles, and had been talking about all these years, was wrong; not just inaccurate, but absolutely wrong.

Even the simplest articles of my beliefs were miles away from the truth. No Australian snake will ever attack unless it is provoked; it invariably runs away. It does this because it is an intensely frightened and fragile creature: one blow on those delicate hairpin-thin bones will instantly break its back. Its poison is its only means of self-defence, and even this is not very effective: among all the varieties of Australian snakes—and there are 140 of them—only five of them are really venomous. The rest can do no more than inflict a sting like a wasp. No lizard is poisonous and none can inflict a wound that will not heal. No python ever dropped on a man out of a tree. Snakes are quite indifferent to music (the snake charming act is a plain fraud), and they hate milk. Moreover they are not in the least slimy or clammy. If you pick one up you will find that it is warm and dry, rather like the feel of a young baby's arm or leg. They are the cleanest of all creatures and they have no smell; you can handle them all day and there is no odour whatever left on your hands.

Worrell, a stocky, bearded man with very strong arms, has about a thousand snakes which he milks for their venom. The thin, pale, golden fluid is dehydrated until it becomes a dry powder (which will keep fresh for a long time) and is ultimately made into a liquid with which horses are injected. When the horses have attained the right amount of immunity their blood is drawn off and is used by the hospitals as an anti-snake-bite serum.

I happened to go down to his farm because I was making a television film about Australian wild life, and much as I hated snakes it seemed only fair that they should be included in the show if only as the villains of the piece. The place was more or less what you might have expected: the tropical snakes in warmed, glassed-in enclosures and the others crawling around by the hundreds in open pits. The only thing that divided the onlooker from the snakes in the pits was a low concrete wall over which one leaned and felt one's flesh creep. Worrell jumped in, picked up a three-foot tiger snake by the tail, and held it out to me.

"Take it."

"No," I said.

"I promise it won't bite you."

"No," I said.

"There's nothing for you to be afraid of."

"I don't care," I said. "I am not going to do it."

Yet he was extraordinarily compelling: his confidence was infectious. While the cameras were being set up he pointed out to me a sheet of corrugated iron that was lying on a low flat mound in the sunshine.

"Under this," he said, "there are about forty black snakes. Now come and sit here and lift it up. It will make an excellent shot."

"What," I asked from my side of the wall, "will happen?"

"They will move quietly away."

"How?"

"Some will go off in that direction. Others will just slither across your lap and disappear."

"No," I said.

"You're not frightened, are you?"

"You bet I'm frightened."

"All right. *I'll* sit here and lift the sheet of iron. You stand alongside me. I tell you, you will not be bitten."

Strangely I felt better after I had climbed over the wall, and felt no real desire to jump back again when he lifted up the iron sheet. There they lay, black, intertwined with one another and gleaming in the sunshine, and with that kind of numbness that overtakes one in a car accident—a sense of fatalistic passivity—I watched them placidly slither away.

We did a good deal of filming that day among both the snakes and the lizards, and I found that, as time went on, I was able to go into their pits so long as Worrell was with me and preferably in front of me. But I could not bear to be left alone even when I was assured that the snakes at my feet were not venomous.

The pythons were a little disappointing since they were all coiled up asleep, and at dinner that night I said to Worrell, "I wonder what they are doing now?"

"Let's go and see."

On the way over to their enclosure we paused to look in on some young tiger snakes Worrell was keeping a special eye on. He picked one up and handed it to me.

"Take it."

We had had a good dinner, and Australian wines these days are almost up to the quality of France. I took it, holding it by the tail and well out from my body, and then quickly handed it back. It was a ridiculously small incident of course, but privately I felt, with elation, that I had crossed some kind of neurotic frontier of the mind, and I went on eagerly to see the pythons.

They were housed in a series of small warmed rooms with glass fronts, and in a gentle artificial light we could see that they had uncoiled themselves from the dead logs and branches on which they had been asleep all day. Their sleek heads and perhaps as much as three or four feet of their bodies swayed to and fro through the air with a strange questing motion. It was as though they were looking beyond us, searching for something in the darkness outside. Back and forth they went in a slow compulsive rhythm. It was exceedingly beautiful and it had a mesmerising effect, an effect that is sometimes produced when one looks down into a rock pool and sees there long strands of seaweed that are drawn first this way and then that by some invisible current.

"Come on," Worrell said. "Let's go inside."

"Have they eaten?"

"As a matter of fact they have. But it wouldn't have mattered anyway."

He unlocked the door of the cage where some half-dozen scrub pythons—it was difficult to tell just how many—were moving about. They took no notice of us at all as we stepped inside, and at least it was reassuring that they moved so deliberately and slowly. On the other side of the glass the television crew were setting up their cameras, and it was an odd business being on the inside looking out. None of the cameramen smiled or waved; they simply peered at us standing there among the slowly writhing bodies as though we were part of the exhibit, and I began to have the feeling that I too ought to be swaying back and forth and putting on some sort of a show.

"Even if I angered one of them," Worrell said, "I could still calm it down again. Look."

He took his handkerchief from his pocket and fluttered it before the head of the nearest python. At once it drew back its head and coiled its great neck in the form of an S, ready to strike. Worrell pocketed his handkerchief and reached his hand forward to take hold of the python behind its head. He was a little too slow. The head darted forward like a piece of elastic that had suddenly been let go, and the two cruel jaws clamped themselves on his hand between his thumb and fingers.

Blood spouted out and it must have been horribly painful, but he calmly prised the jaws apart, and as the python turned away he went after it, murmuring to it, reaching forward to it, stroking it. And the python did in fact subside. Presently Worrell was able to take it up, and it coiled itself round him, settling down comfortably around his waist and shoulders.

Although I had taken no part in these proceedings I had—one searches for a phrase—a good conceit of myself at having been there in the cage and only a couple of feet away when the bite was made, and it was a little galling to discover when we emerged that the cameramen had run out of film and had recorded nothing of the incident.

Next day there was a telephone call from a farmhouse about five miles away. "A snake got into my little boy's bedroom last night," the woman there said. "A big one. Now it's gone out into the shed and it's coiled around the rafters there."

When we arrived at the farm we found an old man leaning over the gate obviously on the lookout for us. He jerked his thumb back in the direction of a large wooden shed in the yard. "He's here," he said.

It was a diamond python, six or seven feet long, and I found that after the experiences of the previous day I could look on it, not as an object of horror, but as a living creature: even more than that, as an object of great beauty. There were marvellous markings on its greenish-yellow head, and its diamond-patterned coils flowed round the rafter like some flowering tropical creeper that had grown up out of the ground.

The woman and the rest of the farmer's family now arrived. "The snake is harmless," Worrell said. "It will not attack your little boy or any of you. On the contrary, it will do a great deal of good around the farm by killing off the vermin."

"Take it away," the woman said.

"You don't want rats and mice around the place do you?" Worrell said.

"Take it away."

He got a sack out of his car and told me to hold it open while he clambered up on to a wooden box and began to disengage the snake from the rafter. It was very neatly done. First one coil was loosened, then the next, and then at the right moment he took the snake by the neck and dropped it into the sack. I fancied I heard a sigh of relief go up from the family.

I had a fellow-feeling for that snake—it really was a very beautiful thing—and I went back to see it in its enclosure at Worrell's place several times that day. Snakes are very sluggish creatures, comfort-loving and not very intelligent. This one had coiled himself down in the warmth and was happy. When they wanted a picture of me with a python I had no hesitation in choosing this one. As with small babies the thing with pythons is to hold them, not gingerly, but firmly. In that way you give them confidence. This one wrapped itself round me two or three times, shifted its position a little until it was comfortable, and then went into a doze. It would be a lie to say I was not frightened, but at least I was not in a panic. I felt I had a certain *rapport* with the creature, and that it was not going to bite me any more than it would have bitten a tree on which it might have chosen to rest.

As I have said, I did not come away from Worrell's farm with the sense of having had a revelation about snakes, but I felt quite certainly that never again would I look on them in quite the same way. From now on they would no longer be an implacable evil, and I would not wish to kill them on sight. I would know that they were not going to attack me, that they had a place in the natural scheme of things, and that, when seen with a detached eye, one would discover that they had much beauty and much grace in all their movements. In short, the myth was broken—the myth which was compounded of so many warnings from my parents, of Kipling's horrific short story *Rikki Tikki Tavi* (the one about cobras), and of so many bad snake dreams and snake fears in my childhood. All this gave me a certain glow of satisfaction, plus, I must admit, a slight feeling of superiority.

And, of course, I was entirely wrong again. One does not recover from ingrained irrational fears quite so easily as this. Not three months after I had left Worrell I came across a little adder one day when I was walking along a dry water-course and instantly habit reasserted itself: I grabbed a stick and beat it to death.

I was sorry afterwards and excused myself on the grounds that it might have bitten someone who had inadvertently stepped upon it in the grass; but then I am not absolutely sure that I would not do the same thing again. Which leads one to the uncomfortable thought that the world must be filled with people who are convinced that mice are going to run up their legs, and that bats will get into their hair, and that spiders will always bite them, and that walls are going to close in on them, and that they are bound to jump off if they look down from a great height, and that God knows how many other fearful delusions bedevil our minds from earliest childhood and that some of us are never really going to get over them.

CONSIDER THIS

★ So, "the myth was broken," Moorehead optimistically believed, but he nevertheless killed yet another snake because of the continuing deep-seated power of the "fearful delusions," delusions that continue to "bedevil our minds from earliest childhood." Charles Lamb, the English writer of the early nineteenth century, believed that we are born with such fears and delusions, that they are inherited: "the archetypes are within us," he argued. How find you?

★ What are your irrational fears or phobias? Who did you learn them from? What can you do to cure them?

★ Have you had the benefit of a similar experience of re-education, of learning to "re-read" something? Who else was involved? Did your re-learning "stick"? Or were its benefits only temporary?

★ "We knew all about snakes." In every culture, you will discover myths and misapprehensions: "facts" that turn out to be mere superstitions; assumptions that have no basis in actuality. An apparently chauvinistic expression for such mis-readings is "old wives' tales": the historical explanation for this term, however, rests on a clear fact—that in transmitting fundamental elements of a culture's "common sense" or "folk wisdom," women (often grandmothers and other female elders) played the primary role in instructing the young. What "old wives' tales" did you hear when you were a child? When did you learn that they were mis-readings? How did you feel when you learned this? What was the equivalent of Moorehead's snakes in your early environment?

★ What has fed and reinforced Moorehead's early attitude toward snakes? Which do you think was the more influential factor in shaping the way he "read" snakes?

★ How many stages does Moorehead's education in re-reading go through? Is it easy to separate them out neatly?

★ Note Moorehead's use of the word *ingrained* in his next-to-the-last paragraph: what is the crucial difference between the meaning of *ingrained* and that of *inborn* or *innate*?

★ Have you noticed people misusing the word *instinct* to refer to attitudes and reactions that they have in fact *learned*, but learned at such an early stage of their life that they have no recollection of having learned it?

MARK TWAIN

Pigeon Season

We have already read of Mark Twain's memories of early pleasures (p. 164). In his autobiography he recalls pigeons as a dramatic part of his childhood, and remembers beating them to death with sticks.

I remember the pigeon seasons, when the birds would come in millions and cover the trees and by their weight break down the branches. They were clubbed to death with sticks; guns were not necessary and were not used. I remember the squirrel hunts and prairie-chicken hunts and wild-turkey hunts, and all that; and how we turned out, mornings, while it was still dark to go on these expeditions, and how chilly and dismal it was and how often I regretted that I was well enough to go. A toot on a tin horn brought twice as many dogs as were needed, and in their happiness they raced and scampered about and knocked small people down and made no end of unnecessary noise. At the word, they vanished away toward the woods and we drifted silently after them in the melancholy gloom. But presently the gray dawn stole over the world, the birds piped up, then the sun rose and poured light and comfort all around, everything was fresh and dewy and fragrant, and life was a boon again. After three hours of tramping we arrived back wholesomely tired, overladen with game, very hungry, and just in time for breakfast.

Take a Chicken to Lunch

In most cultures, people make a categorical distinction between animals that are to be killed and eaten, and animals that are pets. (A friend in Nebraska once had a pet skunk: it was extremely intelligent and its stink gland had been painlessly removed. But the neighbors set their dogs on it and killed it. Was that "the voice of their education"?)

Animals that are to be killed are rarely, if ever, given a name. Pets, conversely, are given a name: by naming a dog or a cat, we bring it into the human community. "Like us," we seem to say, "you are also a member of the family." Ms. Ritsuko Taho, teaching art at Harvard, demolished the crucial distinction between (a) Can kill and (b) Cannot kill (the taboo), and claimed that she would thereby help her students to "expand their imagination and understanding." Was she crazy? Thoughtless? Confused? Cruel? Read on.

An art teacher at Harvard assigned her students to adopt a live chicken for a day, then take it to a slaughterhouse, watch it be processed, and cook and eat it before making a sculpture from the bones.

Ritsuko Taho, a lecturer in the school's visual and environmental studies department who teaches "Fundamentals of Sculpture," said Thursday that the project was intended to reduce the distance between art and object.

"Because they will have eaten it, the chicken will be part of the students' bodies," Ms. Taho said. "This experience will expand their imagination and understanding."

But some students in the class and members of animal rights groups said the project promoted cruelty to animals.

Leah Zuch, executive director of the Cambridge Committee for Responsible Research, an animal rights group, said she thought the project was "disgusting."

Three of the 17 students refused to do the project, said Hannah Gittleman, a senior. She said she could not undertake the project because the chicken "would be like a pet, and to take your pet and have it killed is not a comfortable thing for me."

Ms. Gittleman and two other students took their chickens, which Ms. Taho provided, to an animal shelter. Ms. Gittleman said the episode made her decide not to eat chicken until she could kill one.

Other students approved the project. "It's a very interesting process to watch," said Alexander Kahn, a junior, after witnessing the killing of his chicken on Thursday. "It's something you don't usually see."

Ms. Taho could not be reached today to discuss whether her students had to complete the project.

MARGARET ATWOOD

Song of the Hen's Head

Human beings have language. The judge can pronounce the death sentence. The officer in charge of the firing squad can say "Fire!" So the word itself seems to become an instrument of death. If it is capitalized, "the Word," then it takes on ever stronger authority, for the capitalization claims that this word is not merely a human word but a Fact of Life, Natural, or the Will of God.

After the abrupt collision
with the blade, the Word,
I rest on the wood
block, my eyes
drawn back into their blue transparent   5
shells like molluscs;
I contemplate the Word

while the rest of me
which was never much under
my control, which was always   10
inarticulate, still runs
at random through the grass, a plea
for mercy, a single
flopping breast,

muttering about life   15
in its thickening red voice.

Feet and hands chase it, scavengers
intent on rape:

they want its treasures,
its warm rhizomes, enticing sausages,   20
its yellow grapes, its flesh
caves, five pounds of sweet money,
its juice and jellied tendons.
It tries to escape,
gasping through the neck, frantic.   25

They are welcome to it,

I contemplate the Word,
I am dispensable and peaceful.

The Word is an O,
outcry of the useless head,   30
pure space, empty and drastic,
the last word I said.
The word is No.

So the decapitated head of the chicken continues to cry out, even as the
nervous system of the rest of its body continues to operate, making the legs run,
the wings flap. So the hen discovers that the Word is merely "O"—a cry of
despair, a last gasp, mimicking the O-shape of its severed neck; and the Word is
also "No," the last cry of the dying animal, the last futile plea for mercy, the
Word of Judgment that says "No more life for you!"

SEAMUS HEANEY

The Early Purges

"*Animals are fed and cared for in proportion to their usefulness. . . . Cats are casually
but thoroughly disliked and are given nothing   Dogs are never kindly touched   "
James Agee wrote in his discussion of the tenant-farmers and their animals in Alabama
in 1937. In the next text, Seamus Heaney recalls how his farming neighbors treated
kittens and puppies in the 1940s.*

I was six when I first saw kittens drown.
Dan Taggart pitched them, 'the scraggy wee shits',
Into a bucket; a frail metal sound,

Soft paws scraping like mad. But their tiny din
Was soon soused. They were slung on the snout   5
Of the pump and the water pumped in.

'Sure isn't it better for them now?' Dan said.
Like wet gloves they bobbed and shone till he sluiced
Them out on the dunghill, glossy and dead.

Suddenly frightened, for days I sadly hung   10
Round the yard, watching the three sogged remains
Turn mealy and crisp as old summer dung

Until I forgot them. But the fear came back
When Dan trapped big rats, snared rabbits, shot crows
Or, with a sickening tug, pulled old hens' necks.   15

Still, living displaces false sentiments
And now, when shrill pups are prodded to drown
I just shrug, 'Bloody pups'. It makes sense:

'Prevention of cruelty' talk cuts ice in town
Where they consider death unnatural,   20
But on well-run farms pests have to be kept down.

   In town, people "consider death unnatural," the "I" of the poem claims, and
ends with a no-nonsense, cool, and impersonal "pests have to be kept down"
(rather than, "*I* have to kill them to keep their numbers down.") The "I" has
clearly arrived at this matter-of-fact acceptance of killing as a result of accultur-
ation; the "voice of education" is provided, not by schooling, but by the men of
his community, whom boys have to grow to *resemble* and whose ideology, beliefs,
attitudes, assumptions it is their cultural duty to carry forward into the next
generation. Thus, the sorrow and the sadness of the six-year-old is pared away
and covered, like sensitive skin slowly disappearing under a callus.

PETER MEDAWAR AND JEAN MEDAWAR

Animals and Human Obligations

*Two biologists explain clearly their views on our relationships with animals: what they
are, and what they might be. As they suggest, there are "a number of morally ambiguous
but socially accepted practices that may disadvantage animals unreasonably."*

Peter Medawar (1915–1987), whose fundamental research in immunology paved the way for organ transplants, won a Nobel Prize in 1961; he and Jean Medawar, his wife, collaborated in writing Aristotle to Zoos, A Philosophical Dictionary of Biology, *1983.*

In their text, you will probably encounter—as we did—a few unfamiliar words, outside your range of immediate recognition. We had never before encountered these three words: encephalitides, achondroplasia, dugongid; *but the context helped us to make sense of the second and third, and for the first, we dredged up our memory of* encephalitis, *another name for "sleeping sickness."*

The word "animal" is not mentioned in the Bible, but Jehovah's rulings on the relationship between man and beast are clear enough. Human beings were to have "dominion over the fish of the sea and over the fowl of the air, and over cattle and every creeping thing" (Gen. 1:xxvii). A later verse goes on to reassure man of "dominion over the fowl of the air and over every living thing that moveth upon the earth." Plants rank low in the hierarchy, for to all the animals mentioned "I have given every green herb for meat" (Gen. 1:xxx).

The divine remit did not encourage compassion for animals or any attempt to understand them as animate creatures. The prevailing indifference is understandable, inasmuch as peasants whose own lives were very hard would probably not have thought the beasts so much worse off than themselves.

The changed attitude toward animals may be thought of as a late by-product of the Romantic revival, signaled perhaps by the foundation in England in 1824 of a Society for the Prevention of Cruelty to Animals and perhaps by the publication of a skillfully written and widely popular "autobiography" of a horse—*Black Beauty* by Anna Sewell, published in 1877. The subsequent growth of literacy encouraged proliferation of a nursery literature in which rabbits, cats, foxes, lions, tigers, elephants, and bears all had speaking parts.

To children this seemed quite natural, and they took it in their stride. Our youngest daughter, Louise, as a five-year-old was taken to a zoo; there she saw a large parrot high up in its wire cage. "Hallo!" she said civilly, having been properly brought up. The parrot climbed slowly down from the very top of the cage: beak, claw, beak, claw until it was at the child's eye level. It then thrust its head forward, said " 'allo!" and climbed very slowly back up, leaving Louise elated at the thought that she was now on speaking terms with a parrot.

Our modern concern over the welfare of animals seems to have originated in the general increase of sensibility that followed the Second World War. Perhaps also a factor was the propaganda and persuasive literature of that era, urging upon human beings an awareness of the duties that go with their trusteeship of animate nature. One beneficial result has been the establishment of game preserves and conservation land.

This new awareness has been accompanied by a movement strongly critical of a number of morally ambiguous but socially accepted practices that may disadvantage animals unreasonably.

The first of these practices is experimentation on animals, justified only by the benefits it is rightly believed to confer upon human beings. Those whose affection for animals is so extreme as to encourage an indifference to human welfare that borders on misanthropy advocate a total halt to experimentation on animals. They undermine their own case and lose the confidence of the public by the recklessly inaccurate assertion that experimentation on animals has brought no benefits at all to mankind—a feat of doublethink made possible only by attaching more weight to the encephalitides very rarely caused by whooping cough vaccine than to the combined benefactions of insulin, penicillin, polio vaccine, and transplantation surgery. It is a pity they adopt this attitude, because it weakens and may destroy altogether the valid case for legal regulation of experimentation on animals.

If Samuel Johnson were alive today, he would condone the use of animals for the safety testing of putatively therapeutic drugs, but would scathingly denounce the use of animals to test beauty preparations and cosmetics. No face, he would argue, is so pretty as to justify paining an animal. Furthermore, he would surely insist—as British legislation now does insist—that experimentation on animals should be executed only by those whose training and declared intentions make clear to a panel of impartial judges that they are technically competent. Under no circumstances should experiments ever be performed merely to gratify curiosity or to add to the treasure-house of human knowledge. All experiments must have a specific and declared medical or scientific purpose, always such as to make possible or easier the fulfillment of medical ambitions. All this involves the certification of experimentalists and a continuing review of their activities, supplemented—if thought fit—by unannounced site visits. And, of course, a bureaucratic apparatus that must be large enough, tough enough, and sufficiently well informed to have a cutting edge.

These desiderata are provided for by the regulations currently in force in Great Britain. Most northern European countries exercise some degree of regulation of experimentation on animals (see *New Perspectives in Animal Experimentation*, ed. David Sperlinger [New York, 1981]). The United States, currently impatient with governmental interference, especially by a restrictive bureaucratic machinery, seems to be comparatively backward in these matters, something unexpected in a country which has so often led the way in legislation for the public good.

Although the supervision of animal experiments sounds as if it would be yet another uncalled-for intrusion of officialdom into the lives of respectable private citizens, no competent and humane experimenter should have reason to object to certification or to official supervision or to unannounced inspection visits. Research would be gravely impeded by enforcement of a requirement that each single experiment (such as the injection of one mouse with penicillin) be specifically authorized by high dignitaries of church and state; for the bureaucratic process is well known to feed upon itself and to multiply far beyond the minimum necessary to transact its business. It should be emphasized, though, that the officers of licensing authorities (most of whom do their work conscientiously and expeditiously) can be a source of useful advice.

Once they have official permission, experimenters can make a start at meeting the standards put forward by W. M. S. Russell and R. L. Burch in *The Principles of*

Humane Experimental Technique (London, 1959). Their three Rs are Reduction of the number of animals used, Refinement of experimental procedures, and Replacement of living systems by inanimate ones such as tissue culture.

Blood sports constitute another socially accepted practice that disadvantages creatures lower than man. Killing animals for fun belongs to a tradition so old and so closely associated with what are thought of as manly virtues that it is not counted a malpractice even when some rich and doubtless overweight mechanized vacationer off the coast of Florida whiles away his time by assassinating a shark or some other magnificent sea beast.

It would benefit hunters as well as hunted if sportsmen realized that their considerable exertions to kill animals for fun may eventually coarsen appearance, speech, and manners. It is no wonder that in *A Woman of No Importance* (1893) Oscar Wilde said of "the English country gentleman galloping after a fox" that it was "the unspeakable in full pursuit of the uneatable."

It is not generally known that among the folk most guilty of cruelty to animals— anyhow, to dogs—are professed animal lovers themselves. We have in mind the practice, rapidly dying out under pressure from the veterinary profession, of breeding dogs for perpetuation of the exhibition points that count high in shows. Many of these breeders' points are frank abnormalities. Consider, for example, the sadly crumpled face of the bulldog with its deeply folded and fissured skin, predisposed to dermatitis. The bulldog's difficulty in breathing is due to the skeletal abnormalities of its head, putting one in mind of the mutant abnormality known as *achondroplasia;* the prized "gay" or curly tail is an abnormality of the development of the vertebral column. To these we may add the admired show stance that is made possible by congenital dislocation of the hip. Again, some dogs are bred for the cultivation of a mop of hair that falls over the forehead and causes chronic irritation of the eyeball. Other dogs have hair so thick that in warm weather they have the utmost difficulty in keeping cool by excreting heat and often are thermally distressed. The British Small Animals Veterinary Association classifies all such conditions as enormities and declares that breed societies and show judges are deeply mistaken to connive at their perpetuation. Vanity is at the root of these excesses, as it is also at the root of the deliberate breeding of dogs as toys—as miniatures that will just fit into a deep pocket or handbag, for example. Many of the people that condone or even applaud these malpractices arrogate to themselves the title of dog lover and are among the loudest in denouncing the use of animals in medical research.

Another misuse of animals is now arousing loud self-reproach: the treatment of animals as, in effect, manufactured products—or simply as machines to convert vegetables into meat, as is the case with battery chickens and other animals that can be subjected to mechanized husbandry. Although it is not to be supposed that the animals so treated enjoy the refined sensibilities of a lake poet or that they pine for "daylight and champain," it cannot be denied that the entire proceeding is an affront to one's sense of the fitness of things, and a moral diminishment of man. It seems doubtful that anything short of legislation will bring the practice to an end, for battery farming provides an abundant, commercially profitable source of relatively cheap first-class protein. Moreover, the enterprise has acquired, among people who rate themselves realists, the tawdry glamour associated with anything commercially advantageous, even if the advantage has been secured by somewhat questionable means.

The record of human aggression as it affects other species is a dismal one that records the extinction of roughly three hundred species in the last three hundred years, among them passenger pigeons, that affable dugongid Steller's sea cow, and the Tasmanian wolf. The Tasmanian people, too, have been exterminated (the last native Tasman died in 1876). Jared M. Diamond of the University of California has, however, warned us not to accept too readily the Arcadian legend* that this is mainly the work of mechanized Western man, or that man the hunter-gatherer has always been a shrewd and prudent conserver of whom a modern ecologist could be proud.

That our ancestors have sinned does nothing to excuse the heroic scale on which modern hunters, prompted by commercial interests, have raided nature—something that is rapidly leading to the extermination of whales in spite of the best endeavors of United Nations' agencies. It is a sad note that politicians have passively acquiesced in the notion that commercial advantage excuses almost any enormity and that those who protest and actively express concern for the welfare of animals are dismissed as sentimental cranks, eccentrics, or (in British schoolboy terminology) "wets."

What can be done? Hortatory speeches are not enough and certainly it is inefficacious to call for worldwide refinement of human sensibilities in the interest of plants and animals. What we need is a case for "doing good in minute particulars." Contemplation of the abuses we have cited suggests remedial legislation. All that one asks of human sensibilities is that the issue be taken seriously enough to carry political weight. Nothing is quite so effective a catalyst of legislation as the feeling that it will bring political advantage to the person or party that initiates it. Unhappily, in addition to having no rights in common law, animals generally have no political clout whatsoever.

Pigs, Dogs and People: Clash in Jersey

Clarence Sibert, of New Jersey, is probably the nearest thing to an American equivalent of the type of peasant referred to in the Medawars' text. Here, now, in late 1987, is an account of how the dominant ideology of the American suburb reads him and his life style.

*The assumption that before modern times, people took good care of the land.

For years, Clarence Sibert lived alone on a corner of farmland here, with the pigs he raised and the dogs he kept as pets.

While growing up, Sharon Micinski knew the property, now part of a municipal park, as a good place to hunt pheasant and deer. She also became friends with Mr. Sibert, who the township allowed to live on the property to protect a historic brick house that stands there.

Now Mr. Sibert, 83 years old, can see the manicured lawns of office parks through the bare treetops around his pigpen. And he has become the target of complaints and, most recently, of eviction proceedings from Lawrence Township.

Miss Micinski, 27, is the township's animal-control officer, and a large part of her job lately has involved delivering summonses to Mr. Sibert.

OUT OF FAVOR

"He's just different," she said, as Mr. Sibert stood in the pigpen, scratching the arched back of one of his 700-pound sows while piglets scampered by. "He's used to a different life, one that was acceptable 20 years ago, but not now."

The predicament is a byproduct of rapid development that has engulfed much of Mercer County. As New Jersey's corporate corridor has widened, leading to construction of homes and offices on what was open land, Mr. Sibert's way of life has fallen out of favor with most people living here.

He prefers to let his dogs, who have numbered as many as 32, run loose, but the township has a law against that. He believes in feeding his pigs unadulterated food scraps that he collects from local restaurants, but the state has a law forbidding that.

He keeps one side of his jaw filled with chewing tobacco, eats one meal a day, and wears a faded old Stauffer Chemicals cap. He once sold a piglet for $35 to a group of Princeton alumni, who made her the mascot of their annual "P-rade."

"They put mascara around her eyes, lipstick on her mouth and painted her toenails," he said admiringly. "I went over to Princeton to watch her march down the street."

Until recently, township officials had encouraged Mr. Sibert to live on the park property rent-free, believing his presence would ward off potential vandalism at the historic house.

At first, he lived in the house, said to have belonged to David Brearley, who was among the signers of the Constitution. Three years ago he moved into a trailer the township rents.

"We were always in a nice, symbiotic relationship and everybody profited from it," said the township's health administrator, Daniel DeFrancesco.

In the last year, however, criticism of Mr. Sibert's animals has intensified. The dogs first became a problem, Mr. DeFrancesco said, when executives of Lenox China, which has a pond with Canada geese on its nearby property, complained that the dogs were chasing their geese. Most of the dogs were destroyed after a woman who was bitten in a parking lot filed suit against the township and Mr. Sibert. He has been ordered to keep his five remaining dogs tied up, but has not done so.

"I hope when I pen those dogs up, somebody'll burn that place down," Mr. Sibert said, gesturing toward the historic house.

FOLK HERO STATUS

Mr. DeFrancesco said he alerted the New Jersey Department of Agriculture to Mr. Sibert's pig-feeding style. The state advised Mr. Sibert to either feed his pigs grain or boil the restaurant scraps to rid them of impurities. Mr. Sibert, as is his custom, refused to change his ways.

Last Tuesday, officials tacked a pink quarantine notice to the trunk of a locust tree near Mr. Sibert's trailer, to prevent him from selling his pigs. In the place on the notice reserved for Mr. Sibert's signature acknowledging the quarantine, an official wrote, "Owner refused to sign."

Perhaps most troublesome of all, Mr. DeFrancesco said, is the status Mr. Sibert is gaining.

"What upsets me is that he is getting a reputation as a folk hero, when he is posing a very serious health and safety problem to this township," he said. "The man is a serious liability. One of these days, someone is going to get seriously hurt, either by the dogs, which are not chihuahuas, or with the food source this man is farming. He's the old dinosaur, and civilization is encroaching on him. But our responsibility is to the public."

Mr. Sibert says he is searching for a new place to live. Wherever it is, it will have to be large enough to accommodate his pigs, which he calls "Mommy" or "Hog."

"I'm going to put 'em in the kitchen with me," he said. "They're better than people."

CONSIDER THIS

★ Imagine, now, that Clarence Sibert looks you straight in the eye, extends his hand, and asks you for your support:

How, on the basis of (a) the information in the report and (b) your theory of the world, do you react?

TED HUGHES

Capturing Animals

A "slightly mesmerized and quite involuntary concentration," and a "special kind of excitement . . ." Ted Hughes, the English writer (b. 1930), finds these ways of being in two activities: the first, in his early years, was hunting; the second is writing about something that stirs, arouses, moves, excites him. How far can he press the similarities?

There are all sorts of ways of capturing animals and birds and fish. I spent most of my time, up to the age of fifteen or so, trying out many of these ways and when my enthusiasm began to wane, as it did gradually, I started to write poems.

You might not think that these two interests, capturing animals and writing poems, have much in common. But the more I think back the more sure I am that with me the two interests have been one interest. My pursuit of mice at threshing time when I was a boy, snatching them from under the sheaves as the sheaves were lifted away out of the stack and popping them into my pocket till I had thirty or forty crawling around in the lining of my coat, that and my present pursuit of poems seem to me to be different stages of the same fever. In a way, I suppose, I think of poems as a sort of animal. They have their own life, like animals, by which I mean that they seem quite separate from any person, even from their author, and nothing can be added to them or taken away without maiming and perhaps even killing them. And they have a certain wisdom. They know something special . . . something perhaps which we are very curious to learn. Maybe my concern has been to capture not animals particularly and not poems, but simply things which have a vivid life of their own, outside mine. However all that may be, my interest in animals began when I began. My memory goes back pretty clearly to my third year, and by then I had so many of the toy lead animals you could buy in shops that they went right round our flat-topped fender,* nose to tail, with some over.

I had a gift for modelling and drawing, so when I discovered plasticine my zoo became infinite, and when an aunt bought me a thick green-backed animal book for my fourth birthday I began to draw the glossy photographs. The animals looked good in the photographs, but they looked even better in my drawings and were mine. I can remember very vividly the excitement with which I used to sit staring at my drawings, and it is a similar thing I feel nowadays with poems.

My zoo was not entirely an indoors affair. At that time we lived in a valley in the Pennines in West Yorkshire. My brother, who probably had more to do with this passion of mine than anyone else, was a good bit older than I was, and his one interest in life was creeping about on the hillsides with a rifle. He took me along as a retriever and I had to scramble into all kinds of places collecting magpies and owls and rabbits and weasels and rats and curlews that he shot. He could not shoot enough for me. At the same time I used to be fishing daily in the canal, with the long-handled wire-rimmed curtain mesh sort of net.

All that was only the beginning. When I was about eight, we moved to an industrial town in south Yorkshire. Our cat went upstairs and moped in my bedroom for a week, it hated the place so much, and my brother for the same reason left home and became a gamekeeper. But in many ways that move of ours was the best thing that ever happened to me. I soon discovered a farm in the nearby country that supplied all my needs, and soon after, a private estate, with woods and lakes.

My friends were town boys, sons of colliers and railwaymen, and with them I led one life, but all the time I was leading this other life on my own in the country. I never mixed the two lives up, except once or twice disastrously. I still have some diaries that I kept in those years: they record nothing but my catches.

*Flat-topped fender: a protective metal guard rail in front of an open fireplace.

Finally, as I have said, at about fifteen my life grew more complicated and my attitude to animals changed. I accused myself of disturbing their lives. I began to look at them, you see, from their own point of view.

And about the same time I began to write poems. Not animal poems. It was years before I wrote what you could call an animal poem and several more years before it occurred to me that my writing poems might be partly a continuation of my earlier pursuit. Now I have no doubt. The special kind of excitement, the slightly mesmerized and quite involuntary concentration with which you make out the stirrings of a new poem in your mind, then the outline, the mass and colour and clean final form of it, the unique living reality of it in the midst of the general lifelessness, all that is too familiar to mistake. This is hunting and the poem is a new species of creature, a new specimen of the life outside your own.

I have now told you very briefly what I believe to be the origins and growth of my interest in writing poetry. I have simplified everything a great deal, but on the whole that is the story. Some of it may seem a bit obscure to you. How can a poem, for instance, about a walk in the rain, be like an animal? Well, perhaps it cannot look much like a giraffe or an emu or an octopus, or anything you might find in a menagerie. It is better to call it an assembly of living parts moved by a single spirit. The living parts are the words, the images, the rhythms. The spirit is the life which inhabits them when they all work together. It is impossible to say which comes first, parts or spirit. But if any of the parts are dead . . . if any of the words, or images or rhythms do not jump to life as you read them . . . then the creature is going to be maimed and the spirit sickly. So, as a poet, you have to make sure that all those parts over which you have control, the words and rhythms and images, are alive. That is where the difficulties begin. Yet the rules, to begin with, are very simple. Words that live are those which we hear, like "click" or "chuckle," or which we see, like "freckled" or "veined," or which we taste, like "vinegar" or "sugar," or touch, like "prickle" or "oily," or smell, like "tar" or "onion." Words which belong directly to one of the five senses. Or words which act and seem to use their muscles, like "flick" or "balance."

But immediately things become more difficult. "Click" not only gives you a sound, it gives you the notion of a sharp movement . . . such as your tongue makes in saying "click." It also gives you the feel of something light and brittle, like a snapping twig. Heavy things do not click, nor do soft bendable ones. In the same way, tar not only smells strongly. It is sticky to touch, with a particular thick and choking stickiness. Also it moves, when it is soft, like a black snake, and has a beautiful black gloss. So it is with most words. They belong to several of the senses at once, as if each one had eyes, ears and tongue, or ears and fingers and a body to move with. It is this little goblin in a word which is its life and its poetry, and it is this goblin which the poet has to have under control.

Well, you will say, this is hopeless. How do you control all that. When the words are pouring out how can you be sure that you do not have one of these side meanings of the word "feathers" getting all stuck up with one of the side meanings of the word "treacle,"* a few words later. In bad poetry this is exactly what happens,

---

* Treacle: molasses. Which word is more evocative of stickiness: *treacle* or *molasses*?

the words kill each other. Luckily, you do not have to bother about it so long as you do one thing.

That one thing is, imagine what you are writing about. See it and live it. Do not think it up laboriously, as if you were working out mental arithmetic. Just look at it, touch it, smell it, listen to it, turn yourself into it. When you do this, the words look after themselves, like magic. If you do this you do not have to bother about commas or full-stops* or that sort of thing. You do not look at the words either. You keep your eyes, your ears, your nose, your taste, your touch, your whole being on the thing you are turning into words. The minute you flinch, and take your mind off this thing, and begin to look at the words and worry about them . . . then your worry goes into them and they set about killing each other. So you keep going as long as you can, then look back and see what you have written. After a bit of practice, and after telling yourself a few times that you do not care how other people have written about this thing, this is the way you find it; and after telling yourself you are going to use any old word that comes into your head so long as it seems right at the moment of writing it down, you will surprise yourself. You will read back through what you have written and you will get a shock. You will have captured a spirit, a creature.

After all that, I ought to give you some examples and show you some of my own more recently acquired specimens.

An animal I never succeeded in keeping alive is the fox. I was always frustrated: twice by a farmer, who killed cubs I had caught before I could get to them, and once by a poultry keeper who freed my cub while his dog waited. Years after those events I was sitting up late one snowy night in dreary lodgings in London. I had written nothing for a year or so but that night I got the idea I might write something and I wrote in a few minutes the following poem: the first "animal" poem I ever wrote. Here it is—*The Thought-Fox.*

> I imagine this midnight moment's forest:
> Something else is alive
> Beside the clock's loneliness
> And this blank page where my fingers move,
>
> Through the window I see no star:
> Something more near
> Though deeper within darkness
> Is entering the loneliness:
>
> Cold, delicately as the dark snow,
> A fox's nose touches twig, leaf;
> Two eyes serve a movement, that now
> And again now, and now, and now
>
> Sets neat prints into the snow
> Between trees, and warily a lame

---

* Full-stops: periods.

Shadow lags by stump and in hollow
Of a body that is bold to come

Across clearings, an eye,
A widening deepening greenness,
Brilliantly, concentratedly,
Coming about its own business

Till, with a sudden sharp hot stink of fox
It enters the dark hole of the head.
The window is starless still; the clock ticks,
The page is printed.

    This poem does not have anything you could easily call a meaning. It is about a fox, obviously enough, but a fox that is both a fox and not a fox. What sort of a fox is it that can step right into my head where presumably it still sits . . . smiling to itself when the dogs bark. It is both a fox and a spirit. It is a real fox; as I read the poem I see it move, I see it setting its prints, I see its shadow going over the irregular surface of the snow. The words show me all this, bringing it nearer and nearer. It is very real to me. The words have made a body for it and given it somewhere to walk.

    If, at the time of writing this poem, I had found livelier words, words that could give me much more vividly its movements, the twitch and craning of its ears, the slight tremor of its hanging tongue and its breath making little clouds, its teeth bared in the cold, the snow-crumbs dropping from its pads as it lifts each one in turn, if I could have got the words for all this, the fox would probably be even more real and alive to me now, than it is as I read the poem. Still, it is there as it is. If I had not caught the real fox there in the words I would never have saved the poem. I would have thrown it into the wastepaper basket as I have thrown so many other hunts that did not get what I was after. As it is, every time I read the poem the fox comes up again out of the darkness and steps into my head. And I suppose that long after I am gone, as long as a copy of the poem exists, every time anyone reads it the fox will get up somewhere out in the darkness and come walking towards them.

    So, you see, in some ways my fox is better than an ordinary fox. It will live for ever, it will never suffer from hunger or hounds. I have it with me wherever I go. And I made it. And all through imagining it clearly enough and finding the living words.

    Here, in this next poem, is one of my prize catches. I used to be a very keen angler for pike, as I still am when I get the chance, and I did most of my early fishing in a quite small lake, really a large pond. This pond went down to a great depth in one place. Sometimes, on hot days, we would see something like a railway sleeper* lying near the surface, and there certainly were huge pike in that pond. I suppose they are even bigger by now. Recently I felt like doing some pike fishing, but in circumstances where there was no chance of it, and over the days, as I remembered the extreme pleasures of that sport, bits of the following poem began

---

* Sleeper: wooden tie.

to arrive. As you will see, by looking at the place in my memory very hard and very carefully and by using the words that grew naturally out of the pictures and feelings, I captured not just a pike, I captured the whole pond, including the monsters I never even hooked. Here is the poem which I called *Pike*.*

Pike, three inches long, perfect
Pike in all parts, green tigering the gold.
Killers from the egg: the malevolent aged grin.
They dance on the surface among the flies.

Or move, stunned by their own grandeur,
Over a bed of emerald, silhouette
Of submarine delicacy and horror.
A hundred feet long in their world.

In ponds, under the heat-struck lily pads—
Gloom of their stillness:
Logged on last year's black leaves, watching upwards.
Or hung in an amber cavern of weeds.

The jaws' hooked clamp and fangs
Not to be changed at this date;
A life subdued to its instrument;
The gills kneading quietly, and the pectorals.

Three we kept behind glass,
Jungled in weed: three inches, four,
And four and a half: fed fry to them—
Suddenly there were two. Finally one

With a sag belly and the grin it was born with.
And indeed they spare nobody.
Two, six pounds each, over two feet long,
High and dry and dead in the willow-herb—

One jammed past its gills down the other's gullet:
The outside eye stared: as a vice locks—
The same iron in this eye
Though its film shrank in death.

A pond I fished, fifty yards across,
Whose lilies and muscular tench
Had outlasted every visible stone
Of the monastery that planted them—

---

* If you have never come face to face with a *pike*, count your blessings: it is a large carnivorous freshwater fish with a most terrifying battery of needle-sharp teeth and a powerful jaw.

Stilled legendary depth:
It was as deep as England. It held
Pike too immense to stir, so immense and old
That past nightfall I dared not cast

But silently cast and fished
With the hair frozen on my head
For what might move, for what eye might move.
The still splashes on the dark pond,

Owls hushing the floating woods
Frail on my ear against the dream
Darkness beneath night's darkness had freed,
That rose slowly towards me, watching.

As a boy, Hughes lived two lives: a "tribal" life with other boys in the town and a solitary life in the countryside. Two kinds of lives, two ways of being which simply would not mix: one can imagine the disaster that would occur when he took some boisterous, noisy friends into the country, and how their clamor would drive all animals and birds away.

The crucial shift inside Hughes's mind occurred when he "began to look at them from their own point of view." Another example, surely, of the end of "innocence"—the kind of childish, thoughtless innocence that assumes there is *only one* point of view, one's own.

Notice how easily and unapologetically Hughes admits that his fox poem "does not have anything you could easily call a meaning": if someone asks you what it *means,* you should feel free to reply that it's not a place where meaning is presented or hidden, but a place where something is *felt to happen,* a place where a powerful illusion can offer us a vivid sense of eventfulness. The text is presentational, rather than discursive.

To read well is to read with appropriate expectations. As you read the Medawars, you intuitively recognize what they are doing (you probably wouldn't have done so when you were ten or eleven years old)—they are explaining, proposing a point of view, exploring moral and social issues; they are engaged in the production of a *discursive* text, a text that offers a discussion of an issue or question.

Conversely, most poems do nothing like that; rather, they offer you, through language, an illusion, a sense of "it is as if I also had this experience"; if we ask "*What is the meaning of* having a cheerful conversation, or of being surprised, of being tingly with suspense, or of being excited?" we suspect that you will answer, "That is rather a silly question!" We agree.

MARGARET ATWOOD

The Animals in That Country

In some cultures, the bond between animals and humans is still relatively strong, and animals are endowed with mysterious and religious powers, part-human, part-animal, part-god. But our animals are demystified, desacralized: they are merely the things that get run over.

In that country the animals
have the faces of people:

the ceremonial
cats possessing the streets

the fox run   5
politely to earth, the huntsmen
standing around him, fixed
in their tapestry of manners

the bull, embroidered
with blood and given   10
an elegant death, trumpets, his name
stamped on him, heraldic brand
because

(when he rolled
on the sand, sword in his heart, the teeth   15
in his blue mouth were human)

he is really a man

even the wolves, holding resonant
conversations in their
forests thickened with legend.   20

        In this country the animals
        have the faces of
        animals.

        Their eyes
        flash once in car headlights   25
        and are gone.

        Their deaths are not elegant.

        They have the faces of
        no-one.

    You are now about half-way through the book, so this seems an appropriate place to consider in more detail what exactly *you do* as you are reading. In the Introduction, we quoted part of Frank Smith's account of reading; here he explains how you make predictions and make sense; reading, he argues, is simply one application of what you are doing throughout every day, in all kinds of situations.

FRANK SMITH

Predictions and Intentions—Global and Focal

I have talked as if predictions are made and dealt with one at a time. As we read, a particular prediction may range over a set of alternative meanings, words, or letters. As we drive we may predict the future position of our car with respect to an approaching truck, a pedestrian, or a landmark that we expect to see. But all of this has been oversimplified. Predictions are multiplex; usually we handle more than one at any one time. Some predictions are overriding; they carry us across large expanses of time and space. Other predictions occurring at the same time are far more transient, arising and being disposed of relatively rapidly. Predictions are layered and interleaved.

Consider again the analogy of driving a car downtown. We have a general intention and prediction that we shall reach a certain destination, leading to a number of relatively general predictions about landmarks that will be met along the route. Call these predictions *global*, since they tend to influence the entire journey. No matter how much our exact path might have to be varied because of exigencies that arise on the way, swerving to avoid a pedestrian or diverting down a side street because of a traffic holdup, these overriding global predictions tend to bring us always towards our intended goal.

But while global predictions influence every decisions until out intended goal is reached, we simultaneously make more detailed predictions related to specific events during the course of the journey. Call predictions of this nature *focal*, since they concern us for short periods of time only and have no lasting consequence for the journey as a whole. Focal predictions must be made, usually quite suddenly, with respect to the oncoming truck or the pedestrian or as a consequence of a minor diversion. In contrast to global predictions, we cannot usually be specific about focal predictions before the journey begins. It would be futile to try to predict before starting the specific location of incidents that are likely to occur on the way. Yet while the occasion for a focal prediction is likely to arise out of particular sets of local circumstances, the prediction itself will still be influenced by our global predictions about the journey as a whole. For example, the modified focal predictions that will result if we have to make an unexpected detour will still be influenced by our overriding intention of eventually reaching a particular destination.

Now I want to suggest that we make similar global and focal predictions when we read. While reading a novel, for example, we may handle a number of quite different predictions simultaneously, some global that can persist up to the entire length of the book, others far more focal that can rise and be disposed of as often as every fixation. We begin a book with extremely global predictions about its content from its title and from what perhaps we have heard about it in advance. Sometimes even global predictions may fail—we discover that a book is not on the topic we anticipated. But usually global predictions about content, theme, and treatment can persist throughout the book.

At a slightly more detailed level, there are likely to be expectations still very global that arise and are elaborated within every chapter. At the beginning of the book we may have such predictions about the first chapter only, but in the course of reading the first chapter expectations about the second arise, and so on to the end. Within each chapter there will be rather more focal predictions about paragraphs, each paragraph being a major source of predictions about the next. At lower layers within each paragraph there will be predictions about sentences and within each sentence some predictions about words.

Lower level predictions arise more suddenly; we will rarely make focal predictions about words more than a sentence ahead of where we are reading, nor predictions about sentences more than a paragraph ahead, nor predictions about paragraphs more than a chapter ahead. The more focal the prediction, the sooner it arises (since it is based on more immediate antecedents) and the sooner it is disposed of (since it has fewer long-range consequences). In general, the more focal a prediction, the less it can be specifically formulated in advance. You would be unlikely to predict the content of the present sentence before you had read the previous sentence, although the content of the present chapter as a whole was probably predictable from the previous chapter. On the other hand, predictions at the various layers inform each other. While focal level predictions are largely determined by the particular situation in which they arise, they are also influenced by our more global expectations. Your focal predictions about my next sentence will depend to some extent on your comprehension of the present sentence but also on your expectations about this paragraph, this chapter, and the book as a whole. But similarly, the global predictions that we make at the book and chapter level must be constantly tested and if necessary modified by the results of our predictions at more focal levels. Your comprehension of one sentence could change your view of a whole book. The entire process is at once extremely complex and highly dynamic, but in Figure A I shall try to illustrate it with a considerably simplified and static diagram.

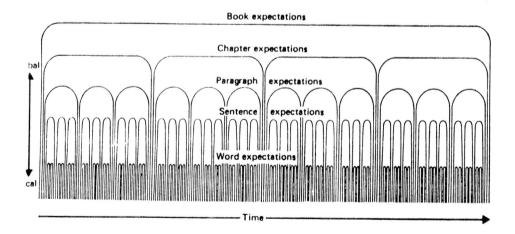

In general, the expectations of Figure A should be regarded as developing from left to right: the past influences our expectations for the future. But it can frequently help at all levels of prediction in reading to look ahead. Meaning can be sought in many ways. Similarly, there should be vertical lines all over the diagram, as the outcomes of focal predictions have their effect on global predictions and the global expectations exert their constant influence on specific focal predictions.

Do not take the diagram too literally. It is not necessary to predict at every level all of the time. We may become unsure of what a book as a whole is about and, for a while, hold our most global predictions to the chapter or even a lower level while we try to grasp where the book might be going. Sometimes we may have so much trouble with a paragraph that we find it impossible to maintain predictions at the chapter level. At the other extreme we may find a chapter or paragraph so predictable, or so irrelevant, that we omit predictions and tests at lower levels altogether. In plain language, we skip. It is only when we can make no predictions at all that a book is completely incomprehensible. It should also not be thought that there are clearly defined boundaries between the different levels of prediction; the global-focal distinction does not describe alternatives but extreme ends of a continuous range of possibilities. A better analogy for reading a novel than my drive downtown might be the weaving of a richly structured tapestry of subtly shaded colors.

In the car-driving analogy I tended to use the words "prediction" and "intention" interchangeably. When we drive, our predictions to a large extent reflect our intentions about where we want to go, how soon we want to get there, and the route we prefer. It is instructive to consider the analysis of prediction in reading that I have just made from the point of view of the intentions of the writer. To some extent, the predictions and intentions can be seen as reflections of each other.

Writers usually begin with global intentions of what the book as a whole shall be about and about the way the subject shall be treated. These global intentions then determine lower-level intentions for every chapter. Within each chapter will be more focal intentions about every paragraph, and within each paragraph, quite detailed focal intentions regarding sentences and words. And just as the more focal predictions of the reader (or the driver) tend to arise at shorter notice and to be dispensed with more quickly, so the more focal intentions of the writer extend over a shorter range in both directions. What I want to say in the present sentence is most specifically determined by what I wrote in the previous one and will, in turn, place a considerable constraint upon how I compose the next sentence. But these focal constraints are at the detailed level. My intention in every sentence that I write is influenced by the more global intentions for the paragraph as a whole, and of course my intention in every paragraph reflects the topic I have selected for the chapter and more generally for the book.

It may be from the perspective of predictions and intentions that one can best perceive the intimate relationship between readers and writers. It might be said that a book is comprehended (from the writer's point of view at least) when the reader's predictions mirror the writer's intentions at all levels. Certainly one important aspect of writing is the intentional manipulation of the reader's predictions. A textbook writer must try to lead readers in a Socratic sense so that the answers to one set of predictive questions set up the succeeding predictions that the readers should make. In a more dramatic context an author may strive for tension by maintaining a particular degree of uncertainty in the reader's predictions at all levels throughout a book. And in a mystery story an author might quite deliberately lead readers into inappropriate predictions so that the inevitable consequence of predictions that fail—surprise—becomes a part of the reading experience.

But readers should also have intentions of their own. When we read a book purely for its literary or even entertainment merit we may willingly submit our expectations to the control of the author or poet. But certainly for textbooks—like the present one, for example—readers should not only be seeking certain information for their own particular ends, quite independently of the intentions of the author, but they should constantly be on guard to resist having their predictions entirely controlled by the author's arguments. The critical mind always reserves some questions of its own. And in all reading, as I have several times reiterated in my assertion that comprehension is relative, there is bound to be an idiosyncrasy in the predictions that readers make at all levels, reflecting their personal interests and purposes and expectations.

Some of the constraints upon authors at all levels are highly conventional. Writers of prose and poetry must temper many of their intentions to the particular stylistic demands of the medium in which they work. In the same way it might be expected that the kinds of predictions that readers make at various levels should also reflect these conventions. Such issues I think lie at the basis of the debates about the "right way" to read poetry or literature. These are difficult questions. On the one hand, I think there is a distinction to be made between what a child has to learn in order to read—a topic which has been a major concern of this book—and what a child is sometimes expected to be able to do as a result of reading. "Drawing inferences" and "evaluating arguments", for example, seem to me to fall into the latter category. Yet I would not want to suggest that there is a clearcut division between the processes and the consequences of reading. I certainly would not want to support a distinction between "reading" on the one hand and "thinking" on the other. Reading should not be regarded as different from thinking or devoid of thinking. Many of the so-called "higher-level skills" associated with the critical reading of literature and poetry seem to me best regarded as specialised questions or predictions that are asked from perspectives beyond the range of this book. Such perspectives do not alter the fundamental nature of reading, but they can add immeasurably to its richness.

YOUR WRITING(S) FOR OTHERS TO READ

1. Do you feel that growing up in an (urban or suburban) environment shaped by earlier generations has cut you off from the natural world? Do you ever fantasize about living in the past—a past of unspoiled natural beauty and grandeur? What are the main features of your ideal lost landscape?
2. Which members of the animal world do you fear or find repulsive? Mice? Rats? Cockroaches? Wasps? Can you account for your feelings?

3. Give an account of your most successful relationship with an animal—a cat, a dog, or other pet. What pleasures do you find in such a relationship that cannot be found in a relationship with another person?
4. How do your attitudes toward animals compare with those of your parents? Your siblings? Your friends? Are you relatively feeling or unfeeling?
5. What part, if any, do animals play in your life?
6. How do you react to the Medawars' arguments? Do you find their tone of voice, their attitudes, more reasonable than that of most people involved in animal welfare? Give an account of your own position on such matters.

Sancho ran to his Dapple, and embracing him, said, " How hast thou done, my dearest Dapple?"

Chapter Eight

Tracks

This is what you shall do: Love the earth and sun and the animals, despise riches, give alms to every one that asks, stand up for the stupid and crazy, devote your income and labor to others, hate tyrants, argue not concerning God, have patience and indulgence toward the people, take off your hat to nothing known or unknown or to any man or number of men, go freely with powerful uneducated persons and with the young and with the mothers of families, read these leaves in the open air every season of every year of your life, re-examine all you have been told at school or church or in any book, dismiss whatever insults your own soul, and your very flesh shall be a great poem and have the richest fluency not only in its words but in the silent lines of its lips and face and between the lashes of your eyes and in every motion and joint of your body . . .

WALT WHITMAN

To be rapt with satisfied attention, like Whitman, to the mere spectacle of the world's presence is one way, and the most fundamental way, of confessing one's sense of its unfathomable significance and importance.

WILLIAM JAMES

> Everything in the universe is in constant interaction with everything else. You cannot say, this is a rock. You can only say, there sits, leans, stands, falls over, lies down, a rock.

> Most of us, I am sure, have forgotten how to play. We've made up games instead. And competition is the force which holds these games together. The desire to win, to beat someone else, has supplemented play—the doing of something just for itself.

ROBYN DAVIDSON

The American psychologist and philosopher William James once explored the possibility of inventing a "moral equivalent" of war: how would it be, to arouse all the energies, all the resourcefulness, all the actively dynamic possibilities of human beings in such a way that they could be harnessed not to destructive but to creative ends? Take all the self-transcendent virtues that people show in wartime, under stress, under pressure, and turn them to good use!

It's still, after almost a hundred years, a great idea, an exciting speculation: but it is indeed more, for our reading tells us that some individuals have actually fulfilled James's hope, have actually achieved his vision. One such—and one of our favorites—is Robyn Davidson: we are disappointed that she is not better known, but make a few amends by devoting this chapter to her. We are confident that her remarkable story would have gratified the heart and mind of William James: you, too, dear reader!

We have chosen to use Robyn Davidson's reflective narrative as the climax to the second section of the book because it raises many of the issues of the section in a vivid, acute, and focused way. It also serves as a bridge to the third section because it rehearses many questions of how we come to recognize and develop our own values by negotiating with other cultures' values, and by renegotiating our relationships with the dominant values of the culture that shaped ourselves.

Why would anyone feel impelled to make a solitary journey across 1700 miles of desert, with only animals for company? That is exactly what Robyn Davidson did. Born in 1950, she was in her late 20s when she went off alone to Alice

Springs in the middle of Australia, to learn how to handle camels and, if possible, to earn the money to buy two or three.

Here, she explains "the reasons and the needs" behind her extravagant plan: first, before she set out:

A couple of years before, someone had asked me a question: "What is the substance of the world in which you live?" As it happens, I had not slept or eaten for three or four days and it struck me at the time as a very profound question. It took me an hour to answer it, and when I did, my answer seemed to come almost directly from the subconscious: "Desert, purity, fire, air, hot wind, space, sun, desert desert desert." It had surprised me, I had no idea those symbols had been working so strongly within me.

I had read a good deal about Aborigines and that was another reason for my wanting to travel in the desert—a way of getting to know them directly and simply.

I had also been vaguely bored with my life and its repetitions—the half-finished, half-hearted attempts at different jobs and various studies; had been sick of carrying around the self-indulgent negativity which was so much the malaise of my generation, my sex and my class.

So I had made a decision which carried with it things that I could not articulate at the time. I had made the choice instinctively, and only later had given it meaning. The trip had never been billed in my mind as an adventure in the sense of something to be proved. And it struck me then that the most difficult thing had been the decision to act, the rest had been merely tenacity—and the fears were paper tigers. One really could do anything one had decided to do whether it were changing a job, moving to a new place, divorcing a husband or whatever, one really could act to change and control one's life; and the procedure, the process, was its own reward.

Secondly, at a moment of crisis during her journey:

I recognized then the process by which I had always attempted difficult things. I had simply not allowed myself to think of the consequences, but had closed my eyes, jumped in, and before I knew where I was, it was impossible to renege. I was basically a dreadful coward, I knew that about myself. The only possible way I could overcome this was to trick myself with that other self, who lived in dream and fantasy and who was annoyingly lackadaisical and unpractical. All passion, no sense, no order, no instinct for self-preservation. That's what I had done, and now that cowardly self had discovered an unburnt bridge by which to return to the past. As Renata Adler writes in *Speedboat*:

> I think when you are truly stuck, when you have stood still in the same spot for too long, you throw a grenade in exactly the spot you were standing in, and jump, and pray. It is the momentum of last resort.

Yes, exactly, only now, after all this time, I had discovered that the grenade was a dud, and I could hop right back to the same old spot which was safety. The excruciating thing was that those two selves were now warring with each other.

Here is how she took her first step:

I arrived in the Alice at five a.m. with a dog, six dollars and a small suitcase full of inappropriate clothes. "Bring a cardigan for the evenings," the brochure said. A freezing wind whipped grit down the platform and I stood shivering, holding warm dog flesh, and wondering what foolishness had brought me to this eerie, empty train-station in the centre of nowhere. I turned against the wind, and saw the line of mountains at the edge of town.

There are some moments in life that are like pivots around which your existence turns—small intuitive flashes, when you know you have done something correct for a change, when you think you are on the right track. I watched a pale dawn streak the cliffs with Day-glo and realized that this was one of them. It was a moment of pure, uncomplicated confidence—and lasted about ten seconds.

Diggity wriggled out of my arms and looked at me, head cocked, piglet ears flying. I experienced that sinking feeling you get when you know you have conned yourself into doing something difficult and there's no going back. It's all very well, to set off on a train with no money telling yourself that you're really quite a brave and adventurous person, and you'll deal capably with things as they happen, but when you actually arrive at the other end with no one to meet and nowhere to go and nothing to sustain you but a lunatic idea that even you have no real faith in, it suddenly appears much more attractive to be at home on the kindly Queensland coast, discussing plans and sipping gins on the verandah with friends, and making unending lists of lists which get thrown away, and reading books about camels.

The lunatic idea was, basically, to get myself the requisite number of wild camels from the bush and train them to carry my gear, then walk into and about the central desert area. I knew that there were feral camels aplenty in this country. They had been imported in the 1850s along with their Afghani and North Indian owners, to open up the inaccessible areas, to transport food, and to help build the telegraph system and railways that would eventually cause their economic demise. When this happened, those Afghans had let their camels go, heartbroken, and tried to find other work. They were specialists and it wasn't easy. They didn't have much luck with government support either. Their camels, however, had found easy street—it was perfect country for them and they grew and prospered, so that now there are approximately ten thousand roaming the free country and making a nuisance of themselves on cattle properties, getting shot at, and, according to some ecologists, endangering some plant species for which they have a particular fancy. Their only natural enemy is man, they are virtually free of disease, and Australian camels are now rated as some of the best in the world.

The train had been half empty, the journey long. Five hundred miles and two days from Adelaide to Alice Springs. The modern arterial roads around Port Augusta had almost immediately petered out into crinkled, wretched, endless pink tracks leading to the shimmering horizon, and then there was nothing but the dry red parchment of the dead heart; god's majestic hidy-hole, where men are men and women are an afterthought. Snippets of railway car conversation still buzzed around in my head.

"G'day, mind if I sit 'ere?"

(Sighing and looking pointedly out the window or at book.) "No."

(Dropping of the eyes to chest level.) "Where's yer old man?"

"I don't have an old man."

(Faint gleam in bleary, blood-shot eye, still fixed at chest level.) "Jesus Christ, mate, you're not goin' to the Alice alone are ya? Listen 'ere, lady, you're fuckin' done for. Them coons'll rape youze for sure. Fuckin' niggers run wild up there ya know. You'll need someone to keep an eye on ya. Tell youze what, I'll shout youze a beer, then we'll go back to your cabin and get acquainted eh? Whaddya reckon?"

I waited until the station had thinned its few bustling arrivals, standing in the vacuum of early morning silence, fighting back my unease, then set off with Diggity towards town.

My first impression as we strolled down the deserted street was of the architectural ugliness of the place, a discomforting contrast to the magnificence of the country which surrounded it. Dust covered everything from the large, dominant corner pub to the tacky, unimaginative shop fronts that lined the main street. Hordes of dead insects clustered in the arcing street lights, and four-wheel-drive vehicles spattered in red dirt, with only two spots swept clean by the wind-screen wipers, rattled intermittently through the cement and bitumen town. This grey, cream and hospital-green shopping area gradually gave way to sprawling suburbia until it was stopped short by the great perpendicular red face of the Macdonnell Range which borders the southern side of town, and runs unbroken, but for a few spectacular gorges, east and west for several hundred miles. The Todd River, a dry white sandy bed lined with tall columns of silver eucalypts, winds through the town, then cuts into a narrow gap in the mountains. The range, looming menacingly like some petrified prehistoric monster, has, I was to discover, a profound psychological effect on the puny folk below. It sends them troppo.* It reminds them of incomprehensible dimensions of time which they almost successfully block out with brick veneer houses and wilted English-style gardens.

I had planned to camp in the creek with the Aborigines until I could find a job and a place to stay, but the harbingers of doom on the train had told me it was suicide to do such a thing. Everyone, from the chronic drunks to the stony men and women with brown wrinkled faces and burnt-out expressions, to the waiters in tuxedos who served and consumed enormous amounts of alcohol, all of them warned me against it. The blacks were unequivocally the enemy. Dirty, lazy, dangerous animals. Stories of young white lasses who innocently strayed down the Todd at night, there to meet their fate worse than death, were told with suspect fervour. It was the only subject anyone had got fired up about. I had heard other stories back home too—of how a young black man was found in an Alice gutter one morning, painted white. Even back in the city where the man in the street was unlikely ever to have seen an Aborigine, let alone spoken to one, that same man could talk at length, with an extraordinary contempt, about what they were like, how lazy and unintelligent they were. This was because of the press, where clichéd images of

*Troppo: crazy, disturbed, as in cabin-fever.

dirty, stone-age drunks on the dole were about the only coverage Aborigines got, and because everyone had been taught at school that they were not much better than specialized apes, with no culture, no government and no right to existence in a vastly superior white world; aimless wanderers who were backward, primitive and stupid.

It is difficult to sort out fact from fiction, fear from paranoia and goodies from baddies when you are new in a town but something was definitely queer about this one. The place seemed soulless, rootless, but perhaps it was just that which encouraged, in certain circumstances, the extraordinary. Had everyone been trying to put the fear of god into me just because I was an urbanite in the bush? Had I suddenly landed in Ku Klux Klan country? I had spent time before with Aboriginal people—in fact, had had one of the best holidays of my entire life with them. Certainly there had been some heavy drinking and the occasional fight, but that was part of the white Australian tradition too, and could be found in most pubs or parties in the country. If the blacks here were like the blacks there, how could a group of whites be so consumed with fear and hatred? And if they were different here, what had happened to make them that way? Tread carefully, my instincts said. I could sense already a camouflaged violence in this town, and I had to find a safe place to stay. Rabbits, too, have their survival mechanisms.

They say paranoia attracts paranoia: certainly no one else I met ever had such a negative view of Alice Springs. But then I was to get to know it from the gutters up, which may have given me a distorted perspective. It is said that anyone who sees the Todd River flow three times falls in love with the Alice. By the end of the second year, after seeing it freakishly flood more often than that, I had a passionate hatred yet an inexplicable and consuming addiction for it.

There are fourteen thousand people living there of whom one thousand are Aboriginal. The whites consist mainly of government workers, miscellaneous misfits and adventurers, retired cattle or sheep station* owners, itinerant station workers, truck drivers and small business operators whose primary function in life is to rip off the tourists, who come by the bus-load from America, Japan and urban Australia, expecting high adventure in this last romantic outpost, and to see the extraordinary desert which surrounds it. There are three major pubs, a few motels, a couple of zed-grade restaurants, and various shops that sell 'I've climbed Ayers Rock' T-shirts, boomerangs made in Taiwan, books on Australiana, and tea towels with noble savages holding spears silhouetted against setting suns. It is a frontier town, characterized by an aggressive masculine ethic and severe racial tensions.

I ate breakfast at a cheap cafe, then stepped out into the glaring street where things were beginning to move, and squinted at my new home. I asked someone where the cheapest accommodation was and they directed me to a caravan park three miles north of town.

It was a hot and dusty walk but interesting. The road followed a tributary of the Todd. Still, straight columns of blue smoke chimneying up through the gum leaves marked Aboriginal camps. On the left were the garages and workshops of industrial Alice—galvanized iron sheds behind which spread the trim lawns and

* Station: ranch.

trees of suburbia. When I arrived, the proprietor informed me that it was only three dollars if I had my own tent, otherwise it was eight.

My smile faded. I eyed the cold drinks longingly and went outside for some tepid tap water. I didn't ask if that were free, just in case. Over in the corner of the park some young folk with long hair and patched jeans were pitching a large tent. They looked approachable, so I asked if I could stay with them. They were pleased to offer me shelter and friendliness.

That night, they took me out on the town in their beat-up panel-van equipped with all the trappings one associates with free-wheeling urban youth—a five million decibel car stereo and even surf-boards . . . they were heading north. We drove into the dusty lights of the town and stopped by the pub to pick up some booze. The girl, who was shy and very young, suddenly turned to me.

"Oo, look at them, aren't they disgusting. God, they're like apes."

"Who?"

"The boongs."

Her boyfriend was leaning up against the bottle-shop, waiting.

"Hurry up, Bill, and let's get out of here. Ugly brutes." She folded her arms as if she were cold and shivered with repulsion.

I put my head on my arms, bit my tongue, and knew the night was going to be a long one.

The next day I got a job at the pub, starting in two days. Yes, I could stay in a back room of the pub, the payment for which would be deducted from my first week's wages. Meals were provided. Perfect. That gave me time to suss out camel business. I sat in the bar for a while and chatted with the regulars. I discovered there were three camel-men in town—two involved with tourist business, and the other an old Afghan who was bringing in camels from the wild to sell to Arabia as meat herds. I met a young geologist who offered to drive me out to meet this man.

The minute I saw Sallay Mahomet it was apparent to me that he knew exactly what he was doing. He exuded the bandy-legged, rope-handling confidence of a man long accustomed to dealing with animals. He was fixing some odd-looking saddles near a dusty yard filled with these strange beasts.

"Yes, what can I do for you?"

"Good morning, Mr. Mahomet," I said confidently. "My name's Robyn Davidson and um, I've been planning this trip you see, into the central desert and I wanted to get three wild camels and train them for it, and I was wondering if you might be able to help me."

"Hrrrmppph."

Sallay glared at me from under bushy white eyebrows. There was a dry grumpiness about him that put me instantly in my place and made me feel like a complete idiot.

"And I suppose you think you'll make it too?"

I looked at the ground, shuffled my feet and mumbled something defensive.

"What do you know about camels then?"

"Ah well, nothing really. I mean these are the first ones I've seen as a matter of fact, but ah . . ."

"Hrrmmph. And what do you know about deserts?"

It was painfully obvious from my silence that I knew very little about anything.

Sallay said he was sorry, he didn't think he could help me, and turned about his business. My cockiness faded. This was going to be harder than I thought, but then it was only the first day.

Next we drove to the tourist place south of town. I met the owner and his wife, a friendly woman who offered me cakes and tea. They looked at one another in silence when I told them of my plan. "Well, come out here any time you like," said the man jovially, "and get to know the animals a bit." He could barely control the smirk on the other side of his face. My intuition in any case told me to stay away. I didn't like him and I was sure the feeling was mutual. Besides, when I saw how his animals roared and fought, I figured he was probably not the right person to learn from.

The last of the three, the Posel place, was three miles north, and was owned, according to some of the people in the bar, by a maniac.

My geologist friend dropped me off at the pub, and from there I walked north up the Charles River bed. It was a delightful walk, under cool and shady trees. The silence was often broken by packs of camp dogs who raced out with their hackles up to tell me and Diggity to get out of their territory, only to have bottles, cans and curses flung at them by their Aboriginal owners, who none the less smiled and nodded at us.

I arrived at the door of a perfect white cottage set among trees and lawns. It was an Austrian chalet in miniature, beautiful, but crazy out there among red boulders and dust devils. The yards were all hand-hewn timber and twisted ropes—the work of a master-craftsman. The stables had arches and geraniums. Not a thing was out of place. Gladdy Posel met me at the door—a small, bird-like woman, middle-aged, with a face that spoke of hardship and worry and unbending will. But there was a suspiciousness in it also. However, she was the first person so far who had not greeted my idea with patronizing disbelief. Or perhaps she just hid it better. Kurt, her husband, was not there so I arranged to come and see him the next day.

"What do you think of the town so far?" she asked.

"I think it stinks," I replied and instantly regretted it. The last thing I wanted to do was to set her against me.

She smiled for the first time. "Well, you might get on all right then. Just remember, they're mostly mad around here and you have to watch out for yourself."

"What about the blacks?" I asked.

The suspiciousness returned. "There's nothing damnwell wrong with the blacks except what the whites do to them."

It was my turn to smile. Gladdy, it appeared, was a rebel.

The next day, Kurt came out to greet me with as much enthusiasm as his Germanic nature would allow. He was dressed in an immaculate white outfit, with an equally crisp white turban. But for his ice-blue eyes, he looked like a bearded, wiry Moor. Standing near him was like being close to a fallen power line—all dangerous, crackling energy. He was dark brown, stringy, with hands calloused and outsized from work and he was certainly the most extraordinary individual I had ever laid eyes on. I had barely got out my name before he had led me to the verandah and begun to tell me exactly how life was to be for the next eight months, grinning, gap-toothed, all the while.

"Now, you vill come to verk for me here for eight months und zen you vill buy vone off my camelts, and I vill teach you to train zem and you vill get two vild vones and dat vill be dat. I haf just de animal for you. He hass only vone eye but, ha, dat does not matter—he is stronk and reliable enough for you, ya."

"Yes, but . . ." I stammered.

"Yes, but vott?" he shouted incredulously.

"How much will he cost?"

"Ah, ya, how much vill he cost. Ya. Let me see. I give him to you for a thousand dollars. A bargain."

A blind camel for a thousand bucks, I thought to myself. I could buy a bloody elephant for that.

"That's very nice of you but you see, Kurt, I have no money."

His grin disappeared like greasy water down a plug-hole.

"But I can work at the pub of course, so . . ."

"Ya. Dat's right," he said. "Ya, you vill vork at de pub and you vill stay here as my apprentice for food and rent beginning tonight and ve vill see vot you are made off, and so it is all settled. You are a very lucky girl dat I do dis for you."

I half understood, through my dazed incredulity, that I was being shanghaied. He led me to my immaculate quarters in the stable and went inside to fetch my new camel-handler's outfit. I climbed into the great swaddling white drapes and perched the ridiculous turban over my pale hair and eyes. I looked like a schizophrenic baker. I laughed helplessly at the mirror.

"Vot's da matter, you too good for it or sometink?"

"No, no," I assured him. "I just never saw myself as an Afghan, that's all."

He led me out to the camels for my first lesson.

"Now, you must start from de bottom and verk up," he said, handing me a dustpan and broom.

Camels shit like rabbits. Neat round little pebbles in copious amounts. Some of it was sitting in the direction of Kurt's pointed finger. It was only then that I realized that on the whole five acres I had not seen a scrap of the stuff, not a particle, and considering Kurt had eight beasts, it was, to say the least, surprising. Hoping to impress my new boss with my diligence, I bent down and carefully scraped every bit into the pan and stood up waiting for inspection.

Something seemed to be wrong with Kurt. He seemed to be having trouble with his lips, and his eyebrows were working up and down his face like lifts. His skin was turning red under the brown. He exploded then like a volcano, blasting me with his spit like hot lava.

"VOTT ISSS DATTTT?"

Confused, I glanced down but could see nothing. I got on my knees but could still see nothing. Kurt threw himself on his knees beside me and there hidden under a blade of clipped couch grass was the most minuscule ancient morsel of camel shit you could image. "Clean it up!" he screamed. "You tink diss iss a bloody holiday or sometink?" I couldn't believe this was happening to me; shaking, I picked up the microscopic flake. It had almost turned to dust over the years. But Kurt was appeased and we continued the rounds of the ranch.

I might have thought twice about staying there after this outburst, but it became apparent very quickly that my new demon friend was a wizard with camels. I will now, once and for all, destroy some myths concerning these animals. They are the most intelligent creatures I know except for dogs and I would give them an I.Q. rating roughly equivalent to eight-year-old children. They are affectionate, cheeky, playful, witty, yes witty, self-possessed, patient, hard-working and endlessly inter-esting and charming. They are also very difficult to train, being of an essentially undomestic turn of mind as well as extremely bright and perceptive. This is why they have such a bad reputation. If handled badly, they can be quite dangerous and definitely recalcitrant. Kurt's were neither. They were like great curious puppies. Nor do they smell, except when they regurgitate slimy green cud all over you in a fit of pique or fear. I would also say that they are highly sensitive animals, easily frightened by bad handlers, and easily ruined. They are haughty, ethnocentric, clearly believing that they are god's chosen race. But they are also cowards and their aristocratic demeanour hides delicate hearts. I was hooked.

Kurt proceeded to outline my duties. Shit seemed to be the major problem. I was to follow the animals around all day and pick up the offending stuff. He then told me how he had once had the bright idea of shoving the inflatable rubber inner bladders of footballs up their anuses, but that during the day they had passed them out with a groan. I looked sideways at Kurt. He wasn't joking.

I was also to catch the animals at four in the morning, unhobble them (they were hobbled by straps and a foot of chain around their front legs to prevent them going too far, too fast) and lead them home in a long line, nose to tail, ready for saddling. Two or three would be used for the day's work, leading tourists around the oval for a dollar a go, while the rest would be kept in the yards. I was to tie the selected three to their feed bins, groom them with a broom, ask them to "whoosh" (an old Afghan word meaning, presumably, sit), then saddle them with the gaudy mock-Arabian saddles of Kurt's design. This was to be the best part of my existence for the next eight months. Kurt threw me right into the thick of things which was excellent. It did not give me time to be frightened of the animals. Most of the rest of the day was spent keeping his sterile domain scrupulously clean, tidy and free of weeds. Not a blade of grass dared grow out of place.

That night, the boy who had been good enough to drive me around town came out to see how I was doing. I informed Kurt that I had a visitor, then took him back to the stables. We sat chatting, watching the iridescent blue and orange glow of late evening. I was exhausted after the day's routine. Kurt had kept me trotting at a brisk scurry from feed shed to camel to yard and back again. I had weeded a garden, trimmed a mile of couch-infested curbing with a pair of scissors, had led countless objectionable tourists around the oval on camel-back and had cleaned, mopped, scraped and lifted until I thought I would collapse. The pace had not slackened for a minute and all the while Kurt had been scrutinizing me and my work, alternately muttering that I might turn out all right and screaming abuse at me, in front of bewildered and embarrassed tourists. While I was working I was too preoccupied to think whether I would be able to stand such treatment for eight months, but as

I talked to my young friend all the anger that I felt towards the man was bubbling away deep down inside. Arrogant prick, I thought. Miserable, lousy, tight, obsessional, whingeing little creep. I hated myself for my infernal cowardice in dealing with people. It is such a female syndrome, so much the weakness of animals who have always been prey. I had not been aggressive enough or stood up to him enough. And now this impotent, internal, angry stuttering. Suddenly, Kurt appeared around the corner—an apparition in white taking giant strides. I could feel his fury before he reached us and stood up to face him. He pointed a shaking finger at my friend and hissed through clenched teeth:

"You, you get out off here. I don't know who de hell you are. No vone iss allowed here after dark. You've probably been sent here by Fullarton to spy out my camel saddle designs."

Then he glared at me. "I heared from my own sources dat you've already been over dere. If you verk for me you don't go near da place—EVER. Do you understand?"

And then I burst. Hell had no fury by comparison. My poor young friend had disappeared, eyes bulging, into the dark and I lashed out at Kurt, calling him every name under the sun and screaming that he had a snowflake's chance in hell of ever getting me to do his dirty work again. I'd die first. I stormed into the room in a passionate rage, ferociously slammed his precious barn-door, the one that had to be handled like glass, and packed my meagre possessions.

Kurt was stupefied. He had sized me up wrongly, and pushed a sucker too far. The dollar signs faded from his eyes. He had lost a patsy and a slave. But he was too proud to apologize and the next morning, early, I moved into the pub.

After eighteen months of strenuous and sometimes dangerous work, being bullied and humiliated by some of the men in Alice Springs—men she couldn't afford to offend—she became reasonably competent at handling camels. She learned the art of piercing their nostrils with a wooden peg, and attaching reins to the peg so that the animals could be controlled and steered. And as she came to know the Aborigines at first hand, and learned to discount white Australians' racist prejudices, she began to understand and appreciate their subtle relationship with nature and to recognize the complexity of their culture. But she also had to admit that generations of white settlers and the implementation of government policies rooted in a supremacist ideology had almost destroyed the Aboriginal soul. As she read in Kevin Gilbert's outspoken book *Because a White Man'll Never Do It*: "It is my thesis that Aboriginal Australia underwent a rape of the soul so profound that the blight continues in the minds of most blacks today. It is this psychological blight that is repeated down the generations."

A sadder and a wiser woman, she finally set off on her journey across the desert; her friends and her pet crow saw her off:

Josephine started bawling which started Andree which started Marg which started Pop, and there were hugs and good lucks and "Watch out for those bull camels like

I told you," from Sallay, and feeble little pats on the back, and Marg looked deep into my eyes and said, "You know I love you, don't you," and Iris was waving, "Goodbye, sweetheart, goodbye, Rob," and I grabbed the nose-line with cold sweaty shaking hands, and walked up over the hill.

"I walk, I lift up, I lift up heart, eyes, to down all the glory of that magnificent heaven."

I could not remember how the rest of it went but the words were dinging around in my head like an advertisement jingle or an Abba tune. It was just how I felt. As if I were made of some fine bright, airy, musical substance and that in my chest was a source of power that would any minute explode, releasing thousands of singing birds.

All around me was magnificence. Light, power, space and sun. And I was walking into it. I was going to let it make me or break me. A great weight lifted off my back. I felt like dancing and calling to the great spirit. Mountains pulled and pushed, wind roared down chasms. I followed eagles suspended from cloud horizons. I wanted to fly in the unlimited blue of the morning. I was seeing it all as if for the first time, all fresh and bathed in an effulgence of light and joy, as if a smoke had cleared, or my eyes been peeled, so that I wanted to shout to the vastness, "I love you. I love you, sky, bird, wind, precipice, space sun desert desert desert."

By a happy coincidence, almost exactly 100 years before, an English priest had written those words that were "dinging around" in her head. She effectively celebrated their 100th birthday by recognizing them, and by acknowledging that they expressed her own exhilaration.

Anyone riding a camel into 1700 miles of desert can hardly be blamed for not getting the words quite right! Gerard Manley Hopkins's actual words read:

> I walk, I lift up, I lift my heart, eyes,
> Down all that glory in the heavens . . .
> —"HURRAHING IN HARVEST"

It is not long before she begins to make discoveries, to see the world in ways that could not happen in the town; she learned, for example, to read the sky:

Stars all made sense to me now that I lived under them. They told me the time when I awoke at night for a piss and a check on the bells. They told me where I was and where I was going, but they were cold like bits of frost. One night, I decided to listen to some music and put Eric Satie into the cassette. But the noise sounded alien, incongruous, so I turned it off and sucked on the whisky bottle instead. I talked to myself, rolling the names of the stars and constellations around on my tongue. Goodnight, Aldebaran. See you, Sirius, Adios, Corvus. I was glad there was a crow in the heavens.

As she moved into the desert, further and further from all the reassurances offered by neighbors, by the taken-for-granted proximity of other people, so her perceptions of the uninhabited world of nature began to change, sometimes verging on the panic of extreme disorientation:

I entered a new time, space, dimension. A thousand years fitted into a day and aeons into each step. The desert oaks sighed and bent down to me, as if trying to grab at me. Sandhills came and sandhills went. Hills rose up and hills slipped away. Clouds rolled in and clouds rolled out and always the road, always the road, always the road, always the road . . . time was different here, it was stretched by step after step and in each step a century of circular thought. I didn't want to think like this, was ashamed of my thoughts but I could not stop them. The moon, cold marble and cruel, pushed down on me, sucked at me, I could not hide from it, even in dream.

And the next day and the next day too, the road and the sandhills and the cold wind sucked at my thoughts and nothing happened but walking.

As the solitude took a hold on her mind, so she began to "hear voices" competing for domination:

The sky was leaden and thick. All day it had been grey, smooth, translucent, like the belly of a frog. Spots of rain pattered on me but not enough to lay the dust.

The sky was washing me out, emptying me. I was cold as I hunched over my meagre fire. And somewhere, between frozen sandhills, in a haunted and forgotten desert, where time is always measured by the interminable roll of constellations, or the chill call of a crow waking, I lay down on my dirty bundle of blankets. The frost clung like brittle cobwebs to the black bushes around me, while the sky turned thick with glitter. It was very still. I slept. The hour before the sun spills thin blood colour on the sand, I woke suddenly, and tried to gather myself from a dream I could not remember. I was split. I woke into limbo and could not find myself. There were no reference points, nothing to keep the world controlled and bound together. There was nothing but chaos and the voices.

The strong one, the hating one, the powerful one was mocking me, laughing at me.

"You've gone too far this time. I've got you now and I hate you. You're disgusting, aren't you. You're nothing. And I have you now, I knew it would come, sooner or later. There's no use fighting me you know, there's no one to help you. I've got you, I've got you."

Another voice was calm and warm. She commanded me to lie down and be calm. She instructed me to not let go, not give in. She reassured me that I would find myself again if I could just hold on, be quiet and lie down.

The third voice was screaming.

Diggity woke me at dawn. I was some distance from camp, cramped, and cold to my bones. The sky was cold, pale blue and pitiless, like an Austrian psychopath's eyes. I walked out into the time warp again. I was only half there, like an automaton. I knew what I had to do. "You must do this, this will keep you alive. Remember." I walked out into that evil whispering sea. Like an animal, I sensed a menace, everything was quite still, but threatening, icy, beneath the sun's heat. I felt it watching me, following me, waiting for me.

I tried to conquer the presence with my own voice. It croaked out into the silence and was swallowed by it. "All we have to do," it said, "is reach Mount Fanny, and there is certain to be water there. Just one step and another, that's all I have to do. I must not panic." I could see what had to be Mount Fanny in the hot blue distance, and I wanted to be there, protected by those rocks, more than anything I'd ever wanted. I knew I was being unreasonable. There was more than enough water to get by on to Wingelinna. But the camels, I'd been so sure they'd do a week comfortably. I hadn't planned on the sudden dryness—the lack of green feed. "But there'll be water there, of course there will. Haven't they told me so? What if there's not? What if the mill's run dry? What if I miss it? What if this thin little piece of string that keeps me tied to my camels breaks? What then?" Walk walk walk, sandhills for ever, they all looked the same. I walked as if on a treadmill—no progress, no change. The hill came closer so slowly. "How long is it now? A day? This is the longest day. Careful. Remember, it's just a day. Hold on, mustn't let go. Maybe a car will come. No cars. What if there's no water, what will I do? Must stop this. Must stop. Just keep walking. Just one step at a time, that's all it takes." And on and on and on went that dialogue in my head. Over and over and round and round.

Late in the afternoon—long creeping shadows. The hill was close. "Please please let me be there before night. Please don't let me be here in the dark. It will engulf me."

It must be over the next sandhill surely. No, then the next one. O.K., all right, the next, no the next, no the next. Please god, am I mad. The hill is there, I can almost touch it. I started to yell. I started to shout stupidly at the dunes. Diggity licked my hand and whined but I could not stop. I had been doing this for ever. I walked in slow motion. Everything was slowing down.

And then, over the last sandhill, I was out of the dunes. I crouched on the rocks, weeping, feeling their substance with my hands. I climbed steadily, up the rocky escarpment, away from that terrible ocean of sand. The rocks were heavy and dark and strong. They rose up like an island. I crawled over this giant spine, where it emerged from the waves, in a fuzz of green. I looked back to the immensity of where I had been. Already the memory was receding—the time, the aching time of it. Already, I had forgotten most of the days. They had sunk away from memory, leaving only a few peaks that I could recall. I was safe.

As she made tracks across the desert, she learned to "read" her camels, the landscape, and herself, discovering things that didn't always reassure or gratify her.

The rest of the time I spent worrying over the camels. Zeleika's suspicious lump was suspiciously bigger. When I inspected her peg, I found the inner knob fractured. Oh no, not again. I tied her down, twisted her head around and inserted a new one. I could hardly hear myself think through her bellowing, and did not notice Bub sneaking up behind me. He nipped me on the back of the head, then galloped away, behind Dookie, as startled as I was by his audacity. Camels stick together.

When we were all rested, and when I thought most of our problems were ironed out, we headed off for Tempe Downs station, forty-odd miles to the south, over an unused path through the ranges. I was a bit windy about my ability to navigate through these hills. The people at Areyonga had sapped my confidence by insisting that I call them on the two-way radio when I made it to the other side. No one had used the track for ten years and it would be invisible at times. The range itself was a series of mountains, chasms, canyons and valleys that ran all the way to Tempe, perpendicular to my direction of travel.

It is difficult to describe Australian desert ranges as their beauty is not just visual. They have an awesome grandeur that can fill you with exaltation or dread, and usually a combination of both.

I camped that first night in a washaway, near the ruin of a cottage. I awoke to the muttering of a single crow staring at me not ten feet away. The pre-dawn light, all pastel misty blue and translucent, filtered through the leaves and created a fairy-land. The character of such country changes wonderfully throughout the day, and each change has its effect on one's mood.

I set off clutching map and compass. Every hour or so, my shoulders would tighten and my stomach knot as I searched for the right path. I got lost only once, ending up in a box-canyon and having to back-track to where the path had been obliterated by a series of cattle and donkey tracks. But the constant tension was sapping my energy and I sweated and strained. This went on for two days.

One afternoon, after our midday break, something dropped off Bub's back and he flew into a flat panic. I now had Zeleika in the lead, because of her sore nose, and Bub at the rear. He bucked and he bucked and the more he bucked, the more bits of pack went flying and the more frenzied he became. By the time he stopped, the saddle was dangling under his quivering belly, and the goods were scattered everywhere. I switched into automatic. The other camels were ready to leap out of their skins and head for home. Goliath was galloping between them and generally causing havoc. There was not a tree in sight to tie them to. If I blew this, they might take off and I would never see them again. I couldn't get back to Bub so I whooshed the lead camel down and tied her nose-line to her foreleg, so that if she tried to get up, she would be pulled down. I did the same with Dook, clouted Goliath across the nose with a branch of mulga so that he took off in a cloud of dust, and then went back to Bub. His eyes had rolled with fear and I had to talk to him and pacify him until I knew he trusted me and wouldn't kick. Then I lifted the saddle with my knees and undid the girth on top of his back. Then I gently took it off and whooshed him down like the others. I found a tree a little further on, and beat the living daylights out of him. The whole operation had been quick, sure, steady and precise, like Austrian clockwork—perfect. But now, whatever toxins had been stirred up by the flow of adrenalin hit my bloodstream like the Cayahogan River. I lay by the tree, trembling as hard as Bub. I had been out of control when I beat him and began to recognize a certain Kurtishness in my behaviour. This weakness, my inability to be terrified with any dignity, came to the forefront often during the trip, and my animals took the brunt of it. If, as Hemingway suggested, "courage is grace under pressure," then the trip proved once and for all that I was sadly lacking in the stuff. I felt ashamed.

I learnt a couple of other things from that incident. I learnt to conserve energy by allowing at least part of myself to believe I could cope with any emergency. And I realized that this trip was not a game. There is nothing so real as having to think about survival. It strips you of airy-fairy notions. Believing in omens and fate is all right as long as you know exactly what you are doing. I was becoming very careful and I was coming right back down to earth, where the desert was larger than I could comprehend. And not only was space an ungraspable concept, but my description of time needed reassessment. I was treating the trip like a nine-to-five job. Up bright and early (oh, the guilt if I slept in), boil the billy, drink tea, hurry up it's getting late, nice place for lunch but I can't stay too long . . . I simply could not rid myself of this regimentation. I was furious with myself, but I let it run its course. Better to watch it now, then fight it later when I was feeling stronger. I had a clock which I told myself was for navigation purposes only, but at which I stole furtive glances from time to time. It played tricks on me. In the heat of the afternoon, when I was tired, aching and miserable, the clock would not move, hours lapsed between ticks and tocks. I recognized a need for these absurd arbitrary structures at that stage. I did not know why, but I knew I was afraid of something like chaos. It was as if it were waiting for me to let down my guard and then it would pounce.

On the third day, and to my great relief, I found the well-used station track to Tempe. I called Areyonga on my radio set, that unwanted baggage, that encumbrance, that infringement of my privacy, that big smudgy patch on the purity of my gesture. I screamed into it that I was all right and got nothing but static as a reply.

Arriving in Tempe, I had a pleasant lunch with the people who ran the station, then filled my canteen with precious sweet rainwater from their tanks and continued on my way.

Periodically, her friend Rick, a photographer, flying in a small plane, had to locate her. He had a map of her intended route, and estimated how much ground she would have covered. Before her trek, she had agreed to write an account of it for the *National Geographic* magazine, in exchange for some financial support. Rick's task was to take photographs of her and her animals at various stages of her journey. The first time he met up with her, he brought photographs of her leaving Alice Springs, her setting out:

Rick showed us the slides of the departure from Alice on his projector. . . . They were gorgeous photos, no complaints there, but who was that *Vogue* model tripping romantically along roads with a bunch of camels behind her, hair lifted delicately by sylvan breezes and turned into a golden halo by the back-lighting. Who the hell was she? Never let it be said that the camera does not lie. It lies like a pig in mud. It captures the projections of whoever happens to be using it, never the truth. It was very telling, to see how the batches of images changed radically as the trip progressed.

At first, I found it difficult to talk, to tell them anything, because it seemed that nothing much had in fact happened to me. I had just walked down a road leading a few camels, that's all. But as we sat together that night, in the heavy air of the caravan, my brain started to crack open sideways, spewing forth bits of cement and chicken wire and I knew that the trip was responsible. It was changing me in a way that I had not in the least expected. It was shaking me up and I had not even noticed. It had snuck up from behind.

From time to time, the route of her journey passed through Aborigine reservations and campsites. Rick, dropping in from the sky, proposed to photograph her in the company of Aborigines; the episode served to clarify her values, almost painfully:

It is amazing to me how human beings can remain calm, controlled and sensible on the surface, when internally they are cracking up, crumbling, breaking down. I can see now that that time in Docker was the beginning of a kind of mental collapse, though I would not have described it in such a way then. I was still functioning after all. The whites there were kind and did their best to entertain and look after me, but they could not know that I needed all my energy just to remain in that caravan and lick my wounds. They could not know that they were gutting me with their invitations that I was too morally weak to resist, that my endless smiles hid an overwhelming despair. I wanted to hide, I slept for hour after hour and when I woke up it was into nothingness. Grey nothingness. I was ill.

Whatever justifications for photographing the Aborigines I had come up with before, now were totally shot. It was immediately apparent that they hated it. They knew it was a rip-off. I wanted Rick to stop. He argued that he had a job to do. I looked through a small booklet *Geographic* had given him to record expenditures. In it was "gifts to the natives." I couldn't believe it. I told him to put down five thousand dollars for mirrors and beads, then hand out the money. I also realized that coverage in a conservative magazine like *Geographic* would do the people no good at all, no matter how I wrote the article. They would remain quaint primitives to be gawked at by readers who couldn't really give a damn what was happening to them. I argued with Rick that he was involved in a form of parasitism, and besides, since everyone saw him as my husband, whatever they felt for him, they felt for me too. They were polite and deferential as always, and they took me hunting and food-gathering, but the wall was always there. He came up with all the old arguments, but was torn, I knew, because he recognized it was true. . . . I didn't know whether to continue. It all seemed rather pointless. I had sold the trip, misunderstood and mismanaged everything. I could not be with Aboriginal people without being a clumsy intruder. The journey had lost all meaning, lost all its magical inspiring quality, was an empty and foolish gesture. I wanted to give up. But to do what? Go back to Brisbane? If this, the hardest and most worthwhile thing I had ever attempted, was a miserable failure, then what on earth would succeed? I left Docker, more unhappy, more negative, more weakened than I had ever been.

One night, shortly after her near-nervous collapse, she was able to say, "I was remembering exactly who I was," but even as she enjoyed the return of a sense of wholeness:

That night, I was about to turn in when I heard cars purr in the distance. Such a foreign, incongruous sound. I didn't need them any more, didn't want them. They would be an intrusion. I was even slightly afraid of them, because I knew I was still half crazy. "Yea or nay for human company tonight, Dig? Well let's let the fire do the talking. But will I make sense to them? What if they ask me questions? What will I say? Best thing is just to smile a lot and keep the trap shut, eh, little dog, what you reckon?" I fossicked around in my head, trying to find the pleasantries of conversation that had been blasted into fragments by the previous week's experience. I muttered them to Diggity. "Oh god, they've seen the fire, here they come." I checked myself nervously for signs of dementia.

Aborigines. Warm, friendly, laughing, excited, tired Pitjantjara Aborigines, returning to Wingelinna and Pipalyatjara after a land rights meeting in Warburton. No fear there, they were comfortable with silence. No need to pretend anything. Billies of tea all round. Some sat by the fire and chatted, others drove on home.

The last car, a clapped-out ancient Holden, chug-a-chugged in. One young driver, and three old men. They decided to stay for the night. I shared my tea and blankets. Two of the old men were quiet and smiling. I sat by them in silence, letting their strength seep in. One I especially liked. A dwarfish man with dancing hands, straight back, and on his feet, one huge Adidas and one tiny woman's shoe. He handed me the best bit of his part-cooked rabbit, dripping grease and blood, fur singed and stinking. I ate it gratefully. I remembered that I had not eaten properly for the past few days.

The one I didn't like so well was the voluble one who could speak a little English and knew all about camels and probably everything else in the world as well. He was loud, egotistical, not composed like the others.

Early in the morning, I boiled the billy and started to pack up. I talked to my companions a little. They decided that one of them should accompany me to Pipal-yatjara, two days' walk away, to look after me. I was so sure it was going to be the talkative one, the one who spoke English, and my heart sank.

But as I was about to walk off with the camels, who should join me but—the little man. "Mr. Eddie," he said, and pointed to himself. I pointed to myself and said "Robyn," which I suppose he thought meant "rabbit," since that is the Pitjantjara word for it. It seemed appropriate enough. And then we began to laugh.

*   *   *

For the next two days Eddie and I walked together, we played charades trying to communicate and fell into fits of hysteria at each other's antics. We stalked rabbits and missed, picked bush foods and generally had a good time. He was sheer pleasure to be with, exuding all those qualities typical of old Aboriginal people—strength, warmth, self-possession, wit, and a kind of rootedness, a substantiality that imme-diately commanded respect. And I wondered as we walked along, how the word "primitive" with all its subtle and nasty connotations ever got to be associated with people like this. If, as someone has said, "to be truly civilized, is to embrace disease," then Eddie and his kind were not civilized. Because that was what was so outstanding in him: he was healthy, integrated, whole. That quality radiated from him and you would have to be a complete dolt to miss it.

By now the country had changed dramatically. I was well away from the dreaded pits and hollows of sandhill country. Vast plains covered in yellow grasses like wheat fields swept up to the foot of chocolate-brown rocky mountains and ranges. These were covered at the base by pale green and yellow spinifex and bushes, which slowly gave way to the bare stony outcroppings at the top. Small washaways contained most of the trees, and every now and then just one single bare red sandhill, stuck up in the middle of the yellow. Bright green peeked out of the valleys and chasms, and all of it capped with that infinite dome of cobalt blue. The sense of space, clean bright limitless space was with me again.

However, after all that had happened to me, all that madness and strain, I desperately needed to talk in depth with someone. Because, while my panic and fear had now been supplanted by a frenetic happiness, I was still shaken to the core. Still teetering, I had to recover my ordinary self and make sense of the experience somehow. I was a third of the way through my trip, and Glendle, the community adviser at Pipalyatjara, would be the first and perhaps last friend I was likely to meet. I was longing to see him, to speak in English about all that had been going on. But Eddie kept telling me he had "gone." I found out later that he attached the word "gone" to the ends of many sentences; it roughly implied direction so I need not have worried. But the thought of Glendle being away was too much to bear.

When Eddie walked a little behind I could feel him looking askance at me—feel his puzzled eyes on the back of my head.

"What's wrong with this woman? What doesn't she just relax, she keeps repeating 'Is Glendle there, Eddie, is he there *now*?'"

"Glendle gooooooone," he said, waving his little hand in the air. Whenever he said that he raised his eyebrows and widened his eyes in a comical look of surprised seriousness, but I found it hard to smile. I turned and walked on, trying to control the trembling chin and the tears that threatened to bounce out of my eyeballs at any second and stream down my face.

She need not have worried, for when they reached Pitjantjara, Glendle was indeed there to greet her and to listen to her:

I got busy making the camels comfortable, and then we three went inside for the inevitable Australian ritual of tea-drinking. I started gibbering then, and I didn't stop raving blessed English for a minute. Or laughing.

That high lasted four days. Glendle was a most perfect, perceptive and loving host. He even gave up his crisp-sheeted bed, while he and Eddie slept outside. He swore he preferred sleeping outside and it was only laziness that prevented him from doing so more often, which was probably true. So I accepted gratefully. Not that I hadn't fallen in love with my swag by then, but experiencing the luxury of a bed again was kind of interesting. Diggity was overjoyed.

That night Glendle cooked tea. Eddie had set up camp outside and old men and women were constantly coming up to see him and talk to Glendle and me. I was once again struck by these old people. They were softly spoken, chuckled constantly and seemed totally in control of their actions. And I wished I understood more Pitjantjara. While I could pick out "camel" often, and get the gist of most conversations, I couldn't pick up on abstracts. But I could tell that there were many camel yarns being swapped there that night.

Throughout the days that followed it seemed that there were always people coming up to the caravan to say hello, borrow cups and billy, share a mug of tea, air and resolve grievances, or discuss policies. It was nice, but I wondered how Glendle ever got anything done. He was burdened with endless paper-work dished out by bureaucrats, and he hated it. A community adviser's job may be enviable in some ways, but is essentially thankless. His major role is to formalize the distribution of money to individuals, which task is usually done through the medium of a store, where the people cash their cheques and buy goods at inflated prices. The profits are used to buy those things for the community that the Aboriginal council thinks should be purchased. Trucks for example, or bore parts. He co-ordinates all the systems such as health and education services and acts as a liaison officer between bureaucrats and the people. This, of course, makes him the primary flak-catcher, because Aborigines have little concept of budgets, how and why the money gets there, and the bureaucrats know nothing about the Aboriginal way of life.

The job has other soul-destroying aspects, as I learnt from Glendle. No white person can fully enter Aboriginal reality and the more you learn, the more you're aware of that vast gap of knowledge and understanding. It takes a long time to perceive the various complications and rules attached to such a position, and by that time you are usually burnt out. Some advisers out there became initiated by the old men. This, they thought, would bring them much closer to the people and an understanding of them. It certainly did, but it also set up other problems. In becoming initiated, they found they had conflicting duties and responsibilities to various groups, thus making it difficult to be fair to all.

The job is made more difficult by the fact that the adviser is more aware than the Aborigines of the possible consequences of their decisions, and wants to protect them. Not becoming a paternal-style protectionist means seeing catastrophic mistakes being made, and not being able to do a thing about it except advise, because you know that the only way the people can learn to deal with the white world is to make such mistakes. There will not always be kind-hearted whitefellas around to save the situation and be a buffer zone. At some point the people must become autonomous. A fine line.

And Glendle was tired—boned out. Trying to get things started, against the pressure of governments and with the lack of money, support and facilities, depressed and frustrated him at times. While he was besotted with the country and its people, and while he enjoyed a mutually respectful relationship with them, the work took its toll, as it does on almost everyone involved for any length of time with Aboriginal rights, whether it be out on some settlement or in a legal office in town. There is always just too much to fight. The positive steps are so minuscule, so piffling in the face of the enormity of what is being done to them.

Pipalyatjara, unlike many other settlements, was lucky in that it did not have a multi-tribal population. It did not have the phenomenon of regularly occurring inter-tribal fights between individuals and groups. Traditionally throughout Australia each tribe had perhaps several tribal neighbours. Some of these were important economic and ritual partners, whilst others were regarded as antagonists because of either a history of conflicts or dissimilar customs and beliefs. Nevertheless, their traditional relationships were not taken into account at all when government field officers established the first outposts and settlements. Here in Pipalyatjara, because of the homogeneity, conflict between individuals was strictly controlled by traditional laws and methods for its resolution. The settlement was originally set up years ago as an outstation—an alternative to Wingelinna which had been a mining centre. It was hoped that other outstations would spring up, like satellites, once Pipalyatjara had been established.

The real importance of this approach to Aboriginal settlement is that it allows groups to get away from the institutionalizing pressure of those areas of maximum Western impact—the mission and government settlements. This movement contains an element of withdrawal; the people go of their own volition back to their traditional life-style and traditional lands, where they are able to enact traditional ceremonies, teach their children traditional skills and knowledge, but at the same time take what they see as important from Western culture, if they so desire. It is a life-style which maximizes identity and pride, and minimizes the problems of cultural conflict. The typical outstation ranges from a camp with no Western artefacts at all, not even a gun, to a camp supplemented with services chosen by the occupants. These may include airstrip, water bore, wireless, and caravans containing teaching and medical facilities with perhaps one to several whites teaching in these. This outstation movement seems to be gaining momentum throughout tribal Australia where it is politically possible.

Whilst in Pipalyatjara, I learnt that the Pitjantjara people were trying to have their land turned from leasehold to freehold. The attitude of the elders at first had been to dismiss the whole question. As far as they were concerned they didn't own the land, the land owned them. Their belief was that the earth was traversed in the dream-time by ancestral beings who had supernatural energy and power. These beings were biologically different from contemporary man, some being a synthesis of man and animal, plant, or forces, such as fire or water.

The travels of these dream-time heroes formed the topography of the land, and their energies remained on earth embodied in the tracks they followed, or in special sites or landmarks where important events had taken place. Contemporary man receives part of these energies through a complex association with and duty towards these places. These are what anthropologists call totems—the identification of individuals with particular species of animals and plants and other natural phenomena. Thus particular trees, rocks and other natural objects are imbued with enormous religious significance for the people who own a particular area of country and have the knowledge of ceremonies and stories for that country.

There is no confusion in the minds of Aboriginal people as to who are the traditional caretakers of country. Land "ownership" and responsibility is handed down through both the patriline and matriline. People also have some claim to the land on which they were born or conceived, and there are other more complex relationships between clans whereby the responsibility for land is shared.

The connection between the dream-time, the country, and the traditional caretakers of country is manifested in the complex ceremonies that are performed by clan members. Some are increase ceremonies, ensuring the continued and plentiful existence of plants and animals and maintaining the ecological welfare of the landscape (indeed of the world); some are specifically for the initiation of young boys (making of men); and some are to promote the health and well-being of the community and so on. This detailed body of knowledge, law and wisdom handed down to the people from the dream-time is thus maintained and kept potent, and handed on through generations by the enacting of ritual. Every tribal person has a knowledge of the ceremonies for his/her country and an obligation to respect the sacred sites that belong to them (or rather, to which they belong).

Ceremonies are the visible link between Aboriginal people and their land. Once dispossessed of this land, ceremonial life deteriorates, people lose their strength, meaning, essence and identity.

Her head was still full of "civilized" ways. She continued to think in terms of schedules and goals, even as she modified her plans and made a decision to go with Eddie into the valleys that he knew like the back of his own hand: "I was being torn by two different time concepts. I knew which one made sense, but the other one was fighting hard for survival. Structure, regimentation, orderedness. Which had absolutely nothing to do with anything." Slowly, however, the turmoil, the conflict, faded:

I relaxed into Eddie's time. He was teaching me something about flow, about choosing the right moment for everything, about enjoying the present. I let him take over.

After a few days, my Pitjantjara was improving but it was still useless in fast conversation. This didn't seem to matter at all. It's amazing how well one can communicate with a fellow being when there are no words to get in the way. Our greatest communication lay in the sheer joy in our surroundings. The sound of birds which he taught me to mimic, the gazing at hills, the laughter at the antics of the camels, the hunting for meat, the discovery of things to eat. Sometimes we would sing together or alone, sometimes we shared a pebble to kick down the road—all this was unspoken and perfectly clear. He would quietly chatter and gesticulate to himself and the hills and plants. Outsiders would have thought us on a par for craziness.

We left the track that evening—Eddie had decided to take me through his country. For a week we wandered through that land, and all the while Eddie seemed to grow in stature with every step. He was a dingo-dreaming man, and his links with the special places we passed gave him a kind of energy, a joy, a belonging. He told me myths and stories over and over at night when we camped. He knew every particle of that country as well as he knew his own body. He was at home in it totally, at one with it and the feeling began rubbing off on to me. Time melted—became meaningless. I don't think I have ever felt so good in my entire life. He made me notice things I had not noticed before—noises, tracks. And I began to see how it all fitted together. The land was not wild but tame, bountiful, benign, giving, as long as you knew how to see it, how to be part of it.

Later, they returned to the road:

Neither of us liked being on the road after our time in the wild country, because we had to deal once again with that strange breed of animal, the tourist. It was very hot one afternoon, stinkingly hot, and the flies were in zillions. I had the three p.m. grumps. Eddie was humming to himself. A column of red dust hit the horizon and swirled towards us, hurtling along at tourist speed. We swerved off into the spinifex, pincushions for feet were better than idiots at this hour of the day. But they saw us, of course, a whole convoy of them, daring the great aloneness together like they were in some B-grade Western. They all piled out with their cameras. I was irritated, I just wanted to get to camp and have a cuppa and be left in peace. They were so boorish, so insensitive, these people. They plied me with questions as usual and commented rudely on my appearance, as if I were a sideshow for their amusement. And perhaps I did look a little eccentric at that stage. I had had one ear pierced in Alice Springs the year before. It had taken months to work up the courage to participate in this barbaric custom, but once the hole was made, I wasn't about to let it close over again. I had lost my stud, so put through a large safety pin. I was filthy and my hair stuck out from my hat in sun-bleached greasy tangles. . . . Then they noticed Eddie. One of the men grabbed him by the arm, pushed him into position and said, "Hey, Jacky-Jacky, come and stand alonga camel, boy."

I was stunned into silence. I couldn't believe he had said that. How dare anyone be so thick as to call someone of Eddie's calibre "boy" or "Jacky-Jacky." I furiously pushed past this fool, and Eddie and I walked together away from them. His face betrayed no emotion but he agreed when I suggested that there'd be no more photos and that they could all rot in hell before we'd talk to them. The last of the convoy arrived a few minutes later. I reverted to my old trick of covering my face with my hat and shouting, "No photographs." Eddie echoed me. But as I went past I heard them all clicking away. "Bloody swine," I shouted. I was boiling, hissing with anger. Suddenly, all five foot four inches of Eddie turned around and strutted back to them. They continued clicking. He stood about three inches from one of the women's faces and put on a truly extraordinary show. He turned himself into a perfect parody of a ravingly dangerous idiot boong, waved his stick in the air and trilled Pitjantjara at them and demanded three dollars and cackled insanely and hopped up and down and had them all confused and terrified out of their paltry wits. They'd probably been told in Perth that the blacks were murderous savages. They backed off, handing him what money they had in their pockets and fled. He walked demurely over to me and then we cracked up. We slapped each other and we held our sides and we laughed and laughed the helpless, hysterical tear-flooded laughter of children. We rolled and staggered with laughter. We were paralysed with it.

The thing that impressed me most was that Eddie should have been bitter and he was not. He had used the incident for his own entertainment and mine. Whether he also used it for my edification I do not know.

Then the time came for her and Eddie to go their separate ways:

When it was time for Eddie to leave me, he looked sideways at me for a moment, held my arm, smiled and shook his head. He wrapped his rifle in a shirt, put it in the back of the truck then changed his mind and put it in the front, then changed it again, and laid it carefully in the back. He waved out the window and then he and Glendle and Glendle's friend *wala karnka* ("fast crow") were swallowed up in the dust.

I spent a week in Warburton, floating with happiness. I could not remember ever associating that emotion with myself before. So much of the trip had been wrong and empty and small, and so much of my life previous to it had been boring and predictable, that now when happiness welled up inside me it was as if I were flying through warm blue air. And a kind of aura of happiness was being generated. It rubbed off on people. It built up and got shared around. Yet nothing of the past five months had been anything like I had imagined. None of it had gone according to plan, none of it had lived up to my expectations. There'd been no point at which I could say, "Yes, this is what I did it for," or "Yes, this is what I wanted for myself." In fact, most of it had been simply tedious and tiring.

But strange things do happen when you trudge twenty miles a day, day after day, month after month. Things you only become totally conscious of in retrospect. For one thing I had remembered in minute and Technicolor detail everything that had ever happened in my past and all the people who belonged there. I had remembered every word of conversations I had had or overheard way, way back in my childhood and in this way I had been able to review these events with a kind of emotional detachment as if they had happened to somebody else. I was rediscovering and getting to know people who were long since dead and forgotten. I had dredged up things that I had no idea existed. People, faces, names, places, feelings, bits of knowledge, all waiting for inspection. It was a giant cleansing of all the garbage and muck that had accumulated in my brain, a gentle catharsis. And because of that, I suppose, I could now see much more clearly into my present relationships with people and with myself. And I was happy, there is simply no other word for it.

So she moved on, with the knowledge that she would have no human companionship for the next month: but there was plenty to keep the mind occupied:

Throughout the trip I had been gaining an awareness and an understanding of the earth as I learnt how to depend upon it. The openness and emptiness which had at first threatened me were now a comfort which allowed my sense of freedom and joyful aimlessness to grow. This sense of space works deep in the Australian collective consciousness. It is frightening and most of the people huddle around the eastern seaboard where life is easy and space a graspable concept, but it produces a sense of potential and possibility nevertheless that may not exist now in any European country. It will not be long, however, before the land is conquered, fenced up and beaten into submission. But here, here it was free, unspoilt and seemingly indestructible.

And as I walked through that country, I was becoming involved with it in a most intense and yet not fully conscious way. The motions and patterns and connections of things became apparent on a gut level. I didn't just see the animal tracks, I knew them. I didn't just see the bird, I knew it in relationship to its actions and effects. My environment began to teach me about itself without my full awareness of the process. It became an animate being of which I was a part. The only way I can describe how the process occurred is to give an example: I would see a beetle's tracks in the sand. What once would have been merely a pretty visual design with few associations attached, now became a sign which produced in me instantaneous associations—the type of beetle, which direction it was going in and why, when it made the tracks, who its predators were. Having been taught some rudimentary knowledge of the pattern of things at the beginning of the trip, I now had enough to provide a structure in which I could learn to learn. A new plant would appear and I would recognize it immediately because I could perceive its association with other plants and animals in the overall pattern, its place. I would recognize and know the plant without naming it or studying it away from its environment. What was once a thing that merely existed became something that everything else acted upon and had a relationship with and vice versa. In picking up a rock I could no longer simply say, "This is a rock," I could now say, "This is part of a net," or closer, "This, which everything acts upon, acts." When this way of thinking became ordinary for me, I too became lost in the net and the boundaries of myself stretched out for ever. In the beginning I had known at some level that this could happen. It had frightened me then. I had seen it as a chaotic principle and I fought it tooth and nail. I had given myself the structures of habit and routine with which to fortify myself and these were very necessary at the time. Because if you are fragmented and uncertain it is terrifying to find the boundaries of yourself melt. Survival in a desert, then, requires that you lose this fragmentation, and fast. It is not a mystical experience, or rather, it is dangerous to attach these sorts of words to it. They are too hackneyed and prone to misinterpretation. It is something that happens, that's all. Cause and effect. In different places, survival requires different things, based on the environment. Capacity for survival may be the ability to be changed by environment.

Changing to this view of reality had been a long hard struggle against the old conditioning. Not that it was a conscious battle, rather it was being forced on me and I could either accept it or reject it. In rejecting it I had almost gone over the edge. The person inside whom I had previously relied on for survival had, out here and in a different circumstance, become the enemy. This internal warring had almost sent me around the bend. The intellectual and critical faculties did everything they could think of to keep the boundaries there. They dredged up memory. They became obsessed with time and measurement. But they were having to take second place, because they simply were no longer necessary. The subconscious mind became much more active and important. And this in the form of dreams, feelings. A growing awareness of the character of a particular place, whether it was a good place to be with a calming influence, or whether it gave me the creeps. And this all linked up with Aboriginal reality, their vision of the world as being something they could never be separate from, which showed in their language. In Pitjantjara and, I suspect, all other Aboriginal languages, there is no word for "exist." Everything in the universe is in constant interaction with everything else. You cannot say, this is a rock. You can only say, there sits, leans, stands, falls over, lies down, a rock.

The self did not seem to be an entity living somewhere inside the skull, but a reaction between mind and stimulus. And when the stimulus was non-social, the self had a hard time defining its essence and realizing its dimensions. The self in a desert becomes more and more like the desert. It has to, to survive. It becomes limitless, with its roots more in the subconscious than the conscious—it gets stripped of non-meaningful habits and becomes more concerned with realities related to survival. But as is its nature, it desperately wants to assimilate and make sense of the information it receives, which in a desert is almost always going to be translated into the language of mysticism.

What I'm trying to say is, when you walk on, sleep on, stand on, defecate on, wallow in, get covered in, and eat the dirt around you, and when there is no one to remind you what society's rules are, and nothing to keep you linked to that society, you had better be prepared for some startling changes. And just as Aborigines seem to be in perfect rapport with themselves and their country, so the embryonic beginnings of that rapport were happening to me. I loved it.

And my fear had a different quality now too. It was direct and useful. It did not incapacitate me or interfere with my competence. It was the natural, healthy fear one needs for survival.

Although I talked constantly to myself, or Diggity or the country around me, I was not lonely—on the contrary, had I suddenly stumbled across another human being, I would have either hidden, or treated it as if it were just another bush or rock or lizard.

As she learned to live in a new way, the values of her own culture and those she was newly discovering engaged in strenuous debate in her mind:

I took out my clock, wound it, set the alarm for four o'clock and left it ticking on the stump of a tree near our dust bath. A fitting and appropriate end for that insidious little instrument, I thought, and that was that preoccupation taken care of. I executed, in celebration, clumsy little steps like a soft-shoe dancer with lead in his feet. I probably looked like a senile old derelict in fact, with my over-large sandals, filthy baggy trousers, my torn shirt, my calloused hands and feet and my dirt-smeared face. I liked myself this way, it was such a relief to be free of disguises and prettiness and attractiveness. Above all that horrible, false, debilitating attractiveness that women hide behind. I pulled my hat down over my ears so that they stuck out beneath it. "I must remember this when I get back. I must not fall into that trap again." I must let people see me as I am. Like this? Yes, why not like this. But then I realized that the rules pertaining to one set of circumstances do not necessarily pertain to another. Back there, this would just be another disguise. Back there, there was no nakedness, no one could afford it. Everyone had their social personae well fortified until they got so drunk and stupid that their nakedness was ugly. Now why was this? Why did people circle one another, consumed with either fear or envy, when all that they were fearing or envying was illusion? Why did they build psychological fortresses and barriers around themselves that would take a Ph.D. in safe-cracking to get through, which even they could not penetrate from the inside? And once again I compared European society with Aboriginal. The one so arche- typally paranoid, grasping, destructive, the other so sane. I didn't want ever to leave this desert. I knew that I would forget.

Her journey involved her not only in a first reading of what she had never before encountered, but also in a re-reading, a re-interpretation, of the familiar. As she got to know Diggity better, she came to some fascinating conclusions:

As if walking twenty miles a day wasn't enough, I often went out hunting or just exploring with Diggity after I had unsaddled the camels of an afternoon. On one such afternoon, I had got myself vaguely lost. Not completely lost, just a little bit, enough to make my stomach tilt, rather than turn. I could, of course, back-track, but this always took time and it was getting dark. In the past, whenever I wanted Diggity to guide me home, I simply said to her, "Go home, girl," which she thought was a kind of punishment. She would flatten those crazy ears to her head, roll her amber brown eyes at me, tuck her tail between her legs and glance over her shoulder, every part of her saying, "Why are you doing this to me. What did I do wrong?" But that evening, she made a major breakthrough.

She immediately grasped the situation: you could see a light bulb flash above her head. She barked at me, ran forward a few yards, turned back, barked, ran up and licked my hand, and then scampered forward again and so on. I pretended I didn't understand. She was beside herself with worry. She repeated these actions and I began to follow her. She was ecstatic, overjoyed. She had understood something and she was proud of it. When we made it back to camp, I hugged her and made a great fuss of her and I swear that animal laughed. And that look of pride, that unmistakable pleasure in having comprehended something, perceived the reason and necessity for it, made her wild, hysterical with delight. When she was pleased over something or someone, her tail did not go back and forward, it whipped round and round in a complete circle and her body contorted into S-bends like a snake.

I am quite sure Diggity was more than dog, or rather other than dog. In fact, I have often thought her father was a vet perhaps. She combined all the best qualities of dog and human and was a great listener. She was by now a black glossy ball of health and muscle. She must have done a hundred miles a day with her constant scampering and bounding after lizards in the spinifex. The trip, of necessity, had brought me much closer to all the animals, but my relationship with Diggity was something special. There are very few humans with whom I could associate the word love as easily as I did with that wonderful little dog. It is very hard to describe this interdependence without sounding neurotic. But I loved her, doted on her, could have eaten her with my overwhelming affection. And she never, not ever, not once, retracted her devotion no matter how churlish, mean or angry I became. Why dogs chose humans in the first place I will never understand.

O.K., you fusty old Freudians, you laudable Laingians,* my psyche is up for grabs. I have admitted a weak point. Dogs.

Animals lovers, especially female ones, are often accused of being neurotic and unable to relate successfully to other human beings. How many times had friends noted my relationship to Diggity, and, with that baleful look usually associated with psychiatrists, said, "You've never thought of having a child, have you?" It's an accusation that brings an explosive response every time because it seems to me that the good lord in his infinite wisdom gave us three things to make life bearable— hope, jokes, and dogs, but the greatest of these was dogs.†

I was by now quite happy about camping by or on the track. The thought of anyone driving down it had long since faded into the impossible. But I had not taken into account madmen and fruit-cakes. I was awakened from my slumber one night by the roar of an engine. I struggled out of deep sleep with Diggity barking in fury, and a voice calling from the dark, "Hey, is that the camel lady, it's the overlander here. Do I have permission to enter camp?"

"What the . . . ?"

An apparition appeared before me, with Dig biting at his trouser legs. The "overlander," as it turned out, was some nut testing a Suzuki vehicle by driving it across the widest part of Australia, over spinifex, sand and gibbers, just as fast as he possibly could. He was breaking some kind of record. He was also manic, and, presumably, out of his mind on speed. His eyeballs hung out on his cheeks and he kept slapping his upper arms, commenting on the cold, and hinting that he wouldn't mind camping here. I most certainly didn't want him camping anywhere near here, and neither did Dig. I made this quite plain without being out and out rude. He sat and raved at me for half an hour, with Dig quietly growling at the foot of my bed, and me pointedly yawning and saying very little except, "Hmm, oh really, that's nice, yawn, hmm, you don't say," and so on. He then informed me that he had been following my tracks for miles, which, considering he was coming from the opposite direction, was no mean feat. He eventually left. I scratched my head for a while,

---

*R. D. Laing was a fashionable psychoanalyst in the 60s and 70s.

†Does Robyn Davidson exaggerate the virtues and talents of her dog? Thomas Keneally, the Australian novelist, who admits that "even as a child I detested the bogus sentimentality of dog stories," insists that Australian cattle dogs are "real colleagues. . . . In the cattle business, dogs are colleagues, and the brightest can talk." One dog owner, who flies a small Cessna plane when herding his cattle, told Keneally, "If ever I snooze off at the controls of the Cessna, she nudges me as soon as the plane gets out of altitude." (*Outback*, p. 102)

and shook it just to make sure I hadn't been hallucinating, and went back to sleep. I forgot about it.

Her solitude, when not broken by intruders, allowed her extraordinary freedom:

It is extraordinary that the two most commonly asked questions about the trip (after "Why did you do it?") are . . . one. What did you do when you ran out of toilet paper? and two (and this is always whispered over in the corner by women who giggle a lot), What did you do when you ran out of Meds?* What on earth do you think I did? Ran to the nearest chemist shop to barter? Well, for all those who remain morbidly curious over body functions, when I ran out of toilet paper, I used smooth rocks, grass and, when lucky, a kindly desert plant known as pussy-cat tails. When I ran out of Meds, I didn't care.

In fact, to this day, I think one of the major breakthroughs I made on that trip was learning the gentle art of farting. I had never farted before. Well, maybe once or twice, but then only pathetic little pfffttts. God knows what happened to all that air. Must have seeped through the pores of my skin at night I suppose. Ah, but now, now I could blart with the best of them—good solid base thrums which spooked the camels and scared flocks of spinifex pigeons into the air. Diggity and I had competitions: she always won for poisonousness, I for sonorousness.

But all good things have to come to an end, and finally she reached her destination, the West coast: soon, she arranged for her camels to retire to a comfortable home, and then she began to try to sum up her reading of the meaning of her extraordinary journey:

I took the camels (all except Zeleika who stubbornly refused even to paddle) for swims; I crunched my way over the beach that was so white it was blinding and gazed at little green and red glass-like plants, and I relaxed in the firelight under bloodshot skies. The camels were still dazed by the water—still insisted that it was drinkable, even after pulling faces and spitting it out time and time again. Often they would come down to the beach at sunset to stand and stare.

And once again, and for the last time, I soared. I had pared my possessions down to almost nothing—a survival kit, that's all. I had a filthy old sarong for hot weather and a jumper and woolly socks for cold weather and I had something to sleep on and something to eat and drink out of and that was all I needed. I felt free and untrammelled and light and I wanted to stay that way. If I could only just hold on to it. I didn't want to get caught up in the madness out there.

*Meds: sanitary napkins.

Poor fool, I really believed all that crap. I was forgetting that what's true in one place is not necessarily true in another. If you walk down Fifth Avenue smelling of camel shit and talking to yourself you get avoided like the plague. Even your best American buddies will not want to know you. The last poor fragile shreds of my romantic naïvety were about to get shrivelled permanently by New York City, where I would be in four days' time, shell-shocked, intimidated by the canyons of glass and cement, finding my new adventuress's identity kit ill-fitting and uncomfortable, answering inane questions which made me feel like I should be running a pet shop, defending myself against people who said things like, "Well, honey, what's next, skateboards across the Andes?" and dreaming of a different kind of desert.

On my last morning, before dawn, while I was cooking breakfast, Rick stirred in his sleep, sat up on an elbow, fixed me with an accusing stare and said, "How the hell did you get those camels here?"

"What?"

"You killed their parents, didn't you?"

He sneered and gloated knowingly for a second then dropped back into unconsciousness, remembering nothing of it later. There was some kind of rudimentary truth hidden in that dream somewhere.

Jan and David arrived with the truck and I loaded my now plump and cheeky beasties on it and took them back to their retirement home. They had many square miles to roam in, people to love and spoil them, and nothing to do but spend their dotage facing Mecca and contemplating the growth of their humps. I spent hours saying goodbye to them. Tearing myself away from them caused actual physical pain, and I kept going back to sink my forehead into their woolly shoulders and tell them how wonderful and clever and faithful and true they were and how I would miss them. Rick then drove me to Carnarvon, one hundred miles north where I would pick up the plane that would wing me back to Brisbane, then to New York. I remember nothing of that car ride, except trying to hide the embarrassingly huge amounts of salt water that cascaded out of my eyeballs.

In Carnarvon, a town about the size of Alice Springs, I suffered the first wave of culture shock that was to rock me in the months ahead, and from which I think I have never fully recovered. Where was the brave Boadicea of the beaches? "Bring on New York," she had said. "Bring on *Geographic*, I'm invincible." But now, she had slunk away to her shell under the onslaught of all those freakish-looking people, and cars and telegraph poles and questions and champagne and rich food. I was taken to dinner by the local magistrate and his wife who opened a magnum bottle of bubbly. Half way through the meal I collapsed and crawled outside to throw up over an innocent fire truck, with Rick holding my forehead saying, "There there, it will all be all right," and me saying, between gasps, "No, no it's not, it's awful, I want to go back."

As I look back on the trip now, as I try to sort out fact from fiction, try to remember how I felt at that particular time, or during that particular incident, try to relive those memories that have been buried so deep, and distorted so ruthlessly, there is one clear fact that emerges from the quagmire. The trip was easy. It was no more dangerous than crossing the street, or driving to the beach, or eating peanuts. The two important things that I did learn were that you are as powerful and strong as you allow yourself to be, and that the most difficult part of any endeavour is taking the first step, making the first decision. And I knew even then that I would forget them time and time again and would have to go back and repeat those words that had become meaningless and try to remember. I knew even then that, instead of remembering the truth of it, I would lapse into a useless nostalgia. Camel trips, as I suspected all along, and as I was about to have confirmed, do not begin or end, they merely change form.

What Do We Have to "Read" in Order to Write Autobiography?

Where were you when you were reading Robyn Davidson's text? Does that strike you as a silly question? If so, let us explain what we are trying to get at.

Obviously, in the common-sense meaning, you were *physically*, actually in a particular place, sitting down or lounging on your bed, possibly with witnesses who would so testify. But what of the distinctive power of your mind to envision itself, to "experience" itself, as being somewhere else—somewhere you may in fact never actually have been? Such is the power of imagining: a means of reconstructing moments of your own past life and of constructing others' lives (represented to your eyes as print, to your mind as meaning) as if you either stood invisibly at their side or even occupied a space behind their eyes.

What, then, is a reader's relationship with such a text? We suspect that it is a delicate and subtle interaction of two ways of being: of being *inside* and of being *outside*. As one becomes gripped by someone's story, involved in it, one moves as if by telepathy into their mind, and construes their experiences through their particular consciousness. This can happen so intensely that, as one becomes oblivious of oneself, it is as if one actually *becomes* the other person: so that one feels their emotions, registers their responses, takes on their point of view.*

Then, at some moment, one's concentration is broken, and one "comes out"— just as Robyn Davidson eventually came out of the events of her journey and transformed them into experiences by thinking, reflecting, evaluating, weighing, judging, sussing out the significances, the gain and loss, the *point* of those events.

After we have "come out of" being inside, so we ourselves in turn can perform the same operations on our experience of Robyn Davidson's text: weighing it, evaluating it, coming to some kind of conclusion—however tentative— about what it meant to us, what it gave us, in what ways it *changed* our minds, extended, deepened, enriched them.

Always there is a gap, a break, between being *inside* the reading and being *outside* it, just as there was a gap for Robyn Davidson between "doing it" and "writing it." We shall never be able to "catch" all that happens to us when we read. Our best hope is probably to choose to refrain from actually lying about it, deceiving both ourselves and others: the better, the richer, the more powerful the experience of reading is, the more difficult it is to represent it to others. (See Judith Condon, p. 164.)

Meanwhile we invite you to consider this: that Robyn Davidson herself went on a journey and also "went" on a "journey"—a journey of exploration—into her own beliefs and assumptions, her values and her ideology; a journey that involved a collision between the values of her own dominant white culture and the values of the increasingly marginal Aboriginal culture. And, as you participated in those two journeys, you also "went" on a "journey," through the inner landscape of your own mind, your own past, and, in so doing, became involved in reading, re-reading, re-interpreting, revising and reevaluating your own assumptions. In some degree, we trust that nothing will ever again be quite the same.

When you sit down with a good friend to tell them something of your past, say of some experience that still seems important to you, what exactly are you doing?

Can you be said to be "reading"? Before you answer that question, let us make a distinction: (a) we can assume that you are simply "making it up," creating a fiction in order to gain your friend's sympathy, or to make yourself appear more "interesting." Conversely, (b) we can assume that you are trying very hard

*Cf. Philip Roth, p. 382.

to tell the "truth." If your story is truthful, where does it exist before you speak the words? Where is it coming from?

It seems to us that the telling or writing of autobiography is a form of *reading*. In shaping our utterance, we are, it seems, involved in reading and re-reading, glancing at images (visual memories), listening to sounds, especially of voices, (auditory memories), generating words to represent them, and almost simultaneously listening to ("reading") our representations—modifying them, extending them, revising them almost as soon as we have discovered them in our minds.

What, then, do we do when we try to tell the "truth" about our past? Most of us probably try to remember as much as possible. Some of this seems to "come to mind," is "recalled" in the form of words: we "hear" our inner speech saying it; and we also experience the illusion of others speaking, as they spoke then, in the past they shared with us. But the past *is* past; it cannot literally be recalled—we cannot call it back into the present moment. Much of what we remember comes to us in the form of fleeting images, visual images, rather like fragments of old movies or snapshots from a family photograph album. If we are going to represent these "scenes" in words, we have to convert, transform, them into language: we have to *reconstruct* them. And this is where telling the truth becomes curiously interesting. Let's assume that we jot these down, as notes, in order not to lose them. What then is on the paper? A collection of jottings: the verbal representation of those primary fleeting images. But even those raw jottings are something other than the "reality," the actuality. As soon as we use language, we are creating a text that is *not* the original fact but, rather, our representation of it. And our representation is shaped, inevitably, by our own needs and desires, which always come into play whenever we *will* ourselves to remember (as opposed to those moments when memories spring unbidden into our consciousness.)

Thus, to think of memory as a storehouse of images, of past sensations—faces, things, seen, heard, touched, smelt—is probably inaccurate; our memories themselves seem to *consist* of language—our language, our version of the past. We remember what we have verbalized, not as a trace of the original event, but rather as our experience translated into language; and when we *recall*, we create *mental* images from what that inner stored language (our own language) tells us. Remembering, then, is not like opening an album and taking out the photographs. It is, rather, a matter of recalling our *stories:* and we tell ourselves stories—represent experiences to ourselves as narratives—*not* while we are having the experience itself, but *afterwards*. Thus what we recall, our story, is itself a *reconstruction* of the experience. When we write a memory down, then, we are reconstructing a reconstruction! And *our* versions, *our* stories, *our* reconstructions will all be shaped in accordance with our "theory of the world," in accordance with the values, beliefs, assumptions that make sense to us.

The powerful trick of good writers is to prevent us from worrying about all this, and to convince us that their representation of past experiences is as reliable as we need it to be. But as soon as we read their "stories" carefully, we see that, unlike memory, they contain no irrelevant matter, nothing that just happens to be there because it *is* there. Our memories, however, are crammed with accidental bits and pieces, fragments that seem to have no meaning that we can discover. The task of the writer's text, however, is to *make* meaning—to select and to shape, so that the text has an effective form or structure: so that each detail *counts* or *tells*, adds its part to the creation of a coherent whole, which will affect its reader in ways that the writer tries to control.

It seems that in every representation and presentation of memory, we may indeed be trying to "tell the truth," but, in order to do so, we have to make it up!

When thou a **Dangerous-Way** *doſt goe,*
Walke ſurely, though thy pace be ſlowe.

ILLVSTR. XIX.   *Book.* I.

YOUR WRITING(S) FOR OTHERS TO READ

1. Give an account of the most important journey you have ever taken. What effects did it have on you? What discoveries did you make about the world? Yourself?
2. If you were to sit down to write your own autobiography, what three or four experiences would you choose as of greatest importance?

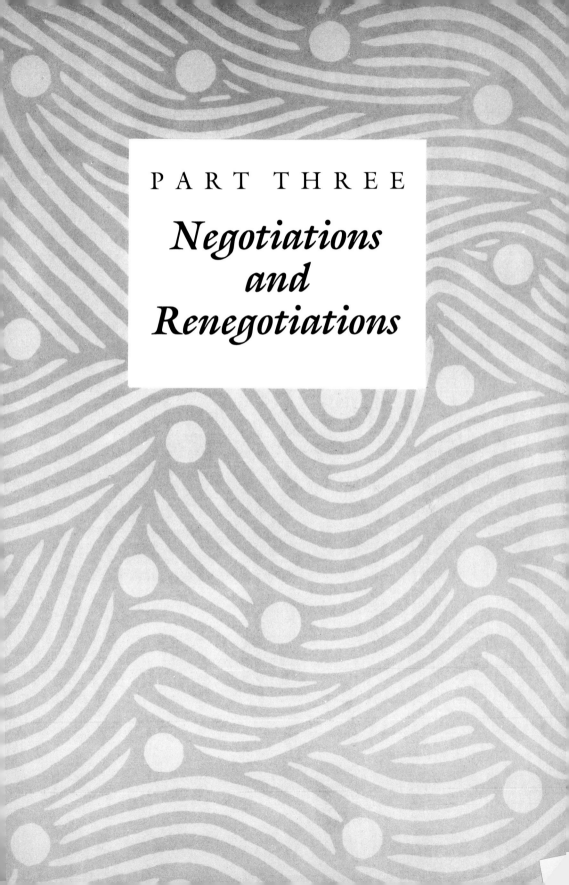

PART THREE

Negotiations and Renegotiations

Chapter Nine

Reading Culture

To the Eyes of a Miser a Guinea is far more beautiful than the Sun, & a bag worn with the use of Money has more beautiful proportions than a Vine filled with Grapes. The tree which moves some to tears of joy is in the Eyes of others only a Green thing which stands in the way. Some see Nature all Ridicule & Deformity, and by these I shall not regulate my proportions; & some scarce see Nature at all. But to the Eyes of the Man of Imagination, Nature is Imagination itself. As a man is, so he sees. As the Eye is formed, such are its Powers.

WILLIAM BLAKE

The face of the water [of the Mississippi] in time became a wonderful book—a book that was a dead language to the uneducated passenger but which told its mind to me without reserve, delivering its most cherished secrets as clearly as if it uttered them with a voice. And it was not a book to be read once and then thrown away. . . .

MARK TWAIN

There is learning "from life," and there is school learning. There are "the old ways," and there are "the new ways." There is conservation (a form of conservatism), and there is progress. There is the familiar, and there is the strange. There is nature, and there is cultivation (culture). There is youthful innocence, and there is adult experience. There is folk culture, and there is urban sophisticated culture.

247

In the interplay of these pairs is the active, sometimes tense movement of lives, of values, of beliefs, of positives, and of negatives. It is this interplay and tension that constitute the dynamic movement within any culture: old values and new, old fashions and new, old people and young, vested interests and innovation—at every moment these are involved in applying pressure, asserting their claim for recognition, for realization.

This chapter begins with a brief recapitulation; we first hear two or three voices that speak for the older claims of nature, but these are quickly displaced by the invasion of culture: with William James's text, the chapter moves irreversibly into the establishment of culture. Some cultures incorporate a sense of intimacy with natural forces into their values; most, however, as they evolve, find less and less space for them. Seamus Heaney's text shows us one individual moving from a folk culture to the more bookish culture institutionalized in schools and colleges.

In this chapter, you will meet texts which show how nature has to yield to the human need for settlements, for a roof over the head, for cultivation, for the million and one bits of paraphernalia, the technologies, the material transformations on which modern cultures have come to depend, and to take for granted.

The process of change is a complicated matter of both gain and loss: how much should we pay for progress? And if x wins, must y lose?

D. H. LAWRENCE

I Think There Are Too Many Trees

In 1921, D. H. Lawrence published an essay, Psychoanalysis and the Unconscious, *his response to the spread of Freud's theory of the unconscious. When it was published, the critics ridiculed it. As a reaction to his critics, Lawrence, living temporarily in the Black Forest, in Germany, wrote his reply,* Fantasia of the Unconscious, *one of the most intelligent and infuriating statements of beliefs about how to raise and educate children.*

He wrote much of it in the open air, and one day the trees around him simply seemed to demand his attention; so he turned aside from his main theme, and gave his attention to the trees.

Oh, damn the miserable baby with its complicated ping-pong table of an unconscious. I'm sure, dear reader, you'd rather have to listen to the brat howling in the crib than to me . . .

But he gets on my nerves. I come out solemnly with a pencil and an exercise book, and take my seat in all gravity at the foot of a large fir-tree, and wait for thoughts to come, gnawing like a squirrel on a nut. But the nut's hollow.

I think there are too many trees. They seem to crowd round and stare at me, and I feel as if they nudged one another when I'm not looking. I can *feel* them standing there. And they won't let me get on about the baby this morning. Just their cussedness. I felt they encouraged me like a harem of wonderful silent wives, yesterday.

It is half rainy too—the wood so damp and still and so secret, in the remote morning air. Morning, with rain in the sky, and the forest subtly brooding, and me feeling no bigger than a pea-bug between the roots of my fir. The trees seem so much bigger than me, so much stronger in life, prowling silent around. I seem to feel them moving and thinking and prowling, and they overwhelm me. Ah, well, the only thing is to give way to them.

It is the edge of the Black Forest—sometimes the Rhine far off, on its Rhine plain, like a bit of magnesium ribbon. But not today. Today only trees, and leaves, and vegetable presences. Huge straight fir-trees, and big beech-trees sending rivers of roots into the ground. And cuckoos, like noise falling in drops off the leaves. And me, a fool, sitting by a grassy wood-road with a pencil and a book, hoping to write more about that baby.

Never mind. I listen again for noises, and I smell the damp moss. The looming trees, so straight. And I listen for their silence. Big, tall-bodied trees, with a certain magnificent cruelty about them. Or barbarity. I don't know why I should say cruelty. Their magnificent, strong, round bodies! It almost seems I can hear the slow, powerful sap drumming in their trunks. Great full-blooded trees, with strange tree-blood in them, soundlessly drumming.

Trees that have no hands and faces, no eyes. Yet the powerful sap-scented blood roaring up the great columns. A vast individual life, and an overshadowing will. The will of a tree. Something that frightens you.

Suppose you want to look a tree in the face? You can't. It hasn't got a face. You look at the strong body of a trunk: you look above you into the matted body-hair of twigs and boughs: you see the soft green tips. But there are no eyes to look into, you can't meet its gaze. You keep on looking at it in part and parcel.

It's no good looking at a tree, to know it. The only thing is to sit among the roots and nestle against its strong trunk, and not bother. That's how I write . . . between the toes of a tree, forgetting myself against the great ankle of the trunk. And then, as a rule, as a squirrel is stroked into its wickedness by the faceless magic of a tree, so am I usually stroked into forgetfulness, and into scribbling this book. My tree-book, really.

I come so well to understand tree-worship. All the old Aryans* worshipped the tree. My ancestors. The tree of life. The tree of knowledge. Well, one is bound to sprout out some time or other, chip of the old Aryan block. I can so well understand tree-worship. And fear the deepest motive.

Naturally. This marvellous vast individual without a face, without lips or eyes or heart. This towering creature that never had a face. Here am I between his toes like a pea-bug, and him noiselessly over-reaching me. And I feel his great blood-jet surging. And he has no eyes. But he turns two ways. He thrusts himself tremen-

*Aryans: Northern Europeans of Indo-European descent.

dously down to the middle earth, where dead men sink in darkness, in the damp, dense undersoil, and he turns himself about in high air. Whereas we have eyes on one side of our head only, and only grow upwards.

Plunging himself down into the black humus, with a root's gushing zest, where we can only rot dead; and his tips in high air, where we can only look up to. So vast and powerful and exultant in his two directions. And all the time, he has no face, no thought: only a huge, savage, thoughtless soul. Where does he even keep his soul? Where does anybody?

A huge, plunging, tremendous soul. I would like to be a tree for a while. The great lust of roots. Root-lust. And no mind at all. He towers, and I sit and feel safe. I like to feel him towering round me. I used to be afraid. I used to fear their lust, their rushing black lust. But now I like it, I worship it. I always felt them huge primeval enemies. But now they are my only shelter and strength. I lose myself among the trees. I am so glad to be with them in their silent, intent passion, and their great lust. They feed my soul. . . .

And I can so well understand the Romans, their terror of the bristling Hercynian wood.* Yet when you look from a height down upon the rolling of the forest—this Black Forest—it is as suave as a rolling, oily sea. Inside only, it bristles horrific. And it terrified the Romans.

The Romans! They too seem very near. Nearer than Hindenburg or Foch or even Napoleon.** When I look across the Rhine plain, it is Rome and the legionaries of the Rhine that my soul notices. It must have been wonderful to come from South Italy to the shores of this sea-like forest: this dark, moist forest, with its enormously powerful intensity of tree life. Now I know, coming myself from rock-dry Sicily, open to the day.

The Romans and the Greeks found everything human. Everything had a face, and a human voice.† Men spoke, and their fountains piped an answer.

But when the legions crossed the Rhine they found a vast impenetrable life which had no voice. They met the faceless silence of the Black Forest. This huge, huge wood did not answer when they called. Its silence was too crude and massive. And the soldiers shrank: shrank before the trees that had no faces, and no answer. A vast array of non-human life, darkly self-sufficient, and bristling with indomitable energy. The Hercynian wood, not to be fathomed. The enormous power of these collective trees, stronger in their somber life even than Rome.

No wonder the soldiers were terrified. No wonder they thrilled with horror when, deep in the woods, they found the skulls and trophies of their dead comrades upon the trees. The trees had devoured them: silently, in mouthfuls, and left the white bones. Bones of the mindful Romans—and savage, preconscious trees, indomitable. . . .

But after bone-dry Sicily, and after the gibbering of myriad people all rattling their personalities, I am glad to be with the profound indifference of faceless trees. Their rudimentariness cannot know why we care for the things we care for. They

* Hercynian wood: Bohemian mountainous forests in Middle Germany.
** Lawrence recalls the leaders of the Germans and the French in World War I, which had virtually wiped out a generation of young men; the war had ended three years before.
† Cf. Margaret Atwood, p. 202.

have no faces, no minds and bowels: only deep, lustful roots stretching in earth, and vast, lissome life in air, and primeval individuality. . . . But they will live you down.

The normal life of one of these big trees is about a hundred years. . . .

One of the few places that my soul will haunt, when I am dead, will be this. Among the trees here near Ebersteinburg, where I have been alone and written this book. I can't leave these trees. They have taken some of my soul.

Excuse my digression, gentle reader. At first I left it out, thinking we might not see wood for trees. But it doesn't much matter what we see. It's nice just to look round, anywhere.

ROBERT FROST

Stopping by Woods on a Snowy Evening

Here, the poet Robert Frost (1874–1963) creates a scene where the "I" is arrested by trees, in this case, by a snowy wood. The poem that follows is one of the best-known in the American canon, that collection of literary texts that constitute the standards, the novels, short stories, and poems, that American college students are expected to meet some time or another in their college careers. No doubt you've met this poem before in a literature anthology.

Whose woods these are I think I know.
His house is in the village though;
He will not see me stopping here
To watch his woods fill up with snow.

My little horse must think it queer   5
To stop without a farmhouse near
Between the woods and frozen lake
The darkest evening of the year.

He gives his harness bells a shake
To ask if there is some mistake.   10
The only other sound's the sweep
Of easy wind and downy flake.

The woods are lovely, dark and deep.
But I have promises to keep,
And miles to go before I sleep,   15
And miles to go before I sleep.

A favorite scene on Christmas cards is snow, trees, a horse-drawn sleigh, a traveler moving toward a lighted window: the coexistence of an obliging nature that provides a pretty background to human civilization, which by nighttime will be safely tucked indoors, before a blazing fire.

Such is the idyllic scene, the pastoral cliché, that Frost quietly transforms into a sober meditation on the *social* dimensions of human culture: social obligations, social responsibilities take us away from the self-indulgent pleasure of imbibing something of the "lovely, dark and deep." And let's make no mistake: these are not the natural, untouched woods of D. H. Lawrence's text; they *belong* to someone, they are *property:* no longer nature, but part of a rural culture. Similarly, the horse itself, however "little" it may be—why, indeed, does Frost describe it as *little?*—has also been acculturated into the constraints and routines of human society: it knows that when it goes about its normal business with its driver, it does not stop *here*.

You may have noticed that Frost's poem is representing, not a *way of being*, but a way of *reflecting* on ways of being, thinking about them, considering them: it is *consideration* of social obligations that prevents the driver from staying longer to enjoy a "way of being" in an uninterrupted way. Frost, in much of his writing, explored exactly these tensions, or contradictions, between play and work, being and considering, freedom and responsibility, the individualistic self ("liberty") and the socialized self ("obligations").

"You can't stand in the way of progress." "What is needed is growth." How often these catch phrases fall from the lips of our leaders, as if they were self-evident, revealed truth, above or beyond dispute or question.

By now, such terms and their appeals are so deeply built into our culture that many people think of them as "natural," a fact of life, rather than as values that our culture has created. (Some historians say that we inherited these values from the Romans: certainly, they have a long history.)

But these values interact with—even collide with—the values and claims of contrary ideologies. Industrialism, the factory system, started about 250 years ago, a twinkling of an eye in the frame of the history of the human race: in that relatively short time, the *natural* world has been altered, extracted, used, mined, exploited, devastated beyond recognition.

Any intense and urgent recognition of this price, this penalty, which we all pay for "progress," began only about 175 years ago. Most of us did not listen, have not listened. Belatedly, it seems to be sinking in, but most of us still want the "blessings," the economic benefits, of "progress." This contradiction runs deep in the contemporary world, and it can be found within most of our minds: we want the best of both worlds; but ecologists and environmentalists often argue that we must make difficult choices.

In the following text, Michael Patrick Doyle explores these issues at a very local level, on a small scale. They probably exist, alas, on your own doorstep.

Michael Patrick Doyle

No Longer Lovely, Nor Dark, Nor Deep

Medina, Ohio—I remember the day a few years ago when I found ominous orange flags running straight through the woods. I followed them, refusing to believe what I knew, up and down the ravines, until they quit at an abandoned field. I followed them back, soaking up that spring day, thinking all the while that these woods would never again exist for me in my life, or for anyone else except the landowners who bought the lots and the bloated houses—expensive, tattered patches of woodland where lawns do not grow because of the shade.

As woods go, it was not much, two old quarter sections left mostly alone for the better part of a century. For this county, in northeastern Ohio, it was a large piece of unbroken trees, about a mile long and half a mile deep, big enough to get lost in for the better part of a day—shaggy-bark hickories, some beech, maple, a few big oaks.

Though it was not far from home, I went there rarely, and for one main reason: *Trillium grandiflorum*. It seemed to grow in uncommon profusion there, covering the steep sides of the wild little valleys with a virginal white, sharing the floor with violets, wild ginger, and mayapple.

I thought it a remarkable place, the beauty too obvious, and hoped, naïvely, that its peacefulness would protect it, that encroachment would pass it by, what with all the flat, worn-out, easily developed old farms nearby just waiting to grow their last and most lucrative crop. The farms still grow scrub. The woods sport wide concrete roads.

The development came too fast for me to absorb the shock of seeing the woods go. When I finally found the courage to survey the damage, I could not feel anything, only remember what used to be, and look for vanished landmarks. How can I go back? How can I remember a fragrant woods in early spring with the sky so warm after a long winter? How can I sit on a favorite log by a small stream to watch the sunlight on new green, and hear in the quiet the call of a hawk? I tell myself that there are other woods. I tell myself that the trillium still grow in abundance somewhere. But I am uneasy about the remnants, and wonder when they might leave us too.

I did not own the woods. I am a trespasser. My vote does not count when there is money to be made. The project stalled. Roads had been built, lots marked, but only a handful of houses went up before the market died. The development is still mostly a fancy sign with landscaping, calling itself, with unintended self-mockery, The Reserve.

I take no pleasure in seeing how badly it has gone, that small avarice was halted by perhaps a larger, inexplicable greed. The houses will be built eventually. I merely, and hollowly, want the trillium to grow undisturbed. I have gone to see people in their thousands and never gained as much as from the trillium in theirs.

I did not ask the bulldozer driver what he thought about the demise of native wildflowers. I did not ask the fortunate carpenter, or the realtor, or the purchaser who could not afford the fine homes. I did not ask the mason who had had no work but found some, pouring "mud" for the new office building that marks the entrance. They are not unfeeling. I did not ask because they only ride out their days, caught in them and mangled by them; "nice flowers, but I need the money." Who am I to tell a man that the trillium can fill his soul better than money while I plot to fill my own pockets? "Tree-hugger," some mutter, and I would say it myself before them. After all, I have not yet met an environmentalist who refuses to drive a car.

I suspect that the world will always have an appetite for trees. The value as an esthetic commodity is well-known. Buyers of an improved acre of natural trees may marvel at the few dozen trillium that poke through. The species is preserved. The woods are safe, tamed, and civilized beyond recognition.

WILLIAM JAMES

On a Certain Blindness in Human Beings

About a hundred years ago, William James (1842–1910), a professor of psychology at Harvard, was traveling in the mountains of North Carolina. The experience, remembered, gave rise to some interesting speculations about how we judge other people's cultures. Like Doyle, James uses a particular experience as a hook on which to hang some large questions.

Our judgments concerning the worth of things, big or little, depend on the *feelings* the things arouse in us. Where we judge a thing to be precious in consequence of the *idea* we frame of it, this is only because the idea is itself associated already with a feeling. If we were radically feelingless, and if ideas were the only things our mind could entertain, we should lose all our likes and dislikes at a stroke, and be unable to point to any one situation or experience in life more valuable or significant than any other.

Now the blindness in human beings, of which this discourse will treat, is the blindness with which we all are afflicted in regard to the feelings of creatures and people different from ourselves.

We are practical beings, each of us with limited functions and duties to perform. Each is bound to feel intensely the importance of his own duties and the significance of the situations that call these forth. But this feeling is in each of us a vital secret, for sympathy with which we vainly look to others. The others are too much absorbed in their own vital secrets to take an interest in ours. Hence the stupidity and injustice of our opinions, so far as they deal with the significance of alien lives. Hence the falsity of our judgments, so far as they presume to decide in an absolute way on the value of other persons' conditions or ideals.

Take our dogs and ourselves, connected as we are by a tie more intimate than most ties in this world; and yet, outside of that tie of friendly fondness, how insensible, each of us, to all that makes life significant for the other!—we to the rapture of bones under hedges, or smells of trees and lamp-posts, they to the delights of literature and art. As you sit reading the most moving romance you ever fell upon, what sort of a judge is your fox-terrier of your behavior? With all his good will toward you, the nature of your conduct is absolutely excluded from his comprehension. To sit there like a senseless statue, when you might be taking him to walk and throwing sticks for him to catch! What queer disease is this that comes over you every day, of holding things and staring at them like that for hours together, paralyzed of motion and vacant of all conscious life? The African savages came nearer the truth; but they, too, missed it, when they gathered wonderingly round one of our American travellers who, in the interior, had just come into possession of a stray copy of the New York *Commercial Advertiser*, and was devouring it column by column. When he got through, they offered him a high price for the mysterious object; and, being asked for what they wanted it, they said: "For an eye medicine,"— that being the only reason they could conceive of for the protracted bath which he had given his eyes upon its surface.

The spectator's judgment is sure to miss the root of the matter, and to possess no truth. The subject judged knows a part of the world of reality which the judging spectator fails to see, knows more while the spectator knows less; and, wherever there is conflict of opinion and difference of vision, we are bound to believe that the truer side is the side that feels the more, and not the side that feels the less.

Let me take a personal example of the kind that befalls each one of us daily:—

Some years ago, while journeying in the mountains of North Carolina, I passed by a large number of "coves," as they call them there, or heads of small valleys between the hills, which had been newly cleared and planted. The impression on my mind was one of unmitigated squalor. The settler had in every case cut down the more manageable trees, and left their charred stumps standing. The larger trees he had girdled and killed, in order that their foliage should not cast a shade. He had then built a log cabin, plastering its chinks with clay, and had set up a tall zigzag rail fence around the scene of his havoc, to keep the pigs and cattle out. Finally, he had irregularly planted the intervals between the stumps and trees with Indian corn, which grew among the chips; and there he dwelt with his wife and babes—an axe, a gun, a few utensils, and some pigs and chickens feeding in the woods, being the sum total of his possessions.

The forest had been destroyed; and what had "improved" it out of existence was hideous, a sort of ulcer, without a single element of artificial grace to make up for the loss of Nature's beauty. Ugly, indeed, seemed the life of the squatter, scudding, as the sailors say, under bare poles, beginning again away back where our first ancestors started, and by hardly a single item the better off for all the achievements of the intervening generations.

Talk about going back to nature! I said to myself, oppressed by the dreariness, as I drove by. Talk of a country life for one's old age and for one's children! Never thus, with nothing but the bare ground and one's bare hands to fight the battle! Never, without the best spoils of culture woven in! The beauties and commodities gained by the centuries are sacred. They are our heritage and birthright. No modern person ought to be willing to live a day in such a state of rudimentariness and denudation.

Then I said to the mountaineer who was driving me, "What sort of people are they who have to make these new clearings?" "All of us," he replied. "Why, we ain't happy here, unless we are getting one of these coves under cultivation." I instantly felt that I had been losing the whole inward significance of the situation. Because to me the clearings spoke of naught but denudation, I thought that to those whose sturdy arms and obedient axes had made them they could tell no other story. But, when *they* looked on the hideous stumps, what they thought of was personal victory. The chips, the girdled trees, and the vile split rails spoke of honest sweat, persistent toil and final reward. The cabin was a warrant of safety for self and wife and babes. In short, the clearing, which to me was a mere ugly picture on the retina, was to them a symbol redolent with moral memories and sang a very pæan* of duty, struggle, and success.

I had been as blind to the peculiar ideality of their conditions as they certainly would also have been to the ideality of mine, had they had a peep at my strange indoor academic ways of life at Cambridge. . . .

WRIGHT MORRIS

My Uncle Harry Said, "Warm Milk from the Titty Made a Cat Purty"

Most of us are now city dwellers, and have little or no direct contact with the crucial phase of American culture when the virgin, natural world was being transformed, irreversibly, into human settlements, a farming society, rural culture. The novelist Wright Morris (b. 1910), in his remarkable book God's Country and My People *(see p. 259 for one of his photographs), taps his own connection with that hinge in time, as it produced Nebraska: through his text we can perceive, vicariously, some of the strengths and limitations of that rural culture.*

On his sand farm near Norfolk my Uncle Harry went in for what he called dry farming. He planted corn, wheat, alfalfa and cottonwood trees. The trees did pretty

*Pæan: A song of praise, joy, triumph.

well. They shaded the path all the way to the pasture, along which, on the canter, I brought in the cows. Most of the year Uncle Harry milked the herd, but during my visits it wasn't worth the trouble. After the run I gave them they all ran a little dry. I brought them in on the gallop, mooing like crazy, their tails up like tassels, their udders heavy with buttermilk on the hoof. In the dark stable the squirt drummed in the pail. The sound of it brought the cats on the double to sit in the doorway, or press against the walls, where Uncle Harry would try to squirt them between the eyes. The smart cats would let it spatter on their fronts, then lick it off. *Warm milk from the titty made a cat purty.* That was what he said. He let the kittens lick the froth from the fingers he dipped in the pail. In the twilight the bats flickered over the yard and the salt lick in the corral gleamed like a snow cake. Across the darkening yard, submerged in the shadows, the croquet post tilted like a grave marker, and I knew where the wickets were trampled in the grass like booby traps. I couldn't see the water pumped into the pail, but I knew when it was full by the sound of it. Because the wire pail handle cut into my palm I would stop and switch hands at the cobhouse, the water I spilled wetting the weeds between the cracks of the stoop. So Harry wouldn't spill her milk Clara would stand waiting for him at the open screen.

He said "sye" for "says I," "see" for "says he," smoked Old Whale on weekdays, Union Leader on Sundays, chewed Mail Pouch, snuffed Copenhagen, suffered from a weight at the pit of his stomach, liked berry pie, oatmeal cooked till you could stretch it, vulcanized eggs, coffee with canned cream, fresh store bread, Senator Capper, barrel candy with the soft centers, Teddy Roosevelt, Billy Sunday, and this big local fellow Dempsey over that little French fellow Carpenteer. He cleaned eggs with his thumbnail, sat on the nails in his pockets, left his spoon in the sugar, left the flies in the dipper, left the mice in the cobs, the apples on the tree, the grapes on the vine, his hat on his head, the harrow in the yard, and the door to the privy standing open, his breath smoking in the winter air, the sun warm on his knees. He paid me ten cents a bushel for shelling his popcorn and once traveled, with other dry farmers, free in both directions, in a private car supplied by the implement dealers, from Omaha to Des Moines, where he gave his opinion that no fool gas tractor would replace the horse. In the summer he liked a straw with a shadow he could stand in, in the winter underwear he could sleep in, but he never gave an inkling if he liked or didn't like the woman he married.

He was like weeds in the spring, corn over the summer, hay in the fall, manure over the winter and a sack of grain after Sunday dinner. He was strong as a horse, stubborn as a mule, slow as molasses, smart as a whip, but what there was that was human in his nature was slow to emerge. His roots were long, but not much showed above the ground. His home-grown virtues were anesthetic: they killed pain by drugging his feelings. His eyes were wide open, but his nerves were numb. He had a good word for horses and other people's children, a knowledge of livestock, a reckoning for dead stock, an elephant's memory, an old hen's bottom and a pullet's scratch. Half an hour before sunrise he heard on the wireless that this fellow Truman had beaten Governor Dewey. At breakfast he said aloud, "He's not my man, but he's my President." After breakfast he did the chores, patched a hole in the screen, patched a hole in a tube, wired the seat of the harrow, straightened a prong of the fork, sharpened the hoe, used the dipper to skim the flies off the pail, filled his pipe with Old Whale and scratched a kitchen match on a lid of her stove.

By now we see that Uncle Harry, for all his many genuine virtues and strengths, lived a *limited*, constricted life: not because he didn't have a TV or a VCR but because his human side, his mind, remained underdeveloped: the point we elicit here is *not* that he lacked refinement, politeness, or social graces but that he lived within narrow horizons.

So Will, his son, represents the next generation, and we acknowledge the stride of "progress"; Will graduated from agricultural college and his farming was more efficient:

Harry's boy, Will, went to the state's Aggie College, where he unlearned what little the old man had taught him. He was like Clara, raw-boned, knobby and stubborn, his Adam's apple so big his neck looked bent. Using a little fertilizer and hybrid corn, Will averaged about forty bushels of corn to the acre. Using the experience of forty-five years and the rheumatism that tipped him off about the weather, Harry averaged up to fifteen bushels to the acre, if the weather was good. Will also managed to build himself a house that Harry said looked like a caboose on a siding. It set up high like that to make room for the furnace he could sit with his feet on most of the winter. In the summer he put a trailer on the rear of his pickup and just let his farm sit while he drove around the country. The kids, of course, liked it. His wife mailed Clara a postcard from Yellowstone Park. Will's wife got along just fine with Harry, but Will never again set foot in the old man's house, ate a bite of his food or borrowed his harrow or corn planter. He said it was easier to buy himself a new one than dig the old one out of the weeds. Through the screen of box elders, on a summer night, you could see Harry reading his *Capper's Weekly*, or turn and see his son Will listening to the Lone Ranger* cry "Heigh-ho, Silver!" That's what comes from sending a boy away to Aggie College or anywhere else.

CONSIDER THIS

★ Continuity or discontinuity? With Harry's withdrawal, what has been lost? Does Will live in a more efficient but diminished world? How can we know that we live in a limited, diminished world unless we know others' worlds? And how, now, do we know those other worlds? Through "Lifestyles of the Rich and Famous"?

★ Note that Morris does not tell us what his sense of the significance of these changes is: not directly, not explicitly. But what is the tone of that last sentence? And whose words are they?

*Cf. p. 83.

WILLA CATHER

A Wagner Matinée

A few generations ago, large prosperous cities often signaled the fact that they had "arrived" by establishing an opera house and/or symphony orchestra. Leisured affluent patrons would go not only to evening performances, but also to matinées, at a time when "ordinary people" were at work.

Willa Cather (1873–1947) knew the cities well, but she also knew the wild prairies of Nebraska, where her family moved when she was ten. In the following story, she takes the prairies to Boston, and has her narrator, Charles, watch his Nebraskan aunt during a concert: he is "in a fever of curiosity" about how she finds the music, but she sits "silent upon her peak in Darien." This is a phrase from Keats's "On First Looking into Chapman's Homer": when Keats first read Chapman's translation, it opened up vast new horizons for him, new worlds to explore, and he felt

> like some watcher of the skies
> When a new planet swims into his ken;
> Or like stout Cortez when with eagle eyes
> He stared into the Pacific—and all his men
> Looked at each other with a wild surmise—
> Silent, upon a peak in Darien!

I received one morning a letter, written in pale ink on glassy, blue-lined note-paper, and bearing the postmark of a little Nebraska village. This communication, worn and rubbed, looking as if it had been carried for some days in a coat pocket that was none too clean, was from my uncle Howard, and informed me that his wife had been left a small legacy by a bachelor relative, and that it would be necessary for her to go to Boston to attend to the settling of the estate. He requested me to meet her at the station and render her whatever services might be necessary. On examining the date indicated as that of her arrival, I found it to be no later than tomorrow. He had characteristically delayed writing until, had I been away from home for a day, I must have missed my aunt altogether.

The name of my Aunt Georgiana opened before me a gulf of recollection so wide and deep that, as the letter dropped from my hand, I felt suddenly a stranger to all the present conditions of my existence, wholly ill at ease and out of place amid the familiar surroundings of my study. I became, in short, the gangling farmer-boy my aunt had known, scourged with chilblains and bashfulness, my hands cracked and sore from the corn husking. I sat again before her parlour organ, fumbling the scales with my stiff, red fingers, while she, beside me, made canvas mittens for the huskers.

The next morning, after preparing my landlady for a visitor, I set out for the station. When the train arrived I had some difficulty in finding my aunt. She was the last of the passengers to alight, and it was not until I got her into the carriage that she seemed really to recognize me. She had come all the way in a day coach; her linen duster had become black with soot and her black bonnet grey with dust during the journey. When we arrived at my boarding-house the landlady put her to bed at once and I did not see her again until the next morning.

Whatever shock Mrs. Springer experienced at my aunt's appearance, she considerately concealed. As for myself, I saw my aunt's battered figure with that feeling of awe and respect with which we behold explorers who have left their ears and fingers north of Franz-Joseph-Land, or their health somewhere along the Upper Congo. My Aunt Georgiana had been a music teacher at the Boston Conservatory, somewhere back in the latter sixties. One summer, while visiting in the little village among the Green Mountains where her ancestors had dwelt for generations, she had kindled the callow fancy of my uncle, Howard Carpenter, then an idle, shiftless boy of twenty-one. When she returned to her duties in Boston, Howard followed her, and the upshot of this infatuation was that she eloped with him, eluding the reproaches of her family and the criticism of her friends by going with him to the Nebraska frontier. Carpenter, who, of course, had no money, took up a homestead in Red Willow County, fifty miles from the railroad. There they had measured off their land themselves, driving across the prairie in a wagon, to the wheel of which they had tied a red cotton handkerchief, and counting its revolutions. They built a dug-out in the red hillside, one of those cave dwellings whose inmates so often reverted to primitive conditions. Their water they got from the lagoons where the buffalo drank, and their slender stock of provisions was always at the mercy of bands of roving Indians. For thirty years my aunt had not been farther than fifty miles from the homestead.

I owed to this woman most of the good that ever came my way in my boyhood, and had a reverential affection for her. During the years when I was riding herd for my uncle, my aunt, after cooking the three meals—the first of which was ready at six o'clock in the morning—and putting the six children to bed, would often stand until midnight at her ironing-board, with me at the kitchen table beside her, hearing me recite Latin declensions and conjugations, gently shaking me when my drowsy head sank down over a page of irregular verbs. It was to her, at her ironing or mending, that I read my first Shakespeare, and her old text-book on mythology was the first that ever came into my empty hands. She taught me my scales and exercises on the little parlour organ which her husband had bought her after fifteen years during which she had not so much as seen a musical instrument. She would sit beside me by the hour, darning and counting, while I struggled with the "Joyous Farmer." She seldom talked to me about music, and I understood why. Once when I had been doggedly beating out some easy passages from an old score of *Euryanthe* I had found among her music books, she came up to me and, putting her hands over my eyes, gently drew my head back upon her shoulder, saying tremulously, "Don't love it so well, Clark, or it may be taken from you."

When my aunt appeared on the morning after her arrival in Boston, she was still in a semi-somnambulant state. She seemed not to realize that she was in the city where she had spent her youth, the place longed for hungrily half a lifetime. She had been so wretchedly trainsick throughout the journey that she had no recollection of anything but her discomfort, and, to all intents and purposes, there were but a few hours of nightmare between the farm in Red Willow County and my study on Newbury Street. I had planned a little pleasure for her that afternoon, to repay her for some of the glorious moments she had given me when we used to milk together in the straw-thatched cowshed and she, because I was more than usually tired, or because her husband had spoken sharply to me, would tell me of the splendid performance of the *Huguenots* she had seen in Paris, in her youth.

At two o'clock the Symphony Orchestra was to give a Wagner program, and I intended to take my aunt; though, as I conversed with her, I grew doubtful about her enjoyment of it. I suggested our visiting the Conservatory and the Common before lunch, but she seemed altogether too timid to wish to venture out. She questioned me absently about various changes in the city, but she was chiefly concerned that she had forgotten to leave instructions about feeding half-skimmed milk to a certain weakling calf, "old Maggie's calf, you know, Clark," she explained, evidently having forgotten how long I had been away. She was further troubled because she had neglected to tell her daughter about the freshly-opened kit of mackerel in the cellar, which would spoil if it were not used directly.

I asked her whether she had ever heard any of the Wagnerian operas, and found that she had not, though she was perfectly familiar with their respective situations, and had once possessed the piano score of *The Flying Dutchman*. I began to think it would be best to get her back to Red Willow County without waking her, and regretted having suggested the concert.

From the time we entered the concert hall, however, she was a trifle less passive and inert, and for the first time seemed to perceive her surroundings. I had felt some trepidation lest she might become aware of her queer, country clothes, or might experience some painful embarrassment at stepping suddenly into the world to which she had been dead for a quarter of a century. But, again, I found how superficially I had judged her. She sat looking about her with eyes as impersonal, almost as stony, as those with which the granite Rameses in a museum watches the froth and fret that ebbs and flows about his pedestal. I have seen this same aloofness in old miners who drift into the Brown hotel at Denver, their pockets full of bullion, their linen soiled, their haggard faces unshaven; standing in the thronged corridors as solitary as though they were still in a frozen camp on the Yukon.

The matinée audience was made up chiefly of women. One lost the contour of faces and figures, indeed any effect of line whatever, and there was only the colour of bodices past counting, the shimmer of fabrics soft and firm, silky and sheer; red, mauve, pink, blue, lilac, purple, écru, rose, yellow, cream, and white, all the colours that an impressionist finds in a sunlit landscape, with here and there the dead shadow of a frock coat. My Aunt Georgiana regarded them as though they had been so many daubs of tube-paint on a palette.

When the musicians came out and took their places, she gave a little stir of anticipation, and looked with quickening interest down over the rail at that invariable grouping, perhaps the first wholly familiar thing that had greeted her eye since she had left old Maggie and her weakling calf. I could feel how all those details sank into her soul, for I had not forgotten how they had sunk into mine when I came fresh from ploughing forever and forever between green aisles of corn, where, as in a treadmill, one might walk from daybreak to dusk without perceiving a shadow of change. The clean profiles of the musicians, the gloss of their linen, the dull black of their coats, the beloved shapes of the instruments, the patches of yellow light on the smooth, varnished bellies of the 'cellos and the bass viols in the rear, the restless, wind-tossed forest of fiddle necks and bows—I recalled how, in the first orchestra I ever heard, those long bow-strokes seemed to draw the heart out of me, as a conjurer's stick reels out yards of paper ribbon from a hat.

The first number was the *Tannhäuser* overture. When the horns drew out the first strain of the Pilgrim's chorus, Aunt Georgiana clutched my coat sleeve. Then it was I first realized that for her this broke a silence of thirty years. With the battle between the two motives, with the frenzy of the Venusberg theme and its ripping of strings, there came to me an overwhelming sense of the waste and wear we are so powerless to combat; and I saw again the tall, naked house on the prairie, black and grim as a wooden fortress; the black pond where I had learned to swim, its margin pitted with sun-dried cattle tracks; the rain gullied clay banks about the naked house, the four dwarf ash seedlings where the dish-cloths were always hung to dry before the kitchen door. The world there was the flat world of the ancients; to the east, a cornfield that stretched to daybreak; to the west, a corral that reached to sunset; between, the conquests of peace, dearer-bought than those of war.

The overture closed, my aunt released my coat sleeve, but she said nothing. She sat staring dully at the orchestra. What, I wondered, did she get from it? She had been a good pianist in her day, I knew, and her musical education had been broader than that of most music teachers of a quarter of a century ago. She had often told me of Mozart's operas and Meyerbeer's, and I could remember hearing her sing, years ago, certain melodies of Verdi. When I had fallen ill with a fever in her house she used to sit by my cot in the evening—when the cool, night wind blew in through the faded mosquito netting tacked over the window and I lay watching a certain bright star that burned red above the cornfield—and sing "Home to our mountains, O, let us return!" in a way fit to break the heart of a Vermont boy near dead of homesickness already.

*   *   *

I watched her closely through the prelude to *Tristan and Isolde*, trying vainly to conjecture what that seething turmoil of strings and winds might mean to her, but she sat mutely staring at the violin bows that drove obliquely downward, like the pelting streaks of rain in a summer shower. Had this music any message for her? Had she enough left to at all comprehend this power which had kindled the world since she had left it? I was in a fever of curiosity, but Aunt Georgiana sat silent upon her peak in Darien. She preserved this utter immobility throughout the number from *The Flying Dutchman*, though her fingers worked mechanically upon her black dress, as if, of themselves, they were recalling the piano score they had once played. Poor hands! They had been stretched and twisted into mere tentacles to hold and lift and knead with;—on one of them a thin, worn band that had once been a wedding ring. As I pressed and gently quieted one of those groping hands, I remembered with quivering eyelids their services for me in other days.

Soon after the tenor began the "Prize Song," I heard a quick drawn breath and turned to my aunt. Her eyes were closed, but the tears were glistening on her cheeks, and I think, in a moment more, they were in my eyes as well. It never really died, then—the soul which can suffer so excruciatingly and so interminably; it withers to the outward eye only; like that strange moss which can lie on a dusty shelf half a century and yet, if placed in water, grows green again. She wept so throughout the development and elaboration of the melody.

During the intermission before the second half, I questioned my aunt and found that the "Prize Song" was not new to her. Some years before there had drifted to the farm in Red Willow County a young German, a tramp cow-puncher, who had sung in the chorus at Bayreuth when he was a boy, along with the other peasant boys and girls. Of a Sunday morning he used to sit on his gingham-sheeted bed in the hands' bedroom which opened off the kitchen, cleaning the leather of his boots and saddle, singing the "Prize Song," while my aunt went about her work in the kitchen. She had hovered over him until she had prevailed upon him to join the country church, though his sole fitness for this step, in so far as I could gather, lay in his boyish face and his possession of this divine melody. Shortly afterward, he had gone to town on the Fourth of July, been drunk for several days, lost his money at a faro table, ridden a saddled Texas steer on a bet, and disappeared with a fractured collar-bone. All this my aunt told me huskily, wanderingly, as though she were talking in the weak lapses of illness.

"Well, we have come to better things than the old *Trovatore* at any rate, Aunt Georgie?" I queried, with a well meant effort at jocularity.

Her lip quivered and she hastily put her handkerchief up to her mouth. From behind it she murmured, "And you have been hearing this ever since you left me, Clark?" Her question was the gentlest and saddest of reproaches.

The second half of the program consisted of four numbers from the *Ring*, and closed with Siegfried's funeral march. My aunt wept quietly, but almost continuously, as a shallow vessel overflows in a rain-storm. From time to time her dim eyes looked up at the lights, burning softly under their dull glass globes.

The deluge of sound poured on and on; I never knew what she found in the shining current of it; I never knew how far it bore her, or past what happy islands. From the trembling of her face I could well believe that before the last number she had been carried out where the myriad graves are, into the grey, nameless burying grounds of the sea; or into some world of death vaster yet, where, from the beginning of the world, hope has lain down with hope and dream with dream and, renouncing, slept.

The concert was over; the people filed out of the hall chattering and laughing, glad to relax and find the living level again, but my kinswoman made no effort to rise. The harpist slipped the green felt cover over his instrument; the flute-players shook the water from their mouthpieces; the men of the orchestra went out one by one, leaving the stage to the chairs and music stands, empty as a winter cornfield.

I spoke to my aunt. She burst into tears and sobbed pleadingly. "I don't want to go, Clark, I don't want to go!"

I understood. For her, just outside the concert hall, lay the black pond with the cattle-tracked bluffs; the tall, unpainted house, with weather-curled boards, naked as a tower; the crook-backed ash seedlings where the dishcloths hung to dry; the gaunt, moulting turkeys picking up refuse about the kitchen door.

The arrival of the letter from Nebraska immediately allows Willa Cather to put her readers "in the picture": she can thereby give us all the information—biographical, cultural, regional—that we need, in order to appreciate the extreme differences between the midwestern plains and the eastern, industrialized city.

Farm life in Nebraska is grim and earnest; a routine of hard manual labor, working to survive, an almost complete absence of amenities, of life's graces, comforts, and pleasures: a severe and demanding rural culture, without frills. Conversely, the city is a place of expensive and sophisticated high culture: a symphony orchestra, an opera house, museums, and art galleries.

The contrasts are extreme, and sharply focused in the perceptions of Clark, the "I" or narrator of the story; especially in his scrutiny of his aunt's reactions to her return, after a quarter century of renunciation and deprivation, to the intense satisfactions she found in music. So he "reads" her, alert for signs of her state of mind and her intense painful emotions. Finally she bursts into tears and sobs, "I don't want to go."

We all live *in* time, and for the last 200 years, the passing of time has been characterized by an unprecedented rate of change in the forms of human culture. We are probably further removed from our parents than our great-great-grandparents were from their ancestors ten generations before them. The steam engine has been invented, come, triumphed, and been displaced: the agricultural era, when *most* of the population lived on and from the land, has been displaced by the machine age, which in turn yielded place to the electronic age.

Harry's son, Will, went to Aggie, and thus underwent transformation and experienced discontinuity. Seamus Heaney went from his parents' farm house in Northern Ireland to boarding school where he picked up some ideas, notions, hopes, and desires profoundly different from those of his father.

SEAMUS HEANEY

Rhymes

A few months ago I remembered a rhyme that we used to chant on the way to school. I know now that it is about initiation but as I trailed along the Lagan's Road on my way to Anahorish School it was something that was good for a laugh:

> "Are your praties dry
> And are they fit for digging?"
> "Put in your spade and try,"
> Says Dirty-Faced McGuigan.

I suppose I must have been about eight or nine years old when those lines stuck in my memory. They constitute a kind of poetry, not very respectable perhaps, but very much alive on the lips of that group of schoolboys, or "scholars," as the older people were inclined to call us. McGuigan was probably related to a stern old character called Ned McGuigan who travelled the roads with a menacing blackthorn stick. He came from a district called Ballymacquigan—The Quigan, for short—and he turned up in another rhyme.

> Neddy McGuigan,
> He pissed in the Quigan;
> The Quigan was hot
> So he pissed in the pot;
> The pot was too high
> So he pissed in the sky;
> Hell to your soul, Neddy McGuigan,　—
> For pissing so high.

And there were other chants, scurrilous and sectarian, that we used to fling at one another:

> Up the long ladder and down the short rope
> To hell with King Billy and God bless the Pope.

To which the answer was:

> Up with King William and down with the Pope

> Splitter splatter holy water
> Scatter the Paypishes every one
> If that won't do
> We'll cut them in two
> And give them a touch of the
> Red, white and blue.

To which the answer was:

> Red, white and blue
> Should be torn up in two
> And sent to the devil
> At half-past two.
> Green, white and yellow
> Is a decent fellow.

Another one which was completely nonsensical still pleases me:

> One fine October's morning September last July
> The moon lay thick upon the ground, the mud shone in the sky.

I stepped into a tramcar to take me across the sea,
I asked the conductor to punch my ticket and he punched my eye for me.

I fell in love with an Irish girl, she sang me an Irish dance,
She lived in Tipperary, just a few miles out of France.
The house it was a round one, the front was at the back,
It stood alone between two more and it was whitewashed black.

We weren't forced to get these lines by heart. They just seemed to spring in our mind and trip off the tongue spontaneously so that our parents would say "If it was your prayers, you wouldn't learn them as fast."

There were other poems, of course, that we were forced to learn by heart. I am amazed to realize that at the age of eleven I was spouting great passages of Byron and Keats by rote until the zinc roof of the Nissen hut* that served for our schoolhouse (the previous school had been cleared during the war to make room for an aerodrome) rang to the half-understood magnificence of:

There was a sound of revelry by night
And Belgium's capital had gathered then
Her beauty and her chivalry, and bright
The lamps shone o'er fair women and brave men.
A thousand hearts beat happily; and when
The music rose with its voluptuous swell . . .

I also knew the whole of Keats's ode "To Autumn" but the only line that was luminous then was "To bend with apples the mossed cottage trees," because my uncle had a small orchard where the old apple trees were sleeved in a soft green moss. And I had a vague satisfaction from "the small gnats mourn/Among the river sallows," which would have been complete if it had been "midges" mourning among the "sallies."

The literary language, the civilized utterance from the classic canon of English poetry, was a kind of force-feeding. It did not delight us by reflecting our experience; it did not re-echo our own speech in formal and surprising arrangements. Poetry lessons, in fact, were rather like catechism lessons: official inculcations of hallowed formulae that were somehow expected to stand us in good stead in the adult life that stretched out ahead. Both lessons did indeed introduce us to the gorgeousness of the polysyllable, and as far as we were concerned there was little to choose between the music with "its voluptuous swell" and the "solemnization of marriage within forbidden degrees of consanguinity." In each case we were overawed by the dimensions of the sound.

There was a third category of verse which I encountered at this time, halfway between the roadside rhymes and the school poetry (or "poertry"): a form known to us as "the recitation." When relations visited or a children's party was held at home, I would be called upon to recite. Sometimes it would be an Irish patriotic ballad:

*Nissen hut: quonset hut.

At length, brave Michael Dwyer, you and your trusty men
Were hunted o'er the mountain and tracked into the glen.
Sleep not, but watch and listen, keep ready blade and ball,
For the soldiers know you hide this night in the Glen of Wild Imall.

Sometimes, a western narrative by Robert Service:

A bunch of the boys were whooping it up in the Malamute Saloon.
The kid that handles the music-box was hitting a ragtime tune.
Back of the bar at a solo game sat Dangerous Dan McGrew
And watching his luck was his light o'love, the lady that's known as Lou.

While this kind of stuff did not possess the lure of forbidden words like "piss" and "hell to your soul," it was not encumbered by the solemn incomprehensibility of Byron and Keats. It gave verse, however humble, a place in the life of the home, made it one of the ordinary rituals of life.

Some of Heaney's learning, then, could take its place comfortably in the home's "ordinary rituals": other paths, however, would lead him into the remoter world of the university and eventually to Harvard, where he recently wrote the "ritual" verse in the Preface. A journey, to put it crudely, from "pissed in the pot" to Keats's ode "To Autumn": from folk verse to the sophisticated American academy; from innocence to experience.

The journey that we all must make from innocence to experience can be "read" in various ways: as Anderson showed, it's a shift from unconsciousness to consciousness, from taking things for granted to taking nothing for granted; from accepting the *status quo*, the world as it is, to questioning it; from accepting our culture as "nature," to construing it as only one of several feasible options; from feeling at home in the world, to feeling exiled; from being rooted, to being uprooted or unrooted. (Cf. Cowley, p. 137.)

However we read this, the move entails a deep shift in our point of view: for it is a move from a stage of one's social growth when others, especially parents, make the decisions for us, to a time when we can take on the responsibility for making our own decisions. And because of all that has modified our theory of the world, and caused it to differ from our parents', it is also often experienced as a move away from home.

Signs

An intense pain in the lower right corner of your stomach may be "read" by your doctor as a *sign* or a *symptom* of appendicitis. If he asks a surgeon to operate on you, but they find no internal evidence of appendicitis, we can say that the doctor mis-read, misconstrued, or misinterpreted the *signs*.

Human culture is itself a very complex, increasingly busy collection of signs. This chapter has offered you a few examples: a new housing development is named "The Reserve," for example. How are likely customers intended to read that sign? What does "the reserve" suggest to you? Something *exclusive*, reserved (just for you)? Something *withdrawn* from the hustle and bustle of business— reserve? Something so good that it can be expressed quietly, understated?

A car is called a "mustang," and becomes a best seller. What *is* a mustang? A horse? A wild horse? A wild horse that may be tamed and ridden (driven) by a skilled rider (driver)? A wild horse with the uncastrated virility and sexual libido of a stallion? We are all suggestible, especially when the suggestions touch on needs or desires that we don't admit even to ourselves or understand. What, then, was suggested by that *sign*—mustang—that appealed to so many men and women?

As we saw in Chapter Five, natural phenomena such as sunsets and clouds, rivers and lakes are often construed as signs: but they are signs which *we*, the spectators, *have invested with meaning;** and they are signs without designs on us. Conversely, the sign-systems of human culture have been created by other human beings to affect those-who-encounter-them in ways that will directly or indirectly be of benefit to those who constructed the signs.

*Probably the same meaning as our parents gave them, since we would learn these from them during our early years.

Robert Frost

Mending Wall

In economic terms, all modern cultures involve some notion of property, of ownership, and of trespass/theft. So culture builds walls, signs which say "This is mine!", "So far, and no further," and "Keep out! Private Property."

  What Frost affirms in "Mending Wall" is that walls are ambivalent: they do indeed "wall in," include; they also "wall out," exclude. Unlike actual walls, the "edges" of any particular culture, whether it is the dominant one, an ethnic culture, regional, occupational, or social class, are fluid, unstable, and blurred. These edges are always open to renegotiation: thus Elvis Presley, regarded for a time as an "outsider," a misfit, an outcast—indecent and disgusting—is finally enshrined inside the temple of American Greats. He started "beyond the pale" and ends up at or near the top of the heap. Cultures, unlike the walls of your classroom, leak; they are porous: infiltrators creep in, old gods are displaced by new ones. Such a process occurs both within the lifespan of anyone's mind, in the development of their own attachments and values; and also at a national, even a supranational level, and over epochs. Some folks, like Frost's neighbor, cling tenaciously to the old values, which made sense in their original context of time and place; that is, they functioned well, even though they have now outlived their usefulness.

Something there is that doesn't love a wall,
That sends the frozen-ground-swell under it,
And spills the upper boulders in the sun;
And makes gaps even two can pass abreast.
The work of hunters is another thing: 5
I have come after them and made repair
Where they have left not one stone on a stone,
But they would have the rabbit out of hiding,
To please the yelping dogs. The gaps I mean,
No one has seen them made or heard them made,   10
But at spring mending-time we find them there.
I let my neighbor know beyond the hill;
And on a day we meet to walk the line
And set the wall between us once again.
We keep the wall between us as we go.   15
To each the boulders that have fallen to each.
And some are loaves and some so nearly balls
We have to use a spell to make them balance:
'Stay where you are until our backs are turned!'
We wear our fingers rough with handling them.   20
Oh, just another kind of outdoor game,
One on a side. It comes to little more:
There where it is we do not need the wall:

He is all pine and I am apple orchard.
My apples trees will never get across   25
And eat the cones under his pines, I tell him.
He only says, 'Good fences make good neighbors.'
Spring is the mischief in me, and I wonder
If I could put a notion in his head:
'*Why* do they make good neighbors? Isn't it   30
Where there are cows? But here there are no cows.
Before I built a wall I'd ask to know
What I was walling in or walling out,
And to whom I was like to give offense.
Something there is that doesn't love a wall,   35
That wants it down.' I could say 'Elves' to him,
But it's not elves exactly, and I'd rather
He said it for himself. I see him there
Bringing a stone grasped firmly by the top
In each hand, like an old-stone savage armed.   40
He moves in darkness as it seems to me,
Not of woods only and the shade of trees.
He will not go behind his father's saying,
And he likes having thought of it so well
He says again, 'Good fences make good neighbors.'   45

The democratic consumerist mass culture of the contemporary United States is a historically new phenomenon: there never was anything like it before. And at its heart lies an interesting contradiction: American individualism will not be hemmed in by constraints or walls; it insists on having freedom to range, and room to grow. But American business practices and American media have produced a remarkably homogenized mass culture in which individual differences are drowned. "Down with the walls!" is the cry. "Let us all be as much alike as possible!" Conversely, the territory of the individual and the territory of the suburban middle class are both jealously guarded, in the name of a great cliché, the American Dream.

The nineteenth century was the century of the city—the era of expanding industries, of millions of people moving into the cities—where the work was—of railway stations like cathedrals and of banks like temples. City-dwellers lived in neighborhoods, crowded, intimate, and lively: they did their shopping at the neighborhood store, on the corner, and paused to chat.

The twentieth century has been the century of the suburb: whereas the culture of the city was brash, boisterous, and communal, the culture of the suburb is an expression of a desire for privacy, for suggestions of country life, for respectability, for signs of status. so the detached house replaced apartments, a house with a lawn smooth and unblemished as a new carpet; and in the driveway, the other dominant element of suburban culture: the automobile.

It was the mass production of relatively cheap cars that made the suburb possible. Quickly the car became the favorite toy of many adults. It also produced traffic jams, pollution, and road accidents.

The culture of the river pilot with his deep attachment to the Mississippi has happily been memorialized by the pen of a remarkable writer, Mark Twain. But the civilization of the "great river" now seems as remote as the dreams of the nineteenth-century romantics: when Philip Roth, the novelist, casts a cold eye on contemporary American culture, he sees mainly "sickness and despair."

Ursula Fanthorpe

Seminar: Felicity and Mr. Frost

Ursula Fanthorpe knows both "Mending Wall" and "Stopping by Woods . . ." (p. 251), and here she frames them within a literature seminar; Mr. Frost's poems have crossed the Atlantic (didn't Frost in fact write them when he was living in England?) because the literary cultures of America and of England are in some respects almost identical for they share a common linguistic, therefore, cultural, past.

  One of the students, a married woman with a young daughter (Felicity), has had to bring Felicity to the class, since she can't leave her at home.

(for Helen and Felicity Clark)

Two truth-tellers are here;
Marigold-headed Felicity (three)
Has come because of a hole in the roof.
Mr. Frost, who is dead, comes in black
On white. He has something to tell us.   5

Both try hard. Felicity
Has drawn a house, silent
As thinking. *Can we have a door?*
She whispers. Mr. Frost has brought a wall

With holes in it. The holes grow   10
Larger and darker as the sun
Walks round the room. Felicity
Opens her mouth in a yawn like a hole.

I didn't understand the story
The man was telling us she says clearly   15
Underneath the table. Mr. Frost
Sticks to his story, but his voice is opaque.

After a cuddle, a thumb-suck, Felicity
Touches the book with her hand,
Gravely. It is snowing now in Mr. Frost.   20
He has written a very short poem

And Felicity has found a jimmy in it
(*Secret world*, her mother explains).
Mr. Frost's world is secret too.
There are woods in it, and miles to go,   25

And snow. It has started to rain
Where we are. Felicity stands on a chair
To look out. *Don't ever have children*,
Her mother smiles at the students.

And miles to go. *You said*   30
Don't have children (Felicity cancels
Her secret world). The students are concerned.
It is still raining. Her mother translates:

I didn't mean it. And snowing.
Mr. Frost is preoccupied. He   35
Has promises to keep. And miles to go.

Our word, *text*, was originally intimately connected with the craft of weaving: the same root gives us also *texture* and *textile:* Ursula Fanthorpe reminds us of this history-in-the-word as she *weaves* Frost and his two poems, along with Felicity and her mother, into one poem.

This allows her to play with the image of "holes," just as Margaret Atwood played with "O" and "No": holes in Frost's wall, in the roof, in Felicity's drawing of a house, in Felicity's yawn. Frost's voice, however, is "opaque" to the child because she is about twelve years too young to be initiated into that stage of the culture (institutionalized as a stage in school or college) which we call "literature." Unlike our students, Felicity (being "innocent") says straight out, "I didn't understand. . . ." Later she will probably learn, through experience of the cultural constraints, the unwritten rules of the classroom, *not* to make such admissions. She will learn to act *as though* she *does* understand.

So, Ursula Fanthorpe plays off the *actual* world of that classroom and the *fictive* world of those poems by Frost: in so doing she herself creates a fictive world (*her* poem, in front of you) which takes its place in *your* actual world, here and now.

Felicity's private word, made up, for a "secret world" is "jimmy"; but the word itself is also a secret, an incomprehensible sign, a signifier without a signified, until Fanthorpe explains, by making the mother explain: "Jimmy" = "Secret World." But a jimmy, or jemmy, is also a tool used to prise things open.

And the "I" of Frost's "Stopping by Woods" (p. 251) stops at the roadside to look in at another "secret world," which remains secret because it's private property, and even if he were allowed to go in, he doesn't have the time.

Felicity turns her back; she stands on a chair and could fall and break a leg; she also looks out beyond the confining *wall* of the classroom; it is at this moment that her mother tells the other students, "Don't ever have children." That presumably is *her* "secret world," a fantasy place where she would be free of motherhood.

How does the mother convey this wry message to the others? It seems that she smiled in a certain way. But Felicity, who should have been walled out of that particular signal, catches it and so catches her mother out. And her mother is forced to translate, that is, deny/cancel, her message: "I didn't mean it." So young Felicity, who has "miles to go" in growing up, is already smart enough, quick enough to make us wonder if we dare label her entirely innocent.

CONSIDER THIS

★ If you re-read our introduction and comments about "Seminar: Felicity and Mr. Frost," you will now see that we made quite a few inferences. For example, we suggested that the mother is a student: but could she not just as well be the teacher? See if there are more of our inferences that you can question.

You were probably not at all surprised or disappointed to discover that there was no *contact* between Mr. Frost (that is, his poem) and Felicity, who, at three, simply did not "understand his story": the wall between them was too high, too thick for her to climb over or knock down.

Now, as a modest experiment, we invite you to see what kind of contact you can establish for yourself with these two poems: be as honest with yourself, and as candid with your instructor, as possible—to admit that a wall exists is *not* to confess to any kind of stupidity on your part.

W. B. YEATS

Down by the Salley Gardens

Down by the salley gardens my love and I did meet;
She passed the salley gardens with little snow-white feet.
She bid me take love easy, as the leaves grow on the tree;
But I, being young and foolish, with her would not agree.

In a field by the river my love and I did stand,   5
And on my leaning shoulder she laid her snow-white hand.
She bid me take life easy, as the grass grows on the weirs;
But I was young and foolish, and now am full of tears.

W. B. YEATS

*The Song of Wandering Aengus**

I went out to the hazel wood,
Because a fire was in my head,
And cut and peeled a hazel wand,
And hooked a berry to a thread;
And when white moths were on the wing,   5
And moth-like stars were flickering out,
I dropped the berry in a stream
And caught a little silver trout.

When I had laid it on the floor
I went to blow the fire aflame,   10
But something rustled on the floor,
And some one called me by my name:
It had become a glimmering girl
With apple blossom in her hair
Who called me by my name and ran   15
And faded through the brightening air.

Though I am old with wandering
Through hollow lands and hilly lands,
I will find out where she has gone,
And kiss her lips and take her hands;   20
And walk among long dappled grass,
And pluck till time and times are done
The silver apples of the moon,
The golden apples of the sun.

Those two poems were written by the Irishman W. B. Yeats (1865–1939)
almost a hundred years ago. Let us now invite you to eavesdrop on another

*There is a fine performance of this song, on a record made by Judy Collins. See if you can track it
down and compare reading to listening (to words *and music*).

seminar, where Yeats's early poetry is being discussed against the backdrop of his life. The students are using a paperback edition of his poems, which has a photograph of the young Yeats on it.

URSULA FANTHORPE

Seminar: Life; Early Poems

Young poet projects identical scowl from five new
Paperback jackets. Face of a man
With narrowed eyes, face of a man with a dream.

Red-hair opens brilliant new briefcase,
Inscribes the date, left-handed,   5
And heads her page: *H. B. Yeats.*

Trouble over by the window: *How d'you say it?*
I thought it was Yeets, like Keats.
A reading-list suppresses him, starred

For quality, like brandy. And dates   10
Silence frivolity: 1865–1939.
Bright sweater notes: *He saw alot of changes.*

'A foreigner writing in English.' They ponder
The foreign-ness of Ireland, poets, the past,
This man, who was *proud of his ancestory,*   15

Who hoped to bring books to the people's doors,
And music too, perhaps. Here he has brought
A load of trouble. *Grew up in Slygo*

(Red-hair again) *where still believed*
In lepry . . . (how d'you spell it?). *Married a median*   20
Who believed in automatic writing

(Whatever that is). Pause to consider
ANIMA MUNDI (caps, for awkward tongues),
Reality of the invisible. 'Does anyone here

Believe this?' *It's a Christian idea*   25
(Snaps SCM) *Th' real world is yet to coom.*
Cowed by infallibility, they license

H.B.'s outré creeds, noting merely
Believed in cycles. So now a poem
Faeryland, talking worms. They resent it   30
                                          worms: dragons

Without knowing why. *He could*
Have made it easier, couldn't he?
The face dreams on. And music too, perhaps.

The students in that classroom did their duty, more or less incompetently: "Red-hair" (female); "Trouble-by-the-window" (male); "Bright sweater" (?); SCM (male? his initials stand for Student Christian Movement—he regards himself as "infallible," incapable of ever getting anything wrong); they made notes (most of them erroneous in trivial or unimportant ways) and their notes reveal the barriers, the walls, between them and late nineteenth-century Ireland.

The central irony seems to be: young Yeats (not much older than these students, than *you*) "hoped to bring books to the people's doors," to enlarge their world, to open up new horizons, to enrich their inner lives. But now, here, his book is failing lamentably to do anything for these young people except to cause confusion and resentment.

So, let's suggest that there's nothing wrong with Yeats and his cultural hopes; and that there's nothing wrong with these young people: the problem lies in the nature of *their encounter*, the meeting, the negative "interaction."*

* Cf. Seamus Heaney, p. 267.

Fanthorpe's cunning poem seems to allow the facts to "speak for themselves," and thereby poses a question for *this* book, the book in which *you now* read these words: how far have we failed to make contact with you? How many texts have we included that you find yourself unable to connect with?

There are many potential barriers between you and Yeats. Almost a century separates you and the poet, and his preoccupations and concerns are different from yours. Is there any *common* ground? His medium is poetry and song: you prefer . . . ? His language is a late nineteenth-century language and often very "poetic": yours is late twentieth century, and . . . ? He *chose* to read and write poetry: do you? Or is it a chore, something "required"? And so on. All of these are invisible walls, separating you from *other* lives, *other* voices, *other* cultures, *other* values. But let's stop to consider: *you* have already climbed over hundreds of such walls—keep climbing!

CONSIDER THIS

★ How many failures of contact can you detect in Ursula Fanthorpe's account of the seminar?

YOUR WRITING(S) FOR OTHERS TO READ

It seems that as children we have to accept the world as it is, as we come to know it: certainly, we have little power to change it, whether it is the "world" of our family or the "world" of school. As we grow older, however, we can begin to negotiate our place in the world, and even create little "worlds" for ourselves; for example, our friendships, our own room, the clothes we wear, the ways we present ourselves.

1. What negotiations have you already accomplished in order to shape your "worlds" according to your needs and desires? What prices are you prepared to pay in order to interact effectively with others? What have you learned of mutual tolerance? Of give-and-take? Of forbearance? Of the need to be assertive without being aggressive?

2. What elements of your present situation are negotiable? Nonnegotiable? (For example, presumably you can *choose* your courses, but have no control over the content of the courses you have chosen to take.)

3. Do you think that the choices you have so far made in your life have been the best choices you could make? What frustrations or denials do you still have to accept or submit to in your life? What kinds of freedoms would you like to gain for yourself, for others?

4. In what ways do you "read" yourself? Others?

Chapter Ten

Reading Differences

Every day our culture changes imperceptibly, as we began to see in Chapter Nine. Even as you read these words, people are dying who regarded the culture of the 1920s as "natural," and babies are being born who will interpret the culture of the 1990s as "natural." Old fashions in all aspects of the culture slowly yield place to new ones, and this change is not like a change in the weather or in the height of the tides; on the contrary, it is the result of human actions.

As we grow, we realize that we don't have to submit to the fashions of the day: as adults, we can renegotiate, holding on to the old while we consider the new. Some people try, with varying degrees of influence and power, to change the culture, and so they work to modify the dominant ideology, nudging, persuading, arguing, contending, pushing, marching, protesting, voting, writing books, sponsoring alternative values. As vocal minorities, they challenge the dominant ideology at all levels, locally, regionally, nationally, and even internationally; for example, through Amnesty International and Greenpeace.

In this chapter, we shall read various peoples' attempts to renegotiate values, received ideas, assumptions, attitudes, and habitual beliefs. In most cases, they have done it through writing, and you will be able to see how they regard their intended readers and how they go about working on them by presenting their views in a persuasive way. In some instances you will read writers' reactions to others' efforts to renegotiate.

KAY BOYLE

It Takes Courage to Say Things Differently

Kay Boyle (b. 1903) is a novelist and poet; she also spent much of her time, before her retirement, teaching English courses at San Francisco State University. Much of her work has been inspired and driven by her passion for justice: her political actions and her writings have expressed her beliefs.

In this essay, she reminds us that fictions are our most vivid and powerful expressions of values and beliefs; and she shows how one of her friends, a prisoner of the most vicious and destructive ideology of the twentieth century, joined with fellow prisoners to create a fantastic scenario, a fiction that expressed their resistance to their jailers and to the institutionalized humiliations of being a prisoner of conscience.

Teenagers and students in their early twenties make teaching an endlessly exciting experience for me. Young people have a particular gift for reviving freshness of thought and language and emotion. Last year, for instance, one of my sixteen-year-old students began a composition with these words:

> All during dinner I was sitting in the Chablis wine bottle, oblivious to what my father was saying. The cool, clear liquid held me up buoyantly, like a turtle on a lake in spring. I saw myself swimming gently, easily, over to the side of the bottle nearest to my father, and I was treading wine. The green glass distorted his face horribly so that his moustache and lips were merged in a snarl which became grotesque every time he moved his mouth to chew.

The picture these sentences evoke is startling in its purity and far more revealing than a long discourse on the lack of communication between a father and his daughter. Words like these make an oasis, richly green and deep with shadows, in the parched wasteland of daily talk.

How to release reluctant students to speech is the first problem for the teacher of writing. At times the young find it as difficult to express their inner thoughts in words as do those whose minds have solidified into all but unbreakable moods. But why, after all, should this inability to speak with the heart as well as with the lips be blamed on "restrictive teaching"? Is it not more a case of restrictive thinking (induced by restrictive living) causing this muteness, which perhaps no teacher can cure? One can suggest reading to such students—great poetry, great novels—to help allay the fear of speaking. But one cannot be sure that the students will dare to understand the words that other men have said. It takes courage to say things differently: Caution and cowardice dictate the use of the cliché.

One can speak of Dylan Thomas crying out in fervor and eagerness, while still in his early teens, "If *Paradise Lost* had not already been written, I would have written it!" One can suggest to one's students that they forget for the moment the daily, insoluble problems of family conflicts, or creative writing courses, or difficulties in transportation, and write of the night mind, of their own night minds. But this does not mean that they will instantly begin to probe beneath their conscious thoughts for the great fortune that is lying there like hidden gold.

Once I quoted to a class of adults André Malraux's statement that to fulfill one's destiny one must never cease converting one's life to wider concepts and wider uses.

"Well, how would you suggest I do that here in this small town?" a gentle old lady student once asked.

"Perhaps each of us has to find the way himself," was the only answer I could give her. "In the Connecticut town where I live, for instance," I added, "I entered into the lives of the men on skid row, tragic derelicts of men who stood all day in doorways, or leaned in huddled groups against a wall, where the sun would warm their blood for a little while. . . ."

And the little old lady asked me then, "Well, if I did that here, what kind of a dress do you think I should wear?"

Most adults, having somehow lost touch with the great simplicities, have forgotten that to write is to speak of one's beliefs. Turning out a typescript with the number of words neatly estimated in the upper right hand corner of the first page has nothing to do with writing. Neither have questions about the prices paid by *Harper's Magazine* or the *Atlantic Monthly* or the *Ladies' Home Journal* or *Esquire*. Writing is something else entirely, as the young instinctively know.

One of the last things Albert Camus averred before his untimely death was that "a man's work is nothing but a long journey to recover through the detours of art the two or three simple and great images which first gained access to his heart." At times I ask my students to write of nothing at all until they can define those images. Only when they have done so are they in some measure prepared for that long journey of which Camus spoke.

For the benefit of one of my students who actually believed that writers must be intellectuals, Robert Frost sat down with me and her and explained the vast difference between the two. "Intellectuals," he said, with a gesture of impatience at the thought of them, "deal in abstractions. It's much safer that way. Writers take risks. They deal in anecdotes and parables. The Bible is written in anecdotes and parables."

It is not always easy to convince students that what Frost said is true. To the recalcitrant who may, quite paradoxically, accept the miracle of Christianity while rejecting the inner world created by the mind of man, I tell the following anecdote:

My friend, a French painter and Resistance fighter, was put in a concentration camp by the Nazis. Every evening during his long incarceration, he and two or three of his fellow prisoners created a world to which their jailers had no access. Entirely by means of conversation and gestures, they dressed for dinner in immaculate white shirts that did not exist, and placed, at times with some difficulty because of the starched material that wasn't there, pearl or ruby studs and cuff links in those shirts. With the greatest gallantry and deference, they helped one another into jackets that were formal or informal, as befitted the restaurant in which they had chosen to dine.

Moreover, these imprisoned men took on different identities every evening, and the conversation therefore differed as they sat down at a table glittering with silver and crystal that their eyes only could perceive. With their varying identities, the menu and the wine also differed. If they were playing the role of distinguished diplomats, the conversation was of wooded alpine regions and the hunt, and they ordered wild boar and pheasant from the waiter who was not there. On occasion, they sent dishes back if the food was not done to their liking.

They drank Châteauneuf-du-Pape throughout the meal and Château d'Yquem with the dessert pastry. At times, after tasting the wine, they found it had not been properly corked and they had it taken away. There were certain restaurants they did not patronize a second time because the lobster had been overcooked or the after-dinner brandy had not been served in the traditional wide-bowled crystal that one could cradle in the hand.

On the evenings that they saw themselves as men of letters, they quoted from the great poets while they dined, reciting all the lines they could remember of Homer, Dante, Milton, and Shakespeare. If they were scientists, at least one among them would be a Nobel prize winner, and they would discuss da Vinci and Spengler and Einstein. The words they spoke were real, if nothing else was, and the lonely courage that other men had expressed gave them the courage to survive.

So to those students who have not found the way to write from inside the bottle of Chablis, one must never cease to offer bottles of even richer, finer wines. And one can ask them as well to listen to the words of a very great young writer of our time, James Baldwin, whose fervent essays put much of contemporary, so-called creative writing to everlasting shame. "Although we do not wholly believe it yet," Baldwin has said, "the interior life is a real life, and the intangible dreams of people have a tangible effect upon the world." If we as writers and as teachers can communicate that quite simple truth to others, then we shall have fulfilled our roles.

"Although we do not wholly believe it yet, the interior life is a real life, and the intangible dreams of people have a tangible effect upon the world." As we

copied these words (December 1987), James Baldwin, who wrote them in the 1960s, had just died in Paris at the age of 63. His legacy is that *his* writings *have* changed peoples' minds, have modified their values, have brought them to see things that they would have preferred to ignore: in so doing, his words undeniably modified the culture.

CONSIDER THIS

★ Kay Boyle quotes the French novelist Albert Camus: "A man's work is nothing but a long journey to recover . . . the two or three simple and great images which first gained access" to the "heart," the place where we think feelingly, where our emotions can be intelligent or otherwise. Do you have any idea what, for you, those "simple and great images" could possibly be?

ADRIAN MITCHELL

The Castaways, or Vote for Caliban

The French prisoners in the Nazi concentration camp reinvented their lives through a beautifully alternative fantasy. In the next text, we see how a group of diverse people, stranded on a desert island, as in Lord of the Flies, *reinvented their lives.*

Adrian Mitchell (b. 1932) borrows some echoes from Defoe's novel, Robinson Crusoe, *which has offered many children one or two great and simple images, and also from Shakespeare's* Tempest, *in which one of the most powerful images is of the half-man, half-animal, Caliban.*

> The Pacific Ocean—
> A blue demi-globe.
> Islands like punctuation marks.
>
> A cruising airliner,
> Passengers unwrapping pats of butter.   5
> A hurricane arises,
> Tosses the plane into the sea.
>
> Five of them, flung on to an island beach,
> Survived.
> Tom the reporter.   10
> Susan the botanist.

Jim the high-jump champion.
Bill the carpenter.
Mary the eccentric widow.

Tom the reporter sniffed out a stream of drinkable
    water.   15
Susan the botanist identified a banana tree.
Jim the high-jump champion jumped up and down
    and gave them each a bunch.
Bill the carpenter knocked up a table for their banana
    supper.
Mary the eccentric widow buried the banana skins.
But only after they had asked her twice.   20
They all gathered sticks and lit a fire.
There was an incredible sunset.

Next morning they held a committee meeting.
Tom, Susan, Jim and Bill
Voted to make the best of things.   25
Mary, the eccentric widow, abstained.

Tom the reporter killed several dozen wild pigs.
He tanned their skins into parchment
And printed the Island News with the ink of squids.

Susan the botanist developed new strains of banana   30
Which tasted of chocolate, beefsteak, peanut butter,
Chicken and bootpolish.

Jim the high-jump champion organized organized games
Which he always won easily.

Bill the carpenter constructed a wooden water wheel   35
And converted the water's energy into electricity.
Using iron ore from the hills, he constructed lampposts.

They all worried about Mary, the eccentric widow,
Her lack of confidence and her—
But there wasn't time to coddle her.   40

The volcano erupted, but they dug a trench
And diverted the lava into the sea
Where it formed a spectacular pier.
They were attacked by pirates but defeated them
With bamboo bazookas firing   45
Sea-urchins packed with home-made nitro-glycerine.

They gave the cannibals a dose of their own medicine
And survived an earthquake thanks to their skill in jumping.

Tom had been a court reporter
So he became the magistrate and solved disputes.   50
Susan the Botanist established
A university which also served as a museum.
Jim the high-jump champion
Was put in charge of law-enforcement—
Jumped on them when they were bad.   55
Bill the carpenter built himself a church,
Preached there every Sunday.

But Mary the eccentric widow . . .
Each evening she wandered down the island's main
    street,
Past the Stock Exchange, the Houses of Parliament,   60
The prison and the arsenal.

Past the Prospero Souvenir Shop,
Past the Robert Louis Stevenson Movie Studios,
Past the Daniel Defoe Motel
She nervously wandered and sat on the end of the pier
    of lava,   65
Breathing heavily,
As if at a loss,
As if at a lover,
She opened her eyes wide
To the usual incredible sunset.   70

Frost remarked, "Writers take risks. They deal in anecdotes and parables." Adrian Mitchell's poem is a series of anecdotes, which "hang together" as a chronological sequence; and he has "taken a risk"—he has not told us explicitly what it is he wants us to take from his story, what moral it is that we should draw. He simply leaves us with Mary, looking out to the "incredible sunset."

CONSIDER THIS

★ The other castaways have reconstructed the world, the culture, they had been cast away from. They have brought their ready-made values with them, and proceed to give them expression in rebuilding society according to those values. Why, then, does Mary not participate? Why, so quietly, so unassertively, does she not join in? What is the point of her subtle *resistance*?

The family is the main agent of continuity and of change. It is in our early dependent lives with our parents (and especially our mothers) that we experience the great and simple images. It is in our early relationships that we become who we are going to be, that we begin to construct our beliefs and values without even realizing it. The moment we realize this fact is the moment we become something other than children, move from innocence to experience, and begin to explore the dimensions of both responsibility and morality: it is then that our *choices* become more interesting, more significant, for inside ourselves we are discovering the exhilarations and the burdens of autonomy. But, before this can happen, for years we have been internalizing the values, the ideology, mediated subtly or obviously, implicitly or explicitly, by the hundreds of thousands of signals that our parents send us, through talk—"Don't pull the cat's ears!" "You *mustn't* lie" and "That was very silly, wasn't it?"—and through action, through interaction: a slap on the wrist, a compulsory hand-washing, being sent to sleep without a bedtime story. All these seemingly trivial moments contribute to our developing belief system, our notions of right and wrong, our sense of social constraints, our distinguishing between "is" and "ought," "may" and "can," "should" and "should not."

ANNA QUINDLEN

A Schism Between Mothers

Here is Anna Quindlen, a journalist, writer, and mother of two children (b. 1953) teasing out a shift in the culture, a rift between women who settle for mothering and those who want/need more in their lives than diapers and running noses. The women's movement has worked hard for the last twenty-five years to change our minds, to challenge long-held assumptions. Women, they say, have been taken for granted for too long: it's time for a change. And now we begin to recognize with Anna Quindlen the tensions, stresses, and strains of this fundamental renegotiation.

The hours between dinner and bedtime seemed very long two summers ago, when my second son was an infant and my stomach and daily routine had not yet flattened out. In the early evenings I would fold out the double stroller and walk to the end of town, and as I did so the people returning from work were walking too, carrying their briefcases, stopping for flowers and take-out food.

I was a woman who had not seen the good end of a mascara wand for weeks, and as I walked the same lines of poetry kept running round my head: "I'm nobody/ Who are you?/Are you nobody, too?" I felt that I had ceased to exist, that those people in suits had contempt for me, or simply did not see me at all.

It was several months later, after I had started writing again, that I met a woman at a party—a lawyer who remembered my double stroller and told me that she had been sick with envy at the sight of my burden, and my freedom; her child, it seemed, had been left home with the sitter.

Of all the schisms that exist in society today, the one that I know best is the one that exists between women who work taking care of their children full time, and women who work outside their homes. It is a schism born of insecurities, and each group has foisted some of it upon the other, with considerable help from interested observers.

Women who stay home have been made to feel defensive because their choice is still undervalued, and so some of them are a little too anxious to advance the opinion that really caring people don't leave their children with someone else while they go to work. Women who leave home to work know about those comments, and some of them are a little too anxious to talk about quality time, and the fulfilled mother leading to the fulfilled child, and other concepts that are sometimes true and sometimes not. In theory, both groups have some right on their side; in practice, I think we are all just trying to find what works best for our children, and for us.

Yet the schism continues, and now it is getting its day in court, in a case about surrogate motherhood. Mary Beth Whitehead contracted to be inseminated with the sperm of William Stern from Tenafly, N.J., and bear a child that would be adopted by his wife, Elizabeth. After she had the baby, a girl, Mrs. Whitehead did not want to give her up. I can understand why, and I can also understand why the Sterns are insisting that she should do so. This is a complicated, sensitive issue, and I had sympathy for both sides until Mrs. Whitehead's lawyer started using code words to make his client's case.

Some weeks ago he suggested that his client was better qualified to raise the baby by saying, "Mrs. Whitehead is a full-time mother, not a career woman." Now he is suggesting that Elizabeth Stern, a pediatrician, had no real need for a surrogate, that she was not infertile and merely wanted someone else to carry her husband's child because she did not want to go to the trouble of interrupting her career. (Since Mary Decker Slaney, the competitive runner, kept up with her running during pregnancy and resumed training a week after her baby was born, and since I personally know that you can chase a toddler only a few days after giving birth, this contention, if true, means Dr. Stern is woefully uninformed.)

I know lawyers do what needs to be done to win their cases, and I am sure Mrs. Whitehead's lawyers could produce experts to say that children thrive with a mother who is home full time. And they would be right. And I am sure the Sterns' lawyers could find experts to say that children do very well even when their mothers work full time. And they would be right, too. I have read so many conflicting studies on this subject that sometimes my head spins. So, here's the result of my own unscientific observations: If there was ever a situational, seat-of-the-pants, ad hoc job created on God's green earth, it is motherhood.

I have seen mothers who devote full time to raising their kids who have built a minute-to-minute relationship with each child that boggles my mind. And I have seen full-time, stay-at-home mothers who seem to react to the minutiae and the stress of the task by lapsing into a semicoma, so that the most stimulating thing they

do with their kids is scream at them. I have also seen working mothers who turn a
scant hour at the end of the day into a magic hour, a perfect meeting of the minds
between them and their child. And I have seen working mothers who look as though
they've been hit over the head with a board at the end of the day, and act like it,
too.

Mostly, I know people in the middle, women spending all day with their kids,
some of it magic, lots of it tedium, and women spending the time before and after
work with their kids, trying their best to make a connection that counts.

And I know this: Being a mother is the toughest thing I've ever tried to do. I've
tried it with one and now I'm trying it with two. I've tried it working full time and
I've tried it not working at all and now I'm trying it working part time. I've tried it
by the book, by the gut, by the mind and by the heart. I could respect Mrs.
Whitehead's stand if she simply said: "This is my daughter. I am good at this. I
have a talent for raising children." But anyone who tries to tell me that mothers who
work outside the home are inferior to mothers who do not had better stay out of
my way, particularly in those difficult hours between dinner and bedtime when
we've all either just finished a hard day with the kids, or just finished a hard day at
the office, or both.

ELLEN GOODMAN

Rating the Kids

*How were you raised? And, how, in not so many years' time, will you raise your
children? How are your older brothers and sisters raising theirs? How important do
you want your children to think success is? And how will you measure it for them?
Consider the journalist Ellen Goodman's (b. 1941) thoughts on these matters.*

The problem was that she had been visiting New York children.

Not that they looked different from other people's children. They didn't. They
were even disguised in blue jeans so that they could pass in Des Moines or Tusca-
loosa. Yet the New York children she met always reminded her of exotic plants
encouraged to blossom early by an impatient owner.

She had spent one night with two thirteen-year-old girls who went to a school
where they learned calculus in French. The next night she met a boy who had
begged his parents for a Greek tutor so he could read the *Iliad*. He was nine.

This same boy came downstairs to announce that the Ayatollah Khomeini had
just come to power. What, he wondered, would happen to Bakhtiar? Or oil imports?

She wondered for a moment whether this person wasn't simply short for his real
age, say, thirty-two. But no, he was a New York child. She'd known many of them
at camp and college. They wrote novels at twelve, had piano debuts at fourteen,
impressed M.I.T. professors at sixteen. (She was, of course, exaggerating.)

The woman was thinking about all this on the plane. She was flying her flu home to bed. Sitting at 16,000 feet, enjoying ill health, it occurred to her that she was guilty of the sin of child rating.

It wasn't New York children; it was other people's children. It wasn't awe, she knew deep in her squirming soul; it was the spoilsport of parenting—comparing.

Her own daughter was reading *My Friend Flicka* while this boy was reading the *Iliad*. Her daughter regarded math as a creation of the Marquis de Sade,* and she was taught in English.

The girl could plot the social relations of every member of Class 5-C with precision, but she couldn't pronounce the Ayatollah to save her gas tank. At ten, she was every inch a ten year old.

The woman hunched down in her seat, wrapping her germs around her like a scarf. When her child was little, the woman had refused to participate in playground competitiveness, refused to note down which child said the first word, rode the first bike. She thought it inane when parents basked in reflected "A's" and arabesques and athletics.

Now she wondered whether it was possible for parents not to compare their children with The Others. Didn't we all do it, at least covertly?

In some corner of our souls, we all want the child we consider so extraordinary to be obviously extraordinary. While we can accept much less, at some point we have all wanted ours to be first, the best, the greatest.

So, we rank them here and there. But we are more likely to notice their relative competence than their relative kindness. More likely to worry about whether they are strong and smart enough, talented enough, to succeed in the world. We are more likely to compare their statistics than their pleasures.

And we are always more likely to worry. She had often laughed at the way parents all seek out new worry opportunities. If our kids are athletic, we compare them to the best students. If they are studious, we worry that they won't get chosen for a team. If they are musical, we worry about their science tests.

If they are diligent, we compare them to someone who is easygoing. And if they are happy, we worry about whether they are serious enough. Perhaps the boy's parents wish he could ski.

We compare our kids to the ace, the star. We always notice, even against our will, what is missing, what is the problem. We often think more about their flaws than their strengths. We worry about improving them, instead of just enjoying them.

She thought about how many parents are disappointed in some part of their children, when they should fault their own absurd expectations.

The woman got off the plane in the grip of the grippe. She got home and crawled into bed. The same daughter who cannot understand why anyone would even want to reduce a fraction brought her soup and sympathy. Sitting at the edge of the bed, the girl read her homework to her mother. She had written a long travel brochure extolling the vacation opportunities of a week in that winter wonderland, the Arctic Circle.

The mother laughed, and felt only two degrees above normal. She remembered

*He gave us the word *sadism*.

that Urie Bronfenbrenner, the family expert, had once written that every child needed somebody who was "just crazy" about him or her. He said, "I mean there has to be at least one person who has an irrational involvement with that child, someone who thinks that kid is more important than other people's kids."

Well, she thought, most of us are crazy about our kids. Certifiably.

When the word *yuppie* was first coined, a new stereotype in the culture was created. In a typical yuppie family, both parents work; they both wear respectably sober suits and crisp shirts; they are probably stockbrokers, lawyers, or accountants: they don't actually *make* anything, except money.

When they plan their family, they ensure that their children will become instant yuppies: at a very early age the children become grown-ups, precocious, anxious, hard-working, and achieving. By the time they are three or four, their competitive spirit is so well developed that you could swear that they have swallowed special additives with their milk: super-child pills!

As a result, they know no childhood; they are not allowed to enjoy a way of being that we would recognize as the appropriate way to be when a child. Dickens wrote about this in the 1840s in his novel *Dombey and Son*; he saw it as a plague of the time. But it had already happened in the 1780s and 1790s, and again in the 1820s.

It seems that it is a recurrent feature of the culture of the ambitious individualist, whose deepest fear is to be found out, discovered to be mediocre.

RUSSELL BAKER

Beset by Mediocrity

If you happen to think some part of the dominant ideology is ridiculous, foolish, misguided, or even wicked, what can you do about it? Mark Twain's answer was irreverence: poke fun, and show it to be ridiculous. "Look, the Emperor has no clothes on!"

Russell Baker, Pulitzer-Prize winning writer (b. 1925), uses these very weapons to good effect in his "Observer" column, which has appeared regularly in The New York Times *since 1962. Baker is always clamoring for renegotiation—for not submitting to the status quo, particularly when it is "beset by mediocrity." His memoir,* Growing Up, *celebrates ordinary people, like his widowed mother, who was not defeated by the America of the Great Depression: she was determined that her children, no matter what, would make something of themselves.*

Wednesday morning it was waking up to the New York Times headline that said "'Tide of Mediocrity' Imperils U.S." Eyes still gummy with sleep and still unable to read the fine print transmitted the headline to the brain.

"I thought it was the window of vulnerability that imperiled U.S.," mumbled the brain.

What an idiot. Just a few days earlier I had told it the Scowcroft commission, reporting to the President on nuclear business, announced that the window of vulnerability did not exist. I reminded the brain of this while shampooing its container.

"Of course," it mused. "So now, without a window of vulnerability to justify buying $30 billion worth of new missiles, the Government needs a new menace. Therefore: the tide of mediocrity. How many missiles do I think it will require to stem the tide of mediocrity?"

What an imbecile. How did I know what it thought until it thought something?

"I just had a terrible thought," it said. "That tide of mediocrity that imperils U.S.—that sounds like it could be us."

"If it is, it's all your fault," I yelled. "How many times have I told you to cut out the mediocrity and buckle down to excellence?" My God, they might already be targeting the missiles on our shower. At least with the window of vulnerability they aimed the things at Russia.

Dripping water, we abandoned the possible target zone and made a closer examination of the newspaper. First, a fuller reading of the headline: "Commission on Education Warns 'Tide of Mediocrity' Imperils U.S." Then, bifocals in place, a study of the article itself.

"Relax," I said. "It's not about us. It's about education."

A quick scan indicated that a Federal commission of 18 learned folk was reporting that American schooling was poor, getting worse and needed a lot more money to keep it from becoming downright shabby.

"The tide of mediocrity, man. Read to me about the tide of mediocrity," said the brain. I read:

"The educational foundations of our society are presently being eroded by a rising tide of mediocrity that threatens our very future as a nation and as a people."

The brain signaled for a halt so it could think. "That sentence shows how bad things are," it said. "If 18 learned folk are writing sentences as mediocre as that, the tide of mediocrity is already lapping at the nation's ankles."

What a trifler. Serious people talking doomsday, and the brain had to play the wise guy.

"I'm not kidding," it protested. "A sentence like that wouldn't be worth more than a C in 10th-grade English. Look at that tired old cliché—foundations being eroded. And that superfluous 'presently' stuck in for no purpose at all."

"This is not about grammar. It's about the potential death of the nation."

"Look," said the brain. "How much better it reads if we remove the pointless 'presently.' Then we get 'foundations of our society are being eroded' instead of 'are presently being eroded.'"

What a nitpicker.

"There's also a grammar error," it went on. "You can't say, 'by a rising tide of mediocrity that threatens our very future.' What they have constructed is a sentence with a nonrestrictive clause. You can't start a nonrestrictive clause with 'that.' You have to start it with a 'which.' If they weren't such mediocre grammarians they would have written 'a rising tide of mediocrity which threatens our very future.'"

Shut up, I suggested.

"Worse than that," it continued, "they have stuck in the most important part of their statement—to wit, that the nation's future is threatened—as an afterthought in a nonrestrictive clause following their unexciting cliché about eroding foundations."

"This is twaddle unworthy of a mind that should be trying to rise above mediocrity," I growled.

"Exactly my point about this fruit of the pen of 18 learned folk," it replied. "In scourging mediocrity in the schools they not only use cliché, deaden their writing with superfluous words like 'presently,' use 'very' as an unnecessary modifier of 'future' and betray an ignorance of the distinction between restrictive and nonrestrictive clauses. But they also bury their main point—that the nation is in danger—so deep in the sentence that many people will go to sleep before reaching it."

No wonder the tide of mediocrity is rising around my house. What a burden, having a brain so arrogant it gives only a C to 18 of its betters.

"That's not fair," the brain protested. "I'm giving them an A-plus in mediocrity."

Russell Baker is a master of the grin that wounds. Ingeniously, he gets "the brain"—not himself—to express opposition, to offer the adversarial voice: the brain knows no politeness, no respect.

The "Commission on Education," its members presumably assume, will be treated with respect; its views will be taken seriously and will influence the culture, for the better, by making others do something, and by scaring parents, who will write to their legislators . . .

But Baker, in effect, replies: who can respect people who express themselves so badly? Their language betrays them: they themselves display obvious symptoms of having caught a bad dose of mediocrity. People who write so badly (about *important* issues) cannot think straught: should we take them seriously?

Thus Baker demystifies and thereby destabilizes the authority of those who stride the corridors of power: at certain times, scepticism, irony, and wit are our best weapons.

Fortunately, you don't have to spend most of your life reading reports from government commissions: so how do you spend it? Our guess is that, apart from sleep, you are involved in interactions, either at work, at college, or in your social life. Whether these are mostly physical, as in tennis or basketball, or mostly verbal, you are involved in exchanging and interpreting signs. Government reports are also signs (to "the nation"), and like your most trivial signs, gestures, words, grunts, or groans, they are an expression of values.

The way we talk to each other, even our tone of voice, signifies our attitudes—affection, contempt, indifference, respect, and so on: and these attitudes are aspects of our values—of what we accept, support, endorse, approve, and conversely of what we deplore, disdain, or resist. When a young Australian tourist addresses an elderly Aborigine as "boy," he thereby reveals something of his ideology, just as a father does when he habitually refers to his daughter as "stupid."

In our next text, Anna Quindlen, in her thirties, homes in on what was signified when Robert called her "baby."

ANNA QUINDLEN

Robert Called Me "Baby"

Robert called me "baby" the other night. "Same old Robert," Donna said. "The only difference was the last time he said it, I was 13 years old and unsure whether I was supposed to be amused, offended or flattered. He was my best boyfriend, with the emphasis on the friend part. We spent hours on the phone together each night deciding which girl deserved his tie clip. I still know the telephone number at his mother's house by heart."

I went to the 20th reunion of my eighth grade class the other night. It was nearly a five-hour drive, there and back. Some people I know thought I was a little crazy: high school, maybe, or college, but grade school? Perhaps they went to a different kind of school.

A couple dozen of us started out together when we were small children and stayed together until we were just entering adolescence. Those were the people with whom I learned the alphabet and the Our Father, how to shoot from the foul line and do a cartwheel. Those were some of the most important years of my life. We know now how important the early years are, but the early years lasted longer then, and while the bedrock on which I am built came from my family, many of my first lessons in friendship, loss, loyalty and love came from a group of people I have not seen for two decades. They have always seemed somehow more real to me than most of the people I have known since.

It was odd, how much the same we all looked. It would have been hard for the women to look worse, or at least worse than our graduation picture, with all of us grouped on the lawn by the convent. Most of us look younger now than we did there, our poor hair lacquered into beehives or baloney curls, our feet squeezed into pumps with pointed toes.

And it was odd how much the same we were, odd how early the raw material had been set. Robert was still the class flirt, Janet still elegant. "Refined," was how I described her in a sixth-grade composition—a funny word for an 11-year-old girl and yet the right one, particularly now that it suited her so. In the photograph Alicia and Susie are sitting together; they drove down together, arrived together, were still friends. In the photograph Donna and I are next to one another, trying not to crack up. "Still inseparable" said Jeff, the class president, looking down on the two of us giggling on the steps. The truth was that we had not seen one another for 15 years and yet the ice was broken within minutes.

I'm not sure that I would have done well at a 10th reunion. If the raw material is laid down in those first 13 years, the next 13 sometimes seem to me to have been given over fruitlessly to the art of artifice, the attempt to hide the flaws beneath a construction as false as those 1966 beehives. Now I am much more who I am, with fewer regrets, apologies and attempts to be something else. To be honest, I am much more like 1966 than I would have been likely to admit 10 years ago. Perhaps it was the beer, but some of the others seemed to be letting down their defenses, too.

Ed remembered that when he had had to think of his most embarrassing moment for a Dale Carnegie course, it was something that had happened in elementary school. ("You're not going to put it in?" he asked plaintively, a lifetime after it happened, and so I said I would not.) And Jim, the host of the party, suddenly said as he saw Robert and me trading wisecracks, "You guys and your clique," making me think, for the first time, really, of how thoughtlessly hurtful we were then, too.

I suppose in a way it was like many reunions. We talked about the time we Crazy-Foamed the gym, went on class picnics to Naylor's Run and dared to go to the public-school canteen. There were children to discuss, and deaths and divorces. Most of the men still lived in the area. Most of the women had moved away. Most of the men came with their wives. Most of the women came alone.

And yet I felt that it was a different kind of occasion, at least for me. Steve had brought photographs from class trips and parties, and in one of them there I was in the front in a plaid dress, my bangs cut too short, my new front teeth a little too big for my face, and it was like looking at one of those photographs of an embryo. On Jim's back porch I looked around and I saw so many prototypes: my first close friendship, my first jealousies, my first boyfriend, all the things that break you in for all the things that are yet to come. I felt a little like Emily in "Our Town."

Robert and I talked a lot about Martha. It turned out that over the years he had never forgotten her. He was crushed that she had not been able to come up from Florida, where she is a teacher. Besides, he said, she still has his tie clip. But it wasn't really Martha he was talking about as much as a basic model he learned then. He liked her and she liked him. It was only later that he, I, all the rest of us learned that that is the basic model, but that sometimes it comes with fins and a sunroof, with games and insecurities and baggage that are just barely burgeoning when you are 13 years old.

On the stereo was a song, a 45, we must have played thousands of times in my living room: "She Loves You" by the Beatles. "With a love like that, you know you should be glad." Robert played the drums. I sang. He made a grab for me, and I slipped past him. "Same old Robert," I said to Donna.

CONSIDER THIS

★ Anna now *reads* Robert's salutation "Baby": at thirteen, she was not sure how exactly to read it: Amusing? Offensive? Flattering? Do the effects of such idioms depend primarily on who it is that is speaking? The situation?

★ How do *you* read "Same old Robert" in the first paragraph and, again, in the last line? Has its significance changed, for you, as a result of what has come between?

It's certain that no two readings of Quindlen's text will be exactly the same. We are not clones or computers, but human beings with particular histories: and "reading" consists of (a) the visual/aural information—what someone has written or said; and (b) nonvisual information. In (b), the word *information* is not altogether satisfactory. Why not? Because what we bring in our minds to any encounter, any interaction with another's words, is our *inner* life, a complex aggregate of needs, desires, expectations, wishes, hopes, beliefs, attitudes, prejudices, knowledges, and so on, all comprising a vast personal iceberg much of which lies beneath or beyond our present awareness: it seems unlikely that the word *information* could ever be an adequate sign for all that.

So every text is interpreted by a variety of readers: each of them negotiates with the words on the page, and these negotiations range from total agreement or identification to total disagreement and rejection, with most of us somewhere between those two extremes. In much the same way we react to strangers' faces: they are open to a variety of interpretations by a variety of spectators. Such variety serves to explain why *stereotypes* are always found in art designed for a mass audience. In the movies, for example, it's usually important that the members of the audience all agree as quickly as possible in identifying the "good guys," on one side, and the "baddies" on the other. So the film industry evolved a set of stereotyped images or signs which would shout (silently), "Hey, this one is the one you're supposed to hate!" These closely resemble the binary morality (good versus bad) which we learn as children: it is a functionally simple, clear, unambiguous morality which shapes the patterns of our primary socialization. We begin to grow up when we say, "But life isn't as simple or neat as that." But don't we all enjoy the occasional indulgence and luxury of regressively slipping back into the fantasy of a simple world—a world of "black and white" even when displayed in color?

ROBYN DAVIDSON

Sheep and Women

Just as commercial advertising agencies invent and propagate stereotypes, so do government agencies. The stereotype promoted by Australian government propaganda designed to encourage immigration from approved countries, ethnic groups, cultures, went like this: Australia was promoted in advertisements as a country where "You can walk tall." Confronted by the seductive simplicity of such slogans, we need to slow down and unpack the implications of the terms. Self-respect? Pride? "Manly" self-confidence?

Status? (If you "walk tall," how exactly are you supposed to relate to the "shorties"?) Push these terms just a bit further, and you verge on assertiveness, "rugged individualism," and your right to believe (perhaps denied) that you also deserve to be on top of the heap.

But how exactly does this stereotypic appeal relate to how Australian men have turned out? Here now is Robyn Davidson's version; first she takes us back, briefly, about 150 years.

By the 1840s it began to dawn on the residents that something was missing—sheep and women. The former they imported from Spain, a stroke of genius that was to set Australia on the economic map; the latter they brought over in boats from the poorhouses and orphanages of England. Since there were never enough to go round (women, that is) one can visualize only too clearly the frenzied rush on the Sydney wharves when the girls came bravely sailing in. Such a traumatic racial memory is hard to blot out in a mere century, and the cult is sustained and revitalized in every pub in the country, especially in the outback where the stereotyped image of the Aussie male is still so sentimentally clung to. The modern-day manifestation is almost totally devoid of charm. He is biased, bigoted, boring and, above all, brutal. His enjoyments in life are limited to fighting, shooting and drinking. To him a mate includes anyone who is not a wop, wog, pom, coon, boong, nigger, rice-eye, kyke, chink, Iti, nip, frog, kraut, commie, poofter, slope, wanker, and yes, shiela, chick or bird.

Here is her account of how it affected her personally:

One night in the pub one of the kinder regulars whispered to me, "You ought to be more careful, girl, you know you've been nominated by some of these blokes as the next town rape case. You shouldn't be so friendly."

I was devastated. What had I done but patted the odd shoulder or helped out the occasional paralytic or listened in silence to some heart-breaking hard luck story. I felt really frightened for the first time.

One another occasion I had taken over from someone in the Inner Bar. There were maybe half a dozen men drinking in there quietly, including two or three policemen. Suddenly an old dishevelled drunken Aboriginal woman came in and started yelling abuse and obscenities at the cops. A big burly policeman went over to her and started banging her head against the wall. "Shuttup and get out, you old gin," he shouted back. I was about to deparalyse my limbs, leap over the bar and stop him, when he dragged her out to the door and shoved her into the street. Not a person moved off their stools and presently everyone went back to their drinks with a few cracks about the stupidity of coons. I shed some tears behind the bar that night when no one was looking, not of self-pity but of helpless anger and disgust.*

Kurt, meanwhile, had overcome his fierce pride and popped in occasionally to talk me into going back. Gladdy, whom I was much more eager to see, came in from time to time, to check on my progress and secretly to urge me to accept. After two or three months at the hotel I had saved enough to make that idea once again feasible, if not attractive. It was obvious that Kurt's was the best place to learn anything and if that meant putting up with his eccentric ways then perhaps it was the best solution. Besides, he had been charming on these visits, and had lulled me into thinking I might have made a tactical mistake.

So I began spending my spare days out there, sleeping the night, this time inside the house at Gladdy's insistence, and going back to work early in the morning. It was on one of these occasions that the pub dealt me its final blow.

I returned to my little dungeon in the wee hours of the morning to find a large, well-moulded lump of excrement snuggling almost lovingly on my pillow. As if it belonged there really. As if it had found its final resting-place at last. I had the most absurd notion that I should address it in some way—let my presence be known as

---

*Just in case you think Robyn Davidson may be exaggerating, here is an account of a bar in Humpty Doo, near Darwin, Northern Australia, written by the celebrated novelist Thomas Keneally: "Its clientele can be eccentric, rowdy, brutal. On her first night serving at the bar, Dee (a young barmaid) saw an Aboriginal woman brained with a wrought-iron chair. Later in the evening, a white woman who owned a local cattle station (ranch) and for whom the Aboriginal woman had worked, turned up in the bar, two revolvers strapped to her waist, screaming to know who'd 'hurt her Bessie.'" (*Outback*, Rand McNally, 1984, p. 66)

if I were the trespasser. Something like, "Excuse me. I think you have the wrong bed." I gazed at it, mouth open, hand poised upon the door, for at least five minutes. My sense of humour, my self-confidence and my faith in humanity were all doing a perceptible fade. I handed in my notice and fled to the relative sanity of the ranch.

And here is how she reacted, how she became another, a new, a more resistant, a tougher self:

I had been in the Alice for almost a year now and I was a changed woman. It seemed I had always been there, that anything I may have been before was a dream belonging to someone else. My grip on reality was a little shaky. I wanted to see my friends again because I was beginning to realize how removed from everything but camels and madmen I had become. The time with Kurt had had a weird effect on me—I was self-protective, suspicious and defensive and I was also aggressively ready to pounce on anyone who looked like they might be going to give me a hard time. Though this may sound like a negative quality, it was essential for me to develop beyond the archetypal female creative who from birth had been trained to be sweet, pliable, forgiving, compassionate and door-mattish. I could be grateful to Kurt for that if nothing else. I also had a reinforced concrete strip down my back which successfully hid the yellow one. It wasn't so much strength I had gained, as tenacity—bulldog tenacity.

PETER APPLEBORNE

Some Say Frontier Is Still There, and Still Different

The cowboy is the major surviving sign/emblem of the mythic American frontier, a place where "men could be men." Let us now see what that frontier is like today: first the view of various spectators.

Aztec, N.M. — Nearly a century after experts pronounced the death of the American frontier, a loosely knit group of academics and public officials are arguing that the death sentence was premature. The frontier is still out there in all its harshness, they say, even if its borders are harder to define.

They say the vast open spaces of the West remain the nation's most misunderstood and dangerous region, and one that needs to be viewed in a light entirely different from the way its rural counterparts elsewhere are perceived. Experts say the rates of violent death among youths in the most isolated parts of the West are higher than those in big-city ghettos, and studies show that residents of the underpopulated areas have worse health conditions and live shorter lives.

Frank J. Popper, chairman of the urban studies department at Rutgers University, said the frontier exists as a distinct region with a view of life that stresses independence, risk-taking and individualism, concepts that remain central to both the American imagination and direction of the West.

"MACHO AND HELL-RAISING"

"I think we've taken a giant wrong intellectual turn in thinking the frontier disappeared in 1890 or whatever," said Dr. Popper, whose writings on the survival of the frontier have attracted the attention of health care professionals in particular. "It's not as big as it was, but it's there, and in some ways it's just as violent and just as macho and hell-raising in 1987."

Over the past two years health planners have increasingly drawn distinctions between generally rural areas and places that are, in effect, on the edge of civilization. Defining the frontier as areas with no more than six people to the square mile, officials note that distance alone provides rare problems in law enforcement and health care.

"When I was in Vietnam, a medic was never more than 10 minutes away," said Lieut. R. L. Stockard, who heads the state police district that includes this northwestern New Mexico town. "Here you can wait by a wreck on the highway for 45 minutes before help gets there."

But more than distance is involved. The frontier is also defined by the West's boom-and-bust economy and dangerous occupations like mining, forestry and oil drilling. Also at play are less tangible factors: the historic machismo of the West, and the transient nature and fragile economies of many Western towns. Some experts contend the combination has produced a far more rootless, violent world than small towns or rural areas elsewhere.

LOTS OF LAND, FEW PEOPLE

"Western towns are more of an aggregate than a community," said Philip A. May, a sociologist at the University of New Mexico. "There is no cultural cohesion. Westerners basically believe in rugged individualism first and the government second."

To people subscribing to the idea of a continuing frontier, its persistence is as clear as the 1980 census. It showed that 394 counties, covering 45 percent of the land area of the United States, including virtually all of Alaska, had six or fewer people per square mile. In all, 2.2 million people live in these counties, which are clustered almost entirely west of the Mississippi River.

Over the past two years consideration of these sparsely populated areas has gained increasing attention from health care professionals. Many, including Gar T.

Elison, director of health planning and analysis of the Utah Department of Health, have argued for a separate designation in assessing health care needs.

"The West has always suffered by being defined by people in the East," said Mr. Elison, who is chairman of the National Frontier Health Care Task Force. "We're always going to have a problem providing services if the frame of reference for rural areas is West Virginia. Standards that make sense in the East are often irrelevant in the West."

He said population and patient census ratios used in evaluating the need for rural health care programs or clinics inevitably short-changed frontier areas. "It's been a way of saying the have-nots will always remain that way, and we resent that," he said.

RARE NEEDS IN REMOTE AREAS

Mr. Elison said that in the past two years some 15 health care organizations had endorsed the basic concept of having different standards for frontier areas. Similarly, he said, a recent health bill in the House of Representatives cited the need for recognizing the underpopulated regions' different needs.

There have been few definitive studies on differences between such areas and places with 6 to 100 people to the square mile, which would be classified as "rural." But recent analyses of statistics in Idaho, Utah, South Dakota, Nebraska and Wyoming indicate residents in the frontier areas have poorer health than those in urban or rural ones.

Mr. Elison said a study of mortality data in Utah showed frontier residents fared the worst in terms of working years of life lost because of several leading causes of death, including suicide, automobile accidents, other accidents and infant diseases. (Working years are defined as the years from the age of 15 to 65, and the figure is derived by subtracting the age of death from 65.)

The figures are 33.5 percent higher in frontier areas than in urban ones, Mr. Elison said.

For academics like Dr. Popper, the frontier designation is less a tool for program planning than a window onto the sparsely populated areas of the West.

He argues that the obscurity of life in those areas has distorted some of the ideas about violence in the United States.

In a paper in The Public Interest this spring, Dr. Popper and two colleagues analyzed violent deaths of American youths from 1939 through 1979. They studied rates for 15-to-24-year-old whites, including Hispanic people, and found that the Western states invariably had the highest death rates and the Northeast the lowest. In the states with the highest death rates, Arizona, Nevada, New Mexico and Utah, the most dangerous counties were the less populated ones.

Typically, those counties had higher death rates among their white population than high-crime cities showed for urban blacks, Dr. Popper said.

"The rural areas of the West, rather than the American urban ghetto, is where youth is far more likely to suffer violent death," Dr. Popper and his colleagues, Michael R. Greenberg and George W. Carey, concluded.

Studies in 1986 by the Federal Centers for Disease Control found that the West had the highest rates for youth suicides and for homicides among both whites and blacks.

Experts cite as reasons for the large number of violent deaths not only dangerous occupations and the individualism of the rural West but also the high number of fatal auto accidents, reflecting both widespread drinking, dangerous roads and the difficulties in providing emergency care in rural areas.

THEY'RE ON THEIR OWN

Law-enforcement officials say the individualism of the West is reflected in what is often a predilection to handle problems outside the law.

"In a lot of these areas, there's really no law enforcement—no police, no sheriff, no state police station," said Lieutenant Stockard, the state police official here. "People prefer to handle their own affairs and disputes by themselves."

He said the problems were compounded by a disparate ethnic mix. His region includes insular Hispanic communities like Cuba, N.M., in the southern part of the district, Indian reservations with high mortality rates and alcohol problems in the middle, and largely white communities dependent on mining and oil and gas to the north.

Mr. Elison said many Western states were involved in efforts to try to gather data on frontier regions. He said most of the available figures probably understated problems there because they did not take into account the economic distress and resultant problems of the past few years throughout the West.

"We're in the midst of an economic crisis that began in 1983, and any earlier numbers are not going to reflect it," he said. "You look at the economy of the West, agriculture is down, oil and gas are down, mining is down, forest industries are down, housing starts are down. All those things are going to have an impact."

GRETEL EHRLICH

About Men

For over eight years, Gretel Ehrlich has lived among the cowboys of Montana: these are men who, she finds, simply don't confirm the myth of the frontier, with its stereotype of macho, freewheeling assertive individualists, fighting for power.

Ehrlich first went to Montana from Los Angeles to make a movie: little did she know that her visit would change her life.

When I'm in New York but feeling lonely for Wyoming I look for the Marlboro ads in the subway. What I'm aching to see is horseflesh, the glint of a spur, a line of distant mountains, brimming creeks, and a reminder of the ranchers and cowboys

I've ridden with for the last eight years. But the men I see in those posters with their stern, humorless looks remind me of no one I know here. In our hellbent earnestness to romanticize the cowboy we've ironically disesteemed his true character. If he's "strong and silent" it's because there's probably no one to talk to. If he "rides away into the sunset" it's because he's been on horseback since four in the morning moving cattle and he's trying, fifteen hours later, to get home to his family. If he's "a rugged individualist" he's also part of a team: ranch work is teamwork and even the glorified open-range cowboys of the 1880s rode up and down the Chisholm Trail in the company of twenty or thirty other riders. Instead of the macho, trigger-happy man our culture has perversely wanted him to be, the cowboy is more apt to be convivial, quirky, and softhearted. To be "tough" on a ranch has nothing to do with conquests and displays of power. More often than not, circumstances—like the colt he's riding or an unexpected blizzard—are overpowering him. It's not toughness but "toughing it out" that counts. In other words, this macho, cultural artifact the cowboy has become is simply a man who possesses resilience, patience, and an instinct for survival. "Cowboys are just like a pile of rocks—everything happens to them. They get climbed on, kicked, rained and snowed on, scuffed up by wind. Their job is 'just to take it,'" one old-timer told me.

A cowboy is someone who loves his work. Since the hours are long—ten to fifteen hours a day—and the pay is $30 he has to. What's required of him is an odd mixture of physical vigor and maternalism. His part of the beef-raising industry is to birth and nurture calves and take care of their mothers. For the most part his work is done on horseback and in a lifetime he sees and comes to know more animals than people. The iconic myth surrounding him is built on American notions of heroism: the index of a man's value as measured in physical courage. Such ideas have perverted manliness into a self-absorbed race for cheap thrills. In a rancher's world, courage has less to do with facing danger than with acting spontaneously—usually on behalf of an animal or another rider. If a cow is stuck in a boghole he throws a loop around her neck, takes his dally (a half hitch around the saddle horn), and pulls her out with horsepower. If a calf is born sick, he may take her home, warm her in front of the kitchen fire, and massage her legs until dawn. One friend, whose favorite horse was trying to swim a lake with hobbles on, dove under water and cut her legs loose with a knife, then swam her to shore, his arm around her neck lifeguard-style, and saved her from drowning. Because these incidents are usually linked to someone or something outside himself, the westerner's courage is selfless, a form of compassion.

The physical punishment that goes with cowboying is greatly underplayed. Once fear is dispensed with, the threshold of pain rises to meet the demands of the job. When Jane Fonda asked Robert Redford (in the film *Electric Horseman*) if he was sick as he struggled to his feet one morning, he replied, "No, just bent." For once the movies had it right. The cowboys I was sitting with laughed in agreement. Cowboys are rarely complainers; they show their stoicism by laughing at themselves.

If a rancher or cowboy has been thought of as a "man's man"—laconic, hard-drinking, inscrutable—there's almost no place in which the balancing act between male and female, manliness and femininity, can be more natural. If he's gruff, handsome, and physically fit on the outside, he's androgynous at the core. Ranchers are midwives, hunters, nurturers, providers, and conservationists all at once. What we've interpreted as toughness—weathered skin, calloused hands, a squint in the eye and a growl in the voice—only masks the tenderness inside. "Now don't go telling me these lambs are cute," one rancher warned me the first day I walked into the football-field-sized lambing sheds. The next thing I knew he was holding a black lamb. "Ain't this little rat good-lookin'?"

So many of the men who came to the West were southerners—men looking for work and a new life after the Civil War—that chivalrousness and strict codes of honor were soon thought of as western traits. There were very few women in Wyoming during territorial days, so when they did arrive (some as mail-order brides from places like Philadelphia) there was a stand-offishness between the sexes and a formality that persists now. Ranchers still tip their hats and say, "Howdy, ma'am" instead of shaking hands with me.

Even young cowboys are often evasive with women. It's not that they're Jekyll and Hyde creatures—gentle with animals and rough with women—but rather, that they don't know how to bring their tenderness into the house and lack the vocabulary to express the complexity of what they feel. Dancing wildly all night becomes a metaphor for the explosive emotions pent up inside, and when these are, on occasion, released, they're so battery-charged and potent that one caress of the face or one "I love you" will peal for a long while.

The geographical vastness and the social isolation here make emotional evolution seem impossible. Those contradictions of the heart between respectability, logic, and convention on the one hand, and impulse, passion, and intuition on the other, played out wordlessly against the paradisical beauty of the West, give cowboys a wide-eyed but drawn look. Their lips pucker up, not with kisses but with immutability. They may want to break out, staying up all night with a lover just to talk, but they don't know how and can't imagine what the consequences will be. Those rare occasions when they do bare themselves result in confusion. "I feel as if I'd sprained my heart," one friend told me a month after such a meeting.

My friend Ted Hoagland wrote, "No one is as fragile as a woman but no one is as fragile as a man." For all the women here who use "fragileness" to avoid work or as a sexual ploy, there are men who try to hide theirs, all the while clinging to an adolescent dependency on women to cook their meals, wash their clothes, and keep the ranch house warm in winter. But there is true vulnerability in evidence here. Because these men work with animals, not machines or numbers, because they live outside in landscapes of torrential beauty, because they are confined to a place and a routine embellished with awesome variables, because calves die in the arms that pulled others into life, because they go to the mountains as if on a pilgrimage to find out what makes a herd of elk tick, their strength is also a softness, their toughness, a rare delicacy.

YOUR WRITING(S) FOR OTHERS TO READ

Differences are what make other people interesting. They are also the source of conflicts, frictions, and misunderstandings. Intolerant minds cannot enjoy others' differences because they construe them as an assertion of excessive freedom: "Why can't these fools (idiots, strangers, foreigners, and so on) be more like me?"

1. Consider the many kinds of differences between you and your siblings; you and your parents; you and your friends; you and your professors. How do you construe these various disparities, dissimilarities? As pleasurable? Interesting? Enlivening? Tiresome? Frustrating?

2. What *kinds* of differences should we be *encouraged* to encourage? What kinds of differences will have to disappear in order to make a better world?

3. What are the *deepest* differences between you and others? Gender? Age? Race? Social Class? Nationality? What kinds of differences are you specially aware of *at this moment?*

Chapter Eleven

Reading Roles and Relationships

Most of the writers in this chapter are women, for our present culture is undergoing reconstruction at all levels as a result of a recent historical shift. In the last thirty years, what is loosely called "the women's movement" has worked to change the dominant culture, to modify its values, and to effect practical and legislative change. In the long run, it seems obvious that equality of the sexes will benefit everyone: but in the short term women have met strenuous, sometimes hysterical, resistance from the men in power locally and nationally. At the center of these moves, negotiations, and struggles are big questions: Can there be a society where men and women exist as equals, be it in their careers or marriages? What is the institution of marriage? Whom does it serve? Who, in an "equal" partnership, is to do the parenting? The cooking? The laundry?

THOM GUNN

Waitress

Every social institution—the home, the café, the filling station, the school, the department store—has a hierarchy, a power structure, similar to those that biologists, ethologists, and anthropologists have recently discovered in animal societies. (The most proverbial of these is the farmyard, over which the most powerful and aggressive rooster has presided as the "Cock of the Walk.")

In Thom Gunn's (b. 1929) text, the office workers who are "pushed around" by their boss escape for lunch and proceed to push the waitress around: this does not go unnoticed.

At one they hurry in to eat.
Loosed from the office job they sit
But somehow emptied out by it
And eager to fill up with meat.
    Salisbury Steak with Garden Peas.   5

The boss who orders them about
Lunches elsewhere and they are free
To take a turn at ordering me.
I watch them hot and heavy shout:
    Waitress I want the Special please.   10

My little breasts, my face, my hips,
My legs they study while they feed
Are not found on the list they read
While wiping gravy off their lips.
    Here Honey gimme one more scoop.   15

I dream that while they belch and munch
And talk of Pussy, Ass, and Tits,
And sweat into their double knits,
I serve them up their Special Lunch: 20
    Bone Hash, Grease Pie, and Leather Soup.

In "Waitress," Gunn has re-invented himself as a woman in a subordinate position: so the voice of the poem speaks to us in the first person—"I" and "me"—and we experience the illusion that we, the readers, can hear (or overhear) what she is speaking inside her mind, speaking her mind.

MARGARET ATWOOD

Backdrop Addresses Cowboy

In the next poem, the author re-invents herself as the backdrop, or scenery, in a cowboy movie; the backdrop then speaks to a cowboy who seems to be quite deaf to what the scenery, speaking for the Earth, tells him. Note that Atwood calls "the West" "almost silly": however silly the plot of a Western may be, however incompetent the acting, there is always the redeeming presence of a great landscape.

Starspangled cowboy
sauntering out of the almost-
silly West, on your face
a porcelain grin,
tugging a papier-mâché cactus   5
on wheels behind you with a string,

you are innocent as a bathtub
full of bullets.

Your righteous eyes, your laconic
trigger-fingers   10
people the streets with villains:
as you move, the air in front of you
blossoms with targets

and you leave behind you a heroic
trail of desolation: 15
beer bottles
slaughtered by the side
of the road, bird-
skulls bleaching in the sunset.

                                                                 20
I ought to be watching
from behind a cliff or a cardboard storefront
when the shooting starts, hands clasped
in admiration,

but I am elsewhere.

                                                                 25
Then what about me

what about the I
confronting you on the border
you are always trying to cross?

I am the horizon
you ride towards, the thing you can never lasso   30

I am also what surrounds you:
my brain

scattered with your
tincans, bones, empty shells,
the litter of your invasions.   35

I am the space you desecrate*
as you pass through.

CONSIDER THIS

★ Does the "backdrop" speak with a feminine voice? (After all, "backdrop,"
"scenery" are names for parts of the landscape, the surface of what used to be
known affectionately as Mother Nature or Mother Earth.) If surrealism had not
existed for the last sixty years or so, we would have more difficulty in visualizing
the landscape as a *mind* through which the cowboy carelessly rides, leaving his
trail of litter. Did you notice how the third stanza ("Your righteous eyes . . .")
set us up, by setting the cowboy up, to see the fantasy-heroics, which lead
straight into the ridiculous anti-climax of the next stanza—"heroic/trail of
desolation"—nothing more than broken beer bottles and dead birds?
★ Why is it that characters like this cowboy are featured in so many cigarette ads
and beer commercials?

ELLEN GOODMAN

Of Roles and Robes

*It is possible that Thom Gunn's text was aroused initially by an episode he witnessed in
his local diner; it is unlikely that Margaret Atwood met a cowboy riding across a movie
set; but it is clear that we should believe Ellen Goodman when she tells us that she had
an encounter in Denver with a telephone repairer. Even if she invented the story, it
surely provides an effective opener for her article: it is amusing to realize that, if your
ideal culture is one in which women do not work and you stick to your principles, you
may never get your telephone repaired!*

When I was in Denver a year ago, I met a telephone repairer of the female persuasion
who told me a very funny story. At least she was laughing.

Several weeks earlier, on a service call, she had rung the doorbell of a customer
and been greeted with, "Oh! good, you're the man from the telephone company."
Well, she was a bit taken aback by that, but proceeded to fix the phone anyway.

---

* Over a hundred years ago, Smohalla, a Nez Perce Indian medicine man, said: "You ask me to plough
the ground. Shall I take a knife and tear my mother's bosom? You ask me to dig for stone. Shall I dig
under her skin for her bones?"

During the entire time, the woman of the house referred to her as "he" and finally praised her as a wonderful "man."

The customer was what you might call a hard-core resister. Apparently it was easier to accept a rather deviant male with silicone implants than a woman who could fix telephones. But there you are.

The majority of us are not quite so immune to reality. The facts tend to change our attitudes more often than the other way around.

There are, of course, those who will never, under any circumstances, accept women in unusual roles. But it's safe to say that they are a minority in the telephone directory or, for that matter, in the congregation.

Which brings me to the subject of women priests. The triennial convention of the Episcopal Church is meeting in Minneapolis until September 24. It will decide the issue of women priests—an issue which has been a divisive one among the three-million-member denomination for a dozen years.

Four years ago, after much pressure, women were finally allowed to become deacons of the church. Since then they have been trying to scramble up the final rung to priesthood.

In 1972 the bishops asserted that they were in favor of women priests "in principle," and the following year the lower clergy continued to forbid them in canon law. Since a dramatic moment in 1974, fifteen women have been ordained in ceremonies that were challenged and unrecognized by the official church. In response, the church officials went so far as to refuse a $600 donation to the World Hunger Campaign because it was raised at a service presided over by "outlaw" women priests.

On Wednesday the House of Bishops finally voted to permit women to be ordained as priests. But this weekend the question will come before the more conservative body, the House of Deputies. This body has based its opposition largely on "tradition," and the idea that the parishes are not ready. In doing so, many have managed to misjudge how the public comes to accept change.

Strong pressure already has built to admit women into "men only" roles and robes. The leaders for change made bold steps by ordaining fifteen women. But the masses generally accept the facts after the fact—whether it's women at West Point or at the altar.

We deal with the *fait accompli* better than with fantasies. In prospect, a *woman priest* is a vague, amorphous threat to tradition. In fact, however, she is a human being with a sincere calling. As a species we are enormously resistant to the idea of change—and remarkably adjustable to its reality.

The horrified alumni of Yale discovered after a few years that the sky did not fall over the female dorms of New Haven. The patrolmen in Washington who were opposed to buddying up with women largely accepted them a year later. The same people who couldn't tolerate the idea of a woman doctor went to Elizabeth Blackwell when they were sick. And West Point marches on.

Many are opposed to women in "men's roles" because they've never seen them, they've never tried them. They regard a woman priest with the suspicion normally directed at raw oysters. The prejudice remains unshakable as long as the experience is unchanged.

The way to effect the change the bishops agreed upon "in principle" four years ago isn't some cop-out, piecemeal compromise, but is to take a stand on that "principle"—to admit women priests, and to let "public acceptance" do what it does best: follow.

"The facts tend to change our attitudes more often than the other way around." That observation is worth discussing, especially by offering instances to support it or otherwise; or, preferably, both!

Don't be in too much of a hurry to make up your mind: a mind made up is often thereby closed or retired. And consider what Keats wrote in his letters: "I shall never be a Reasoner because, when retired from bickering, I care not to be in the right . . ." and "The only means of strengthening one's intellect is to make up one's mind about nothing—to let the mind be a thoroughfare for all thoughts. . . . All the stubborn arguers never begin upon a subject they have not preresolved upon. They want to hammer their nail into you and if you turn the point, still they think you wrong" (1819).

Consider also what Scott Fitzgerald said from a similar point of view: "The test of a first class mind is the ability to hold two opposing ideas in the mind at the same time, and go on functioning."

Whenever we use the word *really*, we are in effect appealing to an authority beyond, outside, transcending our own modest selves. We are claiming that, yes, reality *is* like this or that, that reality *is* just so.

Be on the alert: whenever someone slips *really* into their talking and uses it as an emphasis, see if you can work out exactly what they are up to. It is often a defensive strategy, a way of concealing that they can produce no evidence to support their case, their argument, their point of view. See how neatly Ellen Goodman plays on the word in the following text.

ELLEN GOODMAN

Live-In Myths

"He is not really like that," she said apologetically as her husband left the room.

"Like what?" I asked, wondering which of the many things that had happened that evening she was excusing.

"Well, you know," she said, "cranky."

I thought about that. Cranky. It was typical of the woman that she would choose a gentle, even childish, word for the sort of erratic outbursts of anger which had been her husband's hallmark for the past fifteen years.

He was not really like that. This had been her sentence when they were first dating, when they were living together, and now, since they were married.

When he questioned, minutely, the price tags of her purchases, she would say: "He is really, deep down, very generous." When he disagreed with her politics, veering to the right while she listed to the left, she would cheerily insist that underneath all that he was "basically" liberal.

When he blamed her for the condition of the house, as if he were a lodger, and blamed her for the children's illnesses, as if her negligence had caused their viruses, she would explain, "He is really very understanding."

Even when he was actually his most vital self, amusing and expansive, full of martinis or enthusiasm or himself—and she disapproved—she would forgive him because he wasn't really like that.

This time, dining with them out of town one brief night, I saw that this was the pattern of their lives together—a struggle between realities. His real and her "really."

I had known the wife since college and the husband from their first date. When they met she was a social worker and he was, it seems, her raw material. Was he the case and she the miracle worker? At times she looked at him that way.

Her husband was erratic and difficult, but he had a streak of humor and zaniness as attractive as Alan Arkin's. Over the years, he had grown "crankier" and she more determined in her myth-making.

This trip, for the first time, I wondered what it must be like to be a text living with an interpreter. To be not really like that. And what it must be like for her, living with her myth as well as her man.

I know many other people who live with their ideas of each other. Not with a real person but with a "really." They doggedly refuse to let the evidence interfere with their opinions. They develop an idea about the other person and spend a lifetime trying to make him or her live up to that idea. A lifetime, too, of disappointments.

As James Taylor sings it: "First you make believe / I believe the things that you make believe / And I'm bound to let you down. / Then it's I who have been deceiving / Purposely misleading / And all along you believed in me."

But when we describe what the other person is really like, I suppose we often picture what we want. We look through the prism of our need.

I know a man who believes that his love is really a very warm woman. The belief keeps him questing for that warmth. I know a woman who is sure that her mate has hidden strength, because she needs him to have it.

Against all evidence, one man believes that his woman is nurturing because he so wants her to be. After twenty years, another woman is still tapping hidden wells of sensuality in her mate, which he has, she believes, "repressed."

And maybe they are right and maybe they are wrong, and maybe they are each other's social workers. But maybe they are also afraid that if they let go of their illusions, they will not like each other.

We often refuse to see what we might not be able to live with. We choose distortion.

Leaving this couple, I thought about how much human effort can go into maintaining the "really." How much daily energy that might have gone into understanding the reality—accepting it or rejecting it.

How many of us spend our lives trying to sustain our myths, and how we are "bound to be let down." Because most people are, after all, the way they seem to be.

Really.

CONSIDER THIS

★ "I wondered what it must be like to be a text living with an interpreter." Whose "text" are you? Who is your most persistent interpreter? Who is it that "understands" your "moods," and can interpret them so as to prove that you are not really moody at all? Or greedy? Or extravagant? Or careless? Enough!

★ Did you observe the parallel between Ehrlich's "On Men" and Goodman's text? Each examines a myth and plays it off against the actual, thereby inviting us to criticize the myth.

★ What myths do you live by? Which are the most important? How do they function? Why do you need them?

FIONA PITT-KETHLEY

Spells

At twelve or so, we all thought marriage was more
or less compulsory. Half-seriously,
comparing notes with other girls,
I tried old spells—sleeping on wedding-cake,
throwing an apple's peel at Hallowe'en   5
to form initials and sitting alone
combing my hair out in a darkened room
while I looked for another face in the glass.
I melted lead, too, in the preserving pan,
pouring the molten metal on to water   10
to find the symbols of *his* profession—
I only got a load of balls.

One of my friends was much more practical,
less of a lover of strange rituals.
She planned to wed a lord, then poison him.   15
That way she'd skip the sex, but get to keep
the title and the stately home.

Years later, I met her come from Iran.
She'd crossed Afghanistan alone and brought
a souvenir for all the guests to try—   20
some camel's yoghourt hardened into blocks,
a bit like cakes of paint with hair inside.

ELLEN WILLIS

My Secret Advice

Who is Ann Landers? How long ago was that photograph taken that appears alongside her name in so many of our newspapers? Is she really real? One kind of answer to these questions is to track down a copy of Nathaniel West's novel, Miss Lonelyhearts, but before you rush off to find it, read Ellen Willis's "My Secret Advice."

On a typical day, I buy the *Daily News* and after a brief scan of the front pages turn straight to Ann Landers. The first letter offers With It in Michigan's tips for wedded bliss in the 1980s—items like "Be understanding when he has a headache," and "If you aren't going to be home for dinner, phone." "Thanks for a breezy reminder of how times have changed," Ann replies, friendly but reserved. Aficionados may translate: "I still think you women's lib types are a little far out, but you do have a point." Letter two, from Climbing Out of the Darkness in Newark, is more serious. Climbing is 28: once a suicidal depressive, she has been "doing quite well" with the help of drugs. Her problem is that she hates her job, but her psychiatrist advises her against returning to her more responsible and higher-paying former occupation. So long as she avoids pressure and keeps taking her medication, he says, she can lead a "fairly normal life," but if she takes on too much she will fall apart.

Before looking at Ann's answer, I imagine my own: "Dear Climbing: *Please* don't take your mechanistic doctor's soul-killing advice to settle for a life of permanent drug-taking that will let you function outside a hospital and not much more. Go to a real therapist who can help you get to the root of your problems—maybe you can really get rid of your pain, not just drug it into quiescence." Ann begins, "It sounds as if you're in the hands of a highly competent doctor. Listen to him." Oh, shit. She goes on to enlist the power of positive thinking: reach out to others, make an effort to help yourself. I start my 115th unsent letter to Ann Landers telling her how she's blown it. Actually, I did write to her once. A few years back, during an appearance on the David Susskind show, she said that living together without marriage was a bad idea for women because they got stuck with the housework and ended up feeling exploited. I wrote that this was illogical because if anything, wives were even more likely to get stuck with the housework. I forget to enclose a self-addressed, stamped envelope, so I never got an answer.

While my friends' taste in media potato chips runs to *Miami Vice* and *Dynasty*, I gorge on advice columns and shlock psychology. Besides Ann, I try to keep up with her sister Abby (to my mind, the twin with the Toni) and Dr. Joyce Brothers (a poor substitute for the nonpareil Dr. Rose Franzblau). I love women's magazines and am particularly fond of the *Ladies' Home Journal*'s "Can This Marriage Be Saved?" which each month offers us her side (he beats me, drinks, pays no attention to the children, never takes a bath, and hasn't had a job in 10 years), his side (she won't accept me the way I am), and the counselor's interpretation (Drusilla was still caught up in adolescent fantasies of the perfect husband). That's the way it used to be, anyway—and though the *Journal*'s marriage savers have raised their consciousness (up to a point), I still like to imagine writing a version of the column called "Can This Marriage." But whatever my momentary diversions, Ann Landers is always there, sharing those vulnerable moments when I've just been beaten out for a seat on the subway, or am casting around desperately for an excuse to avoid writing a little while longer.

Ann would have made a terrific first woman vice-presidential candidate. If nothing else, she would have had the world's greatest campaign platform ("Dear Outraged Cardinal: Wake up and smell the coffee!"; "Dear Kicking Ass in Philadelphia: If you think an itchy button finger is the chief requirement for the presidency, you have bran where your brains belong"). I'm surprised, actually, that she was never mentioned as a consensus figure. After all, what else do I, a few million letter writers, and the Albert Lasker Foundation have in common? The Lasker Foundation gives awards for contributions to medicine. This year's recipients, just announced, are two Nobel Prize winners, the surgeon who pioneered lumpectomy, the head of the American Cancer Society, and Ann Landers. A spokesman for the foundation explained to the *News:* "Her push for the 1971 National Cancer Act . . . generated the greatest mail response in the history of Congress. Not even the Vietnam War generated as much mail."

Part of what attracts me to Ann is that she could be my aunt. Like my relatives on my father's side, she's a Jewish midwesterner, a complicated identity. Her midwestern concern with conventions and proprieties sometimes clashes with, sometimes reinforces the pragmatism of a minority that has to get along. Her (secular Jewish) impulses toward enlightenment, modernity, and tolerance run head-on into a sexual conservatism (midwestern and traditionally Jewish both) based not on a sense of sin but on what she sees as women's interest in upholding marriage and monogamy. And her *echt*-Jewish faith in "experts," particularly doctors and therapists, coexists with the upbeat common sense of our heartland.

Like my relatives, too, she's done her best, however unevenly and uneasily, to assimilate the cultural sea changes that have come to pass since she began the column 30 years ago. In the mid-'60s, my leaving my husband "for no good reason" caused a minor scandal in the family; when a cousin's girlfriend got pregnant, the cover story (which no one believed) was that they had been secretly married. Ten years later, several of my cousins were divorced (including the "secretly married" one) and sex outside marriage was a nonevent, though there was still some headshaking over another cousin's interracial relationship. Similarly, Ann once thought divorce could hardly ever be justified and failing marriages were generally the wife's fault; a few years ago, in a tone of rueful bemusement, she announced her own divorce in her column. Her husband had run off with a younger woman; her analysis, delivered on the Susskind show, was that he had lost his sense of direction after selling his business. And no, she had nothing to regret, she had been a good wife. Furthermore, though she had liked being married, she was enjoying the freedom of living alone.

The contemporary Ann approves of women who assert themselves in relationships and gives short shrift to authoritarian husbands. She thinks it's okay for women to have careers and fair that their husbands should do some of the housework. She has defended abortion rights (so has Abby). She assumes most single adults are having sex, and takes it in stride. She opposes discrimination against homosexuals, urges parents of gays to accept their children's way of life, and tells people not to feel guilty about their sexual habits, kinks, and fantasies, so long as they're not imposing on anyone else. She thinks parents who are horrified to discover that their teenage daughter is sexually active should stifle their punitive impulses, keep the lines of communication open, and advise her on birth control.

Still, when it comes to certain subjects the voice of the Jewish/midwestern mother is heard in the land, rising like bubbles from the primordial swamp. Sexual revolution or no, Ann sees it as the woman's job to restrain the irresponsible lust of the male, and those who lie down on the job, so to speak, have only themselves to blame if they get hurt. A recent column set the feminist antirape movement back 10 years. In it, Been Through It in Arizona took up the case of the couple who "repair to some private place for drinks and a little shared affection." In the middle of things, Marcia says, "John, don't." No struggle, just "John, don't." John does. Is this rape? No, said Been: "Unless she has communicated her unwillingness to have sex in a clearly unmistakable manner, she should not be allowed to translate her ambivalence into a felony charge." "Your letter makes an excellent point," said Ann. "And now, at the risk of sounding hilariously square, I'd like to suggest that the woman has . . . by her acceptance of such a cozy invitation, given the man reason to believe she is a candidate for whatever he might have in mind." "Dear Ann," I scribbled to myself, "Say it ain't so. Why is what he might have had in mind more important than what she might have had in mind? How do you know the invitation he thought he was giving was the one she thought she was accepting? Even if it was, doesn't she have the right to change her mind? Why isn't a simple 'no' unmistakable enough? Was she supposed to hit him over the head with a wine bottle? Why isn't he obliged to stop unless she's communicated her *willingness* to have sex in a clearly unmistakable manner?"

Then there's that touchiest of mother-daughter issues, teenage sex. Addressing the mothers, Ann is the soul of rationality and common sense; but when she talks to the daughters, the years fall away and we're back in the high school netherworld of virgins and tramps. How many of my unsent letters have been inspired by Ann's replies to weepy teenage girls who fell in love, wanted to be cool, or simply got tired of being nagged, and "let him," only to be dumped, impregnated, or labeled a slut? Half the time the letter writer is still mooning over the jerk who dropped her, imagining that if she had only proved worthy of his "respect" they would have had a bright future. Stern yet compassionate, Ann admonishes her to learn from her experience, hold her head up, and remember that a "bad reputation" will eventually succumb to impeccable behavior. ("Dear Ann: Your advice to Sorry Now stank. Here's mine: Sorry, be glad you're rid of 'Buddy.' He's an immature, manipulative creep who has Neanderthal attitudes toward women and is obviously incapable of feeling or appreciating honest affection. How dare he condemn you for something you both did? Why should you have to pass some boy's purity test? The only thing you should really be sorry about is sleeping with him because *he* wanted to, not because you did. Trust your own desires next time.")

In all my years of Landers-watching, I've never read a letter that took my view of this matter, nor have I ever seen one from a teenage girl who had sex, liked it, and wasn't punished for it. Well, maybe I just didn't get the paper that day. In general, Ann is pretty good about printing opinions she disagrees with—the column is full of long-running controversies on everything from whether the wife or the other woman has it better, to whether sex is the best thing in life or vastly overrated, to (this one went on for months) whether you should unroll toilet paper from the top or the bottom. Her impulses are antifundamentalist; without making a big deal of it, she simply declines to pander to the mean spirit of the times. And she's not above changing her mind in response to her irate readers or one of her experts. It's this side of her—this "it takes all kinds to make a world, and boy, have I seen them all" side—that allows me to indulge my kinkiest Ann Landers fantasy. "Dear Ann," the letter might go. "If you ever feel like taking off for a while and want a substitute, let me know. I have a very different take on the world. It would really shake up your readers, but after 30 years that might be a good thing. What do you say? Equally Opinionated and Waiting in New York."

Why do we read Ann Landers? Presumably because we enjoy gossip, "true" confessions, voyeurism—peeping into other people's privacy. And *how* do we read her? Ellen Willis reads her as a sign of the times, a way of "reading" ordinary peoples' conflicts about the roles and relationships they find themselves in: how are ordinary men and women faring in a world beset by the women's movement, teenage pregnancy, drugs, incest, violence? And *who* is this voice of advice: what are *her* values, *her* beliefs?

Willis "reads" Landers, the woman behind the column, and her reading reveals a complicated person whose mind, like yours, is inhabited by contradictions: as are all of our minds, once we start to think, to reflect, to interpret, to weigh up, to sort out, to transform mere events into experiences.

The roles and relationships we find ourselves in are shaped by the culture that each of us carries in the mind, but that culture is not a tidy monolith, or a neatly organized and static filing system or catalogue. On the contrary, it is more like a very complicated wrestling match, with hundreds of thousands of participants, all interacting with one another. Some of the wrestlers are mere beginners, and still vulnerable; others are at the peak of their form; and some are "over the hill" and should be quietly urged to retire before they get seriously injured.

Culture is dynamic, fluid, malleable, richly various, unpredictable (who would have predicted Madonna's success? Norman Mailer? Oprah Winfrey? Eddie Murphy? Health clubs? Jogging? McDonald's?), buffeted by cold economic winds, recharged by new possibilities, given to revivals, to circling back to where it was fifty years ago, subject to fashions and fads, and always, whatever its changes, expressive of an ideology, a set of beliefs about what matters, what is desirable, what we need, and above all about who is entitled to have power over us.

No wonder Ann Landers sometimes falls from her tightrope!

Take a peep at some of Ann Landers's columns, and see if you can (a) characterize her position on issues that interest you and (b) account for her longstanding popularity.

What are the fundamental, driving, inescapable *goals* for men and women in the dominant culture? For men, to succeed, to "make it"? For women, to marry? What do you think? Ellen Goodman, the writer and columnist, tackles the issue of women and getting married: is that different from *being married*? Do you *both* agree *and* disagree with Ellen Goodman?

ELLEN GOODMAN

Vowing to Get Married

She is going to get married.

This is not an announcement, you understand. It is, rather, her statement of intent. The poet has honorable intentions.

In fact, she has been going to get married for years now, almost since her divorce. Often across the telephone line that connects one coast and one life to another, the poet has talked out loud to the journalist about singleness as if she were a transient, somehow awkwardly living "between" marriages.

Tonight she says: "If things work out, we'll get married."

The journalist asks her, "Shall I call the caterer?" and they both laugh through the transcontinental echo. You see, they have been here before.

The poet has said three times in six years, "If things work out, we'll get married." The man in her plural has changed. But not her goal . . . and not her single status.

So, with a sigh of self-recognition, she tells the journalist, "Don't buy a dress yet." There is a pause, while the two friends think in tandem.

The poet is the same skeptic who once wrote a rhyme about the headlines that range like graffiti over wedding announcements: "Woman Has Nuptials." They sound, she said, like parts of the anatomy.

Moreover, this woman has not lived like those emotional migrants who set up tents, desperately trying to end their refugee life. She has rested with her children and her life quite comfortably.

The poet knows the difference between the times you have to compromise and the times when you are compromised. She won't discount her needs to bargain in the marriage market.

Nevertheless she is a single woman committed to the ideal marriage. She is going to get married. Someday. The two talk on and on, defying the telephone company, which promised them economy at night rates.

The journalist is not at all sure that her friend wants to mate again and tells her so. There are times she thinks the poet is merely appeasing the gods of her upbringing by assuring them that she, too, wants what she was taught to want. She wonders if the poet is making a bargain—a promise to remarry in the future in return for living as she chooses in the present.

The poet wonders, too. She sees marriage as the question that demands to be answered, even though she knows from experience and observation that it may answer very little.

She knows that marriage carries a weight of its own in our world. If divorce is the context in which we live out our fragile marriages, marriage is the state against which people judge our nonmarriages.

It may be all quite mad, says the poet, but marriage is simply *there*. It is hard, she says, to be unaffected by its powerful presence.

The poet reminds her friend of the times they have told each other, "Everyone we know either gets married or splits." Perhaps it is true; perhaps it is a truism. But it carries with it a self-fulfilling anxiety.

There is just no way to ignore it, says the poet.

The parents of her students get nervous when the children who are living together "premaritally" show no signs of marrying. Her sister asks about her newest love, "How serious is it?" Only marriage is "serious." Every other relationship is, by our social definitions, one which "hasn't worked out yet."

The poet and the journalist have known men who matter more to them than those they were related to by titles. But society takes titles more "seriously" than feelings. An older friend of theirs loved a woman. But when she died, he had no place to mourn. He was not, you see, a widower.

It is odd, living in the State of Flux, with marriages ending in divorces ending in remarriages. No one knows whether the constant is togetherness or aloneness.

The poet on the West Coast believes in the possibility of polishing and perfecting. The journalist on the East Coast believes this: If it is working, don't fix it.

They both see the way the Marriage Issue turns a couple into a ménage à trois: she and he and The Question. The journalist tries to ignore it, which may be absurd. The poet tries to accept it, which may be equally absurd.

Later, after they have spent their budgets and their insights over this long distance, the journalist thinks about her friend's last words: "There is something in me that believes marriage is a more complete commitment. When I look at married people, I don't see it often, yet I keep believing it. What do you do with that?"

Maybe what you do is plan to get married. When, of course, "everything" works out.

> The natural and unconscious community of tradition rapidly disappears from the earth.
>
> W. H. Auden

A few generations ago, our ancestors were preoccupied by the task of growing or earning enough to survive on. As time passed, these primary economic problems fell into the background: we can take many things for granted that were problematic to them. Conversely, questions which they took for granted have become problematic for us.

It is hardly surprising, therefore, that we subscribe to the myth that life then was simpler, easier, more satisfying, *really* satisfying. Certainly, one of the major changes in our culture, a shift rooted in economic change, is that in certain areas we have more options: the result, of course, is that we are more confused, more indecisive, more perplexed. Our liberties come with a high price: for the individual, Auden argued, it means accepting "the loneliness and anxiety of having to choose himself, his faith, his vocation, his tastes." In a "traditional" society, one's life was governed by rules that emanated from the center; in a rapidly changing culture committed to freedom, on the other hand, we all end up living

on what Auden called "The Margin." "The Margin is a hard taskmaster; it says to the individual: 'It's no good your running to me and asking me to make you into someone. You must choose. I won't try to prevent your choice, but I can't and won't help you make it. If you try to put your trust in me, in public opinion, you will become, not someone but no one, a neuter atom of the public" (*The American Scene*).

Auden wrote these words in 1946, just over forty years ago, almost two generations' span. Has the passage of time confirmed the wisdom of his convictions? Is the "State of Flux" not itself turning into a new kind of center? Is the Margin still on the edge?

ANDREW HACKER

U/S and Marriage

If we live, indeed, in the "State of Flux," how exactly do we get our bearings? Is there a compass in the classroom? Probably not, but we can turn to Andrew Hacker, the prime of statisticians, and see how we, our families, and our friends compare with the rest of U/S.*

*Hacker's invention: it means both U.S.A. and "us," as distinct from "them."

> *The great gift of fiction and autobiography lies in its capacity for rendering the texture, the feel, the inwardness of the individual's life-as-a-social life: the privilege is to "see" from the inside. Statistics offer not an* inferior *or a* better *knowledge, but a* different *kind of knowledge: so we don't read them as we would read a novel!*
> *See, then, how U/S looked when Hacker compiled his figures.*

Statistics on marital status deal with the experience of *individuals* as opposed to households. Figures on this subject come from two main sources. First, there are the findings of the Census Bureau's Current Population Survey for 1980. Second, there are figures on marriage and divorce compiled by the National Center for Health Statistics. Some of these statistics are for 1980, but in other cases, we will have to satisfy ourselves with figures from earlier years due to delays in collection and publication.

So far as definitions are concerned, "single" refers to persons who have never been married. "Married" means individuals who are married and currently living with their spouses. "Separated" can mean either a legal separation prior to divorce or married persons living apart for any other reason. "Divorced" means that legal proceedings have been completed and the person has not remarried. "Widowed" means the couple was still married when one of the spouses died. Thus a person stays in the "divorced" category even if his or her ex-spouse dies.

Marital Status: Numbers and Ratios

The following was the marital status of American men and women who were aged 20 and over in 1980:

	MEN		WOMEN	
	Number	*Percentage*	*Number*	*Percentage*
Single	13,626,000	19.5%	10,512,000	13.5%
Married	48,545,000	69.3%	48,013,000	61.7%
Separated	2,046,000	2.9%	3,065,000	3.9%
Widowed	1,972,000	2.8%	10,476,000	13.5%
Divorced	3,869,000	5.5%	5,805,000	7.4%
	70,058,000	100.0%	77,871,000	100.0%

Among persons aged 20 and over, there are 1,296 single men for every 1,000 single women, because more women get married before they are 20. For the same reason, there are slightly more married men than married women: 1,011 to 1,000.

However, there are 668 separated men for every 1,000 separated women, 666 divorced men for every 1,000 divorced women, and only 188 widowers for every 1,000 widows. If these three groups are considered together, there are 408 unattached men for every 1,000 women of similar status.

Are There More Separated Women Than Men? In theory, the number of "separated" men and women should be precisely equal. After all, "separation" means both

spouses are still legally married to each other, and they cannot marry someone else until a divorce has been decreed. How, then, are we to explain the fact that 1,019,000 more women than men say that they are "separated"?

Officials at the Census give three general explanations. First, some men may have married again without bothering with a divorce. Second, some separated men may choose to describe themselves as single. Third, women who have never been married but have children may prefer to say they are separated rather than single. Insofar as this is so, the number of women who really belong in the "single" category should be somewhat larger.

MARRIAGE

The "Marriage Rate." One way to measure the marriage rate is by comparing the number of weddings with the number of unmarried women aged 15 to 44. (In this age range, 93.5 percent of all women's marriages and remarriages occur.)

In 1960 there were 148.0 marriages for every 1,000 unmarried women between 15 and 44. By 1970 the rate was down to 140.2 per 1,000, and in 1979 only 107.9 women got married for every 1,000 in their potential pool.

For 1980 and 1981 we only have marriage rates as measured against the total population. For both those years the rate was 10.6 per 1,000.

Marriage Rates by States

Marriages rates by states are computed on the basis of the overall population. The state with the highest marriage rate is Nevada, which had 156.8 marriages performed in 1980 for every 1,000 persons living in the state.

However, this is a highly inflated figure, because most of the couples marrying there come to Nevada simply for the ceremony and are not residents of the state. (In 1980 there were 121,874 marriages in Nevada, more than the 110,667 in Illinois or the 110,875 in the six New England states together.)*

---

*Nevada also has an abnormally high divorce rate of 18.6 (measured against each 1,000 of its residents), because many people still travel there to dissolve their marriages. Indeed, a considerable number remarry there the same day their decree comes through.

Among the rest of the states, those with the highest marriage rates in 1980 were: South Carolina (18.2 per 1,000 population), Oklahoma (15.8 per 1,000), Wyoming (14.6), Idaho (14.3), and Texas (13.6).

The states with the lowest marriage rates were: New Jersey (7.5 per 1,000), Delaware (7.6), Rhode Island (7.8), New York (8.0), and Pennsylvania and North Carolina (both 8.1).

Marriage and Remarriage

In 1979, of the persons getting married, 70.1 percent were doing so for the first time, and within this group, 50.6 were women and 49.4 percent were men.

Another 26.3 percent of the brides and grooms had been previously divorced, of which 48.1 percent were women and 51.9 percent were men.

And 3.6 percent of the marriage partners were widows or widowers. In this group, 52.2 percent were women and 47.8 percent were men. However, among widowed persons aged 65 or over who remarried, 60.6 percent were men and only 39.4 percent were women.

Month of Marriage

The following are the percentage of marriage ceremonies occurring in each month, according to whether it is the bride's first marriage or if she is remarrying.

If marriages were spread evenly throughout the year, the average would work out to 8.3 percent in every month. Also, these figures vary somewhat from year to year, depending on how many Fridays and Saturdays (when most weddings occur) there are in each month.

BRIDE'S FIRST MARRIAGE		BRIDE REMARRYING	
	Percentage		*Percentage*
June	12.3%	December	10.2%
August	11.1%	July	10.2%
July	10.7%	June	9.7%
September	9.6%	August	8.7%
May	8.9%	April	8.5%
October	8.8%	October	8.5%
April	7.9%	May	8.4%
December	7.4%	November	8.3%
November	7.0%	September	8.1%
March	5.8%	March	6.8%
February	5.4%	February	6.7%
January	5.1%	January	5.9%
	100.0%		100.0%

Day of the Week

Here are the percentage of marriages occurring on the various days of the week: Saturdays (53.0 percent), Fridays (19.7 percent), Sundays (8.0 percent), Thursdays

(5.6 percent), Mondays (5.2 percent), Tuesdays (4.3 percent), and Wednesdays (4.2 percent).

Religious or Civil Ceremonies

When it is the *first* marriage for the bride, 79.2 percent of the weddings are religious ceremonies and 20.8 percent are civil. (When the bride is getting *remarried*, 60.6 percent of the ceremonies are religious and 39.4 percent are civil.)

The following are the states in which the highest proportions of brides' *first* marriages are religious ceremonies: West Virginia (97.9 percent), Indiana (91.0 percent), Missouri (90.0 percent), Delaware (89.6 percent), and Montana (89.0 percent).

Those states that have the lowest percentages of religious ceremonies at brides' *first* marriages are South Carolina (43.7 percent), Georgia (59.1 percent), Alaska (62.9 percent), Florida (65.3 percent), and Wyoming (66.7 percent).

Age at Marriage

The median age of first marriages is 22.1 for the bride and 24.6 for the groom, a difference of 30 months.

The median age at remarriage where the bride has been divorced is 31.9, and for the groom it is 35.3, a difference of 41 months.

And at remarriages for people who have been widowed, the median age for the bride is 55.2 and for the groom is 61.7, a difference of 78 months.

Median Age at Marriage: 1890–1980

The following were the median ages at first marriages for men and women from 1890 through 1980:

	MEN	WOMEN	AGE DIFFERENCE (YEARS)
1980	24.6	22.1	2.5
1970	23.2	20.8	2.4
1960	22.8	20.3	2.5
1950	22.8	20.3	2.5
1940	24.3	21.5	2.8
1930	24.3	21.3	3.0
1920	24.6	21.2	3.4
1910	25.1	21.6	3.5
1900	25.9	21.9	4.0
1890	26.1	22.0	4.1

Age of Marriage for Women: 1970 and 1980

In 1970 altogether 86.0 percent of all women had been married at least once by the age of 25. By 1980 the proportion of women married by 25 was down to 71.6 percent.

Here are figures on how many women were married at various ages in 1970 and 1980:

PERCENTAGES

Age	1970	1980
18	18.0%	12.0%
19	31.2%	22.5%
20	43.1%	33.5%
21	56.1%	40.3%
22	66.5%	51.9%
23	77.6%	58.2%
24	82.1%	66.5%
25	86.0%	71.6%
26	87.8%	77.3%
27	90.9%	77.9%
28	91.1%	84.1%
29	92.0%	85.5%
30–34	93.8%	90.5%
35–39	94.6%	93.8%
40–44	95.1%	95.2%

Age Differences in Marriages

Among American marriages, the husband is younger than the wife among 14.4 percent of the couples; both partners are the same age in another 12.1 percent of the marriages. (This means the same age in terms of years—statistics are not divided by months. Needless to say, except in some very rare cases, one spouse is always older or younger than the other.)

In the 73.4 percent of the marriages where the husband is older, he is 1 to 4 years older among 46.6 percent of the couples; 5 to 9 years older with 19.6 percent; and 10 or more years the wife's senior in 7.2 percent.

Interracial Marriages

In 1980 there were 166,000 married couples in which the partners were black and white.

In 120,000 of these marriages (or 72.3 percent) the husband was black and the wife was white. In the other 46,000 (or 27.7 percent) the wife was black and the husband was white.

When Auden was writing about "The Margin" in 1946, there were quite a few words in the American English language which generally were left unspoken and certainly unwritten: no prizes for guessing what they were; one of them was *rape*.

With the changes signaled by the women's movement, some conventions dissolved, some taboos were eroded. In 1975, Susan Brownmiller published *Against Our Will: Men, Women and Rape*; five years later, Andrea Dworkin published *Pornography: Men Possessing Women*; and Walter Kendrick has recently published (late 1987) a perfectly serious historical survey of pornography in various cultures, *The Secret Museum*. Toward the end of his book, he responds to his reading of Brownmiller and Dworkin.

WALTER KENDRICK

The Secret Museum

The post-pornographic Young Person came of age in the years just after the rejection of the Pornography Commission's *Report*, in a social atmosphere of disgruntlement and stagnation. She was the offspring of several feminist organizations, most notably the Women Against Pornography (WAP), founded in 1976. The events leading up to Nixon's resignation in August 1974, together with the whimpering end of the Vietnam War almost a year later, had lent fresh conviction to the traditional American belief that public authorities, left to themselves, will either do nothing or make matters worse. But the equally endemic faith survived that private activism, operating by strictly legal means, could awaken the sleepy guardians of justice. It was in this spirit that WAP and other organizations set about righting what they saw as the most grievous of social inequities—a sexual tyranny that fostered violence against the minds and bodies of women.

An early statement of their position was provided by Susan Brownmiller's *Against Our Will: Men, Women and Rape*, published in 1975. Brownmiller sought to investigate the entire phenomenon of rape, in all its aspects and throughout Western history; she defined rape broadly and in different terms from those of the law:

> A sexual invasion of the body by force, an incursion into the private, personal inner space without consent—in short, an internal assault from one of several avenues and by one of several methods—constitutes a deliberate violation of emotional, physical and rational integrity and is a hostile, degrading act of violence that deserves the name of rape.

She demonstrated with clarity and precision how traditional definitions of rape, embodied in laws written by men, derived from a conception of women as male property: for all the severity of the punishments they prescribed, such laws were part and parcel of the same system that produced rape itself. She proposed a radical transformation of attitudes and values as the only sure means of rectifying this ancient, pervasive injustice. And she had rather little to say about pornography, treating it as only the most blatant reflection of myths visible everywhere in contemporary culture:

> Pornography, like rape, is a male invention, designed to dehumanize women, to reduce the female to an object of sexual access. . . . The staple of porn will always be the naked female body, breasts and genitals exposed, because as man devised it, her naked body is the female's 'shame,' her private parts the private property of man,

while his are the ancient, holy, universal, patriarchal instrument of his power, his rule by force over *her*.

This is a distinctly post-pornographic definition of "pornography," though one would never know this from Brownmiller herself. Like most writers on the subject, she treated pornography as an ahistorical phenomenon, which had always looked much as it did at the time of writing—in this case, 1975. In fact, however, she relied wholly on the rather recent equation of "pornography" with "worthless trash"; her archetypal pornographic image was that of the stag film, a modern genre in both medium and content, and one that no one had ever tried to defend on aesthetic grounds. Brownmiller's casual employment of the abbreviation "porn"—which, along with "porno," had become almost universal in the post-pornographic era—suggests her assumption that any well-informed reader, male or female, would be familiar with such materials, at least by repute. Twenty years earlier, that familiarity did not exist, but the 1970 *Report* had indicated that 85 percent of adult men and 70 percent of adult women in the United States "have been exposed at sometime during their lives to depictions of explicit sexual material in either visual or textual form." A polysyllabic, technical-sounding word like "pornography" no longer seemed appropriate to such a commonplace article—a curious fate for a concept that had begun its career in the locked cases of museums and libraries. Familiarity, of course, had bred contempt; but it had also produced a contrary tendency that clashed oddly with the insistence that pornography was worthless by definition. Trashy though stag films were, Brownmiller read them in a manner best described as mythic: the raw exposure of a woman's genitals became a statement about her social and political status; a penis became an "ancient, holy, universal, patriarchal instrument." The tacit presupposition that the makers and viewers of these displays were unconscious of their mythic meaning only lent greater impact to Brownmiller's interpretation. Like Freud reading dreams, she was able to find in apparently trivial images a profound significance of which the pornographer, like the dreamer, was unaware.

The mythic reading of pornography also shares with psychoanalysis the advantage (for the interpreter) that its conclusions are irrefutable and always the same. But it is split down the middle by a contradiction that does not trouble psychoanalysis. Freud maintained that dreams were only *apparently* trivial; in fact, they were neither "meaningless" nor "absurd," but rather "psychical phenomena of complete validity." Brownmiller and her followers, in contrast, wished to interpret pornography in the most portentous possible manner, while at the same time maintaining that it was poisonous garbage, worthy only of destruction. The contradiction reached a sort of apotheosis in Andrea Dworkin's *Pornography: Men Possessing Women* (1980), the most vitriolic entry in a genre not noted for self-restraint. There had been anger enough in Brownmiller; in Dworkin there was nothing *but* anger, a scalding flood of it for more than two hundred pages. Dworkin's arguments were much the same as Brownmiller's, padded to bursting with polemic. Her interpretive techniques were similar, too, though she wielded them with a hamhanded brutality that made Brownmiller look namby-pamby by comparison. A virtuoso instance comes early in *Pornography*: a five-page analysis of a photograph from *Hustler* magazine representing two men dressed as hunters, with a naked woman tied spread-eagle to the hood of their Jeep like an animal trophy. From this photograph, its title ("Beaver Hunters"), and a brief accompanying text, Dworkin reads out every feature of the violent male hegemony* that, in her view, has characterized Western culture since its dimmest origins. The reading is ingenious:

> Sex as power is the most explicit meaning of the photograph. The power of sex unambiguously resides in the male, though the characterization of the female as a wild animal suggests that the sexuality of the untamed female is dangerous to men. But the triumph of the hunters is the nearly universal triumph of men over women. . . . The hunters are figures of virility. Their penises are hidden but their guns are emphasized. The car, beloved ally of men in the larger culture, also indicates virility, especially when a woman is tied to it naked instead of draped over it wearing an evening gown. The pornographic image explicates the advertising image, and the advertising image echoes the pornographic image.

Staccato, repetitive, incantatory, Dworkin's style is that of an enraptured demagogue; her aim is not, as Brownmiller's was, to enlighten and persuade, but rather to excite preexisting feelings. Already by 1980, the feminist antipornography campaign had acquired an extremist faction.

Dworkin also went far beyond Brownmiller in insisting upon pornography as not only the clearest depiction but also the cause of violence against women. Her rhetorical repertoire does not include techniques of logical explanation; she never outlines how this causation is supposed to operate. But there is no question of her belief in it: "The woman's sex is appropriated, her body is possessed, she is used and she is despised: the pornography does it and the pornography proves it." The conclusion—unexplicated but very plain throughout the book—is that an entire system of inherited and inculcated values would somehow vanish, or at least become innocuous, if its rudest embodiment were made unavailable. It is not difficult to imagine that pictures like "Beaver Hunters" might reinforce and justify the prejudices of men who look at them; they might also—though this deduction is shakier— encourage those men to act out their prejudices in ways they would not have thought of on their own. Even according to Dworkin's argument, however, it is impossible to conclude that pornography creates attitudes in men who did not have them already. There is a strange incongruity in tracing a violence said to be endemic in Western culture back to some pictures and films that could not have existed a century ago and that have been promiscuously on sale for only about twenty years. The removal of pornography from view would amount only to a kind of window dressing; the supposed attitudes it reflects would then merely go underground, where they might fester.

Nevertheless, it was to this goal that WAP and related organizations turned their attention. Their methods were principally the traditional ones of picketing, protest marches, and the distribution of leaflets, along with the latter-day addition of T-shirts. By 1983, however, they had advanced to a new tactic, the proposal of legislation. A century and more of futility might have taught them that any such

---

*Hegemony: *power over* a weaker group or individual.

law is bound to be ineffectual, even to foster the very thing it would suppress. They might also have seen that their new Young Person—a brutal, low-minded male, or indeed any male at all—was only a weirdly transmogrified version of a fantasy that, in the past, had abetted the oppression of the very people (women) who now wished to appropriate it. But if the antipornography feminists glanced at history, the only lesson they learned was that past procedures had been incorrect, not that the effort itself was both tyrannical and hopeless. With law professor Catharine A. MacKinnon, Dworkin collaborated on the drafting of an ordinance that made its first official appearance before the City Council of Minneapolis, Minnesota, in December 1983. After two days of public hearings, the Council approved it by a one-vote margin; Mayor Donald Fraser vetoed it immediately and did so again a few months later, when a revised version was approved by the Council. Revised again, it was signed into law by Mayor William H. Hudnut III of Indianapolis, Indiana; this time, it was declared unconstitutional by District Judge Sarah Evans Parker. In yet another form, it was voted down by the County Council of Suffolk County, New York. None of these defeats served to convince MacKinnon, Dworkin, and their supporters that the very concept of the ordinance was indefensible, let alone illegal. They persisted in believing that the trouble lay in details, which a little more tinkering would set straight.

In all its incarnations, the MacKinnon-Dworkin ordinance bears little overt resemblance to earlier legislation against pornography. The most striking innovation is that the vicious old circle of synonyms—"lewd," "lascivious," "obscene," and so on—is completely absent from it. The manufacture and distribution of pornography are also no longer criminal offenses; pornography has become a civil matter, specifically a matter of civil rights. As it stood in April 1985, the ordinance (then in "model" rather than practical form) defined pornography as

> the graphic sexually explicit subordination of women through pictures and/or words that also includes one or more of the following: (i) women are presented dehumanized as sexual objects, things, or commodities; or (ii) women are presented as sexual objects who enjoy pain or humiliation; or (iii) women are presented as sexual objects who experience sexual pleasure in being raped; or (iv) women are presented as sexual objects tied up or cut up or mutilated or bruised or physically hurt; or (v) women are presented in postures or positions of sexual submission, servility, or display; or (vi) women's body parts—including but not limited to vaginas, breasts, or buttocks— are exhibited such that women are reduced to those parts; or (vii) women are presented as whores by nature; or (viii) women are presented being penetrated by animals; or (ix) women are presented in scenarios of degradation, injury, torture, shown as filthy or inferior, bleeding, bruised, or hurt in a context that makes these conditions sexual.

This is, no doubt, the longest, most detailed definition of "pornography" ever composed. By any prior standard, it is pornographic in its own right; an enterprising filmmaker might well take it as a blueprint for outraging everybody, even in the jaded late twentieth century. Yet for all its gruesome explicitness, its utter lack of attention to "art" or "value," it is pornography's most aesthetic definition, too. Every clause demands some judgment upon the manufacturer's intentions or the viewer's response, the same dreary problems that used to call "experts" into court. Who but an expert could determine, for example, whether some portrayal of a "bleeding, bruised, or hurt" woman had been placed in "a context that makes these conditions sexual"? Women (and men) bleed and get hurt in an immense variety of contexts, and sexuality is immensely variable. We return once more to our starting point, as we seemed doomed to do.

In mid-1985, yet another official investigation of pornography was launched, this time under the jurisdiction of the Attorney General. Its *Final Report*, issued a year later, seemed designed to obliterate the 1970 *Report*—indeed, the entire twentieth century—and return the United States to the days of Comstockery, though with a few up-to-date flourishes that camouflaged the atavism. Predictably unable to define "pornography," the 1986 Commission nevertheless used the word on virtually every one of its 2,000 pages; unable to establish any definite connection between pornography and antisocial behavior, it nevertheless asserted that the connection was automatic and inescapable. According to the new *Report*, the nature of pornography had changed radically since 1970, exhibiting an intensified focus on violence toward women and the violation of children. Immediate action was therefore necessary, on all levels of government, to halt the advance of this brand-new plague.

Unlike its predecessor, the 1986 *Report* is an unbelievably fatuous document, riddled with false reasoning and bad prose. It is also blatantly pornographic. . . . The *Report* exempts the written or printed word from all prosecution, on the grounds that "the absence of photographs necessarily produces a message that seems to necessitate for its assimilation more real thought and less almost reflexive reaction than does the more typical pornographic item. There remains a difference between reading a book and looking at pictures. . . ." The real difference, of course, had to do with the nature of the Young Person, late-twentieth-century style. He was a functional, if not a total, illiterate; the danger he posed was heightened rather than reduced by this disability.

The *Report*, despite its overall backwardness, reflected the temper of its time when it recognized the impotence of words. It was also timely in maintaining an absolute silence on questions of morality. It speaks instead—following the antipornography feminists—of "harms," by which it means physical or psychological damage wrought upon women and children by the manufacturers and "consumers" of smut. This apparent objectivity merely masked the old desire whose course I have attempted to chronicle: the urge to regulate the behavior of those who seem to threaten the social order. By 1986, though women and children stood in need of as much surveillance as ever, the category of "the poor" had definitively altered from those who lacked money to those who lacked enlightenment; the threat, however, was the same. Women do get raped and battered; pictures of rape and battery often abet these crimes. It remains absurd, however, to suppose that the suppression of the image can prevent the perpetration of the deed. Sexual violence and representations of sexual violence emanate from the identical source, a tangled web of attitudes that cannot possibly be unraveled by setting a few bonfires. Yet the myth persists. Even the most sanguine observer feels the approach of despair at the spectacle of such stubborn ignorance, such stiff-necked denial of history.

Why should we not end this chapter on a happier note? We can think of nothing happier than the way we can lose ourselves in reading fiction. You have seen how columnists and a statistician (another kind of columnist!) deal with what is for most people the most important negotiation of their lives—choosing a mate. Let us, then, see how a novelist and short-story writer, Alice Munro, tackles it. But, first, let us have the novelist Philip Roth (b. 1933) remind us of the distinctive gifts that fiction can give us: he is answering questions put to him by someone else.

PHILIP ROTH

On Reading Fiction

WHAT DO NOVELS DO THEN?

To the ordinary reader? Novels provide readers with something to read. At their best writers change the *way* readers read. That seems to me the only realistic expectation. It also seems to me quite enough. Reading novels is a deep and singular pleasure, a gripping and mysterious human activity that does not require any more moral or political justification than sex.

BUT ARE THERE NO OTHER AFTEREFFECTS?

You asked me if I thought my fiction had changed anything in the culture and the answer is no. Sure there's been some scandal, but people are scandalized all the time; it's a way of life for them. It doesn't mean a thing. If you ask if I *want* my fiction to change anything in the culture, the answer is still no. What I want is to possess my readers while they are reading my book—if I can, to possess them in ways that other writers don't. Then let them return, just as they were, to a world where everybody else is working to change, persuade, tempt, and control them. The best readers come to fiction to be free of all that noise, to have set loose in them the consciousness that's otherwise conditioned and hemmed in by all that *isn't* fiction. This is something that every child, smitten by books, understands immediately, though it's not at all a childish idea about the importance of reading.

ALICE MUNRO

How I Met My Husband

This story by Alice Munro, a Canadian writer, is set in the 1920s, the decade of the barnstormers, when most young men in North America were crazy about flying.

We heard the plane come over at noon, roaring through the radio news, and we were sure it was going to hit the house, so we all ran out into the yard. We saw it come in over the tree tops, all red and silver, the first close-up plane I ever saw. Mrs. Peebles screamed.

"Crash landing," their little boy said. Joey was his name.

"It's okay," said Dr. Peebles. "He knows what he's doing." Dr. Peebles was only an animal doctor, but had a calming way of talking, like any doctor.

This was my first job—working for Dr. and Mrs. Peebles, who had bought an old house out on the Fifth Line, about five miles out of town. It was just when the trend was starting of town people buying up old farms, not to work them but to live on them.

We watched the plane land across the road, where the fairgrounds used to be. It did make a good landing field, nice and level for the old race track, and the barns and display sheds torn down now for scrap lumber so there was nothing in the way. Even the old grandstand boys had burned.

"All right," said Mrs. Peebles, snappy as she always was when she got over her nerves. "Let's go back in the house. Let's not stand here gawking like a set of farmers."

She didn't say that to hurt my feelings. It never occurred to her.

I was just setting the dessert down when Loretta Bird arrived, out of breath, at the screen door.

"I thought it was going to crash into the house and kill youse all!"

She lived on the next place and the Peebles thought she was a countrywoman, they didn't know the difference. She and her husband didn't farm, he worked on the roads and had a bad name for drinking. They had seven children and couldn't get credit at the Hi-Way Grocery. The Peebles made her welcome, not knowing any better, as I say, and offered her dessert.

Dessert was never anything to write home about, at their place. A dish of Jello or sliced bananas or fruit out of a tin. "Have a house without a pie, be ashamed until you die," my mother used to say, but Mrs. Peebles operated differently.

Loretta Bird saw me getting the can of peaches.

"Oh, never mind," she said. "I haven't got the right kind of a stomach to trust what comes out of those tins, I can only eat home canning."

I could have slapped her. I bet she never put down fruit in her life.

"I know what he's landed here for," she said. "He's got permission to use the fairgrounds and take people up for rides. It costs a dollar. It's the same fellow who was over at Palmerston last week and was up the lakeshore before that. I wouldn't go up, if you paid me."

"I'd jump at the chance," Dr. Peebles said. "I'd like to see this neighborhood from the air."

Mrs. Peebles said she would just as soon see it from the ground. Joey said he wanted to go and Heather did, too. Joey was nine and Heather was seven.

"Would you, Edie?" Heather said.

I said I didn't know. I was scared, but I never admitted that, especially in front of children I was taking care of.

"People are going to be coming out here in their cars raising dust and trampling your property, if I was you I would complain," Loretta said. She hooked her legs around the chair rung and I knew we were in for a lengthy visit. After Dr. Peebles went back to his office or out on his next call and Mrs. Peebles went for her nap, she would hang around me while I was trying to do the dishes. She would pass remarks about the Peebles in their own house.

"She wouldn't find time to lay down in the middle of the day, if she had seven kids like I got."

She asked me did they fight and did they keep things in the dresser drawer not to have babies with. She said it was a sin if they did. I pretended I didn't know what she was talking about.

I was fifteen and away from home for the first time. My parents had made the effort and sent me to high school for a year, but I didn't like it. I was shy of strangers and the work was hard, they didn't make it nice for you or explain the way they do now. At the end of the year the averages were published in the paper, and mine came out at the very bottom, 37 per cent. My father said that's enough and I didn't blame him. The last thing I wanted, anyway, was to go on and end up teaching school. It happened the very day the paper came out with my disgrace in it. Dr. Peebles was staying at our place for dinner, having just helped one of our cows to have twins, and he said I looked smart to him and his wife was looking for a girl to help. He said she felt tied down, with the two children, out in the country. I guess she would, my mother said, being polite, though I could tell from her face she was wondering what on earth it would be like to have only two children and no barn work, and then to be complaining.

When I went home, I would describe to them the work I had to do, and it made everybody laugh. Mrs. Peebles had an automatic washer and dryer, the first I ever saw. I have had those in my own home for such a long time now it's hard to remember how much of a miracle it was to me, not having to struggle with the wringer and hang up and haul down. Let alone not having to heat water. Then there was practically no baking. Mrs. Peebles said she couldn't make pie crust, the most amazing thing I ever heard a woman admit. I could, of course, and I could make light biscuits and white cake and a dark cake, but they didn't want it, she said they watched their figures. The only thing I didn't like about working there, in fact, was feeling half hungry a lot of the time. I used to bring back a box of doughnuts made out at home, and hide them under my bed. The children found out, and I didn't mind sharing, but I thought I better bind them to secrecy.

The day after the plane landed Mrs. Peebles put both children in the car and drove over to Chesley, to get their hair cut. There was a good woman then at Chesley for doing hair. She got hers done at the same place, Mrs. Peebles did, and that meant they would be gone a good while. She had to pick a day Dr. Peebles wasn't going out into the country, she didn't have her own car. Cars were still in short supply then, after the war.

I loved being left in the house alone, to do my work at leisure. The kitchen was all white and bright yellow, with fluorescent lights. That was before they ever thought of making the appliances all different colors and doing the cupboards like dark old wood and hiding the lighting. I loved light. I loved the double sink. So would anybody new-come from washing dishes in a dishpan with a rag-plugged hole on an oilcloth-covered table by light of a coal-oil lamp. I kept everything shining.

The bathroom too. I had a bath in there once a week. They wouldn't have minded if I took one oftener, but to me it seemed like asking too much, or maybe risking making it less wonderful. The basin and the tub and the toilet were all pink, and there were glass doors with flamingoes painted on them, to shut off the tub. The light had a rosy cast and the mat sank under your feet like snow, except that it was warm. The mirror was three-way. With the mirror all steamed up and the air like a perfume cloud, from things I was allowed to use, I stood up on the side of the tub and admired myself naked, from three directions. Sometimes I thought about the way we lived out at home and the way we lived here and how one way was so hard to imagine when you were living the other way. But I thought it was still a lot easier, living the way we lived at home, to picture something like this, the painted flamingoes and the warmth and the soft mat, than it was for anybody knowing only things like this to picture how it was the other way. And why was that?

I was through my jobs in no time, and had the vegetables peeled for supper and sitting in cold water besides. Then I went into Mrs. Peebles' bedroom. I had been in there plenty of times, cleaning, and I always took a good look in her closet, at the clothes she had hanging there. I wouldn't have looked in her drawers, but a closet is open to anybody. That's a lie. I would have looked in drawers, but I would have felt worse doing it and been more scared she could tell.

Some clothes in her closet she wore all the time, I was quite familiar with them. Others she never put on, they were pushed to the back. I was disappointed to see no wedding dress. But there was one long dress I could just see the skirt of, and I was hungering to see the rest. Now I took note of where it hung and lifted it out. It was satin, a lovely weight on my arm, light bluish-green in color, almost silvery. It had a fitted, pointed waist and a full skirt and an off-the-shoulder fold hiding the little sleeves.

Next thing was easy. I got out of my own things and slipped it on. I was slimmer at fifteen than anybody would believe who knows me now and the fit was beautiful. I didn't, of course, have a strapless bra on, which was what it needed, I just had to slide my straps down my arms under the material. Then I tried pinning up my hair, to get the effect. One thing led to another. I put on rouge and lipstick and eyebrow pencil from her dresser. The heat of the day and the weight of the satin and all the excitement made me thirsty, and I went out to the kitchen, got-up as I was, to get a glass of ginger ale with ice cubes from the refrigerator. The Peebles drank ginger ale, or fruit drinks, all day, like water, and I was getting so I did too. Also there was no limit on ice cubes, which I was so fond of I would even put them in a glass of milk.

I turned from putting the ice tray back and saw a man watching me through the screen. It was the luckiest thing in the world I didn't spill the ginger ale down the front of me then and there.

"I never meant to scare you. I knocked but you were getting the ice out, you didn't hear me."

I couldn't see what he looked like, he was dark the way somebody is pressed up against a screen door with the bright daylight behind them. I only knew he wasn't from around here.

"I'm from the plane over there. My name is Chris Watters and what I was wondering was if I could use that pump."

There was a pump in the yard. That was the way the people used to get their water. Now I noticed he was carrying a pail.

"You're welcome," I said. "I can get it from the tap and save you pumping." I guess I wanted him to know we had piped water, didn't pump ourselves.

"I don't mind the exercise." He didn't move, though, and finally he said, "Were you going to a dance?"

Seeing a stranger there had made me entirely forget how I was dressed.

"Or is that the way ladies around here generally get dressed up in the afternoon?"

I didn't know how to joke back then. I was too embarrassed.

"You live here? Are you the lady of the house?"

"I'm the hired girl."

Some people change when they find that out, their whole way of looking at you and speaking to you changes but his didn't.

"Well, I just wanted to tell you you look very nice. I was so surprised when I looked in the door and saw you. Just because you looked so nice and beautiful."

I wasn't even old enough then to realize how out of the common it is, for a man to say something like that to a woman, or somebody he is treating like a woman. For a man to say a word like *beautiful*. I wasn't old enough to realize or to say anything back, or in fact to do anything but wish he would go away. Not that I didn't like him, but just that it upset me so, having him look at me, and me trying to think of something to say.

He must have understood. He said good-bye, and thanked me, and went and started filling his pail from the pump. I stood behind the Venetian blinds in the dining room, watching him. When he had gone, I went into the bedroom and took the dress off and put it back in the same place. I dressed in my own clothes and took my hair down and washed my face, wiping it on Kleenex, which I threw in the wastebasket.

The Peebles asked me what kind of man he was. Young, middle-aged, short, tall? I couldn't say.

"Good-looking?" Dr. Peebles teased me.

I couldn't think a thing but that he would be coming to get his water again, he would be talking to Dr. and Mrs. Peebles, making friends with them, and he would mention seeing me that first afternoon, dressed up. Why not mention it? He would think it was funny. And no idea of the trouble it would get me into.

After supper the Peebles drove into town to go to a movie. She wanted to go somewhere with her hair fresh done. I sat in my bright kitchen wondering what to do, knowing I would never sleep. Mrs. Peebles might not fire me, when she found out, but it would give her a different feeling about me altogether. This was the first place I ever worked but I already had picked up things about the way people feel when you are working for them. They like to think you aren't curious. Not just that you aren't dishonest, that isn't enough. They like to feel you don't notice things, that you don't think or wonder about anything but what they liked to eat and how they like things ironed, and so on. I don't mean they weren't kind to me, because they were. They had me eat my meals with them (to tell the truth I expected to, I didn't know there were families who don't) and sometimes they took me along in the car. But all the same.

I went up and checked on the children being asleep and then I went out. I had to do it. I crossed the road and went to the old fairgrounds gate. The plane looked unnatural sitting there, and shining with the moon. Off at the far side of the fairgrounds, where the bush was taking over, I saw his tent.

He was sitting outside it smoking a cigarette. He saw me coming.

"Hello, were you looking for a plane ride. I don't start taking people up till tomorrow." Then he looked again and said, "Oh, it's you. I didn't know you without your long dress on."

My heart was knocking away, my tongue was dried up. I had to say something. But I couldn't. My throat was closed and I was like a deaf-and-dumb.

"Did you want a ride? Sit down. Have a cigarette."

I couldn't even shake my head to say no, so he gave me one.

"Put it in your mouth or I can't light it. It's a good thing I'm used to shy ladies."

I did. It wasn't the first time. I had smoked a cigarette, actually. My girl friend out home, Muriel Lowe, used to steal them from her brother.

"Look at your hand shaking. Did you just want to have a chat, or what?"

In one burst I said, "I wisht you wouldn't say anything about the dress."

"What dress? Oh, the long dress."

"It's Mrs. Peebles'."

"Whose?" Oh, the lady you work for? Is that it? She wasn't home so you got dressed up in her dress, eh? You got dressed up and played queen. I don't blame you. You're not smoking that cigarette right. Don't just puff. Draw it in. Did nobody ever show you how to inhale? Are you scared I'll tell on you? Is that it?"

I was so ashamed at having to ask him to connive this way I couldn't nod. I just looked at him and he saw *yes*.

"Well I won't. I won't in the slightest way mention it or embarrass you. I give you my word of honor."

Then he changed the subject, to help me out, seeing I couldn't even thank him.

"What do you think of this sign?"

It was a board sign lying practically at my feet.

SEE THE WORLD FROM THE SKY. ADULTS $1.00, CHILDREN 50¢. QUALIFIED PILOT.

"My old sign was getting pretty beat up. I thought I'd make a new one. That's what I've been doing with my time today."

The lettering wasn't all that handsome, I thought. I could have done a better one in half an hour.

"I'm not an expert at sign making."

"It's very good," I said.

"I don't need it for publicity, word of mouth is usually enough. I turned away two carloads tonight. I felt like taking it easy. I didn't tell them ladies were dropping in to visit me."

Now I remembered the children and I was scared again, in case one of them had waked up and called me and I wasn't there.

"Do you have to go so soon?"

I remembered some manners. "Thank you for the cigarette."

"Don't forget. You have my word of honor."

I tore off across the fairgrounds, scared I'd see the car heading home from town. My sense of time was mixed up, I didn't know how long I'd been out of the house. But it was all right, it wasn't late, the children were asleep. I got in bed myself and lay thinking what a lucky end to the day, after all, and among things to be grateful for I could be grateful Loretta Bird hadn't been the one who caught me.

The yard and borders didn't get trampled, it wasn't as bad as that. All the same it seemed very public, around the house. The sign was on the fairgrounds gate. People came mostly after supper but a good many in the afternoon, too. The Bird children all came without fifty cents between them and hung on the gate. We got used to the excitement of the plane coming in and taking off, it wasn't excitement any more. I never went over, after that one time, but would see him when he came to get his water. I would be out on the steps doing sitting-down work, like preparing vegetables, if I could.

"Why don't you come over? I'll take you up in my plane."

"I'm saving my money," I said, because I couldn't think of anything else.

"For what? For getting married?"

I shook my head.

"I'll take you up for free if you come sometime when it's slack. I thought you would come, and have another cigarette."

I made a face to hush him, because you never could tell when the children would be sneaking around the porch, or Mrs. Peebles herself listening in the house. Sometimes she came out and had a conversation with him. He told her things he hadn't bothered to tell me. But then I hadn't thought to ask. He told her he had been in the War, that was where he learned to fly a plane, and now he couldn't settle down to ordinary life, this was what he liked. She said she couldn't imagine anybody liking such a thing. Though sometimes, she said, she was almost bored enough to try anything herself, she wasn't brought up to living in the country. It's all my husband's idea, she said. This was news to me.

"Maybe you ought to give flying lessons," she said.

"Would you take them?"

She just laughed.

Sunday was a busy flying day in spite of it being preached against from two pulpits. We were all sitting out watching. Joey and Heather were over on the fence with the Bird kids. Their father had said they could go, after their mother saying all week they couldn't.

A car came down the road past the parked cars and pulled up right in the drive. It was Loretta Bird who got out, all importance, and on the driver's side another woman got out, more sedately. She was wearing sunglasses.

"This is a lady looking for the man that flies the plane," Loretta Bird said. "I heard her inquire in the hotel coffee shop where I was having a Coke and I brought her out."

"I'm sorry to bother you," the lady said. "I'm Alice Kelling, Mr. Watters' fiancée."

This Alice Kelling had on a pair of brown and white checked slacks and a yellow top. Her bust looked to me rather low and bumpy. She had a worried face. Her hair had had a permanent, but had grown out, and she wore a yellow band to keep it off her face. Nothing in the least pretty or even young-looking about her. But you could tell from how she talked she was from the city, or educated, or both.

Dr. Peebles stood up and introduced himself and his wife and me and asked her to be seated.

"He's up in the air right now, but you're welcome to sit and wait. He gets his water here and he hasn't been yet. He'll probably take his break about five."

"That is him, then?" said Alice Kelling, wrinkling and straining at the sky.

"He's not in the habit of running out on you, taking a different name?" Dr. Peebles laughed. He was the one, not his wife, to offer iced tea. Then she sent me into the kitchen to fix it. She smiled. She was wearing sunglasses too.

"He never mentioned his fiancée," she said.

I loved fixing iced tea with lots of ice and slices of lemon in tall glasses. I ought to have mentioned before, Dr. Peebles was an abstainer, at least around the house, or I wouldn't have been allowed to take the place. I had to fix a glass for Loretta Bird, too, though it galled me, and when I went out she had settled in my lawn chair, leaving me the steps.

"I knew you was a nurse when I first heard you in that coffee shop."

"How would you know a thing like that?"

"I get my hunches about people. Was that how you met him, nursing?"

"Chris? Well yes. Yes, it was."

"Oh, were you overseas?" said Mrs. Peebles.

"No, it was before he went overseas. I nursed him when he was stationed at Centralia and had ruptured appendix. We got engaged and then he went overseas. My, this is refreshing, after a long drive."

"He'll be glad to see you," Dr. Peebles said. "It's a rackety kind of life, isn't it, not staying one place long enough to really make friends."

"Youse've had a long engagement," Loretta Bird said.

Alice Kelling passed that over. "I was going to get a room at the hotel, but when I was offered directions I came on out. Do you think I could phone them?"

"No need," Dr. Peebles said. "You're five miles away from him if you stay at the hotel. Here, you're right across the road. Stay with us. We've got rooms on rooms, look at this big house."

Asking people to stay, just like that, is certainly a country thing, and maybe seemed natural to him now, but not to Mrs. Peebles, from the way she said, oh yes, we have plenty of room. Or to Alice Kelling, who kept protesting, but let herself be worn down. I got the feeling it was a temptation to her, to be that close. I was trying for a look at her ring. Her nails were painted red, her fingers were freckled and wrinkled. It was a tiny stone. Muriel Lowe's cousin had one twice as big.

Chris came to get his water, late in the afternoon just as Dr. Peebles had predicted. He must have recognized the car from a way off. He came smiling.

"Here I am chasing after you to see what you're up to," called Alice Kelling. She got up and went to meet him and they kissed, just touched, in front of us.

"You're going to spend a lot on gas that way," Chris said.

Dr. Peebles invited Chris to stay for supper, since he had already put up the sign that said: NO MORE RIDES TILL 7 P.M. Mrs. Peebles wanted it served in the yard, in spite of bugs. One thing strange to anybody from the country is this eating outside. I had made a potato salad earlier and she had made a jellied salad, that was one thing she could do, so it was just a matter of getting those out, and some sliced meat and cucumbers and fresh leaf lettuce. Loretta Bird hung around for some time saying, "Oh, well, I guess I better get home to those yappers," and, "It's so nice just sitting here, I sure hate to get up," but nobody invited her, I was relieved to see, and finally she had to go.

That night after rides were finished Alice Kelling and Chris went off somewhere in her car. I lay awake till they got back. When I saw the car lights sweep my ceiling I got up to look down on them through the slats of my blind. I don't know what I thought I was going to see. Muriel Lowe and I used to sleep on her front veranda and watch her sister and her sister's boy friend saying good night. Afterwards we couldn't get to sleep, for longing for somebody to kiss us and rub up against us and we would talk about suppose you were out in a boat with a boy and he wouldn't bring you in to shore unless you did it, or what if somebody got you trapped in a barn, you would have to, wouldn't you, it wouldn't be your fault. Muriel said her two girl cousins used to try with a toilet paper roll that one of them was the boy. We wouldn't do anything like that; just lay and wondered.

All that happened was that Chris got out of the car on one side and she got out on the other and they walked off separately—him towards the fairgrounds and her towards the house. I got back in bed and imagined about me coming home with him, not like that.

Next morning Alice Kelling got up late and I fixed a grapefruit for her the way I had learned and Mrs. Peebles sat down with her to visit and have another cup of coffee. Mrs. Peebles seemed pleased enough now, having company. Alice Kelling said she guessed she better get used to putting in a day just watching Chris take off and come down, and Mrs. Peebles said she didn't know if she should suggest it because Alice Kelling was the one with the car, but the lake was only twenty-five miles away and what a good day for a picnic.

Alice Kelling took her up on the idea and by eleven o'clock they were in the car, with Joey and Heather and a sandwich lunch I had made. The only thing was that Chris hadn't come down, and she wanted to tell him where they were going.

"Edie'll go over and tell him," Mrs. Peebles said. "There's no problem."

Alice Kelling wrinkled her face and agreed.

"Be sure and tell him we'll be back by five!"

I didn't see that he would be concerned about knowing this right away, and I thought of him eating whatever he ate over there, alone cooking on his camp stove, so I got to work and mixed up a crumb cake and baked it, in between the other work I had to do; then, when it was a bit cooled, wrapped it in a tea towel. I didn't do anything to myself but take off my apron and comb my hair. I would like to have put some make-up on, but I was too afraid it would remind him of the way he first saw me, and that would humiliate me all over again.

He had come and put another sign on the gate: NO RIDES THIS P.M. APOLOGIES. I worried that he wasn't feeling well. No sign of him outside and the tent flap was down. I knocked on the pole.

"Come in," he said, in a voice that would just as soon have said *Stay out.*

I lifted the flap.

"Oh, it's you. I'm sorry. I didn't know it was you."

He had been just sitting on the side of the bed, smoking. Why not at least sit and smoke in the fresh air?

"I brought a cake and hope you're not sick," I said.

"Why would I be sick, Oh—that sign. That's all right. I'm just tired of talking to people. I don't mean you. Have a seat." He pinned back the tent flap. "Get some fresh air in here."

I sat on the edge of the bed, there was no place else. It was one of those fold-up cots, really; I remembered and gave him his fiancée's message.

He ate some of the cake. "Good."

"Put the rest away for when you're hungry later."

"I'll tell you a secret. I won't be around here much longer."

"Are you getting married?"

"Ha ha. What time did you say they'd be back?"

"Five o'clock."

"Well, by that time this place will have seen the last of me. A plane can get further than a car." He unwrapped the cake and ate another piece of it, absent-mindedly.

"Now you'll be thirsty."

"There's some water in the pail."

"It won't be very cold. I could bring some fresh. I could bring some ice from the refrigerator."

"No," he said. "I don't want you to go. I want a nice long time of saying good-bye to you."

He put the cake away carefully and sat beside me and started those little kisses, so soft, I can't ever let myself think about them, such kindness in his face and lovely kisses, all over my eyelids and neck and ears, all over, then me kissing back as well as I could (I had only kissed a boy on a dare before, and kissed my own arms for practice) and we lay back on the cot and pressed together, just gently, and he did some other things, not bad things or not in a bad way. It was lovely in the tent, that smell of grass and hot tent cloth with the sun beating down on it, and he said, "I wouldn't do you any harm for the world." Once, when he had rolled on top of me and we were sort of rocking together on the cot, he said softly, "Oh, no," and freed himself and jumped up and got the water pail. He splashed some of it on his neck and face, and the little bit left, on me lying there.

"That's to cool us off, Miss."

When we said good-bye I wasn't at all sad, because he held my face and he said "I'm going to write you a letter. I'll tell you where I am and maybe you can come and see me. Would you like that? Okay then. You wait." I was really glad I think to get away from him, it was like he was piling presents on me I couldn't get the pleasure of till I considered them alone.

No consternation at first about the plane being gone. They thought he had taken somebody up, and I didn't enlighten them. Dr. Peebles had phoned he had to go to the country, so there was just us having supper, and then Loretta Bird thrusting her head in the door and saying, "I see he's took off."

"What?" said Alice Kelling, and pushed back her chair.

"The kids come and told me this afternoon he was taking down his tent. Did he think he'd run through all the business there was around here? He didn't take off without letting you know, did he?"

"He'll send me word," Alice Kelling said. "He'll probably phone tonight. He's terribly restless, since the War."

"Edie, he didn't mention to you, did he?" Mrs. Peebles said. "When you took over the message?"

"Yes," I said. So far so true.

"Well why didn't you say?" All of them were looking at me. "Did he say where he was going?"

"He said he might try Bayfield," I said. What made me tell such a lie? I didn't intend it.

"Bayfield, how far is that?" said Alice Kelling.

Mrs. Peebles said, "Thirty, thirty-five miles."

"That's not far. Oh, well, that's really not far at all. It's on the lake, isn't it?"

You'd think I'd be ashamed of myself, setting her on the wrong track. I did it to give him more time, whatever time he needed. I lied for him, and also, I have to admit, for me. Women should stick together and not do things like that. I see that now, but didn't then. I never thought of myself as being in any way like her, or coming to the same troubles, ever.

She hadn't taken her eyes off me. I thought she suspected my lie.

"When did he mention this to you?"

"Earlier."

"When you were over at the plane?"

"Yes."

"You must've stayed and had a chat." She smiled at me, not a nice smile. "You must've stayed and had a little visit with him."

"I took a cake," I said, thinking that telling some truth would spare me telling the rest.

"We didn't have a cake," said Mrs. Peebles rather sharply.

"I baked one."

Alice Kelling said, "That was very friendly of you."

"Did you get permission," said Loretta Bird. "You never know what these girls'll do next," she said. "It's not they mean harm so much as they're ignorant."

"The cake is neither here nor there," Mrs. Peebles broke in. "Edie, I wasn't aware you knew Chris that well."

I didn't know what to say.

"I'm not surprised," Alice Kelling said in a high voice. "I knew by the look of her as soon as I saw her. We get them at the hospital all the time." She looked hard at me with her stretched smile. "Having their babies. We have to put them in a special ward because of their diseases. Little country tramps. Fourteen and fifteen years old. You should see the babies they have, too."

"There was a bad woman here in town had a baby that pus was running out of its eyes," Loretta Bird put in.

"Wait a minute," said Mrs. Peebles. "What is this talk? Edie. What about you and Mr. Watters? Were you intimate with him?"

"Yes," I said. I was thinking of us lying on the cot and kissing, wasn't that intimate? And I would never deny it.

They were all one minute quiet, even Loretta Bird.

"Well," said Mrs. Peebles. "I am surprised. I think I need a cigarette. This is the first of any such tendencies I've seen in her," she said, speaking to Alice Kelling, but Alice Kelling was looking at me.

"Loose little bitch." Tears ran down her face. "Loose little bitch, aren't you? I knew as soon as I saw you. Men despise girls like you. He just made use of you and went off, you know that, don't you? Girls like you are just nothing, they're just public conveniences, just filthy little rags!"

"Oh, now," said Mrs. Peebles.

"Filthy," Alice Kelling sobbed. "Filthy little rag!"

"Don't get yourself upset," Loretta Bird said. She was swollen up with pleasure being in on this scene. "Men are all the same."

"Edie, I'm very surprised," Mrs. Peebles said. "I thought your parents were so strict. You don't want to have a baby, do you?"

I'm still ashamed of what happened next. I lost control, just like a six-year-old, I started howling. "You don't get a baby from just doing that!"

"You see. Some of them are that ignorant," Loretta Bird said.

But Mrs. Peebles jumped up and caught my arms and shook me.

"Calm down. Don't get hysterical. Calm down. Stop crying. Listen to me. Listen. I'm wondering, if you know what being intimate means. Now tell me. What did you think it meant?"

"Kissing," I howled.

She let go. "Oh, Edie. Stop it. Don't be silly. It's all right. It's all a misunderstanding. Being intimate means a lot more than that. Oh, I *wondered*."

"She's trying to cover up, now," said Alice Kelling. "Yes. She's not so stupid. She sees she got herself in trouble."

"I believe her," Mrs. Peebles said. "That is an awful scene."

"Well there is one way to find out," said Alice Kelling, getting up. "After all, I am a nurse."

Mrs. Peebles drew a breath and said, "No. No. Go to your room, Edie. And stop that noise. That is too disgusting."

I heard the car start in a little while. I tried to stop crying, pulling back each wave as it started over me. Finally I succeeded, and lay heaving on the bed.

Mrs. Peebles came and stood in the doorway.

"She's gone," she said. "That Bird woman too. Of course, you know you should never have gone near that man and that is the cause of all this trouble. I have a headache. As soon as you can, go and wash your face in cold water and get at the dishes and we will not say any more about this."

Nor we didn't. I didn't figure out till years later the extent of what I had been saved from. Mrs. Peebles was not very friendly to me afterwards, but she was fair. Not very friendly is the wrong way of describing what she was. She never had been very friendly. It was just that now she had to see me all the time and it got on her nerves, a little.

As for me, I put it all out of my mind like a bad dream and concentrated on waiting for my letter. The mail came every day except Sunday, between one-thirty and two in the afternoon, a good time for me because Mrs. Peebles was always having her nap. I would get the kitchen all cleaned and then go up to the mailbox and sit in the grass, waiting. I was perfectly happy, waiting, I forgot all about Alice Kelling and her misery and awful talk and Mrs. Peebles and her chilliness and the embarrassment of whether she had told Dr. Peebles and the face of Loretta Bird, getting her fill of other people's troubles. I was always smiling when the mailman got there, and continued smiling even after he gave me the mail and saw today wasn't the day. The mailman was a Carmichael. I knew by his face because there are a lot of Carmichaels living out by us and so many of them have a sort of sticking-out top lip. So I asked his name (he was a young man, shy, but good humored, anybody could ask him anything) and then I said, "I knew by your face!" He was pleased by that and always glad to see me and got a little less shy. "You've got the smile I've been waiting on all day!" he used to holler out the car window.

It never crossed my mind for a long time a letter might not come. I believed in it coming just like I believed the sun would rise in the morning. I just put off my hope from day to day, and there was the goldenrod out around the mailbox and the children gone back to school, and the leaves turning, and I was wearing a sweater when I went to wait. One day walking back with the hydro bill stuck in my hand, that was all, looking across at the fairgrounds with the full-blown milkweed and dark teasels, so much like fall, it just struck me: *No letter was ever going to come.* It was an impossible idea to get used to. No, not impossible. If I thought about Chris's face when he said he was going to write to me, it was impossible, but if I forgot that and thought about the actual tin mailbox, empty, it was plain and true. I kept on going to meet the mail, but my heart was heavy now like a lump of lead. I only smiled because I thought of the mailman counting on it, and he didn't have an easy life, with the winter driving ahead.

Till it came to me one day there were women doing this with their lives, all over. There were women just waiting and waiting by mailboxes for one letter or another. I imagined me making this journey day after day and year after year, and my hair starting to go gray, and I thought, I was never made to go on like that. So I stopped meeting the mail. If there were women all through life waiting, and women busy and not waiting, I knew which I had to be. Even though there might be things the second kind of women have to pass up and never know about, it still is better.

I was surprised when the mailman phoned the Peebles' place in the evening and asked for me. He said he missed me. He asked if I would like to go to Goderich where some well-known movie was on, I forget now what. So I said yes, and I went out with him for two years and he asked me to marry him, and we were engaged a year more while I got my things together, and then we did marry. He always tells the children the story of how I went after him by sitting by the mailbox every day, and naturally I laugh and let him, because I like for people to think what pleases them and makes them happy.

YOUR WRITING(S) FOR OTHERS TO READ

What is a myth? After reading Chapter Eleven, you may have detected that for us it is "a fiction whereby we justify and make sense of our lives." If the fiction is inadequate, inappropriate, narrow-minded, or perverse (as were Hitler's fictions), then we can use them to justify the less generous or more foolish of our actions.

If, for example, we accept the old myth that women are *inherently* inferior to men, then we will find it difficult to give any individual woman the respect, consideration, and tolerance due to her *as a human being*.

The problem that we all face is that we accept and believe our culture's myths before we are old enough to hold them at arm's length and expose them to our intelligence. It is, therefore, not surprising that many young people *change their views and beliefs* precisely when they begin to use their minds to question, to re-consider, to re-read, to criticize, to evaluate, to distance the traditional assumptions about roles and relationships that shaped the culture in which they grew up.

It seems that we are taking a long time to offer you a suggestion for writing: perhaps, we have already suggested enough.

Chapter Twelve
Interpretations

Let us briefly recapitulate: the act of "reading" others is a primary act, a crucial act, in our lives. Whether or not we trace it to vestigial elements of our evolutionary past, and look for similar actions in the ethological study of animals' interactions, it is clear that our *social* survival, our happiness, our ability to cope with circumstance, all depend on this irresistible act. At the deepest level, it seems to be an affective or *emotional* act, involving a desire to approach others, and a predisposition to accept and to like them, or a converse desire to avoid, to keep one's distance, to turn away. In the many situations in our lives where we are subject to contingencies and imperatives, as we are at work, our ability to "read" others—especially those with control over us—is a crucial part of our survival skills.

Out of an insatiable desire to "read" all manner of people—friends, family, neighbors, and strangers—comes the itch to record one's "readings" or observations, and the speculations, surmises, and fantasies that they feed into: to keep a notebook, a kind of verbal sketchbook, of jottings, of conversations overheard, of idiosyncrasies and quirks noticed, and of the imagined inner life of others.

The *Oxford English Dictionary* gives *twenty-one* distinct, but related, uses of "to read." One of the oldest, and most interesting, is "to make out or discover the meaning or significance of a dream . . ."; another is "to predict"; yet another is "to connect." These ancient examples support our decision to use the word *read*

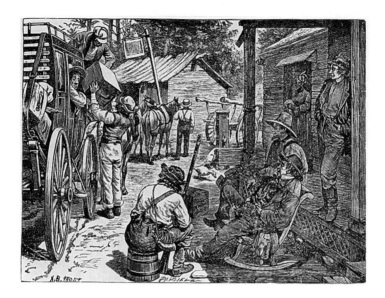

as involving not only comprehending print but also construing *everything* in the world, in order to make sense of it.

Everything in the world? When you glance at friends' faces over lunch, what exactly are you doing? Scanning? Looking for signs of . . . what? Trying to infer (more or less accurately) their mood? Hoping for a smile? When the tennis players walk toward the court and glance up at the sky, what exactly are they doing? Looking for signs that the good weather will hold for at least an hour? What "theory of the world" is in play here?

Consider what happens when you steal a glance at your friend's face—her nose, her chin, her eyes, her ears, her mouth—to try to discern what kind of mood she is in: are you *reading* or *writing*? That sounds like a silly question, but bear with us.

Are you interpreting something—a sign—that is "inscribed" on her face? Or are you "writing" (*not* literally, with a pen or pencil) what you take to be the *meaning* of her lips, the subtle index of mood at each corner? In other words, are you *verbalizing* (producing language) that represents your interpretation of those subtle signs even outside your own awareness?

When we ask, "Are you reading or writing?" we can bring our question nearer home: as you read this text, are you reading or writing? Does the categorical distinction between those two terms begin to break down? And does the idle assumption that reading is *passive*, whereas writing is *active*, also begin to break down?

Curiosity is sometimes construed as rudeness: as children, we have all been rebuked "Don't stare! Mind your own business!" But it seems clear that the act of reading others—whether tactlessly or discreetly will depend on our social training—is a fundamental social necessity. Our social well-being depends on our ability not only to monitor our own actions, learning to use self-control, tact, and discretion, but also to observe and register what exactly other people are up to. So we have to learn to "read" them: their facial expressions, tone of voice, gestures, clothes, manners—all the *signs* they wittingly or unwittingly offer us as a means of interpreting them appropriately. We become aware of these continuous readings most acutely when they break down and someone exclaims, "But you misunderstood!"

Questions About an Image of a Child

How many people have you seen today? In the last week? How many can you see now, as you glance up from this page? How many occupy your head, even when they are not actually present? How do you *read* them?

People who *matter* to us, but who remain in some way mysterious or puzzling, continue to force us to re-read them, to revise our reading of them. On the other hand, we scan or construe most strangers very quickly, partly out of curiosity, and partly to go on feeling secure in the place they share with us, however briefly.

How do *you* read this child? (That is the wrong question; we should have asked: How do *you* read this photograph, this image, of a child?).

The photograph has been reproduced from *Another Way of Telling*, a book that came out of the collaboration of the writer John Berger (b. 1926) and the photographer Jean Mohr. It is especially interesting for its exploration of the

ways in which we "read" photographs: Jean Mohr, for example, takes photographs of a poor old French farmer, develops and prints them, then invites the farmer to criticize them. Mohr then ends up taking the kind of photograph of the old man that the old man himself would like to pass on to his grandchildren as a memorial image of himself.

After Jean Mohr had printed his photograph of that child you have just speculated about, he tried a little experiment:

Was is a game, a test, an experiment? All three, and something else too: a photographer's quest, the desire to know how the images he makes are seen, read, interpreted, perhaps rejected by others. In fact in face of any photo the spectator projects something of her or himself. The image is like a springboard.

I often feel the need to explain my photos, to tell their story. Only occasionally is an image self-sufficient. This time I decided to allot the task of explanation to others. I took a number of photographs from my archives and I went out to look for those who would explain them. Of the ten people I asked, only one refused. He was an old gardener and he said it was too much like a television guessing-game.

All the others agreed to describe what came into their minds when presented with the photo I was showing them. I said nothing myself, simply noting what was said. The choice of people was largely a matter of chance. Some were acquaintances, others I was seeing for the first time.

Here, now, are various responses to Mohr's invitation:

Market gardener: (Laughs) This one makes me think of a little girl who already has a maternal capacity, and who's treating her doll like it was her own baby. All right, the doll is not pretty and is undressed, but it's hers!

Clergyman: An odd photo. Should one protect children from seeing the cruelty of the world? Should one hide certain aspects of reality from them? Her hands over the doll's eyes shouldn't be there. One ought to be able to show everything, to see all.

Schoolgirl: She's crying because her doll hasn't any clothes.

Banker: Well-fed, well-dressed, such a child is probably spoilt. Given the luxury of no material worries, people can give in to any whim or fancy.

Actress: "My baby is crying but doesn't want to show it." What surprises me is how she hides the doll's face. There's a strong sense of identification between the doll and the child. The girl is playing out what is happening to the doll and what the doll feels. The vine in the background is strange . . .

Dance-teacher: She has everything, yet she doesn't realise it, she is crying with her eyes shut. And the tree behind. The doll is as big as she is.

Psychiatrist: It puzzles me. She's crying as if she has pain, and yet she's well. She's crying on behalf of her doll, and she covers the eyes as if there was a sight which shouldn't be seen.

Hairdresser: It's a child and somebody has tried to take her doll, which is precious to her. She's going to hold on to it. Perhaps she's German, she's blonde. It makes me think of myself when I was that age.

Factory worker: It's sweet. It reminds me of my niece when her sister tries to take her doll away from her. She's crying, screaming, because someone wants to take her doll away.

What was happening: Great Britain, in the country. A small girl was playing with her doll. Sometimes sweetly, sometimes brutally. At one moment she even pretended to eat her doll.

In the light of the various and even contradictory interpretations (readings) of the image of the little girl, consider John Berger's observations on the sheer inescapable ambiguity of any photograph:

What makes photography a strange invention—with unforeseeable consequences—is that its primary raw materials are light and time.

Yet let us begin with something more tangible. A few days ago a friend of mine found this photograph and showed it to me [see page 351].

I know nothing about it. The best way of dating it is probably by its photographic technique. Between 1900 and 1920? I do not know whether it was taken in Canada, the Alps, South Africa. All one can see is that it shows a smiling middle-aged man with his horse. Why was it taken? What meaning did it have for the photographer? Would it have had the same meaning for the man with the horse?

One can play a game of inventing meanings. The Last Mountie. (His smile becomes nostalgic.) The Man Who Set Fire to Farms. (His smile becomes sinister.)

Before the Trek of Two Thousand Miles. (His smile becomes a little apprehensive.) After the Trek of Two Thousand Miles. (His smile becomes modest.) . . .

The most definite information this photograph gives is about the type of bridle the horse is wearing, and this is certainly not the reason why it was taken. Looking at the photograph alone it is even hard to know to what use category it belonged. Was it a family-album picture, a newspaper picture, a traveller's snap?

Could it have been taken, not for the sake of the man, but of the horse? Was the man acting as a groom, just holding the horse? Was he a horse-dealer? Or was it a still photograph taken during the filming of one of the early Westerns?

The photograph offers irrefutable evidence that this man, this horse and this bridle existed. Yet it tells us nothing of the significance of their existence.

A photograph arrests the flow of time in which the event photographed once existed. All photographs are of the past, yet in them an instant of the past is arrested so that, unlike a lived past, it can never lead to the present. Every photograph presents us with two messages: a message concerning the event photographed and another concerning a shock of discontinuity.

Between the moment recorded and the present moment of looking at the photograph, there is an abyss. We are so used to photography that we no longer consciously register the second of these twin messages—except in special circumstances: when for example, the person photographed was familiar to us and is now far away or dead. In such circumstances the photograph is more traumatic than most memories or mementos because it seems to confirm, prophetically, the later discontinuity created by the absence or death. Imagine for a moment that you were once in love with the man with the horse and that he has now disappeared.

If, however, he is a total stranger, one thinks only of the first message, which here is so ambiguous that the event escapes one. What the photograph shows goes with any story one chooses to invent.

Nevertheless the mystery of this photograph does not quite end there. No invented story, no explanation offered will be quite as *present* as the banal appearances preserved in this photograph. These appearances may tell us very little, but they are unquestionable.

The first photographs were thought of as marvels because, far more directly than any other form of visual image, they presented the appearance of what was absent. They preserved the look of things and they allowed the look of things to be carried away. The marvel in this was not only technical.

Our response to appearances is a very deep one, and it includes elements which are instinctive and atavistic. For example, appearances alone—regardless of all conscious considerations—can sexually arouse. For example, the stimulus to action—however tentative it remains—can be provoked by the colour red. More widely, the look of the world is the widest possible confirmation of the *thereness* of the world, and thus the look of the world continually proposes and confirms our relation to that thereness, which nourishes our sense of Being.

Before you tried to read the photograph of the man with the horse, before you placed it or named it, the simple act of looking at it confirmed, however briefly, your sense of being in the world, with its men, hats, horses, bridles . . .

*   *   *

The ambiguity of a photograph does not reside within the instant of the event photographed: there the photographic evidence is less ambiguous than any eyewitness account. The photo-finish of a race is rightly decided by what the camera has recorded. The ambiguity arises out of that discontinuity which gives rise to the second of the photograph's twin messages. (The abyss between the moment recorded and the moment of looking.)

A photograph preserves a moment of time and prevents it being effaced by the supersession of further moments. In this respect photographs might be compared to images stored in the memory. Yet there is a fundamental difference: whereas remembered images are the *residue* of continuous experience, a photograph isolates the appearances of a disconnected instant.

And in life, meaning is not instantaneous. Meaning is discovered in what connects, and cannot exist without development. Without a story, without an unfolding, there is no meaning. Facts, information, do not in themselves constitute meaning. Facts can be fed into a computer and become factors in a calculation. No meaning, however, comes out of computers, for when we give meaning to an event, that meaning is a response, not only to the known, but also to the unknown: meaning and mystery are inseparable, and neither can exist without the passing of time. Certainty may be instantaneous; doubt requires duration; meaning is born of the

two. An instant photographed can only acquire meaning insofar as the viewer can read into it a duration extending beyond itself. When we find a photograph meaningful, we are lending it a past and a future.

The professional photographer tries, when taking a photograph, to choose an instant which will persuade the public viewer to lend it an *appropriate* past and future. The photographer's intelligence or his empathy with the subject defines for him what is appropriate. Yet unlike the story-teller or painter or actor, the photographer only makes, in any one photograph, *a single constitutive choice:* the choice of the instant to be photographed. The photograph, compared with other means of communication, is therefore weak in intentionality.

A dramatic photograph may be as ambiguous as an undramatic one.

What is happening? It requires a caption for us to understand the significance of the event. "Nazis Burning Books." And the significance of the caption again depends upon a sense of history that we cannot necessarily take for granted.

All photographs are ambiguous. All photographs have been taken out of a continuity. If the event is a public event, this continuity is history; if it is personal, the continuity, which has been broken, is a life story. Even a pure landscape breaks a continuity: that of the light and the weather. Discontinuity always produces ambiguity. Yet often this ambiguity is not obvious, for as soon as photographs are used with words, they produce together an effect of certainty, even of dogmatic assertion.

In the relation between a photograph and words, the photograph begs for an interpretation, and the words usually supply it. The photograph, irrefutable as evidence but weak in meaning, is given a meaning by the words. And the words, which by themselves remain at the level of generalisation, are given specific authenticity by the irrefutability of the photograph. Together the two then become very powerful; an open question appears to have been fully answered.

Yet it might be that the photographic ambiguity, if recognised and accepted as such, could offer to photography a unique means of expression. Could this ambiguity suggest another way of telling? . . .

*   *   *

Cameras are boxes for transporting appearances. The principle by which cameras work has not changed since their invention. Light, from the object photographed, passes through a hole and falls on to a photographic plate or film. The latter, because of its chemical preparation, preserves these traces of light. From these traces, through other slightly more complicated chemical processes, prints are made. Technically, by the standards of our century, it is a simple process. Just as the historically comparable invention of the printing press was, in its time, simple. What is still not so simple is to grasp the nature of the appearances which the camera transports.

Are the appearances which a camera transports a construction, a man-made cultural artifact, or are they, like a footprint in the sand, a trace *naturally* left by something that has passed? The answer is, both.

The photographer chooses the event he photographs. This choice can be thought of as a cultural construction. The space for this construction is, as it were, cleared by his rejection of what he did not choose to photograph. The construction is his reading of the event which is in front of his eyes. It is this reading, often intuitive and very fast, which decides his choice of the instant to be photographed.

Likewise, the photographed image of the event, when shown as a photograph, is also part of a cultural construction. It belongs to a specific social situation, the life of the photographer, an argument, an experiment, a way of explaining the world, a book, a newspaper, an exhibition.

Yet at the same time, the material relation between the image and what it represents (between the marks on the printing paper and the tree these marks represent) is an immediate and unconstructed one. And is indeed like a *trace*.

The photographer chooses the tree, the view of it he wants, the kind of film, the focus, the filter, the time-exposure, the strength of the developing solution, the sort of paper to print on, the darkness or lightness of the print, the framing of the print—all this and more. But where he does not intervene—and cannot intervene without changing the fundamental character of photography—is between the light, emanating from that tree as it passes through the lens, and the imprint it makes on the film.

It may clarify what we mean by a *trace* if we ask how a drawing differs from a photograph. A drawing is a translation. That is to say each mark on the paper is consciously related, not only to the real or imagined "model," but also to every mark and space already set out on the paper. Thus a drawn or painted image is woven together by the energy (or the lassitude, when the drawing is weak) of countless judgements. Every time a figuration is evoked in a drawing, everything about it has been mediated by consciousness, either intuitively or systematically. In a drawing an apple is *made* round and spherical; in a photograph . . .

Let us reverse the gaze: instead of adults reading a child, let us see how a child reads an adult, an odd, disturbingly incongruous adult, in the following poem by Peter Sharpe (b. 1948).

PETER SHARPE

Waiting for the Idiot to Go Away

The sweet tomato face annealed to itself
in all directions and pressed sloppily
to the car window.
        I sat five years old asking
'why does he do that' and 'why is he like that'.   5
His name was Benji, he was really
35 or 38 years old and he drooled
and was short. I never got
an answer from my father, who

stared straight ahead, his foot tapping   10
nervously on the accelerator pedal,
lips tight and knuckles whitening
on the wheel, 'pretend he isn't there'
he told me.

    I had my first remembered lesson   15
in the social graces: the world
was imperfect, and this was embarrassing.

CONSIDER THIS

★ The five-year-old suddenly felt embarrassed: a bit of "experience" displaces a bit of "innocence." Do you think the five-year-old could have thought "the world is imperfect"? Or do you think that is how the adult writer now reads that long-ago experience?

ARTHUR CONAN DOYLE

Disclosing, Uncovering, Reading, Inferring

Every society has its unwritten rules about how we should look at people: when we look at strangers, glancing is to be preferred to staring.

    In a typical day, we probably don't "register" most of the strangers' faces we see, but if we do register them, economy of mental effort, of cognitive work, probably results in our slotting them into a readymade stereotype, either positive or negative.

    Unless we are artists, private eyes, psychiatrists, or doctors, we are not paid to look closely at others, to do a close reading of all the evidence they offer, signs of age, occupation, social class, personality, background, mood, and so on.

    Here, now, is a case of someone trying to do a close reading of such signs, attempting to come up with a coherent representation of another; he gets as far as making a list of all the possibly useful signs.

1. Knowledge of Literature.—Nil.
2.   "   " Philosophy.—Nil.
3.   "   " Astronomy.—Nil.
4.   "   " Politics.—Feeble.
5.   "   " Botany.—Variable. Well up in belladonna, opium, and poisons gener-
    ally. Knows nothing of practical gardening.
6.   "   " Geology.—Practical, but limited. Tells at a glance different soils from
    each other.

> After walks has shown me splashes upon his trousers, and
> told me by their colour and consistence in what part of London
> he had received them.

7. Knowledge of Chemistry.—Profound.
8.   "   " Anatomy.—Accurate, but unsystematic.
9.   "   " Sensational Literature.—Immense. He appears to know every detail of
                          every horror perpetrated in the century.
10. Plays the violin well.
11. Is an expert singlestick player, boxer, and swordsman.
12. Has a good practical knowledge of British law.

Then, he admitted defeat:

> When I had got so far in my list I threw it into the fire in despair. "If I can only
> find what the fellow is driving at by reconciling all these accomplishments, and
> discovering a calling which needs them all," I said to myself, "I may as well give up
> the attempt at once."

So the observer, before giving up his quest, collected the signs, and tried to
get them to cohere in such a way that he could then draw a major inference
from the whole set. (If someone had first given him the general, unifying explanation, he would then have been able to understand how and where each part
fitted into and contributed to the whole.) He had several bits of concrete evidence—what he could observe with his own senses—but he could not *abstract*
(pull out—as in *tract*or) from that evidence any one secure generalization. He
had plenty of trees, but he couldn't find the wood, the coherent whole.

One morning, Dr. Watson—for *he* was the observer—was waiting for his
landlady to bring his breakfast; to pass the time, he picked up a magazine:

> Then I picked up a magazine from the table and attempted to wile away the time
> with it, while my companion munched silently at his toast. One of the articles had
> a pencil mark at the heading, and I naturally began to run my eye through it.
> Its somewhat ambiguous title was "The Book of Life," and it attempted to show
> how much an observant man might learn by an accurate and systematic examination
> of all that came in his way. It struck me as being a remarkable mixture of shrewdness
> and absurdity. The reasoning was close and intense, but the deductions appeared to
> me to be far-fetched and exaggerated. The writer claimed by a momentary expres-
> sion, a twitch of a muscle or a glance of an eye, to fathom a man's inmost thoughts.
> Deceit, according to him, was an impossibility in the case of one trained to obser-
> vation and analysis. His conclusions were as infallible as so many propositions of
> Euclid. So startling would his results appear to the uninitiated that until they learned
> the processes by which he had arrived at them they might well consider him as a
> necromancer.
> "From a drop of water," said the writer, "a logician could infer the possibility of

an Atlantic or a Niagara without having seen or heard of one or the other. So all life is a great chain, the nature of which is known whenever we are shown a single link of it. Like all other arts, the Science of Deduction and Analysis is one which can only be acquired by long and patient study, nor is life long enough to allow any mortal to attain the highest possible perfection in it. Before turning to those moral and mental aspects of the matter which present the greatest difficulties, let the inquirer begin by mastering more elementary problems. Let him on meeting a fellow-mortal, learn at a glance to distinguish the history of the man, and the trade or profession to which he belongs. Puerile as such an exercise may seem, it sharpens the faculties of observation, and teaches one where to look and what to look for. By a man's finger-nails, by his coat-sleeve, by his boot, by his trouser-knees, by the callosities of his forefinger and thumb, by his expression, by his shirt-cuffs—by each of these things a man's calling is plainly revealed. That all united should fail to enlighten the competent inquirer in any case is almost inconceivable."

"What ineffable twaddle!" I cried, slapping the magazine down on the table; "I never read such rubbish in my life."

"What is it?" asked Sherlock Holmes.

"Why, this article," I said, pointing at it with my egg-spoon as I sat down to my breakfast. "I see that you have read it since you have marked it. I don't deny that it is smartly written. It irritates me though. It is evidently the theory of some arm-chair lounger who evolves all these neat little paradoxes in the seclusion of his own study. It is not practical. I should like to see him clapped down in a third-class carriage on the Underground,* and asked to give the trades of all his fellow-travellers. I would lay a thousand to one against him."

"You would lose your money," Holmes remarked calmly. "As for the article, I wrote it myself."

"You!"

"Yes; I have a turn both for observation and for deduction. The theories which I have expressed there, and which appear to you to be so chimerical, are really extremely practical—so practical that I depend upon them for my bread and cheese."

"And how?" I asked involuntarily.

"Well, I have a trade of my own. I suppose I am the only one in the world. I'm a consulting detective, if you can understand what that is. Here in London we have lots of Government detectives and lots of private ones. When these fellows are at fault, they come to me, and I manage to put them on the right scent. They lay all the evidence before me, and I am generally able, by the help of my knowledge of the history of crime, to set them straight. There is a strong family resemblance about misdeeds, and if you have all the details of a thousand at your finger ends, it is odd if you can't unravel the thousand and first. Lestrade is a well-known detective. He got himself into a fog recently over a forgery case, and that was what brought him here."

"And these other people?"

*Underground: London subway.

"They are mostly sent on by private inquiry agencies. They are all people who are in trouble about something, and want a little enlightening. I listen to their story, they listen to my comments, and then I pocket my fee."

"But do you mean to say," I said, "that without leaving your room you can unravel some knot which other men can make nothing of, although they have seen every detail for themselves?"

"Quite so. I have a kind of intuition that way. Now and again a case turns up which is a little more complex. Then I have to bustle about and see things with my own eyes. You see I have a lot of special knowledge which I apply to the problem, and which facilitates matters wonderfully. Those rules of deduction laid down in that article which aroused your scorn are invaluable to me in practical work. Observation with me is second nature. You appeared to be surprised when I told you, on our first meeting, that you had come from Afghanistan."

"You were told, no doubt."

"Nothing of the sort. I *knew* you came from Afghanistan. From long habit the train of thoughts ran so swiftly through my mind that I arrived at the conclusion without being conscious of intermediate steps. There were such steps, however. The train of reasoning ran, 'Here is a gentleman of a medical type, but with the air of a military man. Clearly an army doctor, then. He has just come from the tropics, for his face is dark, and that is not the natural tint of his skin, for his wrists are fair. He has undergone hardship and sickness, as his haggard face says clearly. His left arm has been injured. He holds it in a stiff and unnatural manner. Where in the tropics could an English army doctor have seen much hardship and got his arm wounded? Clearly in Afghanistan.' The whole train of thought did not occupy a second. I then remarked that you came from Afghanistan, and you were astonished."

Observing, as in Denise Levertov (p. 148) or Mark Twain (p. 166) is a way of *being*, of being rapt by spectacle, by what is seen and heard. (Cf. William James, p. 254). Generally, however, when people earn their living by observing, they are not enjoying simply *being*, they are *doing*. Their doing has a direction, a function, a utility, a practical purpose: it is a necessary part of their work; they will organize and monitor their ways of observing so that the act of scrutiny will yield the desired, appropriate results. Such observers are not driven by normal human curiosity, as we are when we listen in to other peoples' conversations, eavesdropping: they are driven and guided by meeting the demands of a particular *role*—in Sherlock Holmes's case, that of freelance detective.

When Holmes explains this to Watson, all the odd threads of perception that Watson had collected are sewn together, contextualized and explained, by the framework which Holmes offers. The bits and pieces of concrete knowledge have a unifying principle which both ties them together in a meaningful pattern, and explains why they are part of Holmes's equipment. It is partly because the profession of detective was still *relatively uncommon* at that time, that we can understand Watson's inability to make sense of his observations. It's also part of

Conan Doyle's strategy. To highlight or accentuate Sherlock Holmes's brilliance, his sharp capacity for making inferences, for drawing appropriate conclusions, he sets up a contrastive *foil:* Watson's slowness and confusion (with which the reader can obviously identify) are complementary (and complimentary!) to the talented, quick Holmes. If everyone in Doyle's stories were as brilliant as Holmes, then the stories would be much less interesting. We, the readers, have to *experience* the sense of confusion, of being overwhelmed by mystery, so that we can then be enlightened by Holmes. In that sense, Watson, although *in* the text, is a kind of average reader!

"S. Holmes is a great detective" or "Sherlock Holmes is a well-equipped detective" are general statements and valid; but they are not very interesting—they don't offer us much to grasp. Conversely, all the bits and pieces of observation that Watson collected are all very vivid; but, without some cohering framework, they don't mean very much.

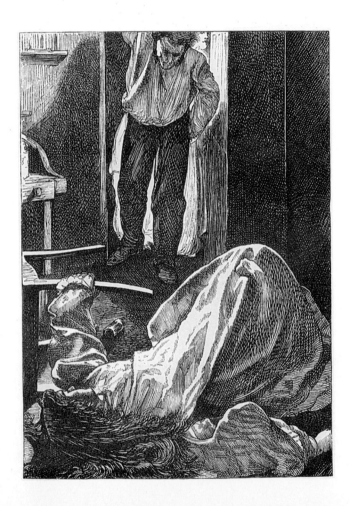

Joseph Bell

How Conan Doyle Learned to Read

At the time that Doyle (1859–1930) was writing his early Sherlock Holmes stories, the most respectable of all the professions that depended on close "reading" of signs was that of medicine, and it was from a doctor, Dr. Joseph Bell, with whom Doyle himself had trained as a medical student, that Doyle derived the idea of detection. By the time Doyle was famous for his Sherlock Holmes stories, Dr. Bell had written the following article.

Dr. Conan Doyle has made a well-deserved success for his detective stories, and made the name of his hero beloved by the boys of this country by the marvellous cleverness of his method. He shows how easy it is, if only you can observe, to find out a great deal as to the works and ways of your innocent and unconscious friends, and, by an extension of the same method, to baffle the criminal and lay bare the manner of his crime . . . every good teacher of medicine or surgery exemplifies every day in his teaching and practice the method and its results. The precise and intelligent recognition and appreciation of minor differences is the real essential factor in all successful medical diagnosis. Carried into ordinary life, granted the presence of an insatiable curiosity and fairly acute senses, you have Sherlock Holmes as he astonishes his somewhat dense friend Watson; carried out in a specialised training, you have Sherlock Holmes the skilled detective.

Dr. Conan Doyle's education as a student of medicine taught him how to observe, and his practice, both as a general practitioner and a specialist, has been a splendid training for a man such as he is, gifted with eyes, memory, and imagination. Eyes and ears which can see and hear, memory to record at once and to recall at pleasure the impressions of the senses, and an imagination capable of weaving a theory or piercing together a broken chain or unravelling a tangled clue, such are implements of his trade to a successful diagnostician. . . . Syme, one of the greatest teachers of surgical diagnosis that ever lived, had a favourite illustration which, as a tradition of his school, has made a mark on Dr. Conan Doyle's method, "Try to learn the features of a disease or injury as precisely as you know the features, the gait, the tricks of manner of your most intimate friend." Him, even in a crowd, you can recognize at once; it may be a crowd of men dressed alike, and each having his complement of eyes, nose, hair, and limbs; in every essential they resemble each other, only in trifles do they differ; and yet, by knowing these trifles well, you make your diagnosis or recognition with ease. So it is with disease of mind or body or morals. Racial peculiarities, hereditary tricks of manner, accent, occupation or the want of it, education, environment of all kinds, by their little trivial impressions gradually mould or carve the individual, and leave finger marks or chisel scores which the expert can recognize. The great broad characteristics which at a glance can be recognized as indicative of heart disease or consumption, chronic drunkenness or long-continued loss of blood, are the common property of the veriest tyro in medicine, while to masters of their art there are myriads of signs eloquent and instructive, but which need the educated eye to detect. A fair-sized and valuable book has lately been written on the one symptom, the pulse; to any one but a trained physician it seems as much an absurdity as is Sherlock Holmes' immortal treatise on the one hundred and fourteen varieties of tobacco ash. . . .

Trained as he has been to notice and appreciate minute detail, Dr. Doyle saw how he could interest his intelligent readers by taking them into his confidence, and showing his mode of working. He created a shrewd, quick-sighted, inquisitive man, half doctor, half virtuoso, with plenty of spare time, a retentive memory, and perhaps with the best gift of all—the power of unloading the mind of all the burden of trying to remember unnecessary details. Holmes tells Watson: "A man should keep his little brain-attic stocked with all the furniture that he is likely to use, as the rest he can put away in the lumber-room of his library, where he can get it if he wants it." But to him the petty results of environment, the sign-manuals of labour, the stains of trade, the incidents of travel, have living interest, as they tend to satisfy an insatiable, almost inhuman, because impersonal curiosity. He puts the man in the position of an amateur, and therefore irresponsible, detective, who is consulted in all sorts of cases, and then he lets us see how he works. He makes him explain to the good Watson the trivial, or apparently trivial, links in his chain of evidence. These are at once so obvious, when explained, and so easy, once you know them, that the ingenuous reader at once feels, and says to himself, I also could do this; life is not so dull after all; I will keep my eyes open, and find out things. The gold watch, with its scratched keyhole and pawnbrokers' marks, told such an easy tale about Watson's brother. The dusty old billy-cock hat revealed that its master had taken to drinking some years ago, and had got his hair cut yesterday. The tiny thorn-prick and fearsome footmark of the thing that was neither a child nor a monkey enabled Holmes to identify and capture the Andaman Islander. Yet, after all, you say, there is nothing wonderful; we could all do the same.

The experienced physician and the trained surgeon every day, in their examinations of the humblest patient, have to go through a similar process of reasoning, quick or slow according to the personal equations of each, almost automatic in the experienced man, laboured and often erratic in the tyro,* yet requiring just the same simple requisites, senses to notice facts, and education and intelligence to apply them. Mere acuteness of the senses is not enough. Your Indian tracker will tell you that the footprint on the leaves was not a redskin's, but a paleface's, because it marked a shoe-print, but it needs an expert in shoe-leather to tell where the shoe was made. A sharp-eyed detective may notice the thumb-mark of a grimy or bloody hand on the velvet or the mirror, but it needs all the scientific knowledge of a Galton† to render the ridges and furrows of the stain visible and permanent, and then to identify by their sign-manual the suspected thief or murderer. Sherlock Holmes has acute senses, and the special education and information that make these valuable; and he can afford to let us into the secrets of his method.

*Tyro: beginner, learner, student.
†Galton: a celebrated Victorian scientist.

JAMES AGEE

Near a Church

One of the most important elements in Holmes's and Bell's work, as detective and as surgeon, was the trained ability to recognize differences: *we know nothing in itself (someone who says, "a dog is a dog," tells us nothing); but we do know, and recognize, anything through a complex and intricate network of differences ("this dog is a retriever" tells us that it is different from two thousand other breeds of dog).*

How well, then, can we read others? Can we ever understand them, represent them justly? How well can we ever hope to read people from a different culture? And what if we want to read them generously and would like them to do the same to us, so that— even while recognizing differences—we might hope to come closer to understanding, even to enjoying each other?

James Agee (see p. 163) here tells of a moment in Alabama, in 1937, when he and his photographer friend, Walker Evans, encountered two strangers.

It was a good enough church from the moment the curve opened and we saw it that I slowed a little and we kept our eyes on it. But as we came even with it the light so held it that it shocked us with its goodness straight through the body, so that at the same instant we said *Jesus.* I put on the brakes and backed the car slowly, watching the light on the building, until we were at the same apex, and we sat still for a couple of minutes at least before getting out, studying in arrest what had hit us so hard as we slowed past its perpendicular.

It lost nothing at all in stasis, but even more powerfully strove in through the eyes its paralyzing classicism: stood from scoured clay, a light lift above us, no trees near, and few weeds; every grain, each nailhead, distinct; the subtle almost strangling strong asymmetries of that which has been hand wrought toward symmetry (as if it were an earnest description, better than the intended object): so intensely sprung against so scarcely eccentric a balance that my hands of themselves spread out their bones, trying to regiment on air between their strengths its tensions and their mutual structures as they stood subject to the only scarcely eccentric, almost annihilating stress, of the serene, wild, rigorous light: empty, shut, bolted, of all that was now withdrawn from it upon the fields the utter statement, God's mask and wooden skull and home stood empty in the meditation of the sun: and this light upon it was strengthening still further its imposal and embrace, and in about a quarter of an hour would have trained itself ready, and there would be a triple convergence in the keen historic spasm of the shutter.

I helped get the camera ready and we stood away and I watched what would be trapped, possessed, fertilized, in the leisures and shyness which are a phase of all love for any object: searching out and registering in myself all its lines, planes, stresses of relationship, along diagonals withdrawn and approached, and vertical to the slightly off-centered door, and broadside, and at several distances, and near, examining merely the ways of the wood, and the nails, the three new boards of differing lengths that were let in above the left of the door, the staring small white porcelain knob, the solesmoothed stairlifts, the wrung stance of thick steeple, the hewn wood stoblike spike at sky, the old hasp and new padlock, the randomshuttered windowglass whose panes were like the surfaces of springs, the fat gold fly who sang and botched against a bright pane within, and within, the rigid benches, box organ, bright stops, hung charts, wrecked hymnals, the platform, pine lectern doilied, pressed-glass pitcher, suspended lamp, four funeral chairs, the little stove with long swan throat aluminum in the hard sober shade, a button in sun, a flur of lint, a torn card of Jesus among children:

While we were wondering whether to force a window, a young negro couple came past up the road. Without appearing to look either longer or less long, or with more or less interest, than a white man might care for, and without altering their pace, they made thorough observation of us, of the car, and of the tripod and camera. We spoke and nodded, smiling as if casually; they spoke and nodded, gravely, as they passed, and glanced back once, not secretly, nor long, nor in amusement. They made us, in spite of our knowledge of our own meanings, ashamed and insecure in our wish to break into and possess their church, and after a minute or two I decided to go after them and speak to them, and ask them if they knew where we might find a minister or some other person who might let us in, if it would be all right. They were fifty yards or so up the road, walking leisurely, and following them, I watched aspects of them which are less easily seen (as surrounding objects are masked by looking into a light) when one's own eyes and face and the eyes and face of another are mutually visible and appraising. They were young, soberly buoyant of body, and strong, the man not quite thin, the girl not quite plump, and I remembered their mild and sober faces, hers softly wide and sensitive to love and to pleasure, and his resourceful and intelligent without intellect and without guile, and their extreme dignity, which was as effortless, unvalued, and undefended in them as the assumption of superiority which suffuses a rich and social adolescent boy; and I was taking pleasure also in the competence and rhythm of their walking in the sun, which was incapable of being less than a muted dancing, and in the beauty in the sunlight of their clothes, which were strange upon them in the middle of the week. He was in dark trousers, black dress shoes, a new-laundered white shirt with lights of bluing in it, and a light yellow, soft straw hat with a broad band of dark flowered cloth and a daisy in the band; she glossy-legged without stockings, in freshly whited pumps, a flowered pink cotton dress, and a great sun of straw set far back on her head. Their swung hands touched gently with their walking, stride by stride, but did not engage. I was walking more rapidly than they but quietly; before I had gone ten steps they turned their heads (toward each other) and looked at me briefly and impersonally, like horses in a field, and faced front again; and this, I am almost certain, not through having heard sound of me, but through a subtler sense. By the time I raised my hand, they had looked away, and did not see me, though nothing in their looking had been quick with abruptness or surreption. I walked somewhat faster now, but I was overtaking them a little slowly for my patience; the light would be right by now or very soon; I had no doubt Walker would do what he wanted whether we had "permission" or not, but I wanted to be on hand, and broke into a trot. At the sound of the twist of my shoe in the gravel, the young woman's whole body was jerked down tight as a fist into a crouch from which immediately, the rear foot skidding in the loose stone so that she nearly fell, like a kicked cow scrambling out of a creek, eyes crazy, chin stretched tight, she sprang forward into the first motions of a running not human but that of a suddenly terrified wild animal. In this same instant the young man froze, the emblems of sense in his wild face wide open toward me, his right hand stiff toward the girl who, after a few strides, her consciousness overtaking her reflex, shambled to a stop and stood, not straight but sick, as if hung from a hook in the spine of the will not to fall for weakness, while he hurried to her and put his hand on her flowered shoulder and, inclining his head forward and sidewise as if listening, spoke with her, and they lifted, and watched me while, shaking my head, and raising my hand palm outward, I came up to them (not trotting) and stopped a yard short of where they, closely, not touching now, stood, and said, still shaking my head (*No; no; oh, Jesus, no, no, no!*) and looking into their eyes; at the man, who was not knowing what to do, and at the girl, whose eyes were lined with tears, and who was trying so hard to subdue the shaking in her breath, and whose heart I could feel, though not hear, blasting as if it were my whole body, and I trying in some fool way to keep it somehow relatively light, because I could not bear that they should receive from me any added reflection of the shattering of their grace and dignity, and of the nakedness and depth and meaning of their fear, and of my horror and pity and self-hatred; and so, smiling, and so distressed that I wanted only that they should be restored, and should know I was their friend, and that I might melt from existence: "I'm *very sorry!* I'm *very* sorry if I scared you! I didn't mean to scare you at all. I wouldn't have done any such thing for anything."

They just kept looking at me. There was no more for them to say than for me. The least I could have done was to throw myself flat on my face and embrace and kiss their feet. That impulse took hold of me so powerfully, from my whole body, not by thought, that I caught myself from doing it exactly and as scarcely as you snatch yourself from jumping from a sheer height: here, with the realization that it would have frightened them still worse (to say nothing of me) and would have been still less explicable; so that I stood and looked into their eyes and loved them, and wished to God I was dead. After a little the man got back his voice, his eyes grew a little easier, and he said without conviction that that was all right and that I hadn't scared her. She shook her head slowly, her eyes on me; she did not yet trust her voice. Their faces were secret, soft, utterly without trust of me, and utterly without understanding; and they had to stand here now and hear what I was saying, because in that country no negro safely walks away from a white man, or even appears not to listen while he is talking, and because I could not walk away abruptly, and relieve them of me, without still worse a crime against nature than the one I had committed, and the second I was committing by staying, and holding them. And so, and in this horrid grinning of faked casualness, I gave them a better reason why I had followed them than to frighten them, asked what I had followed them to ask; they said the thing it is usually safest for negroes to say, that they did not know; I thanked them very much, and was seized once more and beyond resistance with the wish to clarify and set right, so that again, with my eyes and smile wretched and out of key with all I was able to say, I said I was awfully sorry if I had bothered them; but they only retreated still more profoundly behind their faces, their eyes watching mine as if awaiting any sudden move they must ward, and the young man said again that that was all right, and I nodded, and turned away from them, and walked down the road without looking back.

VIRGINIA WOOLF

Strangers on a Train

Agee commits a "crime against nature" by mis-reading character, situation, and cultural values, and by trying too hard to explain. Virginia Woolf (1882–1941), the English writer, sits quietly on a train and imagines the lives of the man and the woman sitting opposite: she turns them into characters, the stuff that novels are made of. Ordinary people are satisfied, she says, with "practical" answers to questions about others they meet: Who are they? How are they related to each other? What do they do for a living? Novelists "go a step further, they feel that there is something permanently interesting in character in itself." We wonder: is it just the novelist who "invents" character out of the strangers they watch in the bus station, the supermarket, the college classroom? (The English novelist Graham Greene once said that all writers are spies).

. . . people have to acquire a good deal of skill in character-reading if they are to live a single year of life without disaster. But it is the art of the young. In middle age and in old age the art is practised mostly for its uses, and friendships and other adventures and experiments in the art of reading character are seldom made. But novelists differ from the rest of the world because they do not cease to be interested in character when they have learnt enough about it for practical purposes. They go a step further, they feel that there is something permanently interesting in character in itself. When all the practical business of life has been discharged, there is something about people which continues to seem to them of overwhelming importance, in spite of the fact that it has no bearing whatever upon their happiness, comfort, or income. The study of character becomes to them an absorbing pursuit; to impart character an obsession. And this I find it very difficult to explain: what novelists mean when they talk about character, what the impulse is that urges them so powerfully every now and then to embody their view in writing.

So, if you will allow me, instead of analysing and abstracting, I will tell you a simple story which, however pointless, has the merit of being true, of a journey from Richmond to Waterloo, in the hope that I may show you what I mean by character in itself; that you may realize the different aspects it can wear; and the hideous perils that beset you directly you try to describe it in words.

One night some weeks ago, then, I was late for the train and jumped into the first carriage I came to. As I sat down I had the strange and uncomfortable feeling that I was interrupting a conversation between two people who were already sitting there. Not that they were young or happy. Far from it. They were both elderly, the woman over sixty, the man well over forty. They were sitting opposite each other, and the man, who had been leaning over and talking emphatically to judge by his attitude and the flush on his face, sat back and became silent. I had disturbed him, and he was annoyed. The elderly lady, however, whom I will call Mrs. Brown, seemed rather relieved. She was one of those clean, threadbare old ladies whose extreme tidiness—everything buttoned, fastened, tied together, mended and brushed up—suggests more extreme poverty than rags and dirt. There was something pinched about her—a look of suffering, of apprehension, and, in addition, she was extremely small. Her feet, in their clean little boots, scarcely touched the floor. I felt that she had nobody to support her; that she had to make up her mind for herself; that, having been deserted, or left a widow, years ago, she had led an anxious, harried life, bringing up an only son, perhaps, who, as likely as not, was by this time beginning to go to the bad. All this shot through my mind as I sat down, being uncomfortable, like most people, at travelling with fellow passengers unless I have somehow or other accounted for them. Then I looked at the man. He was no relation of Mrs. Brown's I felt sure; he was of a bigger, burlier, less refined type. He was a man of business I imagined, very likely a respectable corn-chandler from the North, dressed in good blue serge with a pocket-knife and a silk handkerchief, and a stout leather bag. Obviously, however, he had an unpleasant business to settle with Mrs. Brown; a secret, perhaps sinister business, which they did not intend to discuss in my presence.

"Yes, the Crofts have had very bad luck with their servants," Mr. Smith (as I will call him) said in a considering way, going back to some earlier topic, with a view to keeping up appearances.

"Ah, poor people," said Mrs. Brown, a trifle condescendingly. "My grandmother had a maid who came when she was fifteen and stayed till she was eighty" (this was said with a kind of hurt and aggressive pride to impress us both perhaps).

"One doesn't often come across that sort of thing nowadays," said Mr. Smith in conciliatory tones.

Then they were silent.

"It's odd they don't start a golf club there—I should have thought one of the young fellows would," said Mr. Smith, for the silence obviously made him uneasy.

Mrs. Brown hardly took the trouble to answer.

"What changes they're making in this part of the world," said Mr. Smith, looking out of the window, and looking furtively at me as he did so.

It was plain, from Mrs. Brown's silence, from the uneasy affability with which Mr. Smith spoke, that he had some power over her which he was exerting disagreeably. It might have been her son's downfall, or some painful episode in her past life, or her daughter's. Perhaps she was going to London to sign some document to make over some property. Obviously against her will she was in Mr. Smith's hands. I was beginning to feel a great deal of pity for her, when she said, suddenly and inconsequently:

"Can you tell me if an oak-tree dies when the leaves have been eaten for two years in succession by caterpillars?"

She spoke quite brightly, and rather precisely, in a cultivated, inquisitive voice.

Mr. Smith was startled, but relieved to have a safe topic of conversation given him. He told her a great deal very quickly about plagues of insects. He told her that he had a brother who kept a fruit farm in Kent. He told her what fruit farmers do every year in Kent, and so on, and so on. While he talked a very odd thing happened. Mrs. Brown took out her little white handkerchief and began to dab her eyes. She was crying. But she went on listening quite composedly to what he was saying, and he went on talking, a little louder, a little angrily, as if he had seen her cry often before; as if it were a painful habit. At last it got on his nerves. He stopped abruptly, looked out of the window, then leant towards her as he had been doing when I got in, and said in a bullying, menacing way, as if he would not stand any more nonsense:

"So about that matter we were discussing. It'll be all right? George will be there on Tuesday?"

"We shan't be late," said Mrs. Brown, gathering herself together with superb dignity.

Mr. Smith said nothing. He got up, buttoned his coat, reached his bag down, and jumped out of the train before it had stopped at Clapham Junction. He had got what he wanted, but he was ashamed of himself; he was glad to get out of the old lady's sight.

Mrs. Brown and I were left alone together. She sat in her corner opposite, very clean, very small, rather queer, and suffering intensely. The impression she made was overwhelming. It came pouring out like a draught, like a smell of burning. What was it composed of—that overwhelming and peculiar impression? Myriads of irrelevant and incongruous ideas crowd into one's head on such occasions; one sees the person, one sees Mrs. Brown, in the centre of all sorts of different scenes. I thought of her in a seaside house, among queer ornaments: sea-urchins, models of ships in glass cases. Her husband's medals were on the mantelpiece. She popped in and out of the room, perching on the edges of chairs, picking meals out of saucers, indulging in long, silent stares. The caterpillars and the oak-trees seemed to imply all that. And then, into this fantastic and secluded life, in broke Mr. Smith. I saw him blowing in, so to speak, on a windy day. He banged, he slammed. His dripping umbrella made a pool in the hall. They sat closeted together.

And then Mrs. Brown faced the dreadful revelation. She took her heroic decision. Early, before dawn, she packed her bag and carried it herself to the station. She would not let Smith touch it. She was wounded in her pride, unmoored from her anchorage; she came of gentlefolks who kept servants—but details could wait. The important thing was to realize her character, to steep oneself in her atmosphere. I had no time to explain why I felt it somewhat tragic, heroic, yet with a dash of the flighty and fantastic, before the train stopped, and I watched her disappear, carrying her bag, into the vast blazing station. She looked very small, very tenacious; at once very frail and very heroic. And I have never seen her again, and I shall never know what became of her.

The story ends without any point to it. But I have not told you this anecdote to illustrate either my own ingenuity or the pleasure of travelling from Richmond to Waterloo. What I want you to see in it is this. Here is a character imposing itself upon another person. Here is Mrs. Brown making someone begin almost automatically to write a novel about her. I believe that all novels begin with an old lady in the corner opposite. I believe that all novels, that is to say, deal with character, and that it is to express character—not to preach doctrines, sing songs, or celebrate the glories of the British Empire, that the form of the novels, so clumsy, verbose, and undramatic, so rich, elastic, and alive, has been evolved. To express character, I have said; but you will at once reflect that the very widest interpretation can be put upon those words. For example, old Mrs. Brown's character will strike you very differently according to the age and country in which you happen to be born. It would be easy enough to write three different versions of that incident in the train, an English, a French, and a Russian. The English writer would make the old lady into a "character"; he would bring out her oddities and mannerisms; her buttons and wrinkles; her ribbons and warts. Her personality would dominate the book. A French writer would rub out all that; he would sacrifice the individual Mrs. Brown to give a more general view of human nature; to make a more abstract, proportioned, and harmonious whole. The Russian would pierce through the flesh; would reveal the soul—the soul alone, wandering out into the Waterloo Road, asking of life some tremendous question which would sound on and on in our ears after the book was finished. And then besides age and country there is the writer's temperament to be considered. You see one thing in character, and I another. You say it means this, and I that. And when it comes to writing each makes a further selection on principles of his own. Thus Mrs. Brown can be treated in an infinite variety of ways, according to the age, country, and temperament of the writer.

But now I must recall what Mr. Arnold Bennett says. He says that it is only if the characters are real that the novel has any chance of surviving. Otherwise, die it must. But, I ask myself, what is reality? And who are the judges of reality? A character may be real to Mr. Bennett and quite unreal to me. For instance, in this article he says that Dr. Watson in *Sherlock Holmes* is real to him: to me Dr. Watson is a sack stuffed with straw, a dummy, a figure of fun. And so it is with character after character—in book after book. There is nothing that people differ about more than the reality of characters, especially in contemporary books. But if you take a larger view I think that Mr. Bennett is perfectly right. If, that is, you think of the novels which seem to you great novels—*War and Peace, Vanity Fair, Tristram Shandy, Madame Bovary, Pride and Prejudice, The Mayor of Casterbridge, Villette*—if you think of these books, you do at once think of some character who has seemed to you so real (I do not by that mean so lifelike) that it has the power to make you think not merely of it itself, but of all sorts of things through its eyes—of religion, of love, of war, of peace, of family life, of balls in country towns, of sunsets, moonrises, the immortality of the soul. There is hardly any subject of human experience that is left out of *War and Peace* it seems to me. And in all these novels all these great novelists have brought us to see whatever they wish us to see through some character. Otherwise, they would not be novelists; but poets, historians, or pamphleteers.

CONSIDER THIS

★ ". . . people have to acquire a good deal of skill in character-reading if they are to live a single year of life without disaster." True? No? Can you think of misreadings of others that have caused you problems or distress? How do you account for your errors? Were you reading carelessly?

★ "But, I ask myself, what is reality? And who are the judges of reality?"
"You see one thing in character, and I another. You say it means this, and I that."

These sentences from Virginia Woolf's text could have been overheard in conversation of two people discussing . . . reality? Unreality? Myth? Character? Meaning? How do we read the people we know? How do we read . . . celebrities, people who are in the limelight, and who we see, only, through the mediation of the media: camera, video, the movies, and print? How do we read Elvis Presley?

Here's how Thom Gunn reads one of the most popular images of our time: *Elvis.*

THOM GUNN

Painkillers

The King of rock 'n roll
grown pudgy, almost matronly,
Fatty in gold lamé,
mad King encircled
by a court of guards, suffering   5
delusions about assassination,
obsessed by guns, fearing
rivalry and revolt

popping his skin
with massive hits of painkiller   10

dying at 42.

What was the pain?
Pain had been the colours
of the bad boy with the sneer.

The story of pain, of separation,   15
was the divine comedy
he had translated
from black into white.

For white children too
the act of naming the pain
unsheathed
a keen joy at the heart of it.   20

Here they are still!
the disobedient
who keep a culture alive   25
by subverting it, turning
for example a subway
into a garden of graffiti.

But the puffy King
lived on, his painkillers   30
neutralizing, neutralizing,
until he became
ludicrous in performance.

The enthroned cannot revolt.
What was the pain   35
he needed to kill
if not the ultimate pain

of feeling no pain?

LESTER BANGS

Where Were You When Elvis Died?

Let us now turn back the clock, from that obituary poem on the Elvis who finally killed "the ultimate pain of feeling no pain," to an earlier, happier moment in the emergence of a remarkable celebrity. No, he was more than that, better than that, for as the historian Daniel Boorstin has remarked, celebrities are merely well known for being well known. How good was Elvis? In this essay, taken from his collection, Psychotic Reactions and Carburetor Dung, *Lester Bangs, the rock-critic who died tragically at the age of 33 in 1982, reminds us of the good times, before pop culture was shaken to its roots, and of how good Elvis was: also, alas, of how the business of selling him corrupted him and abused his fans.*

Where were *you* when Elvis died? What were you doing, and what did it give you an excuse to do with the rest of your day? That's what we'll be talking about in the

future when we remember this grand occasion. Like Pearl Harbor or JFK's assassination, it boiled down to individual reminiscences, which is perhaps as it should be,
because in spite of his greatness, etc., etc., Elvis had left us each as alone as he was;
I mean, he wasn't exactly a Man of the People anymore, if you get my drift. If you
don't I will drift even further, away from Elvis into the contemplation of why all
our public heroes seem to reinforce our own solitude.

The ultimate sin of any performer is contempt for the audience. Those who
indulge in it will ultimately reap the scorn of those they've dumped on, whether
they live forever like Andy Paleface Warhol or die fashionably early like Lenny
Bruce, Jimi Hendrix, Janis Joplin, Jim Morrison, Charlie Parker, Billie Holiday.
The two things that distinguish those deaths from Elvis's (he and they having drug
habits vaguely in common) were that all of them died on the outside looking in and
none of them took their audience for granted. Which is why it's just a little bit
harder for me to see Elvis as a tragic figure; I see him as being more like the
Pentagon, a giant armored institution nobody knows anything about except that its
power is legendary.

Obviously we all liked Elvis better than the Pentagon, but look at what a paltry
statement that is. In the end, Elvis's scorn for his fans as manifested in "new" albums

full of previously released material and one new song to make sure all us suckers would buy it was mirrored in the scorn we all secretly or not so secretly felt for a man who came closer to godhood than Carlos Castaneda until military conscription tamed and revealed him for the dumb lackey he always was in the first place. And ever since, for almost two decades now, we've been waiting for him to get wild again, fools that we are, and he probably knew better than any of us in his heart of hearts that it was never gonna happen, his heart of hearts so obviously not being our collective heart of hearts, he being so obviously just some poor dumb Southern boy with a Big Daddy manager to screen the world for him and filter out anything which might erode his status as big strapping baby bringing home the bucks, and finally being sort of perversely celebrated at least by rock critics for his utter contempt for whoever cared about him.

And Elvis was perverse; only a true pervert could put out something like *Having Fun with Elvis on Stage*, that album released three or so years back which consisted *entirely* of between-song onstage patter so redundant it would make both Willy Burroughs and Gert Stein blush. Elvis was into marketing boredom when Andy Warhol was still doing shoe ads, but Elvis's sin was his failure to realize that his fans were not perverse—they loved him without qualification, no matter what he dumped on them they loyally lapped it up, and that's why I feel a hell of a lot sorrier for all those poor jerks than for Elvis himself. I mean, who's left they can stand all night in the rain for? Nobody, and the true tragedy is the tragedy of an entire generation which refuses to give up its adolescence even as it feels its menopausal paunch begin to blossom and its hair recede over the horizon—along with Elvis and everything else they once thought they believed in. Will they care in five years what he's been doing for the last twenty?

Sure Elvis's death is a relatively minor ironic variant on the future-shock mazurka, and perhaps the most significant thing about Elvis's exit is that the entire history of the seventies has been retreads and brutal demystification; three of Elvis's ex-body-guards recently got together with this hacker from the New York *Post* and whipped up a book which dosed us with all the dirt we'd yearned for for so long. Elvis was the last of our sacred cows to be publicly mutilated; everybody knows Keith Richard likes his junk, but when Elvis went onstage in a stupor nobody breathed a hint of "Quaalude. . . ." In a way, this was both good and bad, good because Elvis wasn't encouraging other people to think it was cool to be a walking *Physicians' Desk Reference*, bad because Elvis stood for that Nixonian Secrecy-as-Virtue which was passed off as the essence of Americanism for a few years there. In a sense he could be seen not only as a phenomenon that exploded in the fifties to help shape the psychic jailbreak of the sixties but ultimately as a perfect cultural expression of what the Nixon years were all about. Not that he prospered more then, but that his passion for the privacy of potentates allowed him to get away with almost literal murder, certainly with the symbolic rape of his fans, meaning that we might all do better to think about waving good-bye with one upraised finger.

I got the news of Elvis's death while drinking beer with a friend and fellow music journalist on his fire escape on 21st Street in Chelsea. Chelsea is a good neighborhood; in spite of the fact that the insane woman who lives upstairs keeps him awake all night every night with her rants at no one, my friend stays there because he likes the sense of community within diversity in that neighborhood: old-time card-carrying Communists live in his building alongside people of every persuasion popularly lumped as "ethnic." When we heard about Elvis we knew a wake was in order, so I went out to the deli for a case of beer. As I left the building I passed some Latin guys hanging out by the front door. "Heard the news? Elvis is dead!" I told them. They looked at me with contemptuous indifference. *So what.* Maybe if I had told them Donna Summer was dead I might have gotten a reaction; I do recall walking in this neighborhood wearing a T-shirt that said "Disco Sucks" with a vast unamused muttering in my wake, which only goes to show that not for everyone was Elvis the still-reigning King of Rock 'n' Roll, in fact not for everyone is rock 'n' roll the still-reigning music. By now, each citizen has found his own little obsessive corner to blast his brains in: as the sixties were supremely narcissistic, solipsism's what the seventies have been about, and nowhere is this better demonstrated than in the world of "pop" music. And Elvis may have been the greatest solipsist of all.

I asked for two six-packs at the deli and told the guy behind the counter the news. He looked fifty years old, greying, big belly, life still in his eyes, and he said: "Shit, that's too bad. I guess our only hope now is if the Beatles get back together."

Fifty years old.

I told him I thought that would be the biggest anticlimax in history and that the best thing the Stones could do now would be to break up and spare us all further embarrassments.

He laughed, and gave me directions to a meat market down the street. There I asked the counterman the same question I had been asking everyone. He was in his fifties too, and he said, "You know what? I don't *care* that bastard's dead. I took my wife to see him in Vegas in '73, we paid fourteen dollars a ticket, and he came out and sang for twenty minutes. Then he fell down. Then he stood up and sang a couple more songs, then he fell down again. Finally he said, 'Well, shit, I might as well sing sitting as standing.' So he squatted on the stage and asked the band what song they wanted to do next, but before they could answer he was complaining about the lights. 'They're too bright,' he says. 'They hurt my eyes. Put 'em out or I don't sing a note.' So they do. So me and my wife are sitting in total blackness listening to this guy sing songs we knew and loved, and I ain't just talking about his old goddam songs, but he totally *butchered* all of 'em. Fuck him. I'm not saying I'm glad he's dead, but I know one thing: I got taken when I went to see Elvis Presley."

I got taken too the one time I saw Elvis, but in a totally different way. It was the autumn of 1971, and two tickets to an Elvis show turned up at the offices of *Creem* magazine, where I was then employed. It was decided that those staff members who had never had the privilege of witnessing Elvis should get the tickets, which was how me and art director Charlie Auringer ended up in nearly the front row of the biggest arena in Detroit. Earlier Charlie had said, "Do you realize how much we could get if we sold these fucking things?" I didn't, but how precious they were became totally clear the instant Elvis sauntered onto the stage. He was the only male performer I have ever seen to whom I responded sexually; it wasn't real arousal, rather an erection of the heart, when I looked at him I went mad with desire and envy and worship and self-projection. I mean, Mick Jagger, whom I saw as far back as 1964 and twice in '65, never even came close.

There was Elvis, dressed up in this ridiculous white suit which looked like some studded Arthurian castle, and he was too fat, and the buckle on his belt was as big as your head except that your head is not made of solid gold, and any lesser man would have been the spittin' image of a Neil Diamond damfool in such a getup, but on Elvis it fit. What didn't? No matter how lousy his records ever got, no matter how intently he pursued mediocrity, there was still some hint, some flash left over from the days when . . . well, I wasn't there, so I won't presume to comment. But I will say this: Elvis Presley was the man who brought overt blatant vulgar sexual frenzy to the popular arts in America (and thereby to the nation itself, since putting "popular arts" and "America" in the same sentence seems almost redundant). It has been said that he was the first white to sing like a black person, which is untrue in terms of hard facts but totally true in terms of cultural impact. But what's more crucial is that when Elvis started wiggling his hips and Ed Sullivan refused to show it, the entire country went into a paroxysm of sexual frustration leading to abiding discontent which culminated in the explosion of psychedelic-militant folklore which was the sixties.

I mean, don't tell me about Lenny Bruce, man—Lenny Bruce said dirty words in public and obtained a kind of consensual martyrdom. Plus which Lenny Bruce was hip, too goddam hip if you ask me, which was his undoing, whereas Elvis was not hip at all, Elvis was a goddam truck driver who worshipped his mother and would never say shit or fuck around her, and Elvis alerted America to the fact that it had a groin with imperatives that had been stifled. Lenny Bruce demonstrated how far you could push a society as repressed as ours and how much you could get away with, but Elvis kicked "How Much Is That Doggie in the Window" *out* the window and replaced it with "Let's fuck." The rest of us are still reeling from the impact. Sexual chaos reigns currently, but out of chaos may flow true understanding and harmony, and either way Elvis almost singlehandedly opened the floodgates. That night in Detroit, a night I will never forget, he had but to ever so slightly move one shoulder muscle, not even a shrug, and the girls in the gallery hit by its ray screamed, fainted, howled in heat. Literally, every time this man moved any part of his body the slightest centimeter, tens or tens of thousands of people went berserk. Not Sinatra, not Jagger, not the Beatles, nobody you can come up with ever elicited such hysteria among so many. And this after a decade and a half of crappy records, of making a point of not trying.

If love truly is going out of fashion forever, which I do not believe, then along with our nurtured indifference to each other will be an even more contemptuous indifference to each others' objects of reverence. I thought it was Iggy Stooge, you thought it was Joni Mitchell or whoever else seemed to speak for your own private, entirely circumscribed situation's many pains and few ecstasies. We will continue to fragment in this manner, because solipsism holds all the cards at present; it is a king whose domain engulfs even Elvis's. But I can guarantee you one thing: we will never again agree on anything as we agreed on Elvis. So I won't bother saying good-bye to his corpse. I will say good-bye to you.

LESTER BANGS

Then I Will Be Elvis!

Lester Bangs was, in his time, probably the liveliest writer about rock: some of his best writing has only come to light since his death. For example, in April 1980, he wrote a lively and intelligent review, in the Los Angeles Herald-Examiner, *of Peter Guralnick's* Lost Highway, *a series of portraits of the best performers in blues, rhythm 'n' blues, country and western, and early rock 'n' roll. Since his death, his friend and editor, Greil Marcus, has discovered the notes that Bangs wrote for that review, jottings that became something far more extravagant, manic, surreal, and* bravura *(remember that word?) than a mere book review. In his notes, Bangs left the ground, defied gravity, denied reality, and* became *(!) Elvis Presley—not the earlier one that had exhilarated him, but the later one, the commercialized one, whom he despised. We enter his text just as he is about to take off into his extravaganza of metamorphosis.*

THEN I WILL BE ELVIS! I'll make several dozen unwatchable movies and that number plus a couple dozen more unlistenable albums! I'll know karate so I can kick out the eyeballs of my landlord next time he comes up here to complain I haven't paid the rent in three months! Like I'm sure he's gonna come complaining to Elvis about something as piddling as rent anyway! Ditto for Master Charge, Macy's, all these assholes hounding me for money I don't have and they don't need: I mean, seriously, can you imagine *Elvis* sitting down with his checkbook and a stack of unpaid bills, going through the whole dreary monthly routine, and then balancing his bank account? He'd just go out and buy a car for some colored cleaning lady he'd never met before instead! Then Master Charge would tear up the bill saying "Mr. Presley you are a real humanitarian and since we are too we want to say we feel honored to have you run up as high a tab as you want on us."

Lessee, now, what else can I do? Well, concerts. Kinda boring, tho, since all I've gotta do (all I'm ALLOWED to do if I'm gonna not insult Elvis's memory by breaking with tradition) is just stand there holding a microphone, singing current schmaltz with no emotion, and occasionally wiping the sweat off my brow with one of a series of hankies hidden away in the sleeve of my White Castle studded jacket and then toss the contaminated little rag to whichever female in the first few rows has walked more backs, blackened more eyes and broken more arms and legs in an attempt to get up close to my godly presence. As my whole career has surely borne out, I believe with one hand on my mother's grave that aggressive persistence in the service of a noble cause should be rewarded. Still, all this, ah, don't *you* think it sounds kinda, well, *dull?* I mean, how many hankies can you throw out before you start to go catatonic? At least Sid Vicious got to walk onstage with "GIMME A FIX" written in blood on his chest and bash people in the first row over the head with his bass if he didn't approve of the brand of beercan you were throwing at him.

Sid got to have all the fun.

Let's see, there's GOT to be something else. Well, of course, of course, I can sit around gobbling pills all day, but ANYBODY can do that. You don't have to be Elvis to stay luded-out all the time; if you did, everybody in Washington Square Park is/was Elvis Presley. Which obviously cannot be true, there can only be one, the King, me, not even "and," unless I decide to indulge in a little schizophrenia, but wait, I can't even be schizophrenic because I'm already catatonic and even if it were possible to have two variants of the same malady at once I don't think you should be greedy with your diseases. God knows there's few enough of 'em to go around and more and more people every day who wanna score one, any kind at all, just for some kind of change in the atmosphere. I may have croaked on the commode but I'm not anal retentive.

So. Shit. I thought bein' Elvis was gonna be *fun,* and here I am, stuck, ONCE AGAIN with "nothin' to do and nowhere to go," except now I am sedated beyond my wildest dreams, and that doesn't seem to be making a damn bit of difference. In fact, it feels just like being awake. Guess I could get one of my rifles off the shelf and shoot out a few TV picture tubes. Lemme get the *TV Guide* and see who's on I might wanna shoot: Hmmm, 6:55 Friday night. I've got five minutes left on which to knock off Carol Burnett, Oscar or Felix on "The Odd Couple," whoever the anchorman is on "New Jersey News" or the host on "Tic Tac Dough." There's a bunch of other local news shows just concluding, but fuck them, I can kill them another day. Well, I can't kill Carol or Oscar or Felix 'cause I like all those shows, and killing somebody in a TV show from New Jersey seems like stooping pretty low to conquer, like what's the point, while as far as "Tic Tac Dough" goes one game show host is as obnoxious as another, if I blasted whoever this john is it'd be no special treat, besides which if I killed *him* the other ones might get jealous 'cause of the publicity and start hounding me, and then I'd have to kill Monty Hall and Bill Cullen and Bob Eubanks and Hugh Downs and Chuck Barris and . . . aw, forget it, you can see what a hopeless course that'd turnout to be. I'd probably no sooner blow the smoke outa my barrel as the last one slumped behind his desk than knowing them damn networks I'd look in next week's *TV Guide* and see thirty-five brand new ones I never even heard of before all set and rarin' to go be slaughtered with new shows and everything. One person I definitely wouldn't mind killing would be Rip Taylor. If only "The $1.98 Beauty Show" was on. But it's not. In fact, I don't even know what night it's on. Maybe they canceled it while my back was turned, not too remote a possibility since it (my back) usually is. Maybe Elvis was bad when he was alive and got sent to Hell instead of Heaven—I mean, I definitely don't see his mom around here anywhere, or the brother that died. So I'm gonna have to spend the rest of eternity never getting a chance to kill Rip Taylor. Wait, not only that, but considering what kinda life Rip's probably led he'll get sent down here whenever he croaks from whatever's gonna do him, and HE'LL get to spend the rest of eternity torturing ME. Jeez, this is lookin' blacker by the second. It's now 7:10, which means that murder-wise I have my choice of Walter Cronkite, David Brinkley, and/or John Chancellor, whoever I pick from the cast of "M*A*S*H," Frank Reynolds, that guy who hosts "The Dating Game" or one of the contestants—ah-HA! "Bachelorette Number Two, do you—" BLAM!, anybody from "Happy Days," Fonzie, hmmm, two years ago maybe, now it's not worth the bother, same with "The Dating Game" really: you woulda wanted to kill Bachelorette Number Two in 1971, when you watched the show every day, but hell, by now I haven't seen it in so long I can't even remember what the host's name was/is—Jim Somethingorother. Or "Over Easy": Hugh Downs, Chita Rivera and her daughter. How dreary. Looking ahead to prime time, I find myself confronted with either Bill Bixby or Lou Ferrigno in the "Hulk" hour, except I always kinda liked both those guys for some reason and I bet (I mean, I *know*) so did Elvis; Shirley Jones; some nonentities on something called "B.A.D. Cats"; anybody on the Chicago Black Hawks, the Flames (whatever hockey town they hail from), the New York Arrows, or the Summit Soccer team way down in Houston—but shit, I never was much into sports, I wouldn't know who to shoot first so I guess I'd have to kill both teams whichever game I tuned in; the only guest on Merv Griffin I've ever heard of tonight is Dr. Linus J. Pauling; wait, here, yes, this actually gets my blood up a bit: at 8:30 I can kill *Dick Cavett*, and Mary McCarthy too, depending on my mood by then. Only trouble is my mood by now has gotten so bad I don't feel like killing anybody, not even Dick Cavett, whom I've wanted to kill for years. I seem to have no will whatsoever, in any department or direction. I said catatonia? I think autism now. Perhaps both. Somewhere in the distance of the Bob Lind canyon of my mind I hear Paul Simon singing "I am a rock / I am an island," but it bears no significance or emotional impression positive or negative. Like nullsville, man. And nullsville is dullsville. I think maybe I feel more like a vegetable than a rock anyway. Broccoli, perhaps. In a frozen Stouffer's soufflé. Let's see: I can't eat. I can't sleep. I can't get high. I can't listen to music (it all sounds the same, besides which I made the best records of all time so what's the point?). I can't watch TV cause there's nothing on and if there was I don't have the will to get up, flick it on and maybe even have to (shudder) switch channels. I can't kill. I can't shit or piss. I can't get drunk because Elvis never did because he always remembered what his mama said about how alcohol made Daddy so mean but she never mentioned downers 'cause that's medication. I certainly can't read, except maybe some undoubtedly obscure martial arts text.

Is there anything left? Oh yeah, sex? Well, as I look around my palatial suite in Caesar's Palace here in Vegas then peek through the door and down the hall I see, oh shit, must be at least fifty busty babes that all look like they came outa the centerfolds or the Dallas Cowgirls or "Charlie's Angels." I used to like to jerk off to Playboy every once in a while, just about every night in fact, even the real plastic airline-stewardessy ones, before I was Elvis. Once I even jerked off at a picture of Farrah Fawcett-Majors. At the time I thought it was a really sick thing to do; it was fun. Now I could fuck or get blown by any of these broads and I haven't got the slightest bit of physical inclination. I feel about as sexy as a turnip. I mean I guess I could *make* myself, but what the fuck, you know? Besides, what does Elvis have to prove? What I can't figure out is why, when I used to really dig pulling my pud to pix of 'em in the magazines, and even had my special favorites that always got me hotter while there were others I always avoided because of the way they were posed or they just weren't my type somehow, it was just like girlfriends except lonelier, what I can't understand is why, now, here they all are in the flesh, I could even jerk off at 'em without touching if I had some kind of hangup, or send one out for a copy of *Playboy*, they all look exactly alike to me. The last time that happened was in 1973 when everybody on all the made-for-TV movies started to look like Stefanie Powers post–"Girl from U.N.C.L.E."

But Elvis don't sit around thinking theoretical psychosociological bullshit like that, that's for sure. What does he think about? Beats me. Nothing, I guess. Nothing at all. Himself, maybe. But that's nothing. Like that Billy Preston song: "Nothing from Nothing Leaves Nothing." Jeez, Billy Preston, there's a hep dude, I bet he's sure havin' lotsa fun right now, wherever he is. I wonder if this is how Don Gibson felt when he wrote, "Oh, Lonesome Me." But I don't write songs. I just sing 'em. Sometimes. But how can you even sing 'em when you don't know what any of the lyrics mean cause you don't have any feelings or experiences anymore or all feelings or experiences are equivalent—how can you call yourself an "interpreter" when you've, uh, forgotten the language? So I guess I'm not a singer anymore either. Well, maybe there's some consolation there: that's gotta be the last one to go. Now I can turn into a test pattern. Oh well, sounds peaceful. And if that's the case I'm gonna sign off. Except I don't think I'll be resuming programming at six A.M. or any other time for that matter. I'd sing you the National Anthem, but I'm not a singer anymore, remember? I'm sorry. Wait a second, no I'm not; you're just as much to blame for this hopeless cipherdom as I am, since you made me the biggest star in the world, believed in me, pinned all these false hopes on me I couldn'ta fulfilled even if I'd understood what you meant, that asshole Peter Guralnick and his friends: what the hell did they think I was, a slacker or something? Or even leaving the army out of it, what the hell did people like that really want me to do? Keep on singing rhythm 'n' blues? Why, so I could end up repeating the same tired riffs like Chuck and Jerry Lee and Bo Diddley and the rest of 'em left over from the fifties? So I could open for the Clash? Man, for*get* it. And fuck all the rest of you too, you "true fans" who bought any shit RCA slung out with my name on it and made yourselves love it or say you did or pretend to. *Having Fun With Elvis on Stage*, me babbling and sayin' "WELLLLL" for nigh on an hour, even I'd be embarrassed by an album like that, if I wasn't beyond embarrassment so long ago I can't even remember what it felt like. You think you're paying tribute but that's the world's *worst possible* insult. I'd rather you told me I was shit, some of the time, or even shit all the time. *Anything*. But to say you love everything, indiscriminately, just because it was me or had my name on it—well, that just says to me that you never cared about the music from day one. You couldn't have, or you woulda complained *somewhere* down the line, like maybe by *Harum Scarum*, I dunno, they're all the same to me, too. But if you never cared whether I tried or not, then why in the hell should I? You rock critics and "deep thinkers," you were using me, projecting some fantasy of rebellion on me. I certainly wasn't rebelling against anything, ever. I dressed funny and wore my hair a little different when I was in school, but that wasn't rebelling, like Sam said, that was just . . . *me*. That was just a way of saying I existed, I guess. After I started to get big, I could *feel* it moving in the opposite direction—I don't know when it was, couldn't pinpoint a day, all I know is that, all of a sudden, at a certain point, pretty far before the army too, I started to stop being me. Because, well, everywhere I looked I started seeing me. Every singer, every kid on every streetcorner, everywhere. There was so much me goin' around it just started to look like *Playboy*. Yeah, I was still and always the leader of the pack, but that's not the point. The point is that something I started doing to make people know I existed started rubbing out my existence, a little at a time, day by day, I could feel it going, seeping away, steady and calm . . . and nothin' comin' in to replace it. And I knew nothin' ever would. Maybe if I'da been smart I shoulda gone right then and blown my brains out like Johnny Ace and then there only woulda been those few records and all the critics would be happy and the fans wouldn't know the difference and I'd be a legend. But I was a legend anyway; still am, even more than ever. Shit, I couldn't evena committed suicide! Not for real, because it wouldn't've been for any of the reasons real people use to commit suicide every day. It woulda been cynical, bad faith, trying to prove a point when I didn't have no point to prove. I don't want you to get the idea I'm feelin' sorry for myself. I'm not feelin' *anything* for myself, or anybody else. Except one thing. One last thing. I'm feelin' I wish you all would leave me alone. Go bother Engelbert Humperdinck. Or Gig Young, if you want somebody who's dead. Don't come 'round with your *National Enquirer* or your Peter Guralnicks and Greil Marcuses, not to mention your Geraldo Riveras. Just don't come 'round at all. 'Cause I was nothing for twenty years, and most of you couldn't tell the difference. And then I was dead, and you outdid yourselves thinking up new ways to finish off the job of leaving my corpse humiliated, pissed on, disre-spected, degraded, demythified, lied about, deprived of every last shred of privacy or the most basic human dignities. I'm sure you'll think of some more, and I'm not even that pissed off about it, 'cause that's just the way you are, the way I was: that's your version of *Having Fun With Elvis on Stage*. It's cool; I been there. Besides, I still do take some slight comfort in the fact there's something about me, some weird quality, that you haven't been able to figure out yet, none of you. I never could either. I guess I was something. The only trouble was that when I was somethin', I wasn't me, just like when I was me, I was nothin'. Oh, well. Life's like that. Write any kinda shit you want. I won't be reading it. I'm tunin' out.

The combined effects of the drugs and rotted bodily organs wore off about thirty-six hours later. I came out of a deep and not unrestful sleep feeling disoriented, displaced, vaguely depressed, emotionally numbed, but with mind and body in relatively sound state. After a couple of days I was even able to listen to music again, even his albums. There's just one thing that's different. If they exhume the body again, I don't think they should be worrying about drugs (*I* certainly wouldn't take any more drugs that came outa Elvis Presley's stomach!). I think they should

take him down to a taxidermist's, and have him stuffed, like Trigger. I could say something like "and then have it placed on the steps of the White House," but that would be glib. The trouble is, while I *know* he should be stuffed and put on display somewhere, I don't for the life of me know where that should be. Because I guess he really doesn't belong anywhere, anymore, does he? Does he?

We hope you managed to preserve your sanity while reading this text. If you didn't read it *aloud*, at the top of your voice, on top of a mountain or the Empire State Building, you missed a good opportunity to *realize* the incantatory power, the intoxicating hilarity, the pulsating, enlivening pizzazz of a prose that gets as close to the rhythm of a speaking voice as you are likely to find. Bang's outrageous—deliberately outrageous—tone, his provocative images, his unbuttoned language—all represent ways of dealing with the rage and disappointment that we know he felt as he came to recognize his discovery of sheer *disenchantment*.

One way, then, of *reading* others is to try to *become* them—through language, through stepping into their shoes and trying to see how they fit, through taking on their voice to see how it sounds—through taking on a *role*.

Let Bangs' role-playing continue to resonate in your mind, as you listen in again to Philip Roth, in *Reading Myself and Others*, talking about how writers make fiction:

PHILIP ROTH

It's All the Art of Impersonation

It's all the art of impersonation, isn't it? That's the fundamental novelistic gift. . . . Making fake biography, false history, concocting a half-imaginary existence out of the actual drama of my life *is* my life. There has to be some pleasure in this job, and that's it. To go around in disguise. To act a character. To pass oneself off as what one is not. To *pretend*. The sly and cunning masquerade. Think of the ventriloquist. He speaks so that his voice appears to proceed from someone at a distance from himself. But if he weren't in your line of vision you'd get no pleasure from his art at all. His art consists of being present *and* absent; he's most himself by simultaneously being someone else, neither of whom he "is" once the curtain is down. You don't necessarily, as a writer, have to abandon your biography completely to engage in an act of impersonation. It may be more intriguing when you don't. You distort it, caricature it, parody it, you torture and subvert it, you exploit it—all to give the biography that dimension that will excite your verbal life. Millions of people do this all the time, of course, and not with the justification of making literature. They *mean* it. It's amazing what lies people can sustain behind the mask of their real faces. Think of the art of the adulterer: under tremendous pressure and against enormous odds, ordinary husbands and wives, who would freeze with self-conscious-ness up on a stage, yet in the theater of the home, alone before the audience of the betrayed spouse, they act out roles of innocence and fidelity with flawless dramatic skill. Great, great performances, conceived with genius down to the smallest partic-ulars, impeccably meticulous naturalistic acting, and all done by rank amateurs. People beautifully pretending to be "themselves." Make-believe can take the subtlest forms, you know. Why should a novelist, a pretender by profession, be any less deft or more reliable than a stolid unimaginative suburban accountant cheating on his wife? Jack Benny used to pretend to be a miser, remember? Called himself by his own good name and claimed that he was stingy and mean. It excited his comic imagination to do this. He probably wasn't all that funny as just another nice fellow writing checks to the U.J.A. and taking his friends out to dinner.

Reading, like writing, is also an act of *impersonation*, which is a word that would make its point more effectively if it were spelled *INpersonation*. When successfully impersonating, we can experience an intense and vivid illusion of being in-(another)-person. Like all the relationships that connect us to others, impersonation through reading is a two-way experience: the reader enters into the other person(s) in the fiction, and the other self (or selves) enter(s) into the reader.

Impersonating others through reading and internalizing what is actually out-side our minds is a particular form of a common enough social experience: when a friend makes us laugh for the first time in a week, it must be because *their* laughing mood, their hilarity, has entered into us, just as *we* have entered into their hilarity. Reading, amazingly—though we learn to take it for granted—allows us to do this even when we are actually alone.

EDWIN MORGAN

The Death of Marilyn Monroe

The "decline and fall," such as we read in the story of Presley's life and death, is enough to provoke the primal question, "Why? Why? Why?" And it's in a similar mood of interrogation that Edwin Morgan (b. 1920) begins his elegy for Marilyn Monroe, Hollywood's fabled and mythic counterpart to Presley.

DiMaggio and Miller, just in case you didn't know, were two of her husbands; Strasberg was the director of an acting studio that specialized in a newly authentic kind of acting.

The poem ends with questions, as it began. Who, then, is supposed to answer the closing questions?

What innocence? Whose guilt? What eyes? Whose breast?
Crumpled orphan, nembutal bed,
white hearse, Los Angeles,
DiMaggio! Los Angeles! Miller! Los Angeles! America!
That Death should seem the only protector —   5
That all arms should have faded, and the great cameras and lights
    become an inquisition and a torment —
That the many acquaintances, the autograph-hunters, the
    inflexible directors, the drive-in admirers should become
    a blur of incomprehension and pain —
That lonely Uncertainty should limp up, grinning, with
    bewildering barbiturates, and watch her undress and lie
    down and in her anguish
call for him! call for him to strengthen her with what could
    only dissolve her! A method
of dying, we are shaken, we see it. Strasberg!   10
Los Angeles! Olivier! Los Angeles! Others die
and yet by this death we are a little shaken, we feel it,
America.

Let no one say communication is a cantword.*
They had to lift her hand from the bedside telephone.   15
But what she had not been able to say
perhaps she had said, 'All I had was my life.
I have no regrets, because if I made
any mistakes, I was responsible.
There is now — and there is the future.   20
What has happened is behind. So
it follows you around? So what?' — This
to a friend, ten days before.
And so she was responsible.
And if she was not responsible, not wholly responsible, Los Angeles?
      Los Angeles? Will it follow you around? Will the slow
      white hearse of the child of America follow you around?   25

CONSIDER THIS

★ How, then, do we incorporate such deaths into our normal consciousness? Into our ordinary workaday lives? How do they touch us? How do they affect us?

★ Should we grieve for those we never actually knew? For those whose private selves were hidden behind the showbiz masks? Do we know who we grieve for? What do we "read" when we attend to the showbiz stars: illusion or reality? Fact or fiction?

★ And what of this: "the murder of our children by these men [madmen who intend to destroy this beautifully made planet] has got to become a terror and a sorrow to you, and starting now, it had better interfere with any daily pleasure"? So speaks the woman/narrator in Grace Paley's story "Anxiety" on pages 388–390. Does her remark perhaps put the premature deaths of stars into a saner, more intelligent perspective? Sure, we can lament the deaths of the famous, but what about *all* the people in this whole wide world?

YOUR WRITING(S) FOR OTHERS TO READ

What exactly do we mean by "interpretation"? When musicians interpret a musical score, what exactly do they do? Clearly, they aim to perform all the notes on the page, but even as they do so they also perform expressively, offering their listeners what the music *means for them*—for example, very cheerful, averagely cheerful; lively, very lively, a bit lively; solemn, very solemn; and so on.

Similarly, when we "read" another person, or a book, or an event carefully,

---

*Cantword: Morgan appears to pun on "cantword": a cliché; and "can't word."

and then think about what we have perceived, we are then likely to be ready to say what it *means to us*: we can offer *our* interpretation. Needless to say, "what it means to us" will involve our values, beliefs, attitudes, and assumptions.

As we grow, our minds develop, our beliefs and assumptions become more complicated: we *re*-interpret, achieve an interpretation obviously or subtly different from earlier less mature interpretations.

Give an account of the ways in which your interpretations of people or of events have changed or are even at this moment changing.

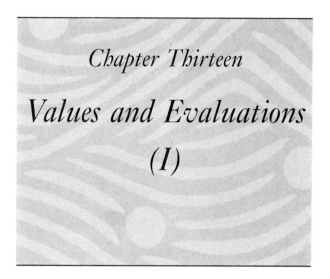

Chapter Thirteen

Values and Evaluations (I)

Y ou will find a few light moments in this chapter—Alan Devenish's answering machine, for example, and the finely honed knives of Oscar Wilde's dialogue; but this is probably the most demanding and most somber chapter in the book; we invite you to tune your expectations accordingly.

The chapter offers a further reading of the various means whereby we read others: the most densely theoretical text is Sapir's essay on fashion, but we have provided our own detailed reading of Sapir, so that you can bounce your own mind *interactively* off both Sapir and us. Russell Hoban's text is also difficult, but in a different sense: it demands that you consciously reexamine your own values and clarify the meanings of those which, secretly or otherwise, run counter to prevailing orthodoxies.

Once you become *critically conscious* of questions of value, whether you construe them in terms of politics, economics, law, or moral philosophy, you can never retreat completely into the lost world of innocence or of unawareness, the world in which children can claim "I didn't know," or "I never realized." As a result of your loss of innocence, you will inevitably find the world a more difficult place to live in, but you will also find it more interesting, more enlivening, more arousing.

GRACE PALEY

Anxiety

The "I" in Grace Paley's "Anxiety" is a compulsive "reader," leaning on her window sill; she is a voyeur of the life in the street. Sometimes what she sees, and what she thinks and feels as a result, compel her to come out of hiding, and to become a participant. Then she has an opportunity to find out whether or not her detective work, her guesswork, her inferences are confirmed by the other person's facts.

The young fathers are waiting outside the school. What curly heads! Such graceful brown mustaches. They're sitting on their haunches eating pizza and exchanging information. They're waiting for the 3 p.m. bell. It's springtime, the season of first looking out the window. I have a window box of greenhouse marigolds. The young fathers can be seen through the ferny leaves.

The bell rings. The children fall out of school, tumbling through the open door. One of the fathers sees his child. A small girl. Is she Chinese? A little. Up u-u-p, he says, and hoists her to his shoulders. U-u-p, says the second father, and hoists his little boy. The little boy sits on top of his father's head for a couple of seconds before sliding to his shoulders. Very funny, says the father.

They start off down the street, right under and past my window. The two children are still laughing. They try to whisper a secret. The fathers haven't finished their conversation. The frailer father is uncomfortable; his little girl wiggles too much.

Stop it this minute, he says.

Oink oink, says the little girl.

What'd you say?

Oink oink, she says.

The young father says What! three times. Then he seizes the child, raises her high above his head, and sets her hard on her feet.

What'd I do so bad, she says, rubbing her ankle.

Just hold my hand, screams the frail and angry father.

I lean far out the window. Stop! Stop! I cry.

The young father turns, shading his eyes, but sees. What? he says. His friend says, Hey? Who's that? He probably thinks I'm a family friend, a teacher maybe.

Who're you? he says.

I move the pots of marigold aside. Then I'm able to lean on my elbow way out into unshadowed visibility. Once, not too long ago, the tenements were speckled with women like me in every third window up to the fifth story, calling the children from play to receive orders and instruction. This memory enables me to say strictly, Young man, I am an older person who feels free because of that to ask questions and give advice.

Oh? he says, laughs with a little embarrassment, says to his friend, Shoot if you will that old gray head. But he's joking, I know, because he has established himself, legs apart, hands behind his back, his neck arched to see and hear me out.

How old are you? I call. About thirty or so?

Thirty-three.

First I want to say you're about a generation ahead of your father in your attitude and behavior toward your child.

Really? Well? Anything else, ma'am.

Son, I said, leaning another two, three dangerous inches toward him. Son, I must tell you that madmen intend to destroy this beautifully made planet. That the murder of our children by these men has got to become a terror and a sorrow to you, and starting now, it had better interfere with any daily pleasure.

Speech speech, he called.

I waited a minute, but he continued to look up. So, I said, I can tell by your general appearance and loping walk that you agree with me.

I do, he said, winking at his friend; but turning a serious face to mine, he said again, Yes, yes, I do.

Well then, why did you become so angry at that little girl whose future is like a film which suddenly cuts to white. Why did you nearly slam this little doomed person to the ground in your uncontrollable anger.

Let's not go too far, said the young father. She *was* jumping around on my poor back and hollering oink oink.

When were you angriest—when she wiggled and jumped or when she said oink?

He scratched his wonderful head of dark well-cut hair. I guess when she said oink.

Have you ever said oink oink? Think carefully. Years ago, perhaps?

No. Well maybe. Maybe.

Whom did you refer to in this way?

He laughed. He called to his friend, Hey Ken, this old person's got something. The cops. In a demonstration. Oink oink, he said, remembering, laughing.

The little girl smiled and said, Oink oink.

Shut up, he said.

What do you deduce from this?

That I was angry at Rosie because she was dealing with me as though I was a figure of authority, and it's not my thing, never has been, never will be.

I could see his happiness, his nice grin, as he remembered this.

So, I continued, since those children are such lovely examples of what may well be the last generation of humankind, why don't you start all over again, right from the school door, as though none of this had ever happened.

Thank you, said the young father. Thank you. It would be nice to be a horse, he said, grabbing little Rosie's hand. Come on Rosie, let's go. I don't have all day.

U-up, says the first father. U-up, says the second.

Giddap, shout the children, and the fathers yell neigh neigh, as horses do. The children kick their fathers' horsechests, screaming giddap giddap, and they gallop wildly westward.

I lean way out to cry once more, Be careful! Stop! But they've gone too far. Oh, anyone would love to be a fierce fast horse carrying a beloved beautiful rider, but they are galloping toward one of the most dangerous street corners in the world. And they may live beyond that trisection across other dangerous avenues.

So I must shut the window after patting the April-cooled marigolds with their rusty smell of summer. Then I sit in the nice light and wonder how to make sure that they gallop safely home through the airy scary dreams of scientists and the bulky dreams of automakers. I wish I could see just how they sit down at their kitchen tables for a healthy snack (orange juice or milk and cookies) before going out into the new spring afternoon to play.

ALAN DEVENISH

After the Beep

The telephone is a very strange technology, once we pause and try not to take it for granted. Only in this century have people been able to talk to each other from separate places, each absent from the other.

The deprivation, which we don't usually notice, is extreme: we cannot see their eyes, their mouth: all the nonverbal signs are obliterated. All the work of interpretation, "getting it right," is thrown onto our ears. So we listen in ways that try to compensate for the absence of other signs, other evidence.

If you hear the following words on the phone—and the transcript doesn't even allow you to hear *them—what impression do you form of the woman on the other end? How do you read her?*

This is the Preston residence
and this is she speaking. Sorry
I'm not broadcasting live but
do leave a message and I
or my machine   5
will get back to you
or your machine. Please wait
until the cannonade
from Tchaikovsky's 1812 Overture
has completed its third volley   10
and the strains of the Marseillaise
stir faintly in the background
before starting your message.
Kindly repress the urge
to be cute or cryptic.   15
On the other hand
don't make it ten years long either.
I would also ask you to refrain
from rhetorical questions
and long subordinate clauses.   20
Just be yourself, keeping in mind
this is the late twentieth century
and literary flourishes
tend to disgust.

Now, if you're the guy I met out jogging,   25
I'm sorry but forget it,
it was all a mistake and anyway
I'm into squash now.
If however this is about an appointment
or interview which could advance   30
my career or in any way redound
to my having more of anything
please speak distinctly
and don't make any decisions
until I can process your message.   35
Lastly, if you've gotten my number

from any other source
except me personally,
you'd better have a good story.
So, until I get back to you,
have a nice day
or, should I decide to ignore your call,
a nice rest of your life.

40

OSCAR WILDE

What a Sweet Name!

Oscar Wilde (1854–1900) was a connoisseur of signs, especially of subtle verbal signs: the kind that don't go in for delivering punches but that nonetheless are designed to inflict damage on another—small very sharp knives. Here we see Cecily and Gwendolen sparring in The Importance of Being Earnest.

ENTER GWENDOLEN

CECILY, *advancing to meet her.*   Pray let me introduce myself to you. My name is Cecily Cardew.

GWENDOLEN.   Cecily Cardew? *Moving to her and shaking hands.* What a very sweet name! Something tells me that we are going to be great friends. I like you already more than I can say. My first impressions of people are never wrong.

CECILY.   How nice of you to like me so much after we have known each other such a comparatively short time. Pray sit down . . .

(Five minutes later)

CECILY.   Mr. Ernest Worthing and I are engaged to be married.

GWENDOLEN, *quite politely, rising.*   My darling Cecily, I think there must be some slight error. Mr. Ernest Worthing is engaged to me . . .

CECILY, *very politely, rising.*   I am afraid you must be under some misconception. Ernest proposed to me exactly ten minutes ago.

GWENDOLYN.   . . . I am so sorry, dear Cecily, if it is any disappointment to you, but I am afraid *I* have the prior claim. . . .

CECILY, *thoughtfully and sadly.*   Whatever unfortunate entanglements my dear boy may have got into, I will never reproach him with it after we are married.

GWENDOLEN.   Do you allude to me, Miss Cardew, as an entanglement? You are presumptuous. . . .

When Oscar Wilde, as a famous playwright and wit, visited America as a celebrity on a lecture tour, he shocked many people by the outlandish extravagance of his dress; his audiences simply didn't know how to *read* his appearance. Was he crazy? Foppish? Effeminate? Decadent? Perverse? One can hear them expressing the fervent hope that their sons and daughters would not rush to adopt Mr. Wilde's sartorial style!

EDWARD SAPIR

Fashion

Edward Sapir (1884–1939), the American anthropologist, was once invited to turn his attention to the increasing importance of fashion in peoples' lives; the year was 1931. This photograph shows what people were wearing that year.

When you have read Sapir's article and our comments, see how far your reading agrees with ours.

1.   The meaning of the term fashion may be clarified by pointing out how it differs in connotation from a number of other terms whose meaning it approaches. A particular fashion differs from a given taste in suggesting some measure of compulsion on the part of the group as contrasted with individual choice from among a number of possibilities. A particular choice may of course be due to a blend of fashion and taste. Thus, if bright and simple colors are in fashion, one may select red as more pleasing to one's taste than yellow, although one's free taste unhampered by fashion

might have decided in favor of a more subtle tone. To the discriminating person the demand of fashion constitutes a challenge to taste and suggests problems of reconciliation. But fashion is accepted by average people with little demur and is not so much reconciled with taste as substituted for it. For many people taste hardly arises at all except on the basis of a clash of an accepted fashion with a fashion that is out of date or current in some other group than one's own.

2.   The term fashion may carry with it a tone of approval or disapproval. It is a fairly objective term whose emotional qualities depend on a context. A moralist may decry a certain type of behavior as a mere fashion but the ordinary person will not be displeased if he is accused of being in the fashion. It is different with fads, which are objectively similar to fashions but differ from them in being more personal in their application and in connoting a more or less definite social disapproval. Particular people or coteries have their fads, while fashions are the property of larger or more representative groups. A taste which asserts itself in spite of fashion and which may therefore be suspected of having something obsessive about it may be referred to as an individual fad. On the other hand, while a fad may be of very short duration, it always differs from a true fashion in having something unexpected, irresponsible or bizarre about it. Any fashion which sins against one's sense of style and one's feeling for the historical continuity of style is likely to be dismissed as a fad. There are changing fashions in tennis rackets, while the game of mah jong, once rather fashionable, takes on in retrospect more and more the character of a fad.

3.   Just as the weakness of fashion leads to fads, so its strength comes from custom. Customs differ from fashions in being relatively permanent types of social behavior. They change, but with a less active and conscious participation of the individual in the change. Custom is the element of permanence which makes changes in fashion possible. Custom marks the highroad of human interrelationships, while fashion may be looked upon as the endless departure from the return to the highroad. The vast majority of fashions are relieved by other fashions, but occasionally a fashion crystallizes into permanent habit, taking on the character of custom.

4.   It is not correct to think of fashion as merely a short lived innovation in custom, because many innovations in human history arise with the need for them and last as long as they are useful or convenient. If, for instance, there is a shortage of silk and it becomes customary to substitute cotton for silk in the manufacture of certain articles of dress in which silk has been the usual material, such an enforced change of material, however important economically or aesthetically, does not in itself constitute a true change of fashion. On the other hand, if cotton is substituted for silk out of free choice as a symbol perhaps of the simple life or because of a desire to see what novel effect can be produced in accepted types of dress with simpler materials, the change may be called one of fashion. There is nothing to prevent an innovation from eventually taking on the character of a new fashion. If, for example, people persist in using the cotton material even after silk has once more become available, a new fashion has arisen.

5.   Fashion is a custom in the guise of departure from custom. Most normal individuals consciously or unconsciously have the itch to break away in some measure from a too literal loyalty to accepted custom. They are not fundamentally in revolt from custom but they wish somehow to legitimize their personal deviation without

laying themselves open to the charge of insensitiveness to good taste or good manners. Fashion is the discreet solution of the subtle conflict. The slight changes from the established in dress or other forms of behavior seem for the moment to give the victory to the individual, while the fact that one's fellows revolt in the same direction gives one a feeling of adventurous safety. The personal note which is at the hidden core of fashion becomes superpersonalized.

6.   Whether fashion is felt as a sort of socially legitimized caprice or is merely a new and unintelligible form of social tyranny depends on the individual or class. It is probable that those most concerned with the setting and testing of fashions are the individuals who realize most keenly the problem of reconciling individual freedom with social conformity which is implicit in the very fact of fashion. It is perhaps not too much to say that most people are at least partly sensitive to this aspect of fashion and are secretly grateful for it. A large minority of people, however, are insensitive to the psychological complexity of fashion and submit to it to the extent that they do merely because they realize that not to fall in with it would be to declare themselves members of a past generation or dull people who cannot keep up with their neighbors. These latter reasons for being fashionable are secondary; they are sullen surrenderers to bastard custom.

7.   The fundamental drives leading to the creation and acceptance of fashion can be isolated. In the more sophisticated societies boredom, created by leisure and too highly specialized forms of activity, leads to restlessness and curiosity. This general desire to escape from the trammels of a too regularized existence is powerfully reenforced by a ceaseless desire to add to the attractiveness of the self and all other objects of love and friendship. It is precisely in functionally powerful societies that the individual's ego is constantly being convicted of helplessness. The individual tends to be unconsciously thrown back on himself and demands more and more novel affirmations of his effective reality. The endless rediscovery of the self in a series of petty truancies from the official socialized self becomes a mild obsession of the normal individual in any society in which the individual has ceased to be a measure of the society itself. There is, however, always the danger of too great a departure from the recognized symbols of the individual, because his identity is likely to be destroyed. That is why insensitive people, anxious to be literally in the fashion, so often overreach themselves and nullify the very purpose of fashion. Good hearted women of middle age generally fail in the art of being ravishing nymphs.

8.   Somewhat different from the affirmation of the libidinal self is the more vulgar desire for prestige or notoriety, satisfied by changes in fashion. In this category belongs fashion as an outward emblem of personal distinction or of membership in some group to which distinction is ascribed. The imitation of fashion by people who belong to circles removed from those which set the fashion has the function of bridging the gap between a social class and the class next above it. The logical result of the acceptance of a fashion by all members of society is the disappearance of the kinds of satisfaction responsible for the change of fashion in the first place. A new fashion becomes psychologically necessary, and thus the cycle of fashion is endlessly repeated.

9.   Fashion is emphatically a historical concept. A specific fashion is utterly unintelligible if lifted out of its place in a sequence of forms. It is exceedingly dangerous

to rationalize or in any other way psychologize a particular fashion on the basis of
general principles which might be considered applicable to the class of forms of
which it seems to be an example. It is utterly vain, for instance, to explain particular
forms of dress or types of cosmetics or methods of wearing the hair without a
preliminary historical critique. Bare legs among modern women in summer do not
psychologically or historically create at all the same fashion as bare legs and bare
feet among primitives living in the tropics. The importance of understanding fashion
historically should be obvious enough when it is recognized that the very essence of
fashion is that it be valued as a variation in an understood sequence, as a departure
from the immediately preceding mode.

10.   Changes in fashion depend on the prevailing culture and on the social ideals
which inform it. Under the apparently placid surface of culture there are always
powerful psychological drifts of which fashion is quick to catch the direction. In a
democratic society, for instance, if there is an unacknowledged drift toward class
distinctions fashion will discover endless ways of giving it visible form. Criticism
can always be met by the insincere defense that fashion is merely fashion and need
not be taken seriously. If in a puritanic society there is a growing impatience with
the outward forms of modesty, fashion finds it easy to minister to the demands of
sex curiosity, while the old mores can be trusted to defend fashion with an affectation
of unawareness of what fashion is driving at. A complete study of the history of
fashion would undoubtedly throw much light on the ups and downs of sentiment
and attitude at various periods of civilization. However, fashion never permanently
outruns discretion and only those who are taken in by the superficial rationalizations
of fashion are surprised by the frequent changes of face in its history. That there
was destined to be a lengthening of women's skirts after they had become short
enough was obvious from the outset to all except those who do not believe that sex
symbolism is a real factor in human behavior.

11.   The chief difficulty of understanding fashion in its apparent vagaries is the
lack of exact knowledge of the unconscious symbolisms attaching to forms, colors,
textures, postures and other expressive elements in a given culture. The difficulty is
appreciably increased by the fact that the same expressive elements tend to have
quite different symbolic references in different areas. Gothic type, for instance, is a
nationalistic token in Germany, while in Anglo-Saxon culture the practically identical
type known as Old English has entirely different connotations. In other words, the
same style of lettering may symbolize either an undying hatred of France or a wistful
look backward at madrigals and pewter.

12.   An important principle in the history of fashion is that those features of fashion
which do not configurate correctly with the unconscious system of meanings characteristic of the given culture are relatively insecure. Extremes of style, which too
frankly symbolize the current of feeling of the moment, are likely to find themselves
in exposed positions, as it were, where they can be outflanked by meanings which
they do not wish to recognize. Thus, it may be conjectured that lipstick is less secure
in American culture as an element of fashion than rouge discreetly applied to the
cheek. This is assuredly not due to a superior sinfulness of lipstick as such, but to
the fact that rosy cheeks resulting from a healthy natural life in the country are one
of the characteristic fetishisms of the traditional ideal of feminine beauty, while

lipstick has rather the character of certain exotic ardors and goes with flaming oriental stuffs. Rouge is likely to last for many decades or centuries because there is, and is likely to be for a long time to come, a definite strain of nature worship in our culture. If lipstick is to remain it can only be because our culture will have taken on certain violently new meanings which are not at all obvious at the present time. As a symbol it is episodic rather than a part of the underlying rhythm of the history of our fashions.

13.   In custom bound cultures, such as are characteristic of the primitive world, there are slow non-reversible changes of style rather than the often reversible forms of fashion found in modern cultures. The emphasis in such societies is on the group and the sanctity of tradition rather than on individual expression, which tends to be entirely unconscious. In the great cultures of the Orient and in ancient and mediaeval Europe changes in fashion can be noted radiating from certain definite centers of sophisticated culture, but it is not until modern Europe is reached that the familiar merry-go-round of fashion with its rapid alternations of season occurs.

14.   The typically modern acceleration of changes in fashion may be ascribed to the influence of the Renaissance, which awakened a desire for innovation and which powerfully extended for European society the total world of possible choices. During this period Italian culture came to be the arbiter of taste, to be followed by French culture, which may still be looked upon as the most powerful influence in the creation and distribution of fashions. But more important than the Renaissance in the history of fashion is the effect of the industrial revolution and the rise of the common people. The former increased the mechanical ease with which fashions could be diffused; the latter greatly increased the number of those willing and able to be fashionable.

15.   Modern fashion tends to spread to all classes of society. As fashion has always tended to be a symbol of membership in a particular social class and as human beings have always felt the urge to edge a little closer to a class considered superior to their own, there must always have been the tendency for fashion to be adopted by circles which had a lower status than the group setting the fashions. But on the whole such adoption of fashion from above tended to be discreet because of the great importance attached to the maintenance of social classes. What has happened in the modern world, regardless of the official forms of government which prevail in the different nations, is that the tone giving power which lies back of fashion has largely slipped away from the aristocracy of rank to the aristocracy of wealth. This means a psychological if not an economic leveling of classes because of the feeling that wealth is an accidental or accreted quality of an individual as contrasted with blood. In an aristocracy of wealth everyone, even the poorest, is potentially wealthy both in legal theory and in private fancy. In such a society, therefore, all individuals are equally entitled, it is felt, so far as their pockets permit, to the insignia of fashion. This universalizing of fashion necessarily cheapens its value in the specific case and forces an abnormally rapid change of fashion. The only effective protection possessed by the wealthy in the world of fashion is the insistence on expensive materials in which fashion is to express itself. Too great an insistence on this factor, however, is the hall mark of wealthy vulgarity, for fashion is essentially a thing of forms and symbols, not of material values.

16.   Perhaps the most important of the special factors which encourage the spread of fashion today is the increased facility for the production and transportation of goods and for communication either personally or by correspondence from the centers of fashion to the outmost periphery of the civilized world. These increased facilities necessarily lead to huge capital investments in the manufacture and distribution of fashionable wear. The extraordinarily high initial profits to be derived from fashion and the relatively rapid tapering off of profits make it inevitable that the natural tendency to change in fashion is helped along by commercial suggestion. The increasingly varied activities of modern life also give greater opportunity for the growth and change of fashion. Today the cut of a dress or the shape of a hat stands ready to symbolize anything from mountain climbing or military efficiency, through automobiling to interpretative dancing and veiled harlotry. No individual is merely what his social role indicates that he is to be or may vary only slightly from, but he may act as if he is anything else that individual phantasy may dictate. The greater leisure and spending power of the bourgeoisie, bringing them externally nearer the upper classes of former days, are other obvious stimuli to change in fashion, as are the gradual psychological and economic liberation of women and the greater opportunity given them for experimentation in dress and adornment.

17.   Fashions for women show greater variability than fashions for men in contemporary civilization. Not only do women's fashions change more rapidly and completely but the total gamut of allowed forms is greater for women than for men. In times past and in other cultures, however, men's fashions show a greater exuberance than women's. Much that used to be ascribed to women as female is really due to woman as a sociologically and economically defined class. Woman as a distinctive theme for fashion may be explained in terms of the social psychology of the present civilization. She is the one who pleases by being what she is and looking as she does rather than by doing what she does. Whether biology or history is primarily responsible for this need not be decided. Woman has been the kept partner in marriage and has had to prove her desirability by ceaselessly reaffirming her attractiveness as symbolized by novelty of fashion. Among the wealthier classes and by imitation also among the less wealthy, woman has come to be looked upon as an expensive luxury on whom one spends extravagantly. She is thus a symbol of the social and economic status of her husband. Whether with the increasingly marked change of woman's place in society the factors which emphasize extravagance in women's fashions will entirely fall away it is impossible to say at the present time.

18.   There are powerful vested interests involved in changes of fashions, as has already been mentioned. The effect on the producer of fashions of a variability which he both encourages and dreads is the introduction of the element of risk. It is a popular error to assume that professional designers arbitrarily dictate fashion. They do so only in a very superficial sense. Actually they have to obey many masters. Their designs must above all things net the manufacturers a profit, so that behind the more strictly psychological determinants of fashion there lurks a very important element due to the sheer technology of the manufacturing process or the availability of a certain type of material. In addition to this the designer must have a sure feeling for the established in custom and the degree to which he can safely depart from it.

He must intuitively divine what people want before they are quite aware of it themselves. His business is not so much to impose fashion as to coax people to accept what they have themselves unconsciously suggested. This causes the profits of fashion production to be out of all proportion to the actual cost of manufacturing fashionable goods. The producer and his designer assistant capitalize the curiosity and vanity of their customers but they must also be protected against the losses of a risky business. Those who are familiar with the history of fashion are emphatic in speaking of the inability of business to combat the fashion trends which have been set going by various psychological factors. A fashion may be aesthetically pleasing in the abstract, but if it runs counter to the trend or does not help to usher in a new trend which is struggling for a hearing it may be a flat failure.

19.   The distribution of fashions is a comparatively simple and automatic process. The vogue of fashion plates and fashion magazines, the many lines of communication which connect fashion producers and fashion dispensers, and modern methods of marketing make it almost inevitable that a successful Parisian fashion should find its way within an incredibly short period of time to Chicago and San Francisco. If it were not for the necessity of exploiting accumulated stocks of goods these fashions would penetrate into the remotest corners of rural America even more rapidly than is the case. The average consumer is chronically distressed to discover how rapidly his accumulated property in wear depreciates by becoming outmoded. He complains bitterly and ridicules the new fashions when they appear. In the end he succumbs, a victim to symbolisms of behavior which he does not fully comprehend. What he will never admit is that he is more the creator than the victim of his difficulties.

20.   Fashions has always had vain critics. It has been arraigned by the clergy and by social satirists because each new style of wear, calling attention as it does to the form of the human body, seems to the critics to be an attack on modesty. Some fashions there are, to be sure, whose very purpose it is to attack modesty, but over and above specific attacks there is felt to be a generalized one. The charge is well founded but useless. Human beings do not wish to be modest; they want to be as expressive—that is, as immodest—as fear allows; fashion helps them solve their paradoxical problem. The charge of economic waste which is often leveled against fashion has had little or no effect on the public mind. Waste seems to be of no concern where values are to be considered, particularly when these values are both egoistic and unconscious. The criticism that fashion imposes an unwanted uniformity is not as sound as it appears to be in the first instance. The individual in society is only rarely significantly expressive in his own right. For the vast majority of human beings the choice lies between unchanging custom and the legitimate caprice of custom, which is fashion.

21.   Fashion concerns itself closely and intimately with the ego. Hence its proper field is dress and adornment. There are other symbols of the ego, however, which are not as close to the body as these but which are almost equally subject to the psychological laws of fashion. Among them are objects of utility, amusements and furniture. People differ in their sensitiveness to changing fashions in these more remote forms of human expressiveness. It is therefore impossible to say categorically just what the possible range of fashion is. However, in regard to both amusements

and furniture there may be observed the same tendency to change, periodicity and unquestioning acceptance as in dress and ornament.

22. Many speak of fashions in thought, art, habits of living and morals. It is superficial to dismiss such locutions as metaphorical and unimportant. The usage shows a true intuition of the meaning of fashion, which while it is primarily applied to dress and the exhibition of the human body is not essentially concerned with the fact of dress or ornament but with its symbolism. There is nothing to prevent a thought, a type of morality or an art from being the psychological equivalent of a costuming of the ego. Certainly one may allow oneself to be converted to Catholicism or Christian Science in exactly the same spirit in which one invests in pewter or follows the latest Parisian models in dress. Beliefs and attitudes are not fashions in their character of mores but neither are dress and ornament. In contemporary society it is not a fashion that men wear trousers; it is the custom. Fashion merely dictates such variations as whether trousers are to be so or so long, what colors they are to have and whether they are to have cuffs or not. In the same way, while adherence to a religious faith is not in itself a fashion, as soon as the individual feels that he can pass easily, out of personal choice, from one belief to another, not because he is led to his choice by necessity but because of a desire to accrete to himself symbols of status, it becomes legitimate to speak of his change of attitude as a change of fashion. Functional irrelevance as contrasted with symbolic significance for the expressiveness of the ego is implicit in all fashion.

Reading "Fashion"

Here, now, is our reading of Sapir's text; see how it compares with yours. Numbers refer to paragraphs in Sapir's essay.

1. Sapir distinguishes between custom, fashion, and fads, on the one hand, and taste on the other. He argues that "taste" is the prerogative of individuals who are relatively independent of social or group approval: whereas taste is a matter of individual choice—a choice freely exercised—custom, fashion, and fads all involve an element of imposition. Do you think that is a fair representation of Sapir's opening argument?

2. Fads, he proposes, have an element of "the unexpected, irresponsible or bizarre," and can be felt to run counter to dominant fashion and can express some kind of social dissent, or disapproval of dominant fashions.

3. In terms of duration or survival, customs last longer than fashions, and fashions last longer than fads. Is it, then, easy to offer examples of these three categories? Presumably, the wearing of shoes is a custom; wearing stiletto-heeled shoes is a fashion; wearing shoes decorated with gold plastic ribbon is a fad. If wearing any shoes at all (as opposed to going barefoot) was at one time a fashion, then it was a fashion that has survived long enough to become a custom. Are Sapir's definitions new to you? If so, how far do they agree with your intuitions?

If one applies Sapir's categories to a recent decade, for example, the Sixties, how well do they apply? Presumably, one can "read" the short-back-and-sides hair of American men as a custom; the long hair of the Sixties as a fashion—it

almost, perhaps, became a custom, lasting well into the Seventies; going without shoes as a fad. What, then, of communes—were they a social fashion or a fad?

4. Can you apply Sapir's discussion of silk and cotton to denim? To washed-out denim? If you apply his categories, "fashion" and "fads," to popular music and rock concerts, what specially would you place in each of those two categories?

5. Sapir seems to see people as balanced somewhere between conformity and nonconformity. We all have an itch, he suggests, to "break away." Breaking away is an assertion of individual freedom, but it is safe to do so because one's peers or contemporaries also break away in the same direction, thus affording the ambiguous and paradoxical pleasure of "a feeling of adventurous safety."

Is it likely that, when a fad occurs, we cannot know it is only a fad until time passes, and it disappears fairly soon into the wastepaper basket of discarded fads? We can recognize last year's fads as fads since they're over, but this year's fads may become fashions. Can you think of examples of these?

10. Sapir's example of long and short skirts offers, he argues, an instance of "sex symbolism" as a factor in human behavior. What, then, is the symbolism of long skirts, of short skirts? What does each category seem to signify?

11. Meanings, Sapir insists, are *local*, not universal. Every particular fashion must be "read" in the context of its time and place, as a part of the larger culture of which it is a part. To "read" any fashion adequately also involves a sensitivity to its unconscious elements—to what its inventors—are revealing without realizing it. Fashion can be said to "give their designers away": we presume you know people whose clothes "give them away."

12. Is Sapir right about the relative meanings of rouge and lipstick, or did he "misread" the signs? How is rouge—or "blush"—read today? *Rouge* is simply the French for red. So what of women reddening their cheeks? Making them "blush"? (We blush when we are aroused.)

13. Differences of culture are revealed in different attitudes toward fashion. In some cultures, fashion does not exist, so powerful is traditional custom. Are there any cultures in America that seem indifferent or resistant to fashion? The Amish, for example?

14. A revolution in the means of production—machines capable of producing mile after mile of material—and demographic changes provided the necessary and sufficient conditions for the emergence of fashion as an element of Western culture.

Without a mass market, supplied through chain stores, mail-order catalogues, and other forms of mass distribution, and without mass producing vast quantities of cheap raw material, fashion would be confined to a very small, very rich elite, the plutocracy.

15. In this paragraph Sapir puts his finger on one of the most distinctive characteristics of American society (and of those societies that have adopted the American pattern): if the crucial social differentiating factor is money and not the inheritance of social power and titles, then anyone is free to believe that they also deserve what the top people have. Thus chain stores provide cheaper imitations of the fashions of the rich and famous, so that "ordinary" people can

enjoy the illusion of equality. The rich are thus forced back to ways of signifying their difference: so they commission one-of-a-kind items from fashionable designers, and insist on *expensive* materials.

16. Massive changes in the means of distribution allow for the wide diffusion of fashionable items; something that is "the latest fashion" sells well and quickly, but its lifespan is limited: it must soon be supplanted by the next fashion that is already looming on the horizon; given more options in life, more leisure, and more money, we can change our clothes and thereby enjoy the illusion of being a different person—more interesting? more glamorous? And women's lives (in 1931) were less constrained, less confined than before. How does this apply to you? Do you change your clothes so as to project a "different self"? If you are a woman, do you feel more psychologically liberated than your grandmother probably felt in 1931 or whenever?

17. Do Sapir's observations still hold true almost sixty years later? Do women still please by "being" and "looking" rather than by doing? Do wives' clothes and jewels still signify their husbands' social and economic status? Do you know men who insist on buying expensive fur coats for their wives? Has the situation that Sapir described in 1931 changed? What of "marked changes" in "woman's place in society"?

18. In this paragraph, Sapir touches on some of the most mysterious elements of fashion; we refer not to his observations on the economics of the fashion industry, but to the ways in which designers and manufacturers are at the mercy of "many masters," and to the fact that designers have to guess or intuit what a feasible fashion for *next* season will look like: to produce a fashion that consumers will consume even though they are not yet conscious of exactly what it is they want. Thus the designer has to "read," as closely as possible, the *unconscious* suggestions that the consumers themselves are offering: she has to "read" the "trend" to determine in which direction she should allow it to nudge her.

19. Sapir concludes this paragraph with a neat paradox: as fashion trends tell us that the clothes we bought last year are now "old hat," we groan; and then we fall into line, and adopt the new fashion, not realizing that our tendency to conform induces the expense of keeping in step. How willing are you to keep up with the trends? Do you know of anyone who resists them?

20. The values that fashion expresses are "both egoistic and unconscious." We do not wish "to be modest"; on the contrary, we wish to be "as expressive— that is, as immodest—as fear allows." How does this generalization apply to you? Can you admit that Sapir is right? When you wish to "be expressive," do you have any idea what it is that you wish to express? Or do you think it is impossible not only to *state* but also to *know* what you are expressing by choosing clothes to wear? Are there things we cannot know about ourselves? And what of Sapir's claim that "the individual in society is only rarely significantly expressive in his [her] own right"? Do you think you match that description? Can you think of someone who is an obvious exception? Elton John? Hulk Hogan? Madonna?

21. "Change, periodicity and unquestioning acceptance" are the three major attributes of fashion, even in matters other than "dress and adornment," such as

games, sport, furniture, houses, bank design, automobiles. . . . When did your grandparents last change their furniture? Your parents?

22. All fashion, Sapir concludes, is characterized by "functional irrelevance"; in other words, whether or not an object performs its utilitarian function better is irrelevant to matters of fashion. A few years ago, women were seen to wear mini-skirts in the middle of winter: can you provide a better example of functional irrelevance?

Sapir argues that beliefs and attitudes are also subject to fashion: if you apply this to American society since 1960, how many changes of fashion can you discover?

We wonder how *you* choose *your* clothes, *your* hairstyle, *your* appearance. When you open a magazine aimed at your particular age group and socioeconomic/ethnic class, do you tend to browse through the advertisements? Do you realize that the fashion and cosmetics business is very interested in you and in how you choose, or may be persuaded, to spend your money? Do you realize that you exist in the files in their market research offices, not as an individual, but as a specific kind of consumer?

Are you wearing the same clothes as you were two years ago? In two years' time will you be wearing today's clothes? If not, why not? In order to persuade you to discard last year's clothes, even if they are perfectly adequate and still in one piece, the rag trade has spawned a vast supplementary industry: clothes-retail advertising, which is itself a multimillion dollar industry.

The market has been systematically broken down into its constituent parts, and the ways in which we now differentiate and describe people by age categories has itself been influenced by fashion advertising and the growth of subgroup magazines (*Seventeen, Cosmopolitan, Self,* and so forth) which provide a well-defined and coherent market for advertisers, and which depend for their survival on advertising revenue. We can argue, indeed, that the "real," the substantial, pages in such publications are the ad pages: the articles are a mere ancillary part put in to prove that the magazine is indeed a magazine, and not just a collection of advertisements.

We have suggested that the activity of reading others can have a variety of purposes: detection, forensic medicine, sheer human curiosity, the pursuit of a specific question (e.g., Sapir on fashion), the control of our social interactions, a deep need to intervene and warn, raw material for fiction, moral enquiry, and so on.

When our reading is driven primarily by natural (nonprofessional) curiosity, it tends to give rise to a simple, necessary, and irresistible consequence: speculation, or surmise.

Our reading of the person(s) observed gives rise to all manner of questions, of thoughts that take off, it seems, out of our control, and take on an energetic life of their own. This is especially the case when our reading involves us in a sense of contradiction, of incongruity, or of tension: something has to be resolved.

In the next text, the expatriate novelist Russell Hoban (b. 1925) starts with a shirtless cyclist he happened to see on the streets of London.

RUSSELL HOBAN

Thoughts on a Shirtless Cyclist, Robin Hood and One or Two Other Things

The other day when I was going to my office in the morning I saw a man without a shirt riding a bicycle in circles at a traffic light and shouting unintelligibly. It was a chilly morning, so he must have been uncomfortable without a shirt on, and he wasn't a hippy. He looked like a workman, and he didn't look drunk. So it seemed to me that he must be having a mental breakdown of some sort.

I thought about it for a while, and then it occurred to me that maybe the man's mind wasn't breaking down. Maybe what had broken down was the system of restraints and conventions inside him that ordinarily made him keep his shirt on and not shout. That system, I think, is part of what could be called an inner society. The inner society has its ballrooms and bedrooms and kitchens, its shops and offices, its narrow alleys and its open places, its figures of authority and rebellion, of usage and surprise, love and hate, should and should not, is and isn't. As in the outer society, some things are done and some are not.

When I had thought that far, my next thought was that on that particular day that particular man's inner society was rioting. The windows of the shops were being smashed, the offices were being deserted, and he was doing what he was doing.

My next thought was that the previous thought had been wrong: he was doing what he was doing because there were no rioters and no provision for riot in his inner society, and so there was no one for the job but him. His trouble, perhaps, was that his inner society was not sufficiently different from the outer one: too many of the same things were done and not done. And having no interior colleague to whom he could assign the task or delegate the responsibility, he himself had to take off his shirt and ride his bicycle in circles at a traffic light and shout. And it must have taken something out of him to do it.

Now my inner society, on the other hand, has always had that shirtless shouting cyclist in it. I know him of old as I know myself, even though I hadn't given him much thought until I actually saw him in the outer world. So it isn't likely that I shall ever have to go out into the street and do that myself; he's always there to take care of it for me. There may, of course, come a day when I shall riotously put on a bowler hat and a neat black suit, buy a tightly furled umbrella, and mingle in wild silence with the brokers in the City. One never knows what will come up.

Which brings me, by cobweb bridges perhaps invisible to the naked eye, to a book I once threw into an incinerator.

The book was *Robin Hood*. My edition, an American one, was bound in what I think was Lincoln Green. I don't remember who it was that wrote that particular version of the story, but it had large black type and was illustrated by an artist named Edwin John Prittie with line drawings and paintings in full colour. I used to read that book up in an old wild-cherry tree, and it was the cosiest reading I can remember.

But there came a time when I got to be eighteen years old, and there was a war, and I was going off to be a soldier, and it seemed to me that I had better stop being a child and be a man altogether. So I took *Robin Hood* and pitched it into the incinerator. It's a crime that I am driven to confess from time to time, as I do now.

When I came home from the war and found myself, surprisingly, alive and having to go on with the business of growing up, I looked for that same edition that I had thrown away. Years later I found a copy. I haven't it with me now; it is gone again, lost in a removal. But I remember how it was when I held it in my hands again. There were all the pictures looking just as good as ever, and that whole dappled word-world of sun and shade with nothing lost whatever—Little John and Robin fighting on the plank bridge with their quarterstaves; the hateful Sheriff of Nottingham in his arrogance and his scarlet cloak; the beautiful Maid Marian and all the merry men in Lincoln Green; Robin in the *capul hide*, standing over the corpse of Guy of Gisborne. I've always liked the sound of the words *capul hide:* the skin of a horse, with the eyes of a man looking out through the eyeholes in the head—the skin of a dead beast hiding a live man, magical and murderous.

Obviously Robin Hood is a part of my inner society and has never stopped being in my thoughts, but it's only recently that I've become fully aware of how much he is to me, of how far the theme of that child's book has gone beyond childhood. Now as I think about him Robin Hood grows deeper and darker and stronger. Constantly he takes on new shadowy identities, and in his *capul hide* he sometimes evokes the dancing *shaman* in the drawing on the cave wall at Les Trois Frères, sometimes Fraser's *Rex Nemorensis*, doomed King of the Wood, the killer waiting for his killer who will be the next king.

In the absence of my found-and-lost again edition I bought Roger Lancelyn Green's Puffin *Robin Hood*. On the title page was a stanza from the Alfred Noyes poem, *Sherwood*, and it gave me gooseflesh when I read it:

> Robin Hood is here again: all his merry thieves
> Hear a ghostly bugle-note shivering through the leaves . . .
> The dead are coming back again, the years are rolled away
> In Sherwood, in Sherwood, about the break of day.

I wanted it to be Sherwood again, about the break of day. I turned the pages, reading with impatience. But it wasn't the same. This book started with Robin Hood's birth, and I didn't want that, I wanted the opening that had been in the cherry-tree book of childhood, and it wasn't there and I couldn't remember it.

Then, on page 19 I found it—the incident in which the Sheriff of Nottingham and his men capture a serf who had killed a royal deer. The beginning of my book came back to me then, just like Proust's Combray—all at once and clear and vivid. "Saxon hind" was what my book called the serf, and I could see the scene again as it first came to me through the words in the cherry tree. I could see that sunlight through the passing leaves, the prisoner trussed up on the sledge like meat, helpless, rolling his eyes in terror as the Sheriff's foresters drag him to his death. Robert Fitzooth, not yet Robin Hood the outlaw, encounters the group and questions the Sheriff's men. The Chief Forester taunts him about the power of the bow he carries, doubts that such a stripling can wield such a weapon. Fitzooth shows his strength and skill with a long shot that brings down one of the King's deer. And with that he has fallen into the forester's trap—like the prisoner, he has forfeited his life with that shot. The Sheriff's men attempt to take him, but he kills some of them and frees the "Saxon hind." They escape into the greenwood, and the outlaw life of Robin Hood begins.

The light and the air of that first encounter have never left my mind, and the sounds of the forest, the hissing of the sledge runners over the grass, the rattle of weapons, the shouts, the whizzing arrows. It is the metaphorical value of that action that has made it so memorable for me: the free and active wild self of the forest, armed and strong, freed the bound and helpless captive self and so became the outlaw self I recognized within me—the self indwelling always, sometimes kept faith with, sometimes betrayed.

Free and savage, the Robin Hood who has always walked the pathways of my inner society has been exemplary—a standard and a reminder to the unfree and unsavage boy that I was who lusted for that greenwood world: excellence was the price of Robin Hood's freedom, his untamedness, and his power. He was able to be what he was only because of his matchless skill; he was the archer who could shoot farther and truer than any other; he was a hero and a winner who had a thing that he could do better than anybody else.

Heroes who can do something well are still considered necessary for children. And if many of today's books for grown-ups offer us a selection of the infirm and the awkward, the losers who lap up defeat like chicken soup ladled out by a Jewish-mother kind of fate, we need those too: the composite hero of the collective, cumulative, juvenile-adult imagination has got to have some antiheroism about him in order to be complete. Certainly anything that closes the gap between the real and the ideal makes the hero more useful for everyday reference—and here I can't help thinking about the god Krishna, who disported himself with fifty or sixty cowgirls at a wonderful party out on the meadows that lasted many nights, during which he made all the cowgirls think he was making love with each of them. But despite his divine powers—or because of them—he did it all with his mind, which I think is charming. A hero no better than the reader, however, will scarcely last a lifetime. And I think that heroes who excel and win all kinds of good things are the best kind. Myself, I can't use a mythology in which there is nothing to win and consequently nothing to lose. I have to have something to try for, and the more excellence I can manage the better I feel. In that respect Robin Hood has been a great help to me all my life.

Reading the Roger Lancelyn Green version, I realize that there was a great deal more to the story and the archetypes than I had thought before. In my edition Marian was simply called Maid Marian, and nothing more was said about it. Once or twice as I grew older and more cynical I may have questioned the validity of her title. She was, after all, presumably sleeping rough like everyone else in the outlaw band, and Robin being her lover, what could have been more natural than for them to sleep together? But Green spells it out and no mistake: Marian *was* a maid; she kept her virginity the whole time that she and Robin lived together in the forest. Although she had pledged herself to him the marriage was not to be consummated until the return of Richard the Lion-Hearted, the true and lawful king.

Robin Hood has no other woman that I ever heard of in any of the stories. So I have to think of him as celibate, as putting off the assumption of a full male role, as being less than a complete, grown-up man. He is asexual and pure, mercurial, airy almost, Ariel-like—a natural innocent, murderous but sweet-natured, light and quick. And he shares with Marian that mystical virtue that chastity confers, so useful for catching unicorns. The male and the female elements, the *yang* and *yin* of this legend, are allied but not conjoined at the peak of their vigour, and when later a legitimate union is formed, they decline.

Robin Hood is more often with Little John than with Maid Marian. He and his giant companion are like a clean-cut, somewhat prim ego and id. They continually test and prove themselves, tempting fate, daring all comers, looking for trouble, never content with safety and boredom. They fight with quarterstaves at their first meeting; they quarrel from time to time; they rescue each other from capture; they compete with each other against the terrible strong beggar with the potent quarter-staff and the bag of meal that blinds the usually cunning Robin. And so they stay young and jolly until King Richard, the lawful ruler, the inevitable mature authority, returns.

And with that return Robin Hood is absorbed into grown-upness and legitimacy. He is pardoned, and no more an outlaw; he is married, and no more a child-man. His best men are called into the service of King Richard. Robin Hood's power is drained off into the power of lawful authority. The outlaw self is assimilated into the lawful self; the puissant* youth becomes the waning man.

I'm no scholar, and I have no idea of the origin of the legend that is Robin Hood. What is inescapable is that the stone of legend is worn into shape by the sea of human perception and need that continually washes over it. Legends, myth and fantasy both ask and tell us how life is, and there seems to be a strong need in us to think about the theme that is in *Robin Hood:* the absorption into law and order of that mysterious, chthonic,† demiurgic power that we vitally need but cannot socially tolerate. We regret the loss of it and we rationalize the necessity of that loss. We say to it, "Yes, be there. But lose yourself in us at the proper time. Grow up." But I wonder what the proper time is, and I wonder if the loss is necessary. And I wonder what growing up is. And I wonder whether young people now are not validly reconsidering and reshaping that theme, reclassifying it as well, so that the values

*Puissant: powerful.
†Chthonic: in or of the earth.

assigned are no longer the same as those agreed upon until now. Maybe what we've always called growing up is sometimes growing down. It bears thinking about.

Robin Hood is only one development of that theme; there must be many others. In *Great Expectations*, for instance, Magwitch, the outlaw self, is content to subsidize anonymously Pip, the lawful self. And it is Magwitch the outlaw who refines what is base and shallow in the respectable youth. Pip thinks that Miss Havisham is financing him, but the money that makes it possible for him to cut a dash as a young gentleman does not come from her decaying beauty, wealth and gentility, but from the starveling and tenacious humanity of what in us is violent, inchoate, unshapen and fit only to be put in prison.

Again, in Conrad's *Secret Sharer*, a young captain, a young lawful authority in his first command, is appealed to by a young man who closely resembles him, a fugitive fleeing trial for killing a mate on another vessel. With characteristic genius Conrad opens his story with the unfledged captain taking the anchor watch alone at night on his ship that is still unfamiliar to him. He looks over the side and sees looking up at him from the water a face like his own, the face of a desperate swimmer. The captain shelters his criminal *doppelganger** aboard his ship during a period of self doubt before putting to sea. But when the barque leaves port the fugitive must be put ashore to take his chances alone. A wide-brimmed hat, given him by the captain as protection against the sun, falls into the water and becomes a sea mark by which the young master gauges the current while negotiating a difficult offing under sail in light and baffling airs.

The fugitive's hat gets the lawful master safely out to sea, but the fugitive cannot go with the ship. Magwitch gives Pip what he can and dies. Robin Hood is killed by the establishment that has no use for him. The predatory church that he has always fought will take him in, ailing and ageing, will bleed him to death at the end by the hand of the treacherous Prioress of Kirkleys Nunnery. Robin Hood, supported by Little John, will loose his last arrow from his deathbed and be buried where it falls. Marian, first magical maid and then magicless woman, will become a nun and Prioress in her turn. Robin in the earth and she in the nunnery will both regain their innocence and power.

After the first reading of the book, the death and the last arrow were always there waiting for Robin Hood and me; he carried that death with him, carried that last arrow in his quiver always. He seems such a year-king! He seems, in his green and lightsome strength, always to hasten toward his sacrificial death that will bring forth from the winter earth another spring. And like a year-king, he must be given up, cannot be kept.

But I cannot give him up entirely. I think that we need our outlaw strength alive and brother to our lawful vigour. The one is not healthy without the other. I keep calling the elements outlaw self and lawful self, but that is unfair, really, to the essence of the thing. Society defines the terms of lawful and unlawful, because society makes the laws. And society is a retarded child with a loaded gun in its hands; I don't completely accept society's terms. Something in us makes us retell that myth; some drive there is in us to find and name the demon in us that is more

Doppelganger: double.

real than laws and conventions that tell us what is right and what is wrong. And that demon is, I think, the radical spirit of life: it is the dark and unseen root system of our human tree whose visible branches are so carefully labelled and scientifically pruned by us. Maybe we think we don't need to know more about that nameless creative chaos, but we do, because in it we must find all real order. Polite gentlemen wearing suits and ties and with neat haircuts sit around tables with the death of the world in their briefcases, and they do not hesitate to tell us what is order. But to me it seems disorder. Other polite gentlemen some years ago sent up human smoke signals from the chimneys of crematoria, and they too defined order with great clarity. I think that fewer definitive definitions and many more tentative ones are needed now.

The fantasy of our legends, myths and stories helps with those new definitions. It is as close as we can get to noumena through phenomena, as close as we can get to the thingness of things through the appearances of things. Fantasy isn't separate from reality; it is a vital approach to the essence of it. As to its importance, it is simply a matter of life and death. If we don't find out more about the truly essential thingness of things, then some future generation, if not this one, won't have anything left to find out about. So we must have fantasy constructed as scaffolding from which to work on actualities. And to work with fantasy is a risky business for the writer: it can change his whole world of actualities.

Which brings me back to the man on the bicycle, shirtless and shouting. I was sorry for that man. I know how he felt. I wish he had been able to do something better with the baffled demon in him. I think he might have found something better to do if he had had more workable material in his mind, more useful people in his inner society. Robin Hood would have helped him, perhaps Captain Ahab too, and Lord Jim and Raskolnikov and goodness knows who else, functioning as surrogate actors-out of extreme and exaggerated degrees of the human condition. They might have taken on for him certain time-consuming and self-defeating tasks. They might have shown him other ways to be, might have freed him to do something more effective than what he was doing, might have helped him to find an identity in that wild surge of random creation that vanished into silence on the indulgent and indifferent air.

Well, you may say, perhaps that man wasn't a reader, and whatever is in books won't help him. But books permeate both the outer and inner societies, moving through readers to non-readers with definitions and provision for societal roles, expectations and probabilities. Always more figures are needed to people our inner societies—personifications of all the subtly different modes of being, *avatars* of the sequential and often warring selves within us. Books in nameless categories are needed—books for children and adults together, books that can stand in an existential nowhere and find a centre that will hold.

A grown man re-reading *Robin Hood?* A grown man *needing Robin Hood?* Russell Hoban's starting point is the moment-in-his-daily-life when he sees the shirtless cyclist "riding in circles at a traffic light and shouting unintelligibly."

We all see such sights, breaking in on our normal lives. The child/narrator in Peter Sharpe's poem "waits for the idiot to go away" (p. 355). Likewise, we in our actual lives move away to avoid any sight that disturbs us, or, if we can't move, we hope and pray *it* will go away, so that we can forget it, and get on with our business.

The shirtless cyclist triggers Hoban's thoughts on a number of questions: his childhood need for Robin Hood; his belief that to be a *man*, he should *incinerate* his copy of *Robin Hood*; his subsequent *re-reading* of what a man (or woman) needs in order to stay sane, to live with the inexorable burdens and pains of twentieth-century life; the fact that "society is a retarded child with a loaded gun in its hand," and that properly dressed, "polite gentlemen" incinerated—in gas ovens—the living flesh of other human beings. We might point our finger at the shirtless cyclist and say, "Madman," but Hoban makes us think twice about the so-called *sane*, civilized, orderly, respectable, polite gentlemen who "sit around tables with the death of the world in their briefcases."

CONSIDER THIS

★ Hoban isn't claiming that books are the cure-all for all social ills, but he does ask us to reflect upon some large questions: What does growing up mean? Must we give up our fantasy lives, our imagination, our capacity to wonder, speculate, dream, to identify with hero(in)es who do the impossible—who defy the *law*? Does growing up mean that inside the dark business suit lurks another dark business suit? Does growing up mean the death of the "outlaw self"? What is the outlaw self? What constitutes "order" in the normal life? And how do we—how can we possibly—reconcile the outer and inner selves, particularly when the outer self has a nine-to-five job, a huge mortgage on the house, and kids who want *everything*?

★ "So, give them Robin Hood for Christmas," Hoban might say. But what good is Robin Hood? What good these legends, myths, and stories? What good fantasy? The dreams of doing other than what is expected—and endorsed? What good the outlaw self? The inner society? When more and more of us (women, as well as men) had better *wear* our shirts, *and* have them neatly tucked into grey flannel business suits, or else . . .? What good any of this when the *center* doesn't seem to be holding?*

★ Who are the Robin Hoods in *your* head? What Robin Hoods do women hold in their heads? Must these figures come from books? What about television, the movies, the comics? What about Batman and Robin?

* Hoban's last line, "Books are needed . . . [to] find a centre that will hold" alludes to a poem by W. B. Yeats, "The Second Coming."

Things fall apart; the centre cannot hold;
Mere anarchy is loosed upon the world,
The blood-dimmed tide is loosed, and everywhere
The ceremony of innocence is drowned;
The best lack all conviction, while the worst
Are full of passionate intensity.

★ "*Why* do we need images of Robin Hood in our heads, when we're grown up?" you ask us. So much of our grown-up lives are governed, controlled, and organized by the processed signs of the dominant culture, that we—little, ordinary, individual selves—can be swallowed whole, unless we can make a place throughout all of our lives (and not only in our childhoods) for the outlaw self: those inner voices within our various public voices that say *no* to all that is expected of us. Through *vicarious* ways of being, by "becoming" these figures, by imagining, and *playing*, we can strike a balance, find compensations— fulfillments and outlets—so that all that is *inside*, the impulses, needs, desires, visions, hopes, aspirations, can breathe. What do you think?

YOUR WRITING(S) FOR OTHERS TO READ

By now you should be ready to negotiate with your instructor the kinds of writing you wish or need to engage in. At this point, then, we can bow out and leave you to work out some kind of realization of what exactly you need or wish to write, in relation to the issues raised by the texts in Chapters 13 and 14.

Chapter Fourteen

Values and Evaluations
(II)

The late twentieth century is a difficult time in which to live, but we who live in the United States are, mostly, relatively fortunate: we know where the next meal is coming from and, if we are students, we are probably quite optimistic about our future prospects. As the people of the Third World say, Americans mostly have "happy problems."

One of the dangers of economic security is to fall into complacency; and one of the dangers of being members of the most powerful country in the world is to fall into the naive belief that everyone else either is like us or ought to be like us. The internationalization of consumer products means, of course, that all peoples of the world face the challenge of homogenization and the obliteration of those cultural differences that constitute the legitimate and enlivening variety of social, moral, political, and aesthetic values.

As Nadine Gordimer shows in her short story, dominant cultures are not therefore morally superior, and there is always a legitimate time and place for making moral judgments, however severe. The political consequences of such judgments are for us, the readers, to think about. Roland Barthes offers a blistering criticism of a world-famous and very popular exhibition of photographs and forces us to think about the ways in which the world of the poor, the deprived, and the oppressed is *not* the same world as that of the prosperous and privileged. And Zbigniew Herbert and Kay Boyle remind us of our responsibility—to read very scrupulously, to attend to particular lives closely and with a clear eye, and to read their particular meanings in their relationships with those in power. Everyone has at least a name: let it be known and recognized; and, if just, memorialized and honored.

NADINE GORDIMER

Six Feet of the Country

Nadine Gordimer lives in South Africa, a country divided by two opposing readings of history and of "human destiny." Most of her great fiction derives its power from the intensity of her response to that division, that contradiction.

Note how closely and carefully the "I" of the story "reads" his wife, Lerice, and so, inescapably, evaluates her. We in turn read the text, and through it we "read" him, and his "reading" of Lerice, and so, equally inescapably, we evaluate him and his values, his attitudes, his ideology. Moreover—so many things happen when we read fiction!— we read his reading of her reading of him! And he admits that he is less interested in a deep reading of their life together than she is: he doesn't want "to go into" it.

My wife and I are not real farmers — not even Lerice, really. We bought our place, ten miles out of Johannesburg on one of the main roads, to change something in ourselves, I suppose; you seem to rattle about so much within a marriage like ours. You long to hear nothing but a deep satisfying silence when you sound a marriage. The farm hasn't managed that for us, of course, but it has done other things, unexpected, illogical. Lerice, who I thought would retire there in Chekhovian sadness for a month or two, and then leave the place to the servants while she tried yet again to get a part she wanted and become the actress she would like to be, has sunk into the business of running the farm with all the serious intensity with which she once imbued the shadows in a playwright's mind. I should have given it up long ago if it had not been for her. Her hands, once small and plain and well-kept — she was not the sort of actress who wears red paint and diamond rings — are hard as a dog's pads.

I, of course, am there only in the evenings and at weekends. I am a partner in a travel agency which is flourishing — needs to be, as I tell Lerice, in order to carry the farm. Still, though I know we can't afford it, and though the sweetish smell of the fowls Lerice breeds sickens me, so that I avoid going past their runs, the farm is beautiful in a way I had almost forgotten — especially on a Sunday morning when I get up and go out into the paddock and see not the palm trees and fishpond and imitation-stone bird bath of the suburbs but white ducks on the dam, the lucerne field brilliant as window-dresser's grass, and the little, stocky, mean-eyed bull, lustful but bored, having his face tenderly licked by one of his ladies. Lerice comes out with her hair uncombed, in her hand a stick dripping with cattle dip. She will stand

and look dreamily for a moment, the way she would pretend to look sometimes in those plays. "They'll mate tomorrow," she will say. "This is their second day. Look how she loves him, my little Napoleon." So that when people come to see us on Sunday afternoon, I am likely to hear myself saying as I pour out the drinks, "When I drive back home from the city every day past those rows of suburban houses, I wonder how the devil we ever did stand it . . . Would you care to look around?" And there I am, taking some pretty girl and her young husband stumbling down to our riverbank, the girl catching her stockings on the mealie-stooks and stepping over cow turds humming with jewel-green flies while she says, ". . . the *tensions* of the damned city. And you're near enough to get into town to a show, too! I think it's wonderful. Why, you've got it both ways!"

And for a moment I accept the triumph as if I *had* managed it — the impossibility that I've been trying for all my life: just as if the truth was that you could get it "both ways," instead of finding yourself with not even one way or the other but a third, one you had not provided for at all.

But even in our saner moments, when I find Lerice's earthy enthusiasms just as irritating as I once found her histrionical ones, and she finds what she calls my "jealousy" of her capacity for enthusiasm as big a proof of my inadequacy for her as a mate as ever it was, we do believe that we have at least honestly escaped those tensions peculiar to the city about which our visitors speak. When Johannesburg people speak of "tension," they don't mean hurrying people in crowded streets, the struggle for money, or the general competitive character of city life. They mean the guns under the white men's pillows and the burglar bars on the white men's windows. They mean those strange moments on city pavements when a black man won't stand aside for a white man.

Out in the country, even ten miles out, life is better than that. In the country, there is a lingering remnant of the pretransitional stage; our relationship with the blacks is almost feudal. Wrong, I suppose, obsolete, but more comfortable all around. We have no burglar bars, no gun. Lerice's farm boys have their wives and their piccanins living with them on the land. They brew their sour beer without the fear of police raids. In fact, we've always rather prided ourselves that the poor devils have nothing much to fear, being with us; Lerice even keeps an eye on their children, with all the competence of a woman who has never had a child of her own, and she certainly doctors them all — children and adults — like babies whenever they happen to be sick.

It was because of this that we were not particularly startled one night last winter when the boy Albert came knocking at our window long after we had gone to bed. I wasn't in our bed but sleeping in the little dressing-room-cum-linen-room next door, because Lerice had annoyed me and I didn't want to find myself softening towards her simply because of the sweet smell of the talcum powder on her flesh after her bath. She came and woke me up. "Albert says one of the boys is very sick," she said. "I think you'd better go down and see. He wouldn't get us up at this hour for nothing."

"What time is it?"

"What does it matter?" Lerice is maddeningly logical.

I got up awkwardly as she watched me — how is it I always feel a fool when I have deserted her bed? After all, I know from the way she never looks at me when she talks to me at breakfast next day that she is hurt and humiliated at my not wanting her — and I went out, clumsy with sleep.

"Which of the boys is it?" I asked Albert as we followed the dance of my torch.

"He's too sick. Very sick," he said.

"But who? Franz?" I remembered Franz had had a bad cough for the past week.

Albert did not answer; he had given me the path, and was walking along beside me in the tall dead grass. When the light of the torch caught his face, I saw that he looked acutely embarrassed. "What's this all about?" I said.

He lowered his head under the glance of the light. "It's not me, baas. I don't know. Petrus he send me."

Irritated, I hurried him along to the huts. And there, on Petrus's iron bedstead, with its brick stilts, was a young man, dead. On his forehead there was still a light, cold sweat; his body was warm. The boys stood around as they do in the kitchen when it is discovered that someone has broken a dish — uncooperative, silent. Somebody's wife hung about in the shadows, her hands wrung together under her apron.

I had not seen a dead man since the war. This was very different. I felt like the others — extraneous, useless. "What was the matter?" I asked.

The woman patted at her chest and shook her head to indicate the painful impossibility of breathing.

He must have died of pneumonia.

I turned to Petrus. "Who was this boy? What was he doing here?" The light of a candle on the floor showed that Petrus was weeping. He followed me out the door.

When we were outside, in the dark, I waited for him to speak. But he didn't. "Now, come on, Petrus, you must tell me who this boy was. Was he a friend of yours?"

"He's my brother, baas. He came from Rhodesia to look for work."

The story startled Lerice and me a little. The young boy had walked down from Rhodesia to look for work in Johannesburg, had caught a chill from sleeping out along the way and had lain ill in his brother Petrus's hut since his arrival three days before. Our boys had been frightened to ask us for help for him because we had never been intended to know of his presence. Rhodesian natives are barred from entering the Union unless they have a permit; the young man was an illegal immigrant. No doubt our boys had managed the whole thing successfully several times before; a number of relatives must have walked the seven or eight hundred miles from poverty to the paradise of zoot suits, police raids and black slum townships that is their *Egoli*, City of Gold — the African name for Johannesburg. It was merely a matter of getting such a man to lie low on our farm until a job could be found with someone who would be glad to take the risk of prosecution for employing an illegal immigrant in exchange for the services of someone as yet untainted by the city.

Well, this was one who would never get up again.

"You would think they would have felt they could tell *us*," said Lerice next morning. "Once the man was ill. You would have thought at least —" When she is getting intense over something, she has a way of standing in the middle of a room as people do when they are shortly to leave on a journey, looking searchingly about her at the most familiar objects as if she had never seen them before. I had noticed that in Petrus's presence in the kitchen, earlier, she had had the air of being almost offended with him, almost hurt.

In any case, I really haven't the time or inclination any more to go into everything in our life that I know Lerice, from those alarmed and pressing eyes of hers, would like us to go into. She is the kind of woman who doesn't mind if she looks plain, or odd; I don't suppose she would even care if she knew how strange she looks when her whole face is out of proportion with urgent uncertainty. I said, "Now I'm the one who'll have to do all the dirty work, I suppose."

She was still staring at me, trying me out with those eyes — wasting her time, if she only knew.

"I'll have to notify the health authorities," I said calmly. "They can't just cart him off and bury him. After all, we don't really know what he died of."

She simply stood there, as if she had given up — simply ceased to see me at all.

I don't know when I've been so irritated. "It might have been something contagious," I said. "God knows." There was no answer.

I am not enamoured of holding conversations with myself. I went out to shout to one of the boys to open the garage and get the car ready for my morning drive to town.

As I had expected, it turned out to be quite a business. I had to notify the police as well as the health authorities, and answer a lot of tedious questions: How was it I was ignorant of the boy's presence? If I did not supervise my native quarters, how did I know that that sort of thing didn't go on all the time? And when I flared up and told them that so long as my natives did their work, I didn't think it my right or concern to poke my nose into their private lives, I got from the coarse, dull-witted police sergeant one of those looks that come not from any thinking process going on in the brain but from that faculty common to all who are possessed by the master-race theory — a look of insanely inane certainty. He grinned at me with a mixture of scorn and delight at my stupidity.

Then I had to explain to Petrus why the health authorities had to take away the body for a post-mortem — and, in fact, what a post-mortem was. When I telephoned the health department some days later to find out the result, I was told that the cause of death was, as we had thought, pneumonia, and that the body had been suitably disposed of. I went out to where Petrus was mixing a mash for the fowls and told him that it was all right, there would be no trouble; his brother had died from that pain in his chest. Petrus put down the paraffin tin and said, "When can we go to fetch him, baas?"

"To fetch him?"

"Will the baas please ask them when we must come?"

I went back inside and called Lerice, all over the house. She came down the stairs from the spare bedrooms, and I said, "*Now* what am I going to do? When I told Petrus, he just asked calmly when they could go and fetch the body. They think they're going to bury him themselves."

"Well, go back and tell him," said Lerice. "You must tell him. Why didn't you tell him then?"

When I found Petrus again, he looked up politely. "Look, Petrus," I said. "You can't go to fetch your brother. They've done it already — they've *buried* him, you understand?"

"Where?" he said slowly, dully, as if he thought that perhaps he was getting this wrong.

"You see, he was a stranger. They knew he wasn't from here, and they didn't know he had some of his people here so they thought they must bury him." It was difficult to make a pauper's grave sound like a privilege.

"Please, baas, the baas must ask them." But he did not mean that he wanted to know the burial place. He simply ignored the incomprehensible machinery I told him had set to work on his dead brother; he wanted the brother back.

"But, Petrus," I said, "how can I? Your brother is buried already. I can't ask them now."

"Oh, baas!" he said. He stood with his bran-smeared hands uncurled at his sides, one corner of his mouth twitching.

"Good God, Petrus, they won't listen to me! They can't, anyway. I'm sorry, but I can't do it. You understand?"

He just kept on looking at me, out of his knowledge that white men have everything, can do anything; if they don't, it is because they won't.

And then, at dinner, Lerice started. "You could at least phone," she said.

"Christ, what d'you think I am? Am I supposed to bring the dead back to life?"

But I could not exaggerate my way out of this ridiculous responsibility that had been thrust on me. "Phone them up," she went on. "And at least you'll be able to tell him you've done it and they've explained that it's impossible."

She disappeared somewhere into the kitchen quarters after coffee. A little later she came back to tell me, "The old father's coming down from Rhodesia to be at the funeral. He's got a permit and he's already on his way."

Unfortunately, it was not impossible to get the body back. The authorities said that it was somewhat irregular, but that since the hygiene conditions had been fulfilled, they could not refuse permission for exhumation. I found out that, with the undertaker's charges, it would cost twenty pounds. Ah, I thought, that settles it. On five pounds a month, Petrus won't have twenty pounds — and just as well, since it couldn't do the dead any good. Certainly I should not offer it to him myself. Twenty pounds — or anything else within reason, for that matter — I would have spent without grudging it on doctors or medicines that might have helped the boy when he was alive. Once he was dead, I had no intention of encouraging Petrus to throw away, on a gesture, more than he spent to clothe his whole family in a year.

When I told him, in the kitchen that night, he said, "Twenty pounds?"

I said, "Yes, that's right, twenty pounds."

For a moment, I had the feeling, from the look on his face, that he was calculating. But when he spoke again I thought I must have imagined it. "We must pay twenty pounds!" he said in the faraway voice in which a person speaks of something so unattainable it does not bear thinking about.

"All right, Petrus," I said, and went back to the living room.

The next morning before I went to town, Petrus asked to see me. "Please, baas," he said, awkwardly, handing me a bundle of notes. They're so seldom on the giving rather than the receiving side, poor devils, they don't really know how to hand money to a white man. There it was, the twenty pounds, in ones and halves, some creased and folded until they were soft as dirty rags, others smooth and fairly new — Franz's money, I suppose, and Albert's, and Dora the cook's, and Jacob the gardener's, and God knows who else's besides, from all the farms and small holdings round about. I took it in irritation more than in astonishment, really — irritation at the waste, the uselessness of this sacrifice by people so poor. Just like the poor everywhere, I thought, who stint themselves the decencies of life in order to ensure themselves the decencies of death. So incomprehensible to people like Lerice and me, who regard life as something to be spent extravagantly and, if we think about death at all, regard it as the final bankruptcy.

The farm hands don't work on Saturday afternoon anyway, so it was a good day for the funeral. Petrus and his father had borrowed our donkey-cart to fetch the coffin from the city, where, Petrus told Lerice on their return, everything was "nice" — the coffin waiting for them, already sealed up to save them from what must have been a rather unpleasant sight after two weeks' interment. (It had taken all that time for the authorities and the undertaker to make the final arrangements for moving the body.) All morning, the coffin lay in Petrus's hut, awaiting the trip to the little old burial ground, just outside the eastern boundary of our farm, that was a relic of the days when this was a real farming district rather than a fashionable rural estate. It was pure chance that I happened to be down there near the fence when the procession came past; once again Lerice had forgotten her promise to me and had made the house uninhabitable on a Saturday afternoon. I had come home and been infuriated to find her in a pair of filthy old slacks and with her hair uncombed since the night before, having all the varnish scraped from the living-room floor, if you please. So I had taken my No. 8 iron and gone off to practise my approach shots. In my annoyance, I had forgotten about the funeral, and was reminded only when I saw the procession coming up the path along the outside of the fence towards me; from where I was standing, you can see the graves quite clearly, and that day the sun glinted on bits of broken pottery, a lopsided homemade cross, and jam-jars brown with rainwater and dead flowers.

I felt a little awkward, and did not know whether to go on hitting my golf ball or stop at least until the whole gathering was decently past. The donkey-cart creaks and screeches with every revolution of the wheels, and it came along in a slow, halting fashion somehow peculiarly suited to the two donkeys who drew it, their little potbellies rubbed and rough, their heads sunk between the shafts, and their ears flattened back with an air submissive and downcast; peculiarly suited, too, to the group of men and women who came along slowly behind. The patient ass. Watching, I thought, you can see now why the creature became a Biblical symbol. Then the procession drew level with me and stopped, so I had to put down my club. The coffin was taken down off the cart — it was a shiny, yellow-varnished wood, like cheap furniture — and the donkeys twitched their ears against the flies. Petrus, Franz, Albert and the old father from Rhodesia hoisted it on their shoulders and the procession moved on, on foot. It was really a very awkward moment. I stood there rather foolishly at the fence, quite still, and slowly they filed past, not looking up, the four men bent beneath the shiny wooden box, and the straggling troop of mourners. All of them were servants or neighbours' servants whom I knew as casual easygoing gossipers about our lands or kitchen. I heard the old man's breathing.

I had just bent to pick up my club again when there was a sort of jar in the flowing solemnity of their processional mood; I felt it at once, like a wave of heat along the air, or one of those sudden currents of cold catching at your legs in a placid stream. The old man's voice was muttering something; the people had stopped, confused, and they bumped into one another, some pressing to go on, others hissing them to be still. I could see that they were embarrassed, but they could not ignore the voice; it was much the way that the mumblings of a prophet, though not clear at first, arrest the mind. The corner of the coffin the old man carried was sagging at an angle; he seemed to be trying to get out from under the weight of it. Now Petrus expostulated with him.

The little boy who had been left to watch the donkeys dropped the reins and ran to see. I don't know why — unless it was for the same reason people crowd around someone who has fainted in a cinema — but I parted the wires of the fence and went through, after him.

Petrus lifted his eyes to me — to anybody — with distress and horror. The old man from Rhodesia had let go of the coffin entirely, and the three others, unable to support it on their own, had laid it on the ground, in the pathway. Already there was a film of dust lightly wavering up its shiny sides. I did not understand what the old man was saying; I hesitated to interfere. But now the whole seething group turned on my silence. The old man himself came over to me, with his hands outspread and shaking, and spoke directly to me, saying something that I could tell from the tone, without understanding the words, was shocking and extraordinary.

"What is it, Petrus? What's wrong?" I appealed.

Petrus threw up his hands, bowed his head in a series of hysterical shakes, then thrust his face up at me suddenly. "He says, 'My son was not so heavy.'"

Silence. I could hear the old man breathing; he kept his mouth a little open, as old people do.

"My son was young and thin," he said at last, in English.

Again silence. Then babble broke out. The old man thundered against everybody; his teeth were yellowed and few, and he had one of those fine, grizzled, sweeping moustaches one doesn't often see nowadays, which must have been grown in emulation of early Empire-builders. It seemed to frame all his utterances with a special validity. He shocked the assembly; they thought he was mad, but they had to listen to him. With his own hands he began to prise the lid off the coffin and three of the men came forward to help him. Then he sat down on the ground; very old, very weak and unable to speak, he merely lifted a trembling hand towards what was there. He abdicated, he handed it over to them; he was no good any more.

They crowded round to look (and so did I), and now they forgot the nature of this surprise and the occasion of grief to which it belonged, and for a few minutes were carried up in the astonishment of the surprise itself. They gasped and flared noisily with excitement. I even noticed the little boy who had held the donkeys jumping up and down, almost weeping with rage because the backs of the grownups crowded him out of his view.

In the coffin was someone no one had seen before: a heavily built, rather light-skinned native with a neatly stitched scar on his forehead — perhaps from a blow in a brawl that had also dealt him some other, slower-working injury that had killed him.

I wrangled with the authorities for a week over that body. I had the feeling that they were shocked, in a laconic fashion, by their own mistake, but that in the confusion of their anonymous dead they were helpless to put it right. They said to me, "We are trying to find out," and "We are still making inquiries." It was as if at any moment they might conduct me into their mortuary and say, "There! Lift up the sheets; look for him — your poultry boy's brother. There are so many black faces — surely one will do?"

And every evening when I got home, Petrus was waiting in the kitchen. "Well, they're trying. They're still looking. The baas is seeing to it for you, Petrus," I would tell him. "God, half the time I should be in the office I'm driving around the back end of the town chasing after this affair," I added aside, to Lerice, one night.

She and Petrus both kept their eyes turned on me as I spoke, and, oddly, for those moments they looked exactly alike, though it sounds impossible: my wife, with her high, white forehead and her attenuated Englishwoman's body, and the poultry boy, with his horny bare feet below khaki trousers tied at the knee with string and the peculiar rankness of his nervous sweat coming from his skin.

"What makes you so indignant, so determined about this now?" said Lerice suddenly.

I stared at her. "It's a matter of principle. Why should they get away with a swindle? It's time these officials had a jolt from someone who'll bother to take the trouble."

She said, "Oh." And as Petrus slowly opened the kitchen door to leave, sensing that the talk had gone beyond him, she turned away, too.

I continued to pass on assurances to Petrus every evening, but although what I said was the same and the voice in which I said it was the same, every evening it sounded weaker. At last, it became clear that we would never get Petrus's brother back, because nobody really knew where he was. Somewhere in a graveyard as uniform as a housing scheme, somewhere under a number that didn't belong to him, or in the medical school, perhaps, laboriously reduced to layers of muscle and strings of nerve? Goodness knows. He had no identity in this world anyway.

It was only then, and in a voice of shame, that Petrus asked me to try and get the money back.

"From the way he asks, you'd think he was robbing his dead brother," I said to Lerice later. But as I've said, Lerice had got so intense about this business that she couldn't even appreciate a little ironic smile.

I tried to get the money; Lerice tried. We both telephoned and wrote and argued, but nothing came of it. It appeared that the main expense had been the undertaker, and after all he had done his job. So the whole thing was a complete waste, even more of a waste for the poor devils than I had thought it would be.

The old man from Rhodesia was about Lerice's father's size, so she gave him one of her father's old suits, and he went back home rather better off, for the winter, than he had come.

So the clash of two cultures, two ideologies—white supremacist settlers and poor black natives—is played out in the death of the brother, the nameless boy. And in the middle stand Lerice and her husband, who find some of the blacks' values incomprehensible (or so he claims). The husband swings erratically, indecisively, on the racial pendulum, now veering right, and now left; and, aston-

ished at a crisis, he reads Lerice and Petrus as identical, "exactly alike . . . impossible." How so?

As for the exiled dead brother, what becomes of him? When do we realize that he has no name? That the story gives him no name; nor does Petrus, nor do the authorities: and his body disappears into "the confusion of the anonymous dead" . . . "Somewhere . . . somewhere . . . a number . . . layers of muscle. . . ."

"He had no identity in this world anyway."

Images of Strangers

Look, now, at these images of strangers on pages 424–425: images that were "taken" in a fraction of a second, so that the people were "arrested" for a moment, and we now see their images removed from their actual lives: we have no knowledge of the lives that preceded the click of the camera, and little knowledge of the places their lives were lived in.

Allowing for all that ignorance (or "innocence"), how, then, do you read their images? What do you think you would *need to know* in order to achieve a better, a fuller, deeper, and more responsible reading?

Those photographs were taken from what is probably the most famous collection of images of people ever assembled—*The Family of Man.* It started life as an exhibition at New York's Museum of Modern Art, then went on an international tour. Subsequently, the exhibition's photographs were reprinted in a best-selling book, *The Family of Man* (1955).

The photographs are presented in *linear* sequence: courtship, marriage, birth (of the next generation), growing up, family life, work, commerce, food, play (music, dancing, games, etc.), aging, famine, and poverty, religion, war, retribution, democracy, children. . . .

That is *our* reading of the sequence, but it's difficult to be sure, since there are very few words in the book. There is, however, an Introduction by the photographer who put it together, Edward Steichen (1879–1973):

I believe The Family of Man exhibition, produced and shown first at The Museum of Modern Art in New York and now being circulated throughout the world, is the most ambitious and challenging project photography has ever attempted.

The exhibition, now permanently presented on the pages of this book, demonstrates that the art of photography is a dynamic process of giving form to ideas and of explaining man to man. It was conceived as a mirror of the universal elements and emotions in the everydayness of life—as a mirror of the essential oneness of mankind throughout the world.

We sought and selected photographs, made in all parts of the world, of the gamut of life from birth to death with emphasis on the daily relationships of man to himself, to his family, to the community and to the world we live in—subject matter ranging from babies to philosophers, from the kindergarten to the university, from primitive

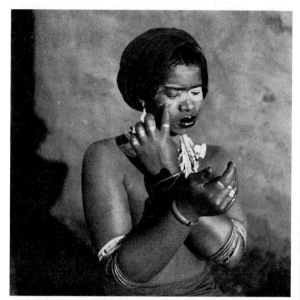

peoples to the Councils of the United Nations. Photographs of lovers and marriage and child-bearing, of the family unit with its joys, trials and tribulations, its deep-rooted devotions and its antagonisms. Photographs of the home in all its warmth and magnificence, its heartaches and exaltations. Photographs of the individual and the family unit in its reactions to the beginnings of life and continuing on through death and burial. Photographs concerned with man in relation to his environment, to the beauty and richness of the earth he has inherited and what he has done with this inheritance, the good and the great things, the stupid and the destructive things. Photographs concerned with the religious rather than religions. With basic human consciousness rather than social consciousness. Photographs concerned with man's dreams and aspirations and photographs of the flaming creative forces of love and truth and the corrosive evil inherent in the lie.

For almost three years we have been searching for these images. Over two million photographs from every corner of the earth have come to us—from individuals, collections and files. We screened them until we had ten thousand. Then came the almost unbearable task of reducing these to 503 photographs from 68 countries. The photographers who took them—273 men and women—are amateurs and professionals, famed and unknown.

All of this could not have been accomplished without the dedicated efforts of my assistant, Wayne Miller, and the tireless devotion of our staff.

The Family of Man has been created in a passionate spirit of devoted love and faith in man.

This is followed by a Prologue written by the 77-year-old Chicago writer, Carl Sandburg (1878–1967):

The first cry of a newborn baby in Chicago or Zamboango, in Amsterdam or Rangoon, has the same pitch and key, each saying, "I am! I have come through! I belong! I am a member of the Family."

Many the babies and grownups here from photographs made in sixty-eight nations round our planet Earth. You travel and see what the camera saw. The wonder of human mind, heart, wit and instinct, is here. You might catch yourself saying, "I'm not a stranger here."

People! flung wide and far, born into toil, struggle, blood and dreams, among lovers, eaters, drinkers, workers, loafers, fighters, players, gamblers. Here are iron-workers, bridgemen, musicians, sandhogs, miners, builders of huts and skyscrapers, jungle hunters, landlords and the landless, the loved and the unloved, the lonely and abandoned, the brutal and the compassionate—one big family hugging close to the ball of Earth for its life and being.

Here or there you may witness a startling harmony where you say, "This will be haunting me a long time with a loveliness I hope to understand better."

In a seething of saints and sinners, winners or losers, in a womb of superstition, faith, genius, crime, sacrifice, here is the People, the one and only source of armies, navies, work-gangs, the living flowing breath of the history of nations, ever lighted by the reality or illusion of hope. Hope is a sustaining human gift.

Everywhere is love and love-making, weddings and babies from generation to generation keeping the Family of Man alive and continuing. Everywhere the sun, moon and stars, the climates and weathers, have meanings for people. Though meanings vary, we are alike in all countries and tribes in trying to read what sky, land and sea say to us. Alike and ever alike we are on all continents in the need of love, food, clothing, work, speech, worship, sleep, games, dancing, fun. From tropics to arctics humanity lives with these needs so alike, so inexorably alike.

Hands here, hands gnarled as thorntree roots and others soft as faded rose leaves. Hands reaching, praying and groping, hands holding tools, torches, brooms, fishnets, hands doubled in fists of flaring anger, hands moving in caress of beloved faces. The hands and feet of children playing ring-around-a-rosy—countries and languages different but the little ones alike in playing the same game.

Here are set forth babies arriving, suckling, growing into youths restless and questioning. Then as grownups they seek and hope. They mate, toil, fish, quarrel, sing, fight, pray, on all parallels and meridians having likeness. The earliest man, ages ago, had tools, weapons, cattle, as seen in his cave drawings. And like him the latest man of our day has his tools, weapons, cattle. The earliest man struggled through inexpressibly dark chaos of hunger, fear, violence, sex. A long journey it has been from that early Family of Man to the one of today which has become a still more prodigious spectacle.

If the human face is "the masterpiece of God" it is here then in a thousand fateful registrations. Often the faces speak what words can never say. Some tell of eternity and others only the latest tattlings. Child faces of blossom smiles or mouths of hunger are followed by homely faces of majesty carved and worn by love, prayer and hope, along with others light and carefree as thistledown in a late summer wind. Faces having land and sea on them, faces honest as the morning sun flooding a clean kitchen with light, faces crooked and lost and wondering where to go this afternoon or tomorrow morning. Faces in crowds, laughing and windblown leaf faces, profiles in an instant of agony, mouths in a dumbshow mockery lacking speech, faces of music in gay song or a twist of pain, a hate ready to kill, or calm and ready-for-death faces. Some of them are worth a long look now and deep contemplation later. Faces betokening a serene blue sky or faces dark with storm winds and lashing night rain. And faces beyond forgetting, written over with faiths in men and dreams of man surpassing himself. An alphabet here and a multiplication table of living breathing human faces.

In the times to come as in the past there will be generations taking hold as though loneliness and the genius of struggle has always dwelt in the hearts of pioneers. To the question, "What will the story be of the Family of Man across the near or far future?" some would reply, "For the answers read if you can the strange and baffling eyes of youth."

> There is only one man in the world
> and his name is All Men.
> There is only one woman in the world

and her name is All Women.
There is only one child in the world
and the child's name is All Children.

A camera testament, a drama of the grand canyon of humanity, an epic woven of fun, mystery and holiness—here is the Family of Man!

❦

Note Sandburg's language: "one big family" . . . "we are all alike" . . . "Alike and ever alike" . . . "so alike, so inexorably alike" . . . "little ones alike" . . . "an epic woven of fun, mystery, and holiness . . ."

The French writer Roland Barthes (1915–1980) saw the exhibition in Paris, where it was entitled *The Great Family of Man*. Here is what he *saw*.

ROLAND BARTHES

The Great Family of Man

A big exhibition of photographs has been held in Paris, the aim of which was to show the universality of human actions in the daily life of all the countries of the world: birth, death, work, knowledge, play, always impose the same types of behaviour; there is a family of Man.

The Family of Man, such at any rate was the original title of the exhibition which came here from the United States. The French have translated it as: *The Great Family of Man*. So what could originally pass for a phrase belonging to zoology, keeping only the similarity in behaviour, the unity of a species, is here amply moralized and sentimentalized. We are at the outset directed to this ambiguous myth of the human "community," which serves as an alibi to a large part of our humanism.

This myth functions in two stages: first the difference between human morphologies is asserted, exoticism is insistently stressed, the infinite variations of the species, the diversity in skins, skulls and customs are made manifest, the image of Babel is complacently projected over that of the world. Then, from this pluralism, a type of unity is magically produced: man is born, works, laughs and dies every-

*What is the effect of reproducing Sandburg's own signature? What effect do you think the promoters of the exhibition hoped it would have?

where in the same way; and if there still remains in these actions some ethnic peculiarity, at least one hints that there is underlying each one an identical "nature," that their diversity is only formal and does not belie the existence of a common mould. Of course this means postulating a human essence, and here is God re-introduced into our Exhibition: the diversity of men proclaims his power, his rich-ness; the unity of their gestures demonstrates his will. This is what the introductory leaflet confides to us when it states, by the pen of M. André Chamson, that *"this look over the human condition must somewhat resemble the benevolent gaze of God on our absurd and sublime ant-hill."* The pietistic intention is underlined by the quotations which accompany each chapter of the Exhibition: these quotations often are "prim-itive" proverbs or verses from the Old Testament. They all define an eternal wisdom, a class of assertions which escape History: *"The Earth is a Mother who never dies, Eat bread and salt and speak the truth,* etc." This is the reign of gnomic truths, the meeting of all the ages of humanity at the most neutral point of their nature, the point where the obviousness of the truism has no longer any value except in the realm of a purely "poetic" language. Everything here, the content and appeal of the pictures, the discourse which justifies them, aims to suppress the determining weight of History: we are held back at the surface of an identity, prevented precisely by sentimentality from penetrating into this ulterior zone of human behaviour where historical alien-ation introduces some "differences" which we shall here quite simply call "injustices."

This myth of the human "condition" rests on a very old mystification, which always consists in placing Nature at the bottom of History. Any classic humanism postulates that in scratching the history of men a little, the relativity of their institutions or the superficial diversity of their skins (but why not ask the parents of Emmet Till, the young Negro assassinated by the Whites, what *they* think of *The Great Family of Man?*), one very quickly reaches the solid rock of a universal human nature. Progressive humanism, on the contrary, must always remember to reverse the terms of this very old imposture, constantly to scour nature, its "laws" and its "limits" in order to discover History there, and at last to establish Nature itself as historical.

Examples? Here they are: those of our Exhibition. Birth, death? Yes, these are facts of nature, universal facts. But if one removes History from them, there is nothing more to be said about them; any comment about them becomes purely tautological. The failure of photography seems to me to be flagrant in this connection: to reproduce death or birth tells us, literally, nothing. For these natural facts to gain access to a true language, they must be inserted into a category of knowledge which means postulating that one can transform them, and precisely subject their natural-ness to our human criticism. For however universal, they are the signs of an historical writing. True, children are *always* born: but in the whole mass of the human problem, what does the "essence" of this process matter to us, compared to its modes which, as for them, are perfectly historical? Whether or not the child is born with ease or difficulty, whether or not his birth causes suffering to his mother, whether or not he is threatened by a high mortality rate, whether or not such and such a type of future is open to him: this is what your Exhibitions should be telling people, instead of an eternal lyricism of birth. The same goes for death: must we really celebrate its essence once more, and thus risk forgetting that there is still so much we can do to fight it? It is this very young, far too young power that we must exalt, and not the sterile identity of "natural" death.

And what can be said about work, which the Exhibition places among great universal facts, putting it on the same plane as birth and death, as if it was quite evident that it belongs to the same order of fate? That work is an age-old fact does not in the least prevent it from remaining a perfectly historical fact. Firstly, and evidently, because of its modes, its motivations, its ends and its benefits, which matter to such an extent that it will never be fair to confuse in a purely gestural identity the colonial and the Western worker (let us also ask the North African workers of the Goutte d'Or district in Paris what they think of *The Great Family of Man*). Secondly, because of the very differences in its inevitability: we know very well that work is "natural" just as long as it is "profitable," and that in modifying the inevitability of the profit, we shall perhaps one day modify the inevitability of labour. It is this entirely historified work which we should be told about, instead of an eternal aesthetics of laborious gestures.

So that I rather fear that the final justification of all this Adamism is to give to the immobility of the world the alibi of a "wisdom" and a "lyricism" which only make the gestures of man look eternal the better to defuse them.

One of the most serious charges that Barthes levels against Steichen is that the exhibition boils down to a ridiculous tautological statement: birth is birth / death is death / work is work / play is play, which leaves us all none the wiser. This allows Steichen to ignore history, politics, social differences, exploitation; it also allows him to transform each photograph (a photo is an image of a *particular* person, place) from a particular to a *universal*: in any photograph people are plucked from their time, place, and culture and set up, *decontextualized*, as Everyman or Everywoman. For all the visual glamour and brilliance, the effect of looking, and of *not* being allowed to read the particular face or body in its context and its history, is a kind of resignation: "That's life!" A shrug of the shoulders. "Only in human affairs inexcusable carelessness reigns supreme—the lack of precise information," as the next text says.

ZBIGNIEW HERBERT

Mr. Cogito on the Need for Precision

Zbigniew Herbert (b. 1924), the Polish writer, has invented a character, Mr. Cogito*: he is a kind of Everyman (Everyperson), an "ordinary guy," Adam, a stereotype.

*Cogito: I think (Latin).

But he does something that those neutralized, anonymous mythic figures never did: he thinks. *As a result, he enquires, he asks awkward questions, he challenges clichés and everything that is taken-for-granted; he wants* a better reading. *The dominant ideology in any society depends for its security, its power, on encouraging people not to attempt a better reading, for those with power prefer their subjects to be "innocent" (that is, kept in ignorance). For every better, closer reading is a* critical *reading: it comes out of "Eh, hold on a minute! What exactly are you (the text, the propaganda, the persuasion) trying to do to me? And what are you hiding?"*

1

Mr. Cogito
is alarmed by a problem
in the domain of applied mathematics

the difficulties we encounter
with operations of simple arithmetic

5

children are lucky
they add apple to apple
subtract grain from grain

the sum is correct
the kindergarten of the world   10
pulsates with a safe warmth

particles of matter have been measured
heavenly bodies weighed
and only in human affairs
inexcusable carelessness reigns supreme   15
the lack of precise information

over the immensity of history
wheels a specter
the specter of indefiniteness

how many Greeks were killed at Troy   20
—we don't know

to give the exact casualties
on both sides
in the battle at Gaugamela
at Agincourt   25
Leipzig
Kutno

and also the number of victims
of terror
of the white   30
the red
the brown
—O colors innocent colors—

—we don't know
truly we don't know   35

Mr. Cogito
rejects the sensible explanation
that this was long ago
the wind has thoroughly mixed the ashes
the blood flowed to the sea   40

sensible explanations
intensify the alarm
of Mr. Cogito

because even what
is happening under our eyes   45

evades numbers
loses the human dimension

somewhere there must be an error
a fatal defect in our tools
or a sin of memory   50

     2

a few simple examples
from the accounting of victims

in an airplane disaster
it is easy to establish
the exact number of the dead   55

important for heirs
and those plunged in grief
for insurance companies

we take the list of passengers
and the crew   60
next to each name
we place a little cross

it is slightly harder
in the case
of train accidents   65

bodies torn to pieces
have to be put back together
so no head
remains ownerless

during elemental   70
catastrophes
the arithmetic
becomes complicated

we count those who are saved
but the unknown remainder   75
neither alive
nor definitely dead
is described by a strange term
the missing

they still have the chance
to return to us
from fire
from water
the interior of the earth

80

if they return—that's fine
if they don't—too bad

85

3

now Mr. Cogito
climbs
to the highest tottering
step of indefiniteness

90

how difficult it is to establish the names
of all those who perished
in the struggle with inhuman power

the official statistics
reduce their number
once again pitilessly
they decimate those who have died a violent death
and their bodies disappear
in abysmal cellars
of huge police buildings

95

100

eyewitnesses
blinded by gas
deafened by salvoes
by fear and despair
are inclined toward exaggeration

105

accidental observers
give doubtful figures
accompanied by the shameful
word "about"

and yet in these matters
accuracy is essential
we must not be wrong
even by a single one

110

we are despite everything
the guardians of our brothers   115

ignorance about those who have disappeared
undermines the reality of the world
it thrusts into the hell of appearances
the devilish net of dialectics
proclaiming there is no difference   120
between the substance and the specter

        therefore we have to know
        to count exactly
        call by the first name
        provide for a journey   125

        in a bowl of clay
        millet poppy seeds
        a bone comb
        arrowheads
        and a ring of faithfulness   130

    amulets*

When you read lines 116–117 of Herbert's poem, "ignorance about those who have disappeared / undermines the reality of the world" and lines 122–125, "therefore we have to know / to count exactly / call by the first name / provide for a journey," think of the mothers of the "disappeared," young people murdered by the military regime in Argentina; think of the hundreds of thousands in mass graves in Uganda after "the butcher," Idi Amin, unleashed a paranoid frenzy of killing; think of the unnamed voters shot down in Haiti as they went to cast their votes; think of the thousand nameless victims of the late Shah of Iran and of his counterpart, the Ayatollah Khomeini. . . .

Ellen Goodman (p. 319), on the East Coast, spoke to her friend (who wanted advice) on the West Coast; likewise, Kay Boyle sends a mailgram from the West Coast, across the United States, to her friend, the East-Coast writer, Babette Deutsch; and in so doing, she achieves exactly what Herbert asks for: "to know / to count exactly / call by the first name." In this instance, the name is "Vida," the name of a young woman who *read* critically the dominant ideology of the Shah's Iran and of its economic consequences: "she had been caught committing research . . . / She had written about peasants / the conditions of their

*"In a bowl of clay . . . amulets" (lines 126–131): examples of the kinds of things that used to be buried with the dead, to help them on their journey in the "other" world; amulets are little charms.

days and nights." The secret police knew what they had to do: that is, to *kill* those who were determined to read critically, and who had to pay with their lives.

KAY BOYLE

A Poem for Vida Hadjebi Tabrizi

A Mailgram for Babette Deutsch

As I write you, discarding for five minutes the names of
    other women and their destinies,
I dismiss as well the vengeance of distance lying
    between us, valley and tree,
Sierras and Rockies, intervening, and the salt white
    breasts of Utah
Barricades in the long drift of sand. But have we not
    called out each other's names,
And on some nights transformed the rocky myth of
    distance into a landscape   5
As light and shimmering as a peacock's open, quivering
    fan?
It was your poem of the gazelle standing "on legs of
    matchstick ivory,"
Your grave words saving us at last, saying that each of us
    carries in her breast
A child, holds a child there as the heart is held, anvil and
    hammer striking and striking
Through a lifetime against the bone ribs of its cage. It
    became   10
The child in your breast calling out to the child in mine
    across the distance,
The voice of "the passionate innocent" we had not
    instructed how to speak,
Crying out to us a total stranger's name. The voices
Of these hidden children summoned her. We had
    nothing to do with it.
Her steps were silent, as if falling on deep moss, each
    velvet spear of that carpet   15
Not bleached by frost as where you are, each short,
    fern-like lancet here,

Under the redwoods, hung with tears of dew; not yours,
    not mine, but tears
Of a woman who had no further use for them, a stranger
    to us, who broke the crystal string
And let them fall. You sensed her presence when you
    wrote of "immense music"
Beyond a closed and bolted door. She is the music,
    prison the bolted iron of the gate.   20
Her name is Vida Tabrizi. And there is more.
It comes from Iran, the fierce invocation, not by cable
    or phone call, not by letter or tongue,
But on the fugitive wind that has slipped through the
    bars. It runs, liquid as mercury,
Down the gutters of alien cities, is cried out through the
    meeting of bleeding palms
In the dark. The words of it are broken like flower
    stems between the teeth.   25
The message is fearful, the meaning hideously clear.

The Deciphered Message

A woman was arrested as she returned home
In the evening. But wait—not a poor woman,
Not disorderly in any way. A young woman, her hair
    black,
Teeth white, she was seen laughing on that final day.   30
She was well-dressed (the broad avenues of the
    residential quarter
Attest to that). She carried a brief case in her hand.
What in the world had she been up to, this woman
    arrested in Teheran?
They say French and English came easily to her tongue,
    as well as Middle Persian,
But she had been caught committing research, not on
    rocks   35
Or the quality of the soil, or on the lava of oil moving
    slowly,
Slow as a caravan of camels creaking across the desert
On their splayed feet. She had written about peasants,
The conditions of their days and nights. That was it.
Iranian palm trees rattled the indictment, vultures had
    the nerve   40
To scream it as they tore at the flesh of the living and the
    dead.

Hyenas, slope-backed in the throne room, laughed in
  high C
About it. That's how the royal family came to know.

The Geography

Tabriz is a city in Iran, home of the Blue Mosques,
Shaken by earthquakes year after year. Tabrizi is a
  woman   45
Who clings with finger-tips turned skeleton-white,
Clings to the edge, and we are the edge to which she
  holds,
And not quite holds, and falls, yet not quite falls,
  clinging
To our flesh and bone as though they were her own.
She is the "immense music" you wrote of behind the
  iron   50
Of a closed and bolted door. "Tabriz?" the curious
  ask,
Finger finding it on the map. Tabriz is a city, a place.
Tabrizi is the syllables of both our names.

What place do the dead occupy in our lives? They will not literally return,
but those who matter to us, those who continue to live in our minds, "appear
in the darkness." Who, exactly, are they? Friends of earlier years, certainly; and
also people we never personally knew, who died, indeed, before we were born.
Yet they, too, can occupy an important place in our hearts and minds; they
were, and are, important to us: they give us something that matters, and therefore
we take them seriously, just as *they* seem to have taken us seriously. Thom Gunn
envisions them, like stars in the night sky, shining, "perfectly embodied," and
"winnowed from failures"—separated out from all those who did not and do not
matter to us. The people who really gave us something of value, some kind of
inspiration, some larger sense of the possibilities of life—as Gatsby did to Nick
in Fitzgerald's novel—now that they are dead, have nothing to gain or lose; their
energy is indeed truly *disinterested*, in the older sense of the word.

In this book we have included some of the writers who are among *our* "sad
captains."*

*In Shakespeare's play *Antony and Cleopatra*, Antony in a fit of depression and weariness of soul says,
"Call to me all my sad captains," i.e., people who could inspire him. "Sad" meant "serious."

Thom Gunn

My Sad Captains

One by one they appear in
the darkness: a few friends, and
a few with historical
names. How late they start to shine!
but before they fade they stand   5
perfectly embodied, all

the past lapping them like a
cloak of chaos. They were men
who, I thought, lived only to
renew the wasteful force they   10
spent with each hot convulsion.
They remind me, distant now.

True, they are not at rest yet,
but now that they are indeed
apart, winnowed from failures,   15
they withdraw to an orbit
and turn with disinterested
hard energy, like the stars.

By the time Thom Gunn sat down to write "My Sad Captains" he already knew Shakespeare's *Antony and Cleopatra*: so he is able to "steal" a phrase from Shakespeare's play and "recycle" it as his title. He does *not* add a footnote to explain his borrowing: the result of his silence on this matter is that readers of his poem will either recognize his allusion or they will not: what do the former gain, and what do the latter lose?

In the body of his poem he plays a second game, rather less obvious than the one of his title: in 1802 Wordsworth wrote a poem in the form of a letter to Milton, the English poet and political writer, who had died in 1674. 1802 was a bad year for England; the government, reacting to the revolutions in America and France, punished political dissent with imprisonment, and corruption in high places was epidemic. If only, Wordsworth wrote to Milton, you were alive now and would speak out: "return to us again / And give us manners, virtue, freedom, power!" And Wordsworth's tribute to Milton included this:

Thy soul was like a star and dwelt apart.

When Thom Gunn produces an "echo" of this line in his own last stanza, "apart . . . like the stars," we cannot know whether this was chosen deliberately, accidentally, or unconsciously.

But the effect is rather like that of family stories, handed down from generation to generation, and changing in the process of telling and retelling. It is, then, possible to read Gunn's category of "sad captains" as including, not only Shakespeare, but also Wordsworth and Milton. In such ways, writers pay their debts to those who have come to inhabit, enrich, and haunt their minds.

WILLIAM STAFFORD

Critique

Whenever the writer John Keats went into a room crowded with people, he felt annihilated, obliterated, wiped out by the sheer pressure of people. It's possible to feel something like that when you go into a bookshop or library; or even when you open a book like this, which contains texts by so many writers. Your privilege, however, is that you can close the book and go back into one of your various other lives.

Let us, then, give William Stafford the last word.

Like a ghost of the writer I read this page.
Every word has cousins; the order is never
arbitrary. All that is not said—
is it near? Why isn't it said?
What is developing? A part of my attention   5
begins to estimate this voice. Is this
an artless song? Am I being used?

Can these lines take a lie detector test?
Can this writer be trusted? When I read
this, who am I supposed to be?—   10
a mother? a father? a lover? a stranger?
Someone who knows as much as the writer?

Do other words wake up? Does this page
give me the feel of arriving where truth is?
The track of this page has diverted my life.   15
Now I turn back to what is my own.

442

Edward Thomas, "Cock-Crow," *Collected Poems*, Faber and Faber Ltd. Reprinted by permission of Myfanwy Thomas.

May Swenson, "Out of the Sea, Early" by May Swensen, reprinted by permission of the author from *New & Selected Things Taking Place*, Copyright © 1966 by May Swenson, first printed in *The New Yorker* magazine.

May Swenson, "How Everything Happens (Based on a Study of the Wave)" by May Swenson, reprinted by persmission of the author from *New & Selected Things Taking Place*, Copyright © 1969 by May Swenson in *The Southern Review*.

From *Black Boy* by Richard Wright. Copyright 1937, 1942, 1944, 1945 by Richard Wright. Reprinted by permission of Harper & Row, Publishers, Inc.

From James Agee, "This Lucky Situation of Joy," from *Let Us Now Praise Famous Men* by James Agee and Walker Evans. Copyright 1939 and 1940 by James Agee. Copyright 1941 by James Agee and Walker Evans. Copyright © 1960 by Walker Evans. Copyright © renewed 1969 by Mia Fritsch Agee and Walker Evans. Reprinted by permission of Houghton Mifflin Company.

From *Autobiography* by Mark Twain. Copyright 1924 by Clara Gabrilowitsch. Reprinted by permission of Harper & Row, Publishers, Inc.

Chapter Seven

D. H. Lawrence, "The Snake," *The Complete Poems of D. H. Lawrence*, ed. Vivian de Sola and F. Warren Roberts. Copyright © 1964, 1971 by The Estate of Frieda Lawrence Ravagli. All rights reserved. Reprinted by permission of Viking Penguin Inc.

Margaret Atwood, "Bad Mouth" (Snake Poems, *Interlunar*) from *Selected Poems II: Poems Selected and New 1976–1986* by Margaret Atwood. Reprinted by permission of Houghton Mifflin Company. © Margaret Atwood 1986; reprinted by permission of Oxford University Press, Canada.

Alan Moorehead, "Snake-Phobia," *The Sunday Times*. Reprinted by permission of Laurence Pollinger Limited on behalf of the Estate of Alan Moorehead.

"Take a Chicken to Lunch," *The New York Times*, November 9, 1987. Reprinted by permission of Associated Press Newsfeatures.

Margaret Atwood, "Song of the Hen's Head," ("Songs of the Transformed"/*You Are Happy*) from *Selected Poems I 1965–1975* by Margaret Atwood. Copyright © 1976 by Margaret Atwood. Reprinted by permission of Houghton Mifflin Company. And from Margaret Atwood's *Selected Poems*, selection © Margaret Atwood; reprinted by permission of the publisher, Oxford University Press, Canada.

Seamus Heaney, "The Early Purges" from *Poems 1965–1975* by Seamus Heaney. Copyright 1966 by Seamus Heaney. Reprinted by permission of Farrar, Straus and Giroux, Inc., and Faber and Faber Ltd.

Jean and Peter Medawar, "Animals and Human Obligations." Reprinted by permission of the publishers from *Aristotle to Zoos: A Philosophical Dictionary of Biology*, by P. B. Medawar and J. S. Medawar, Cambridge, Mass.: Harvard University Press, copyright © 1983 by P. B. Medawar and J. S. Medawar.

"Pigs, Dogs and People: Clash in Jersey," *The New York Times*, December 11, 1987. Copyright © 1987 by The New York Times Company. Reprinted by permission.

Ted Hughes, "Capturing Animals." Excerpts from *Poetry Is* by Ted Hughes. Copyright © 1967 by Ted Hughes. Reprinted by permission of Doubleday, a division of Bantam, Doubleday, Dell Publishing Group, Inc.; and from *Poetry in the Making* by permission of Faber and Faber Ltd.

Margaret Atwood, "The Animals in That Country," from *Selected Poems I 1965–1975* by Margaret Atwood. Copyright © 1976 by Margaret Atwood. Reprinted by permission of Houghton Mifflin Company and from Margaret Atwood's *Selected Poems*, selection © Margaret Atwood; reprinted by permission of the publisher, Oxford University Press, Canada.

From Frank Smith, *Understanding Reading*, Harcourt Brace Jovanovich, Inc. Reprinted by permission of the author.

Chapter Eight

From *Tracks* by Robyn Davidson. Copyright © 1980 by Robyn Davidson. Reprinted by permission of Pantheon Books, a division of Random House, Inc., and by permission of Jonathan Cape Ltd.

Chapter Nine

From D. H. Lawrence, "Fantasia of the Unconscious," from *Psychoanalysis* by D. H. Lawrence. Copyright 1921, 1922 by Thomas Seltzer, Inc. Copyright 1949, 1950 by Frieda Lawrence. All rights reserved. Reprinted by permission of Viking Penguin Inc.

Michael P. Doyle, "No Longer Lovely, Nor Dark, Nor Deep," *The New York Times*, May 8, 1982. Copyright © 1982 by The New York Times Company. Reprinted by permission.

Index of Authors

James Agee 163, 363
Sherwood Anderson 33
Peter Appleborne 299
Margaret Atwood 175,
    186, 202, 307

Russell Baker 290
James Baldwin 111, 128
Lester Bangs 371, 376
Benjamin Barber 146
Roland Barthes 428
Joseph Bell 361
Kay Boyle 280, 436
Rachel Brownstein 112

Willa Cather 259
Colette 41
Johnny Connors 12
Frank Conroy 99
Malcolm Cowley 137

Robyn Davidson 209, 296
Simone De Beauvoir 44
Alan Devenish 390
Charles Dickens 9
Annie Dillard 85
Arthur Conan Doyle 356
Michael Patrick
    Doyle 253

Gretel Ehrlich 302

Ursula Fanthorpe 91,
    272, 276

Winifred Foley 17
Thomas Frosch 83
Robert Frost 251, 270

Ellen Goodman 288, 309,
    311, 319
Nadine Gordimer 414
Thom Gunn 306, 370,
    439

Andrew Hacker 321
Seamus Heaney iii, 78,
    187, 265
Lillian Hellman 24
Zbigniew Herbert 430
Russell Hoban 405
Miroslav Holub 84
Arthur Hopcraft 16
Ted Hughes 195

William James 254

Walter Kendrick 327

D. H. Lawrence 171, 248
Denise Levertov 148, 152

Jean and Peter
    Medawar 188
Steven Millhauser 4, 6,
    109
Adrian Mitchell 283
Alan Moorehead 178
Edwin Morgan xvi, 383

Wright Morris 256
Alice Munro 333

Cynthia Ozick 131

Grace Paley 388
Brian Patten 108
Fiona Pitt-Kethley 40, 96,
    314

Anna Quindlen 143, 286,
    293

Philip Roth 332, 382

Edward Sapir 394
Peter Sharpe 355
Betty Smith 19
Frank Smith 46, 204
William Stafford 97, 440
May Swenson 156, 160

Edward Thomas 156
Mark Twain 164, 166,
    184

Eudora Welty 26, 60, 154
Walt Whitman 158
Oscar Wilde 392
Ellen Willis 314
Virginia Woolf 366
William Wordsworth 136
Richard Wright 120, 162

W. B. Yeats 274, 275

Index of Titles

A bee a noppity: assa question!   6
About Men   302
Advice to a Corkscrew   xvi
After the Beep   390
Animals and Human Obligations   188
The Animals in That Country   202
Anxiety   388
Autobiographical Notes   111

Backdrop Addresses Cowboy   307
Bad Mouth   175
Beset by Mediocrity   290

Captain Murderer   9
Capturing Animals   195
The Castaways, or Vote for Caliban   283
Cock-Crow   156
Critique   440

The Death of Marilyn Monroe   383
Destroying the Roots   137
Did You Have *Our Wonder World?*   26
Disclosing, Uncovering, Reading,
   Inferring   356
Down by the Salley Gardens   274

The Early Purges.   187

Fashion   394
Fifteen   97
The First Book to Impress Me   16
The First Day of School, Washington
   Square, 1946   131

Ghost Stories   40
The Great Family of Man   428
Growing Up   91
Gurshes, Jurbles, Fliffs   4

How Conan Doyle Learned to Read   361
How Everything Happens (Based on a
   Study of the Wave)   160

How I Met My Husband   333
How We Comprehend   46

If I Were King   19
I Had Thought I Understood How a
   Murder Could Happen   33
I Know . . . Green Apples   164
In the Fig Tree I Learned to Read   24
I Sank into Other Streets and
   Universes   109
I Sat Up All Night   78
It's All the Art of Impersonation   382
It Takes Courage to Say Things
   Differently   280
I Think There are Too Many Trees   248
It's Called the Universe   99
I Want to Be an Honest Man   128

Literature   41
Live-in Myths   311
Lone Ranger   83

The Man that Spelt KNIFE was a
   Fool   12
Memories of Waves   158
Mending Wall   270
Mr. Cogito on the Need for
   Precision   430
My Life in Fiction   112
My Sad Captains   439
My Secret Advice   314
My Uncle Harry Said, "Warm Milk from
   the Titty Made a Cat Purty"   256

Near a Church   363
No Longer Lovely, Nor Dark, Nor
   Deep   253

Of Roles and Robes   309
On a Certain Blindness in Human
   Beings   254

On Reading Fiction   332
Out of the Sea, Early   156
O Taste and See   152

Painkillers   370
Pigeon Season   184
Pigs, Dogs and People: Clash in
    Jersey   192
A Poem for Vida Hadjebi Tabrizi   436
Poe's Murders and Corpses Were
    Gathering in Our Kitchen   17
Predictions and Intentions—Global and
    Focal   204
Psalm Concerning the Castle   148

Rating the Kids   288
Reading for Another Life and for
    Liberation   120
Realizing What You Don't Know and
    Never Will   143
Rhymes   265
The River Was Turned to Blood   166
Robert Called Me "Baby"   293

A Schism Between Mothers   286
The Secret Museum   327
Seminar: Felicity and Mr. Frost   272
Seminar: Life; Early Poems   276
Sheep and Women   296
Six Feet of the Country   414
Some Say Frontier Is Still There, and Still
    Different   299
Song of the Hen's Head   186

The Song of Wandering Aengus   275
Snake   171
Snake-Phobia   178
Spells   314
Stopping by Woods on a Snowy
    Evening   251
Strangers on a Train   366
Sunrise   154

Take a Chicken to Lunch   185
Then I Will Be Elvis!   376
This Lucky Situation of Joy   163
Through the Eyes of Men   44
Thoughts on a Shirtless Cyclist, Robin
    Hood and 1 or 2 Other Things   405
Tracks   209
Tragedy   96

Villenelle for an Anniversary   iii
Vowing to Get Married   319

U/S and Marriage   321

A Wagner Matinée   259
Waiting for the Idiot to Go Away   355
Waitress   316
What a Sweet Name!   392
What Do 47-Year-Olds Know?   146
Where Were You When Elvis Died?   371
The Winds   60
The Wonder I Felt (from *Black Boy*)   162
The World is Too Much With Us   136